REMEDIES IN ARBITRATION

Second Edition

REMEDIES IN ARBITRATION.

Second Edition

MARVIN F. HILL, JR.
Professor of Industrial Relations
Northern Illinois University

ANTHONY V. SINICROPI
John F. Murray Professor of Industrial Relations
University of Iowa

The Bureau of National Affairs, Inc. Washington, D.C. 20037

Copyright © 1981, 1991
The Bureau of National Affairs, Inc.

KF
3424
.H54
1990

Library of Congress Cataloging-in-Publication Data

Hill, Marvin
　Remedies in arbitration / Marvin F. Hill, Jr., Anthony V. Sinicropi.—2nd ed.
　　p.　cm.
　Includes bibliographical references and index.
　ISBN 0-87179-658-9
　1. Arbitration, Industrial—United States.　I. Sinicropi, Anthony
V. II. Title.
KF3424.H54 1990
344.73′ 0189143—dc20
[347.304189143]

90-43650
CIP

Published by BNA Books
1231 25th St., N.W., Washington, D.C. 20037

Printed in the United States of America
International Standard Book Number: 0-87179-658-9

Acknowledgements

Our debts are many and like the number of Elvis Presley impersonators (who interestingly have increased exponentially since the first edition of *Remedies in Arbitration* was published in 1981)[1] continue to grow.

We owe thanks to Ellen Lynch and Jeffrey Lenkov, who as law students worked diligently researching legal issues, and Susan Raab and Graham Hill, for their cite checking and library work. A special note of thanks to Lori Brennan who typed the first edition of *Remedies* on computer.

A special thanks to the following arbitrators who took time from busy schedules to provide us with unpublished cases dealing with remedy issues: Reginald Alleyne; Neil Bernstein; Mike Bognanno; Martin Cohen; Joseph Gentile; Harry Graham; Jay Grenig; Gladys Gruenberg; Vern Hauck; I.B. (Beber) Helburn; William Holley, Jr.; Edgar (Ted) Jones, Jr.; Mark Kahn; Walter Kaufman; Sinclair Kossoff; George Larney; Bert Luskin; Richard Mittenthal; William Murphy; Harvey Nathan; Dennis Nolan; Lawrence Schultz; James Sherman; Jesse Simons; Carlton Snow; Byron Yaffe; and Sol Yarowski.

Camille Christie of BNA gets our thanks and respect for her fine editorial skills and, more important, for continuing to laugh at our jokes. We again remind her that intelligent research does not guarantee the accuracy of the findings and that if you find a principle or rule of law that everyone agrees on, it's wrong.

---

[1]Cf. "The Men Who Would Be Elvis," *The New York Times*, Tuesday, June 26, 1990, B1. The authors are split whether there is a cause and effect relationship at work here.

Foreword to the Second Edition

In writing a second edition of *Remedies in Arbitration* we are reminded of Olson's Law (quoted in the 1978 Farmers' Almanac) which holds that every time you buy something, the manufacturer comes out with an improved model for less money. We are also mindful of Sturgeon's Law (noted by C. Lehmann-Haupt in *The New York Times*, December 9, 1970) declaring that 90 percent of everything is junk. With the help of our publisher, we hope to avoid the net of both laws by offering arbitrators, labor-management practitioners, and law students a better text for more money.

To this end we have organized the second edition into three major divisions:

I. Sources of Remedial Authority (which includes chapters on the collective bargaining agreement, the submission, and external law as sources of remedial authority).

II. Remedies in Discharge and Disciplinary Cases (discussing reinstatement; back pay; procedural issues; reduction of discipline; employers' remedies for breach of a no-strike clause; and the arbitrator's authority to issue injunctions and other interim relief).

III. Remedies in Nondisciplinary Cases (discussing subcontracting and improper transfer of operations; overtime; work assignments; vacations; promotions; mistake; punitive remedies; interest, costs, and attorney's fees; and miscellaneous problem areas).

A synthesis follows in the Conclusion.

While we realize that, depending on the particular case, there is overlap between the divisions and chapters, the topics discussed in the 21 chapters fall "more or less" into these broad categories. Unlike the first edition, the second edition makes extensive use of unpublished decisions by arbitrators. After reading a hundred or so unpublished opinions provided mostly by members of the National Academy of Arbitrators, we are convinced that arguments that reported decisions are not indicative of what the arbitral community is actually doing have no basis in fact. As such, our analysis and extensive citations to cases reported by the major services is offered with assurance that when we cite cases and talk about the better weight of authority we are not talking about statistical "outliers."[1]

As in the first edition, the response of the courts to arbitrators' remedies is also considered. Numerous court decisions have issued since 1980 that have an impact on the arbitration process and these cases have been incorporated. Further, we have devoted considerable time discussing remedies in the federal sector, an ever-increasing area of battle between management and labor.

---

[1]Cf. "What everybody echoes . . . as true today, may turn out to be a falsehood tomorrow, mere smoke of opinion." Henry David Thoreau, *Walden*, ch. 1.

Contents

Conclusion

Appendices

Chapter 1

Introduction

The subject of remedies is one of the most controversial and complex topics in labor arbitration. While there is no serious debate, legal or otherwise, with the view that arbitrators can—and should—formulate remedies when they determine that the employer (or, in selected cases, the union) has not complied with the parties' collective bargaining agreement, questions frequently arise regarding the source(s) of arbitrators' remedy power and the extent, or scope, of that power. In addition, there is concern about how the use of remedial authority affects the collective bargaining institution.

As arbitrators and practitioners know, the use of remedy power is situational. Remedial authority depends on a number of factors, including the specific facts of a case, the labor agreement in force at the time, and the statutes and the case law governing the jurisdiction in question. This is especially true for arbitrators who operate in the federal sector. Accordingly, each case and corresponding remedy must be decided on its own merits.

Still, identifiable trends and expectancies in applying remedial power have emerged to form a body of arbitral authority, and from published and unpublished arbitration awards[1] and reported court decisions the authors have at-

---

[1]In relying on published awards we are aware that only a small proportion of arbitration awards are submitted for publication, and only a small proportion of those submitted are, in fact, published. We are not persuaded that reliance on published decisions as indicating what arbitrators in fact do will give undue weight to "outliers." Nor are we convinced that the publishing agencies elect to publish those

1

tempted to determine where those trends are apparent and how such information may be of benefit to the actors involved.

A. Arbitral Remedy Power: Two Views

The subject of remedies in arbitration is an old one, having first been discussed in a 1962 paper by Emmanuel Stein before the National Academy of Arbitrators,[2] and has since been addressed by numerous commentators.[3] The literature outlines two perspectives from which to examine arbitral remedy power. One is based on the "legal" authority of the arbitrator to formulate a specific remedy under the labor agreement. The other is based on a policy foundation, that is, what will be the likely effect, or impact, of a specific remedy on the collective bargaining institution; most conditional remedies fall into this perspective.

A review of the "legal-authority" concept examines the parties' contractual provisions (usually "silent" contracts) as well as state and federal statutes and the common law. In addition, such a review includes the judicial response to remedial determinations because, despite the directive of the

---

decisions that add something new to those already published to the exclusion of well-established norms. See Stieber, Block and Corbitt, *How Representative Are Published Decisions?: Part II*, in Arbitration 1984: Absenteeism, Recent Law, Panels, and Published Decisions, Proceedings of the 37th Annual Meeting, National Academy of Arbitrators, 172 (BNA Books, 1985); *The Publication of Arbitration Awards*, in Arbitration—1975, Proceedings of the 28th Annual Meeting, National Academy of Arbitrators, 208 (BNA Books, 1976).

[2]Stein, *Remedies in Labor Arbitration*, in Challenges to Arbitration, Proceedings of the 13th Annual Meeting, National Academy of Arbitrators, 3 (BNA Books, 1960).

[3]See, e.g., Fleming, *Arbitrators and the Remedy Power*, 48 Va. L. Rev. 1199, 1201 (1962); Stutz, *Arbitrators and the Remedy Power*, in Labor Arbitration and Industrial Change, Proceedings of the 16th Annual Meeting, National Academy of Arbitrators, 54 (BNA Books, 1963); Seitz, *Problems of the Finality of Awards, or Functus Officio and All That—Remedies in Arbitration*, in Labor Arbitration: Perspectives and Problems, Proceedings of the 17th Annual Meeting, National Academy of Arbitrators, 165 (BNA Books, 1964); Wolff, *Power of the Arbitrator to Make Monetary Awards— Remedies in Arbitration*, in Labor Arbitration: Perspectives and Problems, id at 176; Crane, *The Use and Abuse of Arbitral Power*, in Labor Arbitration at the Quarter Century Mark, Proceedings of the 25th Annual Meeting, National Academy of Arbitrators, 66 (BNA Books, 1973); Feller, *Remedies: New and Old Problems: I. Remedies in Arbitration: Old Problems Revisited*, in Arbitration Issues for the 1980s, Proceedings of the 34th Annual Meeting, National Academy of Arbitrators, 109 (BNA Books, 1982); Sinicropi, *Remedies: Another View of New and Old Problems*, in Arbitration Issues for the 1980s, id. at 134.

Supreme Court in the Steelworkers Trilogy,[4] state and federal courts (especially the Fourth and Sixth Circuits) are increasingly accepting invitations to review the merits of arbitrators' awards under the premise of determining contractual restrictions on arbitral authority.[5] As a result, an arbitrator may face the hazard of having his awards overturned based upon the court's own sense of industrial justice.

In analyzing remedial power under the policy concept, it is essential to understand that the focus is not on whether the remedial measure is permissible under the collective bargaining agreement or the law but, instead, on how the measure, if awarded or implemented, might affect the collective bargaining institution. What, for example, is the long-term effect of reinstatement without back pay upon the parties' relationship? What will be the effect of a "punitive" award upon the parties? When, if ever, should the arbitrator be concerned with such considerations when formulating remedies?

It should not be assumed that policy and "legal-authority" concepts are independent. The late Harry Shulman, Dean and Sterling Professor of Law at the Yale Law School, noted in a Holmes Lecture[6] that collective bargaining is not concerned merely with the return for employees' services. Rather, collective agreements are pacts adopted to set up systems of industrial democracy in complex industrial societies. Shulman writes: "No matter how much time is allowed for the negotiation, there is never time enough to think every issue through in all of its possible applications, and never ingenuity enough to anticipate all that does later show up." Dean Shulman went on to state that the parties recognize that all contingencies have not been anticipated and that, in any event, there will be many differences of opinion as to the proper application of

---

[4]Steelworkers v. American Mfg. Co., 363 U.S. 564, 46 LRRM 2414 (1960); Steelworkers v. Warrior & Gulf Navigation Co., 363 U.S. 574, 46 LRRM 2416 (1960); Steelworkers v. Enterprise Wheel & Car Corp., 363 U.S. 593, 46 LRRM 2423 (1960).

[5]See, e.g., St. Antoine, *Judicial Review of Labor Arbitration Awards: A Second Look at* Enterprise Wheel *and Its Progeny*, in Arbitration—1977, Proceedings of the 30th Annual Meeting, National Academy of Arbitrators, 29 (BNA Books, 1978); Christensen, *Judicial Review: As Arbitrators See It—I. The Disguised Review of the Merits of Arbitration Awards*, in Labor Arbitration at the Quarter-Century Mark, supra note 3, at 99. The federal sector advocate is directed to Kagel, *Grievance Arbitration in the Federal Service: Still Hardly Final and Binding?*, in Arbitration Issues for the 1980s, supra note 3, at 178.

[6]*Reason, Contract, and Law in Labor Relations*, 68 Harv. L. Rev. 999 (1955).

the standards used by arbitrators. Shulman recognized that both legal authority and policy factor are present in the collective bargaining arrangement and that the grievance-arbitration mechanism is designed to address and incorporate both of those concepts.

B. The Arbitrator's Function in Formulating Remedies

Any examination of arbitral remedial authority, whether from a legal-authority or policy point of view, must address the question of what the arbitrator's function should be within the "private rule of law" established by the collective agreement. Arbitral opinion is divided on this question.

Some arbitrators and practitioners equate the arbitrator's remedy power with that of a court in a breach-of-contract dispute. This approach has been advanced by Arbitrator Sidney Wolff[7] and has been characterized by Arbitrator David Feller[8] as follows: "What is the proper measure of damages in a suit for breach of a labor agreement which happens to be decided by an arbitrator?"[9] Under this approach, arbitration is viewed as a speedy and informal way of dealing with what is essentially a suit for breach of contract. The basic remedies available in breach-of-contract cases—damages, restitution, and equitable remedies—may, unless proscribed by the agreement, be awarded by the arbitrator, who essentially acts as a surrogate for a judge. Questions concerning the propriety of a specific remedy may readily be understood by reference to Corbin, Williston, or the *Restatement of Contracts*. As one observer has stated, "[T]he never-say-die Willistonian view [is] that a contract is a contract is a contract, and that although some contract rules are too narrow to qualify as full-fledged

---

[7]Wolff, supra note 3, at 176–193.
[8]See Feller, *Remedies in Labor Arbitration: II. The Power of the Arbitrator to Make Monetary Awards: Discussion* in Labor Arbitration: Perspectives and Problems, Proceedings of the 17th Annual Meeting, National Academy of Arbitrators, 193 (BNA Books, 1964).
[9]Id. at 194–195.

principles, the general principles . . . of contract law are always applicable [in arbitration]."[10]

At the other extreme is the view that the arbitrator's only function is to explicate what is implicit in a collective bargaining agreement. Professor David Feller points out that arbitration is not a substitute for judicial adjudication, but a method of resolving disputes over matters which, except for the collective bargaining agreement and its grievance-arbitration machinery, would be subject to no governing adjudicative principles at all. Arbitration is an adjudication against standards, but the standards are not those which would be applied by a court charged with adjudicating a contractual dispute. Labor arbitration requires treatment different from that accorded commercial arbitration cases, Feller contends, since in the commercial setting arbitration is a substitute for litigation, rather than a system to avoid industrial strife.[11]

For this reason arbitration of labor disputes has functions quite different from arbitration under an ordinary commercial agreement. Feller argues that it is important to draw a sharp distinction between the role of the arbitrator in construing and applying the collective bargaining agreement and that of an arbitrator functioning as an adjudicator of contractual controversies subject to resolution under the general law of contracts. In another article he argues:

> [Y]ou must recognize the impropriety of questions such as: "What is the proper measure of damages in a suit or arbitration for breach of contract?" "Can an arbitrator issue an injunction?" "Can he give punitive damages?" All those questions are exactly the same questions that you would address—indeed they are the questions that you *do* address—to a court of law in which you are suing for breach of contract.
>
> When you arbitrate, however, you are not suing through

---

[10]Mueller, *The Law of Contracts—A Changing Legal Environment*, in Truth, Lie Detectors, and Other Problems in Labor Arbitration, Proceedings of the 31st Annual Meeting, National Academy of Arbitrators, 204, 205–206 (BNA, 1979). In Teamsters Local 636 v. J.C. Penney Co., 484 F. Supp. 130, 103 LRRM 2618 (W.D. Pa. 1980), a federal district court, in determining whether an employer was contractually bound to arbitrate, stated: "Although the technical rules of contract do not necessarily control all decisions in labor management cases, normal rules of offer and acceptance are determinative of the existence of a bargaining agreement . . . ." Id., 103 LRRM at 2620.

[11]Feller, *The Coming End of Arbitration's Golden Age*, in Arbitration—1976, Proceedings of the 29th Annual Meeting, National Academy of Arbitrators, 97 (BNA Books, 1976).

an informal domestic tribunal . . . . You are not using an informal tribunal as a substitute for a lawsuit when you establish a system of grievance arbitration. You are establishing a completely different kind of machinery, and it is therefore improper to measure an award as if it were the kind of damage judgment which the courts would render. You should not put the question in that focus or framework at all. The real question is: "What is the proper function of an arbitrator in settling a grievance under a contract?"[12]

According to Feller, an arbitrator's sole function in deciding what remedy should be awarded is to determine what the agreement says about remedy. The arbitrator's task is not to enforce the agreement or to award "damages," but simply to determine what remedy is provided in the agreement and award it. It is a different function than a court is performing when it formulates remedies, such as in a breach-of-contract lawsuit. In that case, the rules involved are external to the agreement, may not correspond to the intentions of the parties, and may in some instances not fully compensate the non-breaching party for the injury suffered. Feller argues that the arbitrator should not consider himself analogous to a court and award the kind of remedies that a court could properly contemplate but, instead, should limit himself to awarding only those remedies which he finds either implicitly or explicitly in the parties' collective bargaining agreement. In the words of Feller:

> The arbitrator's function is not to do justice, even with respect to remedies. His function is to read the contract, including its provision as to remedies, and to tell the parties what those provisions mean as applied to the particular case. Where the agreement is silent, he may find implied in it, as the common law of industrial relations, the kind of remedies customarily provided in collective agreements or by arbitrators. Those remedies are almost universally injunctive in nature and, where the payment of money is involved, based on calculations interior to the agreement. The remedy in a particular case may be more or less than justice. But, as the parties' "contract reader," the arbitrator's function ends when he tells the parties what the remedy provided in their agreement is and directs performance of that remedy.[13]

---

[12]Feller, supra note 8, at 194–195.
[13]Feller, supra note 3, at 132.

Because there is a time gap between the event upon which the grievance is based and the arbitrator's determination that the event constituted a failure of the employer to comply with the agreement, a money award (not "damages") is ordered. If, for example, the arbitrator determines that a grievant was improperly dismissed, an order of reinstatement is issued and the employer is ordered to provide back pay dating from the time of the improper discharge. In this situation a monetary award simply compensates for the time gap between the event and the decision.

The majority view, as argued by Addison Mueller,[14] is probably somewhere between the views of Wolff and Feller, namely, that collective bargaining agreements are special types of contracts[15] with respect to which the principles of ordinary contract law, though not strictly applicable, are nonetheless helpful to arbitrators because they tap the "wisdom of the past." Although the parties are free to make the arbitrator the equivalent of a judge formulating remedies in a contractual dispute, in general the parties do not anticipate that he will act in such fashion. If, as claimed by the Supreme Court, the arbitrator is usually chosen because of the parties' confidence in his knowledge of the "common law of the shop," it is expected that he will draft remedies that may not explicitly be cited within the four corners of the agreement. After all, the Supreme Court, in *Warrior & Gulf*,[16] has stated that "the industrial common law—the practices of the industry and the shop—is equally a part of the collective bargaining agreement although not expressed in it."[17] Justice Black has likewise declared that "a collective bargaining agreement is not an ordinary contract for the purchase of goods and services, nor is it governed by the same old common-law concepts which control such private contracts."[18]

---

[14]Supra note 10. See, e.g., Metal Specialty Co., 39 LA 1265 (Volz, 1962); Coca-Cola Bottling Co., 9 LA 197 (Jacobs, 1947).
[15]In this regard, see Feller, *A General Theory of the Collective Bargaining Agreement*, 61 Calif. L. Rev. 663 (1973).
[16]Steelworkers v. Warrior & Gulf Navigation Co., supra note 4.
[17]Id., 46 LRRM at 2419.
[18]Transportation-Communication Employees v. Union Pacific R.R., 385 U.S. 157, 160, 63 LRRM 2481, 2482 (1966). See also Emery Air Freight Corp. v. Teamsters Local 295, 356 F. Supp. 974, 82 LRRM 2138 (E.D.N.Y. 1972), citing Columbia Broadcasting Sys. v. American Recording & Broadcasting Ass'n, 293 F. Supp. 1400, 69

Whichever view one endorses—the extreme positions may not necessarily be mutually exclusive since an agreement may be explicit in specifying the remedy that is to apply if a violation is found—it is the authors' premise that the parties in the arbitration procedure spend much time on the merits of the dispute, as they should, and sometimes almost as much time on the question of arbitrability, which perhaps they should not. The matter of an appropriate remedy, if addressed at all, is usually noted merely by asking the traditional question: "If so, what shall be the remedy?" While in some cases this will be sufficient, in others the remedy is far from apparent and is not easily determinable.

In view of the potentially great impact of an arbitration decision and the limited judicial review available to the parties, it is puzzling to note the extent to which remedy issues have been ignored by the parties and practitioners alike. This text is designed to provide arbitrators and advocates with a better understanding of the substantive issues concerning an arbitrator's authority to specify remedies once it is determined that the collective bargaining agreement has been violated. The authors believe that most complex remedy issues are sufficiently addressed.[19]

LRRM 2914 (S.D.N.Y. 1968) (stating that "collective bargaining contract not necessarily governed by common-law principles").

[19]Cf. "If you've a melancholy case of the blues, I've got a remedy for you." "Go Into Your Dance," *42nd Street*. Music by Harry Warren, lyrics by Al Dubin.

Part I

Sources of Remedial Authority

Chapter 2

Arbitration Under Common Law and the United States Arbitration Act

Labor arbitration is a matter of contract and, with few exceptions, under current law an arbitrator's power to formulate a specific remedy is limited only by the limits of the parties' bargaining and submission agreement. Prior to an examination of the bargaining contract and submission agreement as a source and limitation of arbitral power, a review of arbitration under common law and the United States Arbitration Act is instructive.

A. Arbitration Under Common Law

The basic tenets of common-law arbitration have been summarized by the U.S. Department of Labor as follows:

> Common law arbitration rests upon the voluntary agreement of the parties to submit their dispute to an outsider. The submission agreement may be oral and may be revoked at any time before the rendering of the award. The tribunal, permanent or temporary, may be composed of any number of arbitrators. They must be free from bias and interest in the subject matter, and may not be related by affinity or consanguinity to either party. The Arbitrators need not be sworn. Only existing disputes may be submitted to them. The parties must be given notice of hearings and are entitled to be present when all the evidence is received. The arbitrators have no power to subpoena witnesses or records and need not conform to legal rules of hearing pro-

11

cedure other than to give the parties an opportunity to present all competent evidence. All arbitrators must attend the hearings, consider the evidence jointly and arrive at an award by a unanimous vote. The award may be oral, but if written, all the arbitrators must sign it. It must dispose of every substantial issue submitted to arbitration. An award may be set aside only for fraud, misconduct, gross mistake, or substantial breach of a common law rule. The only method of enforcing the common law award is to file suit upon it and the judgment thus obtained may be enforced as any other judgment.[1]

Prior to 1957 it was unclear to what extent an agreement to arbitrate could be enforced by a state or a federal court. Initially, no effort was made by the courts to accommodate labor arbitration because it was thought to be competitive with the court system and therefore a process that should be discouraged. This animosity toward arbitration was somewhat paradoxical since some historians assert that the judicial system may have evolved from the arbitration process.[2]

In the early stages of labor arbitration, courts regularly ruled that an agreement to submit a dispute to arbitration was unenforceable by the courts and therefore these agreements could be revoked at will by either party. Parties could revoke the agreement even after the arbitration hearing if they did so prior to the award.[3] Several reasons advanced for refusing to enforce an agreement to arbitrate were summarized as follows in *U.S. Asphalt Refining Co. v. Trinidad Lake Petroleum Co.*:[4]

(a) The contract is in its nature revocable.[5]

---

[1]Ziskind, Labor Arbitration Under State Statutes, 3 (U.S. Dept. of Labor, 1943).

[2]Sturges and Reckeson, *Common Law and Statutory Arbitration: Problems Arising From Their Coexistence,* 46 Minn. L. Rev. 819 (1962).

[3]In England as early as 1609 Lord Coke held that an agreement to submit a dispute to arbitration would be revoked at the will of either party. Vynior's Case, 4 Coke 302, Trinity Term, 7 Jac. 1 (1609). This rule was abandoned in the last century following the enactment of the English Arbitration Act of 1889, 52 & 53 Vict., Ch. 49, §4 (1894). However, the American courts continued to follow the English view until the enactment of arbitration acts by a number of state legislatures and the passage of the United States Arbitration Act, 9 U.S.C. §4 (1947), amended 1954.

[4]222 F. 1006 (S.D.N.Y. 1915).

[5]Professor Archibald Cox has noted that prior to the enactment of § 301 there was grave doubt whether a collective bargaining agreement was enforceable. One view was that a collective bargaining contract was a mere "gentlemen's agreement" without legal effect. Other theories allowed no individual employee, or group of employees independent of the union, to sue the employer as a third-party beneficiary of promises made by the employer to the union. Another view adopted an agency analysis, so that the legal obligation ran directly between the employees and the employer. A

(b) Such contracts are against public policy.

(c) The covenant (agreement) to refer is but collateral to the main contract, and may be disregarded, leaving the contract keeper to his action for damages for breach of such collateral covenant.

(d) Any contract tending to wholly oust the courts of jurisdiction violates the spirit of the laws creating the courts, in that it is not competent for private persons either to increase or diminish the statutory judicial power.

(e) Arbitration may be a condition precedent to suit, and as such valid, if it does not prevent legal action, or seek to determine out of court the general question of liability.[6]

"Agreements to arbitrate were revocable even when they contained an express covenant that neither party to the agreement could revoke because, the courts held, parties could not make irrevocable agreements which were legally revocable."[7] This rule of nonenforceability applied only to an executory agreement to arbitrate.

Today, grievance arbitration has become firmly embedded in our national labor policy as the preferred method for resolving disputes,[8] and is widely accepted by the parties.[9]

---

fourth theory held that the agreement between the employer and the union had the effect of a custom presumed to be incorporated into each individual employment contract unless the presumption was negated. Cox and Bok, Labor Law, Cases and Materials, 598–600 (Foundation Press, 1969).

[6]222 F. at 1008.

[7]See, e.g., Baltimore & Ohio Ry. v. Stankard, 56 Ohio St. 224, 46 N.E. 577 (1897).

[8]See notes 26–61 and accompanying text in Chapter 3.

[9]Two major forces responsible for the increased acceptance of labor arbitration were the War Labor Board in the period 1942 to 1945 and the growth of state arbitration statutes.

Functioning in effect as a tripartite arbitration board of disputes over unresolved contract terms ("rights" arbitration), the War Labor Board laid a foundation for arbitration by consistently rejecting the common-law view that arbitration was to be regarded with hostility because it was against public policy and an attempt by the parties to oust courts from the jurisdiction. Instead, the Board accepted the view that agreements for arbitration of future disputes are to be favored. Besides consistently urging the parties to use voluntary arbitration procedures, it ordered the adoption of contract clauses providing for arbitration. This practice was a major factor in making arbitration the terminal point of the grievance procedure. In addition, the Board pioneered many of the criteria used by arbitrators today. See Freidin and Ulman, *Arbitration and the National War Labor Board,* 58 Harv. L. Rev. 309 (1945).

State laws pertaining to arbitration include laws specifying the subjects, conditions, and agreements upon which valid arbitrational steps may be taken so as to be enforced by the courts. Some state statutes merely codify the common law, while others go further and seek to aid arbitration by providing for finality of awards. Arbitrator Russell Smith classifies arbitration statutes into three categories: (1) general statutes used principally in commercial disputes, but often applicable to labor disputes; (2) statutes designed specifically for labor disputes, presenting arbitration procedures for judicial review and providing for enforcement of awards; and (3) statutes which merely "promote" arbitration by directing state officials to encourage its

B. The United States Arbitration Act

The United States Arbitration Act[10] provides that any maritime, international, or interstate contractual obligations between the parties "shall be valid, irrevocable, and enforceable, save upon such grounds as exists at law or in equity for the revocation of any contract."[11] The possible applicability of the Act to collective bargaining agreements is of interest because it may provide a statutory standard for review that could preempt any judicial standard. More important, from the standpoint of arbitral remedial power, the statute authorizes judicial involvement in actions where the procedural integrity of the arbitration process is impaired or, alternatively, where the arbitrator, in formulating a remedy, has exceeded his authority.[12] Indeed, four circuits, the First, Second, Sixth, and Seventh, have expressly held the Act applicable to suits involving the arbitration of collective bargaining disputes.[13] Other

---

use. See Smith, Merrifield, and Rothschild, Collective Bargaining and Labor Arbitration (Bobbs-Merrill Co., 1970); Matto, *The Applicability of State Arbitration Statutes to Proceedings Subject to LMRA Section 301*, 27 Ohio St. L.J. 692 (1966). At present there is substantial question with respect to the significance of state common law and statutory provisions relating to the arbitration process in the private sector in view of the development of federal substantive law under §301 of Taft-Hartley. See Fairweather, Practice and Procedure in Labor Arbitration, 2d ed., 1–9 (BNA Books, 1983).

[10]9 U.S.C. §§1–14 (1970). The principal provisions of the Act are found in §§1, 2, 3, and 4. The Act provides for the enforcement of (a) agreements to arbitrate future controversies arising out of (1) "any maritime transaction or a contract evidencing a transaction involving commerce," or (2) "the refusal to perform the whole or any part" of the transaction or contract; and (b) a written agreement to submit to arbitration an existing controversy "arising out of such contract or transaction, or . . . refusal." Excluded from the Act are "contracts of employment of seamen, railroad employees, or any other class of workers engaged in foreign or interstate commerce." If the issue involved in any suit or proceeding instituted in a federal court is "referable to arbitration under an agreement in writing for such arbitration" the suit or proceeding may be stayed pending arbitration by a motion under §3 of the Act. If one party to the contract or transaction fails, refuses, or neglects to proceed to arbitration, the aggrieved party may petition, under §4 of the Act, for an order directing arbitration. See Appendix C.

[11]9 U.S.C. §2 (1970).

[12]Construction and application of §10(a–d) of the United States Arbitration Act of 1947 (9 U.S.C. §10(a–d)), providing grounds for vacating arbitration awards, may be found by reference to 20 A.L.R. Fed. 295 (1974).

[13]See Derwin v. General Dynamics Corp., 719 F.2d 484, 114 LRRM 3076 (1st Cir. 1983) (holding that the Act may be consulted in formulating federal substantive law but it is not binding in cases arising under §301); Teamsters Local 251 v. Narragansett Improvement Co., 503 F.2d 309, 87 LRRM 2279 (1st Cir. 1974); Electronics Corp. of Am. v. Electrical Workers (IUE) Local 272, 492, F.2d 1255, 85 LRRM 2534 (1st Cir. 1974); T.C. Vaer, Inc. v. Iron Workers Local 580, 813 F.2d 562 (2d Cir. 1987); Bell Aerospace Co., Div. of Textron v. Automobile Workers Local 516, 500 F.2d 921, 923, 86 LRRM 3240 (2d Cir. 1974); Machinists, Auburn Elecs. Local 967 v. General Elec.

circuits are in conflict,[14] having rejected the applicability of the Act,[15] or have reserved judgment on the issue.[16]

The Act specifically provides that arbitration awards are to be vacated:

(a) Where the award was procured by corruption, fraud, or undue means.

(b) Where there was evidence of partiality or corruption in the arbitrators, or either of them.

(c) Where the arbitrators were guilty of misconduct in refusing to postpone the hearing, upon sufficient cause shown, or in refusing to hear evidence pertinent and material to the controversy; or of any other misbehavior by which the rights of any party have been prejudiced.

(d) Where the arbitrators exceeded their powers or so imperfectly executed them that a mutual, final, and definite award upon the subject matter submitted was not made.[17]

The Act also calls for modification of an award:

(a) Where there was an evident material miscalculation of figures or an evident material mistake in the description of any person, thing, or property referred to in the award.

Co., 406 F.2d 1046, 70 LRRM 2477 (2d Cir. 1969); American Broadcasting Cos. v. Television & Radio Artists, Washington-Baltimore Local, 412 F. Supp. 1077, 92 LRRM 2599 (S.D.N.Y. 1976); Makress Lingerie v. Ladies' Garment Workers, 395 F. Supp 110, 89 LRRM 2552 (S.D.N.Y. 1975); Mailers Local 92 (Chattanooga) v. Chattanooga News-Free Press, 524 F.2d 1305, 90 LRRM 3000 (6th Cir. 1975); Miller Brewing Co. v. Brewery Workers Local 9, 739 F.2d 1159, 116 LRRM 3130 (7th Cir. 1984), cert. denied, 469 U.S. 1160, 118 LRRM 2192 (1985); Typographical Union No. 23 (Milwaukee) v. Newspapers, Inc., 639 F.2d 386, 106 LRRM 2317 (7th Cir.), cert. denied, 454 U.S. 838 (1981); Pietro Scalzitti Co. v. Operating Eng'rs Local 150, 351 F.2d 576, 60 LRRM 2222 (7th Cir. 1965). See also Mine Workers Local 2424 v. Consolidation Coal Co., 682 F. Supp. 399, 400 (S.D. Ill. 1988) (citing Act and holding that "only where there is a bona fide dispute over the award, limited to the statutory basis, may a district court review an otherwise valid award.").
[14]See Service Employees Local 36 v. Office Center Servs., 670 F.2d 404, 406 n.6, 109 LRRM 2552 (3d Cir. 1982) (recognizing conflict in earlier Third Circuit cases and concluding that other decisions by Third Circuit reflect advancing lifelessness of the Act in labor arbitration).
[15]See Sine v. Teamsters Local 992, 644 F.2d 997, 1001–1002, 107 LRRM 2089 (4th Cir.), cert. denied, 454 U.S. 965, 108 LRRM 2923 (1981) (rejecting applicability of the Act to collective bargaining agreements); Carpenters District Council (San Diego County) v. G.L. Cory, Inc., 685 F.2d 1137, 1141, 111 LRRM 2222 (9th Cir. 1982) (deciding that exclusion by the Act of contracts of employment suggests that Congress did not intend the Act to be used to review arbitration awards involving collective bargaining agreements).
[16]See Teamsters Local 767 v. Standard Brands, 579 F.2d 1282, 1294 n.9, 99 LRRM 2377 (5th Cir. 1978) (reserving decision for another case); Electrical Workers (UE) Local 1139 v. Litton Microwave Cooking Prods., 704 F.2d 393, 395 n.2, 113 LRRM 2015 (8th Cir. 1983) (identifying conflicts among circuits and noting that Eighth Circuit has not squarely decided issue).
[17]9 U.S.C. §10 (1970).

(b) Where the arbitrators have awarded upon a matter not submitted to them, unless it is a matter not affecting the merits of the decision upon the matter submitted.

(c) Where the award is imperfect in matter of form not affecting the merits of the controversy.[18]

Whether the United States Arbitration Act applies to collective bargaining agreements is a question that has not yet been resolved by the Supreme Court. One difficulty is created by the Act's language in Section 1 that "nothing herein contained shall apply to contracts of employment of seamen, railroad employees, or any other class of workers engaged in foreign or interstate commerce." Most of the appellate courts that have considered the issue have limited this provision to cases where the union or the employer is actually engaged in the transportation industry.[19] The Court, however, has indicated in dictum that the Act does not apply but is available to use as a guide when fashioning a "federal common law" of arbitration.[20] The Act's legislative history and language also support the conclusion that it is inapplicable to labor arbitrations generally. Accordingly, when reviewing the remedy power of an arbitrator, one should consider the cited provisions for vacating awards as authoritative (but not dispositive) guidelines.

---

[18]9 U.S.C. §11 (1970).

[19]See Machinists, Auburn Elecs. Local 967 v. General Elec. Co., supra note 13. In General Elec. Co. v. Electrical Workers (UE) Local 205, 353 U.S. 547, 548, 40 LRRM 2119 (1957), the Court enforced, under §301 of the LMRA, an agreement to arbitrate which the Second Circuit had enforced under the United States Arbitration Act, noting that the Second Circuit had taken "a different path . . . though we reach the same result." The Court again suggested that the United States Arbitration Act was to be a guiding analogy.

[20]Paperworkers v. Misco, Inc., 484 U.S. 29, 126 LRRM 3113, 3118 n.9 (1987) (explaining, in dictum, that the Act "does not apply to 'contracts of employment of . . . workers engaged in foreign or interstate commerce,' . . . but the federal courts have looked to the Act for guidance in labor arbitration cases . . .").

Chapter 3

The Collective Bargaining Agreement

A starting point for understanding judicially imposed limits placed upon the arbitrator's power to fashion a remedy is the parties' collective bargaining agreement. With few exceptions, the arbitrator's remedy will not be disturbed by a reviewing court simply because the court's reading of the parties' labor agreement or submission is different from the arbitrator's. It is black letter law that if arbitrators have jurisdiction over the subject matter of the grievance (i.e., the dispute is substantively arbitrable), they have the power to render an award and fashion a remedy "sufficiently grounded in the agreement," even though the agreement is silent on the issue of remedial authority. To hold otherwise would subvert and render meaningless the entire grievance-arbitration process. What follows is a review of the relationship between courts and arbitrators and the limits of both to interpret a collective bargaining agreement and issue an appropriate remedy.

A. Background

Section 1 of the National Labor Relations Act of 1935,[1] also known as the Wagner Act, declares that it is the purpose

---

[1] 49 Stat. 449 (1935), as amended, 61 Stat. 136 (1947), 63 Stat. 601 (1951), 72 Stat. 945 (1958), 73 Stat. 541 (1959); 29 U.S.C. §§151–168 (1970).

17

and policy of the Act to "encourage practices fundamental to the friendly adjustment of industrial disputes arising out of differences as to wages, hours, or other working conditions."[2] Yet prior to the Labor Management Relations Act of 1947 (Taft-Hartley)[3] Congress had consistently refrained from providing for federal enforcement of collective bargaining agreements. Nothing in the Wagner Act authorized the National Labor Relations Board to enforce such agreements, nor could the breach of a labor contract be treated as an unfair labor practice. One problem in enforcing the terms of a collective agreement against a union which had breached the contract was the difficulty of subjecting the union to process. The great majority of unions are unincorporated associations, and at common law voluntary associations are not suable as such.[4] In the absence of a statute,[5] unincorporated labor unions could not be sued in their own names. Instead, each individual member of the union had to be named and be made party to the suit, making it virtually impossible to enforce the terms of a collective agreement.

The Norris-LaGuardia Act of 1932[6] had also insulated

---

[2]Id. at 29 U.S.C. §141.

[3]61 Stat. 136 (1947), as amended, 73 Stat. 519 (1959); 29 U.S.C. §§141–197 (1970).

[4]See Wilson v. Airline Coal Co., 215 Iowa 855, 246 N.W. 753 (1932).

[5]Some states had enacted statutes which subjected unincorporated associations to the jurisdiction of courts, but the statutes were hardly uniform, some pertaining to fraternal societies, welfare organizations, associations doing business, etc. See Report of the Senate Committee on Labor and Public Welfare, S. Rep. No. 105, 80th Cong., 1st Sess. 15–18 (1947).

[6]47 Stat. 70 (1932), 29 U.S.C. §§101–115 (1970). Section 1 of the Act declared that "no court of the United States . . . shall have jurisdiction to issue any restraining order or temporary or permanent injunction in a case involving or growing out of a labor dispute, except in strict conformity with the provisions of this Act. . . . " Section 13 defines a labor dispute in such broad terms as to preclude emasculation by the judiciary, as was the case when Congress attempted via the Clayton Act to place conditions upon the issuance of labor injunctions by the federal courts. Section 4 provides that in any case involving or growing out of a "labor dispute," no order may be issued by a federal court restraining or enjoining any of the union activities meticulously defined in that section. Even when violence or fraud is involved, making §4 unavailable, an order restraining such conduct may be issued only after a hearing and finding of facts specified in §7. The requisite findings must be based upon "the testimony of witnesses in open court (with opportunity for cross examination)." Two of these findings are that "as to each item of relief granted greater injury will be inflicted upon defendants by the granting of relief," and that "the public officers charged with the duty to protect complainant's property are unable or unwilling to furnish adequate protection." The hearing required by §7 must be preceded by "due and personal notice . . . to all known persons against whom relief is sought." Section 7 permits the issuance of a temporary restraining order "effective for no longer than five days" upon a showing that substantial and irreparable damage will result to complainant's property and posting of bond to "recompense those enjoined for any

labor unions against liability for breach of contract. Federal courts held that strikes, picketing, or boycotting, when carried on in breach of a collective agreement, involved a "labor dispute" under Norris-LaGuardia, thus making the activity immune to injunctions absent a showing of the requirements which conditioned the issuance of an injunction under the Act.[7] In addition, a number of states enacted anti-injunction statutes modeled after Norris, and the courts of many of these jurisdictions held that a strike in violation of a collective agreement was a "labor dispute" and could not be enjoined.

1. Labor Management Relations Act of 1947—Section 301

In 1947 Congress passed the Labor Management Relations (Taft-Hartley) Act,[8] and included Section 301, which has had a profound effect on the legal status of arbitration in federal and state courts. Section 301 of the Act provides:

> Sec. 301. (a) Suits for violation of contracts between an employer and a labor organization representing employees in an industry affecting commerce as defined in this Act, or between any such labor organizations, may be brought in any district court of the United States having jurisdiction of the parties, without respect to the amount in controversy or without regard to the citizenship of the parties.
>
> (b) Any labor organization which represents employees in an industry affecting commerce as defined in this Act and any employer whose activities affect commerce as defined in this Act shall be bound by the acts of its agents. Any such labor organization may sue or be sued as an entity and in behalf of the employees whom it represents in the courts of the United States. Any money judgment against a labor organization in a district court of the United States shall be enforceable only against the organization as an entity and against its assets, and shall not be enforceable against any individual member or his assets.[9]

---

loss, expense or damage caused by the imprudent or erroneous issuance of such order or injunction," including court costs and attorney fees.

[7] Wilson & Co. v. Birl, 105 F.2d 948, 4 LRRM 544 (3d Cir. 1939).

[8] Supra note 3.

[9] The remainder of §301 reads as follows:

(c) For the purposes of actions and proceedings by or against labor organizations in the district courts of the United States, district courts shall be deemed to have jurisdiction of a labor organization (1) in the district in which such organization maintains its principal offices or (2) in any district in which its duly authorized officers or agents are engaged in representing or acting for employee

The inclusion of Section 301 in Taft-Hartley did not immediately resolve the problems of enforcing collective bargaining agreements since Congress did not provide any guidelines as to the substantive law applicable to labor contracts brought before the courts. The common question was as follows—what law was to be applied, state law, as had been the previous practice, or some undetermined federal law? There was also the issue of state versus federal jurisdiction under Section 301. The question of whether issues could be arbitrated prior to a court determination of the merits was also an unresolved problem. In *Machinists v. Cutler-Hammer, Inc.*,[10] for example, the New York State Court of Appeals ruled that it is for the court to determine whether the contract contains a provision for arbitration of the dispute tendered, and in the exercise of that jurisdiction the court must determine whether there is such a dispute. The court declared that if the meaning of the provision of the contract sought to be arbitrated is beyond dispute, there cannot be anything to arbitrate and the contract cannot be said to provide for arbitration.

In 1957 the *Lincoln Mills* case[11] provided a foundation for developing a system of federal substantive law on arbitration and enforcement of a collective bargaining agreement. A discussion of the Lincoln Mills decision should be preceded by an account of the decision in *Westinghouse Salaried Employees v. Westinghouse Electric Corp.*,[12] the court's first encounter with Section 301.

2. Pre-*Lincoln Mills*—Section 301 and Union Access to the Federal Courts: The *Westinghouse* Case

The *Westinghouse* case resulted from a dispute over a contractual provision which provided that salaried employees

---

members.
　　(d) The service of summons, subpena, or other legal process of any court of the United States upon an officer or agent of a labor organization, in his capacity as such, shall constitute service upon the labor organization.
　　(e) For the purpose of this section, in determining whether any person is acting as an "agent" of another person so as to make such other person responsible for his acts, the question of whether the specific acts performed were actually authorized or subsequently ratified shall not be controlling.
[10]271 App. Div. 917, 67 N.Y.S.2d 317, 19 LRRM 2232 (1947).
[11]Textile Workers v. Lincoln Mills, 353 U.S. 448, 40 LRRM 2113 (1957).
[12]348 U.S. 437, 35 LRRM 2643 (1955).

were to receive full pay even if a working day was missed. The labor union charged that the company had violated the labor agreement, and filed a Section 301 suit in federal court, after the employer deducted a day's pay from the salaries of some 4,000 employees who had missed work on a particular day. The trial court ruled that the union had a cause of action under Section 301.[13] On appeal, the case was dismissed, the court holding that the union was without authority to sue for its employees.[14] Unions could sue on behalf of employees only if specific provisions of the agreement between the union and the employer affected union rights exclusive of those of employees. On appeal to the Supreme Court, a divided Court sustained the court of appeals but employed different reasoning. A majority held that Section 301 did not confer jurisdiction over such a suit in the federal courts. Section 301 was merely to provide procedural directions to the federal courts; that is, it gave the federal courts jurisdiction over the parties but left undisturbed applicable state law. Accordingly, the majority held that Section 301 did not give the federal courts jurisdiction over the wage claims. Although the Supreme Court avoided the constitutional objections decided in *Lincoln Mills*, in dictum the Court noted that if it were to construe Section 301 as giving the federal courts power to fashion a body of substantive law to apply in Section 301 suits, it would then be subject to constitutional objections since Section 301 did not explicitly provide or define the new substantive rights created. The effect of this decision was to place the Court's imprimatur on the refusal to abide by arbitration awards.[15]

3. *Textile Workers v. Lincoln Mills*—The Emergence of the Federal Judiciary in Labor Arbitration

The essential facts of *Lincoln Mills*[16] are not complicated. The union and the employer entered into a collective bar-

---

[13]217 F. Supp. 622, 53 LRRM 2204 (W.D. Pa. 1963).

[14]283 F.2d 93, 46 LRRM 3084 (3d Cir. 1960).

[15]Five years after the *Lincoln Mills* decision, in Smith v. Evening News Ass'n, 371 U.S. 195, 199, 51 LRRM 2646 (1962), the Court declared that *Westinghouse* was "no longer authoritative as precedent."

[16]Supra note 11. *Lincoln Mills* controlled three cases: Goodall-Sanford, Inc. v. Textile Workers Local 1802, 353 U.S. 550, 40 LRRM 2118 (1957); General Elec. Co. v. Electrical Workers (UE) Local 205, 547, 40 LRRM 2119 (1957); Textile Workers v. Lincoln Mills, supra note 11.

gaining agreement which provided that there would be no strikes and no work stoppages and that grievances would be handled under a specified grievance procedure. The last step in the grievance procedure—a step that could be taken by either party—was arbitration. A dispute arose over work loads and work assignments. Grievances were processed through various steps of the grievance procedure, and, when no settlement was reached, the union requested arbitration. The employer refused, declaring the issues nonarbitrable; consequently the union brought suit in federal district court seeking specific enforcement of the arbitration provision. Under Section 301 (a),[17] the district court concluded it had jurisdiction and ordered the employer to comply with the grievance and arbitration sections of the collective bargaining agreement.[18] The court of appeals reversed.[19]

Speaking for the majority of the Supreme Court, Justice Douglas affirmed three basic principles:

1. Under Section 301 either party could sue in the federal courts for enforcement of a collective bargaining agreement. No constitutional problem existed.[20]

2. Section 301 (a) is more than jurisdictional in that it authorizes federal courts to fashion a body of federal substantive law for the enforcement of collective bargaining agreements. An agreement to arbitrate future disputes is enforceable in federal courts under federal substantive law rather than state courts under state law.[21]

---

[17]Equity jurisdiction was also invoked under §301 and under the Arbitration Act, 9 U.S.C. §§1–14 (1952).

[18]36 LRRM 2361 (N.D. Ala. 1955).

[19]230 F.2d 81, 37 LRRM 2462 (5th Cir. 1956).

[20]In the Court's words: "There is no constitutional difficulty. Article III, §2 extends the judicial power to cases 'arising under . . . the Laws of the United States. . . .' The power of Congress to regulate these labor-management controversies under the Commerce Clause is plain. NLRB v. Jones & Laughlin Steel Corp., 301 U.S. 1, 1 LRRM 703 (1937). A case or controversy arising under §301(a) is, therefore, one within the purview of judicial power as defined in Article III." 353 U.S. 448, 457, 40 LRRM 2113, 2116 (1957).

For a discussion of the constitutional problems of §301, see Bickel and Wellington, *Legislative Purpose and the Judicial Process: The* Lincoln Mills *Case*, 71 Harv. L. Rev. 1 (1957).

[21]"We conclude that the substantive law to apply in suits under §301(a) is federal law which the courts must fashion from the policy of our national labor laws. . . . The Labor Management Relations Act expressly furnishes some substantive law. It points out what the parties may or may not do in certain situations. Other problems will lie in the penumbra of express statutory mandates. Some will lack express statutory sanction but will be solved by looking at the policy of the legislation and

3. That the Norris-LaGuardia Act, which limits the issuance of injunctions by federal courts in labor disputes, does not apply to a suit seeking enforcement of an agreement to arbitrate.[22]

In a dissenting opinion Justice Frankfurter reiterated his position, set forth in Westinghouse, that Section 301 was merely procedural and could not be "transmuted into a mandate to the federal courts to fashion a whole body of substantive federal law appropriate for the . . . problems raised by collective bargaining."[23] He further argued that there are severe limits of "judicial inventiveness," even for the most imaginative judges. "The law," noted Justice Frankfurter, "is not a 'brooding omnipresence in the sky' . . . and it cannot be drawn from there like nitrogen from the air."[24]

4. Summary and Policy Implications

The effect and importance of *Lincoln Mills* in supplying legal sanctions for arbitration agreements is clear. For the first time the Supreme Court gave judicial recognition and sanction to effective collective bargaining. Contrary to the situation prior to *Lincoln Mills*, in 1957 the Supreme Court declared that agreements to arbitrate were enforceable in the federal courts under Section 301. The judicial remedy now available effectively prevents a union or an employer with

---

fashioning a remedy that will effectuate that policy. The range of judicial inventiveness will be determined by the nature of the problem. . . . Federal interpretation of the federal law will govern, not state law. . . . But state law, if compatible with the purpose of §301, may be resorted to in order to find the rule that will best effectuate the federal policy. . . . Any state law applied, however, will be absorbed as federal law and will not be an independent source of private rights." 353 U.S. at 456–457, 40 LRRM at 2116.

[22]"The question remains whether jurisdiction to compel arbitration of grievance disputes is withdrawn by the Norris-LaGuardia Act, 47 Stat. 70, 29 U.S.C. §101. Section 7 of that Act prescribes stiff procedural requirements for issuing an injunction in a labor dispute. The kinds of acts which had given rise to abuse of the power to enjoin are listed in §4. The failure to arbitrate was not a part and parcel of the abuses against which the Act was aimed. Section 8 of the Norris-LaGuardia Act does, indeed, indicate a congressional policy toward settlement of labor disputes by arbitration, for it denies injunctive relief to any person who has failed to make 'every reasonable effort' to settle the dispute by negotiation, mediation, or 'voluntary arbitration.' Though a literal reading might bring the dispute within the terms of the Act . . . , we see no justification in policy for restricting §301 (a) to damage suits, leaving specific performance of a contract to arbitrate grievance disputes to the inapposite procedural requirements of that Act." 353 U.S. at 457–458, 40 LRRM at 2116–2117.

[23]Id. at 461, 40 LRRM at 2120.

[24]Id. at 461, 40 LRRM at 2121.

overwhelming economic power from imperiously violating its contractual obligations. More important, the "law of collective bargaining" is no longer state law in any practical sense, as it was prior to *Lincoln Mills*. By requiring the judiciary to develop a federal substantive law of collective bargaining, the Court prevented the development of a patchwork system of labor policy, which might have resulted if the Court had allowed state law to be controlling.[25] Three years later the Court issued the landmark Trilogy decisions, which remain the most significant and highly controversial decisions on the subject of judicial accommodation and deference to the arbitral process.

B. Arbitration and the Federal Courts

Section 301 of Taft-Hartley does not establish standards for the review of arbitration awards, including the remedies that arbitrators order when a violation of a collective bargaining agreement is found. Indeed, Section 301 does not mention arbitration. It is only because Section 301 establishes a federal remedy for breaches of labor agreements, and because many such agreements contain an arbitration clause, that the refusal to comply with an award becomes a breach of contract upon which a Section 301 suit may be brought.

On June 20, 1960, the Supreme Court handed down three decisions commonly referred to as the *Steelworkers Trilogy*.[26] In each of these cases the Steelworkers requested the courts

---

[25]The jurisdiction of the courts was later clarified in Charles Dowd Box Co. v. Courtney, 368 U.S. 502, 49 LRRM 2619 (1962), where the Court held that §301 does not divest the state courts of jurisdiction. Section 301 provides that suits of the kind described "may" be brought in the federal district courts, not that they must be. Id. at 506. The Court noted that "nothing in the concept of our federal system prevents state courts from enforcing rights created by federal law." Id. at 507. In Teamsters Local 174 v. Lucas Flour Co., 369 U.S. 95, 49 LRRM 2717 (1962), the Court held that where local laws are incompatible with the principles of federal law, the former must yield to the latter. The Court noted that "the existence of possibly conflicting legal concepts might substantially impede the parties' willingness to agree to contract terms providing for final arbitral or judicial resolution of disputes." Id. at 104, 49 LRRM at 2721. "In enacting §301 Congress intended doctrines of federal labor law uniformly to prevail over inconsistent local rules." Id.

[26]Steelworkers v. American Mfg. Co., 363 U.S. 564, 46 LRRM 2414 (1960); Steelworkers v. Warrior & Gulf Navigation Co., 363 U.S. 574, 46 LRRM 2416 (1960); Steelworkers v. Enterprise Wheel & Car Corp., 363 U.S. 593, 46 LRRM 2423 (1960).

either to order arbitration[27] or to enforce an arbitration award.[28] Although the final case specifically addressed the remedial authority of an arbitrator, a discussion of all three decisions is necessary to understand the relationship to the judiciary to the arbitral institution and the special place that arbitration has occupied since the *Trilogy*. More important, a review of the *Trilogy* cases will provide a framework for understanding the judicially imposed limits placed upon the arbitrator's power to fashion a remedy.

1. The *Steelworkers Trilogy*

In *Steelworkers v. American Manufacturing Co.*,[29] a dispute arose concerning the reinstatement of an employee, determined by his physician to be 25-percent permanently disabled. The union argued that (1) the employee was entitled to reinstatement because his physician had stated that he was able to perform his job, and (2) the seniority provision of the collective bargaining agreement mandated his return. The employer defended on the ground that (1) the union was prohibited from making the claim because the employee had previously accepted a settlement in a workmen's compensation claim against the company, (2) the employee was not physically able to do the work, and (3) the dispute was not arbitrable under the collective bargaining agreement.

The agreement provided that during its term there would be no strikes, unless the employer refused to abide by a decision of the arbitrator. The agreement also set out a detailed grievance procedure with a provision for arbitration of all disputes between the parties "as to the meaning, interpretation and application of the provisions of this agreement." The contract reserved to management the power to suspend or discharge any employee "for cause." Moreover, the agreement contained a provision requiring the employer to employ and promote employees on the principle of seniority "where ability and efficiency are equal."

Unable to resolve the dispute, the union requested arbi-

---

[27]Steelworkers v. American Mfg., Co. and Steelworkers v. Warrior & Gulf Navigation Co., supra note 26.
[28]Steelworkers v. Enterprise Wheel & Car Corp., supra note 26.
[29]Supra note 26.

tration, and, when the employer refused, the union brought suit in district court to compel arbitration. The lower court held that since the employee had accepted a settlement on the basis of his permanent partial disability, he was estopped to claim any seniority or employment rights. The court of appeals affirmed,[30] but for different reasons. After reviewing the evidence, it held on the merits that the grievance was "a frivolous, patently baseless one, not subject to arbitration under the collective bargaining agreement." The appellate court assumed that no arbitrator could find for the union because the contract contained a provision which gave preference in the filling of vacancies to employees based on seniority only if their abilities were relatively equal.[31] On appeal to the Supreme Court, Justice Douglas, writing for the majority, rejected the logic and the holding of *Machinists v. Cutler Hammer, Inc.*[32] "The agreement," said Justice Douglas, "is to submit all grievances to arbitration, not merely those the court will deem meritorious."[33] At the same time Douglas declared that there was no exception in the "no-strike clause and none therefore should be read into the grievance procedure, since one is the quid pro quo for the other.

Delineating the role of the federal courts when called upon to enforce an agreement to arbitrate, Justice Douglas stated:

> The function of the court is very limited when the parties have agreed to submit all questions of contract interpretation to the arbitrator. It is then confined to ascertaining whether the party seeking arbitration is making a claim which on its face is governed by the contract. Whether the moving party is right or wrong is a question of contract interpretation for the arbitrator. In these circumstances the moving party should not be deprived of the arbitrator's judgment, when it was his judgment and all that it connotes that he bargained for.[34]

Justice Douglas went on to say that "the courts therefore have no business weighing the merits of the grievance, [or] considering whether there is equity in the particular claim . . . ."[35] Further, "the processing of even frivolous claims may

---

[30]264 F.2d 624, 43 LRRM 2757 (6th Cir. 1959).
[31]Id. at 628.
[32]271 App. Div. 917, 67 N.Y.S. 2d 317, 19 LRRM 2232 (1947).
[33]363 U.S. at 567–68, 46 LRRM at 2416.
[34]Id. at 568, 46 LRRM at 2415.
[35]Id. at 568, 46 LRRM at 2415–16.

have therapeutic values which those who are not a part of the plant environment may be quite unaware."[36]

The dispute in *Warrior & Gulf*[37] involved the "lay-off" of employees between 1956 and 1958, thus reducing the bargaining unit from 42 to 36. The reduction was due in part to the employer's contracting maintenance work, previously done by unit employees, to other companies. The collective agreement had both a "no-strike" and a "no-lockout" provision and a grievance procedure with arbitration as the final step. The agreement was silent on the subject of subcontracting.

Grievances were filed challenging the action by the company and alleging a partial lockout in violation of the contract. The grievances remained unsettled and when the employer refused arbitration, a suit was commenced by the union requesting the court to issue an order forcing the employer to arbitrate. The district court granted the company's motion to dismiss the complaint.[38] It held after hearing the evidence, much of which concerned the merits of the grievance, that the agreement did not "confide in an arbitrator the right to review the defendant's business judgment in contracting out work."[39] It further held that "the contracting out of repair and maintenance work . . . is strictly a function of management not limited in any respect by the labor agreement involved here."[40] The court of appeals affirmed, the majority holding that the collective agreement had withdrawn from the grievance procedure matters which are strictly a function of management and that contracting fell within that exception.[41] The Supreme Court reversed.

Justice Douglas, joined by six members of the Court, presented a detailed analysis of (1) the nature of the collective bargaining agreement, (2) the role of the arbitrator in interpreting the agreement, and (3) the scope of the judiciary in a labor agreement where there is doubt as to the arbitrability of a grievance.

---

[36]Id. at 568, 46 LRRM at 2416.
[37]Supra note 26.
[38]168 F. Supp. 702, 43 LRRM 2328 (S.D. Ala. 1958).
[39]Id. at 705.
[40]Id.
[41]269 F.2d 633, 44 LRRM 2567 (5th Cir. 1959).

a. Nature of the Agreement

Discussing the nature of the agreement, Justice Douglas cited from an article written by Archibald Cox:[42]

> "[I]t is not unqualifiedly true that a collective-bargaining agreement is simply a document by which the union and employees have imposed upon management limited, express restrictions of its otherwise absolute right to manage the enterprise, so that an employee's claim must fail unless he can point to a specific contract provision upon which the claim is founded. There are too many people, too many problems, too many unforeseeable contingencies to make the words of the contract the exclusive source of rights and duties. One cannot reduce all the rules governing a community like an industrial plant to fifteen or even fifty pages. Within the sphere of collective bargaining, the institutional characteristics and the governmental nature of the collective-bargaining process demand a common law of the shop which implements and furnishes the context of the agreement. We must assume that intelligent negotiators acknowledged so plain a need unless they stated a contrary rule in plain words."
>
> . . .
>
> Apart from matters that the parties specifically exclude, all of the questions on which the parties disagree must therefore come within the scope of the grievance and arbitration provisions of the collective agreement. The grievance procedure is, in other words, a part of the continuous bargaining process. It, rather than a strike, is the terminal point of a disagreement.[43]

b. Role of the Labor Arbitrator

The Court went on to endorse the concept of arbitration as a "means of solving the unforeseeable by molding a system of private law for all the problems which may arise. . . ."[44] It delineated the role of the arbitrator, citing the words of the late Dean Shulman:

> "A proper conception of the arbitrator's function is basic. He is not a public tribunal imposed upon the parties by superior authority which the parties are obliged to accept. He has no general charter to administer justice for a community which

---

[42]Cox, *Reflections upon Labor Arbitration*, 72 Harv. L. Rev. 1482, 1498–1499 (1959).

[43]363 U.S. at 578–580, 46 LRRM 2418, 2419.

[44]Id. at 581, 46 LRRM at 2419.

transcends the parties. He is rather part of a system of self-government created by and confined to the parties. . . . "

The labor arbitrator performs functions which are not normal to the courts; the considerations which help him fashion judgments may indeed be foreign to the competence of courts. . . . The labor arbitrator is usually chosen because of the parties' confidence in his knowledge of the common law of the shop and their trust in his personal judgment to bring to bear considerations which are not expressed in the contract as criteria for judgment. The parties expect that his judgment of a particular grievance will reflect not only what the contract says but, insofar as the collective bargaining agreement permits, such factors as the effect upon productivity of a particular result, its consequence to the morale of the shop, his judgment whether tensions will be heightened or diminished. For the parties' objective in using the arbitration process is primarily to further their common goal of uninterrupted production under the agreement, to make the agreement serve their specialized needs. The ablest judge cannot be expected to bring the same experience and competence to bear upon the determination of a grievance, because he cannot be similarly informed.[45]

c. Scope of Judicial Review

Discussing the scope of judicial review, the court reasoned that in Section 301 of the Labor-Management Relations Act Congress had assigned the courts the duty of determining whether a party has breached its promise to arbitrate. "[A]rbitration," noted the Court, "is a matter of contract and a party cannot be required to submit to arbitration any dispute which he has not agreed so to submit."[46]

Yet, to be consistent with congressional policy in favor of settlement of disputes by the parties through the machinery of arbitration, the judicial inquiry under §301 must be strictly confined to the question whether the reluctant party did agree to arbitrate the grievance or agreed to give the arbitrator power to make the award he made. An order to arbitrate the particular grievance should not be denied unless it may be said with positive assurance that the arbitration clause is not susceptible to an interpretation that covers the asserted dispute. Doubts should be resolved in favor of coverage.[47]

---

[45]Id. at 581–82, 46 LRRM at 2419.
[46]Id. at 582, 46 LRRM at 2419.
[47]Id. at 582–83, 46 LRRM 2419–20 (footnote omitted).

With that, the Court held that the contracting out of work was not necessarily exempted under a provision that "matters which are strictly a function of management shall not be subject to arbitration." Here the grievance procedure also provided that if differences arose or if any local trouble of any kind arose, the grievance procedure should be applicable. Accordingly, the lower court's decision was reversed and the company was ordered to arbitrate the grievance.[48]

The third case, *Steelworkers v. Enterprise Wheel & Car Corp.*[49] centered on enforcement of an actual arbitration award which the company refused to implement. A group of employees left their jobs in protest against the discharge of an employee. Grievances were filed when the employer refused to reinstate the employees until the dispute was settled. When the company refused to arbitrate, a suit was brought for specific enforcement of the arbitration provisions of the agreement. The district court ordered arbitration. When the grievance was later heard by the arbitrator, he awarded reinstatement with back pay, minus pay for a 10-day suspension and such sums as the employees received from other employment (it was the arbitrator's view that the facts warranted at most a suspension of the men for 10 days each). After the discharge but before the arbitration award the collective bargaining agreement had expired. Holding that the agreement imposed an unconditional obligation on the employer, the arbitrator rejected the contention that expiration of the agreement barred reinstatement of the employees.

The company refused to comply with the award. The district court, on petition from the union, directed the employer to comply.[50] The court of appeals reversed.[51] While agreeing that the district court had jurisdiction to enforce an arbitration award under a collective bargaining agreement, it went on to hold that any award for back pay subsequent to the date of termination of the agreement could not be enforced. It also held that the requirement for reinstatement of the discharged employees was likewise unenforceable because the collective bargaining agreement had expired.

---

[48]Id. at 585, 46 LRRM 2421.
[49]363 U.S. 593, 46 LRRM 2423 (1960).
[50]168 F. Supp. 308, 43 LRRM 2291 (S.D. W. Va. 1958).
[51]269 F.2d 327, 44 LRRM 2349 (4th Cir. 1959).

Reversing the court of appeals, the Supreme Court further defined the role of the federal courts in enforcing an arbitration award. Awards should be enforced as long as the arbitrator stays within the scope of the submission agreement and the award is based on his construction of the agreement:

> The refusal of courts to review the merits of an arbitration award is the proper approach to arbitration under collective bargaining agreements. The federal policy of settling labor disputes by arbitration would be undermined if courts had the final say on the merits of the awards.[52]

In this case the Court stated that the opinion of the arbitrator is ambiguous:

> It may be read as based solely upon the arbitrator's view of the requirements of enacted legislation, which would mean that he exceeded the scope of the submission. Or it may be read as embodying a construction of the agreement itself, perhaps with the arbitrator looking to "the law" for help in determining the sense of the agreement. A mere ambiguity in the opinion accompanying an award, which permits the inference that the arbitrator may have exceeded his authority, is not a reason for refusing to enforce the award. Arbitrators have no obligation to the court to give their reasons for an award. To require opinions free of ambiguity may lead arbitrators to play it safe by writing no supporting opinions.[53]

Finally the Court concluded:

> [T]he question of interpretation of the collective bargaining agreement is a question for the arbitrator. It is the arbitrator's construction which was bargained for; and so far as the arbitrator's decision concerns construction of the contract, the courts have no business overruling him because their interpretation of the contract is different from his.[54]

What can be gleaned from the *Trilogy* cases, particularly with regard to remedies? All opinions of the Supreme Court, argues Arbitrator David Feller, must be read in the light of the function they must perform.[55] What function did the Supreme Court have in mind in these cases? According to Feller,

---

[52]363 U.S. at 596, 46 LRRM 2425.
[53]Id. at 597–598, 46 LRRM 2425.
[54]Id. at 599, 46 LRRM 2426.
[55]Feller, *Recent Supreme Court Decisions and the Arbitration Process: Discussion*, in Arbitration and Public Policy, Proceedings of the 14th Annual Meeting, National Academy of Arbitrators, 18 (BNA Books, 1961).

it was not simply to say that the grievances in *American* and *Warrior* were arbitrable, or in the *Enterprise* decision, to say that the award should be enforced. The function was, at least equally, to provide guidance to the lower courts in the hundreds of other cases which the Supreme Court would not be able to review. According to Feller, the problem facing the Court was that lower courts had assumed that they as judges were better able to decide which grievances are foolish and which subjects are covered by the collective bargaining agreement than arbitrators. In Arbitrator Feller's words, "They had, frankly, to be hit over the head."[56]

BNA reports that approximately 96 percent of all collective bargaining agreements contain procedures for the settlement of disputes through arbitration—99 percent in manufacturing and 98 percent in nonmanufacturing.[57] These provisions are among those which may be enforced under Section 301 of Taft-Hartley. Moreover, the Supreme Court has made it clear that Section 301 authorizes the courts to fashion a body of federal common law for the enforcement of collective bargaining contracts and, more specifically, the enforcement of promises to arbitrate. Furthermore, Congress has provided that "final adjustment by a method agreed upon by the parties is declared to be the desirable method for settlement of grievances disputes." As cited by the Court in *American Manufacturing*, this congressional policy can be effectuated only if the means chosen by the parties for settlement of their differences under the agreement is given full play.

It is beyond dispute that the *Steelworkers Trilogy* established labor arbitration as the preferred method of resolving grievances arising from the collective bargaining agreement. Unlike other adjudicators, as noted by Justice Douglas in *Warrior & Gulf*, all doubts are resolved in favor of arbitral jurisdiction. More important, from the standpoint of understanding the remedial power of an arbitrator, an arbitral decision, unlike those of courts, is in theory[58] subject to only the most

---

[56]Id. at 23.

[57]BNA reports that grievance and arbitration procedures are found in 100% of the 400 contracts sampled in a recent study. Basic Patterns in Union Contracts, 33 (BNA Books, 1989).

[58]Christensen, *Judicial Review: As Arbitrators See It—I. The Disguised Review*

limited form of judicial review.[59] The decision of the arbitrator, acting within the power granted him by the agreement, is final, and not reviewable on the merits by any court, unless the party attacking the decision can demonstrate fraud, partiality, or misconduct on the part of the arbitrator.[60] So great is the presumption in favor of the finality and validity of the

---

of the Merits of Arbitration Awards, in Labor Arbitration at the Quarter-Century Mark, Proceedings of the 25th Annual Meeting, National Academy of Arbitrators, 99 (BNA Books, 1973).

[59]Feller provides an excellent example of the significance of according arbitral authority a presumption in favor of finality and validity. A judicial holding adverse to the "reserve clause" in professional football (binding a player to a particular team) can be appealed "all the way to the Supreme Court." But Arbitrator Peter Seitz's decision in the Andy Messersmith case, which achieved for the major-league baseball players almost the same result they sought unsuccessfully to achieve in the Supreme Court in Flood v. Kuhn, 407 U.S. 258 (1972), is, as the owners quickly discovered, virtually unreviewable. See Feller, *The Coming End of Arbitration's Golden Age*, in Arbitration—1976, Proceedings of the 29th Annual Meeting, National Academy of Arbitrators, 97 (BNA Books, 1976).

[60]In *Teamsters Local 767 v. Standard Brands*, 579 F.2d 1282, 1292 n.8, 99 LRRM 2377, 2384 n.8 (5th Cir. 1978), the Fifth Circuit has outlined the "few" recognized situations where an arbitrator's award may be vacated:

An award may be vacated where it is shown that there was fraud, partiality or other misconduct on the part of the arbitrator, see, e.g., Commonwealth Coatings Corp. v. Continental Casualty Co., 393 U.S. 145, 89 S.Ct. 337, 21 L.Ed.2d 301 (1968); or because the award was too vague or ambiguous for enforcement, see, e.g., United Steelworkers v. Enterprise Wheel & Car Corp., 363 U.S. 593, 599, 80 S.Ct. 1358, 4 L.Ed.2d 1424, 46 LRRM 2423 (1960); Bell Aerospace Co. Division of Textron, Inc. v. Local 516, UAW, 2 Cir. 1974, 500 F.2d 921, 923, 86 LRRM 3240; Hanford Atomic Metal Trades Council, AFL-CIO v. General Electric Co., 9 Cir. 1965, 353 F.2d 302, 61 LRRM 2004; or where the award conflicted with the demands of a statute, see Banyard v. NLRB, 1974, 164 U.S.App.D.C. 235, 505 F.2d 342, 87 LRRM 2001 (award authorizing company to violate state law held void as against public policy); Associated Milk Dealers, Inc. v. Milk Drivers Local 753, 7 Cir. 1970, 422 F.2d 546, 553, 73 LRRM 2435 (arbitration would not be ordered if clause to be interpreted violated antitrust laws); Nursing Home Union Local 1115 v. Hialeah Convalescent Home, 348, F. Supp. 405, 411, 81 LRRM 2312 (S.D. Fla. 1972) (conflict with national wage-price control policy).

Arbitrator Theodore St. Antoine has noted that, in addition to the above reasons, many courts feel compelled to test an arbitral award against some minimum standard of rationality. See *Judicial Review of Labor Arbitration Awards: A Second Look at Enterprise Wheel and Its Progeny*, in Arbitration—1977, Proceedings of the 30th Annual Meeting, National Academy of Arbitrators, 29 (BNA Books, 1978). Professor Bernard Meltzer has put it this way: "In short, under the Trilogy, arbitrators have jurisdiction to be wrong but not goofy. Judges, experienced as they are with judicial, arbitral, and academic writing, appreciate the haziness of that distinction." See *After the Labor Arbitration Award: The Public Policy Defense*, Vol. 10–24 Indus. Rel. L.J. 241, 243 (1988).

An award may also be vacated because of "gross error" (i.e., where the central fact underlying an arbitrator's decision is erroneous). See, e.g., Kalish v. Illinois Educ. Ass'n, 116 Ill. Dec. 816, 818, 519 N.E.2d 1031, 1033 (Ill. App. 1st Dist. 1988) ("gross errors of judgment in law or mistake of fact can be used to vacate an award where the mistakes or errors are apparent on the face of the award"). Vacation may also result when the union did not fairly represent the employees in the arbitration proceeding. Hines v. Anchor Motor Freight, 424 U.S. 554, 91 LRRM 2481 (1976).

award that the Court has held that the finality provision has sufficient force to surmount even instances of mistake.[61]

2. *Paperworkers* v. *Misco, Inc.*: A Reaffirmation of the *Trilogy* Standard of Review

The Supreme Court has recently reaffirmed arbitration as the preferred method of dispute settlement in the labor field. In *Misco*[62] the Supreme Court reversed a Fifth Circuit decision[63] which had refused to enforce an arbitrator's award reinstating (with back pay and full seniority) an employee fired for violating a company rule against possessing intoxicants and controlled substances on company premises. The grievant, Isiah Cooper, was apprehended by police in the backseat of someone else's car in the employer's parking lot with marijuana smoke in the air and a lighted marijuana cigarette in the front-seat ashtray. A police search of Cooper's own car on the lot revealed a plastic scales case and marijuana gleanings, although the company did not learn of this until just five days before the hearing. The fact did not become known to the union until the hearing began. Cooper was discharged for violating a rule against possession or use of controlled substances on company property. Cooper then filed a grievance which proceeded to arbitration on the stipulated issue whether the company had just cause for the discharge under the rule and, if not, what should be the appropriate remedy. The arbitrator upheld the grievance and ordered Cooper's reinstatement, finding that the cigarette incident was insufficient proof that Cooper was using or possessed marijuana on company property. Because, at the time of the discharge, the employer was not aware of, and thus did not rely upon, the fact that marijuana had been found in Cooper's own car, the arbitrator refused to accept this fact into evidence. The District Court vacated the award and the Court of Appeals for the Fifth Circuit affirmed, ruling that reinstatement would violate a public policy against the operation of dangerous machinery by persons under the influence of drugs or alcohol. Speaking

---

[61]See Hines v. Anchor Motor Freight, supra note 60.
[62]484 U.S. 29, 126 LRRM 3113 (1987).
[63]768 F.2d 739, 120 LRRM 2119 (5th Cir. 1985).

through Justice White, the Court again acknowledged the great deference usually accorded arbitration awards by the courts. In the words of the Court:

> Because the parties have contracted to have disputes settled by an arbitrator chosen by them rather than by a judge, it is the arbitrator's view of the facts and of the meaning of the contract that they have agreed to accept. Courts thus do not sit to hear claims of factual or legal error by an arbitrator as an appellate court does in reviewing decisions of lower courts. To resolve disputes about the application of a collective-bargaining agreement, an arbitrator must find facts and a court may not reject those findings simply because it disagrees with them.[64]

Stating that, normally, an arbitrator is authorized to disagree with the sanction imposed for employee misconduct, the Court had this to say about the power of an arbitrator to fashion a remedy.

> So, too, where it is contemplated that the arbitrator will determine remedies for contract violations that he finds, courts have no authority to disagree with his honest judgment in that respect.[65]

Prior to *Misco*, the circuit courts had been in disagreement over whether an arbitration award must require the violation of a positive law before a reviewing court may refuse to enforce the award based on the public policy exception. Some courts had taken a broad view of the public policy exception,[66] while

---

[64]126 LRRM at 3117.

[65]Id.

[66]See Oil Workers Local No. 4-228 v. Union Oil of Cal., 818 F.2d 437, 442–443, 125 LRRM 2630 (5th Cir. 1987) (finding that reinstatement of employee fired for use and sale of drugs after employee failed postarbitration drug test could violate public policy; case remanded for reconsideration by arbitrator); E.I. Du Pont de Nemours & Co. v. Grasselli Employees Indep. Ass'n of E. Chicago, 790 F.2d 611, 616, 122 LRRM 2217 (7th Cir. 1986), cert. denied, 470 U.S. 853, 123 LRRM 2592 (1986); (enforcing award reinstating employee discharged after suffering mental breakdown, but rejecting narrow view of public-policy exception requiring violation of a positive law); Postal Serv. v. Postal Workers, 736 F.2d 822, 826, 116 LRRM 2870 (1st Cir. 1984) (award requiring reinstatement of employee convicted of embezzling funds was unenforceable as violative of public policy); Meat Cutters Local 540 v. Great W. Food Co., 712 F.2d 122, 124–125, 114 LRRM 2001 (5th Cir. 1983) (award reinstating truck driver who admittedly consumed alcohol while on duty violative of public policy); Meat Cutters Local P-1236 v. Jones Dairy Farm, 680 F.2d 1142, 110 LRRM 2805 (7th Cir. 1982) (refusing to enforce award that found company valid requiring employees to first report all USDA violations to management rather than USDA inspectors.

others had taken a narrow focus.[67] The Court ruled that for a court to refuse to enforce an arbitrator's interpretation of a collective bargaining agreement, the "contract as interpreted [must] violate 'some explicit public policy' that is 'well defined and dominant, and is to be ascertained by reference to the laws and legal precedents and not from general considerations of supposed interests.' "[68] The Court found that the reinstatement of the discharged employee would not create an explicit conflict with other laws and legal precedents and the appellate court's public policy formulation based on "general considerations of supposed public interest" was insufficient to justify the court's refusal to enforce the award.

Since the *Misco* Court did not specifically address whether a court may refuse to enforce an arbitrator's award on public policy grounds only when the award itself violates a positive law or requires unlawful conduct by the employer, the courts[69]

---

[67]See Professional Admr's v. Kopper-Glo Fuel, 819 F.2d 639, 643–644, 125 LRRM 3010 (6th Cir. 1987) (award permitting trustees of pension and welfare funds to unilaterally increase contribution rates contrary to public policy where federal law made wages and benefits mandatory bargaining issue); Lithographers Local 1 v. Stearns & Beale, 812 F.2d 763, 769–770, 124 LRRM 2809 (2d Cir. 1987) (award based on conclusion directly in conflict with NLRB ruling unenforceable as violative of public policy); Postal Serv. v. Letter Carriers, 810 F.2d 1239, 1241, 124 LRRM 2644 (D.C. Cir. 1987) (enforcing award reinstating postal carrier convicted of unlawful delay of mail where award did not compel unlawful action or violate clearly defined statutory or case law); Northwest Airlines v. Air Line Pilots, 808 F.2d 76, 78, 124 LRRM 2300 (D.C. Cir. 1986), cert. denied, 486 U.S. 1014, 128 LRRM 2296 (1988) (enforcing award reinstating pilot who consumed alcohol prior to flying where award did not require violation of any clear statutory or case law); Bevles Co. v. Teamsters Local 986, 791 F.2d 1391, 1392, 122 LRRM 2666 (9th Cir. 1986), cert. denied, 56 USLW 3414, 127 LRRM 2048 (1987) (upholding award of reinstatement and back pay to two undocumented aliens where award did not subject employer to criminal or civil liability); Postal Workers v. Postal Serv., 789 F.2d 1, 8, 112 LRRM 2094 (D.C. Cir. 1986) (enforcing award reinstating employee after arbitrator refused to accept evidence received from employee without issuance of *Miranda*-type warnings, rejecting public policy basis for reversing arbitrator; court reasoned that it is not clear that reference to "public policy" denotes anything more than what courts have said over years construing *Enterprise Wheel*); Painters Dist. Council 48 (Orange Belt) v. Kashak, 774 F.2d 985, 990, 120 LRRM 3036 (9th Cir. 1985) (enforcing award requiring employer to turn over books and records as not violative of public policy).

[68]126 LRRM at 3119, quoting W.R. Grace & Co. v. Rubber Workers Local 759, 461 U.S. 757, 766, 113 LRRM 2641, 2645 (1983).

[69]Some circuits have retained a broad interpretation of the exception. See Daniel Constr. Co. v. Electrical Workers (IBEW) Local 257, 856 F.2d 1174, 1182–83, 129 LRRM 2429 (8th Cir. 1988), cert. denied, 57 USLW 3551, 130 LRRM 2656 (1989) (enforcing award of back pay to employees of nuclear plant dismissed for failure to pass psychological test which allegedly screened security risks; applying *Misco*, court stated that public policy requires that unstable employees be denied access to sensitive areas of nuclear plant); Postal Serv. v. Letter Carriers, 847 F.2d 775, 777, 128 LRRM 2842 (11th Cir. 1988) (approving, in dictum, district court's refusal to enforce arbitrator's award reinstating employee convicted of stealing from mail on public

and the commentators remain in conflict over the correct application of *Misco*.[70] While the *Misco* Court placed the public policy defense against labor arbitration awards within the general traditions of contract law, in the end the Court provided little guidance regarding the scope of that defense.

What is important for this analysis is that the *Misco* Court specifically rejected, as exceeding a reviewing court's authority under the *Trilogy* standard, techniques employed by the district court, including: (1) asserting a public policy without substantiating its existence within existing laws and legal precedents, thereby failing to distinguish an explicit and "well defined and dominant" policy as opposed to a "general consideration of supposed public interests"; (2) second-guessing the arbitrator's fact-finding function by drawing on factual inferences not made by the arbitrator; and (3) assailing the arbitrator's reasonable construction of the "just cause" provision, and of the rules of evidence and procedure appropriate to that function under the parties' collective bargaining agreement.

---

policy grounds, but affirming decision on other grounds); Iowa Elec. Light & Power Co. v. Electrical Workers (IBEW) Local 204, 834 F.2d 1424, 1427 n.3, 127 LRRM 2049 (8th Cir. 1987) (vacating award reinstating machinists discharged for intentionally violating federal nuclear power safety rules and finding that court need not find award illegal before public-policy exception is applicable). Other courts have applied the narrow view. Stead Motors Walnut Creek v. Machinists Lodge 1173, 843 F.2d 357, 358–359, 127 LRRM 3213 (9th Cir. 1988) (vacating award reinstating employee discharged for improperly tightening wheel's lug bolts on two occasions as against public policy because award violated specific section of California Vehicle Code); Delta Air Lines v. Air Line Pilots, 861 F.2d 665, 130 LRRM 2014 (11th Cir. 1988) (System Board of Adjustment's award that airline lacked just cause for discharging pilot who flew while intoxicated violated well-established public policy, reasoning that established public policy condemns performance of employment activities in manner engaged in by employee); Georgia Power Co. v. Electrical Workers (IBEW) Local 84, 707 F. Supp. 531, 130 LRRM 2419 (N.D. Ga. 1989) (finding well-defined and dominant public policy against operation of hazardous equipment by employees under influence of drugs). Still other courts have expressly declined to join the debate. Postal Serv. v. Letter Carriers, 839 F.2d 146, 150, 127 LRRM 2593 (3d Cir. 1988) (expressly declining to reach issue of whether award must first require violation of positive law or require unlawful conduct before public policy exception is applicable).

[70]The general trend is in favor of interpreting *Misco* as approving the more traditional narrow view of the public-policy exception. See Note, *Judicial Deference to Grievance Arbitration in the Private Sector: Saving Grace in the Search for the Well-Defined Public Policy Exception*, 42 U. Miami L. Rev. 767, 798 (1988); Note, *The Public Policy Exception to Judicial Deferral of Labor Arbitration Awards—How Far Should Expansion Go?*, 39 S.C.L. Rev. 465, 491 (1988); Note, *Public Policy Exception to the General Rule of Judicial Deference to Labor Arbitration Awards: United Paperworkers International Union v. Misco, Inc., 108 S.Ct. 364 (1987)*, 57 U. Cin. L. Rev. 819, 831 (1988).

The application and implication of the *Trilogy* and *Misco* as applied to the general remedial power of an arbitrator is examined below.

C. The Collective Bargaining Agreement and the Arbitrator's Power to Formulate Remedies

Unlike the executory agreements to arbitrate that were at issue in *American Manufacturing* and *Warrior & Gulf*, *Enterprise Wheel* directly addressed the question of a court's role in reviewing an arbitrator's interpretation of a collective bargaining agreement. The Court stated that "[the arbitrator's] award is legitimate only so long as it draws its essence from the collective bargaining agreement. When the arbitrator's words manifest an infidelity to this obligation, courts have no choice but to refuse enforcement of the award."[71] At the same time, however, the Court realized that labor arbitration must remain flexible in order to function effectively in an industrial relations setting. Accordingly, the Court concluded that the arbitrator must have wide latitude in formulating remedies:

> When an arbitrator is commissioned to interpret and apply the collective bargaining agreement, he is to bring his informed judgment to bear in order to reach a fair solution of a problem. *This is especially true when it comes to formulating remedies.* There the need is for flexibility in meeting a wide variety of situations. The draftsmen may never have thought of what specific remedy should be awarded to meet a particular contingency. Nevertheless, an arbitrator is confined to interpretation and application of the collective bargaining agreement; he does not sit to dispense his own brand of industrial justice. [Emphasis added.][72]

The same theme of wide remedial power was again stressed by the Court in *John Wiley & Sons v. Livingston.*[73] According to the Court, the "collective bargaining agreement is not an ordinary contract . . . . Central to the peculiar status and function of a collective bargaining agreement is the fact . . . that it is not in any real sense the simple product of a consensual

---

[71]Steelworkers v. Enterprise Wheel & Car Corp., 363 U.S. 593, 597, 46 LRRM 2423, 2425 (1960).
[72]Id. at 597, 46 LRRM at 2425.
[73]376 U.S. 543, 55 LRRM 2769 (1964).

relationship."[74] Therefore the Court directed arbitrators to operate "within the flexible procedures of arbitration" to fashion solutions "which would avoid disturbing labor relations."[75]

The basic philosophy of *Enterprise Wheel* was to elevate the arbitrator to a special status by emphasizing that there would be no interference with his award simply because a reviewing court differed with him in his interpretation of the contract. At the same time, as noted by the Third Circuit, the Supreme Court held a "checkrein" on the arbitrator, confining his zone of action to the "four corners of the collective bargaining agreement."[76] Writing for the Seventh Circuit, Judge Richard Posner has astutely noted the problem with the "essence" test:

> It might in retrospect have been better if the Court had not said "draws its essence from the collective bargaining agreement," arresting as this formula is (it has displaced all its rivals in the marketplace of judicial formulas), but instead had made the test simply whether the arbitrator had exceeded the powers delegated to him by the parties. That is the test in the federal arbitration statute, see 9 U.S.C. §10(d), and the Railway Labor Act is quite similar, see 45 U.S.C. §153 First (q). In meaning if not in words, the test is the same under all three statutes.[77]

Judge Posner goes on to argue that the problem with the expression "draws its essence from the collective bargaining agreement" is that it invites setting aside awards "because the judge is not satisfied that the award has a basis in a particular provision of the contract."[78]

One problem that has become apparent from the cases that have followed *Enterprise* is that of formulating a consistent and workable standard to be used by arbitrators and by the courts in exercising its function of review. An arbitrator cannot, "simply by making the right noises—noises of contract interpretation— . . . shield from judicial correction an outlandish disposition of a grievance."[79]

The *Enterprise* Court does note that in formulating rem-

---

[74]Id. at 550.
[75]Id. at 551–552 n.5.
[76]Ludwig Honold Mfg. Co. v. Fletcher, 405 F.2d 1123, 70 LRRM 2368 (3d Cir. 1969).
[77]Ethyl Corp. v. Steelworkers, 768 F.2d 180, 119 LRRM 3566, 3568 (7th Cir. 1985).
[78]Id., 119 LRRM at 3568.
[79]Id. at 3570.

edies the arbitrator "may . . . look for guidance from many sources. . . ."[80] Moreover, in *Warrior & Gulf*, the Court further explains that "the labor arbitrator's 'source of law' is not confined to the express provisions of the contract, since the industrial common law—the practices of the industry and the shop—is equally a part of the collective bargaining agreement although not expressed in it." The arbitrator, in his task of interpreting the parties' agreement, is entitled to take into account "such factors as the effect upon productivity of a particular result, its consequences to the morale of the shop, [and] his judgment whether tensions will be heightened or diminished."[81] Yet, again, the decision must "draw its essence" from the collective bargaining agreement. "It is only when the arbitrator *must* have based his award on some body of thought, or feeling, or policy, or law that is outside the contract . . . that the award can be said not to 'draw its essence from the collective bargaining agreement.' "[82]

Noting this state of ambivalence between the presumption of finality and the "essence test,"[83] one commentator has correctly stated that the name of the game is determining what constitutes a construction or interpretation of the contract.[84] And while no set standards exist for determining when an award and a corresponding remedy will draw their essence from the agreement, the courts have made attempts to flesh out and make meaningful the *Enterprise* rule. Thus, the Third Circuit has explained the "essence test" as follows:

> [A] labor arbitrator's award does "draw its essence from the collective bargaining agreement" if the interpretation can in

---

[80]363 U.S. at 596, 46 LRRM 2415.

[81]Steelworkers v. Warrior & Gulf Navigation Co., 363 U.S. 574, 46 LRRM 2416 (1960).

[82]Ethyl Corp. v. Steelworkers, supra note 77.

[83]Arbitrator Theodore St. Antoine has argued that *Enterprise Wheel* exhibits an ambivalence about how far it wishes to go in embracing finality: "In insisting that an enforceable award must 'draw its essence from the collective bargaining agreement,' and must not, for example, be based solely upon 'the requirements of enacted legislation,' the Court plainly appears to authorize *some* substantive examination. This is a risky invitation, because a number of courts will inevitably seize upon any opening to intervene in cases of alleged 'gross error' in construction." St. Antoine, Supra note 60, at 40.

Arbitrator Tom Christensen has contended that the bench mark that the award must "draw its essence from the contract" has become only a basis for the very judicial review of the merits of a dispute which Enterprise attempts to prohibit. Christensen, supra note 58, at 106.

[84]Christensen, supra note 58, at 103.

any rational way be derived from the agreement, viewed in the light of its language, its context, and any other indicia of the parties' intention; only where there is a manifest disregard of the agreement, totally unsupported by principles of contract construction and the law of the shop, may a reviewing court disturb the award.[85]

Similarly, the Ninth Circuit has stated that "if on its face, the award represents a plausible interpretation of the contract in the context of the parties' conduct, judicial inquiry ceases and the award must be affirmed."[86] In another decision, the Ninth Circuit declared that an award drew its essence from the agreement where it is "possible for an honest intellect to interpret the words of the contract and reach the result the arbitrator reached."[87] The Fifth Circuit has likewise refused to disturb an award unless it is "so unfounded in reason and fact, so unconnected with the wording and purpose of the collective bargaining agreement as to 'manifest an infidelity to the obligation of the arbitrator.' "[88] The Court of Appeals for the Sixth Circuit has declared that "if an examination of the record before the arbitrator reveals no support whatever for his determination, his award must be vacated."[89] And in *Misco* the Supreme Court stated that:

> Even in the very rare instances where an arbitrator's procedural aberrations rise to the level of affirmative misconduct, as a rule the court must not foreclose further proceedings by settling the merits according to its own judgment of the appropriate result, since this step would improperly substitute a judicial determination for the arbitrator's decision that the parties bargained

---

[85]Ludwig Honold Mfg. Co. v. Fletcher, supra note 76, 70 LRRM at 2371.

[86]Holly Sugar Corp. v. Distillery Workers, 412 F.2d 899, 71 LRRM 2841, 2844 (9th Cir. 1969).

[87]Newspaper Guild, San Francisco-Oakland v. Tribune Publishing Co., 407 F.2d 1327, 70 LRRM 3184 (9th Cir. 1969). See also Safeway Stores v. Bakery & Confectionery Workers Local 111, 390 F.2d 79, 82, 67 LRRM 2646, 2648 (5th Cir. 1968) ("so palpably faulty that no judge, or group of judges could ever conceivably have made such a ruling"); Timken Co. v. Steelworkers Local 1123, 482 F.2d 1012, 83 LRRM 2814 (6th Cir. 1973) ("unless the award manifests a clear infidelity to the arbitrator's obligation of drawing the 'essence' of the award from the bargaining agreement a court must refuse to substitute its judgment on the merits for that of the arbitrator"); Teamsters Local 784 v. Ulry-Talbert Co., 330 F.2d 562, 55 LRRM 2979 (8th Cir. 1964) (authority must be found or legitimately assumed from terms of arbitration agreement).

[88]Railroad Trainmen v. Central of Ga. Railway, 415 F.2d 403, 415, 71 LRRM 3042 (5th Cir. 1969), cert. denied, 396 U.S. 1008, 73 LRRM 2120 (1970).

[89]Storer Broadcasting Co. v. Television & Radio Artists, 600 F.2d 45, 101 LRRM 2497, 2499 (6th Cir. 1979), cert. denied, 454 U.S. 1099, 108 LRRM 3152 (1981).

for in the collective-bargaining agreement. Instead, the court should simply vacate the award, thus leaving open the possibility of further proceedings if they are permitted under the terms of the agreement. The court also has the authority to remand for further proceedings when this seems appropriate.[90]

At the very least the reported decisions indicate that a particular remedy should not be disturbed merely because the courts' reading of the agreement is different from that of the arbitrator. As Justice Douglas noted, the question of the interpretation of an agreement is a question for the arbitrator. It is his construction that was bargained for, and so far as the arbitrator's decision concerns the construction of the contract, the courts should not overrule him because their interpretation of the contract is different from his.[91] The arbitrator can be wrong, or even clearly wrong, so long as he is not doing something other than interpreting the parties' collective bargaining agreement.[92]

1. Arbitrator's Power to Specify Remedies When the Contract Is Silent

While a contract may contain provisions detailing what remedies should be applied to compensate for a particular violation,[93] collective bargaining agreements commonly omit such provisions. With few exceptions, arbitrators[94] and

---

[90]Paperworkers v. Misco, Inc., 484 U.S. 29, 126 LRRM 3113, 3118 n.10 (1987).

[91]Steelworkers v. Enterprise Wheel & Car Corp., 363 U.S. 593, 599, 46 LRRM 2423 (1960).

[92]Ethyl Corp. v. Steelworkers, 768 F.2d 180, 119 LRRM 3566, 3569 (7th Cir. 1985) ("all this just amounts to saying that the arbitrator may have been wrong, maybe even clearly wrong; it does not show that he was doing something other than interpreting the contract.").

[93]See, e.g., Operating Eng'rs Local 9 v. Shank-Artukovich, 751 F.2d 364, 118 LRRM 2157, 2158 (10th Cir. 1985) (where contract provided that if no individual is found entitled to damages for employer's violation of manning provision, company must pay damages to union training fund).

[94]See, e.g., Crane, *The Use and Abuse of Arbitral Power*, in Labor Arbitration at the Quarter-Century Mark, Proceedings of the 25th Annual Meeting, National Academy of Arbitrators, 66, 72 (BNA Books, 1973) ("When a labor agreement is silent about an arbitrator's power to formulate a remedy if he finds a violation, he presumably has the power to formulate what he deems a proper remedy 'so long as it draws its essence from the collective bargaining agreement,' according to what Mr. Justice Douglas said when he spoke for the U.S. Supreme Court in the *Enterprise Wheel & Car Corp.* case."); Gorske, *Arbitration Back-Pay Awards*, 10 Lab. L.J. 18, 19 (1959) ("We do find in the reported cases of arbitrators not only consistent assertions of implied jurisdiction to award back pay and to fashion remedies, but also strong statements to the effect that this is essential to the process itself."). See also Interstate

courts[95] uniformly agree that an arbitral appointment carries with it the inherent power to specify an appropriate remedy. Perhaps the best explanation of the policy reasons for concluding that the power to formulate a remedy is implied from the appointment comes from Arbitrator W. Willard Wirtz in the much-quoted *International Harvester Co.* decision:[96]

> The conclusion that no money arbitration award is proper regarding contract provisions which do not specifically provide for it would have two effects. The first would be the substitution of some other method of settlement in the place of arbitration. The second would be the cluttering up of the contract with a lot of "liquidated damage" provisions which would invite more trouble than they could ever be expected to prevent. It will be unfortunate if collective bargaining agreements develop along the lines of the revenue laws, with provision necessarily being made for every little hair-line question which may arise between adverse parties presenting conflicting interests. They will lose their effectiveness when they become so involved that laymen cannot follow or understand them. It would contribute dangerously to that tendency if it were required that every contract clause had to include a damages provision. This is the kind of thing which it must be assumed the parties intended would be handled in the light of the applicability of a particular clause to the particular problems that might arise under it.[97]

Indus., 46 LA 879, 881 (Howlett, 1966) ("If arbitrators lacked power to require affirmative action unless specifically so authorized, many arbitration awards would be nullified."); Aetna Portland Cement Co., 41 LA 219, 222 (Dworkin, 1963) (absent contract language controlling arbitrator's authority, precise form of relief must rest with arbitrator's judgment and discretion); Lucky Stores, 70-1 ARB ¶8271, at 3902 (Feller, 1969).

[95]See, e.g., Electrical Workers (IUE) v. Peerless Pressed Metal Corp., 489 F.2d 768, 82 LRRM 3089 (1st Cir.), cert. denied, 414 U.S. 1022, 84 LRRM 2683 (1973); (fact that agreement is silent as to remedy cannot be of note in claim for vacation of award); Children's Hosp. v. Minnesota Nurses Ass'n, 265 N.W.2d 649, 98 LRRM 2614 (Minn. 1978) (arbitrators did not exceed authority under clause providing that "any controversy" arising over "interpretation or the adherence" of contract terms was subject to binding arbitration; reinstatement with back pay is proper notwithstanding absence in agreement as to remedies to be provided; arbitrators are free to fashion remedy which they deem appropriate in exercise of discretion); Safeway Stores v. Teamsters Local 70, 80 Cal.App.3d 998, 746 Cal. Rptr. 139, 98 LRRM 2795 (1978) (72-hour notice requirement ordered by arbitrator was sustained notwithstanding any reference in agreement; "just cause" not defined and, therefore, what constitutes just cause is for arbitrator to determine); Lynchburg Foundry Co. Div. v. Steelworkers Local 2556, 404 F.2d 259, 69 LRRM 2878 (4th Cir. 1968); Machinists Lodge 12 v. Cameron Iron Works, 292 F.2d 112, 48 LRRM 2516 (5th Cir. 1961), cert. denied, 368 U.S. 926, 49 LRRM 2173 (1961); Kroger Co. v. Teamsters Local 661, 380 F.2d 728, 65 LRRM 2573 (6th Cir. 1967); Steelworkers v. Northwest Steel Rolling Mills, 324 F.2d 479, 54 LRRM 2552 (9th Cir. 1963); Electric Specialty Co. v. Electrical Workers (IBEW) Local 1069, 222 F. Supp. 314, 55 LRRM 2574 (D. Conn. 1963).

[96]9 LA 894 (Wirtz, 1947).

[97]Id. at 896.

Arbitrator William Eaton has likewise observed:

> It is often the case in industrial disputes . . . that the fashioning of a remedy appropriate to a right is required. The necessity for this is founded in the common law maxim that where there is a right, there is a remedy. That maxim, in turn, is derived from the simple realization that where a right is purportedly granted, but where no remedy is awarded when that right is violated, the right itself is meaningless.[98]

Arbitrator C. Allen Foster, in awarding a union $400 in "damages" for the employer's improper assignment of work to another craft, has also found authority to fashion a remedy even though the agreement is silent:

> The Company may complain that I lack explicit authority under the contract to make such an award. This criticism may be levied against any award that goes beyond a statement that one party has violated the contract. The contract is silent on the subject of remedies for its breach. It contains no explicit authority for the award of back pay, the reinstatement of improperly discharged workers or the issuance of injuctions. Yet arbitrators routinely make these awards. An arbitrator is more than an authoritative reader of a contract: he is an impartial arbiter of industrial disputes, empowered to make binding adjudications within the intent, as well as the strict letter, of the contract.[99]

In *Phillips Chemical Co.*,[100] Arbitrator Clyde Emery declared that "[t]he power merely to decide that the Agreement has been violated, without power to redress the injury, would be futility in the extreme. . . . jurisdiction means the power to grant relief."

Likewise, Arbitrator Robben Fleming has observed that in most instances an arbitrator's remedy power is implied, rather than specific, since most agreements do not specifically bestow such power upon the arbitrator.[101] Arbitrators have quite uniformly held, writes Fleming, that the parties were not engaging in an academic exercise in seeking a ruling as to whether the contract has been violated, and that the power

---

[98]Air Line Pilots Ass'n and Northwest Airlines, ALPA Case No. CHI-60-73-F (Eaton, 1975).
[99]Celanese Fiber Co., 72 LA 271, 276 n.2 (Foster, 1972).
[100]17 LA 721, 722 (Emery, 1951).
[101]*Arbitrators and the Remedy Power*, 48 Va. L. Rev. 1199 (1962).

to decide the contract violation must therefore carry with it the power to award a remedy.

David Feller, in an address before the National Academy of Arbitrators, has reflected what we feel is the better perspective as follows:

> My argument ... has been only that the arbitrator, in awarding remedies, should award only those which he finds implicit in the agreement. That does not advance us very far if we assume that the parties normally intend to provide implicitly in their agreement that the arbitrator shall have authority to award damages or, to put it in the words used by those arbitrators who have awarded damages, "by necessary implication the parties contracted for arbitration on the implied condition that if a violation were found an arbitrator could frame an appropriate remedy to undo the wrong that has been done." Or, as an arbitrator in a second case put it, "It has always been the law that where there is a wrong there must be a remedy; and absent a specific limitation on possible remedies, a Court or arbitrator should order a remedy which is based on principles of equity and justice." If a collective agreement can be read as authorizing an arbitrator to "frame an appropriate remedy to undo the wrong that has been done," or, as in the second case quoted, to "order a remedy which is based on the principles of equity and justice," then my first proposition does not advance the inquiry very far, but simply changes the locus of the source of the arbitrator's authority.[102]

While at one time courts may have been averse to recognizing arbitral power to fashion remedies where no explicit jurisdictional grant appears in the agreement,[103] clearly this

---

[102]Feller, *Remedies: New and Old Problems: I. Remedies in Arbitration: Old Problems Revisited*, in Arbitration Issues for the 1980s, Proceedings of the 34th Annual Meeting, National Academy of Arbitrators, 109, 116 (BNA Books, 1982), quoting Schott's Bakery, 69-1 ARB ¶8118 (Jenkins, 1968), at 3397–3398, and Vallejo Times-Herald, 76-2 ARB ¶8746 (Walsh, 1976), at 6720, respectively.

[103]See, e.g., Refinery Employees v. Continental Oil, 268 F.2d 447, 44 LRRM 2388 (5th Cir.), cert. denied, 361 U.S. 896, 45 LRRM 2131 (1959) (where agreement contained provision for arbitration of differences which related to interpretation or performance of agreement but was silent as to remedy for misassigned overtime work and as to arbitrators' power to provide a remedy or impose a penalty, remedy was not a matter of interpretation or performance, and, therefore, arbitrators lacked authority to award damages for misassigned overtime and to thereby contravene management's policy of paying only for work performed); Retail Clerks Local 782 v. Sav-On Groceries, 508 F.2d 500, 88 LRRM 3205 (10th Cir. 1975) (back-pay award vacated where parties only submitted issue of whether employer exercised fairness in judging qualifications of grievant); Leather Goods Workers Local 66 v. Neevel Luggage Mfg. Co., 325 F.2d 992, 55 LRRM 2153 (8th Cir. 1964) (portion of award (back pay) denied enforcement where parties submitted only issue of whether layoff was proper).

is no longer the prevailing view. Writing for the Seventh Circuit, Judge Posner outlined the thinking of the courts as follows:

> Collective bargaining agreements often say little or nothing about the arbitrator's remedial powers; yet it cannot be that he has none; and since he derives all his powers from the agreement, the agreement must implicitly grant him remedial powers when there is no explicit grant.[104]

Judge Posner pointed out that the Supreme Court in *Enterprise Wheel* went on to uphold the arbitrator's remedy—an award of back pay after the expiration of the collective bargaining agreement—even though the remedy had not been mentioned in the agreement.[105]

Citing the language of the Supreme Court in *Enterprise Wheel*, the Fourth Circuit, in *Tobacco Workers Local 317 v. P. Lorillard Corp.*,[106] stated that part of what the parties bargain for when they include an arbitration provision in the agreement is the "informed judgment" the arbitrator can bring to bear on a grievance. Although the agreement was silent as to remedies, the court of appeals, reversing the lower court, held that the fashioning of an appropriate remedy was not an "addition" to the contract. Attention is called to the court's reasoning:

> The Company argues that retroactive pay for unjustly denying an employee a promotion is an "obligation not explicity [sic] provided for in this Agreement." But the agreement contains no provision for any kind of remedy in cases involving promotions. Carried to its logical conclusion, the Company's argument would mean that an arbitrator would have jurisdiction to determine that the Company had violated the seniority provisions with respect to promotions, but would have no authority to direct the Company to correct its violation. Arbitration would thus be rendered meaningless.[107]

In *Minute Maid Co. v. Citrus Workers Local 444*[108] an

---

[104]Miller Brewing v. Brewery Workers Local 9, 739 F.2d 1159, 1163, 116 LRRM 3130, 3133 (7th Cir. 1984), cert. denied, 469 U.S. 1160, 118 LRRM 2192 (1985).
[105]Id. at 1163.
[106]448 F.2d 949, 78 LRRM 2273 (4th Cir. 1971), reversing 314 F. Supp. 513, 75 LRRM 2437 (M.D.N.C. 1970).
[107]Id., 78 LRRM at 2278.
[108]331 F.2d 280, 56 LRRM 2095 (5th Cir. 1964). In an earlier case, Machinists Lodge 12 v. Cameron Iron Works, supra note 95, 48 LRRM at 2520, The Fifth Circuit

arbitrator, concluding that an employee had been improperly discharged, ordered reinstatement with back pay. The employer argued that because the agreement did not provide for a back-pay remedy, the award should not be enforced. Finding that the contract at issue did not exclude from the arbitrator's jurisdiction either the subject matter or the remedy adopted by the arbitrator, the Court of Appeals for the Fifth Circuit rejected the employer's contention that the arbitrator exceeded his authority under the agreement.

Similarly, the Fifth Circuit, in *Steelworkers v. United States Gypsum Co.*,[109] upheld an arbitrator's award ordering a "successor" employer who had refused to negotiate, pursuant to a wage-reopener clause, to pay to a union the increases in wages that would have been agreed to had negotiations occurred. Although nothing in the agreement explicitly authorized payment of wages that would have been negotiated, the court of appeals, in upholding the award, stated that the nexus between the violation of the reopener clause and the method selected to remedy that violation was sufficient to support a finding that the remedy "drew its essence from the contract."[110]

Unless there is clearly restrictive language withdrawing the subject matter or a particular remedy from the jurisdiction of the arbitrator, courts will generally hold that the arbitrator possesses the power to make the award and fashion a remedy even though the agreement is silent on the issue of remedial authority. This is not to say that any remedy the arbitrator formulates will pass muster by the courts. A remedy ordered by an arbitrator must, pursuant to the *Trilogy* standard, "draw its essence from the agreement." The problem, of course, is

---

stated:
> [W]hether it is thought to be a part of the substantive right or more a part of the grievance procedure in the absence of clearly restrictive language, great latitude must be allowed in fashioning the appropriate remedy constituting the arbitrator's 'decision.' When an arbitrator is commissioned to interpret and apply the collective bargaining agreement, he is to bring his informed judgment to bear in order to reach a fair solution of a problem. This is especially true when it comes to formulating remedies. ... And particularly should latitude in fashioning the remedy be allowed when the grievance itself comprehends both for reinstatement and back pay so that on its face the controversy is a "difference ... as to the meaning, application or interpretation" of the agreement.

[109]492 F.2d 713, 85 LRRM 2962 (5th Cir.), cert. denied, 419 U.S. 998, 87 LRRM 2658 (1974).
[110]Id., 85 LRRM at 2976.

determining when a particular remedy is sufficiently grounded in the agreement so as to withstand judicial scrutiny. Bernard Dunau has posed the resulting dilemma for arbitrators and advocates alike:

> The agreement is the source of an arbitrator's authority; within the scope of authority, his award is final, but outside that scope it has no legal basis. The elemental judicial role is therefore to confine the arbitrator to action which does not exceed his authority.
>
> The syllogism is, however, deceptively simple. A dispute over the existence of a contractual limitation on authority is itself a question of contract interpretation.[111]

What is clear is that an arbitrator is confined to the agreement, but no hard and fast rules exist whereby one can predict when a specific remedy "draws its essence" from a "silent" contract. As noted by Arbitrator Tom Christensen,

> In the application of [the *Enterprise* standards], depending upon the court in which one finds oneself (as well as the presence or absence of resources for procuring appellate review), the final result is predictable only in terms of the palatability of the arbitral process and its result to the reviewing judge.[112]

Both arbitrators and the courts have established that if the arbitrator has jurisdiction of the subject matter, he also has implicit power to fashion an appropriate remedy sufficiently grounded in the contract, even though the agreement is silent as to remedies.

2. Contractual Limitations on Arbitral Power and Discretion

a. Substantive Arbitrability

Arbitration is a matter of contract and it is clear that a party cannot be required to submit to arbitration any dispute which it has not agreed to so submit.[113] As the Supreme Court

---

[111]Dunau, *Three Problems in Labor Arbitration*, 55 Va. L. Rev. 427 (1969).
[112]Christensen, supra note 58, at 106.
[113]Steelworkers v. Warrior & Gulf Navigation Co., 363 U.S. 574, 582, 46 LRRM 2416, 2419 (1960).

stated in *AT&T Technologies*,[114] "this axiom recognizes the fact that arbitrators derive their authority to resolve disputes only because the parties have agreed in advance to submit such grievances to arbitration."[115] It follows that the parties are free to limit arbitral authority in the area of remedies by simply removing any subject area they wish from the arbitrator's jurisdiction. For example, where a contract expressly reserved to the employer the "absolute right to hire, promote, suspend, discharge or lay off employees at its discretion," Arbitrator Edgar A. Jones, Jr., in *Reynolds Electrical & Engineering Co.*,[116] held that a grievance protesting the suspension of an employee for telling an ethnic joke was not arbitrable. Similarly, the Court of Appeals for the Second Circuit, in *Communications Workers v. New York Telephone*,[117] upheld a lower court decision denying arbitration of a dispute involving the criteria to be used in deciding which employees to promote where the agreement provided that "in no event shall any grievance or dispute arising out of [promotion] . . . be subject to the arbitration provisions of this agreement."[118]

When attempting to exclude particular subject matter from the arbitrator's jurisdiction, the strong presumption in favor of arbitrability must be recognized. As stated by Justice Douglas in *American Manufacturing*, when a party presents a claim of arbitrability before the courts, a court's function is confined to ascertaining whether the party seeking arbitration "is making a claim which on its face is governed by the contract."[119] More important, in *Warrior & Gulf*, the court demanded an

---

[114]AT&T Technologies v. Communication Workers, 475 U.S. 643, 121 LRRM 3329 (1986). The Court went on to state that unless the parties clearly and unmistakably provide otherwise, "the question of arbitrability—whether a collective-bargaining agreement creates a duty for the parties to arbitrate a particular grievance—is undeniably an issue for judicial determination." Id., 121 LRRM at 3331. However, "in deciding whether the parties have agreed to submit a particular grievance to arbitration, a court is not to rule on the potential merits of the underlying claim." Id. at 3332.

[115]Id., 121 LRRM at 3331.

[116]72 LA 1012 (Jones, 1979).

[117]327 F.2d 94, 55 LRRM 2275 (2d Cir. 1964).

[118]Id., 55 LRRM at 2276. See also United Aircraft Corp. v. Machinists Lodge 971, 360 F.2d 150, 62 LRRM 2299 (5th Cir. 1966); Electrical Workers (IBEW) Local 278 v. Jetero Corp., 496 F.2d 661, 88 LRRM 2184 (5th Cir. 1974); Frederick Meiswinkel, Inc. v. Laborers Local 261, 744 F.2d 1374, 117 LRRM 2649, 2650 (9th Cir. 1984) (agreement permitting arbitration of "[a]ny dispute concerning the interpretation or application of this Agreement, other than a jurisdictional dispute . . . .").

[119]Steelworkers v. American Mfg. Co., 363 U.S. 564, 567–568, 46 LRRM 2414, 2415 (1960).

"express provision excluding a particular grievance from arbitration" or "the most forceful evidence of a purpose to exclude the claim from arbitration"[120] before the presumption in favor of arbitrability could be overborne. This presumption favoring arbitrability is equally applicable to disputes involving interest arbitration.[121] Accordingly, it is fair to conclude that unless it can be proven with some assurance that the arbitration clause is not susceptible to an interpretation that covers the asserted rights or interest dispute, arbitration will be ordered. Any doubts are to be resolved in favor of arbitrability.[122] Under standard labor arbitration clauses providing for arbitration of any "difference" or "dispute" between the parties "arising out of or relating to the agreement or its interpretation or application," virtually every grievance will be arbitrable unless the contract contains a clear and unambiguous clause of exclusion. As a result, commonly used management rights clauses granting the employer "exclusive" right to make certain decisions, or arbitration clauses merely limiting arbitration to the "express terms" of the agreement, will generally not preclude arbitral jurisdiction unless there is clear language to the effect that a grievance about a certain subject matter is beyond the authority of the arbitrator.

The above-stated principle was applied by the First Cir-

---

[120]Steelworkers v. Warrior & Gulf Navigation Co., 363 U.S. 574, 585, 46 LRRM 2416, 2420 (1960).

[121]In Printing Pressmen No. 318 v. Piedmont Publishing Co. of Winston-Salem, 393 F.2d 221, 67 LRRM 2939 (4th Cir. 1968), the court considered whether the collective bargaining agreement provided a proper basis for compelling the employer to submit the terms of a new contract to arbitration. Reasoning that the role of the courts in a §301 action is "limited to ascertaining 'whether the party seeking arbitration is making a claim which on its face is governed by the contract'," the court concluded that the interest clause required arbitration of a new contract. The appellate court rejected the employer's argument that if the courts enforce interest arbitration procedures, never-ending contracts would result. The court stated that "it is immaterial that the contract might be of indeterminate duration—if that is what the parties bargained for." Id. at 227. See also Graphic Arts Local 23 (Milwaukee) v. Newspapers, Inc., 586 F.2d 19, 99 LRRM 3033 (7th Cir. 1978); Mailers Local 92 (Chattanooga) v. Chattanooga News-Free Press Co., 524 F.2d 1305, 90 LRRM 3000 (6th Cir. 1975); A. Seltzer & Co. v. Livingston, 361 F.2d 218, 62 LRRM 2079 (2d Cir. 1966); Builders Ass'n of Kansas City v. Greater Kansas City Laborers Dist. Council, 326 F.2d 867, 55 LRRM 2199 (8th Cir. 1964); M.K.&O. Transit Lines v. Transit Union Div. 892, 319 F.2d 488, 53 LRRM 2662 (10th Cir.), cert. denied, 375 U.S. 944 (1963).

[122]The positive assurance test enunciated by Mr. Justice Douglas has recently been applied by the Fourth Circuit in Lever Brothers v. Chemical Workers Local 217, 554 F.2d 115, 95 LRRM 2438 (4th Cir. 1976).

cuit in *Mobil Oil v. Oil Workers Local 8-766*.[123] In this case the union filed a grievance after Mobil had unilaterally decided to subcontract all delivery of fuel oil and gasoline at its Bangor, Maine, facility. Mobil argued that the dispute was not arbitrable because there was no express provision regarding subcontracting in the collective bargaining agreement and the arbitration clause in the contract limited the scope of the arbitrator's power to the "express provisions of the agreement." Finding that the subcontracting could undercut the express terms of the agreement dealing with recognition, seniority, job classification, and wage scales, the arbitrator determined that the dispute was arbitrable. Mobil commenced an action in federal court to vacate the award. The district court denied the motion, and the court of appeals affirmed the decision and applied the *Warrior & Gulf* rationale as follows:

> [A] dispute is arbitrable unless it can be said "with positive assurance that the arbitration clause is not susceptible of an interpretation that covers the asserted dispute" the unless there is an "express provision excluding a particular grievance from arbitration."[124]

Since the arbitration clause did not expressly exclude subcontracting from arbitration, the dispute was deemed arbitrable.

Of particular note in the substantive arbitrability area is the wording of the grievance procedure. For example, the Second Circuit, in *Rochdale Village v. Public Service Employees Local 80*,[125] stated that if the parties have agreed to submit to arbitration grievances "of any nature or character," or simply "any and all disputes," all questions will properly be consigned to the arbitrator. If, however, the arbitration clause covers only "employee grievances," the court indicated that it should not compel arbitration of an issue involving contract termination.

b. Limiting Arbitral Discretion

As an alternative to removing an entire subject matter from the arbitrator's jurisdiction, the parties may attempt to

---

[123]600 F.2d 322, 101 LRRM 2721 (1st Cir. 1979).
[124]Id., 101 LRRM at 2725.
[125]603 F.2d 1296, 102 LRRM 2476 (2d Cir. 1979).

control the arbitrator's remedy power by placing specific limitations on his discretion when interpreting the contract, or by explicitly designating a particular remedy to be applied for a violation of the agreement. As an example of the first option, in *Koehring Co. v. Electrical Workers (IUE) Local 699*,[126] a federal district court vacated an arbitrator's award granting back pay to reinstated employees who had violated a no-strike agreement by engaging in a wildcat strike. The court found that an award of back pay was expressly prohibited by an agreement that provided that "employees not found innocent by an Arbitrator of violating [the no-strike clause] will not receive back pay."

In *Amanda Bent Bolt Co. v. Automobile Workers Local 1549*,[127] an arbitrator reinstated 28 employees who had been discharged for striking in violation of a no-strike agreement. In reinstating the employees, the arbitrator stated that the employer's notice of discharge coupled with an offer to reemploy the grievants as new hires was a punitive measure and was at variance with the contract. The arbitrator also cited the "indiscriminate application of the discharge penalty" as unusually harsh and severe. The collective bargaining agreement, in relevant part, provided that any violation of the no-strike clause "may be made the subject of disciplinary action, including discharge." In addition, the agreement provided that "the right to . . . discharge for cause . . . is the sole responsibility of the Company." Based upon these two provisions, the Sixth Circuit concluded that the determination of the penalty was exclusively reserved to the employer and that the arbitrator exceeded his authority in making an award "contrary to the terms of the collective bargaining contract."

While it can be argued that the Sixth Circuit conducted a review on the merits,[128] it is of greater importance to realize that it is extremely difficult to draft language that will assure

---

[126]87 LRRM 2472 (S.D. Ohio 1974).

[127]451 F.2d 1277, 79 LRRM 2023 (6th Cir. 1971).

[128]The arbitrator's decision of the arbitrator in *Amanda Bolt* does not "manifest a clear infidelity to the arbitrator's obligation of drawing the 'essence' of the award from the bargaining agreement." There is nothing in the language of the agreement that mandates only discharge and not a lesser penalty. Moreover, it is not at all clear that the language cited by the court of appeals removes from the arbitrator's jurisdiction the determination of penalties, especially where the arbitrator found that the employer had indiscriminately applied the discipline.

that the courts, when called upon to review whether an arbitrator exceeded his jurisdiction, will not conduct a de facto review of the merits and, in the process, misread (or even invent) contractual limitations.[129]

Another form of attempted limitation on arbitral discretion was the subject of discussion in *White v. NLRB*,[130] a decision by the Fifth Circuit. In that case the employer had insisted on a "no-strike" clause and a provision that matters going to arbitration must be decided in the company's favor if there was any evidence that the employer's position was not arbitrary or capricious. The court of appeals noted that such a limitation on arbitration would leave the union "hamstrung" in a dispute with the company, since the union would effectively be precluded from securing a full review on the merits by an arbitrator.

An extreme attempt to circumvent arbitral authority is illustrated in *Automobile Workers Local 342* v. *TRW*,[131] where, in an apparent attempt to alter the traditional role of a court when reviewing an arbitrator's award, the parties drafted the following language:

> The arbitrator shall not have the power to add to or subtract from or modify any of the terms of this Agreement or any agreement supplemental hereto. . . . The arbitrator shall be bound by the provisions of this Agreement. Any decision by an arbitrator contrary to such provisions shall not be binding on either party and shall not be enforceable through legal proceedings except upon a determination by the court de novo that the arbitrator's decision is not contrary to the provisions of the Agreement.[132]

The employer argued that the court was not bound by the usual rules of judicial review but rather must examine the merits of the controversy, considering the agreement anew and applying its own contractual interpretation. In rejecting this argument, the court reasoned that the cited language is merely an express acknowledgment by the parties of the gen-

---

[129]See, e.g., Clinchfield Coal Co. v. Mine Workers Dist. 28, 736 F.2d 998, 116 LRRM 2884, 2885 (4th Cir. 1984) (holding that arbitrator improperly concluded that employer violated agreement proscribing layoffs, reasoning that arbitrator failed to recognize the "common law" of the industry expressed in past arbitral decisions).
[130]255 F.2d 564, 42 LRRM 2001 (5th Cir. 1958).
[131]65 LRRM 2597 (M.D. Tenn. 1967), rev'd on other grounds, 402 F.2d 727, 69 LRRM 2524 (6th Cir. 1968), cert, denied, 395 U.S. 910, 71 LRRM 2253 (1969).
[132]Id. at 2598. See also Haynes v. United States Pipe & Foundry Co., 363 F.2d 414, 62 LRRM 2389 (5th Cir. 1966) (arbitration not part of grievance procedure).

eral principle of arbitral enforcement enunciated by the Supreme Court in *Enterprise Wheel*, where it was held that an arbitrator's award is never final and binding if he exceeds the limitations imposed upon him by the bargaining agreement. The court concluded that to hold otherwise would subvert and render meaningless the arbitration process.

From the narrow perspective of limiting arbitral discretion to formulate a remedy, *Automobile Workers Local 342* suggests that the parties might attempt, through carefully drafted language, to vest the arbitrator merely with power to issue an advisory opinion, with final review on the merits reserved to the courts. It is unlikely, however, that many labor organizations would agree to a no-strike clause in return for something so illusory as advisory grievance arbitration.

c. Stipulated Remedies

There are instances where the parties will mandate a specific remedy for a violation of the labor agreement. When this is the case the arbitrator must accordingly award the parties' agreed-upon remedy once a violation is found. Illustrative of this rule is *Operating Engineers Local 9 v. Shank-Artukovich*.[133] The terms of the parties' contract provided that compressors at a tunnel entrance be manned by operating engineers. Following a hearing, the arbitrator held that the employer violated the agreement by not manning the compressors. He ordered that in the future the compressors be manned, but ordered no remedy for the past violation. The union requested and received a clarification of the award. The arbitrator concluded that there were no damages, and, accordingly, an award for the past violation was not warranted. The union then brought an action to set aside the decision not to award damages. On a stipulated record, the district court ordered the case remanded to the arbitrator to award damages consistent with the agreement which, in relevant part, provided:

> "If violations of the manning provisions . . . are found by . . . the Arbitrator and if an individual(s) is found entitled to back pay, the same shall be paid by the violator, but if no individual is

---

[133]751 F.2d 364, 118 LRRM 2157 (10th Cir. 1985).

THE COLLECTIVE BARGAINING AGREEMENT 55

found entitled to damages the violator shall remit such damages to the Trustees of the Colorado Journeymen and Apprentice Training Fund for Operating Engineers."[134]

The Tenth Circuit affirmed, concluding that the award did not draw its essence from the collective bargaining agreement, even though the parties' submission to the arbitrator provided as follows: " 'Did the employer violate the collective bargaining agreement by not manning the compressors . . . . If so, what is the appropriate remedy?' "[135]

Another case where the arbitrator failed to award the remedy mandated by the parties for a particular violation is *Food & Commercial Workers Local 1119 v. United Markets.*[136] The parties' contract required that there be no more than two general clerks on duty at any time. If United violated this provision more than twice, the agreement provided that the employer would lose the classification, and food clerk rates would be applied to the general clerks in the store where the violation occurred. United violated the agreement twice by using three general clerks at one time and the union grieved. Arbitrator Sam Kagel found for the union and required *all* general clerks to be paid at a higher rate than provided for in the agreement. He further provided that a third violation would cause United to lose the general clerk classification for the duration of the agreement. Upon the union's urging, the arbitrator modified the award to apply only to those employees of the store where the violation occurred, but did not further alter the award.

The union accordingly filed suit to vacate the award since the monetary relief exceeded the scope of the agreement and it failed to remove the general clerk classification. The district court vacated the award as exceeding the arbitrator's authority, and ordered United not to use the general clerk classification. The court of appeals concurred that the award did not draw its essence from the agreement since it did not deny United the general clerk classification for the entire agreement period but only for five months and it gave United a third chance at correcting its violations, instead of two, both

---

[134]Id., 118 LRRM at 2158.
[135]Id.
[136]784 F.2d 1413, 121 LRRM 3338 (9th Cir. 1986).

required by the agreement. The court also ruled that since the arbitrator's award was such a clear derivation from the agreement, remand was not required of the district court.

What is of note is that the Ninth Circuit found no justification for the arbitrator's remedy, which was based both on the inadvertence of the violations and United's good-faith attempts to cure the "oversight" once it was notified of the violations. The parties' designated remedy would take precedence over the arbitrator's informed judgment.

The difficulty of specifying remedies for a particular breach of the agreement is illustrated in a case decided by the Fourth Circuit.[137] The relevant contract language provided that "should it be decided under the rules of the agreement that an injustice has been dealt the discharged employee, the Company shall reinstate such employee to his former position and pay full compensation for time lost."[138] An employee was dismissed for inaccuracy in keeping records in the course of his duty as an instrument reader. A grievance was filed and the arbitrator subsequently ordered reinstatement, but without back pay. The arbitrator found that the employee engaged in "culpable conduct," but that the sanction of discharge was not justified under the circumstances.

The employer brought suit in federal district court to set aside the award, claiming that the arbitrator, upon finding the employee guilty of misconduct, had no authority to modify the discipline imposed. The employer argued that the contract leaves the arbitrator with only a narrow choice—reinstatement with full back pay or no relief at all—and that the arbitrator exceeded his authority in ordering reinstatement without also awarding full back pay. The district court vacated the award and the court of appeals reversed.[139] Rejecting the employer's argument, the Fourth Circuit stated that the employer's rigid interpretation of the arbitrator's scope of authority was not warranted and would be acceptable only if the agreement expressly forbade the arbitrator to exercise any discretion in the fashioning of the award. The issue, reasoned

---

[137]Lynchburg Foundry Co. Div. v. Steelworkers Local 2556, 404 F.2d 259, 69 LRRM 2878 (4th Cir. 1968).
[138]Id., 69 LRRM at 2878.
[139]Lynchburg Foundry Co. Div. v. Steelworkers Local 2556, 285 F.Supp. 59, 68 LRRM 2379 (W.D. Va. 1968).

the court of appeals, is whether reinstatement with full back pay represents the sole remedy for an employee who has suffered an injustice, or whether it merely marks the outer limits within which an arbitrator may fashion a remedy appropriate to the circumstances. The court further stated that "full compensation for time lost" is not necessarily the equivalent of full back pay. The use of the more general term "full compensation" may reasonably be viewed as indicating an intent that the employee be awarded whatever back pay would compensate him for time unjustly lost from work. In the absence of language showing a clear intent to deny the arbitrator latitude of judgment, the court declared that it is for the arbitrator to answer this question.

d. Agreed Remedies—Liquidated Damages and Labor Arbitration

Liquidated damage provisions are contract provisions in which the parties designate a specific sum to be awarded to the injured party in the case of a breach of contract. In the area of contract law, these remedies are enforceable only if reasonable, and not out of proportion to the loss or injury actually sustained or reasonably to be anticipated. In addition, liquidated damage provisions are enforceable only when actual damages are impossible or difficult to ascertain at the time the agreement is made.[140]

The difficulty of calculating damages may lead the parties to incorporate a liquidated damage provision in their collective bargaining agreement. And although the better rule of authority would mandate that an arbitrator, as the parties' official contract reader, should respect such language when a breach is found, conflicts with a reviewing court may result. For example, in *Retail Clerks v. Food Employers Council*,[141] an arbitrator, in accordance with a formula specified in the agreement, awarded double damages for a work violation. Despite the reliance on the letter of the agreement, a California court of appeals vacated the award on the grounds that it

---

[140]Hillman, Contract Remedies, Equity, and Restitution, 144 (Iowa Law School, Continuing Legal Education, 1979).
[141]85 Cal.App.3d 286, 99 LRRM 3255 (1978).

constituted a provision for liquidated damages, in violation of a state statute providing that any contract in which the amount of damages paid is determined in anticipation of a contractual breach is void. The court noted that the statute provided an exception where, from the nature of the case it would be impracticable or extremely difficult to fix actual damages, but this was not such a case. In support of this decision, the court stated that the liquidated damages provision is not supported by any evidence that the parties ever discussed the impracticability of measuring damages in cases of successive violations by the employer.

e. Settlement Agreements and Limitations of Arbitral Authority

An agreement settling a dispute precludes an arbitrator from exercising jurisdiction over the same grievance. The Code of Professional Responsibility for Arbitrators of Labor-Management Disputes, in relevant part, provides:

> An arbitrator must observe faithfully both the limitations and inclusions of the jurisdiction conferred by an agreement or other submisssion under which he or she serves.
> A direct settlement by the parties of some or all issues in a case, at any stage of the proceedings, must be accepted by the arbitrator as relieving him or her of further jurisdiction over such issues.[142]

The Sixth Circuit has outlined as follows the analysis to take when an arbitrator is alleged to have ignored the parties' settlement agreement in formulating a remedy:

> The policy in favor of the finality of arbitration is but one part of a broader goal of encouraging informal, i.e., non-judicial, resolution of labor disputes.
> "It is not arbitration per se that federal policy favors, but rather final adjustment of differences by a means selected by the parties. If the parties agree that a procedure other than arbitration shall provide a conclusive resolution of their differ-

---

[142]See Code of Professional Responsibility for Arbitrators of Labor-Management Disputes, approved by the Joint Steering Committee of the National Academy of Arbitrators (composed of representatives from the Academy, the American Arbitration Association, and the Federal Mediation and Conciliation Service) in November 1975, published April 1975, amended May 1985.

ences, federal labor policy encourages that procedure no less than arbitration."

. . .

Parties who reach a settlement pursuant to a formal grievance procedure have not bargained for an arbitrator's construction of the collective bargaining agreement: they have bargained for their own construction.

When a party claims that a prior settlement agreement controls the parties' obligations, the policy in favor of the finality of arbitration must yield to the broader policy in favor of the parties' chosen method of non-judicial dispute resolution. When the former policy gives way to the latter, the rule restricting our scope of review—a rule designed to implement the former policy—necessarily loses its foundation.[143]

The court reasoned that to rule otherwise would mean that a party who became unhappy with a settlement agreement would have every incentive to breach the agreement and then submit the controversy to an arbitrator. In the case at issue, pursuant to a third-step grievance settlement, the grievant's suspension was rescinded by the company provided that he follow the recommendations of an alcohol treatment program, attend weekly meetings of Alcoholics Anonymous, take antiabuse pills, and continue total abstinence from alcohol. By its terms the agreement stated, "Failure to comply with any of the [stated conditions] or any alcohol related infractions at work will result in dismissal." The agreement was signed by management, the union, and the grievant. The grievant was ultimately discharged when he did not attend treatment sessions for two weeks. A grievance was filed and the case moved to arbitration. Calling the agreement "reasonable and humanitarian," the arbitrator concluded that just cause existed for the discharge but nevertheless held the penalty too severe. The arbitrator accordingly reinstated the grievant on the condition that he be bound by an agreement, the terms of which were substantially identical to the parties' prior settlement agreement.

The company refused to reinstate the grievant, and the union sought enforcement of the arbitrator's award in district court. The court enforced the award, and the Sixth Circuit reversed, reasoning that even if the settlement agreement is

---

[143]Bakers Local 326 v. ITT Continental Baking Co., 749 F.2d 350, 117 LRRM 3145, 3147–3148 (6th Cir. 1984).

not final and binding in the sense that it can be enforced in federal court without first having been submitted to an arbitrator, the parties' settlement agreement is binding on the arbitrator. The court did note, however, that the presumption binding an arbitrator to a settlement agreement may be overcome by a contrary, unambiguous provision in the parties' collective bargaining agreement.

Does the same analysis apply when a grievance is withdrawn? The issue whether the withdrawal of a grievance (or other conduct) constitutes a "settlement" so as to preclude later arbitration on the merits is a question of contract interpretation and is properly resolved by the arbitrator.[144] Likewise, where the issue is the preclusive effect of a prior withdrawal of a grievance or, alternatively, the effect of a prior award, case law indicates that the matter is one of procedural significance and for the arbitrator to decide under the parties' agreement.[145]

Suppose management's conduct gives rise to a grievance and a claim under Title VII of the Civil Rights Act and the grievant enters a settlement agreement but without union participation. Can the grievant's union pursue a remedy in the arbitral forum? Subsequent to an EEOC settlement (which, in part, provided that there would be no reimbursement of pay due to the grievant's suspension for an alleged failure to meet production expectations) the employee's bargaining agent, at the request of the grievant, filed a grievance requesting reimbursement of the days lost to suspension. Under these facts Arbitrator James Sherman, in a 1988 unpublished decision, held that the grievant's decision to settle her EEOC claim cannot preclude her bargaining agent from pursuing the grievance in arbitration. Sherman stated that there are

---

[144]Machinists Lodge 862 v. Safeguard Powertech Sys. Div., 623 F. Supp. 608, 123 LRRM 3058 (D.S.D. 1985). See also Office & Professional Employees Local 9 v. Industrial Workers (AIW), 397 F. Supp. 688, 692, 90 LRRM 2129 (E.D. Wis. 1975), aff'd, 535 F.2d 1257, 93 LRRM 2019 (7th Cir. 1976), (issue of whether settlement reached constitutes dispute over interpretation of collective bargaining agreement and therefore question for arbitrator).

[145]Little Six Corp. v. Mine Workers Local 8332, 701 F.2d 26, 112 LRRM 2922 (4th Cir. 1983) (rejecting argument that prior arbitration precluded rearbitration of grievance, holding that preclusive effect of prior award was itself question for arbitrator); Electrical Workers (IUE) Local 103 v. RCA Corp., 516 F.2d 1336, 1339, 89 LRRM 2487 (3d Cir. 1975) (declaring that it is not the function of a court to decide whether the same question or issue had been the subject of arbitration within meaning of collective bargaining agreement).

two separate and distinct sets of rights involved in the case, those which emanate from the labor agreement and those mandated by Congress in the Civil Rights Act. It does not follow, reasoned Sherman, that what happens in one forum does not concern, or have an effect upon, the other. With respect to the grievant's back-pay claim, Sherman held that the probability of a decision awarding back pay is almost zero because the grievant waived the right to back pay when she agreed to drop the grievance. Arbitrator Sherman further ruled:

> [T]he arbitrator can think of several reasons why a grievant would not be awarded backpay under these circumstances. The first is a generally recognized principal called "estoppel" which states that a litigant will not be permitted to take inconsistent positions in two forums. The second reason is based on the widely accepted theory that arbitration closely resembles the common law Courts of Equity. And these Courts steadfastly refused to grant relief if the plaintiff "did not come before the court with clean hands."

Sherman concluded that inducing management to settle the EEOC complaint with a promise that the grievant did not intend to keep would not be considered "clean hands." Arbitrator Sherman also cited "public policy" reasons for denying the relief sought by the grievant:

> In simple terms, public policy favors settlement over adjudication in all types of forums. And it would undermine the EEOC's ability to settle complaints if the complaintant were permitted to benefit, as the grievant here seeks to do, by subterfuge—trading something that is worthless, a false promise, for something of obvious value, namely, a clean record.

Suppose the grievant desires to withdraw a grievance pursuant to an EEOC settlement with management? Denying management's motion for a bench decision declaring a grievance not arbitrable because the grievant accepted the remedy offered by the agency during an EEO hearing, Arbitrator James Sherman, in a 1989 unpublished case, explained that the union had a right to proceed "because it had a legitimate interest in the outcome and, indeed, it 'owned' the grievance once it was designated as [Grievant's] agent." While the grievant did not seek additional relief in arbitration (indeed, the grievant urged the union to drop the case), Sherman posed the issue this way: "What is a proper remedy when management, for the most ulterior of motives, causes this type of disruption [grievant was reassigned 80 miles from her present location to a midnight shift] to an employee's life?" Sherman ordered the Grievant reinstated to a full-time position formally denied and compensated for the time spent on the road to and from work. The grievant had informed the union that she was satisfied with the remedy initially offered by management: the next available full-time position at a location close to her home. Sherman fashioned a remedy for the individual grievant other than the one she already agreed to in settlement of an EEOC complaint.

f. Summary

Most arbitrators take the view that broad remedy power is implied from the appointment. If the parties fear that an arbitrator may fashion a remedy that is inappropriate, they can limit the scope and reach of arbitral authority by carefully drafting limitations in the agreement. This may be accomplished by removing the subject matter in its entirety from the jurisdiction of the arbitrator (substantive arbitrability). As an example, it is not uncommon for an agreement to provide that an arbitrator is prohibited from reviewing management's determination in rating the comparative abilities of employees for purposes of promotion. Given the presumption in favor of arbitrability as established by the Supreme Court in *American Manufacturing* and *Warrior & Gulf*, the contract must clearly exclude the subject matter from the scope of the arbitrator's jurisdiction; otherwise a reviewing court or an arbitrator is likely to find the issue arbitrable.

As an alternative to excluding a particular subject from the arbitrator's authority altogether, the parties may attempt merely to limit arbitral discretion. For example, an arbitrator may be limited to a reinstatement remedy only if he finds that the party involved was not guilty of any misconduct. Some agreements provide that an arbitrator, in a discharge case, is limited to only two choices—reinstatement with full back pay, or complete affirmance of the termination. Still other contracts will specify the remedy to be applied for a particular breach, leaving it to the arbitrator to determine only if in fact a breach occurred.

One arbitrator has stated that a parallel exists between the complexities of society at large and the complexities of the industrial relations society in which arbitrators function as decision makers.[146] Despite the best efforts of labor and management to develop objective rules and standards, experience demonstrates the impossibility of putting into words specific rules and standards to cover all circumstances for violations of collective bargaining agreements. Arbitrators undoubtedly welcome unequivocal instructions as to remedy determinations; however, the drafting and implementation of such instructions are not without difficulties. More important, the parties necessarily sacrifice some flexibility when specific remedies or limitations are placed in the agreement. Hard cases may indeed make bad law in both the arbitral and judicial forum and there is merit in retaining flexibility as to remedies when disputes are submitted for arbitral resolution.

---

[146]Alexander, *Discretion in Arbitration*, in Arbitration and the Public Interest, Proceedings of the 24th Annual Meeting, National Academy of Arbitrators, 84 (BNA Books, 1971).

Chapter 4

The Submission Agreement and the Remedial Authority of an Arbitrator

Where the parties have not negotiated a grievance procedure calling for arbitration, they may enter into a submission (sometimes called a stipulation or an agreement to arbitrate).[1] Such an agreement is necessary when (1) the parties are arbitrating a dispute over future contract terms (interest disputes), or (2) the contract provides for arbitration only if both parties agree to submit a specific dispute. More common, a submission specifies in writing the issue to be resolved, generally formulating it as a question or questions before the arbitrator. The submission will frequently designate the relief desired, and it will generally grant to the arbitrator jurisdiction over the specific subject matter of the dispute. Sometimes it will contain considerable detail over the procedures to be implemented at the hearing. Elkouri and Elkouri cite the following reasons for executing a submission even where the collective bargaining agreement contains an arbitration provision covering the dispute:

1. To expand or diminish the authority of the arbitrator more than provided by the collective agreement.

---

[1]See, e.g., Elkouri and Elkouri, How Arbitration Works, 4th ed., 183 (BNA Books, 1985); Fairweather, Practice and Procedure in Labor Arbitration, 2d ed. (BNA Books, 1983) at 9; Prasow and Peters, Arbitration and Collective Bargaining, 17 (McGraw-Hill, 1970).

  2. To state precisely the issue to be decided by the arbitrator, and thus to indicate the scope of his jurisdiction more precisely.
  3. To state procedural details where the parties desire to control them and the collective agreement contains little or no detail in regard thereto.
  4. In arbitration under a statute, to complete any statutory requirements not met by the arbitration clause of the collective argreement.
  5. In cases not covered by state or federal law making agreements to arbitrate future disputes specifically enforceable, to provide a contract after the dispute has materialized. Contracts to arbitrate existing disputes are the basis of damage actions under the common law of some jurisdictions and sometimes are made specifically enforceable by statute even where agreements to arbitrate future disputes are not.
  6. To confirm the arbitrability of the particular dispute.
  7. To provide an additional opportunity to settle the dispute—in negotiating on a submission the parties may find that they are not too far apart for a negotiated settlement of the basic dispute.[2]

The Elkouris go on to argue that "the use of a submission depends upon the particular case, and that the particular contents and form of submissions which are used will vary greatly from case to case."[3]

Arbitrator Emanuel Stein has noted that a number of arbitrators have suggested that the submission is especially well suited to the definition of the arbitrator's authority on remedies and that, indeed, some arbitrators make it a practice to have the parties include in the submission their respective views on the remedies.[4] Not only are the parties better disposed to moderation on the appropriate remedy before the award is issued but also, if the submission contains a clause as to remedies, they are less likely to be surprised at the result.

A. Using the Submission to Expand or to Diminish an Arbitrator's Authority

In his concurring opinion in *Enterprise Wheel,* in which he was joined by Justice Harlan, Justice Brennan observed

---

[2]Elkouri and Elkouri, supra note 1, at 226–227 (footnotes omitted).
[3]Id. at 227.
[4]Stein, *Remedies in Labor Arbitration,* in Challenges to Arbitration, Proceedings of the 13th Annual Meeting, National Academy of Arbitrators, 3 (BNA Books, 1960).

that "the arbitration promise is itself a contract," and that "[t]he parties are free to make that promise as broad or narrow as they wish for there is no compulsion in law requiring them to include any such provision in their agreement."[5] Accordingly, when the subject matter jurisdiction and/or the remedial authority of the arbitrator has been defined in the agreement, either in broad or limited terms, the parties are free to revise that authority by a carefully drafted submission agreement since both the contract and the submission define the arbitrator's authority. An award that exceeds that submission is subject to reversal by a reviewing court.[6]

The Fifth Circuit, in *Piggly Wiggly Operators' Warehouse*,[7] made clear that the agreement to arbitrate a dispute may be dependent upon the submission agreement as well as upon the arbitration clause in the collective bargaining agreement. The arbitration concerned an employee-driver who was discharged because he had been declared uninsurable by the employer's insurance carrier. In support of its action, the employer relied upon Section z, Article 21, of the collective bargaining agreement, which provided that " 'any driver who becomes uninsurable by any of the Company's insurance carriers will be subject to immediate discharge.' " The union questioned the validity of that clause and filed a grievance which, in part, alleged that " 'purported Section (z) of Article 21 of the contract is not a valid term of the contract.' "

---

[5]Steelworkers v. Enterprise Wheel & Car Corp., 363 U.S. 593, 46 LRRM 2423, 2427 (1960).

[6]Oil Workers Local 2-477 v. Continental Oil Co., 524 F.2d 1048, 90 LRRM 3040 (10th Cir. 1975), cert. denied, 424 U.S. 936, 91 LRRM 3081 (1976) (arbitrator exceeded authority in considering two grievances where one was not submitted pursuant to contractual procedure); Delta Lines v. Teamsters Local 85, 409 F. Supp. 873, 93 LRRM 2037 (N.D. Cal. 1976) (no presumption for finding scope of arbitrator's authority to decide issues is determined by authority to find facts; award vacated where arbitrator decided issues not submitted by parties); Wright-Austin Co. v. Automobile Workers Local 212, 422 F. Supp. 1364, 94 LRRM 2714 (E.D. Mich. 1976) (award vacated where arbitrator ordered reinstatement of employee who was determined by arbitrator to have lost seniority; submission held to contemplate reinstatement only if arbitrator found that employee did not lose seniority); Retail Clerks Local 782 v. Sav-On Groceries, 508 F.2d 500, 88 LRRM 3205 (10th Cir. 1975) (back-pay award vacated where parties did not include remedy of back pay in submission to arbitrator); Lee v. Olin Mathieson Chem. Corp., 271 F. Supp. 635 (W.D. Va. 1967) (under agreement providing that "the arbitrator's jurisdiction to make the award shall be limited by the submission and confined to the interpretation or application of the provisions of this Agreement," award was vacated where arbitrator considered and found violations of portions of agreement that were not submitted to arbitration).

[7]Piggly Wiggly Operators' Warehouse v. Independent Truck Drivers Local 1, 602 F.2d 134, 103 LRRM 2646 (5th Cir. 1980).

The parties selected an arbitrator and submitted the grievance without entering into a separate submission agreement. The arbitrator concluded that the discharge was improper, reasoning that Article 21 (z) was not a part of the contract because the clause in question had never been submitted to the union for consent. The employer moved to vacate the award, the district court granted the motion to vacate then reversed itself and confirmed the award.

Rejecting management's argument that the arbitrator effectively rewrote the terms of the agreement, the court of appeals stated that the scope of an arbitrator's authority is not always controlled by the collective agreement alone, and that before arbitration could proceed it would be necessary for the parties to "supplement the agreement to arbitrate by defining the issue . . . and by explicitly giving him authority to act."

The court further discussed the difference between arbitrating with and without a submission. The court noted that when the parties enter into a submission agreement, this later "contract" is the substitute for legal pleadings before the arbitrator; it joins the issue between the parties and empowers the arbitrator to decide them. In the words of the court: "The arbiter's jurisdiction is then not limited to the issue that the parties could have been compelled to submit; the parties may agree on this method of resolving disputes that they were not compelled to submit to arbitration."

In contrast, when the parties do not agree on a submission, they may ask the arbitrator to decide the written grievance as it has been posed in the grievance steps prior to arbitration. "When they do so," according to the court, "they have in effect empowered him to decide the issues stated in the grievance." The court stated that it is then up to the arbitrator to decide the issue, and the written grievance and the contract define the limits of the arbitrator's authority. "Arbitration is a matter of contract . . . but the initial contract to arbitrate may be modified by the submission agreement or grievance."[8]

It is noteworthy that the court of appeals stressed that at no time had the employer contended that the grievance or any part of it was not a proper subject for arbitration. The decision stands as a warning to the parties that where there is no

---

[8]Id. at 2648.

separate submission agreement and one party disagrees with the statement of the issue to be submitted to arbitration, it is incumbent on that party to put its objection before the arbitrator lest it waive its position and discover that it has broadened the scope of arbitrability under the agreement.[9]

In *Ottley v. Schwartzberg*,[10] the Second Circuit relied upon the following quotation for the proposition that an arbitrator does not have authority to review compliance with his own award:

> "[T]he scope of authority of arbitrators generally depends on the intention of the parties to an arbitration, and is determined by the agreement or submission. Such an agreement or submission serves not only to define, but to circumscribe, the authority of arbitrators."[11]

A classic case that presented the issue of an arbitrator's authority to fashion a remedy (numerous remedies in this instance, including interest and attorneys' fees), and whether limitations are to be applied based upon the submission, the collective bargaining agreement, and a prior arbitration award is *Synergy Gas Co. v. Sasso*,[12] a decision by the Second Circuit. The facts are simple but the procedural history of the case is convoluted. James Brown, a cylinder truck driver employed by Synergy Gas Co., was discharged on October 24, 1980. Arbitration proceedings were initiated by the Teamsters. Arbitrator James Cashen found that Synergy failed to show just cause for the discharge, and in an award dated October 5, 1981, provided a " 'lump sum back pay award equal to the difference between what grievant would have received in full employment with [the employer] during the period in question minus any amounts actually earned from other employment or received as unemployment insurance during the period.' " The employer commenced an action on October 27, 1981, by petitioning the Supreme Court, Suffolk County, New York, to vacate the Cashen award. The court confirmed the award, but the Appellate Division reversed and remanded and ordered a

---

[9]See Morris, *Report of the Committee on Law and Legislation*, in Decisional Thinking of Arbitrators and Judges, Proceedings of the 33d Annual Meeting, National Academy of Arbitrators, 382, 387 (BNA Books, 1981).

[10]819 F.2d 373 (2d Cir. 1987).

[11]Id. at 376, quoting 5 C.J.S. Arbitration §69 at 280–281 (1975).

[12]853 F.2d 59, 129 LRRM 2041, 2042, 2044–2045 (2d Cir.), cert. denied, 57 USLW 3412, 129 LRRM 3072 (1988).

hearing on the merits. The State Supreme Court thereafter confirmed the award, which was later affirmed by the Appellate Division.

Management still refused to reinstate Brown or to grant him any back pay, alleging that subsequent events, including the decline of Brown's health, did not warrant the Cashen remedy. The union then filed a new grievance seeking a determination of " '[h]ow much money and what other relief are James Brown and Local 282 and [its] affiliated funds entitled to receive pursuant to the arbitration award of James Cashen dated October 5, 1981.' " The stipulated submission read as follows: " 'What relief, if any, is James Brown entitled to pursuant to the Arbitration award of James Cashen dated October 5, 1981.' "

Although the Cashen award and the stipulated submission expressly limited remedial relief to James Brown only, Arbitrator Jesse Simons, on June 15, 1987, awarded the grievant back pay of $57,285 plus accrued interest, minus the amount of union dues that would have been deducted from Brown's wages. The award also directed Synergy to make certain contributions to the Pension Trust Fund and to pay to the union reasonable attorney's fees incurred as a result of litigating management's refusal to comply with Cashen's award. Arbitrator Simons retained jurisdiction to determine the amount of union dues and attorney's fees.

In December of 1987 the employer moved for summary judgment in the federal district court. The district court granted summary judgment and confirmed Simons' award in its entirety and remanded to the arbitrator the determination of the amount of attorney's fees and union dues. On July 26, 1988, the Second Circuit affirmed the order of the district court. The appellate court recognized "the longstanding rule that any doubt concerning the scope of the submission is to be resolved in favor of coverage," and found that Arbitrator Simons had the authority under the stipulated submission to decide whether to award payments other than back pay, such as pension fund contributions, union dues and attorney's fees.

In *Railway & Steamship Clerks v. Universal Carloading & Distributing Co.*[13] a submission was employed to expand the terms of the agreement. The agreement provided that if

---

[13]1 Cal.App.3d 145, 72 LRRM 2798 (1969).

the charges against an employee were not sustained, all of his records should be cleared and the employee should be reinstated and paid for all time lost, less an amount earned elsewhere. The arbitrator ordered reinstatement, but without back pay. Refusing the union's motion for correction of the award, the court pointed out that the submission provided that the issue for the arbitrator was whether the employer acted properly in terminating the grievance and, if not, what remedy was ordered. The parties could have submitted to the arbitrator only the issue of unlawful termination, reserving for the future any question of remedy. Alternatively, they could have submitted the issue of unlawful termination and the issue of what remedy the contract afforded. But, as stated by the court, they did neither:

> They submitted to the arbitrator the broad and general issue: "... what remedy is ordered?" Having thus mutually invited him to frame his own remedy according to his own conscience, neither [party] can now object that he framed a remedy not to its liking.[14]

A contrary position was taken by a New York court. In *O'Rourke v. Hickey Co.*,[15] an arbitrator refused to sustain a discharge and ordered reinstatement without back pay. Although the submission authorized the arbitrator, if he found the discharge unjustified, to decide what the remedy should be, the contract provided that if an employee is found to have been wrongfully discharged, the employee " 'shall be reinstated with back pay for time lost.' "[16] The court modified the award, holding that the submission did not empower the arbitrator to disregard the contractual provision.

This line of thinking was not followed by the Eighth and Ninth Circuit. In *Carpenters' District Council v. Anderson*,[17] the Eighth Circuit ruled that even if the arbitrator exceeded his authority under a collective bargaining agreement by reinstating an employee found guilty of misconduct, the submission (providing that the arbitrator could fashion a remedy) gave him authority to award to order reinstatement and back

---

[14]Id., 72 LRRM at 2800.
[15]31 LA 765 (N.Y. Sup. Ct. 1958).
[16]Id.
[17]619 F.2d 776, 104 LRRM 2188 (8th Cir. 1980).

pay. Similarly, the Ninth Circuit, in *High Concrete Structures v. Electrical Workers (UE) Local 166*,[18] stated that the parties may agree to allow an arbitrator to go beyond the express terms of the collective bargaining agreement, either by providing in the contract for interest arbitration, or by agreeing, separately, to submit specific issues to arbitration. Thus, where the submission asked for a resolution of whether the " 'CAP on disability retirement credited years of service [should] be 25 or 30 years,' " it was permissible for the arbitrator to decide that management was required to credit a maximum of 30 years even though the express terms of the agreement provided only for 25 years, and the arbitrator acknowledged that the language was unambiguous. The court of appeals made it clear (correctly, we think) that in determining the arbitrator's authority, the court must look not only at the text of the agreement but also at the agreed submission.

B. Drafting the Submission

The importance of carefully drafting the submission is indicated in *Kroger Co. v. Teamsters Local 661*,[19] a decision by the Sixth Circuit. In that case the employer had denied an employee's request for an additional leave of absence. Grievance proceedings were initiated, terminating in the submission of the following issues for consideration by the arbitrator:

"(1) Whether or not the Company had the right to refuse to extend [the employee's] leave; and
"(2) Thereafter apply the remaining provisions of this contract which resulted in the severance of her employment."[20]

On the first issue, conceded by the union from the outset, the arbitrator found that the employer had the right to refuse to extend the employee's leave. With respect to the second issue, the arbitrator held that the company had in fact given the grievant a day-to-day extension of her leave. As a remedy he ordered the employer to grant back pay without prejudice to the grievant's seniority and profit-sharing rights.

---

[18]879 F.2d 1215, 131 LRRM 3152 (3d Cir. 1989).
[19]380 F.2d 728, 65 LRRM 2573 (6th Cir. 1967).
[20]Id., 65 LRRM at 2574.

Although the employer reinstated the grievant, management refused to honor that part of the award granting back pay and reinstatement in the profit-sharing plan, on the grounds that these issues had not been submitted to the arbitrator. The district court granted summary judgment for the employer, and the court of appeals reversed. The court stated that the submission, proposed by the employer's representative, was "reasonably susceptible of a construction that threw open for consideration and determination by the arbitrator the entire contract and all issues arising under it with respect to [the grievant]."[21] Moreover, the court noted that the union had discussed the propriety of an award of back pay at the arbitration hearing, while the employer had failed to discuss any issue of remedies. In the court's view, the question of the entire contract and its interpretation were presented to the arbitrator; the court held therefore that it could not conclude that the award was not to be found within the four corners of that contract.

An arbitrator can bind the parties only on issues they agree to submit to arbitration. How is it determined "what the parties have agreed to submit"? The Eighth Circuit has pointed out that in determining the scope of a submission, courts have considered a number of factors to be relevant: "clarity and scope of the submission language; correspondence between the parties; description and discussion of the issues during arbitration; and evidence of confusion, uncertainty, or dissent in the record,"[22] Not arguing the applicability of a contractual provision may give rise to a court decision vacating an award that interprets the provision.[23]

C. Changing the Submission

The difficulties of changing a submission is illustrated in *Defense General Supply Center.*[24] In that decision the arbitrator held that he had authority to continue hearing a dispute

---

[21]Id. at 2575–2576.
[22]Lackawanna Leather Co. v. Food & Commercial Workers Dist. 271, 692 F.2d 536, 540 n.5, 111 LRRM 3031, 3034 n.5 (8th Cir. 1982).
[23]Id.
[24]63 LA 901 (Di Stefano, 1974).

involving a claim of qualification for promotion, even though the employer objected that the issue before the arbitrator involved only the processing of a grievance. The record indicated that the parties had jointly framed the issue as one dealing with promotion, but subsequently cited "the processing of a grievance" as the issue for arbitration. The arbitrator determined that the employer was responsible for the mix-up in submissions and, accordingly, held that the promotion question was properly before him.

D. Failure to Agree on Scope of Submission

As noted, it is not always possible for the parties to reach agreement concerning the scope of the submission to the arbitrator. Suppose, for example, an employee is convicted of gambling activities (possession of policy slips) in his place of employment and subsequently discharged. The facts indicate that the grievant possessed 24 years of seniority, was 3 years from retirement, had four children, and notwithstanding his gambling conviction, produced a letter attesting to his good character from the grievant's parish priest. Finally, the record indicates that the employer had reinstated four other employees arguably involved in the same gambling activities.[25] Consider the remedial power of the arbitrator under the following stipulations:

Did the employer discharge the grievant for just cause and, if not, what shall be the remedy?

Did the employer act reasonably in concluding that the grievant was guilty of wrongdoing so as to justify a discharge?

Was the penalty imposed on the grievant too severe in view of all the facts and circumstances of the case and, if so, shall the grievant be reinstated with full compensation?

Is the employer required to reinstate employees that have been convicted of gambling?

Did the employer violate the terms and conditions of the

---

[25]See Otis Elevator Co. (unpublished, 1961) (cited in Cox, Bok and Gorman, Labor Law: Cases and Materials, 585 (Foundation Press, 1977)), rev'd sub nom. Electrical Workers (IUE) Local 453 v. Otis Elevator Co., 314 F.2d 25, 52 LRRM 2543 (2d Cir.), cert. denied, 373 U.S. 949, 53 LRRM 2394 (1963).

contract in discharging the grievant and not the other employees involved in gambling activities?

It is not expected that the parties will agree on the scope of the issue before the arbitrator but, as should be clear from the above examples, an arbitrator's authority to fashion a remedy may vary, depending upon which particular submission agreement is adopted. In many cases the task of determining scope will be left to the arbitrator; indeed, the courts have recognized that such disputes over the scope of submission are themselves to be resolved by the arbitrator.[26] The Second Circuit has held that "[a]ny doubts about the scope of the submission agreement should be resolved in favor of coverage," noting that "[t]he language of arbitration demands should not be subjected to the same strict standards of construction that would be applied in formal court proceedings."[27] The Third Circuit has remarked that "the deference that is accorded to an arbitrator's interpretation of the collective bargaining agreement should also be accorded to an arbitrator's interpretation of the issue submitted."[28] And the Fourth Circuit has held that "the agreement to arbitrate particular issues need not be expressed. It may be implied or established by the conduct of the parties."[29]

What is the proper course to follow when the parties cannot agree on a statement of the issue to be arbitrated? The better rule in this regard is outlined as follows: Unless otherwise stated in the parties' collective bargaining agreement, the recalcitrance of a party to agree on the framing of the issue submitted will not divest the arbitrator of subject-matter

---

[26]Warehousemen Local 767 v. Standard Brands, 560 F.2d 700, 96 LRRM 2682 n.9 (5th Cir. 1977), citing Steelworkers v. United States Gypsum Co., 492 F.2d 713, 732, 85 LRRM 2962 (5th Cir. 1974). Where the agreement provided that "the statement of the question to be arbitrated shall be mutually agreed upon," one court held that this provision required only that the parties make a reasonable effort to agree on the statement of the issue to be submitted. Socony Vacuum Tanker Men's Ass'n v. Socony Mobil Oil Co., 254 F. Supp. 897, 63 LRRM 2037 (S.D.N.Y 1966), aff'd, 369 F.2d 480, 63 LRRM 2590 (2d Cir. 1966). See also Olympia Brewing Co., 72 LA 20 (Madden, 1978) (purpose of arbitration should not be frustrated by lack of agreement as to appropriate framing of issue for submission).
[27]Kurt Orban Co. v. Angeles Metal Systems, 573 F.2d 739, 740 (2d Cir. 1978).
[28]Mobil Oil Corp. v. Oil Workers Local 8-831, 679 F.2d 299, 302, 110 LRRM 2620, 2622 (3d Cir. 1982).
[29]Chemical Workers Local 566 v. Mobay Chem. Corp., 755 F.2d 1107, 1110, 118 LRRM 2859, 2861 (4th Cir. 1985).

jurisdiction. To hold otherwise would frustrate the provisions of agreements calling for final and binding arbitration.[30]

E. Summary

While many cases come before arbitrators without a formal submission agreement, agreeing in advance to the issues and remedies appropriate in a case will not only reduce delays in the arbitration process but will also place the parties on a clear track as to any limitations or directives that the parties desire to place upon the arbitrator.[31] Although a grievance may serve as a submission, a grievance is not the same as the submission. A grievance is a complaint generally alleging that the collective bargaining agreement has been violated. It is made by one party without the agreement or even knowledge of the other party. It is not contractual in nature, only a complaint.[32] The submission agreement, coupled with the contract, defines the outer limits of the arbitrator's authority. In many cases, the parties will submit to arbitration only a part of the issues actually involved in a particular dispute, since they agree that the issues not submitted will be resolved by mutual agreement once the key issue is decided. Alternatively, the parties may conclude that, in connection with a particular dispute, they need an arbitral decision on an issue which the contract had not contemplated. In the latter case,

---

[30]Stauffer Chem. Co. v. Rubber Workers, 116 LRRM 2738, 2740–2741 (S.D. W.Va. 1983).

[31]In Social Sec. Admin., 72 LA 387, 391 (Wahl, 1979), Arbitrator Marvin Wahl focused on the importance of the submission in relation to arbitral authority. In the arbitrator's words:

> Although the parties have agreed that grievances and arbitration may deal with certain policies and regulations of the Administration, as well as matters involving their specific written Agreement, their joint submission deals only with their General Agreement. The submission is clear, containing no ambiguity which justifies interpretation. It is not within the Arbitrator's province to assume that the parties meant anything other than that which they said, even if the reasons therefor are not readily apparent. Thus, it is my conclusion that, by virtue of the joint submission, I am confined to the four corners of the Agreement and cannot look to any regulation or policy unless it can be shown that it is part of the Agreement.

[32]"A grievance is a complaint . . . . It is not a submission agreement." Haddon Craftsmen v. Bookbinders Local 97, 281 A.2d 713, 78 LRRM 2525 (Pa. Sup. Ct. 1971), citing Steelworkers v. Westinghouse Elec. Corp., 413 Pa. 358, 196 A.2d 857, 55 LRRM 2201 (1964).

the submission agreement is in effect the parties' bargaining agreement for purposes of defining the arbitrator's jurisdiction.

A review of arbitration awards and court decisions makes it clear that a carefully drafted submission enables the parties to limit or expand the arbitrator's power and accordingly affect his ultimate authority to formulate a remedy. Although the courts are receptive to inferring broad power to formulate a remedy based merely on a submission to rule on the substantive issue, there are selected instances where courts have vacated awards based on claims that an arbitrator exceeded his authority in formulating a remedy that was not authorized or explicitly called for in the submission.[33] The parties are accordingly advised to take care when making use of submission agreements to state precisely the particular issues and, at minimum, to vest in the arbitrator the power to formulate an appropriate remedy if the parties so desire.[34] If care is not exercised in drafting the question to be resolved and the relief requested, the award may not resolve the dispute and the stage will be set for additional litigation.[35]

---

[33]See, e.g., Courier-Citizen Co. v. Boston Electrotypers Union Local 11, 702 F.2d 273, 281, 112 LRRM 3122, 3129 (1st Cir. 1983) (refusing to allow back pay to person adversely affected by layoff (Sparks) where submission before arbitrator was: "Did the Company violate the contract by placing Richard Grant in the laborer's job . . . . If so, what shall be the remedy?").

[34]Rule 9 of the Voluntary Rules of the American Arbitration Association provides:
Initiation Under a Submission—Parties to any collective bargaining agreement may initiate an arbitration under these Rules by filing at any Regional Office of the AAA two copies of a written agreement to arbitrate under these Rules (Submission), signed by the parties and setting forth the nature of the dispute and the remedy sought.

[35]See Fairweather, supra note 1, at 12.

Chapter 5

External Law as a Remedy

Frequently, either at the parties' request or even on his own motion, an arbitrator will fashion a remedy consistent with or patterned after external law. Indeed, in the federal sector, remedies must conform to the mandates of law and agency regulations.[1] Although arbitrators have decided questions of external law for years, until recently the decisions were few and involved issues not central to the employment relationship.[2] However, with the passage of several statutes regulating the terms and conditions of employment,[3] dupli-

---

[1]Cornelius v. Nutt, 472 U.S. 648, 119 LRRM 2905 (1985) (holding that federal-sector arbitrators are required to follow the "harmful error" rule contained in 5 U.S.C. §7701(c)(2)(A)). See also National Weather Serv. 83 LA 689 (Gaunt, 1984) (applying harmful error rule and Title VII); Veterans Admin. Medical Center, 81 LA 286 (Bailey, 1983) (federal probationary employee precluded from utilizing grievance procedure where D.C. Circuit reversed FLRA ruling).

[2]Feller, *The Coming End of Arbitration's Golden Age*, in Arbitration—1976, Proceedings of the 29th Annual Meeting, National Academy of Arbitrators, 97, 115 (BNA Books, 1976).

[3]See, e.g., Equal Employment Opportunity Act of 1972, Pub. L. No. 92-621, 86 Stat. 103 (1972); Occupational Health and Safety Act of 1970, Pub. L. No. 91-596, 84 Stat. 1590 (1970); Employment Retirement Income Security Act of 1974, Pub. L. No. 93-406, 80 Stat. 829 (1974); Age Discrimination in Employment Act of 1967, Pub. L. No. 90-202, 81 Stat. 602, as amended by Pub. L. No. 95-256, 92 Stat. 189 (1978); Equal Pay Act of 1963, Pub. L. No. 88-38, 77 Stat. 56 (1963); Vocational Rehabilitation Act of 1973, Pub. L. No. 93-112, 87 Stat. 390, as amended by Pub. L. No. 95-602, 92 Stat. 2955 (1978); Veteran's Readjustment Act of 1974, 38 U.S.C. §42 (1974); Fair Labor Standards Act of 1938, Pub. L. No. 75-718, 52 Stat. 1060 (1938); Labor-Management Relations Act, Pub. L. No. 101 ch. 120, 61 Stat. 136 (1947) (current version at 29 U.S.C. §§141–197 (1970 & Supp. V, 1975)).

See, e.g., In re City of Detroit, 73 LA 717 (Daniel, 1979) (federal constitution); Thrifty Corp., 72 LA 898 (Barrett, 1979) (child labor laws); Southwest Power Admin., 72 LA 31 (Schedler, 1978) (Executive Order 11491); Veterans Admin., 72 LA 57 (Goodman, 1978) (Freedom of Information Act); Bethel School Dist., 71 LA 314 (Beck,

cative remedies now exist in several areas of labor-management relations, particularly in discipline and discharge cases that may also involve violations of the Labor-Management Relations (Taft-Hartley) Act or Title VII of the Civil Rights Act of 1964. The increased overlap between contractual rights and those rights existing under statutes have created problems for the arbitrator who decides questions cognizable in both the arbitral and judicial or administrative forums. Does an arbitrator have greater authority to fashion a remedy in those cases that are cognizable in more than one forum? Can the arbitrator go outside the agreement and formulate a remedy when it is demonstrated that there is a conflict between what the contract provides and what the law mandates? Does an arbitrator's authority to issue a remedy depend upon whether the case arises in the public sector? There is much debate about the proper role of the arbitrator in reconciling the provisions of the contract with the mandates of external law; accordingly, in addition to a review of reported court and arbitration cases, this section will capsulize the various schools of thought on this issue. Our thesis is that there are times and circumstances where it is appropriate for an arbitrator to *consider* external law in formulating remedies, both in the private and public sector.

A. Background

The obligation and authority of a labor arbitrator to interpret and apply the law when resolving grievances has been the subject of much discussion and litigation, both in the legal and arbitral forum.[4] Two situations are to be distinguished.

1978) (application of First Amendment Rights); Delta Concrete Prods., 71 LA 538 (Bailey, 1978) (Garnishments & Truth in Lending Act of 1971); City of San Antonio, 69 LA 541 (Caraway, 1977) (state constitution).

[4]See generally Sovern, *When Should Arbitrators Follow Federal Law?* in Arbitration and the Expanding Role of Neutrals, Proceedings of the 23rd Annual Meeting, National Academy of Arbitrators, 29 (BNA Books, 1970); Mittenthal, *The Role of Law in Arbitration*, in Developments in American and Foreign Arbitration, Proceedings of the 21st Annual Meeting, National Academy of Arbitrators, 42 (BNA Books, 1968); Meltzer, *The Role of Law in Arbitration: A Rejoinder*, id. at 58; Howlett, *The Role of Law in Arbitration: A Reprise*, id. at 64; St. Antoine, *Role of Law in Arbitration: Discussion*, id. at 75; Meltzer, *Ruminations About Ideology, Law, and Labor Arbitration*, in The Arbitrator, the NLRB, and the Courts, Proceedings of the 20th Annual Meeting, National Academy of Arbitrators, 1 (BNA Books, 1967); How-

In the first situation, the contractual and statutory standards are not in conflict, but overlap. Few argue that arbitrators should ignore external law when a contractual provision is ambiguous and can be interpreted in two ways—one consistent with the law and one inconsistent therewith. Arbitrator Bernard Meltzer[5] argues that in such a situation, there is not necessarily an incompatibility between the statutory and contractual standard. Meltzer argues that arbitrators, like judges, should seek to avoid a construction that would be invalid "under a higher law" and thus, "where a contractual provision is susceptible to two interpretations, one compatible with, and the other repugnant to, an applicable statute, the statute is a relevant factor for interpretation."[6]

The second, and more difficult, situation involves a conflict between the agreement and a statute. The orthodox position is that an arbitrator's decision is constrained by the collective bargaining agreement, and when there is conflict the arbitrator should respect the agreement and ignore the law. Meltzer, the leading exponent of this traditional view, has argued that arbitrators should respect the agreement, which is the source of their authority, leaving the courts or other official tribunals to determine whether the agreement contravenes a specific statute. Otherwise, arbitrators would be deciding issues beyond the scope not only of the submission agreement, but also of arbitral competence.[7] Meltzer does state that the arbitrator is justified in resolving a legal question if the parties have requested the arbitrator to issue an additional advisory opinion[8] or if they intended to incorporate legal standards into the agreement.[9]

Absent these special circumstances, Meltzer believes that an arbitrator who invokes the law to defeat the negotiated contract exceeds the authority conferred by the submission agreement.[10] In defending this stand Meltzer points out, how-

---

lett, *The Arbitrator, the NLRB, and the Courts*, id. at 67; Cox, *The Place of Law in Labor Arbitration*, in The Profession of Labor Arbitration, Selected Papers From the First Seven Annual Meetings of the National Academy of Arbitrators, 1948–1954, 76 (BNA Books, 1957).

[5]Meltzer, *Ruminations About Ideology, Law, and Labor Arbitration*, supra note 4.
[6]Id. at 15.
[7]Id. at 16.
[8]Id. at 31.
[9]Id. at 15.
[10]Id. at 16–17.

ever, that when addressing the competence of arbitrators he is talking about their institutional competence as distinct from their personal competence, since some arbitrators would have great personal competence to interpret the law.[11]

A contrary position is taken by Arbitrator Robert Howlett,[12] who argues that "arbitrators should render decisions on the issues before them based on both contract language and law."[13] This position is based on the following considerations: (1) The rationale that "each contract includes all applicable law," which becomes "part of the 'essence [of the] collective bargaining agreement' to which Justice Douglas has referred in [*Enterprise Wheel*]";[14] (2) the policy of the NLRB, first enunciated in *Spielberg* (and other cases), favoring the arbitral determination of legal issues;[15] and (3) the notion that

---

[11]Id.

[12]Howlett, *The Arbitrator, the NLRB, and the Courts*, supra note 4.

[13]Id. at 83.

[14]Id., citing Steelworkers v. Enterprise Wheel & Car Corp., 363 U.S. 593, 46 LRRM 2423 (1960).

[15]Id. at 79, citing Spielberg Mfg. Co., 112 NLRB 1080, 36 LRRM 1152 (1955). In *Spielberg*, as part of a settlement of a strike, the employer and the union agreed to arbitrate the question whether four strikers should be reinstated. The arbitration award held that the employer was not obligated to reinstate these four employees. In finding that the employer's refusal to reinstate the strikers violated the Act, the trial examiner rejected the defense based on the arbitrator's award. The Board agreed with the trial examiner that as a matter of law the Board is not bound by the award; however, the Board reversed the trial examiner's ruling and held that the employer did not violate the Act when, in accordance with the award, it refused to reinstate the strikers. The Board found that (1) the proceedings were fair and regular, (2) all parties had agreed to be bound by the decision, and (3) the decision was not repugnant to the purpose and policies of the Act. Id. at 1082. Subsequently, in International Harvester Co., 138 NLRB 923, 51 LRRM 1155 (1962), enf'd sub nom. Ramsey v. NLRB, 327 F.2d 784, 55 LRRM 2441 (7th Cir.), cert. denied, 377 U.S. 1003, 56 LRRM 2544 (1964), the Board refined these criteria in upholding an arbitration award that was not "palpably wrong" and where the proceedings were not "tainted by fraud, collusion, unfairness, or serious procedural irregularities." Id. at 929. Still later, in Banyard v. NLRB, 505 F.2d 342, 87 LRRM 2001 (D.C. Cir. 1974), the court added two new standards to the original *Spielberg* criteria: (1) that the arbitrator must have clearly decided the issue which the Board is asked to defer, and (2) that the arbitrator be competent to decide the issue. See also Suburban Motor Freight, 247 NLRB 146, 102 LRRM 1113, 1114 (1980) (Board "will no longer honor the results of an arbitration proceeding under Spielberg unless the unfair labor practice issue before the Board was both presented to and considered by the arbitrator").

In Olin Corp., 268 NLRB 573, 115 LRRM 1056, 1058 (1984), the Board adopted one more standard. Dissatisfied with the extent to which current deferral doctrine encouraged arbitration, the Board expressly reaffirmed the *Spielberg* criteria and further provided:

> We would find that an arbitrator has adequately considered the unfair labor practice if (1) the contractual issue is factually parallel to the unfair labor practice issue, and (2) the arbitrator was presented generally with the facts relevant to resolving the unfair labor practice. In this respect, differences, if any, between the contractual and statutory standards of review should be weighed by the Board

"an arbitrator who decides a dispute without consideration of legal issues disserves his management-union clients."[16] Indeed under Howlett's view, an arbitrator is not only under a duty to apply substantive law, but is also under an affirmative duty to probe for a statutory violation. In Howlett's words: "Unless he does so, neither the General Counsel nor the Board will 'defer' to the arbitrator's decision."[17]

Several commentators have proposed solutions somewhere between the Meltzer and Howlett positions. Archibald Cox has argued that an arbitrator should look to the statutes to avoid rendering an award the would require the parties to violate the law.[18] Cox states that this position does not suggest that an arbitrator should pass upon all parties' legal rights and obligations, nor does it suggest that an arbitrator should refuse to give effect to a contract provision merely because the courts would not enforce it. Moreover, it does not imply that an arbitrator should be guided by judge-made rules of evidence or contract interpretations. According to Cox, the principle "requires only that the arbitrator look to see whether sustaining the grievances would require conduct the law forbids or would enforce an illegal contract; if so, the arbitrator should not sustain the grievance."[19]

In an address before the National Academy of Arbitrators in 1968, Arbitrator Richard Mittenthal, asserting that, on balance, the relevant considerations support Cox's view,[20] nevertheless refined Cox's position as follows:

---

as part of its determination under the Spielberg standards of whether an award is "clearly repugnant" to the Act. And, with regard to the inquiry into the "clearly repugnant" standard, we would not require an arbitrator's award to be totally consistent with Board precedent. Unless the award is "palpably wrong," i.e., unless the arbitrator's decision is not susceptible to an interpretation consistent with the Act, we will defer.

Finally, we would require that the party seeking to have the Board reject deferral and consider the merits of a given case show that the above standards for deferral have not been met. Thus, the party seeking to have the Board ignore the determination of an arbitrator has the burden of affirmatively demonstrating the defects in the arbitral process or award.

In those cases in which no award has issued, the Board's guidelines have been less clear. At times the Board has dealt with the unfair labor practice claim, and at others it has left the parties to their contractual remedies. See Collyer Insulated Wire, 192 NLRB 837, 77 LRRM 1931 (1971).

[16]Howlett, The Arbitrator, the NLRB, and the Courts, supra note 4, at 79.
[17]Id. at 92.
[18]Cox, supra note 4, at 78.
[19]Id. at 79.
[20]Mittenthal, supra note 4.

The arbitrator should "look to see whether sustaining the grievance would require conduct the law forbids or would enforce an illegal contract; if so, the arbitrator should not sustain the grievance." This principle, however, should be carefully limited. It does not suggest that "an arbitrator should refuse to give effect to a contract provision merely because the courts would not enforce it." Thus, although the arbitrator's award may permit conduct forbidden by law but sanctioned by contract, it should not require conduct forbidden by law even though sanctioned by contract.[21]

Mittenthal cited several examples that demonstrate the rationale behind his position, including the following, which was first proposed by Cox. After World War II a conflict developed between provisions of the Selective Service Act and contractual provisions of collective bargaining contracts dealing with seniority. The Supreme Court interpreted the Act to require employers to give veterans preference over nonveterans in the event of layoffs during the first year after their discharge from the armed forces,[22] while the common collective bargaining contract gave veterans only the seniority they would have had if they had not been drafted. The other example concerned a problem arising under the National Labor Relations Act. Without prior discussion with the union, an employer advanced starting time at the plant pursuant to a contract granting the employer "sole jurisdiction over all matters concerning the management of the plant subject only to the terms of the agreement." In the first example, the union filed a grievance when the employer released a nonveteran who had more contract seniority than a veteran. In the second, the union charged that statutory rights and duties are part of the contract and that the unilateral action was a violation of Section 8(a)(5) of the LMRA, which makes it an unfair labor practice for an employer to refuse to bargain collectively with representatives of its employees.

Mittenthal would apply the Supreme Court's ruling in the first example and deny the grievance because such an award would require the employer to engage in conduct forbidden by law. In the second hypothetical, he would deny the

---

[21]Id. at 50.
[22]Fishgold v. Sullivan Drydock & Repair Corp., 328 U.S. 275, 18 LRRM 2075 (1946).

grievance if there were no contract violations, for even if the employer's actions were contrary to law, the award would merely permit and not require illegal action. Arbitrator Mittenthal supports his position by reasoning that contracts contemplate "final and binding" awards, and that an award compelling unlawful conduct cannot really be "final and binding" since "the dispute over the contract, over the award itself, would continue into the courts."[23] However, Mittenthal realizes that the arbitrator should, for the same reason, enforce statutory obligations because failure to do so would likely result in a court suit:

> When an arbitrator refuses to enforce a statutory obligation, his award is "final and binding" with respect to the contract. The grievant has no contract question to take to court. He may pursue his statutory rights in the appropriate forum, but such a suit has nothing to do with the contract.[24]

Michael Sovern[25] offers a more detailed compromise to the debate, listing the following criteria that should be satisfied before an arbitrator entertains a legal issue:

1. The arbitrator is qualified.
2. The question of law is implicated in a dispute over the application or interpretation of a contract that is also before him.
3. The question of law is raised by a contention that, if the conduct complained of does violate the contract, the law nevertheless immunizes or even requires it.
4. The courts lack primary jurisdiction to adjudicate the questions of law.[26]

Sovern notes that in a Title VII case, the fourth criterion is

---

[23]Mittenthal, supra note 4, at 52 n.37.

[24]Id. The authors take the position that Mittenthal's distinction between "permitting" and "requiring" a violation of the law is not functionally useful. As Meltzer notes, "[I]f the arbitrator is viewed as 'enforcing' contracts, he 'enforces' an illegal contract equally whether he causes an employer to engage in an act prohibited by statute or, by denying a remedy, condones the prohibited act already executed by the employer." Meltzer, *The Role of Law in Arbitration: A Rejoinder*, supra note 4, at 60.

[25]Sovern, supra note 4.

[26]Id. at 38.

not met, since the courts have primary jurisdiction to decide Title VII questions.[27]

Similar to Sovern, Scheinholtz and Miscimarra argue that it is not instructive to ask whether arbitrators should or shouldn't consider statutory issues. Rather, if arbitration is to be preserved as a practical, expeditious, and final method of dispute resolution under the parties' labor agreement, the more helpful query is "whether and under what circumstances is the consideration of statutory issues appropriate."[28] Noting that it is impossible to formulate a single answer to the question of whether statutory issues should be considered by an arbitrator, the authors maintain the four guiding principles should be considered when determining whether an arbitrator should consider external law: (1) the authority of the arbitrator (Do the parties explicitly indicate in their labor agreement that an arbitrator cannot consider issues of external law?); (2) arbitral expertise (Is the arbitrator competent to resolve the statutory issue?); (3) arbitration hearing procedures (Will the parties' procedure enable a fair resolution of the issue?); and (4) the finality or "nonredundancy" of the procedure (Does an arbitrator ever perform a service by handing down an award that is predestined not to be enforced?). Consideration of statutory issues will vary depending on a balancing of these factors.

B. Arbitral Experience

An examination of arbitration and court decisions shows wide differences on the questions of applying law when issuing awards and formulating remedies. While situations vary from case to case, a number of patterns emerge depending upon whether the parties have granted the arbitrator the authority to consider statutory issues, whether the contract is silent on

---

[27]Id. at 45. In Alexander v. Gardner-Denver Co., 415 U.S. 36, 7 FEP Cases 81 (1974), the Supreme Court limited the influence of arbitration decisions in civil rights matters by holding that an arbitral award does not bar a concurrent or subsequent suit in federal court alleging discrimination under Title VII. See Hill, *The Authority of a Labor Arbitrator to Decide Legal Issues Under a Collective Bargaining Contract: The Situation After* Alexander v. Gardner Denver, 10 Ind. L. Rev. 899 (1977).

[28]Scheinholtz and Miscimarra, *The Arbitrator as Judge and Jury: Another Look at Statutory Law in Arbitration*, 40 Arb. J. No. 2, at 55 (1985).

matters of external law, and whether the award will cause or require unlawful conduct by a party.

1. Granting the Arbitrator Authority to Consider External Law

Frequently the parties explicitly incorporate external law into the agreement or, alternatively, by submission empower the arbitrator to rule on a legal issue. In such cases, arbitrators, with few exceptions, have not hesitated to "apply the law" when interpreting the agreement.

a. Incorporating Legal Standards Into the Collective Bargaining Agreement

Arbitrator Jack Clarke, in *Combustion Engineering*,[29] held an employee's discharge was improper because the employer denied the employee's request that a union steward be present at a meeting where the grievant was questioned for his alleged misconduct. The arbitrator found that it was appropriate to apply standards enunciated by the Supreme Court in *NLRB v. Weingarten*,[30] where the contract, in relevant part, provided that "[a]ny part of this Agreement which is or may become in violation of or in conflict with the laws of the United States or of the State of Tennessee shall be null and void, and shall be made to conform to such laws without voiding any other part of this Agreement."[31]

Similarly, Arbitrator Bruce Boals, in *Southern Gage Co.*,[32] applied the EEOC's guidelines and applicable case law under Title VII when holding that an employer violated a contract provision barring discrimination based on sex by denying family health-care coverage to a married female employee. The arbitrator found that the agreement was "tantamount to the incorporation of applicable statutory and administrative law" where the contract contained a provision applying its terms to all employess "without discrimination on account of race,

---

[29]67 LA 349 (1976).
[30]420 U.S. 251, 88 LRRM 2689 (1975).
[31]67 LA at 349–350.
[32]68 LA 755 (1977).

color, national origin, sex, or creed."[33] "Why else," stated the arbitrator, "would it be in the Agreement?"

In *Chrysler Corp.*,[34] Arbitrator Gabriel Alexander found that where the contract provided that reemployment rights of employees and probationary employees "will be limited by applicable laws and regulation," it would be permissible for the arbitrator to rule on an employee's claim that his constitutional rights to free speech had been infringed upon by the employer. Arbitrator Alexander did state, however, that in the absence of a special grant of authority of the sort mentioned, "arbitrators should not depart from the contractual frame of reference in which they function."[35]

And Arbitrator Philip Marshall, in *FSC Paper Corp.*,[36] declared:

> I have always been of the view that all applicable provisions of State and Federal Law impress themselves upon *all* contracts, including collective bargaining agreements, and that therefore arbitrator[s] cannot give their exclusive attention to those matters which are specifically set forth within the four corners of a collective bargaining contract.[37]

The arbitrator went on to note that the parties' agreement contained an antidiscrimination clause which, in the arbitrator's opinion, incorporated by reference applicable provisions of federal law. Arbitrator Marshall went on to hold that there was no basis to sustain a charge of race discrimination.

Taking a narrow view of his authority to apply law, Arbitrator Samuel Kates, in *Stark County Engineer*,[38] ruled that decisions under the National Labor Relations Act do not constitute "applicable law" with which the construction of the

---

[33]Id. at 758.
[34]62 LA 161 (1974).
[35]Id. at 164. See also Apollo-Ridge School Dist., 68 LA 1235 (LeWinter, 1977) (arbitrator's duty to examine general law to determine meaning of contract where parties have incorporated by reference state and federal laws as to maternity leaves); County of Los Angeles, 68 LA 1132 (Richman, 1977) (agreement integrating Fair Labor Standards Act); Frazer & Johnston Co., 66 LA 250 (Killian, 1976) (proper to consider NLRB and court rulings on issue of employer obligation to discharge employee for failure to tender union dues where contract language is identical to statutory provisions in LMRA); Virginia Elec. & Power Co., 61 LA 844 (Murphy, 1973) (proper to consider public law of equal employment where agreement provides that all provisions are to be applied to all employees without regard to sex, race, color, religious creed, or national origin).
[36]65 LA 25 (1975).
[37]Id. at 27.
[38]88 LA 497 (1986).

agreement must be consistent under language providing that "[t]he arbitrator's decision shall be consistent with applicable law." Arbitrator Kates pointed out that this provision must be read with language providing that "[t]he arbitrator shall limit his decision *strictly* to the interpretation, application or enforcement of those *specific* articles and/or sections of this Agreement in question."

How far can arbitrators venture in determining that the parties' agreement incorporates external law? Suppose they apply the law incorrectly? The limit is unknown, but case law indicates that arbitrators' decisions are entitled to great deference. In *Postal Workers v. Postal Service*,[39] Judge Harry Edwards, a former arbitrator, delivered a unanimous opinion in which the D.C. Circuit upheld an arbitration award that applied *Miranda*-type warnings to the Postal Service. The grievant, a postal window and supply clerk, had been discharged for alleged dishonesty in handling postal transactions. As part of an investigation, a postal inspector interviewed the grievant regarding the suspected theft. After approximately one hour and twenty minutes of questioning, the inspector read the employee his *Miranda* rights and presented him with a waiver. The grievant then signed two statements admitting dishonesty in the handling of postal transactions.

At the grievant's criminal trial, the court excluded the grievant's statements, ruling that they were the result of interrogation prior to the recitation of *Miranda* warnings and, therefore, were obtained in violation of the fifth amendment. The grievant was acquitted.

Hearings were later held before an arbitrator, who refused to admit into evidence the grievant's statements given to the federal authorities during the interrogation. The arbitrator ruled the statements inadmissible in a civil removal proceeding because the grievant had not been given his *Miranda*-type warnings. The grievant's dismissal was reversed because the grievant's excluded statements were the only evidence of theft. Substituting its judgment for that of the arbitrator, the district court vacated the award.

Reversing the district court, Judge Edwards noted that the parties' collective bargaining agreement specified that the

---

[39]789 F.2d 1, 122 LRRM 2094 (D.C. Cir. 1986).

discharge of a Postal Service employee must be "consistent with applicable laws and regulations." The *Miranda* rule, said Edwards, "is surely within the realm of 'applicable law' when interrogation by federal law enforcement officers leads to the discharge of an employee." It did not matter whether the arbitrator's construction and application of the *Miranda* rule was correct as a matter of law. Judge Edwards concluded that the district court's decision was contrary to the legal principles enunciated by the Supreme Court in *Enterprise Wheel* and *W. R. Grace & Co.*[40] The court stated that an award will not be vacated even though the arbitrator may have made errors of fact and law, "unless it 'compels the violation of law or conduct contrary to accepted public policy.' "[41]

b. Submission Agreements

As an alternative to drafting a labor agreement incorporating applicable law, special submission agreements may be executed authorizing arbitrators to render a decision on legal, as distinct from contractual, grounds. A decision by Arbitrator Joseph Shister illustrates using submission in such fashion. In *Michigan Consolidated Gas Co.*,[42] the parties submitted the issue of whether the employer had violated the ninth and fourteenth amendments of the Constitution or, if not, the Taft-Hartley Act in establishing grooming standards for employees. In executing the submission, the parties agreed that, if the arbitrator found a violation of both of the above, a hearing date would be set to consider the merits of the grievance in question. The arbitrator found that he could not rule on the question of whether the employer's grooming standard was a reasonable application of the agreement, since the sole issue submitted was the constitutionality or legality of the employer's action.[43]

---

[40]W. R. Grace & Co. v. Rubber Workers Local 759, 461 U.S. 757, 113 LRRM 2641, 39 FEP Cases 1409 (1983).

[41]789 F.2d at 7. See also Postal Serv. v. Letter Carriers, 789 F.2d 18, 122 LRRM 2101 (D.C. Cir. 1986) (sustaining award holding that language in parties' labor agreement subjecting exercise of management rights to applicable laws and regulations included Tennessee statute entitling all employees to regular wages while serving on jury).

[42]58 LA 1058 (1972).

[43]Id. at 1060.

Arbitrator Thomas Roberts considered a claim that an employer's elimination of outside phone service was both a violation of the collective bargaining agreement and of the employer's obligation to bargain under Section 8(a)(5) of Taft-Hartley. Although the union had filed charges with the NLRB and the regional director had advised the parties that he would defer action on the complaint until completion of the grievance-arbitration process, Arbitrator Roberts nevertheless stated that the "arbitral submission is unique in that the parties request not only a consideration of the import of the collective bargaining agreement but also an adjudication of the pending unfair labor practice charge in consonance with the purposes and policies of the Labor-Management Relations Act."[44] Although the arbitrator found both a violation of the statute and of the agreement, he stated that the remedy usually granted by the Board in such a case would be an order calling upon the employer to now bargain in good faith regarding the change in telephone capability. This remedy, reasoned the arbitrator, would not afford the affected employees redress for the contractual violation. Arbitrator Roberts accordingly ordered restoration of the telephone service.[45]

In *General Foods Corp.*,[46] Arbitrator Eaton Conant stated that the case before him was not complicated by any of the problems arbitrators might encounter in discrimination cases with respect to whether law external to the agreement should intrude into the decision-making process. The parties had specifically framed the issue to indicate whether the grievant's rights under the agreement and Title VII of the Civil Rights Act were violated.[47] The contract also provided: "In the application of this Agreement and in accordance with applicable Federal and State laws, there shall be no discrimination against employees because of race, color, religion, sex, age or national origin."[48]

---

[44]Universal City Studios, 71 LA 325, 327 (1978).

[45]Id. at 328.

[46]72 LA 505 (1979)

[47]Id. at 508.

[48]Id. at 507. See also Sterling Regal, Inc., 69 LA 513 (Kaplan, 1977) (submission pursuant to *Collyer* of issue whether union violated §§8(b)(4)(i) and (ii)(B) of LMRA's secondary boycott provisions); Doces Sixth Ave., Inc., 66 LA 1143 (Beck, 1976) (submission whether fines levied by union are enforceable under applicable labor law); Richard La Chance, 63 LA 640 (Laybourne, 1974) (parties agree to make arbitrator "referee" and decide case as though issue had been submitted to judge in Common

c. The Significance of "No Discrimination" and "Savings" Clauses

Arbitrator David Feller has argued that it has become almost standard practice to insert into the collective bargaining agreement a no-discrimination provision, of one of three varieties: (1) those that provide that the employer shall not discriminate in the application of the provisions of the collective bargaining agreement on any of the forbidden bases; (2) provisions that the employer shall not discriminate on any of the forbidden grounds involving wages, hours, or working conditions; and (3) provisions where the parties explicitly incorporate into the agreement the provisions of the external law governing the question of discrimination.

Feller argues that since discriminatory application of a provision of a collective bargaining agreement would, in any case, be found to be a violation of the agreement, the first type of provision adds nothing to the agreement but "protective coloring." The second type of antidiscriminatory provision is important because it is potentially applicable to questions within the scope of the employment relationship that are not dealt with either specifically or impliedly in the agreement. According to Feller, arbitrators who encounter this type of no-discrimination provision may look to decisions or guidelines issued by agencies charged with administering antidiscrimination statutes in determining grievances that arise under such a provision and do not implicate any other provisions of the collective agreement. But in so doing, arbitrators would still be adjudicators of what the parties intended to govern their relationships with each other, rather than expounders of the meaning and application of external law.

An example of the third type is an agreement that not only forbids race discrimination by the company or the union, but also declares that both parties will abide by and comply with all applicable federal laws banning discrimination in regard to hiring, promotion, and job assignment. Clearly, under such a provision the arbitrator is designated as "an expounder of the meaning and application of external law."[49]

Pleas Court); North Am. Mfg., 62 LA 1219 (Hutcheson, 1974) (issue whether employer's no-discrimination rules are valid under LMRA).
[49]Feller, supra note 2, at 117–118.

Owen Fairweather has also argued that where the agreement contains an express clause to the effect that any provision found to be illegal shall be unenforceable—a so-called "savings" provision—the arbitrator should apply external law.[50]

In the absence of an explicit directive not to consider matters of external law, the authors' view is that all the above situations provide a contractual basis (some more so than others) for considering statutory issues. Similarly, standard just-cause provisions provide the basis for arbitral consideration of unfair labor practice arguments under the Labor-Management Relations Act. Finally, "savings" clauses also clothe the arbitrator with the authority to consider external law.

2. Interpreting the Agreement Consistent With External Law

When the contract is silent on incorporation of external law in formulating awards and remedies, most arbitrators, while not announcing that their decision is based upon legal doctrine, will not ignore the mandates of law, but rather will issue an award consistent with the law. This position, of course, is consistent with both the Meltzer and Howlett views that an arbitrator should not ignore law where a contractual provision is ambiguous and can be interpreted in two ways—one consistent and one inconsistent with law. Thus, Arbitrator Charles Morris, in *South Central Bell Telephone Co.*,[51] while not basing his award and remedy upon the mandates of external law, nevertheless found that NLRB decisions represented "pertinent authority" in finding that an employer violated the contract in unilaterally eliminating a past practice. Similarly, Arbitrator Adolph Koven, in *County of Santa Clara*,[52] stated that a grievance alleging sex discrimination in the classification of employees was "in accord with Title

---

[50]See Fairweather, Practice and Procedure in Labor Arbitration, 2d ed.; 449–450 (BNA Books, 1983); but see Feller supra note 2, at 118 (such provision doubtfully incorporates into the agreement the provisions of antidiscrimination statutes). See also Clarion-Limestone Area School Dist., 90 LA 281 (Creo, 1988) (enforcing separability clause); PPG Indus., 87 LA 74 (Duff, 1986) (interpreting savings clause).
[51]72 LA 333 (1979).
[52]71 LA 290 (1978).

VII case law," and such preferential treatment was "permitted under Title VII."[53]

Arbitrator David Feller submits that in a substantial number of cases arbitrators mention and discuss statutes and administrative decisions by agencies such as the NLRB, but they do so only by analogy as an aid in construing and applying the collective bargaining agreement.[54] In this respect, Feller further notes:

> [A]n arbitrator faced with a grievance implicating questions under the NLRA, which is being heard because the Board has deferred to the arbitrator, can make it clear that he is not deciding any questions under the NLRA but simply determining whether, on the facts presented, it can be said that the employer violated the terms of the collective bargaining agreement.[55]

Feller points out that an often-forgotten example of this position is Milton Schmidt's decision in *Enterprise Wheel*, which, after the employer refused to comply with the award, turned up as the subject matter of the third case in the *Steelworkers Trilogy*. Arbitrator Schmidt decided that he had the authority to order reinstatement with back pay to wrongfully discharged employees, even though by the time the award was made the collective bargaining agreement had expired and was not renewed. His decision noted that the NLRB provided such a remedy in similar situations. Feller asserts, however, that the arbitrator did not purport to base his award upon the NLRA. His decision was enforced on the theory that it was a permissible interpretation, not of the NLRA, but of the collective bargaining agreement.[56]

Some arbitrators take the position that even where the agreement is susceptible to two interpretations—one consistent and the other inconsistent with the law—the arbitrator should not enter the field of legalities and attempt to interpret the law. Such a view was arguably taken by Arbitrator George Young in *St. Regis Paper Co.*[57] In that decision an employee claimed sickness and accident benefits which she argued were due during her pregnancy leave. Finding that the agreement

---

[53]Id. at 294–295.
[54]Feller, supra note 2, at 115.
[55]Id. at 122.
[56]Id. at 115.
[57]65 LA 802 (1975).

was silent on disability for pregnancy unaccompanied by other physical problems, the arbitrator held that the grievant was not entitled to such benefits. The arbitrator did note, however, that this decision did not end the matter, since she could be entitled to the remedy she sought from another source, specifically Title VII of the Civil Rights Act. On this issue, the arbitrator stated that he was expressing no opinion because of his belief that "the interpretation of Federal laws and regulations is not the proper function of an arbitrator who is empowered only to interpret the language of the Agreement and not to add to it or to change it."[58] Arbitrator Young declared that if an award is to be based on external law, the arbitrator's authority should stem from the statute or rule and not a stipulation of the parties.

3. Conflict Between Contract and Law

Where a true conflict is determined to exist between the terms of the agreement and the requirements of enacted legislation, the reported cases indicate divergent views on whether the contract or the law should prevail.

a. Decisions Applying External Law

Where a company refused an employee's request for union representation during an investigatory conference and discharged him for failing to cooperate, Arbitrator David Dolnick, in *Illinois Bell Telephone Co.*,[59] held firm to the view that when a public law is in direct conflict with an express or implied provision of a collective bargaining agreement, the law takes precedence. In Dolnick's words, "[f]or all intents and purposes such a public law establishes public policy which an arbitrator should not ignore." He went on to note, however, that there are public laws that only appear to be in conflict with contractual terms, and these laws need to be interpreted and clarified. Where no interpretation of external law by a designated public agency or by a court exists, an arbitrator may properly interpret the contract provision in relation to

---

[58]Id. at 803.
[59]63 LA 968 (1974).

such a public law. In the case where no definitive decision is made by an agency or court having jurisdiction to interpret and apply the law, "then an arbitrator is obliged to accept and apply such an interpretation and decision even though it may be in direct conflict with the express or implied terms in the contract."[60] Finding that the U.S. Courts of Appeals had refused to enforce NLRB decisions requiring union representation during investigatory interviews, and that the Supreme Court was about to rule on the issue, Arbitrator Dolnick accordingly ruled that the company was not required under the contract to afford union representation and, thus, the discharge was sustained.

International Paper Co.[61] reports a decision where an arbitrator was confronted with an agreement that was apparently in conflict with an affirmative action program. In considering the validity of awarding an apprenticeship job to a black employee instead of a senior white employee, Arbitrator Jay Taylor held that he could not just look to the contract that was "clear and unequivocal," but must also consider applicable remedial programs:

> I fully recognize that an Arbitrator is a creature of the Contract. His powers are created in the Contract and are limited by the Contract. And I have asked myself the questions—Does the arbitrator have greater authority to fashion a remedy in discrimination cases other than what is set forth in the Collective Bargaining Agreement? Can the Arbitrator go outside the Collective Bargaining Agreement and apply the law if there is a conflict? My answer must be: When a group of employees, as is clearly evident in this case, has been found to be the victims of past discrimination, and the Company through its Affirmative Action Program has fashioned a remedy to alleviate the problem, then I must conclude that this remedy is exempt from Contractual obligations.[62]

Although the contract provided that the position would be awarded on the basis of "seniority consistent with ability," the arbitrator nevertheless denied the grievance of the senior employee because of the obligations placed upon the employer pursuant to an affirmative action program.

---

[60]Id. at 976.
[61]69 LA 857 (1977).
[62]Id. at 860–861.

Where a federal court found that a union had used a contractually authorized referral system, a hiring hall, in a discriminatory fashion,[63] Arbitrator Jay Kramer found that a multiemployer association was excused from compliance with that provision. Citing a nondiscrimination requirement in the agreement, the arbitrator reasoned that the court's mandate under Title VII and other civil rights legislation could never be achieved under the present exclusive hiring-hall language.[64]

In an unpublished 1989 arbitration between a company that chartered and operated coastal and seagoing tankers and a union representing seamen, Arbitrator Jesse Simons ruled that he could not provide a monetary remedy for breach of a recognition clause when the employer improperly failed to apply the terms of the collective bargaining agreement to some tug-barges acquired after the parties signed their labor agreement. The NLRB had determined that the tug-barge seamen did not accrete to the union-represented unit and, therefore, management argued that the arbitrator was foreclosed from finding that the agreement was applicable to the tug-barges.

Rejecting the employer's argument that the determination of questions of representation, accretion, and appropriate unit do not depend upon contract interpretation, Arbitrator Simons found that the employer had a contractual obligation to recognize and negotiate with the union regarding the seamen working the tug-barges. Simons also found that management violated the agreement when it failed to secure certain tug-barge personnel through the union hiring hall. With respect to the remedy issue (as a remedy the union sought not "performance" by accretion, but payment of all monies due employees and benefit funds for employees who would have been employed under the agreement), the arbitrator concluded that "he is required by extrinsic law to abstain from awarding the remedy sought by the Union for [management's] breach of the Agreement." Two reasons were cited by Simons:

> The first is that my review of all of the court decisions cited by both parties, taken together with the fact pattern . . . has

---

[63]See Commonwealth of Pa. v. Operating Eng'rs Local 542, 469 F. Supp. 329, 18 FEP Cases 1560 (E.D. Pa. 1978).

[64]Operating Eng'rs Employers, 72 LA 1223 (1979).

caused me to conclude that I am without the authority to direct payment of the sums sought as [a] remedy by the Union. The Undersigned is of the view that in the exercise of his arbitral function, he is required also to act in accordance with the law and public policy as enunciated by the NLRB and/or the Federal Courts.

The second reason for abstaining from directing a remedy is the conclusion that it probably would be an exercise in futility to do otherwise because it would result in a motion to vacate the Award, which motion might well be upheld in Federal Court.

What is noteworthy is that the Arbitrator, citing a decision from the Second Circuit[65] and other case law, was convinced that awarding the union simple "damages" for management's failure to apply the terms of the agreement to the tug-barges would clearly violate federal labor law, as would an award of specific performance. Simons accordingly rejected the union's argument that "the Arbitrator is not authorized to consider matters extraneous to the language of the Agreement . . . ."

b. Decisions Ignoring External Law

Evans Products Co. v. Millmen's No. 550[66] is a classic case illustrating the dilemma faced by arbitrators when an award based solely on the contract will not be enforced by a court because it compels an employer to contravene a statute. Adrian Landers was dispatched by the union to fill a vacancy pursuant to a nonexclusive hiring hall. The parties' contract required Evans to hire individuals referred to it by the union if qualified to do the job. The agreement also prohibited discrimination "against any employee or applicant for employment on the basis of age." Evans refused to hire Landers, who was 17 years old at the time, solely because the position required that he perform duties specifically declared to be hazardous by the Secretary of Labor and thereby illegal under the child labor provisions of the Fair Labor Standards Act (FLSA). After his selection, but before the arbitration hearing,

---

[65]Masters, Mates & Pilots v. Trinidad Corp., 803 F.2d 69, 123 LRRM 2792 (2d Cir. 1986) (holding that if arbitrator's specific enforcement of collective bargaining agreement requiring employer to apply its terms to subsidiary would violate NLRA, award of damages would also violate statute).

[66]159 Cal.App.3d 815 (1984).

the arbitrator informed the parties in writing of his view that his function was confined to the interpretation of the agreement. Before the hearing the arbitrator reiterated his view that he did not have the authority to consider the application of "external" child labor laws unless the parties stipulated to such an extension of his jurisdiction. The parties refused (the union was willing to have the arbitrator decide the factual issue and leave the legal issue for another tribunal), and the arbitrator ruled that Evans' refusal to employ Landers violated the age clause of the agreement.

Ruling that the arbitrator's decision would compel Evans to contravene the child labor provisions of the FLSA, a California Appellate Court held that the award was not enforceable on grounds of illegality alone.

Another case illustrating allegiance to the contract rather than to the mandates of external law is *Jackson Purchase Rural Electric Cooperative Ass'n v. Electrical Workers (IBEW) Local 816*.[67] The parties' contract was silent on the issue of checking off union dues, but for 16 years Jackson Purchase deducted dues from employee paychecks and paid them over to Local 816 without written authorization from the affected employees. When management unilaterally terminated this practice, the union filed a grievance and the matter was submitted to arbitration. The arbitrator found that the practice violated federal law, specifically Section 302 of the Labor Management Relations Act. However, the arbitrator concluded that the legality was relevant only between "the federal government and each of the parties separately and should not affect [the] consensual relationship between [employer and union]." As to the relationship between the parties the arbitrator concluded that the fact that the practice continued for 16 years created an implied agreement to check off union dues, and this agreement had become a part of the collective bargaining agreement. He ordered Jackson to continue to check off union dues upon receipt of proper authorization cards from the employees. A federal district court set aside the award, holding that since the check-off violated the Act it could not be enforced, and this decision was affirmed by the Sixth Circuit.

---

[67]646 F.2d 264, 107 LRRM 2181 (6th Cir. 1981).

The award, said the appellate court, depended on the illegal past practice, and thus was not based on the collective bargaining agreement.

Adopting a Meltzer-type position, Arbitrator Gabriel Alexander, in *Chrysler Corp.*,[68] stated:

> I think that as Chairman I should confine my deliberations and rulings to issues of contract meaning and application, and that where the applicable agreement is plain on its face, I should not ignore or nullify it even if I were convinced that it was not enforceable at law.[69]

In that decision, Arbitrator Alexander cited the similar views of Umpire Ralph Seward in a veterans seniority case at General Motors:

> The Umpire in his official capacity is a creature of the Agreement. His power is derived from it. His jurisdiction is defined by it. His only function is to interpret and apply it. So far as his official rulings are concerned, therefore, he must assume the Agreement's validity, for to do otherwise would be to question the very authority under which those rulings are issued.
>
> To the parties, their right under the law to do the things to which they have agreed, should be of great concern. It cannot concern the Umpire. His duty is to decide disputes between them as to the meaning and application of their Agreement. He cannot be relieved of that duty by the possibility that their Agreement is void as contrary to law.[70]

Similarly, Arbitrator Geraldine Randall, in *Alameda-Contra Costa Transit Dist.*,[71] considered an employee's claim that he had a constitutional right to a hearing prior to his suspension, notwithstanding a contractual provision giving the employer the right to suspend without any such hearing. The union argued that since the employer was a public agency, the grievant was protected under the Constitution and that his constitutional rights were violated when he was suspended without a hearing. In rejecting this argument, the arbitrator stated that even assuming the Constitution does in fact require such a hearing, it does not follow that the arbitrator must, or even may, apply constitutional rather than contrac-

---

[68]62 LA 161 (1974).
[69]Id. at 164.
[70]Id. at 164, citing Decision D-31, May 17, 1946.
[71]71 LA 889 (1978).

tual standards. The arbitrator reasoned that to apply the contractual standards is not to find that the employee's
constitutional rights have been waived. Arbitrator Randall
noted that the employee was not required to use the contractual grievance procedure, but elected to do so. If the grievant
wished to assert constitutional rights, there was an alternative forum for that purpose. Finally, the arbitrator found that
to uphold the position of the grievant would have required a
decision outside the submission agreement—in this case, the
collective bargaining agreement—and thus an "amendment"
to the agreement, which the contract explicitly prohibited.[72]

In announcing that he was taking a "middle position,"
Arbitrator Arthur Porter, in *Eaton Corp.*,[73] could not conclude
that an employer engaged in sex discrimination when it assigned a male machine tender to fill in for an absent employee
in another department, instead of assigning such work to a
female machine tender. The arbitrator stated that a decision
supporting the grievant would be based on definitions outside
the normal concepts of discrimination, and that the arbitrator
did not have the authority to make such application. Arbitrator Porter noted that such application must be rendered by a
duly authorized federal or state judicial body, and not the
arbitrator.[74]

---

[72]Id. at 892. See also George A. Hormel & Co., 90 LA 1246, 1248 (Goodman, 1988)
("Arbitrators have no authority to interpret law even though an arbitrator might be
well qualified to do so."); Minnesota Dep't of Corrections, 88 LA 535, 538 (Gallagher,
1987) ("right created by the labor agreement must prevail unless that right is made
subservient to the Consent Decree either by some binding provision of external law
or by the consent of *both* parties to the labor agreement"); Kentile Floors, 66 LA 933
(Larkin, 1976) ("[I]f one is claiming a violation of the Civil Rights Act of 1964, the
matter should be taken to the EEOC rather than to arbitration"; while arbitrators
must respect external law, it is not arbitrators' function to administer law); Union
Tank Car Co., 55 LA 170, 181 (Platt, 1970) ("I must decline to decide the legal question
raised. It need hardly be added that, in doing so, those questions . . . are left for
resolution, in the parties' discretion, in a forum which has responsibility for dealing
with such specialized matters."); Studebaker Corp., 49 LA 105, 109 (Davey, 1967)
("clear in unmistakable terms that [arbitrator] is not commissioned to interpret Title
VII . . . . [S]ole responsibility is decision of disputes over the interpretation or application of . . . agreement"); Pitman-Moore Div., 49 LA 709, 718 (Seinsheimer, 1967)
("I do not intend to judge whether the procedure or practice that has been followed
is discriminatory or not. It may well have been, or may be, a violation of the Civil
Rights Act, but it is my opinion that it is not up to the Arbitrator to interpret the
Federal Law. My responsibility has only to do with determining if the Company has
violated provisions of the Contract.").
[73]73 LA 729 (1979).
[74]Id. at 732.

Arbitrator Russell A. Smith, in *Globe-Democrat Publishing Co.*,[75] adopted a similar middle position:

> I recognize, however, that the authority to decide these legal questions is vested in the Board and courts, not in the Arbitrator. The parties have agreed that my task has been to interpret their agreement. This I have done. My only concern, with respect to the legal issues . . . has been whether my award will have the effect of ordering the Company to perform an illegal act. Since, at best, this conclusion is in doubt, I feel that I should discharge my primary function, and enter an award which in my view is justified as a matter of contract interpretation.[76]

A major reason for sticking to the collective bargaining agreement, even when it is apparent that the agreement may conflict with external law, is illustrated in *Hunter Engineering Co.*,[77] a case reported by Arbitrator Reginald Alleyne. The parties' contract protected union officials from layoff so long as there was work they were able to perform. The grievant, a union vice president, was laid off at a time when there was work available for him. The employer argued that the provision in question was illegal under a decision of the NLRB. Finding no assistance from a "savings" or "separability" provision (this provision simply declared that if a portion of the contract is illegal, the remainder remains intact), Arbitrator Alleyne found the arbitral forum inappropriate to resolve statutory issues. Alleyne reasoned that a court could reverse the NLRB or the NLRB could even reverse itself, as it has done in the past on this very issue. Taking the better view, Alleyne found that "the grievance-arbitration procedure is best served when arbitrators adhere to areas of conventional contract interpretation, leaving pure questions of contract legality to those authorized by law to resolve such questions."[78]

Similarly, Arbitrator I.B. Helburn, in a 1989 unpublished decision involving a dispute over payment of union dues by employees who resigned from the union, found the following language of a separability clause not applicable to an NLRB ruling: "Any provision of this Agreement which may be ad-

---

[75]41 LA 65 (1963).
[76]Id. at 75.
[77]82 LA 483 (1984).
[78]Id. at 485. See also Bi-State Dev. Agency, 88 LA 854 (Brazil, 1987) (noting that external law "too indefinite" to apply).

judged by a court of final jurisdiction to be in conflict with any Federal, State or Local Law shall become inoperative to the extent and duration of such conflict." Holding that the NLRB is not a court of final jurisdiction, Helburn stated that "in light of established Supreme Court doctrine and the fact that the arbitrator in the instant case draws his authority from the negotiated Agreement, the award must honor and give life to the contract." Helburn enforced the parties' collective bargaining agreement and ignored past and pending NLRB rulings bearing on the grievance. Accordingly, management's argument that external law should be applied so that the company will not be subjected to inconsistent rulings from the arbitrator and the NLRB was rejected.

c. W.R. Grace & Co.: Enforcing Awards That Conflict With External Law

There is indication that the courts will enforce an award that gives legal effect to a collective bargaining agreement even though the agreement conflicts with external statutory rights or determinations.[79] The facts of *W.R. Grace & Co.*[80] are complex and not easily summarized. Faced with the prospect of liability for violations of Title VII in its hiring practices, W.R. Grace entered into a conciliation agreement with the EEOC that conflicted with the seniority provisions of the parties' collective bargaining agreement (the union had declined to participate in the negotiations leading to the conciliation agreement). While conciliation was proceeding, the labor agreement expired and failed negotiations led to a strike. The company hired strike replacements, some of whom were women who assumed jobs never before held by women. The strike was settled with the signing of a new agreement that continued the plant seniority system specified by the expired agreement. The strikers returned to work and, significantly, the women

---

[79]See generally Christensen, *W.R. Grace and Co.: An Epilogue to the Trilogy?*, in Arbitration 1984: Absenteeism, Recent Law, Panels, and Published Decisions, in Proceedings of the 37th Annual Meeting, National Academy of Arbitrators, 21 (BNA Books, 1985): Note, *Judicial Deference to Grievance Arbitration in the Public Sector: Saving* Grace *in the Search for a Well-Defined Public Policy Exception*, 42 U. Miami L. Rev. 767 (1988).

[80]W.R. Grace & Co. v. Rubber Workers Local 759, 461 U.S. 757, 39 FEP Cases 1409 (1983).

replacements were assigned to positions ahead of men with greater seniority. Specifically, management prevented men from exercising the shift preference seniority (to which they were entitled under the agreement) to obtain positions held by women strike replacements. Grievances were filed and arbitration sought.

The company, refusing to arbitrate, sought an injunction prohibiting arbitration and, while such actions were pending before the court, negotiated a conciliation agreement with the EEOC which supported the shift preference granted the women strike replacements. In addition, the conciliation agreement provided that in the event of layoffs, the company would maintain the existing proportion of women in the plant's bargaining unit. Layoffs were subsequently effected, more grievances filed and, after complex legal maneuvering on both sides, a federal district court found that the terms of the conciliation agreement prevailed over those of the contract. Two years later the Fifth Circuit, reversing the lower court, ordered arbitration.[81]

In response to the decision, management reinstated the male employees. Grievances seeking back pay were then submitted to arbitration. The first to reach arbitration was that of a male employee who had been demoted. Arbitrator Anthony Sabella concluded that although the grievant was entitled to an award under the collective bargaining agreement, it would be inequitable to penalize the company for conduct that complied with an outstanding district court order in favor of the conciliation agreement. He thus denied the grievance. Rather than filing an action to set aside the award, the union elected to contest Sabella's reasoning in later arbitrations.

The union subsequently arbitrated a second set of grievances before Arbitrator Gerald Barrett, who ruled for the union. Although the arbitrator acknowledged that the Sabella arbitration resolved the same contractual issue, he nevertheless concluded that the collective bargaining agreement did not require him to follow Sabella's award. Finding that the agreement made no exception for good-faith violations of the sen-

---

[81]W.R. Grace & Co. v. Rubber Workers Local 759, 652 F.2d 1248, 107 LRRM 3251 (5th Cir. 1981).

iority provisions, Barrett ruled that the company had acted at its own risk in breaching the agreement.

The employer then brought an action to vacate the Barrett award. The lower court, granting summary judgment in favor of the company, found that public policy prevented enforcement of the collective bargaining agreement during the period prior to the court of appeals' reversal. The Fifth Circuit reversed.

The Supreme Court upheld the validity of the second award. Stating that "[t]he sole issue before the Court is whether the Barrett award should be enforced," a unanimous Court, true to the *Enterprise* standard of review, nevertheless enforced Barrett's award that in no uncertain terms reversed a prior award that credited a determination of statutory rights over the seniority provisions of the contract. Arbitrator Barrett found that Arbitrator Sabella had no jurisdiction to fashion a decision based entirely upon equity unrelated to any provision of the contract. The Employer's decision to follow the lower court's order in favor of the conciliation agreement proved costly.

4. *Alexander v. Gardner-Denver* and the Arbitrator's Jurisdiction to Interpret and Apply the Law[82]

In *Alexander v. Gardner-Denver*,[83] the Supreme Court held that the arbitration of a discrimination claim did not preclude a subsequent suit under Title VII, and that the plaintiff-grievant was entitled to a trial de novo in a federal court. It is especially noteworthy that throughout the opinion the Court focused on the role of arbitration "in a system of industrial government,"[84] as well as some of the institutional deficiencies of the arbitration process. The Court felt that the arbitral institution was a comparatively inappropriate forum for final resolution of Title VII rights. This conclusion was based on the following considerations: (1) the role of the arbitrator is to effectuate the intent of the parties; (2) since the arbitrator's

---

[82]This section is, in part, taken from Hill, supra note 27.
[83]415 U.S. 36, 7 FEP 81 (1974).
[84]Id. at 52.

source of authority is the collective bargaining agreement, any conflict between Title VII and the agreement must be resolved in favor of the agreement;[85] (3) the specialized competence of arbitrators lies primarily in the law of the shop, not in the law of the land;[86] (4) arbitral fact-finding is not equivalent to judicial fact-finding;[87] (5) the record of the arbitration proceeding is generally incomplete compared to the rights and procedures common to civil trials, such as discovery, compulsory process, cross-examination, and testimony under oath, which are often severely limited or unavailable in arbitration;[88] (6) arbitrators have no obligation to the court to give reasons for their awards;[89] (7) the general informality of the arbitration procedure relative to the court system makes it a less appropriate forum for final resolution of Title VII issues;[90] and (8) the interests of an individual employee may be subordinated to the collective interests of all employees in an arbitration hearing.[91]

The *Alexander* decision has resolved little of the Meltzer-Howlett debate. The Court, in dicta, merely cited the dicta in *Enterprise Wheel* and stated that the arbitrator has authority to resolve only questions of contractual rights.[92] Presumably, under *Alexander*, no legal infirmity would result in the situation where an arbitrator, faced with an ambiguous contract, looks to Title VII, or other relevant external law, for guidance in resolving a grievance. Indeed the Supreme Court in *Enterprise Wheel* contemplated that the arbitrator would look for guidance from many sources, including the law.[93]

Where the question does not require choosing one of two interpretations of an ambiguous provision—one consistent with the law, the other inconsistent—arbitrators are entitled to rest their decision squarely on the law if the parties have granted the arbitrator such authority, either by contract or

---

[85]Id. at 56–57.
[86]Id.
[87]Id. at 57.
[88]Id. at 57–58.
[89]Id. at 58.
[90]Id.
[91]Id. n.19.
[92]Id. at 53–54.
[93]Steelworkers v. Enterprise Wheel & Car Corp., 363 U.S. 593, 597, 46 LRRM 2423 (1960).

by a submission agreement.[94] In this regard, Arbitrator David Feller has stated:

> An arbitrator is, after all, the servant of the parties, and if they make it clear that they want what must inevitably be an advisory opinion from him in the hope that, when rendered, it will resolve the dispute and no one will seek to contest in court, he must oblige.[95]

Moreover, the *Alexander* Court states that when the collective bargaining agreement contains a nondiscrimination clause similar to Title VII, arbitration may well produce a satisfactory settlement.[96]

In the difficult situation where the arbitrator has not been given the authority to apply external law, and he feels that the arbitral award would conflict with Title VII (or another statute) if he were to follow the agreement instead of the law, *Alexander* appears to mandate that the arbitrator follow the agreement. The Court states that "where the collective bargaining agreement conflicts with Title VII, the arbitrator must follow the agreement."[97]

Applying *Alexander*, in *Roadmaster Corp. v. Laborers Local 504*,[98] the Court of Appeals for the Seventh Circuit made it clear that an arbitrator's authority derives from the parties' contract, and that an arbitrator is not to stray from his obligation to interpret the labor agreement. Because *Roadmaster* breached Section 8(d)(2) of the National Labor Relations Act, the arbitrator concluded that the employer's letter to the union was insufficient notice under the applicable contract to terminate the current labor agreement. Citing *Alexander*, the court declared:

> His [the arbitrator's] source of authority is the collective bargaining agreement, and he must interpret and apply that agreement in accordance with the "industrial common law of the shop" and the various needs and desires of the parties. *The arbitrator, however, has no general authority to invoke public laws that conflict with the bargain between the parties:*

---

[94]See Fairweather, supra note 50, at 454–458.
[95]Feller, supra note 2, at 123.
[96]415 U.S. at 55.
[97]Id. at 57.
[98]851 F.2d 886, 129 LRRM 2449 (7th Cir. 1988).

> [A]n arbitrator is confined to interpretation and application
> of the collective bargaining agreement; he does not sit to
> dispense his own brand of industrial justice. He may of
> course look for guidance from many sources, yet his award
> is legitimate only so long as it draws its essence from the
> collective bargaining agreement. When the arbitrator's words
> manifest an infidelity to this obligation, courts have no
> choice but to refuse enforcement of the award. *United Steel-*
> *workers of America v. Enterprise Wheel & Car Corp.*, 363
> U.S. 593, 597 [46 LRRM 2425] (1960).

If an arbitral decision is based "solely upon the arbitrator's view
of the requirements of enacted legislation," rather than on an
interpretation of the collective bargaining agreement, *the ar-*
bitrator has "exceeded the scope of the submission," and the award
will not be enforced.[99]

In no uncertain terms, the Seventh Circuit stated that it
is "plainly wrong" for arbitrators to base a decision upon their
view of the requirements of enacted legislation. With regard
to applying law, the court had this to say: "Arbitrators should
restrict their considerations to the contract, even if such a
decision conflicts with federal statutory law."[100] The court accordingly set aside the arbitration award.

The authors submit that this position represents the better weight of authority among arbitrators—and for good reason. Arbitrator Feller correctly points out that questions of
external law are not the kind which are supposed to be within
the area of arbitrators' special competence, and arbitrators
have done poorly in interpreting and applying that external
law.[101] The following case illustrates the problems that may
arise when an arbitrator renders an award based upon external law.

In *General Telephone Co. of Pennsylvania v. Locals 1635,*
1636, & 1637,[102] the collective bargaining agreement explicitly excluded benefits for absence due to pregnancy from a
general sick-pay benefits program. The arbitrator found that
such exclusion in the contract was "unenforceable as creating

---

[99]Id. at 889, 129 LRRM at 2451.
[100]Id. See also U.S. Steel and Carnegie Pension Fund, 759 F.2d 269 (3d Cir. 1985)
(vacating award that was based on interpretation under ERISA rather than contractual pension plan).
[101]Feller, supra note 2, at 118.
[102]427 F. Supp. 398, 14 FEP Cases 1654 (W.D. Pa. 1977).

an unlawful, discriminatory employment practice."[103] The arbitrator relied upon Title VII and the Pennsylvania Human Relations Act of 1955 in ruling that disabilities due to pregnancy should be treated as other temporary disabilities to avoid unlawful sex discrimination. It is noteworthy that in this decision the arbitrator correctly interpreted the findings of an overwhelming majority of the U.S. district courts and the unanimous holdings of the U.S. courts of appeals that had considered the issue. The arbitrator, however, did not anticipate the holding of the Supreme Court in *General Electric Co. v. Gilbert*,[104] where the Court held that it was not gender-based discrimination for an employer to exclude pregnancy-related disabilities from a general disability program. Accordingly, citing the decision in *Gilbert*, the district court in *General Telephone* reversed the decision of the arbitrator, stating that his award was "in manifest disregard of the law."[105]

While the district court ruled that the arbitrator's decision was in "manifest disregard of the law," the court also held that the arbitrator had exceeded his powers under the collective bargaining agreement by going outside the agreement to determine the legality of the provision. The court, citing language in *Alexander*, stated that "if an arbitral decision is based 'solely on the arbitrator's view of the requirements of enacted legislation,' rather than on the interpretation of the collective-bargaining agreement, the arbitrator has 'exceeded the scope of his submission,' and the award will not be enforced."[106]

Although *Alexander* indicates that the arbitrator can resolve "only questions of contractual rights, and this authority remains regardless of whether certain contractual rights are similar to or duplicative of, the substantive rights secured by Title VII,"[107] an arbitrator who is not explicitly granted the power by a collective bargaining agreement to apply the law and is faced with a contract which "requires" or "permits" a violation of Title VII (or arguably other statutes) must, under *Alexander*, follow the agreement. This is not to say that under

---

[103]Id., 14 FEP Cases at 1655.
[104]429 U.S. 125, 13 FEP Cases 1657 (1976).
[105]Id.
[106]Id.
[107]415 U.S. at 53–54.

Alexander the arbitrator cannot resolve the dispute consistent with external law. The arbitrator who determines that the agreement, in fact, incorporates "the law" may well resolve the dispute consistent with external law on the theory that the parties did not intend to negotiate an agreement that is contrary to law. However, in drafting the opinion, the arbitrator must be especially cognizant of the dicta in *Enterprise Wheel*:

> [T]he award is legitimate only so long as it draws its essence from the collective bargaining agreement. When the arbitrator's words manifest an infidelity to this obligation, courts have no choice but to refuse enforcement of the award.[108]

Absent explicit authority from the parties to incorporate external law in the remedy, the arbitrator, under the dicta of *Alexander* and *Enterprise Wheel*, must make it clear that his award is based upon the collective bargaining agreement, and not upon his application of external law. Of course, under *Enterprise Wheel* the arbitrator may look to the law for help in determining the sense of the agreement. Such "reaching out" for the law by the arbitrator is likewise permitted by *Alexander*, but again, the arbitrator must carefully word the opinion so as to indicate that his decision is, in fact, "based upon" or "draws its essence" from the agreement.

C. Summary

Arbitration is a private institution in which the arbitrator receives his authority from the parties. As the late Dean Harry Shulman wrote:

> A proper conception of the arbitrator's function is basic. He is not a public tribunal imposed upon the parties by superior authority which the parties are obliged to accept. He has no general character to administer justice for a community which transcends the parties. He is rather part of a system of self-government created by and confined to the parties. He serves their pleasure only, to administer the rule of law established by their collective agreement.[109]

---

[108]363 U.S. at 597.
[109]Shulman, *Reason, Contract, and Law in Labor Relations*, 68 Harv. L. Rev. 999, 1016 (1955), reprinted in Management Rights and the Arbitration Process, Proceeding of the 9th Annual Meeting, National Academy of Arbitrators, 169 (BNA Books, 1956).

Although the arbitrator is generally not hired to interpret external law, the arbitrator frequently cannot escape the legal framework that surrounds the parties' "system of self government." While no hard-and-fast rules exist with respect to the role of the arbitrator in reconciling the provisions of the agreement with external law, the following points are offered by way of analysis and summary:

The many issues involving external law and the collective bargaining agreement cannot be separated into nicely segmented compartments. The question is not whether arbitrators should consider external law but, rather, whether and under what circumstances is consideration of statutory issues appropriate. In this regard it is useful to distinguish between factual determinations (which may or may not have legal consequences) and the legal determination itself. The significance of this distinction should not be overlooked.

To cite an example given at the Proceedings of the 25th Meeting of the National Academy of Arbitrators: an employer terminates an employee because he or she wears an Afro hair style. At an arbitration hearing the employer argues "just cause," while the employee defends by arguing that wearing an Afro is a protected activity under the Civil Rights Act.[110] The arbitrator makes a factual determination as to why the employee was terminated and whether the reasons constituted "just cause" in the industrial setting. Whether the arbitrator should decide, either on his own motion or the motion of a party, that the wearing of an Afro is protected under Title VII of the Civil Rights Act, and thus issue an appropriate remedy based on that determination, is subject to debate.

David Feller submits that the tendency of some arbitrators to reach out, without agreement from the parties, to engage in the process of public-law adjudication can, in the end, only be fatal to the posture of the arbitral profession.[111] Robert Howlett has argued that an award that does not consider the law may result in error.[112] While at times these two positions

---

[110]See Bernstein, *The Use and Abuse of Arbitral Power: Comment*, in Labor Arbitration at the Quarter-Century Mark, Proceedings of the 25th Annual Meeting, National Academy of Arbitrators, 76, 94 (BNA Books, 1973).

[111]Feller, supra note 2, at 110.

[112]See text accompanying notes 12–17, supra. See also Warren Consol. School Dist., 67-1 ARB ¶8228 (Howlett, 1967).

may not be contradictory, the important point is that the overlap between the contract and external law does not imply or mandate that the arbitrator is precluded from exercising jurisdiction over the contractual issue and cannot, at the very least, make factual determinations that may affect the outcome in another forum.[113] Again, one need only recall the Supreme Court's statement in *Alexander* that the "special nature of . . . contractual and statutory rights is not vitiated merely because both were violated as a result of the same factual occurrence,"[114] and that a court may properly accord an arbitral determination great weight, especially where the issue is solely one of fact.[115] An arbitrator should not, therefore, refuse to rule on an issue simply because the matter may be cognizable in another forum.

In an attempt to avoid the multiplicity of remedies available under the agreement and external law, the parties may attempt to limit the grievance-arbitration mechanism only to

---

[113]See the discussion of Arbitrator Edgar Jones, Jr., in Stardust Hotel, 61 LA 942 (1973). In Carey v. Westinghouse Elec. Corp., 375 U.S. 261, 55 LRRM 2042 (1964), the Supreme Court held that neither §10(k) nor §9(c) of the National Labor Relations Act deprives a state court of jurisdiction to compel arbitration of a grievance questioning the performance of bargaining-unit work by employees in a unit represented by another labor organization. The opinion by Justice Douglas noted that §10(k) not only tolerates but actively encourages voluntary settlements of work-assignment controversies between unions, and, accordingly, a grievance arbitration procedure would further the policies of the Act.

Although the superior authority of the NLRB was recognized along with the possibility of direct conflict in orders, the Court concluded that arbitration should be ordered:

> Should the Board disagree with the arbiter, by ruling, for example, that the employees involved in the controversy are members of one bargaining unit or another, the Board's ruling would, of course, take precedence; and if the employer's action had been in accord with that ruling, it would not be liable for damages under §301. But that is not peculiar to the present type of controversy. Arbitral awards construing a seniority provision . . . or awards concerning unfair labor practices, may later end up in conflict with Board rulings . . . [but] the possibility of conflict is no barrier to resort to a tribunal other than the Board.

> However the dispute be considered—whether one involving work assignment or one concerning representation—we see no barrier to use of the arbitration procedure. If it is a work assignment dispute, arbitration conveniently fills a gap and avoids the necessity of a strike to bring the matter to the Board. If it is a representational matter, resort to arbitration may have a persuasive, curative effect even though one union is not a party.

> By allowing the dispute to go to arbitration its fragmentation is avoided to a substantial extent; and those conciliatory measures which may be dispositive of the entire dispute are encouraged. The superior authority of the Board may be invoked at any time. Meanwhile the therapy of arbitration is brought to bear in a complicated and troubled area.

Id. at 2044.
[114]415 U.S. at 49.
[115]Id. at 60 n.21.

those grievances which do not allege or involve an issue of external law. For example, Arbitrator Ernest Marlatt, in *Woodward Co.*,[116] held that a grievance was not arbitrable where an employee has filed a similar action with the EEOC. In that case the contract provided that "if any subject matter which is or might be alleged as a grievance is instituted in any administrative action before a governmental board or agency, then such administrative procedure shall be the sole remedy, and a grievance under this agreement shall no longer exist."[117]

While it is true that the parties generally can limit the scope of the grievance procedure, it should not be assumed that the courts would hold that limiting the scope of grievances is permissible whatever the reason advanced by the parties. It is the position of the authors that failure to make discrimination claims grievable under the contract constitutes a separate violation of the Civil Rights Act.[118] Accordingly, it may be extremely difficult to eliminate the multiplicity of remedies that may frequently be available to an employee arising out of a single factual occurrence.

As a general rule arbitrators will confine and limit themselves to interpreting, construing, and applying existing contractual provisions, either negotiated by the parties, or otherwise determined to be in effect.[119] Most arbitrators probably agree that where the submission or the agreement makes it clear that the parties want an advisory opinion as to the law, such an opinion is within the arbitrator's role and accordingly it would be proper for the arbitrator to fashion a remedy grounded on external law. Likewise, most arbitrators would agree that when a contractual provision is susceptible to two interpretations, one compatible with and the other repugnant to external law, arbitrators will seek to avoid a construction that would invalidate contractual language.

Neither arbitrators nor legal scholars agree on the extent to which arbitrators, in resolving grievances, should rely upon external law rather than the agreement when the two conflict.

---

[116]61 LA 259 (1973).

[117]Id.

[118]Hill and Sinicropi, *Excluding Discrimination Grievances From Grievance and Arbitration Procedures: A Legal Analysis*, 33 Arb. J. 16 (1978).

[119]Monsanto Co., 68 LA 101 (Dworkin, 1977).

The positions range from always (Howlett), sometimes (Mittenthal), to never (Meltzer) and the Supreme Court has not definitively resolved the debate other than offering additional dicta.[120] Perhaps the most that can be offered is to merely quote Arbitrator Milton Edelman's declaration that "an arbitrator's position on this matter of law versus agreement must rest on his conception of the arbitration process, the clarity of the law, and the role ascribed to arbitration by the legislature and the courts."[121]

As argued by David Feller, "[T]o the extent that an arbitrator decides disputed questions of external law, he necessarily relinquishes his right to claim immunity from review by the bodies that external law has established."[122] Although the arbitrator is accorded wide discretion in the formulation of remedies, where issues of external law are present his choice is often Draconian, for he is subject to reversal by courts for fashioning remedies that are repugnant to statutes[123] and is also subject to reversal under the *Enterprise* standard for formulating a remedy based upon his view of the requirements of enacted legislation.[124] And while arbitrators remain split over the issue, we feel that the better weight of authority is expressed by Arbitrator Edgar Jones, Jr.:

> It seems the course of prudence at least, if not wisdom, that arbitrators should protect their awards by rooting them in the contract whenever that is possible, even though there undoubtedly will be cases in which the parties expressly submit issues

---

[120]But see W.R. Grace & Co. v. Rubber Workers Local 759, 461 U.S. 757, 113 LRRM 2641, 39 FEP Cases 1409 (1983), where the Court enforced an award that gave legal effect to a contract that conflicted with external statutory rights.

[121]Hollander & Co., 64 LA 816, 819 (1975).

[122]Feller, supra note 2, at 111.

[123]See, e.g., Douglas Aircraft Co. v. NLRB, 609 F.2d 352, 102 LRRM 2811 (9th Cir. 1979) (conditioning award of back pay on surrender of unfair labor practice charge before NLRB by discharged employee repugnant to statute); Teamsters Local 767 v. Standard Brands, 579 F.2d 1282, 99 LRRM 2377 (5th Cir. 1978) (for award to be enforced there must be (1) agreement to arbitrate and parties must be covered by that agreement; (2) award which draws its "essence" from agreement and does not exceed scope of issues presented to arbitrator; and (3) award which is not "repugnant" to the NLRA), id., 99 LRRM at 2384; Banyard v. NLRB, 505 F.2d 342, 87 LRRM 2001 (D.C. Cir. 1974) (award authorizing employer to violate state law held void); Associated Milk Dealers v. Teamsters Local 753, 422 F.2d 546, 73 LRRM 2435 (7th Cir. 1970) (arbitration "ill-equipped" to interpret antitrust laws and will not be ordered if clause to be interpreted would violate laws); Carey v. Westinghouse, supra note 113, at 271 (arbitration procedure must be fair and not repugnant to NLRA).

[124]Steelworkers v. Enterprise Wheel & Car Corp., 363 U.S. 593, 597, 46 LRRM 2423 (1960).

for arbitral decision framed in and requiring answers from statutory terms. Even in that latter context, however, it seems vital to bear in mind that arbitration remains consensual in nature, not statutory, and that the arbitrator's decisional life is tied, not to Congress or the Labor Board, but to the contracting parties.[125]

---

[125]Farmer Bros., 64 LA 901, 904 (1975).

Chapter 6

Contract Termination and the Arbitrator's Remedy Power

The Supreme Court has consistently recognized that the duty to arbitrate is a matter of contract, and before a party can be required to arbitrate any dispute there must be a finding that the parties in fact agreed to arbitrate.[1] Since the duty to arbitrate does not extend to a period where the parties are no longer contractually bound to arbitrate, it follows that the arbitrator would have no power to formulate a remedy where the contractual obligation has expired. It should not be assumed, however, that the obligation to arbitrate necessarily expires with the collective bargaining agreement. Under certain circumstances, the duty to arbitrate can survive the expiration of the agreement.

Similar to those situations where actions to compel or enjoin arbitration are at issue, two conflicting principles are

---

[1]AT&T Technologies v. Communications Workers, 475 U.S. 643, 121 LRRM 3329 (1986); Nolde Bros. v. Bakery & Confectionery Workers Local 358, 430 U.S. 243, 94 LRRM 2753 (1977); Gateway Coal Co. v. Mine Workers, 414 U.S. 368, 85 LRRM 2049 (1974); Operating Eng'rs Local 150 v. Flair Builders, 406 U.S. 487, 80 LRRM 2441 (1972); John Wiley & Sons v. Livingston, 376 U.S. 543, 55 LRRM 2769 (1964); Atkinson v. Sinclair Ref. Co., 370 U.S. 238, 50 LRRM 2433 (1962); Steelworkers v. Warrior & Gulf Navigation Co., 363 U.S. 574, 46 LRRM 2416 (1960).

See generally Krupman, *Arbitration After Contract Expiration*, in A Review of the NLRA Interpretations and Current Case Law, 211 (ABA Committee on Development of Law Under the NLRA, 1984); Geslewitz, *Case Developments Since* Nolde Brothers: *When Must Post-Contract Disputes Be Arbitrated?*, 35 Lab. L. J. 225 (1984); Krikscium, *Post-Contract Arbitrability Since* Nolde Brothers, 54 U. Colo. L. Rev. 103 (1982); Leonard, *Post-Contractual Arbitrability after* Nolde Brothers: *A Problem of Conceptual Clarity*, 28 N.Y.L. Sch. L. Rev. 257 (1983).

balanced in dealing with issues of arbitrability and the expiration of an agreement. The first principle is the strong presumption in favor of arbitration of labor disputes; the second is the bar against requiring a party to arbitrate a dispute it has not agreed to arbitrate. In accommodating these two principles, the courts have made it clear that unless a collective bargaining agreement clearly manifests a contrary intent, the court, and not the arbitrator, has the ultimate authority to decide whether the parties have agreed to arbitrate.[2] An exception to this general rule is where the parties have agreed to arbitrate issues of arbitrability.[3] Consent to grant the arbitrator such authority may be implied from the conduct of the parties at the hearing.[4]

While the issue of contract expiration or termination is generally resolved judicially, an arbitrator's decision is, as observed by the Second Circuit, often one of substantial aid to a court in determining arbitrability,[5] and, accordingly, it is useful to examine both court and arbitral authority. In this regard the following situations should be distinguished:

---

[2]In AT&T Technologies v. Communications Workers, supra note 1, the Supreme Court reaffirmed four principles established in the *Steelworkers Trilogy* (discussed in Chapter 3, at notes 4-5, and accompanying text) to guide courts in determining whether a labor dispute is arbitrable. First, the parties must have contracted to submit the grievance to arbitration before arbitration will be ordered. Second, the court determines whether the contract provides for arbitration of the grievance in question. Third, while determining if the dispute is arbitrable, the court may not decide the merits of the grievance. Fourth, if the contract contains an arbitration clause, a presumption of arbitrability arises. The court should not decline to order arbitration "unless it may be said with positive assurance that the arbitration clause is not susceptible of an interpretation that covers the asserted dispute." Id. at 650, 121 LRRM at 3332, quoting Steelworkers v. Warrior & Gulf Navigation Co., supra note 1, 363 at 582–583, 46 LRRM at 2419–2420.

See also Mobil Oil Corp. v. Oil Workers Local 8-766, 600 F.2d 322, 101 LRRM 2721 (1st Cir. 1979); Ladies' Garment Workers v. Ashland Indus., 488 F.2d 641, 85 LRRM 2319 (5th Cir. 1974); Automobile Workers Local 998 v. B. & T. Metals Co., 315 F.2d 432, 52 LRRM 2787 (6th Cir. 1963); Procter & Gamble Indep. Union v. Procter & Gamble Mfg. Co., 312 F.2d 181, 51 LRRM 2752 (2d Cir. 1962), cert. denied, 374 U.S. 830, 53 LRRM 2544 (1963).

[3]Automobile Workers Local 125 v. IT&T, 508 F.2d 1309, 88 LRRM 2213 (8th Cir. 1975), citing Electrical Workers (IBEW) Local 4 v. Radio Thirteen-Eighty, 469 F.2d 610, 81 LRRM 2829 (8th Cir. 1972).

[4]On this issue see the discussion of Arbitrator Paul Rothschild in MGM Grand Hotels, 86 LA 765 (1986) and the decision of the Ninth Circuit in George Day Constr. Co. v. Carpenters Local 354, 722 F.2d 1471, 115 LRRM 2459 (9th Cir. 1984) (which found arbitrable a grievance involving use of nonunion subcontractors where dispute arose after expiration of collective bargaining agreement but before impasse was reached, and employer impliedly consented to arbitrator deciding both arbitrability question and merits).

[5]F & M Shaefer Brewing Co. v. Brewery Workers Local 49, 420 F.2d 854, 73 LRRM 2298 (2d Cir. 1970).

(1) where the claim arose before the contract expired, but arbitration takes place after expiration; (2) where the grievance arose after expiration but is based on a right that "vested" prior to termination, and (3) where the grievance arose after expiration and depends upon an extracontractual agreement subsequent to expiration of the contract.[6]

A. Grievance Arises During Life of Agreement but Demand to Arbitrate Occurs After Expiration

When the grievance arises during the contract term but arbitration is not demanded until after its termination, an order to arbitrate will usually issue, for otherwise a party could merely stall the arbitration hearing until after the expiration of the contract and thus not be bound by the award. As stated by the Supreme Court in *Nolde Brothers v. Bakery & Confectionery Workers Local 358*:[7]

> Our prior decisions have indeed held that the arbitration duty is a creature of the collective-bargaining agreement and that a party cannot be compelled to arbitrate any matter in the absence of a contractual obligation to do so. Adherence to these principles, however, does not require us to hold that termination of a collective-bargaining agreement automatically extinguishes a party's duty to arbitrate grievances arising under the contract. Carried to its logical conclusion that argument would preclude the entry of a post-contract arbitration order even when the dispute arose during the life of the contract but arbitration proceedings had not begun before termination. The same would be true if arbitration processes began but were not completed, during the contract's term. Yet it could not seriously be contended in either instance that the expiration of the contract would terminate the parties' contractual obligation to resolve such a dispute in an arbitral, rather than a judicial forum.[8]

---

[6]See Nolan, Labor Arbitration Law and Practice, 191–194 (West Publishing Co., 1979).

[7]Supra note 1.

[8]Id. at 2756. See also Steelworkers v. Enterprise Wheel & Car Corp., 363 U.S. 593, 46 LRRM 2423 (1960), where the Supreme Court enforced Arbitrator Milton Schmidt's decision directing the employer to reinstate and pay back pay to discharged employees for the period before and after the expiration of the collective bargaining agreement. After the discharge, and before the arbitration award had issued, the collective bargaining agreement had expired. See notes 66–68, infra, and accompanying text.

Arbitrator Arthur Talmadge, in *Shieldalloy Corp.*,[9] ruled arbitrable a grievance involving entitlement to vacation pay based on a formula in an expired contract, and summarized the thinking of arbitrators this way:

> It is generally agreed that if a grievance arises prior to the termination of the collective bargaining agreement, the matter is arbitrable, even though the demand for arbitration is not made until the termination of the agreement. Further, even if the grievance arises following termination of the agreement, and if the grievance is based on a right established by the contract, such as vacation pay or the right to a fringe benefit, the grievance is arbitrable. There is a wide currency of labor arbitrators' opinion that certain right[s] growing out of the agreement have been effectively "vested"—and when these rights are at issue in arbitral proceedings, arbitrability will be found.[10]

Similarly, if a grievance arises and the arbitrator is designated prior to the expiration of the agreement, the arbitrator does not lose his authority to render an award should the agreement expire before the award issues. One commentator has stated that in these cases the right of access to the grievance procedure is deemed "vested" as of the date the facts giving rise to the grievance occur.[11] It follows, therefore, that when the facts giving rise to the grievance occur after expiration or termination of the agreement, absent a consent to arbitrate the matter, no arbitral jurisdiction exists. For example, in *Oil Workers Local 7-210 v. American Maize Products Co.*,[12] the Seventh Circuit held a grievance contesting an employer's lockout on August 1 not arbitrable where the agreement expired after midnight on August 1. And in *In re Globe Seaways*,[13] the Second Circuit held that a federal district court correctly refused to confirm arbitration awards, issued ex parte, in favor of union members who were discharged for engaging in strike-related activities during the hiatus between two agreements.

This principle was again affirmed in *Procter & Gamble Independent Union v. Procter & Gamble*,[14] where the Second

---

[9]81 LA 489 (1983).
[10]Id. at 492.
[11]Gorman, Basic Text on Labor Law, 564 (West Publishing Co., 1976).
[12]492 F.2d 409, 86 LRRM 2438 (7th Cir.), cert denied, 417 U.S. 969, 86 LRRM 2687 (1974).
[13]451 F.2d 1159, 79 LRRM 2067 (2d Cir. 1971).
[14]Supra note 2.

Circuit held that grievances for strike-related activities were not arbitrable where the activities on which the discipline was based, the disciplinary measures which the union sought to arbitrate, and the filing of the grievances all occurred in the interval between the termination date of the old agreement and the effective date of the new agreement.[15]

B. Grievance Arises After Expiration but Is Based on Right "Vested" Before Termination

In *Nolde Brothers*,[16] the Supreme Court considered the arbitrability of a dispute arising after termination of the collective bargaining agreement. Nolde Brothers entered into a collective bargaining agreement with Local 358 of the Bakery and Confectionery Workers, which, in relevant part, provided for arbitration of "any grievance" not satisfactorily adjusted in the grievance procedure. In addition, the contract contained a provision that provided for severance pay on termination of employment for all employees having three or more years of active service. By its terms, the contract was to remain in effect until July 21, 1973, and thereafter, until such time as either a new agreement was executed between the parties, or the existing agreement was terminated upon seven days' written notice by either party. Negotiations concerning modification of the agreement began in May 1973, and continued beyond the July expiration date without settlement. On August 20, the union gave written notice of cancellation; thus termination became effective August 27, 1973.

Despite the contract's cancellation, negotiations continued. They ended, however, on August 31, when Nolde, faced by a threatened strike after the union had rejected its last offer, informed the union of its decision to close its bakery permanently, effective that day. Operations at the plant ceased shortly after midnight on August 31. Although Nolde paid employees accrued wages and vacation pay under the canceled agreement, plus wages for work performed between the termination of the contract and the closing of the bakery, the

---

[15]Id., 51 LRRM at 2753.
[16]Nolde Bros. v. Bakery & Confectionery Workers Local 358, 430 U.S. 243, 94 LRRM 2753 (1977).

employer rejected the union's demand for arbitration of the severance-pay claim, arguing that the obligation to arbitrate terminated with the collective bargaining agreement.

The union filed a suit in federal court under Section 301 seeking to compel Nolde to arbitrate the severance-pay issue or, in the alternative, judgment for the severance pay. The district court granted Nolde's motion for summary judgment on both issues. It concluded that since the union had voluntarily terminated the contract on which the right to severance pay was founded, any entitlement to severance pay was thereby destroyed. The lower court noted that to hold that severance pay was a "vested" or "earned" right would be to "breathe into it an existence apart from the collective bargaining agreement," thus upsetting the congressionally created balance between union and employer.[17] The Fourth Circuit reversed on the question of arbitrability but expressed no decision on the merits.[18] The circuit court criticized the lower court for deciding the case on the merits without first determining whether the dispute was subject to arbitration. The court of appeals held that, if the dispute was subject to arbitration, it was within the exclusive province of the arbitrator to hear the merits of the dispute. The Supreme Court, in a 7-to-2 decision written by Chief Justice Warren Burger, affirmed the decision of the Fourth Circuit.

In *Nolde Brothers* the Court made it clear that the duty to arbitrate need not expire with the collective bargaining agreement that brought it into existence. Furthermore, in holding that the union's claim for severance pay under the expired agreement was subject to resolution under the arbitration provisions of that agreement, the Court stated that the presumption favoring arbitrability is also applicable even when the facts giving rise to the grievance occur after termination of the agreement. The Court declared: "In short, where the dispute is over a provision of the expired agreement, the presumptions favoring arbitrability must be negated expressly or by clear implication."[19] Noting that the parties had

---

[17]Bakery & Confectionery Workers Local 358 v. Nolde Bros., 382 F. Supp. 1354, 87 LRRM 2646, 2648 (E.D. Va. 1974).

[18]Bakery & Confectionery Workers, Local 358, v. Nolde Bros., 530 F.2d 548, 91 LRRM 2570 (4th Cir. 1975).

[19]Nolde Bros. v. Bakery & Confectionery Workers Local 358, Supra note 16, 94

clearly expressed a general preference for arbitration, the Court found that the intent of the parties was to arbitrate even those disputes arising after the contract's termination. The Court presumed that because the parties' evidenced an intent to arbitrate during the terms of the agreement, they would not change their opinion about the advantages of arbitration after the contract expired.

The decision in *Nolde* is consistent with *John Wiley & Sons v. Livingston*.[20] The parties' labor agreement provided for arbitration of "any differences, grievance or dispute between the Employer and the Union arising out of or relating to this agreement, or its interpretation or application, or enforcement." During the term of an agreement, Interscience Publishers merged with John Wiley & Sons and ceased to do business as a separate entity. The Court held that a package of wage, pension, severance, and vacation pay rights was arbitrable even after the original company merged with a new corporation and terminated the agreement. In reaching this decision, the Court focused not on whether the right "accrued" before or after the agreement expired, but rather on preserving the original intent of the parties when circumstances have arisen that were unanticipated when the agreement was drafted.[21] Because the package of rights would have been "plainly arbitrable" if the unanticipated merger had not occurred, the Court assumed that the parties intended the same result post merger as well.

A review of arbitration awards indicates that arbitrators have been receptive to crediting arguments that certain rights growing out of the agreement have effectively "vested" or "ac-

---

LRRM at 2757. As to the presumption of arbitrability, see Teamsters Local 703 v. Kennicott Bros. Co., 771 F.2d 300, 303, 120 LRRM 2306, 2308 (7th Cir. 1985), where the Seventh Circuit, finding that a postcontract dispute over retroactive pay issues was not arbitrable, stated: "Although it may be reasonable to presume that parties intend to arbitrate grievances arising shortly after the expiration of a contract, the presumption weakens as the time between expiration and grievance events increases. A contrary holding would mean that parties to a collective-bargaining agreement would be presumed to intend that any dispute arising between them years or even decades after the expiration of the agreement would be arbitrable." See also Teamsters Local 238 v. C.R.S.T., 795 F.2d 1400, 122 LRRM 2993, 2996 (8th Cir.), cert. denied, 479 U.S. 1007, 123 LRRM 3192 (1986) (passage of almost one year between expiration of contract and employee's discharge makes application of *Nolde* presumption of doubtful propriety).

[20]376 U.S. 543, 55 LRRM 2769 (1964).

[21]Id. at 554, 55 LRRM at 2774. See generally Goetz, *Arbitration After Termination of a Collective Bargaining Agreement*, 63 La. L. Rev. 693 (1977).

crued," and where those rights are at issue in an arbitral proceeding, arbitrability will be found despite the expiration or termination of a collective bargaining agreement.[22] For example, where rights to payment were at issue, Arbitrator W. Willard Wirtz, in *Brooklyn Eagle*,[23] stated:

> So far as can be determined, the developing case law is virtually uniform in its recognition of payment rights arising under a collective bargaining agreement and measured by service already performed as being enforceable even where the event upon which their enforceability depends occurs after the termination of the agreement.[24]

Arbitrator Milton O. Talent, in *Bunn-O-Matic Corp.*,[25] held that an employer was obligated to pay severance pay when it closed its plant following a strike at the expiration of the agreement. Citing the decision in *Nolde Brothers*, the arbitrator found that the rationale behind the severance-pay clause (accrual of benefits on the basis of length of service), together with the broad language used by the parties in that provision (the language did not indicate that the right to severance pay died with the agreement), demonstrated an intent to permit the accrual of rights during the term of the agreement.[26]

Arbitrator C. Chester Brisco, in *Bekins Moving & Storage Co.*,[27] ruled that a grievance alleging that strikers were entitled to be paid for birthday holidays that fell during a strike where there was no collective bargaining agreement in effect was not arbitrable, at least in the situation where the new contract did not provide for retroactivity and there was no past practice of providing fringe benefits during contract interregnums.[28]

---

[22]Besides the cases discussed in this section, see Clow Corp., 90 LA 969, 972 (Cohen, 1988) (discharge grievance arbitrable where all employer's contract proposals contained grievance-arbitration procedure); Westwood Prods., 77 LA 396 (Peterschmidt, 1981) (holding discharge grievance not arbitrable where no contract was in existence when events giving rise to grievance occurred and there was no agreement that the obligation to arbitrate continue).

[23]32 LA 156 (1959).

[24]Id. at 163.

[25]70 LA 34 (1977).

[26]Id. at 41.

[27]81 LA 1198 (1983).

[28]See also Gates Canada Inc., 82 LA 480, 481 (Brown, 1984) (grievance requesting indemnity benefits for employee who had surgery after agreement expired not arbitrable under insurance agreement provision providing dispute may be taken by grievance under "the collective labour agreement then in effect.").

Are employees, upon termination of the collective bargaining agreement, relegated to a status of employment at will? Where an employer discharged employees for strike misconduct after an agreement had expired but before a new agreement was negotiated, Arbitrator Thomas Roberts, in *Bell Foundry Co.*,[29] held that the rationale of *Nolde Brothers* was inapplicable and therefore the grievances were not arbitrable. The arbitrator reasoned that the decision in *Nolde Brothers* does not disturb the existing concept that grievances not involving claims of "vested" rights are not arbitrable if they arise after an agreement has expired. He stated that to hold otherwise would result in a finding that an employer would be obligated for all time to arbitrate the discharge of an employee after the expiration of an agreement.[30]

Reading *Nolde* narrowly, the Supreme Court of Michigan ruled that a county deputy sheriff's "just cause" grievance did not survive the expiration of the collective bargaining agreement, even though the discharge may have been based, in part, on conduct which took place while her "just cause" right was viable. *Nolde*, reasoned the court, should be limited to grievances regarding contract rights which can vest or accrue while a collective bargaining agreement is in effect. The right to be reappointed except for just cause is not the kind of right which could accrue over time or vest upon a particular contingency.[31]

The Eighth Circuit, in *Teamsters Local 238 v. C.R.S.T.*,[32] likewise found that a discharge, based on events occurring

---

[29]73 LA 1162 (1979).

[30]Id. at 1166. See also Boeing Co. v. Machinists, 381 F.2d 119, 65 LRRM 2961 (5th Cir. 1967).

[31]County of Ottawa v. Jaklinski, 423 Mich. 1, 377 N.W.2d 668, 120 LRRM 3260 (1985). See also Oil Workers Local 4-23 v. American Petrofina Co. of Tex., 586 F. Supp. 643, 117 LRRM 2034 (E.D. Tex. 1984), (limiting *Nolde* only to accrued rights and benefits, and holding discharge not arbitrable), rev'd, 759 F.2d 512, 119 LRRM 2395 (5th Cir. 1985) (question whether discharge arbitrable must itself be submitted to arbitration); Garland Coal & Mining Co. v. Mine Workers Dist. 21, 596 F. Supp. 747, 120 LRRM 3507 (W.D. Ark. 1984) (denying arbitration where (1) arbitrators served only for "duration of agreement," (2) express provision made in contract for postexpiration of selected benefits, and (3) union sought clause in prior negotiations allowing arbitration of benefits on basis of events occurring prior to effective date of contract, indicating union's acknowledgment that arbitration would not be available otherwise); Teamsters Local 636 v. J.C. Penney Co., 484 F. Supp. 130, 132, 103 LRRM 2618 (W.D. Pa. 1980) (denying arbitrability of just-cause grievance where agreement defined "grievance" as a dispute arising "during the term of the Agreement").

[32]759 F.2d 1400, 122 LRRM 2993 (8th Cir.), cert, denied, 479 U.S. 1007, 123 LRRM 3192 (1986).

some twelve months after the agreement had expired, was not arbitrable. The union's position was that the existence of a grievance procedure could be inferred because the employer's impasse schedule, unilaterally implemented in the interim, called for resolving seniority disputes by grievance. Since no procedure had been settled upon by the parties, the union urged that the procedures in the expired agreement remained in force. The court ruled that the facts did not reveal any events subject to arbitration had occurred prior to the contract termination and, therefore, the presumption of arbitrability as outlined in *Nolde* was inapplicable. The dissent, arguing that there was a continuing duty to arbitrate, pointed out that the employer stated in its unilaterally implemented schedule that it was continuing other terms and conditions of employment consistent with its final offer, and this final offer included a grievance procedure.

Where the acts giving rise to a dismissal occur prior to the expiration, however, the *Nolde* presumption of arbitrability should operate.[33]

C. Grievance Arises After Expiration With Subsequent Agreement to Continue Rights Established in Contract

The Ninth Circuit, in *Ficek v. Southern Pacific Co.*,[34] stated that "an agreement to arbitrate a particular issue need not be express—it may be implied from the conduct of the parties."[35] Accordingly, even if the contract has expired, an agreement to arbitrate may be inferred from the actions of the parties after expiration. If the parties act as if there is an agreement, either by their conduct in the interim or their past practice, an arbitrator may properly conclude that one exists.[36]

When does an agreement exist? The Eighth Circuit found an interim agreement to arbitrate grievances existed when

---

[33]Glover Bottled Gas Corp. v. Teamsters Local 282, 711 F.2d 479, 113 LRRM 3211 (2d Cir. 1983) (holding discharge arbitrable where all acts leading to discharge occurred before termination of contract).

[34]338 F.2d 655, 57 LRRM 2573 (9th Cir. 1964), cert. denied, 380 U.S. 988, 60 LRRM 2284 (1965).

[35]Id., 57 LRRM at 2574.

[36]Ryan-Walsh Stevedoring Co., 89 LA 831 (Baroni, 1987); Santa Cruz City School Dist., 73 LA 1264 (Heath, 1979).

the employer, after the termination of a prior agreement, sent the union a letter declaring that the terms of employment, including grievance procedures, as set out in a draft agreement, would be in effect until the union had the opportunity to negotiate any change.[37] In *Teamsters Local 610 v. VDA Moving & Storage,*[38] a federal district court enforced an arbitration award that ordered the reinstatement of employees determined to have been improperly discharged and placed on layoff. Although the agreement had expired and no new agreement had been reached when the arbitrator made his award, the court found that the employer had indicated a consent to arbitrate when it proceeded to arbitration without challenging the arbitrator's jurisdiction.

Similarly, the Ninth Circuit, in *Holly Sugar Corp. v. Distillery Workers,*[39] declared that there is no inherent prohibition against arbitration awards which are based upon a violation of an expired agreement. The arbitrator found that grievances were arbitrable under an expired agreement, where the employer failed to comply with the contract's terms specifying that the union be notified of the grievant's employment status in a job classification. Both the arbitrator and the court agreed that under these facts the employer was estopped from asserting nonarbitrability of grievances under the expired contract.[40]

Arbitrator Dale Allen, Jr., in *Mason County Road Commission,*[41] concluded that the discharge of an employee following the termination of an agreement but before consummation of a new contract was arbitrable where the parties' actions continued on a normal level and under conditions provided in the old contract. Even though no formal memorandum of agreement was ever written, Arbitrator Allen noted that, by their own actions, there was an implied understanding that the conditions of the old agreement were to be extended during the hiatus period between labor con-

---

[37]Taft Broadcasting Co. v. NLRB, 441 F.2d 1382, 77 LRRM 2257 (8th Cir. 1971).
[38]447 F. Supp. 439, 98 LRRM 2066 (E.D. Mo. 1978).
[39]412 F.2d 899, 71 LRRM 2841 (9th Cir. 1969).
[40]See also Culinary Workers Local 226, Local Executive Bd. of Las Vegas, v. Royal Center, 754 F.2d 835, 119 LRRM 2958 (9th Cir. 1985) (holding arbitrable grievance involving carryover of contract after closure of business where arbitration clause covered "all grievances").
[41]70 LA 234 (1978).

tracts.[42] It is interesting that Arbitrator Allen cited a contractual provision that allowed an arbitrator to proceed ex parte and make an award in the event that one party refused to participate in the arbitration hearing. This, argued Allen, was evidence that the negotiators placed faith in the arbitration process as a means of resolving labor-contract differences and thus supported the decision to uphold arbitrability in the present case.

Similarly, Arbitrator Thomas Gallagher, in *Martin Podany Associates*,[43] rejected an employer's argument that expiration of the agreement precluded arbitration. While the parties were in the process of negotiating a new agreement, the employer sold its assets on December 3, 1981. The next day Martin Podany notified its work force that they would be permanently terminated, along with all union agreements. The new buyer notified the dismissed employees that they could apply for employment, but that the terms and conditions of employment would not be the same as those that had prevailed when working for Podany. The previous labor agreement, by its terms, expired on June 30, 1981. Arbitrator Gallagher reasoned that the continuing operation of the parties implied an intention that the grievance procedure established in the expired agreement should also continue in effect.

Finally, a strike settlement agreement may effectively serve as a "submission" and form the basis for arbitral jurisdiction for acts occurring during the hiatus between agreements.[44] In *Knollwood Cemetery Association v. Steelworkers*,[45] employees began a strike after the parties' collective bargaining agreement expired. Several months later the employees returned to work although no new agreement had been reached. Knollwood then discharged the grievant for punching out another employee's time card. The union requested arbitration which was denied, the company asserting that it had no duty to arbitrate because no agreement was in effect. In settlement

---

[42]Id. at 237.

[43]80 LA 658 (1983).

[44]See, e.g., the discussion of Arbitrator Alex J. Simon in Walker Mfg. Co., 60 LA 269 (1973). See also Carus Corp., 71 LA 624 (Kossoff, 1978) (grievance seeking benefits under medical plan for striker who sustained injury following expiration of agreement, where parties entered into strike settlement agreement requiring insurance to continue during strike).

[45]789 F.2d 367, 122 LRRM 2103 (6th Cir. 1986).

of an unfair labor practice action brought by the union, Knollwood agreed to arbitrate, later bringing an action in federal court to vacate an award by Arbitrator Peter Di Leone in favor of the grievant, which had ordered reinstatement with back pay. The district court granted the union's motion to dismiss, and the Sixth Circuit refused to vacate the award, reasoning that Knollwood independently agreed to arbitrate the dispute, employing the prevailing grievance and arbitration procedure. The court, quoting the Supreme Court in *W.R. Grace*,[46] rejected management's argument that even when the arbitrator is given authority to rule on matters of substantive arbitrability, the district court is required to make an independent ruling on the arbitrability of the dispute:

> "Because the authority of arbitrators is a subject of collective bargaining, just as in any other contractual provision, the scope of the arbitrator's authority is itself a question of contract interpretation that the parties have delegated to the arbitrator."[47]

D. Policy Under Taft-Hartley

Section 8(a)(5) of the Taft-Hartley Act makes it an unfair labor practice for an employer to refuse to bargain collectively with the representatives of its employees. An employer violates the statute when it makes a midterm change in any provision of the collective bargaining agreement relating to a mandatory subject of bargaining,[48] and the Board has firmly established that a grievance/arbitration procedure is a "term or condition of employment" and a mandatory subject of bargaining within the meaning of Section 8(a)(5).[49]

In *Hilton-Davis Chemical Co. Div.*,[50] the Board held that an employer's refusal to honor an expired contract's arbitration provision did not violate the statute. The Board reasoned

---

[46]W.R. Grace & Co. v. Rubber Workers Local 759, 461 U.S. 757, 765f, 113 LRRM 2641 (1983).

[47]122 LRRM at 2105. See also Johnston Boiler Co. v. Boilermakers Local 893, 753 F.2d 40, 43 118 LRRM 2348, 2351 (6th Cir. 1985) ("we do hold that the presumption of authority that attaches to an arbitrator's award applies with equal force to his decision that his award is within the submission.").

[48]Allied Chem. & Alkali Workers Local 1 v. Pittsburgh Plate Glass Co., 404 U.S. 157, 78 LRRM 2974 (1971).

[49]NLRB v. Independent Stave Co., 591 F.2d 443, 100 LRRM 2646 (8th Cir.), cert. denied, 100 U.S. 55, 102 LRRM 2360 (1979).

[50]185 NLRB 241, 75 LRRM 1036 (1970).

that during the hiatus between the expiration of the old agreement and the negotiation of a new contract, absent mutual consent the parties revert to the statutory scheme of free collective bargaining. While the parties must continue to meet and confer in good faith, not only over terms and conditions of a new agreement but also over employee grievances, the Board nevertheless held that it does not follow that during such hiatus the parties are required by law to submit to arbitration any grievance arising after the expiration of the agreement.

Although the *Hilton-Davis* reasoning is found in numerous arbitration decisions where contract expiration is at issue, the validity of this decision after *Nolde Brothers* is questionable. In *American Sink Top & Cabinet Co.*,[51] a three-member panel of the Board, applying *Nolde Brothers*, ruled that the duty to arbitrate survived expiration of the contract, and ordered the employer to arbitrate the grievance of an employee discharged after the expiration of an agreement.[52] Similar to the reasoning of the Court in *Nolde Brothers*, the three-member panel stated that there was no evidence that the parties intended to exclude such claims from the grievance-arbitration procedure. More important, the grievance arguably related to events that occurred in part before the contract expired. *Nolde* made it clear that "it could not be seriously contended" that contract expiration would terminate the contractual obligation to arbitrate disputes based on preexpiration disputes.

In a 1987 decision, the full Board clarified the postexpiration duty to arbitrate in light of *Nolde*, and declared that it was reaffirming the principles expressed in *Hilton-Davis* "that the arbitration commitment arises solely from mutual consent and that Congress did not intend the National Labor Relations Act to operate to create a statutory obligation to arbitrate."[53] Citing *Warrior & Gulf Navigation Co.*[54] and *Gateway Coal*,[55]

---

[51] 242 NLRB 408, 101 LRRM 1166 (1979).

[52] See also ESB, Inc., 246 NLRB 325, 102 LRRM 1507 (1979).

[53] Indiana & Mich. Elec. Co., 284 NLRB 53, 125 LRRM 1097, 1101 (1987).

[54] Steelworkers v. Warrior & Gulf Navigation Co., 363 U.S. 574, 582, 46 LRRM 2416, 2419 (1960) (stating that "arbitration is a matter of contract and a party cannot be required to submit to arbitration any dispute which he has not agreed so to submit").

[55] Gateway Coal Co. v. Mine Workers, 414 U.S. 368, 374, 85 LRRM 2049, 2051 (1974) ("[n]o obligation to arbitrate a labor dispute arises solely by operation of law.

as well as the legislative history of Section 203(d) of the Labor Management Relations Act, the Board concluded that the decision in *Hilton-Davis* is in accord with the legislative history of the Act and Supreme Court decisions, *Nolde* included. The Board nevertheless stated that the holding in *Hilton-Davis* that an employer is free to abandon the arbitration procedure during a contractual hiatus must be modified in light of *Nolde*. In certain circumstances the arbitration commitment survives the expiration of the collective bargaining agreement, as in the case where a broad arbitration clause exists which does not contain language sufficient to negate the presumption in favor of arbitration. The Board concluded by holding that a postexpiration event "arises under" the contract within the meaning of *Nolde* "only if it concerns contract rights capable of accruing or vesting to some degree during the life of the contract and ripening or remaining enforceable after the contract expires."[56] Accordingly, where a company took the position that it was no longer bound by the arbitration provisions and refused to arbitrate all grievances during the hiatus, rather than limit its refusal to arbitrate a particular grievance or class of grievances, the Act was violated.

E. Contract Expiration and the Arbitrator's Remedy Power

In a situation where the grievance arises after the expiration of the collective bargaining agreement, such as *Nolde Brothers*, the parties' obligation to arbitrate is not necessarily extinguished. Chief Justice Burger has declared that there is a presumption that all grievances arising out of the contractual relationship are arbitrable, even if they arise after the contract has expired, at least in the case where the parties' agreement provides for arbitration of "any grievance," and there is no express language excluding claims arising after expiration from the grievance-arbitration procedure.

The decision in *Nolde*, however, left unanswered the question of the effect of contract termination on the arbitrator's

---

The law compels a party to submit his grievance to arbitration ony if he has contracted to do so.").

[56]Indiana & Mich. Elec. Co., supra note 53, 125 LRRM at 1103.

remedial power. Although *Nolde* clearly provides that termination does not automatically affect the arbitrability of a dispute (the Court failed to reveal the conditions where termination of the contract agreement would result in termination of the duty to arbitrate, other than the case where the parties explicitly so provide), some reported court decisions indicate that the arbitrator's remedial power may be limited. In *Teamsters Local 610 v. VDA Moving & Storage*,[57] a federal district court modified an arbitrator's remedy when it was shown to require action past the court's determination of the agreement's expiration date. The agreement had initially expired on February 28, 1976, and arbitration took place on November 22, 1976, concerning grievances that occurred in June and July. Holding that the awards were valid even assuming that the contract had expired, the court nevertheless found that the parties, by their conduct, had actually extended the agreement to December 1976. When the arbitrator ordered reinstatement with back pay for one of the grievants, the court held that back pay would be proper only from the date of the discharge to the December date of termination. In addition, the court held that the reinstatement remedy was mooted, since the December date had now passed.

Similarly, in *Steelworkers v. Overly Manufacturing Co.*,[58] the federal district court held that in view of the expiration of the agreement under which an award was entered, together with the subsequent decertification of the bargaining representative, the controversy with respect to reinstatement was moot. The court found that there was no possibility of reinstatement, in part, because no new agreement had been executed.

This view was rejected, however, by the Ninth Circuit. In *Longshoremen (ILA) Local 142 v. Land & Construction Co.*,[59] the Court of Appeals held that an arbitrator did not exceed his jurisdiction in holding that a terminated collective bargaining agreement neither (1) deprived him of jurisdiction to rule of the merits of a grievance arising prior to the expiration, nor (2) required that a back-pay award be limited to that

---

[57]Supra note 38.
[58]438 F. Supp. 922, 96 LRRM 2999 (W.D. Pa. 1977).
[59]498 F.2d 201, 86 LRRM 2874 (9th Cir. 1974).

accruable as of the date of the contract's termination, even though plaintiff union had been replaced as a bargaining representative by a different union. In enforcing an award of reinstatement with back pay, the Ninth Circuit stated that there was no provision limiting back pay to a period ending with the expiration of the contract. The court pointed out that the only provision dealing with back pay relates to improper disciplinary suspensions and not to layoffs, and even that provision limits back pay only to that pay "lost because of the discharge or suspension." It follows that back pay because of improper suspension or discharge could exceed that which accrues to the date of termination of the agreement.[60]

The Seventh Circuit, in *Mogge v. Machinists District 8*,[61] has also rejected a claim that an arbitrator exceeded his authority by ordering reinstatement and back pay where, at the time of the award, the contract had expired and had not been renewed. In holding that the award should be enforced, the court of appeals noted that the question of the effect of the expiration of the agreement had never been presented to the arbitrator. The burden was on District 8 (the "employer" in this case) to prove to the arbitrator that the contract had expired so that he could take this into account in fashioning a remedy. Absent any showing that these facts were unavailable at that time, the union-employer could not complain that the award was unjustified.

More important, the court of appeal stated that, even assuming that the contract had expired, the arbitrator did not exceed his contractual authority in ordering back pay for a period past the expiration of the agreement. The Seventh Circuit, citing *Enterprise Wheel*, declared:

> The dispute in this case arose during the term of a valid agreement which provided for arbitration but left it to the arbitrator to fashion an appropriate remedy. Unlike matters before the Labor Board, the parties to an arbitration proceeding have privately agreed to that procedure to settle their disputes. The contract . . . did not provide for a specific remedy in the case of a wrongful discharge, nor did it contain any restriction on the arbitrator.[62]

---

[60]Id., 86 LRRM at 2876.
[61]454 F.2d 510, 78 LRRM 2939 (7th Cir. 1971).
[62]Id., 78 LRRM at 2942. Accord Burt Bldg. Materials Corp. v. Teamsters Local 1205, 277 N.Y.S.2d 399, 64 LRRM 2137 (N.Y. Ct.App. 1966).

The Seventh Circuit's decision in *Mogge* was followed by the federal court for the Western District of Virginia in *Food & Commercial Workers Local 400 v. Marval Poultry Co.*,[63] where the court held that arbitration awards granting reinstatement and back pay to two employees remained in effect beyond the expiration of the agreement, notwithstanding a strike and a change in bargaining representative. The court pointed out that the agreement was silent as to the employer's obligations after expiration and that back pay is particularly appropriate where the employees have a continuing expectation of employment, because the expiration does not place employees in jeopardy of losing their jobs. As noted by the court:

> Even though Marval's employees went on strike after the expiration of the bargaining agreement, many of its employees continued to enjoy the same wages and benefits beyond the expiration of the contract. While this court may have felt disinclined to fashion quite so broad a remedy as that rendered by the arbitrator, "a federal court may not overrule an arbitrator's decision simply because the court believes its own interpretation of the contract would be a better one . . . ."[64]

The court also declared that the "most forceful factor in favor of upholding the arbitrator's remedy of back pay and reinstatement is simply that the company failed to raise the issue of the expiration of the collective bargaining agreement during the pendency of the arbitration proceedings."[65]

Finally, in *Steelworkers v. Enterprise Wheel & Car Corp.*,[66] one of the three landmark Steelworkers Trilogy cases, the Supreme Court upheld an arbitrator's award for reinstatement after the expiration of a contract (which was subsequently renewed). In *Enterprise*, a group of employees were discharged because they had walked off the job in protest against the discharge of another employee. When the union sought arbitration of the matter, the employer refused. Less than three months after the termination, the contract expired. After the expiration date, the union filed suit in federal court

---

[63]645 F. Supp. 1174, 123 LRRM 2819 (W.D. Va. 1986).
[64]Id. at 1180, 123 LRRM at 2823, quoting W.R. Grace & Co. v. Local 759, 461 U.S. 757, 764, 113 LRRM 2641, 2644 (1983).
[65]645 F. Supp. at 1180, 123 LRRM at 2823.
[66]363 U.S. 593, 46 LRRM 2423 (1960). *Enterprise Wheel* is discussed at length in Chapter 3 at notes 49–54, and accompanying text.

and won a court order requiring arbitration. The arbitrator subsequently ordered reinstatement with back pay, less 10 days' pay and earnings from other employment. The district court ordered specific performance of the arbitrator's award. On appeal, the Fourth Circuit[67] held that upon expiration of the contract the right to reinstatement had disappeared. The court of appeals also modified the district court's order to allow back pay only for the period following the termination of employment but prior to the expiration of the contract.

The Supreme Court reversed the Fourth Circuit. In so doing, the Court found no infirmity in formulating a remedy of back pay beyond the collective bargaining agreement's expiration, along with reinstatement. The Court's reasoning is particularly noteworthy:

> The opinion of the arbitrator in this case, as it bears upon the award of back pay beyond the date of the agreement's expiration and reinstatement, is ambiguous. It may be read as based solely upon the arbitrator's view of the requirements of enacted legislation, which would mean that he exceeded that scope of the submission. Or it may be read as embodying a construction of the agreement itself, perhaps with the arbitrator looking to "the law" for help in determining the sense of the agreement. A mere ambiguity in the opinion, accompanying an award, which permits the inference that the arbitrator may have exceeded his authority, is not a reason for refusing to enforce the award. . . . Moreover, we see no reason to assume that this arbitrator has abused the trust the parties confided in him and has not stayed within the areas marked out for his consideration. It is not apparent that he went beyond the submission. The Court of Appeal's opinion refusing to enforce the reinstatement and partial back pay portions of the award was not based upon any finding that the arbitrator did not premise his award on his construction of the contract. It merely disagreed with the arbitrator's construction of it.
>
> . . .
> It is the arbitrator's construction which was bargained for; and so far as the arbitrator's decision concerns construction of the contract, the courts have no business overruling him because their interpretation of the contract is different from his.[68]

It can accordingly be argued that *Enterprise* establishes

---

[67]Steelworkers v. Enterprise Wheel & Car Corp., 269 F.2d 327, 44 LRRM 2349 (4th cir. 1969).
[68]363 U.S. at 597–599, 46 LRRM at 2425–2426.

the broad principle that the arbitrator is the one to decide whether a collective bargaining agreement, despite its expiration, permits a postexpiration remedy and that a reviewing court should not engage in interpretation of the contract in the course of determining whether an arbitrator has exceeded his power in this regard.

F. Summary

One court has suggested that the disparity between the actual holding of *Nolde Brothers* (the event that triggered a severance-pay grievance, the closing of a plant, occurred four days after expiration of the contract) and the Court's broad language has been a source of confusion to the lower federal courts. [69] Notwithstanding the dicta in *Nolde*, there is no question that if employers wish to avoid the effects of the decision, they will have to bargain specifically for explicit limitations in grievance arbitration provisions or clearer statements of the nonvesting nature of such items as pension, disability, vacation, or severance benefits.[70] Without such an *express* exclusion, the duty to arbitrate will be presumed, especially where a contractual no-strike clause survives the expiration of the collective bargaining agreement and the rights at issue can vest or accrue during the life of the agreement.

A review of reported court and arbitral decisions indicates that the obligation to arbitrate need not expire with the collective bargaining agreement, and, accordingly, arbitrators are not without jurisdiction to issue an award even though the contract has expired. A grievance may in fact "arise under the agreement," even though the facts giving rise to the grievance arose after the contract's termination. Courts and arbitrators have been imaginative in holding that certain rights, such as pension, vacation and severance pay, effectively "vest" or "accrue" during the agreement, and are thus subject to

---

[69]County of Ottawa v. Jaklinski, 423 Mich. 1, 377 N.W.2d 668, 120 LRRM 3260 (1985).

[70]Edwards, *Labor-Law Decisions of the Supreme Court, 1976–77 Term* in Labor Relations Yearbook—1977, 91 (BNA Books, 1978).

arbitral jurisdiction and remedies.[71] In those cases where the rights at issue are not "vested," agreements to arbitrate have been inferred from the conduct of the parties during the hiatus between agreements.

The better weight of authority makes it clear that where the agreement is not explicit concerning the power of an arbitrator to fashion a remedy after the expiration of the collective bargaining agreement, consistent with *Enterprise Wheel* the arbitrator will have wide latitude in fashioning a remedy, even for a period after the contract has expired.

---

[71]Teamsters Local 238 v. C.R.S.T., 795 F.2d 1400, 1403–1404, 122 LRRM 2993 (8th Cir.), cert. denied, 479 U.S. 1007, 123 LRRM 3192 (1986) (right to be discharged for cause does not arise under agreement); Nibbs v. Felix, 726 F.2d 102, 104, 117 LRRM 2674 (3d Cir. 1984) (holding grievance over failure to promote "arises under" expired contract only if eligibility list structured or prepared under agreement); Teamsters Local 807 v. Brink's, Inc., 744 F.2d 283, 286, 117 LRRM 2306 (2d Cir. 1984) (dispute over postexpiration withdrawal of recognition did not "arise under" expired agreement); Federated Metals Corp. v. Steelworkers, 648 F.2d 856, 107 LRRM 2271 (3d Cir.), cert. denied, 454 U.S. 1031, 108 LRRM 2924 (1981) (ordering arbitration of pension benefits dispute); Steelworkers v. Fort Pitt Steel Casting Div., 635 F.2d 1071, 105 LRRM 3232 (3d Cir. 1980), cert. denied, 452 U.S. 985, 107 LRRM 2384 (1981) (presumption of arbitrability not overcome by clause in contract defining "employees" as workers from whom union acted as representative "during life of this agreement," and employer ordered to arbitrate severance-pay dispute); Ladies Garment Workers Local 589 v. Kellwood Co., 592 F.2d 1008, 100 LRRM 2750 (8th Cir. 1979) (scope of employer's obligation under expired contract to "maintain" pension benefits "in effect" arbitrable under *Nolde*).

Part II

Remedies in Discharge and Disciplinary Cases

Chapter 7

Reinstatement

A. Background

During the eighteenth and nineteenth centuries, employers, in effect, had total discretion in directing the work force. Under an 1877 legal principle, the employment relationship was one which was "at will" unless the parties otherwise provided. Professor Clyde Summers points out that the American rule was apparently announced 100 years ago by a treatise writer who cited, as authority, court decisions that did not support this principle.[1] As a practical matter, however, the "at will" principle meant that the employment relationship existed solely at the will of the employer, since few employees had any bargaining leverage.[2]

With the passage of protective labor legislation,[3] and the flourishing of unionization and collective bargaining, the "at will" doctrine was significantly modified. Unions demanded and obtained contract language requiring employers to have

---

[1]Summers, *Arbitration of Unjust Dismissal: A Preliminary Proposal*, in The Future of Labor Arbitration in America, 159, 168–169 (American Arbitration Association, 1976). See also Blades, *Employment at Will vs. Individual Freedom: On Limiting the Abusive Exercise of Employer Power*, 67 Colum. L. Rev. 1404 (1967); Note, *Implied Contract Rights to Job Security*, 26 Stan. L. Rev. 335 (1974).

For a comprehensive review of the common-law "at-will" rule, see Wagenseller v. Scottsdale Memorial Hosp., 710 P.2d 1025, 119 LRRM 3166 (Ariz. 1985) and Magnan v. Anaconda Indus., 193 Conn. 558, 117 LRRM 2163 (1984).

[2]Blumrosen, *Strangers No More: All Workers Are Entitled to "Just Cause" Protection Under Title VII*, 2 Indus. Rel. L.J. 519, 521 (1978).

[3]National Labor Relations Act, 29 U.S.C. §§151–169 (1970 & Supp. V, 1975); Fair Labor Standards Act of 1938, §6, 29 U.S.C., §206 (1970 & Supp. V, 1975); Civil Rights Act of 1964, 42 U.S.C. §2000 (1970 & Supp. V, 1975); Occupational Safety and Health Act, 29 U.S.C. §§651–678 (1970).

a good reason to take actions adverse to an employee's economic interest.[4] Indeed, recent survey reports by The Bureau of National Affairs, Inc., reveal that discharge and discipline provisions are found in 96 percent of the contracts analyzed— 99 percent in manufacturing and 92 percent in nonmanufacturing.[5] Moreover, disciplinary cases constitute the largest single category of grievances that are brought before arbitrators. A recent report by the Federal Mediation and Conciliation Service reveals that almost one out of every three grievances decided by arbitrators is in this category.[6] In this same regard, BNA also reports grounds-for-discharge provisions, found in 94 percent of their sample, are generally of two types—discharge for "cause" or "just cause" (found in 86 percent of the agreements), or discharge for a specific offense (found in 75 percent of the contracts in the database).[7]

Despite the high frequency of arbitration cases dealing with discharge and discipline, few, if any, contracts contain a definition of "just cause." Although there is no uniform definition of what constitutes just cause, a review of published arbitration awards reveals a "common law" set of guidelines that may be applied to the facts of any particular case. Arbitrator Harry Platt, in a 1947 case, had this to say on the function of an arbitrator in discipline cases:

> It is ordinarily the function of an Arbitrator in interpreting a contract provision which requires "sufficient cause" as a condition precedent to discharge not only to determine whether the

---

[4]Summer H. Slichter, James J. Healy, and E. Robert Livernash argue that "few areas of personnel policy have been more significantly affected by collective bargaining than management's administration of employee discipline." The Impact of Collective Bargaining on Management, 624 (Brookings Inst., 1960).

[5]Basic Patterns in Union Contracts, 12th ed., 7 (BNA Books, 1989).

[6]Federal Mediation and Conciliation Service, Fortieth Annual Report—Fiscal Year 1987, 23 (Government Printing Office, 1987). FMCS reports 4,753 cases in 1987; 1,993 in the discharge and discipline category. The downward trend from 1982 is noteworthy:

	1982	1983	1984	1985	1986	1987
Total cases:	8,348	7,066	6,866	5,380	11,205	4,753
Discharge & Discipline	3,253	2,764	2,747	2,050	4,375	1,993

[7]Basic Patterns in Union Contracts, supra note 5, at 7. Grounds most frequently referred to in BNA sample agreements are: violation of leave provisions (37%), participation in unauthorized strikes (34%), unauthorized absence (30%), dishonesty or theft and violation of company rules (21% each), intoxication (20%), insubordination (17%), incompetence or failure to meet standards (16%), failure to obey safety rules (14%), misconduct (12%), and tardiness (9%). Id.

employee involved is guilty of wrongdoing and, if so, to confirm the employer's right to discipline where its exercise is essential to the objective of efficiency, but also to safeguard the interests of the discharged employee by making reasonably sure that the causes for discharge were just and equitable and such as would appeal to reasonable and fair-minded persons as warranting discharge. To be sure, no standards exist to aid an Arbitrator in finding a conclusive answer to such a question and, therefore, perhaps the best he can do is to decide what reasonable man, mindful of the habits and customs of industrial life and of the standards of justice and fair dealing prevalent in the community ought to have done under similar circumstances and in that light to decide whether the conduct of the discharged employee was defensible and the disciplinary penalty just.[8]

Generally, to establish that just cause exists in the termination context requires a significant showing, which includes a demonstration of evidence connecting the conduct complained of to the responsibilities of the individual grievant. One arbitrator declared that "[t]he question of 'just cause' is nothing less than the question of justice, placed in an industrial setting. True, it is not legal justice; it is not social justice—it is industrial justice."[9] Another arbitrator expanded on this concept this way:

> [Just cause mandates] not merely that the employer's action be free of capriciousness and arbitrariness but that the employee's performance be so faulty or indefensible as to leave the employer with no alternative except to discipline him.[10]

Perhaps the most often-quoted statement of the criteria used in these guidelines is in the form of a series of questions provided by Arbitrator Carroll Daugherty (the full text of Arbitrator Daugherty's guidelines is reprinted in Appendix E):

> 1. Did the company give to the employee forewarning or foreknowledge of the possible or probable disciplinary consequences of the employee's conduct?
> . . .
> 2. Was the company's rule or managerial order reasonably

---

[8]Riley Stoker Corp., 7 LA 764, 767 (1947).
[9]Lear Seigler, Inc., 63 LA 1157, 1160 (McBrearty, 1974).
[10]Platt, *Arbitral Standards in Discipline Cases*, in The Law and Labor-Management Relations, 223, 234 (Univ. of Mich. 1950). See also Koven and Smith, Just Cause: The Seven Tests (Kendall/Hunt, 1985); Smith, Merrifield, and Rothschild, Collective Bargaining and Labor Arbitration, 347 (Bobbs-Merrill, 1970).

related to (a) the orderly, efficient, and safe operation of the company's business and (b) the performance that the company might properly expect of the employee?

. . .

3. Did the company, before administering discipline to an employee, make an effort to discover whether the employee did in fact violate or disobey a rule or order of management?

. . .

4. Was the company's investigation conducted fairly and objectively?

. . .

5. At the investigation did the "judge" obtain substantial evidence or proof that the employee was guilty as charged?

. . .

6. Has the company applied its rules, orders, and penalties evenhandedly and without discrimination to all employees?

. . .

7. Was the degree of discipline administered by the company in a particular case reasonably related to (a) the seriousness of the employee's proven offense and (b) the record of the employee in his service with the company?[11]

Arbitrator Daugherty states that a "no" answer to any one or more of the above questions signifies that just and proper cause for discipline did not exist.

In an address before the National Academy of Arbitrators in 1989,[12] Arbitrator John E. Dunsford offered an insightful criticism of the Daugherty Seven Tests while simultaneously proposing that just cause essentially is a concept that requires "judgment and discretion" on the part of the arbitrator. Dunsford nodded respectfully to the contributions of Daugherty but stopped short of accepting the Seven Tests formula as arbitral common law. He instead stressed that just cause requires the arbitrator to exercise judgment and discretion, neither of which can be fully applied if limited by the Daugherty criteria.

The authors feel that Daugherty's Seven Tests may be a good starting point for the uninitiated or the novice, but as maturity and understanding of the arbitral process and just cause is achieved, the "judgment and discretion" concept should direct the arbitrator's decision making.

---

[11]Enterprise Wire Co., 46 LA 359, 363–364 (1966). See also McCall Printing Co., 64 LA 584, 588 (Lubic, 1975); Sunshine Biscuits, 60 LA 197 (Roberts, 1973).

[12]Dunsford, *Arbitral Discretion: The Tests of Just Cause*, in Arbitration 1989: The Arbitrator's Discretion During and After the Hearing, Proceedings of the 42nd Annual Meeting, National Academy of Arbitrators, 27–45 (BNA Books, 1990).

A reading of arbitral rulings in the just cause area reveals that any determination of just cause requires two separate considerations: (1) whether the employee is guilty of misconduct, and (2) assuming guilt, whether the discipline imposed is a reasonable penalty under the circumstances of the case. The universal rule in grievance arbitration is that the employer must carry the burden in a discharge case.

Even if no "just cause" provision is contained in the agreement, the better weight of authority holds that absent a clear indication to the contrary, a just cause standard is implied in the contract.[13] For example, Arbitrator M.S. Ryder rejected management's argument that, since there was no provision in the parties' collective bargaining agreement with respect to the discharge of employees, management was free to discharge or suspend where it acted in good faith and was "motivated by sincere reasons." The arbitrator's reasoning, as follows, is especially instructive:

> The fact that the applicable labor agreement does not deal with the subject matter of disciplinary discharge or suspension— which factual circumstance is hereby so found—does not give an employer the right to effect such kinds of severances from employment solely under the standards advanced here as correspondingly contractually proper by the Company. It is no modification of, or addition to the instant labor agreement, or a distortion of its meaning or misapplication of its mutual intent to require that beyond the bona fides, lack of arbitrariness or capriciousness and where there is sincerity of reason . . . the moving cause must also have the ingredient of justifiability. No labor agreement that purports to effect and maintain uninterrupted operations while at the same time promoting sound labor relations, as the instant agreement describes in its preamble, can eschew such a principled concept as that good or just cause should govern an employment severance bottomed on a disciplinary motivation.[14]

Similarly, a federal court, in *Food & Commercial Workers Local 634 v. Gold Star Sausage Co.*,[15] held that it was per-

---

[13]See generally, Hill and Sinicropi, Management Rights: A Legal and Arbitral Analysis, 102–104 (BNA Books, 1986) and citations therein. See also Shell Oil Co., 90 LA 112, 114–15 (Massey, 1988) ("In the absence of any express standard for discipline or discharge, the Arbitrator will apply the basic principle of just cause."); Clow Corp., 90 LA 969, 972 (Cohen, 1988) (finding just-cause provision continued during hiatus between contracts).

[14]B.F. Goodrich Tire Co., 36 LA 552, 556 (1961).

[15]487 F. Supp. 596, 104 LRRM 2252 (D. Colo. 1980).

missible for an arbitrator to imply a just-cause provision where the parties' agreement provided for certain forms of job security. The court reasoned as follows:

> If the [employer] had the power to fire employees at will, the seniority provisions and other benefits under the contract would be meaningless. Job security, a fundamental aspect of collective bargaining agreements, would be non-existent. By adhering to these principles, the arbitrator could reasonably infer that a just cause restriction was enmeshed in the fabric of the Agreement.[16]

And Arbitrator David Feller has likewise argued:

> It is now well established that, at least if the agreement contains a seniority provision, the "just cause" limitation is implicit in the agreement and may be enforced, although there is not a shred of language indicating that there is any such limitation. The arbitrator, in reading a collective bargaining agreement, not only reads the words of that agreement but also incorporates the commonly accepted standards to which the parties are assumed to have agreed. The authority to act as the parties' "contract reader" includes the authority to read into the contract those provisions which the arbitrator reasonably assumes the parties intended even if they fail to signify it by words.[17]

Arbitrator Aaron Wolff, in *A. Finkl & Sons*,[18] suggested that the traditional just-cause standards may be different once the labor agreement expires and the parties are engaged in economic warfare:

> "Whatever 'just cause' encompasses in a peaceful industrial setting where the employees are at work under a collective bargaining agreement, the concept of 'just cause' is broader [sic; should read 'narrower'] when the contract has expired and the parties are engaged in 'economic warfare.' While not to be condoned, certain conduct which might sustain a discharge during peacetime will not do so in wartime. For example, use of obscene or abusive language toward working fellow employees or supervisors while a contract is in effect may result in 'capital punishment' but not if used against non-striking employees during a strike. . . . Even 'Scuffling, jostling and occasional blows on the picket line between pickets and working employees [which] is a common result in labor disputes' may not justify dis-

---

[16]Id., 104 LRRM at 2255.
[17]Feller, *The Remedy Power in Grievance Arbitration*, 5 Indus. Rel. L.J. 128, 134–35 (1982).
[18]90 LA 502 (1988).

charge. . . . Similarly, apparent intimidation by carrying a rifle near the picket line may not be cause for discharge. . . ."[19]

Does the just-cause standard apply to a probationary employee or an employee dismissed pursuant to a "last-chance" agreement? The answer to both queries depends on the specific language of the parties' agreement. Many agreements preclude access to the grievance procedure for a probationary employee and, accordingly, a remedy for an improper discharge may not be accorded under such language. Similarly, if the specific terms of a last-chance agreement limits the employee's right to grieve, the limitation must be honored by the arbitrator. As pointed out by one arbitrator, however, most arbitrators do not broadly interpret waivers by employees of important rights under the collective bargaining agreement, including the right to grieve:

> In order for such waivers to be effective, the Company must prove the validity of the agreement by clear and convincing evidence. . . . For a waiver to be proper, the following conditions must be met: (1) the waiver must be specific, (2) the employee have full knowledge as to the rights he is giving up, (3) the employee must receive a substantial benefit in return, and (4) the Union must participate and consent, either expressly or impliedly, to the waiver, since the Union negotiated the contractual rights and the waiver by one employee may affect others.[20]

Applying this test, Arbitrator Timothy Heinsz found that a dismissal made pursuant to a last-chance agreement was not arbitrable under language providing if the grievant's attendance is unsatisfactory "for any time during the probationary period, he shall be subject to immediate termination." Another arbitrator, however, ruled a last-chance grievance arbitrable where, by its terms, the agreement was indefinite as to its duration and unclear as to the meaning of the term "disciplinary problems."[21]

Arbitrator William Daniel, in *BASF Corp.*,[22] discussed at

---

[19]Id. at 508, quoting County Line Cheese Co. (unpublished), FMCS Case No. 83K-01117 (Wolff, 1983).
[20]Atlantic Richfield Co., 81 LA 1193, 1195–96 (Heinsz, 1983), citing Lady Baltimore Bakery Co., 47 LA 8, 10 (Koven, 1966); United States Borax & Chem. Corp., 41 LA 1200, 1203 (Lennard, 1963); Mosaic Tile Co., 13 LA 949, 950 (Cornsweet, 1950).
[21]Ozalid Corp., 80 LA 1061 (Denson, 1983).
[22]90 LA 460 (1987).

length last-chance agreements and argued that they should
be strictly construed by an arbitrator:

> [Last-chance agreements] usually arise when an employee has
> come to the point of discharge by [un]disputed violations and
> offenses connected to substance abuse. Such agreement is a last
> chance because it not only sets forth the problem in writing but
> also details very specific steps to be taken and conditions to be
> met. The key to such agreements is the provision that failure
> to comply will immediately result in termination. These agree-
> ments are regularly signed by the three parties involved—the
> company, the union and the individual. In most cases, the union,
> by encouraging the employee to enter into these agreements, is
> saving the person's employment for otherwise, most assuredly,
> termination would result. Employers, who take the last step of
> entering into such agreements as a last chance, are entitled to
> strict enforcement by arbitrators for, otherwise, there would be
> no motivation to enter into such pacts for other employees. Ar-
> bitrators reviewing such cases arising under such last chance
> agreements should construe them strictly as long as the pro-
> visions are not unconscionable or in violation of some other
> contractual right.[23]

Where a finding is made that the employer did not have
cause for imposing discipline or discharge, the arbitrator is
left with the task of formulating a remedy. Similarly, even in
the case where an arbitrator's opinion indicates that cause
existed for assessing some discipline, a remedy may still be
forthcoming because mitigating circumstances exist.[24]

A review of both published and unpublished awards indicates that arbitrators have demonstrated no uniformity in
formulating remedies in the disciplinary area. The late Arbitrator Peter Seitz, commenting on the complexity of the

---

[23]Id. at 462.

[24]A study of published discharge grievances in the Bureau of National Affairs'
Labor Arbitration Reports (May 1971 through January 1974) reveals that management had its disciplinary action reduced or eliminated in approximately 58% (231
or 400 cases) of the awards. See Jennings and Wolters, *Discharge Cases Reconsidered*,
31 Arb. J. 164 (1976). See also Fogel, *Court Review of Discharge Arbitration Awards*
37 Arb. J. 22, No. 2 (1982); Stone, *Why Arbitrators Reinstate Discharged Employees*,
92 Monthly Lab. Rev. 49 (1969); Jones, *Ramifications of Back-Pay Awards in Suspension and Discharge Cases*, in Arbitration and Social Change, Proceedings of the
22nd Annual Meeting, National Academy of Arbitrators, 163, 166–167 (BNA Books,
1970); Summers, *Arbitration of Unjust Dismissal: A Preliminary Proposal*, in The
Future of Labor Arbitration in America, 161 (American Arbitration Association,
1976); Holly, *The Arbitration of Discharge Cases: A Case Study*, in Critical Issues in
Labor Arbitration, Proceedings of the 10th Annual Meeting, National Academy of
Arbitrators, 1, 16 (BNA Books, 1957); Note, *Discharge in the "Law" of Arbitration*,
20 Vand. L. Rev. 81 (1966).

problem, had this to say on the difficulty of formulating standards:

> Dispensing justice is an awesome responsibility; and it is much more so when the decision maker is afforded no more precise criterion than "just cause." The search for precise standards of decision making in industrial jurisprudence is likely to be illusory and in vain. Disputants probably will always have to depend on the exercise, by their arbitrator of sound judgment, an informed conscience, and that vague attribute that, for want of a better label, is called "common sense." The arbitrator, however much he seeks objective standards for decision making, seems to have no better standard than the Chancellor is said to have had in Equity: the size and configuration of his foot.[25]

The following sections review several aspects of the remedies that arbitrators have devised in the discipline and discharge area.

B. Reinstatement Orders

An order of reinstatement should be expected to be issued where a discharge is held not to be for "just cause." However, that condition has not always been the case. In *Practice and Procedure in Labor Arbitration*,[26] Owen Fairweather reports that as a matter of historical interest, courts, as late as 1936, held that reinstatement orders could not be enforced because the common law would not order the specific performance of an employment contract (i.e., force an employee to work for a particular employer, or force an employer to employ a particular employee). Professor Dallas L. Jones notes that the reinstatement element of a "just cause" concept is unique to the American system of industrial relations. In most West European countries, if a labor court finds that a discharge was not for just cause, the individual employee is entitled to damages but not to an equitable order of reinstatement. The rationale for this view is that an employer should not be required

---

[25]Seitz, *Substitution of Disciplinary Suspension for Discharge (A Proposed "Guide to the Perplexed" in Arbitration)*, 35 Arb. J. 27, 29 (1980).
[26]Fairweather, Practice and Procedure in Labor Arbitration, 2d ed., 499–500 (BNA Books, 1983).

to retain an employee whom it finds undesirable.[27] Jones notes
that American unions insisted upon an equitable remedy of
reinstatement rather than damages because of the high discharge rate in many American firms prior to the rise of mass
unionism in the 1930s. In addition, the labor movement's emphasis on job security made it impossible for organized labor
to accept a system that did not provide for reinstatement.[28]

Section 12(a)(5) of the Uniform Arbitration Act,[29] adopted
by the National Conference of the Commissioners on Uniform
State Laws, provides, in relevant part, that "the fact that the
relief was such that it could not or would not be granted by
a court of law or equity is not ground for vacating or refusing
to confirm the award." Although a court of equity will not
ordinarily order specific performance of a contract for personal
services,[30] it is clear that no rule of law limits an arbitrator
from ordering the reinstatement of an employee who has been
discharged without good cause. Accordingly, it is well established that an arbitrator may grant equitable-type relief, including reinstatement, without regard to whether a court of
equity would do so.[31]

C. Conditional Reinstatement

A review of awards and court cases indicates that an award
of reinstatement may be conditional. For example, an arbitrator may provide that an employee is to be reinstated, but
not until the occurrence of some future event (condition precedent); or, an arbitrator may order reinstatement, but if some
event or condition materializes in the future, the order of

---

[27] Jones, supra note 24 at 163.
[28] Id. at 164.
[29] See Appendix D.
[30] See 49 Am. Jr. 1st 151–161, Specific Performance §§134–137 (1943).
[31] See *Power of an Arbitrator to Award Injunction or Specific Performance*, 70
A.L.R.2d 1055 (1960). In its early decisions the NLRB did not order reinstatement
to wrongfully discharged employees who had obtained equivalent employment elsewhere. In re Rabhor Co., 1 NLRB 470, 481, 1 LRRM 31 (1936); In re Jeffery-De Witt
Insulator Co., 1 NLRB 618, 628, 1 LRRM 428 (1936). As stated by the Supreme Court
in Phelps Dodge Corp. v. NLRB, 313 U.S. 177, 8 LRRM 439 (1941), the Board apparently focused on the absence of loss of wages in determining the applicable remedy.
In that case the Court further stated: "[W]ithout such a remedy [reinstatement]
industrial peace might be endangered because workers would be resentful of their
ability to return to jobs to which they may have been attached and from which they
were wrongfully discharged." Id. at 443.

reinstatement shall no longer be binding on the employer (condition subsequent). Although there may be overlap, some common examples of both types of conditional remedies are noted below.

1. Proof of Physical or Mental Capacity

Where it is demonstrated that the basis of a discharge was due not to an intentional individual fault of the grievant but rather to a defect in mental or physical capacity to perform the job,[32] arbitrators have not hesitated to order reinstatement conditioned upon a proper showing of mental or physical fitness. Remedies in this area may range from requiring the employee to submit to a psychological or physical exam as a condition of continued employment[33] to undertaking serious

---

[32]See, e.g., Sears, *Use of Experts in Arbitration—III.: Observations on Psychiatric Testimony in Arbitration*, in Arbitration and Social Change, supra note 24, 151; Fairweather, supra note 26, at 221; Elkouri and Elkouri, How Arbitration Works, 4th ed., 722, 724 (BNA Books, 1985); Miller, *The Use of Experts in Arbitration—I.: Expert Medical Evidence: A View From the End of the Table*, in Arbitration and Social Change, supra note 24, at 135; Volz, *Health and Medical Issues in Arbitration, Employee Benefit Plans and the Doctor's Office: I.: Medical and Health Issues in Labor Arbitration*, in Truth, Lie Detectors, and Other Problems in Labor Arbitration, Proceedings of the 31st Annual Meeting, National Academy of Arbitrators, 156 (BNA Books, 1979).
 In addition to the cases discussed in this section, recent examples include: Ashland Oil Inc., 90 LA 681 (Volz, 1988) (grievant reinstatement conditioned upon active participation in aftercare program); S.E. Rykoff & Co., 90 LA 233 (Angelo, 1987) (employee dismissed after six "no shows" reinstated on "last-chance" agreement on condition that he furnish written professional certification that grievant no longer subject to emotional distress that caused attendance problems); U.C. Agricultural Prods. Co., 89 LA 432 (Anderson, 1987) (grievant who made unprovoked assault on co-worker while suffering psychotic episode reinstated provided she undergo physical and mental exam; grievant to be immediately dismissed without recourse upon any future act or threat of violence occurring in workplace within one year); Kelly-Springfield Tire Co., 88 LA 201 (Dean, 1986), (employee given two months to show earnest effort to improved productivity); Kroger Co., 88 LA 463 (Wren, 1986) (employee, discharged for one-time use of cocaine, reinstated with no back pay but full seniority on condition that he submit to maximum of six drug tests at employer's discretion during next six months, with immediate nongrievable dismissal permitted upon positive test result for any drug).
 [33]Hill and Sinicropi, supra note 12, at 165–190, discuss at length the authority of management to order an employee to undertake a mental or physical examination. With respect to conditional remedies in this area, see Benzie County Sheriff's Dep't, 81 LA 858, 861 (Keefe, 1983) (holding "Grievant's dexterity in attaining mobility is to be reevaluated upon medical certification by the attending physician. . . . Disputes over such claims are subject to the arbitrator's review and decision."); East Hartford Bd. of Educ., 81 LA 769 (Johnson, 1983) (requiring doctor's certificate); Olin Corp., 80 LA 797 (Denson, 1983) (requiring medical certification); National Steel Corp., 76 LA 103 (Roberts, 1981) (reinstatement conditioned on physical exam); Atlas Metal Parts Co., 67 LA 1230 (Kossoff, 1977) (reinstatement conditioned upon grievant making himself available for examination by physician selected by employer); Lever

long-term mental therapy. As an example, Arbitrator Aaron Wolff, in *Greenlee Brothers & Co.*,[34] found that a discharge for excessive absenteeism was improper because the employee demonstrated that his poor attendance record was due to an alcohol problem. As a remedy the arbitrator converted the discharge to a disciplinary layoff and, effective the date of the award, ordered the grievant immediately to place himself in the care of a hospital rehabilitation center and carry out whatever recommendations it should make, including submission to long-term hospital treatment and/or Alcoholics Anonymous. Arbitrator Wolff also directed the employer to reinstate the grievant unconditionally within six months provided that the rehabilitation center certified that the grievant was able to work. If the conditions were not met, the arbitrator declared that the grievant could be treated as if he had voluntarily quit. The arbitrator further provided that, if after his unconditional reinstatement the grievant "falls off the wagon," management could apply whatever disciplinary action is appropriate.

Arbitrator Harry Casselman was called upon to consider the discharge of an employee who was diagnosed as a manic-depressive with no clear prognosis. In reversing the discharge, Arbitrator Casselman stated:

> Although cause for discharge is not *always* based on fault on the employee's part, it normally requires such a finding. For example, cases of chronic illness, lack of requisite skill in job performance and the like are not normally analyzed in terms of fault; yet, in such cases inability to do the work, or continuous unreliable attendance, are regarded as disqualifying conditions over a period of time.
>
> . . . Fault has no place in this situation. Since Grievant was helpless to prevent what he did *while mentally ill* and since Management could not reasonably be expected to tolerate his conduct, it would seem more reasonable to remove him from the work place until one of two things occur.
>
> 1. He fully recovers and can establish his recovery to the reasonable satisfaction of Management's physicians, or to a board of those psychiatrists chosen jointly by a physician selected by Management and a physician designated by the Union on Grievant's behalf.

Bros., 66 LA 211 (Bernstein, 1976) (grievant directed, as express condition to receipt of sums provided for in award, to furnish company with itemized statement of outside earnings).
[34]67 LA 847 (1976).

2. He reaches retirement age.

If he reaches retirement age first, he should be retired under the pension plan then current. . . .[35]

Arbitrator Duane Traynor converted a discharge into a two-year suspension where the record indicated that the employee was schizophrenic. The arbitrator found that the discharge was inappropriate, in part, because it would result in the grievant seeking employment elsewhere and merely passing the problem on to another employer. Ordering an indefinite suspension not to exceed two years from the date of the award, the arbitrator attached the following conditions:

> 1. The Grievant places himself under the care and treatment of a qualified psychiatrist for treatment of his mental illness.
> 2. That when at any time within the two-year period the Grievant's psychiatrist declares the Grievant recovered, or that his illness is and can be controlled so that he can function in a factory environment without engaging in disruptive conduct attributed to his illness, the Union and Management are to agree on an independent psychiatrist, or in the absence thereof, a Board of three psychiatrists, consisting of one selected by the Company, one by the Union, and a third selected by the two psychiatrists selected by the parties, for the purpose of evaluating the Grievant. Such independent psychiatrist or Board's evaluation shall be determinative of the issue herein and if favorable to the Grievant's employment, he is to be reinstated without back pay but with full seniority and other contractual benefits as if he had been on a leave of absence. If unfavorable to the Grievant, the suspension to be converted into a discharge.[36]

Arbitrator Sid Braufman, in *Bucklers, Inc.*,[37] converted the discharge of an employee inflicted with AIDS to an involuntary unpaid medical leave of absence. As part of the remedy the arbitrator directed that the grievant be examined by a jointly selected physician who specialized in AIDS. The grievant would be permitted to resume active duty when the physician certified the grievant fit to perform the duties of a machine operator.

The question of an arbitrator's authority to condition an

---

[35]Consolidated Foods Corp., 58 LA 1285, 1288 (1972).
[36]Johns-Manville Penlite Corp., 67 LA 1255, 1260–1261 (1977).
[37]90 LA 937 (1987).

award on the outcome of a medical examination, ordered *sua sponte* by the arbitrator at the parties' expense after the hearing was closed, was considered by the Ninth Circuit in *Sunshine Mining Co. v. Steelworkers Local 5089*.[38] The grievant was dismissed for insubordination. Arbitrator Carlton J. Snow concluded that there was a question concerning the grievant's mental stability at the time of the incident giving rise to his discharge (in 1981 the grievant had received a head injury while working as an underground miner and at the arbitration hearing claimed that he suffered from "spells" which caused him to "feel strange"). Finding that the employee had been insubordinate, Arbitrator Snow reasoned that if the grievant were mentally ill at the time he was insubordinate, the illness (under certain circumstances) would preclude a finding of just cause for discharge. Snow declared there was insufficient evidence in the record to determine whether the grievant's mental instability was temporary or permanent:

> A critical issue in this case is the mental condition of the grievant at the time of the incident. If mentally ill at the time of the incident, the grievant's condition would constitute an extenuating circumstance that deserves consideration in determining the appropriateness of the penalty imposed by the Employer. For the grievant to be guilty of insubordination, he must have been responsible for his conduct. If he was mentally ill at the time, he could not have been in control of his own actions and, accordingly, could not be held responsible for the insubordination.
>
> . . .
> . . . There was sufficient evidence to determine whether or not mental instability experienced by the grievant would be sufficient to cause him to be unable to perform the duties of his job. If he is unable to do the work because of a mental illness, it is clear that the Employer is not obligated to retain him.

Arbitrator Snow stated that he needed more than a lay person's opinion about the grievant's mental disability. In his words, "some of the most unique awards in arbitral literature can be found in cases involving mental illness. It is the arbitrator's belief that much of their uniqueness has been caused by the desire of arbitrators to follow the dictates of the evidence while at the same time attempting to protect the in-

---

[38]823 F.2d 1289, 124 LRRM 3198 (1987).

terests of both the grievant, fellow employees, and the company itself." Arbitrator Snow ordered the parties to mutually select a psychiatrist to examine the grievant; expenses of the examination would be borne equally by the parties. If the psychiatrist concluded that the grievant suffered from no mental illness, the discharge was to be sustained. If the psychiatrist concluded that the grievant was mentally ill at the time of the incident, and his prognosis for recovery would preclude underground mining work, the discharge would similarly be sustained. However, if the psychiatrist determined that the grievant was mentally ill at the time of the incident, but had recovered sufficiently to work underground, the grievant was to be reinstated without back pay but with seniority. Arbitrator Snow retained jurisdiction for 60 days following issuance of the psychiatric report.

Arguing that the arbitrator had no authority to reopen the record for posthearing evidence, or to require the employer to pay part of the costs of the examination, management moved to vacate the award in district court. The district court, concluding that the arbitrator's conditional award was not final and binding as required by the agreement, ruled in favor of management. The court also ruled that the parties had been denied due process by the arbitrator's conditioning his award, after closing the record, on a conclusion to be reached by a psychiatrist. It further held that the arbitrator acted beyond his authority in ordering a psychiatric examination, which it deemed to be an improper delegation of the arbitrator's fact-finding function.

The Ninth Circuit reversed. The appellate court held that consideration of the grievant's mental condition was well within the arbitrator's authority. The issue, said the court, was whether the grievant was dismissed for just cause, and it was permissible for the arbitrator to interpret "cause" to encompass a mental fault element. The appellate court further ruled that structuring the award to make it conditional on the results of a future psychiatric examination rendered it a partial or interim award, even though it was not so designated. Consistent with the Supreme Court's declarations in *Enterprise Wheel* regarding the function of the courts when reviewing awards, the Ninth Circuit upheld the arbitrator's authority to issue a preliminary award.

With respect to the arbitrator's order that the grievant

submit to a psychiatric examination to be paid for by the parties, the court reasoned that the order "cannot be said to render the arbitration fundamentally unfair." Further, there was no improper delegation of decision-making authority to the psychiatrist. In the words of the appellate court, "[s]imply requesting production of evidence that the arbitrator believes germane or necessary to resolution of the issue submitted is not an improper delegation, as long as the arbitrator carefully evaluates and weighs that evidence himself." The Ninth Circuit found no infirmity in ordering the examination paid for by the parties because the record was already closed. "It is common practice in arbitration proceedings for arbitrators to request the production of evidence if there is a reasonable basis to believe that it is germane to the case."[39]

Sunshine Mining clearly affirms the arbitrator's power to (1) direct that the record be reopened for both the creation and production of further posthearing evidence, and (2) require a party to pay part of the cost of creating and producing such evidence in aid of the adverse party's case. The Ninth Circuit also reaffirmed that the concept of just cause is not limited to a determination of the information management had available to it at the time it made the decision to terminate the employment of the grievant. Rather, it is permissible for the arbitrator to take an objective view of just cause.[40]

In an example of a remedy conditioned upon an event subsequent to reinstatement, Arbitrator Wilbur Bothwell considered the discharge of an employee who allegedly concealed on his employment application his problem with hand eczema. Finding that the condition was not work related, the arbitrator reinstated the grievant but placed him on probation for five years, with the provision that if at any time during that period the grievant was unable to perform a full schedule, including overtime, he should immediately be terminated.[41]

Where it was shown that an employee's weight problem placed undue restrictions on his capacity to perform assigned

---

[39]Id. at 1295, 124 LRRM at 3202.
[40]Accord Mobil Oil Corp. v. Oil Workers Local 8-831, 679 F.2d 299, 110 LRRM 2620 (3d Cir. 1982) (permissible for arbitrator to interpret "cause" to mean "objective" cause, rather than only those factors known to employer at time of discharge).
[41]64 LA 1129, 1132 (1975).

work, Arbitrator Bothwell in *Reynolds Metals Co.*,[42] sustained a discharge, with the following conditions:

> If the grievant undertakes a program to reduce his weight under the care of his physician, and is successful within a period of one year in reducing his weight within the normal and optimum limits for an adult male of his age and height, as determined by the Company Medical Director, and can produce a medical certificate that he can work without restrictions, he shall be reinstated to the laborer classification with his seniority as of the date of his termination. If he is so reinstated he will be on probation for attendance for one year. If his absences exceed the average for all employees at the plant he may be terminated. . . . The arbitrator retains jurisdiction to decide any questions as to this award.[43]

In *Newkirk Sales Co.*,[44] Arbitrator Kent Hutcheson found that an employer did not have just cause to discharge an employee who had a proven disability. Although the employee had been restricted by his doctor from lifting in excess of 200 pounds—after the employer's workers' compensation insurance carrier had determined that he had suffered a permanent partial disability of 16 percent—Arbitrator Hutcheson nevertheless held that the standard of "just and sufficient cause" presupposes some wrongful act on the part of the grievant. The arbitrator refused to reinstate the grievant to his old position even though the employee had performed his old duties for eight weeks after his return to work. The arbitrator reasoned that there was no evidence that his reinstatement would not create a risk to himself, to his fellow workers, and to customers. Absent evidence that the grievant would not recover sufficiently to perform the required tasks, the arbitrator ordered the employer to carry the grievant on a "suspended" status for a period of three years, or until such time as medical proof was established that he could perform all the requirements of his job.

Arbitrator Timothy Heinsz, in *Mead Corp.*,[45] found that an employee, suffering from diabetes, was improperly dismissed for being a safety risk. Reasoning that the grievant

---

[42]71 LA 1099 (1978).
[43]Id. at 1102.
[44]61 LA 1144 (1973).
[45]81 LA 1000 (1983).

took positive steps to resolve his domestic situation and that his medical condition had stabilized, Arbitrator Heinsz formulated both a condition precedent and condition subsequent. As part of the remedy, the Grievant, was to obtain a medical release from his physician and, if the company desired, a release from a physician of its choosing. After his reinstatement, the Grievant was ordered to submit medical verification on a quarterly basis for a period of one year past the date of reinstatement. The arbitrator retained jurisdiction for the one-year period to resolve any disputes between the parties concerning the award.

2. Occurrence of Similar Acts or Conduct

Arbitrators have frequently ordered reinstatement conditioned upon the nonrecurrence of the conduct giving rise to the initial disciplinary penalty. Often referred to as "last chance" remedies, they are applied in a variety of situations. For example, in cases where an employee is discharged for excessive absenteeism, an arbitrator may find mitigating circumstances and order reinstatement, but condition it upon some satisfactory level of attendance in the future. Thus, Arbitrator Stanley Michelstetter, in *East Ohio Gas Co.*,[46] found that an employee was improperly dismissed for excessive absenteeism primarily caused by depression that had been caused by a serious illness and a gang rape, but conditioned her return on the following:

> 1. Grievant shall promptly execute a written statement expressly accepting the terms of this award, including all of the conditions subsequent, which statement shall be executed before the Employer shall reinstate the Grievant.
> 2. For the first three months of her re-employment, Grievant shall not exceed two occasions totalling one-day absence per month for sickness and for personal reasons combined.
> 3. For the next two years thereafter, Grievant shall maintain on a quarterly basis an attendance record (number of days and number of occurrences for both sickness and personal time) which does not exceed one-quarter of her department's average of 1981 (excluding her attendance record's effect) for the comparable figure (full days, partial days, number of occurrences, all for sick or personal time).
> 4. If Grievant fails to meet conditions 1, 2, or 3, then this

---

[46]78 LA 71 (1982).

remedy shall be rescinded, the instant grievance dismissed, and the Grievant's right to employment ended.[47]

In this same regard, Arbitrator William Belshaw, in *Barnes Drill Co.*,[48] ordered reinstatement of an employee upon condition that he be placed on probation for one year and maintain an absenteeism rate of two percent or less, determined at three-month intervals. In the event that the absentee rate did not exceed the indicated percentage for the probationary period, the arbitrator provided that the grievant should unqualifiedly be reinstated and the employer should then make full restitution to the grievant for all lost earnings between the initial date of discharge and the date of reinstatement.[49]

Similarly, Arbitrator George Roumell, Jr., in *Menasha Corp.*,[50] conditioned a reinstatement order on the fact that if within the 12-month period from the date of reinstatement the grievant was again charged with habitual absenteeism, it would be considered a third offense and he would be subject to the usual contractual provisions. The arbitrator considered the initial discharge for absenteeism as a suspension and accordingly designated it as equivalent to a second offense under the agreement.

In yet another absenteeism case, Arbitrator Malcolm Hall stated that a common remedy where discipline is upheld, but discharge is found to be too severe, is to reduce the penalty to a suspension, and to place the grievant on permanent probation in case of future offenses, thus placing the burden and responsibility on the employee if he or she wants to retain employment.[51]

Arbitrator Charles LaCugna, in *Intalco Aluminum Corp.*,[52] ordered conditional reinstatement of an employee who was discharged after pleading guilty, in a criminal proceeding, to unlawful delivery of marijuana. Finding no evidence that the employee's conduct had adversely affected the employer, the arbitrator nevertheless stated that he would fashion a remedy

---

[47]Id. at 74.
[48]62 LA 875 (1974).
[49]Id. at 878.
[50]71 LA 653 (1978).
[51]Stevens Shipping & Terminal Co., 70 LA 1066, 1072 (1978). See also Microdot, Inc., 66 LA 177 (Kelliher, 1976).
[52]68 LA 66 (1977).

to ensure the legal rights of the grievant and to protect the employer's right to pursue its objectives with minimal interruption and disturbance. The grievant was ordered to be reinstated without back pay and with loss of seniority from his discharge to the date of reinstatement. In addition, the reinstatement was conditioned upon the following:

> (a) [I]f the Grievant is found to possess marijuana on Company property, the Company is free to discharge him at will.
> (b) [I]f the Grievant is again found guilty of selling or buying marijuana outside the Company premises by a court, the Company is free to discharge at will.[53]

The arbitrator further provided that the grievant would lose all further protection under the just cause provision of the contract in criminal matters, absenteeism, and tardiness.[54]

Another arbitrator actually "stayed" for one year an employee's discharge for missing more than 50 percent of work days during an eight-month period for a documented medical problem on condition that she not exceed annual paid sick leave. Absenteeism in excess of this amount would result in her termination. After the one-year stay, the grievant's initial termination would be considered a final warning that future absenteeism could result in her termination.[55]

3. Special Act or Promise by Grievant

Numerous arbitrators have reinstated employees on condition of a special act or promise by the Grievant. Possibilities in this area are limited only by the imagination of the parties and/or the arbitrator. Arbitrator Peter Kelliher, for example, in *Microdot, Inc.*,[56] declaring authority for arbitrators to condition remedies upon acts or promises of grievants, ordered the reinstatement of an employee who was discharged for calling in sick during a period when he was attending to his private garage business. In reinstating the grievant, the ar-

---

[53]Id. at 67.
[54]Id. See also Barry-Wehmiller Co., 78 LA 1055 (O'Reilly, 1982) (ordering that grievant acknowledge full and final settlement of all grievances and complaints arising from discharge); Inmont Corp., 58 LA 15 (Sembower, 1972) (any recurrence of disruptive activity); United Tel. Co., 58 LA 1256 (Seinsheimer, 1972) (company rules).
[55]Board of Supervisors, 90 LA 469, 471 (Riker, 1988).
[56]66 LA 177 (1976).

bitrator nevertheless designated that the following conditions had to be maintained for a period of one year after reinstatement:

> The Grievant shall waive in writing any sick and accident benefits during the period prior to his reinstatement.
> The Grievant prior to reinstatement is to cease and desist from any outside business or employment and continue to do so during said one (1) year period. The Grievant shall furnish the Company with an affidavit that he has discontinued his business.[57]

Similarly, Arbitrator Milton Friedman in a case involving a conflict of interest of a sports reporter, reinstated an employee provided he disposed of all interest in a co-owned racehorse.[58]

Where an employee who worked in mining operations was discharged for refusing to submit to a "pat-down" search for smoking materials, Arbitrator Marlin Volz, in *Wisconsin Steel Coal Mines*,[59] ordered the employee to be reinstated provided that he agree to the "pat-down" method of search before entering the mines. The arbitrator found no infirmity in conditioning reinstatement upon such consent where it was established that employers could make reasonable searches of employees and discharge had been upheld by arbitrators for refusing to submit to such a search.[60]

Arbitrator Ferrin Mathews reports a case where he ordered a grievant to execute a document reflecting that he was being reinstated on the promise that he would not violate the company's rules and, upon management's determination that a rule violation occurred, he would not contest such determination and the subsequent discharge.[61] Another arbitrator, after finding that a chemical dependency counselor was properly dismissed for having sexual relations with a residential client, nevertheless ordered reinstatement provided she executed a sworn affidavit that she had ended the relationship and that the client no longer lived with her.[62]

---

[57]Id. at 180.
[58]New York Post Corp., 62 LA 225 (1973).
[59]67 LA 84 (1976).
[60]Id. at 87.
[61]United States Plywood Corp., 88 LA 275 (1986).
[62]Minnesota Dep't of Human Servs., 90 LA 320, 324 (Gallagher, 1987).

4. Conditional Remedies, Just Cause, and the "Troubled" Employee[63]

Thomas Miller and Susan Oliver, in a paper entitled *Just Cause and the Troubled Employee*,[64] query whether arbitrators apply traditional concepts of just cause to troubled employees who engage in misconduct or unsatisfactory job performance. They point out that troubled employees traditionally argue that they would not have engaged in the misconduct warranting discipline, but for their alcohol- or chemical-dependency problem. Also, troubled employees maintain that their successful treatment following termination should justify mitigation of the discharge penalty. The authors note that a review of airline arbitration decisions indicates that there is a divergence of opinion among arbitrators as to whether the alcohol- or chemical-dependent employee who has engaged in misconduct should be subject to the traditional just-cause standard. Miller and Oliver, citing Denenberg and Denenberg,[65] submit that many arbitrators have adopted three approaches in deciding discharge cases where alcohol or chemical dependency is asserted as a defense:

1. *Traditional Corrective Discipline Model*. Arbitrators using this approach uphold discipline or discharge without regard to an employee's claimed alcoholism or chemical dependency as long as the employer has properly adhered to all pertinent disciplinary requirements.

2. *Therapeutic Model*. Under this model alcoholism or chemical dependency is viewed as an illness warranting opportunities to recover, including leaves of absence and rehabilitation. An employee's subsequent failure to refrain from misconduct or to correct performance deficiencies is not viewed as cause for discipline, but as a need for additional treatment.

3. *A Modified Corrective Discipline Model*. This approach takes a middle ground between the traditional corrective discipline and the therapeutic model. These arbitrators view al-

---

[63]This section is an expanded discussion of a presentation by the authors at the 1988 Continuing Educational Conference, National Academy of Arbitrators, Milwaukee, Wis., October 28–30, 1988.

[64]Miller and Oliver, *Just Cause and the Troubled Employee: II. A Management Viewpoint* in Arbitration 1988: Emerging Issues for the 1990s, Proceedings of the 41st Annual Meeting, National Academy of Arbitrators, 34 (BNA Books, 1989). See also Collins, *Just Cause and the Troubled Employee*, in Arbitration 1988, id. at 21.

[65]Denenberg and Denenberg, Alcohol and Drugs: Issues in the Workplace, 3 (BNA Books, 1983).

coholism or chemical dependency as an illness, and routinely allow one "second chance" after there has been some opportunity for rehabilitation. However, should there be a subsequent failure to correct the behavior, the employee will be held fully accountable.[66]

Miller and Oliver assert that arbitrators adjudicating airline cases appear to limit their approach to either the traditional corrective discipline or the modified corrective discipline models. Our research suggests that arbitrators reach the same result in nonairline cases.

Under what circumstances will arbitrators grant a second- or third-chance remedy to a "troubled" or "distracted" employee? When will an arbitrator accept an employee's argument that rehabilitation is an appropriate remedy? If an employee claims successful rehabilitation subsequent to dismissal, will an arbitrator credit this postdisciplinary evidence and order reinstatement? Suppose rehabilitation is under way but not yet completed at the time of the hearing? Does management have a continuing obligation to rehabilitate an employee incapacitated by an "illness"?

In *Crewe v. Office of Personnel Management*,[67] the court of appeals considered a claim under the Rehabilitation Act of 1973,[68] and concluded that there can be little doubt that alcoholism is a handicap for the purposes of the Act. In the same opinion the court pointed out that, in determining whether to hire persons with a prior history of alcohol abuse, the federal government has adopted the following policy:

> "In considering applicants for federal employment who have a history of alcoholism . . . the Office of Personnel Management will make its determination on the basis of whether or not the applicant is a good employment risk. In such cases, the length of time since the last abuse of alcohol . . . is less important than the steps taken by the applicant to obtain treatment of his or her illness through medical care, rehabilitation, and similar actions."[69]

Arbitrators have likewise recognized the potential for successfully overcoming the debilitating effects of alcoholism or

---

[66]Miller and Oliver, supra note 64, at 41.
[67]834 F.2d 140, 45 FEP Cases 555 (8th Cir. 1987).
[68]29 U.S.C. §§701–794.
[69]45 FEP Cases at 557.

other chemical dependencies, even after repeated relapses by the employees. For example, in *Thrifty Drug Stores Co.,*[70] a 23-year employee had a 14-year history of disciplinary problems relating to alcohol abuse. There was even an incident when a fellow-employee was killed in a car accident possibly because of the grievant's alcohol problem. On returning to work after a two-day unexcused absence, the company gave the grievant a three-day suspension and granted him a leave of absence to enroll in a rehabilitation program. Two months later the employee returned to work while continuing with outpatient treatment. However, a few weeks later he returned to drinking and after a four-day absence was terminated. The employee's doctors told the Company that there was progress in his case and asked that the employee be given a six-month leave of absence and be returned to work on probation. The company offered a "last leave of absence" without a "second chance." The Union refused the company's proposal, but the employee agreed to the "no second chance" conditions and returned to work after six months. After two months on the job, the employee was found drinking and was subsequently fired. At the arbitration hearing where the union requested that the employee be returned to work, the arbitrator agreed that relapses in the treatment of chronic alcoholism were a common occurrence and that the main problem in alcohol treatment was getting the patient to accept that he or she had a problem. Arbitrator Edward Peters ruled that "the grievant should be given yet another opportunity to demonstrate that he has managed to acquire an acceptable control over his problem." What is particularly interesting is that the arbitrator did not formulate a conditional remedy of any kind, but simply reinstated the grievant with all contractual benefits, but without back pay. He noted, however, that if the employee still retained the illusion that he could handle one or two drinks, "then the outcome of this arbitration will accomplish no more than to defer for a few weeks or months his inevitable termination."[71]

In *City of Buffalo,*[72] the grievant, an account clerk ste-

---

[70]56 LA 789 (Peters, 1971).
[71]Id. at 794.
[72]59 LA 334 (Rinaldo, 1972).

nographer and a 15-year employee, was found intoxicated at work and given a leave of absence to be hospitalized, after which she enrolled in Alcoholics Anonymous (AA). She was then discovered drunk at work again and discharged. In reducing the penalty to a two-month suspension, the arbitrator wrote:

> A person undergoing a program consisting of regular attendance could successfully rehabilitate themselves after a period of years. It is not uncommon for an alcoholic to have periods of remission, a falling off the wagon, as it is referred to, before eventual rehabilitation.
>
> B— admits that she is an alcoholic and indicates a desire to rehabilitate herself. Since attending the hospital in Rochester, she has attended Alcoholics Anonymous at least three times a week.
>
> . . .
>
> Her request [to continue employment] should not be refused in light of her 15 years employment record with the City. To deny B— this opportunity, would be unwarranted considering that since returning to work [after the first hospitalization], only two incidents have been established which it was proven interfered with B—'s ability to properly perform. This is not sufficient cause to warrant discharge of an employee faced with a serious drinking problem where there is a willingness and indication for rehabilitation.[73]

The arbitrator concluded:

> Taking into consideration B—'s employment and her willingness to faithfully attend Alcoholics Anonymous and group therapy with the Alcoholism Clinic, the penalty of discharge is too severe.[74]

In *Chrysler Corp.*,[75] an employee was dismissed for reporting to work under the influence. The record indicated that the grievant had been repeatedly admonished and penalized for alcohol abuse at work. Arbitrator Gabriel N. Alexander, in overturning the dismissal, credited the grievant's postdischarge rehabilitation and reasoned:

> [The] evidence shows clearly that *since* he was discharged, Grievant has done the sort of things that an alcoholic should do. He placed himself under the care of his physician. He joined

---

[73]Id. at 336, 337.
[74]Id. at 337.
[75]40 LA 935 (Alexander, 1963).

Alcoholics Anonymous, and has regularly attended its sessions. He has taken help from a church, and from an alcoholic treatment center maintained by the City of Detroit. Representatives of those agencies and his doctor have issued written statements to the effect that he is doing well. No contradictory evidence was submitted on that point. Accordingly, the Chairman concludes that Grievant has been making progress on the road towards control of his addiction.[76]

The arbitrator rejected the employer's plea that the employee had ample opportunity to reform his conduct before he was dismissed and that, therefore, no mitigating significance should be accorded his subsequent efforts:

> The remaining question, then, is to what extent if at all such [postdischarge] events justify modification of Grievant's discharge. The Corporation argues with reason that he had ample opportunity to attempt to rehabilitate himself *before* he was discharged, and that therefore no mitigating significance should be accorded his subsequent efforts in that direction. On the other hand the Union emphasized, also with reason that one of the characteristic features of alcoholism is a psychological *inability* on the part of the person afflicted to face up to the rigors of rehabilitation until some drastic consequence such as discharge befalls him. Consideration of that fact, the Union reasons, justifies a conclusion that Grievant be reinstated and reimbursed for some portion of his lost time.
>   The close balance between these conflicting considerations is tilted slightly in Grievant's favor, the Chairman believes, by (a) his long seniority, (b) his reputation as a good worker, and (c) the fact that his prior conduct record is clear except for the mentioned instances of discipline for intoxication. The Chairman's conclusion, limited of course to the particular facts of the case, is the Grievant should be reinstated, but without back pay.[77]

No conditional remedy was ordered by Arbitrator Alexander although the facts arguably called for one.

In all these cases reinstatement was ordered after the employee suffered a relapse.

In *Armstrong Cork Co.*[78] an employee's demonstration of a strong desire to rehabilitate was shown to affect the arbitrator's award. The employee was discharged after his third

---

[76]Id. at 936.
[77]Id.
[78]56 LA 527 (Wolf, 1971).

absence from work because of a drinking problem. The arbitrator ruled that:

> The violation occurred not because of an indifference toward the Company rules but because [the Grievant] was emotionally and physically sick. He testified that he was an alcoholic and this fact must be taken into account in assessing the punishment. . . .
>
> Alcoholism is, of course, not a virtue but neither is it a wholly voluntarily condition subject to the will-power of the victim. It is now fairly well recognized as an illness which affects certain people who start drinking as a social matter and find themselves gripped in its clutches. Of course, an employer is not required to put up with an alcoholic indefinitely but this does not mean that an alcoholic is to be treated as a pariah and shunned without further responsibility. The Employer owes an employee, especially an honorable and long-standing employee, the obligation of making at least one attempt to get him to rehabilitate himself.
>
> The purpose of a disciplinary penalty is, first and foremost, the rehabilitation of an employee. It is only when there is enough evidence to believe that rehabilitation is no longer a reasonable prospect that discharge should be invoked. Absent in this case is any attempt on the part of the Employer to give the employee an opportunity to rehabilitate himself. . . .
>   . . .
> Since the discharge, the uncontradicted evidence is that B— not only has joined Alcoholics Anonymous but has regularly attended its meetings and has not had a drop to drink. In view of the fact that it is now more than eight months since his discharge this is impressive evidence of a serious effort at self-rehabilitation.[79]

In ordering reinstatement, the arbitrator imposed the following conditional remedy:

> B— is directed to supply the Company Personnel Manager with written verification from his Alcoholics Anonymous group chairman of his attendance at Alcoholics Anonymous meetings. This will be done on a monthly basis for six months.
>
> If B— is AWOL during said six months period, the full history upon which the Company relied in this case shall be considered in imposing punishment notwithstanding any Company policy to remit penalties occurring beyond the allowed time limits.
>
> At the end of six months without being on AWOL, B— is

---

[79]Id. at 529–530.

to be treated in the normal way under the contract and Company rules.[80]

In *Texaco, Inc.*,[81] a 20-year employee with two prior alcohol-related suspensions was discharged for showing for work under the influence. Following the discharge he met with a physician, attended AA, and was given medication. He had eight months of sobriety before the arbitration hearing. In ordering reinstatement, Arbitrator Paul Prasow stated that there was no quick cure for alcoholism and that the alcoholic needed support. Though there was a risk, the possibility of recovery could provide great benefits to the alcoholic, his family, the company, and society. The arbitrator had this to say about postdischarge attempts at rehabilitation:

> It is true that in most grievance arbitrations, the basic issue to be determined is whether management's action was proper based upon the facts known at the time the action was taken. Normally the clock stops at that moment, and anything that occurs subsequently is irrelevant. However, there are occasions, especially in discharge cases, where events occurring after the incident giving rise to the grievance are given some weight by arbitrators. For example, the conduct of an employee after he has been discharged may be considered significant either for its mitigating or aggravating influence in determining whether the penalty should be modified.
>
> It is a well accepted principle in arbitration and industrial relations that the primary purpose of industrial discipline is not to inflict punishment for wrongdoing, but to correct individual faults and behavior and to prevent further infractions. Both the Company and the employee lose when the employee is terminated. It is for this reason that discharge is normally invoked only as a last resort, after it has become abundantly clear that corrective measures will not succeed.
>
> X— has a social-problem disease called alcoholism, for which there are no dramatic and quick cures. Current therapy focuses on attempts to arrest the disease and restore the person to a useful and respected role in society. This is no easy task, and most of the effort must come from the affected person himself. He must become aware of the problems that induced the disease; he must believe strongly that he has the ability to remain sober; and he must practice rigorous self-discipline in his personal habits and his relations with others. The chances of successful rehabilitation are increased if the person has the understanding

---

[80]Id. at 530–531.
[81]42 LA 408 (Prasow, Chair., 1963).

and cooperation of family, friends, and society itself. Some risks are certainly involved, but the gains from success are of such inestimable value to the person, his family, to the Company, and to society as a whole that they seem worth the effort. It is for this reason that the Review Board, or a majority thereof, believes that a modification of the discharge penalty is warranted.[82]

While not forming a conditional remedy (the arbitrator simply ordered reinstatement without back pay), Chairman Prasow nevertheless noted in his opinion that he hoped the grievant would continue his rehabilitation, and "that any future deviation from the strict sobriety on the job will warrant immediate termination."[83]

Similarly, in *Pacific Northwest Bell Telephone*,[84] the arbitrator noted that postdischarge efforts at rehabilitation are relevant in evaluating whether just cause for discharge exists and the severity of the penalty. In the arbitrator's words:

> [I]f the discharged employee proves after this discharge that he has a significant chance for recovery, the officials must have misjudged him and have given him too severe a penalty. The arbitrator even if he upholds the officials' charge, may reduce the penalty to give the offender another chance.[85]

Arbitrator Lafayette Harter went on to cite with approval a decision by Arbitrator Louis Kesselman as follows:

> Arbitrator Louis Kesselman, in American Synthetic Rubber Corporation, 73-1 ARB 8070 (1973) states that "The alcoholic person has come to be regarded by medical experts as suffering from a disease which causes him to become a compulsive drinker . . ." Yet he also states:

>> [I]t is also generally recognized that there are limits to what a company can and should do to help an alcoholic employee overcome his problem. It is unreasonable to expect any company to carry indefinitely an employee whose chronic overindulgence presents a potential danger to himself, fellow employees or plant equipment or who, because of his drinking problem, cannot perform his work duties in a responsible manner.

> Before an alcoholic is disciplined or discharged Kesselman would require:

---

[82]Id. at 411.
[83]Id. at 412.
[84]66 LA 965 (Harter, Chair., 1976).
[85]Id. at 973.

1) that the employee be informed as to the nature of his illness.
(2) he must be directed or encouraged to seek treatment.
(3) he must refuse treatment or
(4) he must fail to make substantial progress over a considerable period of time.[86]

The remedy was drafted as follows:

. . . [T]he Employer may have the option to retire the Grievant on a service pension.
. . . [T]he Employer may restore the Grievant to duty subject to involuntary retirement if he should miss work because of drinking, if he should drink on the job, or if he should be arrested for driving under the influence of alcohol.[87]

A case of special note is *Northwest Airlines v. Air Line Pilots Association*,[88] where a 16-year pilot was discharged for violating company alcohol regulations within 24 hours of flight duty. The employer's investigation indicated that the grievant actually piloted a flight with a blood-alcohol level at .13 percent (FAA regulations prohibit any person from serving as a crew member with a blood-alcohol level of .04 percent or more), although (to the grievant's credit) he had asked to be replaced on his scheduled flight. Admitting that he had a 10-year history of alcoholism, but had not sought treatment, the grievant, after being discharged, successfully completed a comprehensive alcohol treatment program.

A system board of adjustment held that the discharge was without just cause and that the grievant, who was found by the board to suffer the illness of alcoholism, should be offered reinstatement, without back pay or benefits, including sick pay and medical benefits, at such time as the Federal Air Surgeon certified that he met the standards of 14 C.F.R. §67.13(d)(1)(i)(c) (1986). That section provides that a pilot may not have an established medical history or clinical diagnosis of "alcoholism, unless there is established clinical evidence, satisfactory to [the] Federal Air Surgeon, of recovery, including sustained total abstinence from alcohol for not less than the preceding two years." The circuit court noted that the "Board took pains to point out that its decision 'should not

---

[86]Id.
[87]Id. at 975.
[88]808 F.2d 76, 124 LRRM 2300, 2303 (D.C. Cir. 1986).

be construed to mean that the Company cannot, under its present policy, terminate rule violators who are found to be alcoholics.' " Northwest had filed a complaint in district court seeking to set aside the award. Reasoning that the board's remedy impermissibly impinged on the employer's duty to ensure airline safety, the district court had granted the employer's motion for summary judgment.[89]

Reversing the district court, the court of appeals held that the arbitration board had authority to review the pilot's discharge for violating the 24-hour alcohol rule, and that the decision requiring the airline to reinstate the pilot if and when recertified by the FAA as fully fit was was not unlawful.

What is important in *Northwest* is that the appellate court found no infirmity in the board's conditional reinstatement remedy based, in part, on the grievant's successful postdischarge completion of an alcohol treatment program.

There is no question that postdischarge rehabilitation is a determinative factor in reinstating a discharged alcoholic or drug abuser. In short, and as illustrated by the *Northwest* case, even if the grievant took no rehabilitative efforts before his termination, where the misconduct at issue occurs because of a condition subject to "cure" rather than from willful misconduct, arbitrators will generally consider whether the grievant has taken the necessary steps to be "cured" and use this as a mitigating factor in determining whether discharge is appropriate.[90]

Of what effect is an offer of an Employee Assistance Program? A difficult case is where the troubled grievant is offered an Employee Assistance Program (EAP) before his conduct

---

[89]Northwest Airlines v. Air Line Pilots, 633 F. Supp. 779, 122 LRRM 2311 (D.D.C. 1985).

[90]Koven and Smith, Just Cause: The Seven Tests, 216–217 (Kendall-Hunt, 1985). See also Bacharach Instrument Co., 85-2 Arb ¶9558 (Hewitt, 1985) (reinstating 13-year employee, reasoning that grievant recognized problem by postdischarge enrollment in AA); Veterans Admin. Medical Center, 83 LA 51 (Denson, 1984) (under Alcohol Abuse Act employer required to provide opportunity for alcoholic employees to obtain treatment of their drinking problems before disciplinary action); Greenlee Bros., 67 LA 847 (Wolff, 1976) (ordering conditional remedy of reinstatement and six-month leave of absence so employee can place himself in rehabilitation center); Land O'Lakes, 65 LA 803 (Smythe, 1975) (grievant reinstated provided he undertake treatment to cure drinking problem; failure to resolve drinking problem negates reinstatement); Monte Mart-Grand Auto Concession, 56 LA 738 (Jacobs, 1971) (holding discharge for just cause, but according grievant medical leave for alcohol treatment).

resulted in termination but refuses management's help. Generally, an employee has less of a chance of getting a sympathetic ear from an arbitrator if he was offered help by management but rejected it.[91] Some arbitrators hold that the employee must be reinstated, with the condition that the employee participate in an EAP. Other arbitrators rule that, once an employee has been terminated, he or she may not use the employer's rehabilitation program as a crutch to regain employment. The best case for a troubled employee can be made when his conduct should have generated some inquiry by management as to its cause.[92]

To what extent must an employee cooperate with management in admitting that he or she has an alcohol or drug problem? In *General Telephone Co. of Illinois*,[93] Arbitrator John Sembower held that a telephone serviceman who would not admit that he was an alcoholic was not refusing to cooperate with the alcohol rehabilitation program he had agreed to attend as a condition of an earlier reinstatement. Interesting is the question posed by Arbitrator Sembower and the implications for an arbitrator who, as a condition to reinstatement, orders the grievant to attend Alcoholics Anonymous:

> [T]he theorem of those who work with alcoholics rehabilitation, particularly Alcoholics Anonymous, that it is an essential prerequisite to any effective treatment that a patient acknowledge that he is an alcoholic is put to the acid test. It is all very well with those individuals who voluntarily subscribe to a program such as Alcoholics Anonymous be required to acknowledge at the onset that they are alcoholics, but what of the person who, like this Grievant, is precipitated into such a program somewhat or wholly against his will. Must he also be required to admit that he is an alcoholic as an indicia of his "cooperation" with such rehabilitative efforts?[94]

If an arbitrator is convinced that the grievant has a reasonable chance of success of becoming a useful employee (the term often used is "salvageable"), a conditional remedy may

---

[91]See Koven and Smith, Alcohol-Related Misconduct, 144-152 (Kendall-Hunt, 1984); Loomis, *Employee Assistance Programs: Their Impact on Arbitration and Litigation of Termination Cases*, Employee Rel. L.J., Vol. 12, No. 2, at 275–288, 277 (1987).

[92]See, e.g., Midwest Grain Prods., 87-1 ARB ¶8052 (Yarowsky, 1986) (noting grievant's "obvious march to discharge").

[93]77-2 ARB ¶8481 (1977).

[94]Id. at 5088.

be issued. Similar to cases involving employees who are not "troubled," reinstatement may be conditioned upon the occurrence of a future event (condition precedent). Thus, an employee may be reinstated after successfully completing an alcohol abuse or EAP program. Alternatively, an arbitrator may provide for reinstatement, but if some event or condition materializes in the future (e.g., the grievant fails to continue professional counseling), the remedy is no longer binding on management (condition subsequent). Arbitrators who issue conditional remedies (and practitioners who ask for them) must make clear the exact nature of the condition—whether a condition precedent or subsequent is being imposed. Sometimes, an arbitrator will form a remedy with both conditions. Thus, Arbitrator Jeffrey Winton, in *General Telephone Co. of Indiana*,[95] issued the following remedy for an employee who had been accused of reporting under the influence:

> The grievant will be reinstated to his job on the day he meets the following conditions and his continued employment will be dependent on continuing them:
> 1. Proof of enrollment in a hospital administered alcoholism program.
>   A. It will be either an inpatient or outpatient program as the hospital recommends and he will continue with the program until release by the hospital.
> 2. Weekly attendance at Alcoholics Anonymous (AA) meetings for one year.
> 3. Reporting to work under the influence of alcohol even if it causes very limited physical or mental impairment, shall be cause for immediate discharge.[96]

5. Conditional Reinstatement—Policy Considerations

Although conditional reinstatement is commonly used in arbitration, a neutral ought to proceed with caution before formulating such a remedy. A conditional reinstatement may, in the abstract, be a suitable way of dealing with an industrial problem but when applied to a particular fact pattern create operational problems for the parties. The parties must implement the award and, in the process, it is not uncommon that the conditions imposed by the arbitrator will cause another

---

[95]86-1 ARB ¶8103 (1985).
[96]Id. at 3057.

round of litigation in the arbitral forum,[97] which, in turn, may create continued antagonism between the parties. The arbitrator, rather than acting as the parties' "contract reader," instead becomes a "legislator" and an important and sometimes unwanted fixture in the grievance process.

Another problem involves the terms of the conditions themselves. If the conditions are deemed to be repugnant to a statute or some public policy, the award is subject to reversal if appealed. To illustrate, in *Douglas Aircraft Co. v. NLRB*,[98] the Ninth Circuit considered an award where back pay was denied for two reasons: (1) a pattern of abusive and uncivil conduct by the grievant and (2) the grievant's refusal to agree to a settlement worked out by the union and the employer, which called for reinstatement, arbitration of the back-pay issue, and withdrawal of an unfair labor practice charge. The general counsel of the NLRB issued a complaint alleging that the discharge was an unfair labor practice and that the arbitrator's award was repugnant to the National Labor Relations Act. The company and the union then requested the arbitrator to clarify his decision. The arbitrator responded that there was no evidence that the grievant's union activities were a reason for his firing, and that the two reasons for denying back pay were each independent and sufficient. Although an administrative law judge recommended deference to these arbitral findings and dismissal of the unfair labor practice charge, the NLRB found that the arbitrator's award was clearly repugnant to the purposes and policies of the statute and refused to defer to it. The Ninth Circuit, while agreeing with the Board that the conditioning of an award of back pay on surrender of an unfair labor practice charge is repugnant to the Act, nevertheless held that the NLRB abused its discretion in not deferring since the two reasons given for denying back pay were independent and not cumulative.

Finally, arbitration-reporting services publish numerous awards where reinstatement is conditioned upon a designated period of "probation" or "good behavior." Such conditions are ambiguous and potentially troublesome. For example, if an

---

[97]See, e.g., Kunz Kashch, Inc., 68 LA 677 (Imundo, 1977); Story Chem Corp., 65 LA 1257 (Daniel, 1976); Bethlehem Steel Corp., 54 LA 1090 (Porter, 1970); Taystee Bread Co., 52 LA 677 (Purdom, 1969).
[98]609 F.2d 352, 102 LRRM 2811 (9th Cir. 1979).

employee is reinstated and placed on probation, does this indicate that the employee is to be treated as a "probationary
employee" (however those employees are treated under the
parties' agreement),[99] or does it mean that if the reinstated
employee is found to have engaged in any violation of the
agreement (as opposed to similar disciplinary offenses), he is
subject to discharge with full access to the grievance/arbitra-
tion procedure? Not only are the parties faced with administering their negotiated agreement but also with the possibility
that the conditions imposed by the arbitrator may themselves
be subject to interpretation.

D. Limiting the Effect of a Reinstatement Remedy

In ordering an employee reinstated, an arbitrator may
condition or otherwise limit the effect of his award pending
an outcome in another forum. This limitation is especially
found in cases where an employee is discharged as a result of
a collateral criminal proceeding.[100] For example, in *In re Bamberger's*,[101] an employee was discharged one day after he had
been arrested for selling marijuana on the employer's premises. Before a hearing could be held, a grand jury handed down
an indictment charging the grievant with distribution of narcotics, based on the same marijuana episode. The employer
thereafter filed an application with the arbitrator requesting
that the arbitration be postponed until the trial in the criminal
matter was completed. Arbitrator Morris Glushien, in ruling
that the application for continuance should be denied, stated
that the grievant was entitled to a reasonably prompt hearing
to resolve his job status and economic rights. After a hearing
on the merits, the arbitrator held that the employer had not
sufficiently proved that the grievant had been involved in the
sale of drugs, and accordingly ordered reinstatement. An added
caveat, however, was that in the event that the grievant was

---

[99]See, e.g., Caterpillar Tractor Co., 81 LA 1165 (Traynor, 1983) (discussing issue
whether employee discharged for unsatisfactory attendance and reinstated on condition that he participate in AA meetings is entitled to arbitrate subsequent dismissal
under agreement precluding grievance of "probationary employees."
[100]See Hill and Sinicropi, *Collateral Proceedings*, in Evidence in Arbitration, 369–
385 (BNA Books, 1987).
[101]59 LA 879 (Glushien, 1972).

convicted in the criminal case, the opinion and the award were not intended to have any bearing upon the propriety of a subsequent action.[102]

Likewise, Arbitrator Joseph McKenna, in *Donaldson Co.*,[103] reinstated an employee after he had been indicted for being implicated in a conspiracy to commit arson with two other employees who admitted setting fire to company property. While the arbitrator held that an indictment indicated only a presumption of guilt, he nevertheless denied back pay, in part, because of the grievant's negligence in the matter. The arbitrator did indicate that the award was without prejudice to the employer should it wish to take further action against the grievant upon resolution of the case before the civil courts.

In *K.L.M. Royal Dutch Airlines*,[104] Arbitrator Bertram Kupsinel held that the penalty of discharge was too severe for an airline service agent who had been placed on probation by a court for possession of marijuana. While the arbitrator ordered the company to withdraw the discharge, he nevertheless conditioned this order on the grievant satisfying all the requirements of his court-imposed probation. Should the court determine that the grievant had not fulfilled the conditions, the arbitrator provided that the discharge would stand, and the grievance accordingly would be dismissed.

E. Reinstatement With Demotion or Transfer

Generally where arbitrators have ordered reinstatement to a lower position the facts have not indicated an intent to impose a punitive sanction, but rather an effort to place an employee in a position commensurate with his abilities. Arbitrator Marlin Volz, in an address before the 31st Meeting of the National Academy of Arbitrators, cited numerous situations where this remedy might be appropriate:

In some instances an employee may be discharged where the evidence is persuasive that an unsatisfactory work performance or defective workmanship was not due to carelessness, indiffer-

---

[102]Id. at 883.
[103]60 LA 1240 (1973).
[104]66 LA 547 (1975). See also Greyhound Lines-W., 61 LA 44 (Block, 1973) (employer not obligated to reinstate employee following acquittal of criminal charge).

ence, poor attitude, or lack of conscientious application, but rather to a lack of physical or mental ability consistently to achieve the result obtainable by the average employee. In this type of case, demotion or transfer, unless prohibited by the contract, is a more appropriate remedy than discipline, assuming that a job exists to which the employee may be demoted or transferred.[105]

Elkouri and Elkouri likewise assert:

> In disciplinary discharge cases where the arbitrator concludes that the grievant should be reinstated but that some strong reason exists for denying him his former job (such reason may involve his physical condition, or a need to screen him from contacts with the public, or personality conflicts, or the like), reinstatement may be ordered to some other job which does not involve the conditions or impediments that disqualify him for his former job.[106]

Arbitrator George Roberts, in *Sunshine Biscuits*,[107] found that an additional and more severe suspension could not be expected to achieve a corrective purpose in the case of a "head mixer" who had been discharged for omitting essential ingredients in bakery products. In holding that the grievant should be reinstated and demoted at the discretion of the employer, Arbitrator Roberts stated:

> The grievant had performed several other jobs in a satisfactory manner, consequently, he could be expected to do so again if reassigned to another position which he had previously held. Because the job of Head Mixer was one of the highest paid in the production line, such reassignment would necessarily mean a demotion. The Union Contract makes no provision for or references to demotion. This does not prohibit a company from effectuating demotions, as it is an inherent right of management.
> . . .
> In considering the position to which the grievant should be demoted, the rights of other employees as protected by the Union Contract must be considered. To insure that these rights are not violated, the only position to which the grievant can be assigned is that of General Helper which is the entrance position to most departments.[108]

---

[105]Volz, supra note 32, at 156–157.
[106]Elkouri and Elkouri, supra note 32, at 691.
[107]60 LA 197 (1973).
[108]Id. at 205.

In this case the arbitrator awarded back pay from the date of discharge, but at the lower general helper rate. He also indicated that once the grievant was assigned to the position, he was entitled to exercise all bidding rights and benefits that his seniority granted under the agreement.[109] A problem one might have with the latter aspect of this award is that it may permit the grievant at some future date to bid again on the job he was considered incapable of doing in the instant case. The ramifications of this consequence are indeed far-reaching.

In another case an insurance carrier excluded a driver from further insurance coverage, due to citations for traffic violations, and Arbitrator Henry Wilmoth, in *Inland Lumber Co.*,[110] granted the grievant reinstatement to a nondriver position as a proper remedy.

Under circumstances where a discharged employee demonstrated that her supervisor had made sexual advances, Arbitrator Michael Beck, in *Osborn & Ulland*,[111] ordered the grievant to be reinstated to a position equivalent to her former position with full seniority rights, but at another store.[112]

Arbitrator M. David Keefe, in *Parke Davis*,[113] ruled that an employee was improperly dismissed after he and his wife were convicted of several criminal acts (forgery, kiting checks) relating to a Ponzi-like pyramid scheme. Beset by delusions of beating the Michigan Lottery, the grievant's wife apparently extracted some $500,000 from banks and merchants only to squander the proceeds on lottery tickets (her net take was $32,290). Citing the illegal activities of the couple, management argued that the grievant posed a security risk relating to the production of drugs. Arbitrator Keefe ordered the grievant reinstated to the first nonsensitive job "to which he has entitlement." The arbitrator further ordered that the parties negotiate the possibility of relaxing transfer or bidding rules to allow the employee access to a nonsensitive job.

---

[109]Id. at 206.
[110]62 LA 1150 (1974).
[111]68 LA 1146 (1977).
[112]See also Penn Traffic Bi-Lo Mkts., 91 LA 1087, 1089 (Duff, 1988) (grievant reinstated, demoted, and awarded back pay and benefits he would have earned had he been given option of demotion pending outcome of grievance); Corns Truck & Tractor, 63 LA 828 (Cowan, 1974); Hawaiian Tel. Co., 44 LA 218 (Tsukiyama, 1965) (incompetent employee ordered demoted).
[113]86 LA 935 (1985).

F. Removal From Union Office

While there are reported cases to the contrary,[114] the better rule is that an arbitrator should not formulate a remedy disqualifying an employee from holding union office. This view is perhaps best articulated by Arbitrator Louis Crane:

> [T]he parties have a right to expect that an arbitrator will not encroach upon their contractual or other rights in formulating a remedy for what he finds to be a violation of the labor agreement. For example, however obstreperous a union steward may be and whatever disciplinary action may be imposed against him as an employee, an arbitrator would be intruding upon the internal affairs of the union if he dealt with the right of that employee to hold union office.[115]

In *Allis-Chalmers Corp.*,[116] a three-member panel of the NLRB held that an employer committed an unfair labor practice by conditioning the reinstatement of an employee who was terminated for sleeping on the job on his resignation as union representative. Absent evidence showing that the employee's duties as grievance representative interfered with his job responsibilities, the Board found that the natural and foreseeable consequences of this conduct were to discourage employees from serving as union grievance representative and to discourage active membership in the union by other employees.

G. Reinstatement With Loss of Seniority

Some arbitrators have reinstated employees, but without seniority for the period between termination and reinstatement, reasoning that it would be inappropriate to permit accumulation of seniority for the time that the grievant has been

---

[114]Farm Pac Kitchens, 59 LA 251 (Sartain, 1972) (reinstated employee ordered ineligible for union office for approximately two years); Consolidated Edison Co., 54 LA 488 (Crowley, 1969) (reinstatement conditioned upon grievant not holding union office for three years). See generally Elkouri and Elkouri, supra note 32, at 691 n. 202; Fairweather, supra note 11, at 281–282.

[115]Crane, *The Use and Abuse of Arbitral Power*, in Labor Arbitration at the Quarter-Century Mark, Proceedings of the 25th Annual Meeting, National Academy of Arbitrators, 66; 75 (BNA Books, 1973).

[116]231 NLRB 1207, 96 LRRM 1257 (1977).

away from work.[117] While rare, arbitrators have even ordered reinstatement to an entry-level position with loss of seniority.[118]

H. Reinstatement to Positions
Subsequently Eliminated

Reinstatement raises problems when the grievant's former position has been eliminated for economic reasons or otherwise has been converted to a nonunit position. In *Chemical Workers Local 227 v. BASF Wyandotte Corp.*,[119] the arbitrator reinstated a grievant with back pay to the janitorial position he held under the collective bargaining agreement at the time of his wrongful discharge. The arbitrator, however, handed down the decision before the new collective bargaining agreement eliminated the grievant's position. What is the effect of the award under the new agreement? The Second Circuit reasoned that reinstatement would have placed the grievant in a position similar to that of the other janitorial staff at BASF. Accordingly, the grievant was subject to any changes agreed to by the parties. The arbitrator's award of reinstatement did not guarantee the grievant "perpetual job security," but simply restored him to the status as a janitor under the old labor agreement with the same rights as any other janitor.

A different result was reached where Arbitrator Robert Howlett ordered Field Enterprises "to return [the grievant] to work at the beginning of the payroll period following receipt of [the] Award." The Seventh Circuit noted that even if it were to accept the employer's contention that the award required only that the grievant be restored to the position he would have been in had he not been terminated, the same result

---

[117]Burton Mfg. Co., 82 LA 1228, 1237 (Holley, 1984) (reinstating grievant without back pay and without any seniority rights which would have accumulated during disciplinary suspension); Baker Store Equip. Co., 81 LA 1077, 1083 (Richard, 1983) (ordering loss of seniority for period of suspension); Nugent Sand Co., 81 LA 988, 994 (Daniel, 9183) ("It would be more inappropriate to permit the grievant to accumulate seniority credit for the time that he has been away from work, and so it is further directed that his seniority date be adjusted, calculating such seniority as he had at the time of his termination and adding to it seniority as he will commence accruing after his return to work."

[118]Cincinnati Gas & Elec. Co., 90 LA 841, 844 (Katz, 1988) (reinstating grievant to entry-level position without opportunity for promotion).

[119]774 F.2d 43, 120 LRRM 2711 (2d Cir. 1985).

would be reached since management acknowledged that it would be impossible to establish that the grievant would have been laid off due to the demise of the Chicago Daily News where the layoffs were not carried out by seniority.[120] In dictum the Seventh Circuit stated that even if Field were able to prove that the grievant would have been laid off, the court could not credit the argument because it was not presented to the arbitrator.[121]

A similar situation arose when a nurse was discharged from her position as supervising head nurse. An arbitrator ruled that her conduct did not merit dismissal and converted the discharge to a six-week suspension without pay, thus awarding the employee back pay for 7 of the 13 weeks she missed. The hospital was ordered to immediately reinstate the grievant. Before the award was issued, the grievant's position was reclassified as a supervisory position and, thus, excluded from the bargaining unit. The hospital refused reinstatement, but complied with the award by paying the grievant seven weeks' back pay plus one additional day's pay. The court held that because the employee's position was no longer a unit position, she could be discharged at any time after her reinstatement as an employee-at-will. According to the court, the practical effect of paying her one day's wages, in addition to seven weeks pay, was to "reinstate" her.[122]

A study of case law reveals that compliance with an arbitrator's reinstatement order is to be gleaned from the specific words used in the award, as well as the facts and circumstances of each case. An employee "reinstated to his former

[120]Newspaper Guild (Chicago) v. Field Enters., 747 F.2d 1153, 117 LRRM 2937 (7th Cir. 1984).

[121]Citing Steelworkers v. Smoke-Craft, 652 F.2d 1356, 1360, 108 LRRM 2218 (9th Cir. 1981), cert. denied, 455 U.S. 1021, 109 LRRM 3104 (1982) (failure to raise certain claims before arbitrator waives them in confirmation proceeding); Cook Indus. v. C. Itoh & Co., 449 F.2d 106, 107–108 (2d Cir. 1971), cert. denied, 405 U.S. 921 (1972) (failure to object to arbitrator's bias waives objection on appeal; Newspaper Guild Local 35 (Washington-Baltimore) v. Washington Post Co., 367 F. Supp. 917, 919, 84 LRRM 3003 (D.D.C. 1973) (failure to raise defense as set-off before arbitrator bars employer from asserting it to resist enforcement); Machinists Local 701 v. Holiday Oldsmobile, 356 F. Supp. 1325, 1328, 84 LRRM 2200 (N.D. Ill. 1972) (failure to raise issue of oral agreement between parties before arbitrator waives argument in enforcement proceeding).

[122]Service Employees Local 144 v. Metropolitan Jewish Geriatric Center, 94 LRRM 3151 (S.D.N.Y. 1977). Cf. Diamond Match Co., 87-2 ARB ¶8574 (Miller, 1987) (reinstatement to position improperly denied to senior job bidder impossible where, between denial and arbitration, a more senior employee bumped into position).

position" or "reinstated to his employment"[123] may be subject to any adverse consequences associated with the former job classification. A grievant may fare better, as in *Field Enterprises*, when management is ordered to "'reinstate him to employment." When an employee is reinstated for a token period of time and subsequently dismissed, the employer's conduct should not be evaluated independently of the reinstatement order. To rule otherwise may invite abuse by an unscrupulous employer.[124]

I. Reinstatement to Disability Leave

Arbitrator Jonathan Dworkin, in *East Ohio Gas Co.*,[125] ordered reinstatement to disability leave for a nondisciplinary discharge. Finding that he could not reinstate the grievant to his former position because he could not determine whether the grievant was medically fit, the arbitrator ordered reinstatement to disability leave (with wages and benefits he would have received had he remained on disability leave up to and beyond the date of the award) because the company's decision was based on dated medical evidence. In *Bucklers, Inc.*,[126] an AIDS victim was similarly reinstated to an involuntary leave of absence when, by his own admission, he was physically incapable of performing his regular job. Directing the grievant to an AIDS specialist, the arbitrator ruled that the grievant shall continue on medical leave "subject to the terms and conditions of the pertinent provisions of the labor agreement and/or customary practice or the parties."

---

[123]Teamsters Local 100 v. Liquid Carbonic Corp., 562 F. Supp. 825, 116 LRRM 2184 (S.D. Ohio 1983) (holding that award ordering employee "reinstated to his employment" required employer to restore employee to position he would have held had he not been discharged, which was on layoff status).
[124]See, e.g., Aluminum Workers Local 250 v. Chromalloy Am. Corp., 489 F. Supp. 536, 105 LRRM 2084 (N.D. Miss. 1980) (finding no compliance with arbitral order of reinstatement when management "simultaneously" and retroactively reinstated and discharged employee for absenteeism occurring prior to arbitration award); Staffman's Org. Comm. v. Steelworkers, 399 F. Supp. 102, 92 LRRM 2007 (W.D. Mich. 1975) (noting chilling effect on grievants if aware that after enduring three years of contract grievance procedures and winning, they could be transferred to farthest of district and be forced to start over again).
[125]91 LA 366, 374 (1988).
[126]90 LA 937, 939 (Braufman, 1987).

J. Reinstatement and Retroactive Bidding Rights

Does a reinstated employee have retroactive bidding rights to a job posting that occurs during the period from the date of discharge to the date of reinstatement? The normal make-whole remedy is that the grievant is entitled to be placed in the same position the grievant would have occupied had the improper discharge not been effected. Some arbitrators direct reinstatement without making a determination to which job the grievant should be returned. Realizing that it is impracticable for employees who are discharged to bid on vacancies during the time of the resolution of their dismissals, the better course is to order reinstatement to the position the employee held at the time of dismissal, with the understanding that this means the position in relationship to other employees in the bargaining unit by seniority. If there had been a reduction in force during the period of dismissal and the grievant's seniority was insufficient to maintain the former position, management would not be required to alter the agreement in order to place the grievant in his old position. Just as an order of reinstatement does not tenure the grievant in his old position, a make-whole reinstatement remedy should not preclude the grievant from assuming a position he would have bid but for the improper discharge.[127]

---

[127]See, e.g., the discussion of Arbitrator Thomas Hewitt in Georgia Pac. Corp., 88-2 ARB ¶8435 (1988) (holding that employee was entitled to job he would have successfully bid had he not been wrongfully discharged for misconduct on picket line).

Chapter 8

Back Pay

This chapter will focus on the complexities that exist in formulating back-pay awards in discipline and discharge cases. Although back-pay remedies are discussed in discipline and discharge situations, many of the principles noted are equally applicable in cases where arbitrators have found back pay an appropriate remedy in nondisciplinary cases.

A. Back-Pay Considerations

At common law, a basic policy of contract remedial law is to encourage contract formation by protecting the reasonable expectations of the parties. A contract secures the stability of promise, and society is benefited by the specialization that contract making permits. Accordingly, expectancy is reinforced by placing the nonbreaching party in as favorable a position as if the contract had been performed.[1] To this end the general contract rule for determining damages was stated by the Supreme Court as follows:

> [W]hen a wrong has been done, and the law gives a remedy, the compensation shall be equal to the injury. The latter is the standard by which the former is to be measured. The injured

---

[1]See Hillman, Contract Remedies, Equity, and Restitution, 125–126 (Iowa Law School, Continuing Legal Educ., 1979).

180

party is to be placed, as near as may be, in the situation he would have occupied if the wrong has not been committed.[2]

Similarly, in the area of labor relations it is uniformly recognized that the purpose of a back-pay award is to indemnify the employee by making him whole for loss of earnings incurred by reason of the employer's contract violation. This loss of earnings is generally measured by the wages that he would have earned during the period they were denied. The amount owed is usually reduced by the income that the employee received from substitute employment, or by the amount that he would have received if a reasonable effort had been made to find interim employment.[3] Other setoffs will, at times, be imposed, and these will be discussed in subsequent sections.

1. Power of Arbitrator to Make a Back-Pay Award

There is no genuine issue concerning the power of an arbitrator to make a monetary award of back pay,[4] either in the private or the public sector.[5] Even where this power is not

---

[2]Wicker v. Hoppock, 73 U.S. (6 Wall.) 94, 99 (1867).

[3]Falls Stamping & Welding v. Automobile Workers, 485 F. Supp. 1097, 109 LRRM 2987, 2991 (N.D. Ohio 1979) ("In the employment contract context, the employee is entitled to the amount of money he would have received if he had continued to work for the company. The amount owed under the contract or collective bargaining agreement must be reduced by the income that the employee received from substitute employment or by the amount that he or she would have received if a reasonable effort had been made to find interim employment.").

[4]See "Arbitrator's Power to Specify Remedies When the Contract Is Silent," in Chapter 3, at notes 93–112 and accompanying text.

[5]5 U.S.C. §5596(b)(1)(A)(i) (1982), in relevant part, provides:

(b)(1) An employee of an agency who, on the basis of a timely appeal or an administrative determination (including a decision relating to an unfair labor practice or a grievance) is found by appropriate authority under applicable law, rule, regulation, or collective bargaining agreement, to have been affected by an unjustified or unwarranted personnel action which has resulted in the withdrawal or reduction of all or part of the pay, allowances, or differentials of the employee—

(A) is entitled, on correction of the personnel action, to receive for the period for which the personnel action was in effect—

(i) an amount equal to all or any part of the pay, allowances, or differentials, as applicable which the employee normally would have earned or received during the period if the personnel action had not occurred, less any amounts earned by the employee through other employment during that period; . . . .

expressly provided in the collective bargaining agreement,[6] or expressly requested in the parties' written submission to the arbitrator, arbitrators have held that the power to decide the disciplinary issue includes the power to formulate an appropriate remedy including, but not limited to, full or partial back pay. It must be remembered, however, that the parties may, through contractual language, limit the amount of back pay that may be awarded by an arbitrator. For example, Arbitrator Donald Leach, in *Columbus Show Case Co.,*[7] ruled that a back-pay award must be limited where the contract provided that "awards or settlements shall in no event be made retroactive beyond the date on which the grievance was first presented by the employee to his foreman." Similarly, Arbitrator Richard O'Connell, in *Yellow Taxi of Minneapolis,*[8] ordered reinstatement with only 10 days' back pay pursuant to an agreement which limited any make-whole compensation to 10 days' pay.

Even where the contract specifically designates or limits the amount of back pay that is to be awarded in a disciplinary case, there are reported decisions indicating that arbitrators have not always adhered to such constraints.[9]

2. Back Pay Without Reinstatement

When an arbitrator finds that discharge was improper, a range of remedies is to grant reinstatement with full, partial, or no back pay. Infrequently, an arbitrator may award back pay but not order the grievant reinstated. Thus, in one case, Arbitrator William Gould held that reinstatement was inappropriate where the grievant's behavior was not correctable. Although the contract provided that an employee may not be discharged except for just cause, the arbitrator pointed out

---

[6]BNA reports that reinstatement with back pay for employees improperly discharged is required in 43% of the contracts surveyed—44% of the manufacturing agreements and 40% of collective bargaining agreements in nonmanufacturing. Of these provisions, BNA states that 63% grant full back pay, 34% leave the amount awarded to the arbitrator's discretion, and 4% place a limitation on the amount awarded. In some instances unemployment compensation or money earned from other jobs is deducted from back pay. Basic Patterns in Union Contracts, 12th ed., at 9 (BNA Books, 1989).

[7]64 LA 1148 (1975).

[8]68 LA 26 (1977).

[9]See Chapter 3, notes 128–129 and accompanying text.

that such a remedy would be justified since nothing in the parties' bargaining history, contract language, or other precedent precluded him from ordering back pay without reinstatement. Attention is called to his reasoning:

> It is important to note that the Agreement is silent with regard to any mandated remedy. Neither party quarrels with the view that the Arbitrator has the authority under the Agreement to provide for reinstatement with back pay with interest. But what is significant is that the Arbitrator under this Agreement is not mandated to fashion any particular remedy. The parties could have bargained for such a contractual provision. Limitations upon arbitral remedial discretion are not unknown to American labor-management contractual relationships. But under this collective bargaining agreement, the Arbitrator was provided remedial flexibility.[10]

The arbitrator also found that the discharge was not for cause, since "procedural due process" guarantees were violated. Specifically, Gould found that the agreement provided that "[b]efore a regular employee is discharged for incompetency or failure to perform work as required, he shall receive a written warning (with a copy to the Union), and be given an opportunity to improve his work."[11] Since the union did not receive copies of the written warnings until five days before the discharge, it was denied the opportunity to counsel with the employee, as is clearly provided in the agreement. Accordingly, back pay without reinstatement was ordered.

In another situation where an employee, found to have been improperly discharged, had secured employment elsewhere and did not desire to be reinstated, Arbitrator Kenneth McDonald, in *American Building Maintenance Co.*,[12] found a back-pay remedy appropriate. Noting that the agreement spoke only in terms of reinstatement, and was silent about relief where the discharged employee had secured alternate work, the arbitrator nevertheless held that the failure of the parties to include this contingency in the agreement should not work to the detriment of an otherwise improperly discharged employee.[13]

---

[10]Safeway Stores, 64 LA 563, 570 (1974).
[11]Id. at 567–568.
[12]58 LA 385 (1972).
[13]Id. at 397.

Still other arbitrators have ordered back pay without reinstatement when the dismissal was for cause but the employer engaged in procedural infirmities in effecting the discharge.[14]

Back pay without reinstatement was upheld by one federal court as a remedy for wrongfully laid off employees who could not be reinstated because the employer licensed out its coal mining operations.[15] In another case, the Seventh Circuit upheld an arbitrator's award ordering back pay to the date of the award but no reinstatement where the employee's post-discharge conduct "revealed a motivation that disqualified [the grievant] as an employee."[16]

When, if ever, should an arbitrator order back pay without reinstatement? William Gould had argued that arbitrators, following the position of the NLRB in connection with unfair labor practice jurisdiction, generally believe that if a violation of the collective bargaining agreement is found, automatic reinstatement is mandated. Gould further maintains that arbitrators' inflexibility about the remedies they devise prompts excessive judicial review of labor arbitration awards. Specifically, courts have reacted against reemployment of workers they perceive as harmful to the employment relationship, especially where the arbitrator has not made findings with regard to the potential for rehabilitation. Gould maintains that where reinstatement is not ordered, but rather some other form of relief is fashioned, the concerns of a reviewing court ought to diminish. "Remedial flexibility," says Gould, "is intrinsically desirable and arbitrators ought to exercise it more often."[17]

We believe that Gould's position is well taken especially

---

[14]Virgin Islands Water & Power Auth., 87-2 ARB ¶8473 (Watkins, 1987) (procedurally flawed discharge remedied by offering employer choice between paying employee eight months' wages and allowing discharge to stand, or reinstatement of grievant); Hiland Dairy, 87-1 ARB ¶8101 (Belcher, 1986) (finding fault on both sides, parties offered two options: no reinstatement but separation pay, or discharge converted to suspension without back pay).

[15]Big Bear Mining Co. v. Mine Workers Dist. 17, 579 F. Supp. 1072, 116 LRRM 2882 (S.D. W.Va. 1983).

[16]Yellow Cab Co. v. Democratic Union Org. Comm. Local 777, 398 F.2d 735, 68 LRRM 2812, 2813 (7th Cir. 1968).

[17]Gould, *Judicial Review of Labor Arbitration Awards—Thirty Years of the* Steelworkers Trilogy: *The Aftermath of* AT & T *and* Misco, 64 Notre Dame L. Rev. 464, 492–493 (1989).

where procedural infirmities are present in a case that would otherwise warrant the dismissal of an employee.

3. Conditioning Back-Pay Awards

Where it appears that there is some question concerning an employee's sincerity in maintaining employment, an arbitrator may condition a back-pay award upon a grievant's acceptance and completion of a specified length of employment. For example, Arbitrator W. Gowan, in *Fabsteel Co.*,[18] reinstated an employee with full back pay for all time lost during the period of termination (less any amounts earned through other employment or received as a result of unemployment compensation or relief) with the provision that the grievant accept an offer of reinstatement. The arbitrator further stated that the employer need not tender back pay in a lump sum, but rather would have the option to pay it at weekly intervals, making allowance first for the amounts earned and received during the period of termination.

In yet another example where back pay may be conditional, Arbitrator Burton Turkus, in *Raytheon Co.*,[19] held that an employer was not justified in suspending an employee pending resolution of a homicide incident. While the arbitrator reinstated the employee, he nevertheless reserved consideration on the grievant's entitlement to back pay until the determination of the criminal charge, at which time the back-pay issue would be determined in a supplemental award.

In *Colgate-Palmolive Co.*,[20] Arbitrator Duane Traynor ordered six months of back pay, provided that the reinstated employee satisfactorily performed her job during a probationary period. Similarly, in *American Airlines*,[21] Arbitrator Peter Seitz conditioned an award of back pay upon completion of 75 compensable days of service.

---

[18] 62 LA 672 (1974).
[19] 66 LA 677 (1976).
[20] 64 LA 293 (1975).
[21] 48 LA 705 (1967).

4. Option to Remand Back-Pay Issue

Once it is determined that a back-pay award is appropriate, an arbitrator may remand the task of computation to the parties. Such a remedy is usually, but not always, accompanied by retention of jurisdiction by the arbitrator in the event that there is a subsequent dispute over the amount. Some examples include the following:

> "The employer is directed to reinstate to their jobs those employees who were [laid] off . . . and to reimburse each of them for the wages lost by them because of the wrongful layoffs under the contract.
> "In the event that the parties can not agree on the payments due and owing by the Employer and to whom those payments are forthcoming under this Award, the undersigned arbitrator shall retain jurisdiction of this matter in order to hear and determine only those issues."[22]
> The amount of back pay is a more difficult problem. As previously indicated, there was a long hiatus, for reasons unknown to the arbitrator, between the initial demand for arbitration and the further progress of the case. In addition, [the grievant] has been receiving unemployment insurance benefits. Conceivably he has also had some outside earnings. These factors and perhaps others bearing upon the problem, some of which may be unknown to the arbitrator but available to the parties, indicate that full back pay may be inappropriate.
> Because of these considerations, the arbitrator directs that the parties promptly confer and attempt to agree upon the appropriate amount of back pay . . . .
>   . . .
> [T]he arbitrator hereby retains jurisdiction to rule upon this question [back pay] . . . .[23]

In *Hart v. Overseas National Airways*,[24] the Third Circuit considered, in an enforcement proceeding, the following award:

> "His [grievant's] termination shall be set aside and stricken from his personal record and he should be made whole for any and all wages, benefits and/or rights to which he is or would have been entitled had he not been wrongfully discharged."[25]

A lower court had found that the award was "fatally uncertain

---

[22]UFI Razor Blades v. Distributive Workers Dist. 65, 610 F.2d 1018, 102 LRRM 2759, 2760 (2d Cir. 1979).

[23]Bamberger's, 59 LA 879, 883 (Glushien, 1972).

[24]541 F.2d 386, 93 LRRM 2103 (3d Cir. 1976).

[25]Id., 93 LRRM at 2107.

and therefore incapable of enforcement."[26] While the Third Circuit agreed that the award was too indefinite to enforce, the court nevertheless held that the entire award need not be set aside merely because of the indefiniteness of the damage provision. Given no other infirmities, the damage portion of the award should, held the court, be remanded to the arbitrator for clarification and additional findings.[27]

Similarly, the Fifth Circuit held that where an employee was ordered to be reinstated and paid for his "time lost," the award was too indefinite to be enforced. In remanding to the arbitration board, the court of appeals, stating what appears to be the better rule, declared:

> We conclude that where the award is ambiguous, but can be clarified by reference to extrinsic evidence not involving the special expertise of the board . . . , the district court may proceed to resolve the conflict in an enforcement proceedings. However, where, as here, the award is too indefinite to be enforced, and cannot be made definite by considering nonspecialized extrinsic evidence, then the court should remand to the board for clarification of the award.[28]

Another federal court has likewise ruled that it is appropriate for an arbitrator to retain jurisdiction for a peripheral aspect of a case, such as computing the amount of back pay. Ruling that it was proper under a just cause provision for an arbitrator to award tips to a dismissed waiter as part of a back-pay award, the court held that the award was not rendered incomplete by the arbitrator's retention of jurisdiction to determine the amount of tips to be paid. In the court's words, "[r]ather than having the parties go through all the steps of the grievance procedure again to obtain a determination of this matter through another arbitration case, it was proper, for the sake of procedural economy, to retain jurisdiction for this peripheral aspect of the case."[29]

---

[26]Id. See the discussion at 93 LRRM 2106.

[27]See Hart v. Overseas Nat'l Airways, 94 LRRM 3133 (E.D. Pa. 1977), where the court, on remand, remanded the issue to an impartial referee.

[28]United Transp. Union v. Southern Pac. Transp. Co., 529 F.2d 691, 693, 91 LRRM 3057, 3058 (5th Cir. 1976).

[29]Hilton Int'l Co. v. Union de Trabajadores Local 610, 600 F. Supp. 1446, 1451, 119 LRRM 2011, 2015 (D.P.R. 1985). Accord American Standard v. Electrical Workers (UE) Local 610, 133 LRRM 2985 (3d Cir. 1990) (holding that federal district court that enforced arbitration award, which sustained discharged employees' grievance, ordered make-whole remedy, and directed parties to negotiate remedy, had jurisdic-

In general, where the parties present the remedy question as part of the overall merits of the dispute, they necessarily invite construction of the remedy by the arbitrator and any questions regarding the scope of the remedy are properly returned to the arbitrator for further consideration. When a remedy determination is remanded to the parties for further consideration, the arbitrator has not adjudicated an issue which has been submitted and, thus, the arbitrator has not exhausted his function. It accordingly remains open for him, and not a reviewing court or a new arbitrator, for subsequent determination should the parties not reach agreement on the financial or other implications of a particular remedy. However, where a collateral dispute arises from an award that is not self-executing, it may be more appropriate to channel the dispute back through the entire grievance machinery.[30]

Although it is clear that an award will not be vacated merely because the damage portion is unspecified or incomplete, not all arbitrators agree that a neutral should leave unspecified the components of a back-pay award. Indeed, some have even maintained that the arbitrator should compute the actual amount due. Thus, Arbitrator Sidney Wolff has argued:

> I would like to refer to those awards where the arbitrator directs payment of back pay, less outside earnings, and leaves to the parties the computation of the actual figures. I suggest this is erroneous and, unless specifically authorized by the parties, ought not to be done. I recognize this is the procedure of the National Labor Relations Board but, as arbitrators, we have the obligation to order final and definite awards on the controversy submitted. We should not inaugurate a make-work project for arbitrators.[31]

---

tion under §301 of LMRA over union's postmotion for order returning dispute concerning remedial issues to same arbitrator who sustained grievance); Automotive, Petroleum & Allied Indus. Employees Local 618 v. Sears, Roebuck & Co., 581 F. Supp. 672 (E.D. Mo. 1984) (holding arbitrator properly permitted to testify as to meaning of phrase "regular straight time hourly rate" in back-pay award); Electrical Workers (IBEW) Local 2222 v. New England Tel. & Tel. Co., 628 F.2d 644, 105 LRRM 2211 (1st Cir. 1980) (ruling that union not required to resort anew to grievance arbitration procedure before filing §301 action for order compelling employer to resubmit dispute concerning computation of discharged employee's loss of earnings to board of arbitration that originally heard dispute; dispute concerning loss of earnings encompassed by parties' original submission).

[30]La Vale Plaza v. R.S. Noonan, Inc., 378 F.2d 569, 573 (3d Cir. 1967) ("where the award does not adjudicate an issue which had been submitted, then as to such issue the arbitrator has not exhausted his function and it remains open to him for subsequent determination.").

[31]Wolff, Remedies in Arbitration: II. The Power of the Arbitrator to Make Monetary

In support of his contention, Arbitrator Wolff notes that one of the issues before the Supreme Court in the *Enterprise Wheel* decision concerned an "incomplete" award. In *Enterprise* the arbitrator directed reinstatement with back pay, less monies earned elsewhere. The Supreme Court agreed that the failure to specify the amounts to be deducted rendered the award unenforceable and accordingly directed the parties to complete the arbitration "so that the amounts due the employees may be definitely determined by arbitration."[32]

A review of arbitration awards indicates that arbitrators generally refrain from specifying the amount due when back-pay awards are made. And with good reason. Rarely do the parties present relevant data, either at the hearing or in post-hearing briefs, that would enable the arbitrator to compute a specific dollar sum. This posture is not unexpected. The parties may not desire to engage in protracted arguments concerning the components and amounts due as a back-pay remedy where the issue may eventually be mooted by an award adverse to the grievants.

At the same time, however, an arbitrator who orders rein-statement with "all monies due" may be planting the seeds for a further round of litigation, especially if jurisdiction is not retained. Rather than attempt to designate specific dollar amounts, some arbitrators will instead draft a back-pay award specifying the components and leaving it to the parties to work out the exact amounts. For example, Arbitrator Edgar A. Jones, Jr., in *Farmer Brothers Co.*,[33] issued the following award:

> The Award is that F— and R— were wrongfully discharged by the Employer. They shall be reinstated effective October 5, 1974, without loss of pay, computed on the basis of the straight-time hours they would otherwise have worked but for their wrongful separation from the payroll. Any monies received by them in lieu of their wages, including unemployment compensation, shall be deducted from the sum due them, and they shall submit sworn statements of such earnings to the Employer as a condition precedent to receipt of back pay.[34]

Awards, in Labor Arbitration: Perspectives and Problems, Proceedings of the 17th Annual Meeting, National Academy of Arbitrators, 176, 181–182 (BNA Books, 1964).
    [32]Steelworkers v. Enterprise Wheel & Car Corp., 363 U.S. 593, 46 LRRM 2423, 2426 (1960).
    [33]64 LA 901 (1975).
    [34]Id. at 906.

Arbitrator Jones retained jurisdiction to dispose of any problems in the administration of the award.

Where an employee was found to have been improperly discharged for distributing union cards during working hours in violation of a no-distribution rule, Arbitrator Jerome Brooks, in *Messenger Corp.*,[35] drafted the following back-pay award:

> Because the Act also is being vindicated by the Arbitrator's decision, it is further directed that the policies and rules followed by the NLRB in making back pay awards shall apply in the determination by the Company of the amount of back pay due Grievant. In this respect [citations] . . . are noteworthy relative to the computation of back pay on a quarterly basis and the payment of interest on the quarterly sum due.[36]

While arbitrators and parties are not of the same view regarding the specificity of the back-pay remedy and the retention of jurisdiction by the arbitrator, it is the authors' view that when the remedy can be specifically formulated, it should be; and, when this is inappropriate, the arbitrator, with concurrence from the parties, should retain jurisdiction for a specified period of time, and such jurisdiction should be exercised only in the event the parties cannot reach accord on the extent of the remedy. Further, retention of jurisdiction by the arbitrator should be initiated only if both parties agree to such a procedure. The arbitrator has an obligation to attempt to make the award final. Courts will remand the case to the arbitrator for clarification or even vacate the award if it is not clear and specific. The arbitrator's fidelity to finality requires that he make a complete assessment of all aspects of the award and be as specific as possible including, when possible, designating the remedy.

5. Computing Back Pay

(1) Background—experience under NLRA. The National Labor Relations Act vests the National Labor Relations Board (NLRB) with discretion to remedy unfair labor practices:

> If . . . the Board shall be of the opinion that any person named in the complaint has engaged in . . . any such unfair labor prac-

---

[35]72 LA 865 (1979).
[36]Id. at 874.

tice, then the Board shall state its findings of fact and shall issue and cause to be served on such person an order requiring such person to cease and desist from such unfair labor practice, and to take such affirmative action . . . as will effectuate the policies of . . . [the Act].[37]

The Supreme Court has consistently recognized the great breadth of discretion given the Board in remedial matters, including back pay.[38] The Court has also pointed out that the Board's remedial "conclusions may 'express an intuition of experience which outruns analysis and sums up many unnamed and tangled impressions.' "[39]

In computing back pay, the principle of "make whole" relief for an employee who was wrongfully discharged has been uniformly applied by the Board and the courts where an unfair labor practice has been found. Thus the Supreme Court has declared: "[A]n order requiring reinstatement and back pay is aimed at 'restoring the economic status quo that would have obtained but for company's wrongful refusal to reinstate.' "[40]

Similarly, the Eighth Circuit has stated:

> The amount which serves as the basis for the back pay award is the amount which the employee discriminated against would have earned but for the discriminatory act. It is grounded upon the rate of compensation normally to be expected during the period.[41]

The Fifth Circuit has voiced this principle as follows:

> [T]he "make whole" concept does not turn on whether the pay was wholly obligatory or gratuitous, but on the restoration of the *status quo ante.* . . . The Board's discretion to take such affirmative *remedial* action as will effectuate the purposes of the Act includes more than placing the employee in position to assert contractual or legally enforcible obligations. "Back pay" . . . includes the moneys, whether gratuitous or not, which it is

---

[37]29 U.S.C. §160(c).
[38]Phelps Dodge Corp. v. NLRB, 313 U.S. 177, 8 LRRM 439 (1941).
[39]NLRB v. Seven-Up Bottling Co. of Miami, 344 U.S. 344, 348, 31 LRRM 2237, 2239 (1953).
[40]Golden State Bottling Co. v. NLRB, 414 U.S. 168, 84 LRRM 2839, 2847 (1973), citing NLRB v. J.H. Rutter-Rex Mfg. Co., 396 U.S. 258, 263, 72 LRRM 2881 (1969).
[41]NLRB v. Columbia Tribune Publishing Co., 495 F.2d 1385, 86 LRRM 2078, 2084 (8th Cir. 1974).

reasonably found that the employee would actually have received in the absence of the unlawful discrimination.[42]

The Court of Appeals for the District of Columbia has stated the policy reasons for allowing back pay as "make whole" relief:

> The purpose of requiring that the employer make the discriminatee whole in such a case has a two-fold objective. First, the back pay remedy reimburses the innocent employee for the actual losses which he has suffered as a direct result of the employer's improper conduct; second, the order furthers the public interest advanced by the deterrence of such illegal acts.[43]

(2) Arbitral rulings. Arbitrators have borrowed from court and Board decisions and applied similar "make whole" concepts when ordering back-pay relief. Indeed, one federal court has declared that "[t]he arbitrator may look for guidance in the Labor Management Relations Act in applying the correct back pay computation."[44] Arbitrator Rankin Gibson, in *Alliance Manufacturing Co.,*[45] advanced the following principle for awarding back pay:

> The theory upon which back pay is awarded a discharged employee upon reinstatement is the same theory upon which courts of law award damages for breach of contract of employment, viz., to make the employee whole for the loss sustained by reason of his discharge. The purpose is to put him in exactly the same position financially that he would have been in had the discharge not occurred.[46]

In this same regard, Arbitrator Ralph Seward has stated:

> The ordinary rule at common law and in the developing law of labor relations is that an award of damages should be limited to the amount necessary to make the injured party "whole." Unless an agreement provides that some other rule should be followed, this rule must apply.[47]

Arbitrator Archibald Cox, while recognizing make-whole

---

[42]W.C. Nabors Co. v. NLRB, 323 F.2d 686, 54 LRRM 2259, 2262 (5th Cir. 1963). See also Segarra v. Sea-Land Serv., 581 F.2d 291, 99 LRRM 2198 (1st Cir. 1978).
[43]NLRB v. Madison Courier, 472 F.2d 1307, 80 LRRM 3377, 3382 (D.C. Cir. 1972).
[44]Hilton Int'l Co. v. Union de Trabajadores Local 610, supra note 29, 600 F. Supp. at 1451, 119 LRRM at 2015.
[45]61 LA 101 (1973).
[46]Id. at 103.
[47]International Harvester Co., 15 LA 1, 1 (1950).

concepts, has observed that back-pay awards are punitive as well as compensatory:

> [T]he company pays twice when it improperly discharges a man or violates his seniority. It pays back wages and also pays the person who took the grievant's place. And the "only justification for an award of back pay is that there is no method of doing perfect justice." Thus the dilemma lies in being forced to choose between denying the employee an adequate remedy or forcing the employer to pay twice for the same work. When the employer causes the loss, however innocently, it is more just that he should bear the cost of making the employee whole than that the employee should be forced to suffer a denial of contract rights without a remedy.[48]

Some practitioners, however, have questioned whether "make whole" relief can ever be fully effectuated in the arbitral forum. Ben Fischer, in an appearance before the National Academy, has argued:

> You never make a discharged employee whole by putting him back to work. In this day and age, when workers are developing dignity and status in the community and in their family, and you operate almost in an industrial goldfish bowl, you can't make him whole. He was offended; he was embarrassed; his family was embarrassed. "I saw your husband the other day. Isn't he working? What's the matter?" Do you reply, "He was fired"? Or, "He's ill"? Or, what do you do to avoid the stigma? How do you make that whole? What do you do about the guy who loses his car, whose TV is picked up, who has to borrow money and pay interest, who loses his home? We've had those cases. How do you make him whole?[49]

Although arbitrators are by no means legally or otherwise bound to apply damage principles developed by the Board and the courts under Taft-Hartley,[50] there is no dispute that many

---

[48]Electric Storage Battery Co., AAA Case No. 19-22 (Cox, 1960), as cited in Fairweather, Practice and Procedure in Labor Arbitration, 2d ed., at 513 (BNA Books, 1983).

[49]See Fischer, *Implementation of Arbitration Awards—The Steelworker's View*, in Arbitration and the Public Interest, Proceedings of the 24th Annual Meeting, National Academy of Arbitrators, 126, 133–134 (BNA Books, 1971).

[50]In J.H. Rutter-Rex Mfg. Co. v. NLRB, 399 F.2d 356, 68 LRRM 2916, 2922 (5th Cir. 1968), the court stated that "[a] backpay proceeding is designed to enforce a public, not a private right. The purpose of a backpay award is to deter unfair labor practices and not to enforce the private rights of the employees," citing NLRB v. Mooney Aircraft, 366 F.2d 809, 63 LRRM 2208 (5th Cir. 1966). See also W.C. Nabors Co. v. NLRB, 323 F.2d 686, 54 LRRM 2259, 2263 (5th Cir. 1963); Virginia Elec. & Power Co. v. NLRB, 319 U.S. 533, 543, 12 LRRM 739, 744 (1943).

of the concepts and policy reasons applicable under the Act have been incorporated by arbitrators in formulating "make whole" relief for a breach of a collective bargaining agreement. Therefore, where relevant, reference will be made to various remedies applicable in the legal sector, especially those applied by the NLRB where violations of Taft-Hartley have been established. This is not to assert that the functions of an arbitrator are the same as those of the Board or a court. They are not. If, however, a remedy has some basis in the contract an arbitrator may properly direct it, even though he "borrows" from the Board or courts in arriving at back pay or some other remedy.

a. The Period of Back Pay

A review of arbitration awards and of NLRB and court decisions indicates that a variety of periods may be used in computing back pay. Some examples include:

(1) Back pay that would normally have been earned from the date of discharge to the date of an offer of reinstatement. The NLRB's first published order awarded back-pay wages which normally would have been earned during the period from the date of discharge to the date an offer of reinstatement was made, less any amounts earned subsequent to discharge.[51] Under this approach, back pay is calculated on a continuous basis; that is, the amount of loss is determined by computing the difference between what the employee would normally have earned in his old job, less what he earned from other sources during the whole period starting with the date of discharge and ending with an offer of reinstatement.

The Board followed this approach for 15 years until 1950 when, in *F.W. Woolworth Co.*,[52] the Board concluded that this form of relief falls short of effectuating the purposes and policies of the Act. Under the old formula, if an employee, sometime after discharge, obtained a better paying job than the one he was discharged from, it became profitable for the employer to delay an offer of reinstatement as long as possible,

---

[51]Pennsylvania Greyhound Lines, 1 NLRB 1, 1 LRRM 303 (1935), enforced sub nom, NLRB v. Pennsylvania Greyhound Lines, 303 U.S. 261, 2 LRRM 600 (1938).
[52]90 NLRB 289, 26 LRRM 1185 (1950).

since every day the employee worked the better paying job the more the employer's back-pay liability was reduced. In addition, employees who obtained higher paying jobs elsewhere were faced with diminishing back-pay returns. As a consequence these employees would waive their right to reinstatement in order to toll the running of back pay and to safeguard the amount owed to them at that time.[53]

(2) Back pay computed on the basis of each separate calendar quarter. Under this formula (commonly referred to as the "Woolworth formula") established by the NLRB and approved by the Supreme Court,[54] the loss of pay is computed on the basis of each separate calendar quarter or portion thereof during the period from the discriminatory act (i.e., discharge, improper transfer, etc.) to the date of an offer of reinstatement. Loss of pay is determined by deducting quarterly net earnings in other employment, if any, from what the employee would have earned for each such quarter. Earnings in one particular quarter have no effect upon the back-pay liability for any other quarter.[55] Under this approach:

> The liability for each quarter may be determined by reference to factors then current, and not subject to subsequent fluctuation. Thus, both employee and employer will be in a position to know with some precision the amount that will be due at the end of each 3-month period, if discrimination should ultimately be found.[56]

Application of this method also protects an employee's right to Social Security benefits, which are based on the number of quarterly contributions from an employee's wages. Thus, the formula serves the remedial purposes of labor law and retirement law.[57]

(3) Other relevant back-pay periods. There is nothing magic about the period that one selects for purposes of measuring

---

[53]Daykin, *Back Pay Under the National Labor Relations Act*, 39 Iowa L. Rev. 104, 123 (1953).

[54]NLRB v. Seven-Up Bottling Co. of Miami, supra note 39.

[55]See, e.g., NLRB v. Rutter-Rex Mfg. Co., 396 U.S. 258, 72 LRRM 2881 (1969); NLRB v. Mercy Peninsula Ambulance Serv., 589 F.2d 1014, 100 LRRM 2769 (9th Cir. 1979); NLRB v. Pilot Freight Carriers, 604 F.2d 375, 102 LRRM 2579 (5th Cir. 1979); Golay & Co. v. NLRB, 447 F.2d 290, 77 LRRM 3041 (7th Cir. 1971). (The quarters established by the Board were: January 1, April 1, July 1, October 1.)

[56]F.W. Woolworth Co., supra note 52 at 293, 26 LRRM at 1186.

[57]City of Great Falls v. Young, 686 P.2d 185, 119 LRRM 2682 (Mont., 1984).

back-pay computation. One could validly use a monthly, bi-weekly, weekly,[58] or even daily[59] period for computing back-pay liability.

(4) Significance of selecting a specific period for computation of back pay. The significance of selecting a particular period for computational purposes may be demonstrated by a fact pattern cited by Arbitrator Patrick Fisher in an address before the National Academy of Arbitrators:

> E was terminated on September 1. On November 1 he obtained a higher-paying job. On January 1 an arbitrator reinstated E with back pay for the period from September 1 to November 1. Then the company claimed that the amount due E from September 1 to November 1 should be reduced by the extra amount E earned from November until the date of the award. Let's say E earned $300.00 a month from the company and $400.00 a month from his new employer. The arbitration award determined that the company had to pay E $600.00 for the months of September and October when he was out of work. The company now says that it should get a $200.00 credit on that obligation because E earned that much more in November and December. How would you handle that one?[60]

For the purposes of computing back pay, if the relevant benchmark period is September 1 (date of discharge) to January 1 (date of reinstatement), then the employer's liability is $400 ($1,200 for the four months the grievant was severed from the payroll, less $800 in interim earnings for the last two months). If, however, the remedy is formulated using each month as a separate "back-pay period," the employer's liability is clearly $600. In effect, an award of $600 will make the grievant more than "whole" only if the reference point is considered from the four-month period taken as one computational period.

To further illustrate the complexities of this computational problem, in *Conner Manufacturing Co.*,[61] Arbitrator Thomas Mulhall reinstated an employee with back pay even though, until the hearing date, the grievant had suffered no

---

[58]New York Shipbuilding Corp., 22 LA 851 (Dash, 1954).
[59]Pacific Mills, 3 LA 141 (McCoy, 1946).
[60]Fisher, *II. Ramifications of Back Pay in Suspension and Discharge Cases*, in Arbitration and Social Change, Proceedings of the 22d Annual Meeting, National Academy of Arbitrators, 175, 179 (BNA Books, 1969).
[61]63 LA 1102 (1974).

loss of earnings. The record indicated that the discharge occurred on August 6. At the September 24 hearings the grievant admitted that his earnings from August 6 to October 22 were actually in excess of the amount that he would have earned from his first employer for that same period. Moreover, in its posthearing brief, the union admitted that the grievant suffered no loss of earnings from the date of discharge to November 12, 1974. The arbitrator, nevertheless, ordered back pay from November 12 to the date of reinstatement (or offered reinstatement), less any monies earned during this period. The award was dated December 4.

In *American Wood Products Co.*,[62] Arbitrator Charles Livengood refused to order back pay where an employee's earnings for the entire discharge period were at least equal to what he would have earned during such period had he not been discharged. The arbitrator rejected the union's contention that earnings in one week should not be offset against earnings lost in another week. Arbitrator Livengood stated that he did not consider the Board's Woolworth policy of computing back pay on a quarterly basis as precedent for going still further and computing it on a weekly basis.[63]

b. Determining "What the Grievant Would Have Earned"

After the designation of a computational period, formulating an appropriate back-pay award under the "make whole" principle mandates a determination, either by the arbitrator or the parties, of the wages that the grievant would have earned but for the discharge. In computing back pay of an employee who is discriminatorily denied employment, attention is called to the policy of the NLRB. The board may estimate damages by reference to another employee who performed the same kind of work the claimant performed or would have performed.[64] Under this method, the employee

---

[62] 17 LA 419 (1951).

[63] Id. at 423, citing F.W. Woolworth Co., supra note 52. See also Reynolds Metals Co., 54 LA 1187 (Purdom, 1970) (" 'interim earnings' includes earnings from all sources by quarter during the period for which back pay is and has been awarded").

[64] See, e.g., NLRB v. Toppino & Sons, 358 F.2d 94, 61 LRRM 2655 (5th Cir. 1966); East Tex. Steel Castings Co., 116 NLRB 1336, 38 LRRM 1470, 1474 (1956), enforced, 255 F.2d 284, 42 LRRM 2109 (5th Cir. 1958).

who replaced the improperly discharged employee is a "representative employee" for the purpose of computing back pay. Thus, the money earned is taken as an estimate of what the grievant would have made.[65]

Another method used by both the Board and arbitrators is the "projection of average earnings" formula.[66] Back pay is based on an estimate of the employee's "average earnings" for some specified period prior[67] to discharge. This formula generally takes into account overtime and other monies that would have been received during that period but for the improper discharge. Adjustments are also made for normal absences of the employee.

(1) Adjusting for lost overtime opportunities. It is generally held that the computation of back pay for an employee who has been improperly discharged may properly be computed to include lost overtime opportunities. Arbitrator Whitley McCoy gave the rationale for this principle in *Masonite Corp.*:[68]

> Ordinarily such pay [overtime] would be denied on the ground that the matter is purely conjectural. In this case it is not conjectural. By the Company's own admission [grievant] would have been required to work, and would have been subject to discipline had he refused. All the other men in his crew worked the extra hours, including the man who took his place. [Grievant] himself had worked all the hours offered him during the shutdown previous to this one. The facts remove the matter entirely from the field of conjecture.[69]

Similarly, Arbitrator George Fleischli, in *Milwaukee Sewerage Commission*,[70] stated:

> Since it is undisputed that the three employees would have been scheduled to work certain overtime hours . . . the loss of those

---

[65]New Albany Concrete Serv., 76 LA 44, 46 (Fitch, 1981) (reinstated employee entitled to back pay based upon number of hours worked by replacement, excluding two weeks spent in county jail for shooting incident).

[66]See, e.g., Ohio Hoist Mfg. Co., 202 NLRB 472, 82 LRRM 1789 (1973), enforced, 496 F.2d 14, 86 LRRM 2135 (6th Cir. 1974).

[67]George Webel d/b/a Webel Feed Mills & Pike Transit Co., 229 NLRB 178, 96 LRRM 1203 (1977) (appropriate period for measuring average weekly wages of discriminatorily discharged employee is year prior to discharge rather than quarter, in view of business' seasonal operations).

[68]10 LA 854 (1948).

[69]Id. at 856.

[70]66 LA 539 (1976).

potential overtime earnings is far from speculative. It is appropriate under these circumstances to make the boat operators whole for the loss of earnings that they apparently suffered by reason of the violation.[71]

Arbitrator Rankin Gibson, in *Alliance Manufacturing Co.,*[72] considered a grievance which, in part, involved a claim for overtime between the date of discharge and the date a strike commenced. The union contended that reinstatement "with backpay" means pay for all hours the grievant would have worked or all work which would have been offered, including overtime hours. In contrast, the employer argued that the grievant was not entitled to any money for overtime since such an award would be speculative absent proof (1) that overtime would have been offered and (2) that the grievant would have worked overtime if offered.

In holding that it would be speculative to make any allowance for overtime during the five-month period of the grievant's discharge, Arbitrator Gibson pointed out that by practice employees are free to decline overtime work. In addition, some of the employees in the grievant's department worked no overtime. Finally the arbitrator found that no evidence was introduced to show how much overtime the grievant herself would have accepted or declined.

Where an employee failed to establish at the hearing or in a posthearing brief that he expected to earn overtime, Arbitrator Samuel Nicholas, in *Standard Brands,*[73] denied such benefits:

> Your Arbitrator is well aware of the fact that the concept back wages may include overtime pay and fringe benefits, as well as direct earnings.
> . . . In the instant case nothing was said at the Hearing to evidence that the Grievant was expecting overtime pay. The Grievant's post-Hearing brief also fails to mention the possibility of the Grievant being denied expected overtime. While it might be argued that the matter was implicit, I am of the thought that the matter must be explicit. For example, if the grievant would have made an argument for back wages and relegating said wages to his past earnings record, including overtime; the overtime earnings record of workers in the same department;

---

[71]Id. at 542.
[72]61 LA 101 (1973).
[73]57 LA 448 (1971).

length and time of production schedules with the payment of overtime, and seasonal fluctuations in production; then your Arbitrator would have some basis to include overtime pay in the Award.[74]

In *Air Treads of Atlanta*,[75] Arbitrator Dorothy Yancy formulated the following test which, in her words, "removes the issues of overtime from the realm of pure conjecture, . . . to a level of reality":

1. Does the grievant have a good attendance record?
2. Did employees in the grievant's classification and work area work overtime during the period in question?
3. Was the grievant available to work overtime in the past?
4. Does the contract language require employees to work overtime?[76]

According to the arbitrator, affirmative responses to the above questions will be necessary for an award of overtime.[77]

The best way to remove the issue from conjecture is to outline in the parties' agreement the elements of make whole relief. Thus, in *Yoh Security, Inc.*,[78] Arbitrator Steven Goldsmith ruled that under a provision that "all awards of back wages shall be limited to the amounts of wages the employee would have earned from his straight-time employment . . . less any unemployment compensation," he was precluded from considering lost overtime in computing back pay. Arbitrator Goldsmith reasoned that the parties, in negotiating this language, were concerned with the involvement of "mythical time" in computing the grievant's back wages.

In *Darby Printing Co.*,[79] Arbitrator George Savage King considered an argument that, since the grievant's job was filled by an employee who performed the same work the griev-

---

[74]Id. at 450. Compare to Norris Indus., 70-1 ARB ¶8207 (Edelman, 1969) (back pay awarded to employee improperly passed over for promotion was to include overtime wanted by employee who was promoted to that position). Dare Pafco, Inc. 73-2 ARB ¶8478 (High, 1973) (proper test is overtime grievant would have worked under "make whole" principle, notwithstanding that grievant did not request benefit).
[75]85 LA 155 (1985).
[76]Id. at 158.
[77]Other arbitrators have followed suit. See, e.g., Sparklett Devices, 88-2 ARB ¶8388 (Fowler, 1988); Menasha Corp., 90 LA 427, 431 (Clark, 1987) (awarding overtime compensation for each month during back-pay period equal to overtime received by grievant in corresponding month of previous year, provided overtime work available during back-pay period).
[78]85 LA 196, 197 (1985).
[79]68-1 ARB ¶8138 (1967).

ant had performed, the measure of back pay should be the hours worked by the employee—both regular and overtime—less the amount earned by the grievant in the interim. The employer asserted that the agreement neither guaranteed overtime to an employee nor required its assignment on the basis of seniority or an equal distribution among any group of employees. In the alternative, the employer asserted that if overtime was to be awarded, the grievant should not be compared to his replacement, because the grievant was a slow employee and would not have been given similar overtime.

Arbitrator King, in holding that some overtime was due, stated that he was not persuaded that the grievant would necessarily have worked the same amount of overtime, or even the same straight-time hours, that his replacement had. The arbitrator instead found that the most equitable method of calculating back pay was to use the average number of hours per week, both straight time and overtime, that the grievant worked in the 50 weeks prior to his discharge.

Similarly, in *Retail Clerks Local 37 v. Five Star Food Center*,[80] a federal district court upheld an arbitrator's award of back pay with an allocation for overtime, even though the contract provided for a basic workweek of 40 hours, with assignment of overtime at management's discretion. The court, agreeing with the arbitrator's formula, stated that in measuring the loss due to an improper discharge, the relevant fact is not how many hours the employer was required to work the grievant, but how many hours the grievant would have worked but for the discharge.

In summary, while arbitrators differ on the calculation of overtime, when it is clear that the employee was entitled to (and would have worked) overtime if not wrongfully discharged, the grievant is usually granted such benefits upon reinstatement. The better rule is not how many hours the employer was required to employ the grievant, but how many hours the grievant would have worked but for the improper discharge.

(2) Adjusting for absenteeism. Arbitrators have ruled that the computation of back pay for an employee who has been

---

[80]103 LRRM 2252 (N.D. Ill. 1979).

improperly discharged should reflect a poor attendance record prior to her discharge.[81] This principle is well illustrated by Arbitrator Ralph Seward in *Bethlehem Steel.*[82] In a supplemental decision, Arbitrator Seward considered the back-pay claim of an employee who had previously been reinstated. The union submitted that back pay should be computed on the assumption that the employee would have worked at his old job all the time he was scheduled to work, thus crediting him with 40 hours a week at straight time plus any applicable overtime, shift differential, incentive, and vacation pay. The employer argued that the back-pay calculation should be based on the assumption that the employee would have worked no more than he usually had in the past. In this regard the employer pointed out that during the 66 weeks preceding his discharge the employee worked an average of only 22.57 hours per week; all other hours between 22.57 and 40.00 were missed because of absenteeism. Since this figure was less than the grievant actually made as interim earnings, the employer argued that no back pay was due.

The arbitrator concluded that both parties carried their positions to unjustified extremes:

> The Union would have [grievant's] prior record of unjustified absenteeism completely disregarded and have [grievant's] back pay computed on the assumption that if he had not been discharged his attendance record . . . would have been perfect. The Company, on the other hand, includes among the "absences" charged against [grievant] in computing his average attendance, many absences for which he is considered to have had an acceptable excuse (days of illness, when a doctor's excuse was presented; certain days when he was required to be in court; etc.); a week of vacation and a number of holidays on which he was not scheduled to work; and other [times] . . . where he was off pending a disciplinary investigation which resulted in his

---

[81]Kansas Power & Light Co., 87-1 ARB ¶8038 (Belcher, 1986), at 3157 (back pay with deduction "for anticipated time lost for all reasons, but not less than equal to [grievant's] absences for 12 months preceding [date of discharge]."); Bethlehem Steel Corp. 71 LA 1003 (Strongin, 1978) (period of "total disability" excluded as nonrecurring period of absence); McCreary Tire & Rubber Co., 77-1 ARB ¶8218 (Lewinter, 1977); Fairchild Engine & Airplane Corp., 33 LA 146 (Sugerman, 1959); Oklahoma Furniture Mfg. Co., 24 LA 522 (1955) (average number of hours/week); Ford Motor Co., 20 LA 13 (Schulman, 1952); Weber Aircraft, 19 LA 166 (Spaulding, 1952); Universal Dishwashing Mach. Co., 17 LA 737 (Reynolds, 1952) (back pay computed at 80 percent to reflect attendance record); Neon Prods., 13 LA 204 (Lehoczky, 1949); Bell Aircraft Corp., 1 LA 281 (Griffin, undated).
[82]57 LA 536 (1971).

reinstatement with full pay. The Umpire can accompany neither side in its extreme and (in both cases) somewhat punitive approach to this issue.[83]

The best evidence, stated Seward, of what the grievant's attendance would have been, had he not been discharged, was the record of his actual attendance at the job he obtained after being discharged. Finding that the grievant would have been present 96 percent of the time, Arbitrator Seward held that the employee should receive 96 percent of the straight and overtime pay, shift differential, and incentive and vacation pay he would have received but for the discharge.[84]

A "projected absence" figure was computed by Arbitrator Rankin Gibson in *Alliance Manufacturing*.[85] In formulating a back-pay award, the arbitrator noted that in the first eight months of 1972, during which time the grievant took two weeks of vacation, she was absent 11 additional days. Using seven and one-half months as a base, the grievant's average absence per month was 1.357 days. Based upon this figure, the arbitrator projected her loss of earnings for a six-month back-pay period.

Robert Gorske has summarized this area as follows:

Though they rest sheerly on speculation, the reported cases which reveal consideration of the question appear uniform in providing for some deduction if the employer can show a prior pattern of absenteeism. However, since these cases proceed upon the mere assumption that the employee would have continued the same attendance pattern during the contested period, it would seem clear that the employee rebut his assumption by evidence showing that the cause of absenteeism (for example, illness or care of a sick relative) had disappeared or diminished during such period.[86]

(3) Bonuses, insurance, pension contributions, vacation and holiday pay, and other monetary relief. A review of Board, court, and arbitral decisions indicates that "make whole" relief may, but need not, include any of the following:

A special bonus (Christmas, merit, etc.) or wage increase received in grievant's department, section, or plant,

---

[83]Id. at 537–538.
[84]Id. at 538.
[85]Supra note 72.
[86]Gorske, *Arbitration Back-Pay Awards*, 10 Lab. L.J. 18, 27 (1959).

which, but for the improper dismissal, grievant would have received.[87]

Any expenses incurred by reason of removal from any insurance benefit program. In this respect, a back-pay award may properly include any hospital or medical expenses incurred at a time that the improperly terminated employee would have been covered by the employer-maintained program.[88]

Contributions or "credits" to a pension or welfare retirement fund that were not made on behalf of the employee during the discriminatory discharge.[89]

Lost seniority credits.[90]

Adjustments made in connection with a supplementary unemployment benefit fund. Lost credits or, alternatively, credits that were "used up" may be corrected to reflect "make whole" relief.[91]

---

[87]Lizdale Knitting Mills, 232 NLRB 592, 97 LRRM 1565 (1977) (15-cent/hour increase in federal minimum wage); NLRB v. Madison Courier, Inc., 472 F.2d 1307, 80 LRRM 3377 (D.C. Cir. 1972); Golay & Co., 184 NLRB 241, 76 LRRM 1110 (1970); NLRB v. United States Air Conditioning Corp., 336 F.2d 275, 277, 57 LRRM 2068 (6th Cir. 1964); W.C. Nabors Co. v. NLRB, 323 F.2d 686, 690, 54 LRRM 2259 (5th Cir. 1963), cert. denied, 376 U.S. 911, 55 LRRM 2455 (1964); Brass-Craft Mfg. Co., 61-3 ARB ¶8743 (Kahn, 1961).

[88]NLRB v. Laborers Local 38, 748 F.2d 1001, 118 LRRM 2062 (5th Cir. 1984) (only medical expenses that qualify under employer's plan recoverable as make-whole remedy); DeLorean Cadillac, 231 NLRB 329, 96 LRRM 1347 (1977); NLRB v. Rice Lake Creamery Co., 365 F.2d 888, 892–893, 62 LRRM 2332 (D.C. Cir. 1966) (NLRB warranted in allowing hospital and medical expenses to employees, after deducting amounts equal to premiums employees would have paid, where employees would have recovered such expenses under group insurance plan had employer not violated Act); Deena Artware, 112 NLRB 371, 36 LRRM 1028 (1955), enforced, 228 F.2d 871, 37 LRRM 2231 (6th Cir. 1955) (medical maternity benefits payable under terms of group insurance policy included in back pay.

See also Amshu Assocs., 234 NLRB 791, 97 LRRM 1360 (1978) (reimbursement for insurance premiums); American-International Aluminum Corp., 49 LA 728 (Howlett, 1967); American Chain & Cable Co., 40 LA 312 (McDermott, 1963).

[89]NLRB v. Rice Lake Creamery Co., 365 F.2d 888, 62 LRRM 2332 (D.C. Cir. 1966) (pension contributions); Sioux Falls Stock Yards Co., 236 NLRB 543, 99 LRRM 1316 (1978) (pension fund contributions to union); Merchants Home Delivery Serv., 234 NLRB 1040, 97 LRRM 1419 (1978) (health and welfare contributions); Cowlitz Redi-Mix, 85 LA 745, 753 (Boedecker, 1985) (awarding holiday and pension payments); Evening News Ass'n, 68 LA 1318 (Volz, 1977) (contributions for pension and sick-leave fund).

[90]While most reinstatements will be with full seniority, there are a few select cases where arbitrators have not credited an employee with full seniority upon reinstatement. See, e.g., Alabama Power Co., 66 LA 220 (Caraway, 1976) (10-month suspension without pay and loss of seniority during suspension); University of Cal., 63 LA 314 (Jacobs, 1974) (reinstatement without back pay or accrual of seniority from date of discharge to date of reemployment).

[91]Brass-Craft Mfg. Co., supra note 87.

Wages and tool allowances uniformly made available to similarly situated employees.[92]

Reasonable expenses incurred in seeking and maintaining interim employment.[93]

Credits for holiday and vacation pay.[94]

Shift differentials.[95]

Promotions.[96]

6. Federal Sector

An employee who meets the requirements of the Back Pay Act, 5 U.S.C. §5596, is entitled to receive, for the period the improper agency action was in effect, an amount equal to all or part of the employee's pay, allowances, or differentials and leave recreditation, as applicable, that normally would have been earned had the wrongful action not occurred.[97] In computing back pay for the period covered by the corrective action, the following items may (but need not) be included:

Premium Pay.

Changes in pay rates by reason of wage surveys, administrative action, law, or other changes of general application.

Within-grade or step increases which would otherwise have become due "but for" the improper removal.

Changes in pay caused by changes in assigned working shifts.

---

[92]Nelson-Hershfield Elecs., 188 NLRB 26, 77 LRRM 1013 (1971).

[93]Aircraft & Helicopter Leasing & Sales, 227 NLRB 644, 94 LRRM 1556 (1976); Famet, Inc., 222 NLRB 1180, 91 LRRM 1473 (1976); Braniff Airways, 31 LA 1018 (Schedler, 1958); Northland Greyhound Lines, 23 LA 277 (Levinson, 1954) (transportation expenses to hearing).

[94]Westinghouse Elec. Corp., 237 NLRB 1209, 99 LRRM 1184 (1978); Sioux Falls Stock Yards Co., supra note 89; Alliance Mfg. Co., 61 LA 101 (Gibson, 1973); Dare Pafco, Inc., supra note 74; American-International Aluminum Corp., supra note 88; Darby Printing Co., 49 LA 828 (King, 1967); Heckman Furniture Co., 39 LA 1148 (Cole, 1963); Pittsburgh-Des Moines Steel, Co., 38 LA 148 (Wood, 1962); Logan-Long Co., 63-2 ARB ¶8722 (Warns, 1962); R.C. Williams & Co., 33 LA 428 (Knowlton, 1959); North Range Mining Co., 29 LA 724 (Howlett, 1957); Cone Mills Corp., 29 LA 346 (McCoy, 1957).

[95]McCreary Tire & Rubber Co., supra note 81; Rohr Indus., 65 LA 778 (Hardbeck, 1975); Towmotor Corp., 66-3 ARB ¶9028 (Kates, 1966); Cities Serv. Petroleum Co., 37 LA 888 (Edes, 1961).

[96]Underwood Mach. Co., 95 NLRB 1386, 28 LRRM 1447 (1951); Dinion Coil Co., 96 NLRB 1435, 29 LRRM 1049 (1951).

[97]5 U.S.C. §5596(b)(1)(A)(i)(1982).

Changes in employee's leave-earnings rate.

Any other changes which would affect the amount of pay, allowances, differentials, or leave which the employee would have earned had it not been for the action.

Living quarters allowance (where employee would have received allowance "but for" improper removal). Training costs where incurred after removal and agency would have paid costs "but for" unjustified removal).[98]

Since 1987, interest is allowed on back pay in the federal sector.

Authority is also provided under federal law to restore health insurance benefits to employees reinstated under the Back Pay Act. There is no authorization, however, for reimbursement to restored employees for commercial health insurance purchased during periods when unjustified or unwarranted removals or suspensions were in effect.[99] Thus, an employee who obtains private health insurance during a period of improper removal will not be reimbursed the cost of that insurance. Following an improper suspension or removal, an employee is permitted to enroll in a health insurance program as a new employee or, alternatively, the employee may elect to have the original insurance restored.

Must an arbitrator award back pay for all or even part of the time that an improper discharge was in effect? In *Government Employees (AFGE) Local 2718 v. Immigration & Naturalization Service*,[100] the Federal Circuit, applying the same standard of appeals from Merit System Protection Board cases,[101] held that an arbitrator is not mandated by the Back Pay Act to award back pay for a period greater than that encompassed by a 15-day suspension. Unable to find any provision in the Act which precludes an arbitrator from denying back pay as part of a mitigated penalty, or which limits a denial of back pay to a period of suspension, the Federal Circuit effectively adopted the private-sector model.

---

[98]See Guest, *The Remedial Authority of Arbitrators in the Federal Sector*, in Grievance Arbitration in the Federal Service, 63–113 (FPMI, 1987). See also *Remedies Available and Not Available in the Federal System: A Synthesis*, in Federal Civil Service Law and Procedure: A Basic Guide 383–391, 2d ed. (BNA Books, 1990).

[99]5 U.S.C. §§8908 & 5596.

[100]768 F.2d 348 (Fed. Cir. 1985).

[101]Cornelius v. Nutt, 472 U.S. 648, 119 LRRM 2905 (1985).

B. Reductions in Back Pay

Should earnings from a second job be deducted from a back-pay award? Suppose the employee earned more at the second job during the interim period? What if the employee worked two jobs? Or suppose the grievant earned more at the new job because he worked overtime or worked Saturdays and Sundays? Should unemployment compensation, union benefits, or welfare payments be deducted? Suppose the grievant never looked for work? Does a discharged employee have a duty to seek other employment?

As a starting point, the usual period for calculating back pay typically begins to run at the time of the discharge and ends when the employee's reinstatement becomes effective. This remedial period can be reduced if there is proof of mitigating circumstances. The law is clear that actual interim earnings and willfully incurred losses will be deducted from an order of back pay issued by the NLRB. Thus in *Phelps Dodge Corp. v. NLRB*,[102] the Supreme Court, in ruling on the issue of "make whole" relief, stated:

> Making the workers whole for losses suffered on account of an unfair labor practice is part of the vindication of the public policy which the Board enforces. Since only actual losses should be made good, it seems fair that deductions should be made not only for actual earnings by the worker but also for losses which he willfully incurred.[103]

The burden is on the employer to prove such earnings or losses.[104] Failure to mitigate damages by a refusal to search for alternative work or by a refusal to accept substantially equivalent employment is an affirmative defense and, if proven, will result in a corresponding reduction in a back-pay award.[105] However, as stated by the Fifth Circuit, the employer does not

---

[102]313 U.S. 177, 8 LRRM 439 (1941).
[103]Id., 8 LRRM at 448.
[104]Id. at 449; NLRB v. Pilot Freight Carriers, 604 F.2d 375, 102 LRRM 2579 (5th Cir. 1979); Dayton Tire & Rubber Co. v. NLRB, 591 F.2d 566, 100 LRRM 2549 (10th Cir. 1979); NLRB v. Avon Convalescent Center, 549 F.2d 1080, 95 LRRM 2368 (6th Cir. 1977); NLRB v. Carpenters Local 1913, 531 F.2d 424, 91 LRRM 2542 (9th Cir. 1976).
[105]Alfred M. Lewis, Inc. v. NLRB, 681 F.2d 1154, 110 LRRM 3280 (9th Cir. 1982) (upholding NLRB's determination that job offered employee was not "equivalent" employment because it paid only $2.35/hour as opposed to $6.40/hour received in prior job; NLRB v. Mooney Aircraft, 366 F.2d 809, 63 LRRM 2208 (5th Cir. 1966); NLRB v. Miami Coca-Cola Bottling Co., 360 F.2d 569, 62 LRRM 2155 (5th Cir. 1966).

meet its burden merely by proving that the employee failed to find interim employment. The law requires only "reasonable exertions" in this regard, not the highest standard of diligence.[106]

1. Interim or Outside Earnings

With few exceptions[107] arbitrators, like the courts and the NLRB, will deduct "interim earnings" from an award of back pay. The reason for taking into account money earned in other employment is that such wages could not have been earned if the employee had not been discharged. Accordingly, a reinstated employee that was allowed to keep interim earnings would be placed in a better position than if there had been no discharge. Arbitrator John Sembower, in *Universal Producing Co.*,[108] has explained the policy as follows:

> The basic idea which the common law has followed is that such a claimant is entitled to "damages" measured by what they would have earned. During the period of their idleness, said the courts, they did not need to make an extraordinary effort to obtain compensating employment, but if they did, in fact, accomplish earnings of any sort these were to be deducted from the award of "full back pay." That is, the claimant (or Grievant, in this instance) should not be "unjustly enriched" by receiving an award which would constitute a windfall by giving them more money than they otherwise would have received, if they had never been terminated. This requires, of course, a deduction from the award of "back pay" of the earnings which they received from other sources during the pendency of their dispute.[109]

Arbitrator Sembower goes on to state that deducting the outside pay from other sources will be simple in most cases:

> It simply calls for the Grievant to supply a statement of the

---

[106]NLRB v. Pilot Freight Carrier, supra note 104, 102 LRRM at 2580, citing NLRB v. Arduini Mfg. Corp., 394 F.2d 420, 68 LRRM 2129 (1st Cir. 1968). See also Heinrich Motors v. NLRB, 403 F.2d 145, 69 LRRM 2613 (2d Cir. 1968); NLRB v. Brown & Root, 311 F.2d 447, 52 LRRM 2115 (8th Cir. 1963).

[107]ESB, Inc. 70-1 ARB ¶8172 (Amis, 1969) (question not one of actual damages suffered, but of employer's contractual obligation to reinstate without loss of pay); Dubuque, Lorenz, Inc., 66 LA 1245 (Sinicropi, 1976).

[108]57 LA 1072 (1971).

[109]Id. at 1073.

earnings which they received from other employers while their claim was pending against the instant Company.[110]

Where an arbitrator awarded "straight pay for all time lost as the result of [grievant's] discharge" without deducting interim earnings, one federal court, in enforcing the award, stated that a setoff should be effected. According to the court:

> In enforcing the arbitrator's award this court must assure that the grievant receives just compensation. Although the award makes no specific mention as to a deduction of interim earnings actually received by grievant, this court finds that to allow grievant to recover back pay without deducting interim earnings would be unfair, inequitable and not within the intent of a compensatory award. The court therefore finds that as a matter of law the grievant is entitled to back pay with a reasonable deduction for interim earnings.[111]

a. Secondary Employment as "Interim Earnings"

Arbitrator Whitley McCoy, in *Martin Co.*,[112] stated the following principle that is often followed in computing "interim earnings" as an offset to back pay:

> It is a principle or rule of the law of damages that for breach of a contract of employment recovery may only be had of the sum lost *by reason of the breach*, i.e., the wages or salary lost by reason of the firing. If another job has been secured *in lieu of the one discharged from*, or if by reasonable diligence the discharged man could have secured a suitable job in place of the one discharged from, then the deduction is to be made. That is the law.[113]

Although the contract provided that any award of back pay should exclude "benefits or other compensation for personal services received from any source during the period in question," Arbitrator McCoy, in refusing to deduct monies earned from "moonlighting," reasoned that if the parties had intended

---

[110]Id.

[111]Operating Eng'rs Local 675 v. Trumbull Corp., 98 LRRM 2406, 2406 (S.D. Fla 1978). It is noteworthy that the court also awarded interest on the unpaid back pay, but denied the union attorney's fees "[s]ince there is not sufficient evidence to indicate that the defendant acted in bad faith . . . ." See also Segarra v. Sea-Land Serv., 581 F.2d 291, 99 LRRM 2198 (1st Cir. 1978).

[112]49 LA 255 (1967).

[113]Id. at 257 (emphasis in original).

a different measure of damages than that prescribed by the law, they could have expressly so stated.[114]

In *American-International Aluminum Corp.*,[115] an employee, during the interim of his discharge, expanded his farming operations. Arbitrator Robert Howlett, in ruling that only the extra, or additional, income from farming could be used to mitigate damages, stated:

> While there are some cases which hold that discharged employees who "elect recklessly to embark on a risky business venture of their own," have not complied with the requirement to mitigate damages, these cases are not applicable here. . . .
>
> If grievant had started farming after his discharge . . . [these cases] might apply. Grievant, however, was engaged in farming at the time of his discharge and had experienced a successful year in 1965. Thus a decision to increase his farming operations, rather than seek a factory job, was bona fide self-employment. . . .[116]

To the extent that grievant worked during his regular working hours and thus increased his profit, Arbitrator Howlett held that these monies should decrease the employer's liability. In view of the employee's failure to keep adequate records of his farming operations, the case was again returned to the parties to attempt to determine the amount due the grievant.

Similarly, Arbitrator Thomas McDermott stated that a deduction for earnings in other employment may be made only if the employees, during that period, engaged in regular employment as distinguished from odd jobs or part-time employment. The arbitrator's reasoning was that income from odd jobs or part-time employment could be earned even during an employee's regular working periods.[117]

Arbitrator J. Earl Williams, in *Markle Manufacturing*

---

[114]It is noteworthy that the stated reason for discharge in *Martin Co.* was unrelated to the grievant's secondary employment.

[115]49 LA 728 (1967).

[116]Id. at 730.

[117]American Chain & Cable Co., 40 LA 312 (1963). Besides the cases discussed in this section, see American Iron & Mach. Works Co., 19 LA 417 (Merrill, 1952); United Eng & Foundry Co., 37 LA 1095 (Kates, 1962); Wilshire Indus., 71 LA 56, 58 (Mueller, 1978); Golay & Co, 184 NLRB 241, 76 LRRM 1110 (1970) (earnings from "moonlighting" normally earned not included in "interim earnings"); Max Factor & Co., 47 LA 378 (Jones, 1966); Alcan Aluminum Corp., 90 LA 16, 20 (Volz, 1987) (employee dismissed for moonlighting while on leave reinstated without back pay where grievant had earnings from moonlighting).

Co.,[118] considered the difficulties involved when a part-time job becomes a full-time job. In that case the grievant, working as a part-time taxi driver, earned an average of $169.76 per quarter while still employed for Markle. After his discharge, the employee averaged $665.38 per quarter as a full-time driver. Since the percentage of part-time to full-time income was 25.5 percent, the employee argued that 25.5 percent of his income should not be counted as "interim earnings" for purposes of reducing the employer's back-pay liability.

While acknowledging that it is generally held by arbitrators that wages from part-time employment will not be used to mitigate the employer's liability if the grievant was engaged in those activities while employed full-time, Arbitrator Williams nevertheless found that this rule was inapplicable in this case since the grievant did not work to the same extent he had in his old position. Although the grievant worked approximately the same number of hours in both jobs, the arbitrator found that the employee worked only four to five days in his "new" job, as compared to six and one-half days per week while at Markle. Williams held that all the grievant's reported earnings should accordingly be used to mitigate the employer's liability.

b. *"Overtime" Earnings During Interim Period*

The NLRB has held that overtime earnings in interim employment are similar to supplemental pay or earnings from "moonlighting," and thus should not be deducted from back-pay orders.[119] This position, however, has not always been accepted by appellate courts. For example, in *McCann Steel Co. v. NLRB*,[120] the Sixth Circuit held that "substantially equivalent employment" refers to the hours worked for the interim employer as well as the nature of the work there:

> Thus [grievant] refused to accept "substantially equivalent employment" when he refused to work the same number of hours

---

[118]73 LA 1292 (1980).
[119]McCann Steel Co., 224 NLRB 607, 93 LRRM 1365 (1976); United Aircraft Corp., 204 NLRB 1068, 83 LRRM 1616 (1973); Southeastern Envelope Co., 206 NLRB 933, 84 LRRM 1577 (1973) (overtime pay excluded from interim earnings where gross back-pay computation does not include overtime).
[120]570 F.2d 652, 97 LRRM 2921 (5th Cir. 1978).

at his interim employer as he had worked at McCann. This was a willful loss of earnings. The NLRB should calculate a constructive interim earnings figure based upon the amount of pay [grievant] would have received at his interim employer had he always worked the same number of hours, including overtime, he averaged at McCann to the extent those hours were available at the interim employer. The NLRB should then deduct the new constructive interim earnings figure from the amount [grievant] would have earned at McCann in calculating the back pay award.[121]

In *Caterpillar Tractor Co.*,[122] Arbitrator John Larkin held that an employer had no monetary liability where an employee's interim earnings from other employment exceeded what he would have made at his regular job. Although a substantial part of such interim earnings came from overtime work the employee would not have earned had he not been discharged, the arbitrator nevertheless stated that overtime earnings should be counted as "interim earnings" where the past practice of the employer had been to compute retroactive payment in this manner.

c. Strike Benefits or Other Assistance Payments as "Interim Earnings"

Where monetary or other "in kind" benefits flow from the association with the union or some other "non-employer," the authors, similar to the Board, take the position that these benefits should not be used as a "setoff" in computing the employer's back-pay liability if they are not "earned."[123]

---

[121]Id., 97 LRRM at 2923. The Sixth Circuit also held that the employer had the burden of proof to show a willful loss of earnings as an affirmative defense to its back-pay liability. This burden was met when McCann showed grievant's procurement of interim employment and the ready availability of overtime there.

[122]39 LA 910 (1962).

[123]Florence Printing Co. v. NLRB, 376 F.2d 216, 65 LRRM 2047 (4th Cir.), cert. denied, 389 U.S. 840, 66 LRRM 2307 (1967) (benefits paid from union trust fund during strikes, lockouts, and shutdowns excluded from "earnings") NLRB v. Rice Lake Creamery Co., 365 F.2d 888, 62 LRRM 2332 (D.C. Cir. 1966) (union strike benefits excluded where picketing was not absolute requirement); NLRB v. Braschear Freight Lines, 127 F.2d 198, 199, 10 LRRM 578 (8th Cir. 1942) (employer not entitled to deduct, from back pay, value of groceries that union furnished to discharged employee who was engaged in picketing, absent a showing that groceries were furnished for performing picket duty); Florida Steel Corp., 234 NLRB 1089, 98 LRRM 1080 (1978) (strike benefits included as interim earnings where condition of receiving benefits was picket duty). See also NLRB v. Madison Courier, 472 F.2d 1307, 80 LRRM 3377, 3386 n.51 (D.C. Cir. 1972); Chemical Leaman Tank Lines, 57 LA 538 (Cahn, 1971) (welfare benefits included in "interim earnings").

In this regard, in *Sears Roebuck & Co.*,[124]Arbitrator Arthur Miller held that an employer violated the agreement in discharging employees for refusing to cross a picket line of another union. As a remedy the arbitrator ordered back pay based on an average weekly-earnings figure for a 52-week period. Insofar as assistance payments were made by the union, Arbitrator Miller determined that the employees were to be made whole by the employer without deduction for such assistance payments. At the same time, the arbitrator held that it would be a patent duplication to award the aggregate of the assistance payments to the union as compensatory damages for the employer's breach of the agreement.

Similarly, Arbitrator Samuel Nicholas, Jr., reports a decision in which he ruled that social security disability payments are not "earnings" for purposes of mitigating damages awarded in a make-whole order of reinstatement.[125] But where public assistance or welfare benefits are paid in lieu of wages, an arbitrator may order a setoff.[126]

d. "In-Kind" Income

Should an arbitrator allow a setoff for "in-kind" income? Arbitrator Sidney Wolff cited a situation where a successful grievant, during an interim layoff, did not seek alternative employment but, rather, decided to paint his house. In computing the employer's liability, Arbitrator Wolff deducted $400 that the employee saved by not paying a painting contractor.[127] Arbitrator Wolff's position is the minority view.

e. Spousal Income as Interim Earnings

Can a spouse's income serve as a setoff to an employer's back-pay liability? An employee is dismissed and during the

---

[124]35 LA 757 (1960).

[125]Boise Cascade Corp., 90 LA 748 (1988).

[126]United States Steel, 52 LA 1210, 1212 (Dybeck, 1969); Orlando Transit Co., 71 LA 897, 903 (Serot, 1978) (ordering deduction for unemployment compensation but not G.I. Bill benefits, reasoning that G.I. benefits not compensation for work performed within employer-employee relationship).

[127]Wolff, supra note 31, at 178. See also Olson Bros., 61-3 ARB ¶8855 (Jones, 1961) (no compensation due where employee built house during interim period); Mixon v. Rossiter, 223 S.C. 47, 74 S.E.2d 46 (1953) (setoff of estimated value of employee's work done on his own home not required).

relevant back-pay period the employee's spouse, to make up the loss in income, takes a job while the grievant remains home with the pets and children. Under these circumstances the authors see no infirmity in reducing the employer's back-pay liability by the amount the spouse earned. But for the grievant's dismissal, the spouse would not have entered the labor market. Thus, a setoff is consistent with make-whole relief. If, however, the grievant's spouse already had a job and additional income was not realized *as a result of the discharge*, a setoff is not appropriate.

Suppose the grievant's 13-year-old daughter, eager to do her part to help the family cause, earned some extra babysitting money during the back-pay period? Dispensing our own brand of industrial justice, absent explicit contract language to the contrary, we would draw the line at the spouse's income.

2. The Duty to Mitigate Damages

An alternative approach, and one that appears to be preferred by most (but not all) arbitrators, is simply to reduce the employer's liability for the grievant's failure to mitigate damages.[128] In this respect, except in unusual circumstances, arbitrators require that an aggrieved employee has a duty to attempt to mitigate any loss he might suffer as a result of the employer's improper assessment of discipline. Arbitrator Sidney Wolff has stated this principle as follows:

---

[128]The Restatement of Contracts §336 (1932) expresses the requirement that a plaintiff mitigate damages as follows:
  Section 336. Avoidable Harm; Losses Incurred In Efforts to Avoid Harm. (1) Damages are not recoverable for harm that plaintiff should have foreseen and could have avoided by reasonable effort without undue risk, expense or humiliation. (2) Damages are recoverable for special losses incurred in a reasonable effort, whether successful or not, to avoid harm that the defendant had reason to foresee as a probable result of his breach when the contract was made. Comment d to §336 declares:
  d. It is not infrequently said that it is the "duty" of the injured party to mitigate damages so far as that can be done by reasonable effort on his part. Since his legal position is in no way affected by his failure to make this effort, however, it is not desirable to say that he is under a "duty." His remedy will be exactly the same, whether he makes the effort and avoids harm or not. But if he fails to make the reasonable effort with the result that his harm is greater than it would otherwise have been, he cannot get judgment for the amount of this avoidable and unnecessary increase. The law does not penalize his inaction; it merely does nothing to compensate him for the harm that a reasonable man in his place would have avoided.

I believe, in a discharge or similar situation, that the employee is obligated to minimize his damages; he is required to make reasonable efforts to obtain gainful employment; he may not sit at home "licking his chops" in anticipation of the large money award that may be in the offing.[129]

Under a contract providing that an unjustly discharged employee shall be . . . paid for all time lost," Arbitrator Lewis Solomon held:

It is commonly and generally recognized that the purpose of a contract provision calling for payment of "all time lost", when disciplinary action or discharge has been found to be without justifiable cause is to compensate and indemnify the injured employee and make him whole for loss of earnings suffered by him as a result of the inappropriate exercise of judgment by the Company. The loss of earnings is usually to be measured by the wages he would have earned for the period they were improperly denied to him, subject, however, to a recognized duty and responsibility reposed in the employee to mitigate, so far as reasonable, the amount of that loss. If, as a result of employee's action or inaction, he has failed to mitigate the loss, then to the degree of such failure he is himself partially responsible.[130]

And Arbitrator Edgar Jones has likewise declared:

A grievant has the responsibility of lessening his damages, if possible. He cannot fairly expect to sit back and reject the economic resources at hand to tide him over the period of his dispute with his employer. Here, [G.] chose to undertake a four months project of building his home. It would hardly be equitable to allow him to compel his employer to underwrite that project.[131]

The contrary position is raised by Arbitrator David Feller. After conceding that arbitrators often speak in terms of the duty to mitigate damages, Feller argues that there is no duty to "mitigate damages" because the arbitrator does not award damages. According to Feller:

There is, or should be, therefore, no requirement that the em-

---

[129]Wolff, supra note 31, at 178.
[130]Love Bros., 45 LA 751, 756 (1965).
[131]Olson Bros., supra note 127, at 6878. See also Sparklett Devices, 90 LA 910 (Fowler, 1988) (reinstated employee who may not have been most persistent job seeker is entitled to back pay despite claim that he did not use due diligence to find employment, where he applied for work at considerably lower level than that from which he was fired, reported periodically to unemployment office, answered job advertisements, and applied directly for jobs).

ployee seek other employment ('gnt, and no deduction from the employee's back pay because of his failure to do so. . . . [T]he cases in which an employer raises this defense are, at least in my experience, rare, as are the agreements providing for such a duty. The fact indicates to me that the parties do not really regard this as an element to be considered in determining the appropriate arbitral remedy in a discharge case.[132]

We believe that the better rule is articulated by Arbitrators Wolff, Solomon, and Jones.[133] A discharged employee should be required to make a reasonable effort to mitigate "damages" by seeking substantially equivalent employment. The reasonableness of his effort should be evaluated in light of the individual's qualifications and the relevant job market. His burden is not onerous, and does not require that he be successful in mitigating his "damages." Further, the burden of proving lack of diligence or an honest, good faith effort on the employee's part is on management. The employee's expenses in securing alternative employment may properly be included in a back-pay award.

a. Willful Loss of Employment

A difficult issue within the employment context is determining what constitutes "willful loss of employment." Court

---

[132]Feller, *The Remedy Power in Grievance Arbitration*, 5 Indus. Rel. L.J. 128, 145 (1982). Arbitrators adopting this view include: American Bakeries Co., 77 LA 531 (Modjeska, 1981) (acknowledging propriety of deducting sums actually earned, but holding no authority to impose a duty to mitigate damages in absence of contractual mandate); Shakespeare & Shakespeare Prods. Co., 9 LA 813, 817–818. (Platt, 1948) (proper to deduct from back-pay award sums actually earned by employee before reinstatement, including unemployment compensation; no authority to penalize employee financially for failing to have earnings).

[133]Other arbitrators have adopted this same view. See, e.g., Niemand Indus., 88-1 ARB ¶8070 (Sergent, 1987), at 3340 (grievant who did not apply for employment more than six weeks after occurrence of discharge denied back pay for that period, reasoning that "it is a well-recognized arbitral principle that a discharged employee has a duty to mitigate the damages he or she incurs by actively seeking comparable employment."); Aerol Aircraft Employees Ass'n & Cleveland Pneumatic Co., 88-1 ARB ¶8116 (Sharpe, 1987), at 3563 ("grievant's failure to seek alternative employment during the period between his discharge and reinstatement reflects 'willful idleness' that the mitigation doctrine attempts to correct."); Kansas Power & Light Co., 87-1 ARB ¶8038 (Belcher, 1986), at 3157 ("amount of back pay is to be further reduced if it is found that the Grievant did not earnestly seek other employment during the period following termination so as to mitigate 'damages.'"); Orlando Transit Co., 71 LA 897, 900 (Serot, 1978) ("dischargee cannot sit idly by and let back pay accumulate, taking a vacation, as it were, at the expense of the employer. . . . [but] is obligated to make reasonable efforts to seek other employment and thereby mitigate the losses.").

decisions, Board rulings, and arbitration awards reveal that an employee is not entitled to back pay to the extent that he fails to remain in the labor market, refuses to accept substantially equivalent employment, fails to search for alternative work, or voluntarily quits alternative employment without good reason.[134] Further, a company's attempt to assert willful loss of earnings in order to reduce a back-pay award is an affirmative defense. Management accordingly bears the burden of persuasion in this regard.[135]

Particularly troublesome is determining what constitutes similar employment which, if not accepted, will constitute failure to avoid loss and, thus, a reduction in back pay. The Court of Appeals for the District of Columbia has declared:

> A discriminatee need not seek *or* accept employment which is "dangerous, distasteful or essentially different" from his regular job. . . . Similarly, he is not necessarily obligated to accept employment which is located an unreasonable distance from his home.
>
>   . . .
>
> [T]here is no requirement that such a person seek employment which is not consonant with his particular skills, background, and experience.[136]

The Fifth Circuit has likewise stated:

> In order to be entitled to backpay, an employee must at least make "reasonable efforts to find new employment which is substantially equivalent to the position [which he was discriminatorily deprived of] and is suitable to a person of his background and experience."[137]

The First Circuit has ruled that the principle of mitigation of damages does not require success but only an honest, good faith effort, and the employee is held "only to reasonable exertions in this regard, not the highest standard of diligence."[138] The reasonableness of the effort to find substantially

---

[134]NLRB v. Mastro Plastics Corp., 354 F.2d 170, 174 n.3, 60 LRRM 2578 (2d Cir. 1965), cert. denied, 384 U.S. 972, 62 LRRM 2292 (1966).

[135]NLRB v. Laborers Local 38, 748 F.2d 1001, 118 LRRM 2062, 2065 (5th Cir. 1984).

[136]NLRB v. Madison Courier, 472 F.2d 1307, 80 LRRM 3377, 3384–3385 (D.C. Cir. 1972).

[137]NLRB v. Miami Coca-Cola Bottling Co., 360 F.2d 569, 575, 62 LRRM 2155, 2158 (5th Cir. 1966).

[138]NLRB v. Arduini Mfg. Corp., 394 F.2d 420, 422–423, 68 LRRM 2129 (1st Cir. 1968).

equivalent employment should be evaluated in light of the individual characteristics of the employee and the job market.[139] The definition of similar work is enlarged if the employee has several skills or trades.[140]

The extent to which a court may venture in applying the mitigation doctrine is illustrated in *Roy Stone Transfer Corp. v. Teamsters Local 22*,[141] a case reported by the Third Circuit. After upholding the decision of an arbitrator reinstating an employee, a lower court nevertheless limited the back-pay period from the date of the discharge (October 27, 1981) to the date of the employer's offer of transfer to another city (late January 1982), even though the arbitrator (in an award dated January 12, 1982) ordered the employee be made whole "for all wages lost." The Third Circuit found that the district court had a "sound basis" for changing the date of the back-pay period to the date on which a job transfer proposal was made to the grievant (the grievant rejected the transfer). The dissent pointed out that the test under *Enterprise Wheel*[142] for setting aside an award is not whether a district court has a sound basis for its action but, rather, whether the award "draws its essence" from the collective bargaining contract.

Applying the mitigation principle, Arbitrator Thomas Christopher, in *Albertson's, Inc.*,[143] stated that even those arbitrators who recognize a duty to mitigate damages may not require the employee to use more than "ordinary diligence" to obtain other work. In that decision an assistant manager in a retail food store was discharged after he refused to give up his interest in an outside business venture. Before dismissing the grievant, however, the employer had given him the option of accepting a clerk's position if he insisted on retaining his interest in his business. Granting the grievant full back pay,[144] the arbitrator held that the mitigation rule does

---

[139]Rasimas v. Michigan Dep't of Mental Health, 714 F.2d 614, 624, 32 FEP Cases 688 (6th Cir. 1983), cert. denied, 466 U.S. 950, 34 FEP Cases 1096 (1984).

[140]Holloway and Leech, Employment Termination: Rights and Remedies, 408 (BNA Books, 1985).

[141]752 F.2d 949, 118 LRRM 2159 (4th Cir. 1985).

[142]Steelworkers v. Enterprise Wheel & Car Corp., 363 U.S. 593, 46 LRRM 2423 (1960), discussed in Chapter 3, notes 49–54 and accompanying text.

[143]65 LA 1042 (1975).

[144]The arbitrator did not provide that if the grievant received outside income from the date of the hearing to the date of his reimbursement, such income should be deducted from the back-pay liability of the employer. Id. at 1048. City of West Haven,

not require an employee to accept unsuitable or "lower rated work" and that, since the grievant received a large income as assistant manager, it would have been difficult for him to secure the same or substantially equivalent position in the immediate labor market.

This principle was again voiced by Arbitrator Edgar A. Jones, Jr., in *Crowell-Collier Broadcasting Co.*,[145] where Jones held that a radio disc jockey, improperly discharged because of poor station ratings, could not be faulted for not searching for alternative employment.[146]

At some point in the mitigation process employees may be reasonably required to lower their expectations concerning alternative employment. As the Sixth Circuit noted in *NLRB v. Southern Silk Mills*,[147]

> We are of the opinion, however, that the usual wage earner, reasonably conscious of the obligation to support himself and family by suitable employment, after inability over a reasonable period of time to obtain the kind of employment to which he is accustomed, would consider other available, suitable employment at a somewhat lower rate of pay "desirable new employment." The fact that a married woman employee is being supported by her husband during the discharge period should not relieve her of the obligation to accept suitable employment. The failure . . . under the conditions existing in the present case, to seek or take other suitable, available employment, although at a lower rate of pay, over a period of approximately three years, constitutes to some extent at least loss of earnings "willfully incurred."[148]

One caveat, however, has been noted by the Court of Appeals for the District of Columbia Circuit:

> If the discriminatee accepts significantly lower-paying work too soon after the discrimination in question, he may be subject to a reduction in back pay on the ground that he willfully incurred a loss by accepting an "unsuitably" low-paying position. On the other hand . . . if he fails to "lower his sights" after the passage of a "reasonable period" of unsuccessful employment searching,

---

70-2 ARB ¶8663 (Silverstone, 1970) (failure to apply for unemployment compensation).

[145]45 LA 635 (1965).

[146]See also Honeywell, Inc., 51 LA 1061 (Elson, 1968); McLouth Stell Corp., 23 LA 640 (Parker, 1954); Airquipment Co., 10 LA 162 (Aaron, 1948).

[147]242 F.2d 697, 700, 39 LRRM 2647 (6th Cir.), cert. denied, 355 U.S. 821, 40 LRRM 2680 (1957).

[148]Id. at 700, 39 LRRM at 2649.

he may be held to have forfeited his right to reimbursement on the ground that he failed to make the requisite effort to mitigate his losses.[149]

b. Mitigation and Offers of Reinstatement Without Back Pay

Cases have arisen where an employee rejects an offer of reinstatement without back pay and thereafter pursues the matter in the arbitral forum. Should refusal to accept reinstatement preclude the employee from receiving an award of back pay past the period where the employee refused employment?

Arbitrator George Savage King considered this problem in *Cagles, Inc.*[150] In that decision the employer offered to reinstate the grievant, without back pay, two weeks after her discharge. The grievant refused and, in a subsequent arbitration, was reinstated without back pay from the date she refused reinstatement until the date of the award. Because the employer made an offer of reinstatement albeit without back pay, the arbitrator reasoned that this was effectively a "two-week layoff for which it had just cause." The grievant's refusal was accordingly used to mitigate the employer's back-pay liability.

Arbitrator Alfred Kamen, in *Weyerhaeuser Co.*[151] also reduced the employer's liability where the employees involved refused an offer of reinstatement without back pay. In making the award the arbitrator reasoned that, since the employer stated that the offer was not conditional upon a waiver of any back-pay grievance the union might wish to present, any monetary award must be reduced by the employees' failure to mitigate losses.

In *MGM Grand Hotel*,[152] Arbitrator Leo Weiss ordered reinstatement of an employee dismissed for failing to follow procedures regarding the method of bill payment for dining customers. Back pay was ordered but only from the date of discharge to the date the employer had offered "conditional"

---

[149]NLRB v. Madison Courier, 472 F.2d 1307, 80 LRRM 3377, 3385 (D.C. Cir. 1972).
[150]48 LA 972 (1967).
[151]49 LA 47 (1967).
[152]68 LA 1284 (1977).

reinstatement. The employee would be returned to her position if she paid the amount of a bill ($68.00) that her customer had failed to pay, leaving her the option of filing a grievance to recover the money. The arbitrator stated that when the grievant refused to accept this alternative she disregarded her obligation to take reasonable steps in mitigation of the employer's back-pay liability.[153]

Likewise, Arbitrator Harry Platt, in *Simplicity Pattern Co.*,[154] ruled that an employee who was wrongfully denied reinstatement after a leave of absence was not entitled to back pay for the period between the time an offer of rehire as a new employee was first made and the time it was withdrawn. Arbitrator Platt reasoned that the grievant was obligated to accept the proffered employment pending settlement of the grievance.[155]

Arbitrator Thomas Gallagher similarly ruled that refusing available work with a successor employer that did not assume the labor agreement did not constitute failure to mitigate damages when the employees were on strike to protest the breach of the successor clause, which required the assumption of the agreement. The arbitrator reasoned that if the opportunity for the grievants' employment came from an employer other than the company that improperly refused to honor the agreement, mitigation of damages would be required. Arbitrator Gallagher ruled that when the employees' duty to work conflicts with their right to refuse support to the cause of their damages, the duty to mitigate should give way.[156]

Such a decision is more difficult in a case where the employer offers the employee unconditional reinstatement without back pay, the offer is rejected, and the employee is subsequently reinstated by an arbitrator. In a case similar to the above, Arbitrator Platt, declaring what appears to be the better rule, held that the employer could not mitigate a back-pay obligation where an employee refused an improper trans-

---

[153]See also Automobile Workers Local 509 and N.I. Indus., 88-1 ARB ¶8069 (Weckstein, 1987), at 3333 ("Company should not have to bear the burden of back pay during the period from which the Grievant denied the offer of conditional reinstatement or in which the Union may have delayed processing of the case for arbitration.").
[154]14 LA 462 (1950).
[155]See also Kroger Co., 12 LA 1065 (Blair, 1949) (no retroactive pay beyond date of reimbursement offer).
[156]Martin Podany Assocs., 84-2 ARB ¶8469 (Gallagher, 1984).

fer to a lower paying job at a time when the employee could not subsequently challenge the action:

> Having held that the transfer . . . was unjustified, it necessarily follows that she should be made whole for her full loss unless she was obligated to accept the transfer and thereby to mitigate her damages. Under the peculiar facts here, however, I cannot find that she was so obligated. My conclusion on this might be different if, at the time of the incident, the parties had been bound by a collective bargaining contract which included a grievance procedure affording her protection in securing a retroactive adjustment of her monetary loss while continuing at work in her new job. But there was no such contract in existence at the time and had she accepted the transfer to an inferior job, it would clearly have constituted a full settlement of her grievance, as she had no right, nor was she given the opportunity by the Company to accept the transfer conditionally. As testified by the Company, the only alternative[s] she had were to accept the transfer or to terminate her employment.[157]

Arbitrator Platt, citing a decision from the Tenth Circuit, went on to state that in similar circumstances, where an employee had refused an undesirable job offer by the employer, there had been no mitigation of the employer's liability:

> They (the employees) were in effect discharged from the jobs they were entitled to hold. Under the circumstances, their refusal to accept the discriminatory jobs was not willful. While they should be charged with earnings actually received and with earnings not received because of the unjustifiable refusal to take desirable new employment, they should not, in our opinion, be charged with the earnings they would have received at the discriminatory jobs proffered them.[158]

The better rule, as we see it, is reflected by Holloway and Leech as follows: "The employer is not entitled to create a 'catch 22' situation for the employee by offering the same or similar work after a wrongful discharge on the condition that the employee give up his claim."[159]

A bona fide settlement agreement whereby an employee, as consideration for reinstatement, waives any claim to back pay or other benefits is binding on the parties and should be

---

[157]Gardner-Richardson Co., 11 LA 957, 962 (1948).
[158]Id., citing NLRB v. Armour & Co., 154 F.2d 570, 17 LRRM 592 (10th Cir. 1945).
[159]Holloway and Leech, supra note 140, citing Smith v. Concordia Parish School Bd., 387 F. Supp. 887 (W.D. La. 1975) and Punkar v. King Plastics Corp., 290 So.2d 505 (Fla. Dist. Ct. App. 1974).

respected by the arbitrator.[160] For example, where negotiations ended in an understanding that an employee would be returned to work on a specific date, Arbitrator Daniel Dykstra, in *Eimco Corp.*,[161] ruled that the employer would not be liable for back pay from the date of the settlement agreement to the date of the grievant's return to employment.

3. Interim Periods Where Back Pay May Be Suspended

In general, the improperly discharged employee is entitled to "make whole" relief of back pay from the time the grievance is filed,[162] to the date reinstatement is either offered by the employer or ordered by the arbitrator. Arbitrators, similar to the Board and the courts, will not order back pay for any period where the employee is not available for work. Common situations where the back-pay period may be tolled include: (1) any period of a strike occurring during the "back-pay" period, (2) a seasonal slack or layoff period, and (3) periods of illness or other incapacity to work.

a. Strikes

In *Acme Markets of Tazewell, Va.*,[163] Arbitrator Francis Flannagan conducted a second hearing to determine the back-pay obligation of an employer previously ordered to reinstate an employee and pay her "for all time off." The arbitrator stated that his award of back pay was to make the grievant whole and not to penalize the company, and that if he had known at the time of the award that the union was on strike

---

[160]See Comaco, Inc., 68-1 ARB ¶8156 (Krimsly, 1968).

[161]41 LA 1184 (1963).

[162]In Lebanon Steel Foundry, 4 LA 94 (1946), Arbitrator Joseph Brandschain stated: "The well-established rule in arbitration is that retroactive pay is not to be awarded back farther than the date of the filing of the grievance." Accord National Torch Tip Co., 77-2 ARB ¶8432 (LeWinter, 1977); Wilco Food Center, 70-1 ARB ¶8091 (Larkin, 1969) (back pay limited from time union notified employer); National Steel & Shipbuilding Co., 67-1 ARB ¶8041 (Roberts, 1966); Eaton Mfg. Co., 66-3 ARB ¶9089 (Kates, 1966) (time union objected); American Welding & Mfg. Co., 45 LA 812 (Dworkin, 1965); General Cable Corp., 15 LA 910 (Kaplan, 1950); Inland Steel Co., 2 LA 655 (Gilden, 1945). But see Publicker Indus., 69-2 ARB ¶8491 (Duff, 1969) (reimbursement for improper assignments limited to 60 days prior to date grievance was filed).

[163]66 LA 960 (1976).

"he would only have awarded back pay to the time of the strike, absent some showing that the Grievant would have worked during the period of the strike." To permit otherwise, reasoned the arbitrator, would be to award the employee something in the nature of punitive damages. Arbitrator Flannagan ruled that the employer's back-pay liability was tolled during the strike period, since the grievant admitted at the hearing that she would not have crossed the picket line during the strike.

Similarly, Arbitrator J. Earl Williams, in *Markle Manufacturing Co.*,[164] declared that the historic rationale for deducting wages earned in interim employment is to arrive more precisely at the employer's "make whole" obligation to the employee. Since it is assumed that the improperly dismissed employee would have been employed during the period in question, Arbitrator Williams held:

> [T]here can be no deduction of wages earned during the strike period unless it is also assumed that the Company was obligated to pay the gross wages of the employees during the strike period. On the other hand, if the analysis concludes that there is no back pay obligation of the employer during the period of the strike, the entire period should be excluded from all calculations related to back pay, just as would be true of any other period in which the employer has no obligation.[165]

In concluding that the employer was obligated to include in its calculation of back-pay liability the gross earnings that the reinstated employees would have received had they been employed, the arbitrator cited the practice of the NLRB to resolve any uncertainty against the employer where there is a question whether the employees would have worked:

> In computing back pay for employees who have been wrongfully discharged before an economic strike is called, the Board normally refuses to exclude the period of a subsequent economic strike. In the Board's view, the employer's burden of proof is not met merely by establishing the fact of the strike, for it remains a matter of speculation and conjecture whether the employees would have gone out on strike if still in the employer's employ and, as the Board sees it, that uncertainty must be resolved against the wrongdoing employer who made it impos-

---

[164]73 LA 1292 (1980).
[165]Id. at 1295.

sible to ascertain what they would have done had they not been unlawfully discharged.[166]

The arbitrator noted that in the *Markle* case no offer of reinstatement was ever made and opposition to the return of the grievants was so great it would be a futile gesture to speculate as to the grievants' reaction to any offer. More important, the arbitrator stated that the grievants were engaged in mitigating the employer's liability during the strike in that both were working at other jobs.

We think the better rule is that an employee wrongfully discharged before an economic strike is presumptively entitled to back pay accruing during the strike. Since the employer's own conduct often makes it impossible to determine whether the improperly dismissed employee would have joined the strike, absent evidence to the contrary an employer should not be allowed to benefit from the uncertainty caused by its own conduct.

b. *Production Shutdown or Economic Layoff*

Where it can be demonstrated that, for reasons unconnected with the improper discharge, the employee would not have been employed, back pay may be reduced accordingly. For example, a showing that an employee would have been laid off or dismissed during a seasonal slack period may properly mitigate the employer's back-pay liability.[167] Any monies earned by the improperly dismissed employees during these periods should not be considered "interim earnings" to be used as a setoff against the employer's back-pay obligation. The burden is generally placed upon the employer to show facts

---

[166]Id. at 1296, citing Rogers Mfg. Co., 178 NLRB 429, 72 LRRM 1132 (1969).

[167]See, e.g., NLRB v. United Contractors, 614 F.2d 134, 103 LRRM 2581 (7th Cir. 1980); Florsheim Shoe Store Co. v. NLRB, 565 F.2d 1240, 96 LRRM 3273 (2d Cir. 1977) ("phasing out" of job held by discriminatee); Rex Printing Co., 227 NLRB 1144, 94 LRRM 1401 (1977) ("back pay period" from date of unlawful discharge to date employer could have lawfully discharged employee when it learned of his solicitation of business for competing printing operation); Midland-Ross Corp., 239 NLRB 323, 100 LRRM 1020 (1978) (employer which unlawfully closed one of its plants and terminated plant employees ordered to pay amount each would have earned from date of plant closing to date employer would have closed plant solely for economic reasons).

that would mitigate its liability to a given employee.[168] Similarly, back pay may properly be reduced for any period past a plant shutdown.[169]

c. Physical Inability to Work

The physical availability of a reinstated employee for employment during the discharge or back-pay period is an important consideration in computing an employer's back-pay liability. Following NLRB practice,[170] arbitrators will toll the back-pay period for any period where an employee is not available for work. For example, Arbitrator Erwin Ellman, in *American Air Filter Co.*,[171] ruled that it would be inappropriate to direct reimbursement for time not worked by an employee during the period he was shown to be physically unfit to return to work. Similarly, Arbitrator Carroll Martin, in *Edward Kraemer & Sons*,[172] held that a laid-off employee, who improperly was not recalled to work, was not entitled to back pay for the period during which a physical injury would have prevented his performance of the required work if recalled, even though the employer had no knowledge of the employee's injury at the time it recalled another employee.[173]

In cases involving pregnancy and other temporary disabilities, back-pay liability may be limited during the period a pregnant employee would normally have been on a maternity leave. In the case of pregnancy, liability may be properly assessed from the time of the improper discharge to the date

---

[168]NLRB v. Brown & Root, 311 F.2d 447, 454, 52 LRRM 2115 (8th Cir. 1963); Center Fuel Co., 65 LA 1291 (Gratz, 1976).

[169]See, e.g., NLRB v. Master Slack, 773 F.2d 77, 120 LRRM 2514 (6th Cir. 1985) (back-pay awards that extend past plant shutdowns do not further any policy under NLRA and will not be enforced).

[170]See, e.g., Sure-Tan v. NLRB, 467 U.S. 883, 116 LRRM 2857 (1984) (denying back pay to undocumented workers who were outside the United States in back-pay period); Gifford-Hill & Co., 188 NLRB 337, 76 LRRM 1349 (1971) (denying back pay for incarcerated employee); American Mfg. Co. of Tex., 167 NLRB 520, 66 LRRM 1122 (1967) (no back pay for periods of illness or accident incurred in interim employment); New Albany Concrete Serv., 76 LA 44 (Fitch, 1981) (employee entitled to back pay based on number of hours worked by replacement, excluding two weeks spent in county jail for shooting neighbors). But see Ladies' Garment Workers Local 512 v. NLRB, 795 F.2d 705, 122 LRRM 3113 (9th Cir. 1986) (denying enforcement of NLRB decision conditioning payment of back pay to laid-off workers upon proof of legal immigration status).

[171]63 LA 1277 (1974).

[172]72 LA 684 (1979).

[173]Accord Alameda Contra-Costa Transit Dist., 77-1 ARB ¶8101 (Koven, 1977).

the woman would have left work, and from the time she would have been available for work to the date of the order or offer of reinstatement.[174] A reinstated employee who suffers a disability during the back-pay period would not be entitled to back pay until the date of medical release.[175]

In *Taylor v. Safeway Stores*,[176] the Tenth Circuit confronted a similar issue when a discharged employee enrolled in college after first looking for employment. The district court excluded from its back-pay award the period during which the employee was in college. Affirming the lower court, the Tenth Circuit stated:

> If a discharged employee accepted employment elsewhere, there is little doubt that this would cut off any back pay award. If not, the employee would be receiving a double benefit for the same period of time. Likewise, when an employee opts to attend school, curtailing present earning capacity in order to reap greater future earnings, a back pay award for the period while attending school also would be like receiving a double benefit.[177]

Back pay has also been reduced during the period an employee was incarcerated. As stated by one arbitrator:

> Back pay is a species of damages aimed at providing compensation for the injury sustained. Even had the grievant been employed by the Company, he would not have been paid for the time during which he was incarcerated since he was unavailable for work. It would have been impossible for him to perform his duties at the plant. . . . A requirement that the Company pay grievant for his period of incarceration would be to go beyond

---

[174]See, e.g., Avon Convalescent Center, 219 NLRB No. 191, 90 LRRM 1264 (1975) (employee who was pregnant at time of discharge did not incur willful loss of interim earnings during period preceding last trimester of her pregnancy, since she signed up with unemployment authorities and, on her own, sought other work; employee did not incur willful loss of employment during period beginning three months after her child was born, since no effort was made to obtain work during that period); Harper v. Thiokol Chem. Corp., 619 F.2d 489, 23 FEP Cases 61, 64 (5th Cir. 1980).

[175]See, e.g., Communication Corp. of Am., 87-2 ARB ¶8496 (Barron, 1987), at 5983 (ordering back pay, less interim earnings and unemployment compensation received from date grievant released for work by doctor to date of reinstatement or date employer's offer of reinstatement expires; grievant required to submit evidence when he was released to work, and evidence requested by employer necessary to determine interim wages and unemployment compensation received).

[176]524 F.2d 263, 11 FEP Cases 449 (10th Cir. 1975).

[177]Id. at 268, 11 FEP Cases at 451. For a contrary position, see Hanna v. American Motors Corp., 724 F.2d 1300, 1307, 115 LRRM 2393, 2543 (7th Cir. 1984) and Cook v. 84 Lumber Co., 118 LRRM 2639 (N.D. Ohio, 1984) (pointing out that employer produced no evidence that it would not have been possible for employee to attend classes, complete assignments, and maintain full-time employment).

making him whole and take on the attributes of a punitive remedy against the Company.[178]

4. Exclusions and Deductions in Back-Pay Computation in the Federal Sector

In the federal sector, the period included in a recomputation of back pay may not extend beyond (1) the date of the employee's death, or (2) the date on which the employee was properly separated from the agency if the separation would have been effected regardless of the wrongful act. In addition, a recomputation may not include any period during which the employee (1) was not ready and able to perform the job, and (2) this unavailability was not related to or caused by the wrongful action.

Any amounts the employee earned from other employment during the recomputation period must be deducted from an award of back pay. If, however, the employee had earnings from an outside job he would have held even if not dismissed, he is entitled to the full amount of back pay for that period.

Finally, amounts designated as reimbursement for expenses the employee would have incurred in performance of the job, but which were not incurred due to the improper action, may not be included as allowances.

5. Unemployment Compensation

Arbitrators are split over the question of whether unemployment compensation benefits received during a period of layoff or suspension should be deducted from a back-pay award.[179] Under one view such benefits, paid out of a fund to which only the employer contributes, are the equivalent of

---

[178]Bell Helicopter Textron, 71 LA 799, 801 (Johannes, 1978). Cf. General Portland Cement Co., 74-1 ARB ¶8012 (Davidson, 1974).

[179]See generally Fairweather, supra note 48, at 515–516; Gorske, supra note 86, at 26–27; Wolff, supra note 31; Gray, *Back Pay Awards and Unemployment Insurance Benefits*, 4 Arb. J. n.s. 268 (1949); Elkouri and Elkouri, How Arbitration Works, 4th ed., 408–409 (BNA Books, 1985).

outside compensation and therefore should be deducted from an award of back pay.[180]

Other arbitrators have treated unemployment compensation as a collateral benefit and have not deducted such benefits from back-pay awards.[181] Illustrative of this view is a decision by Arbitrator Martin Wagner in *National Rejectors, Inc.*[182] Although the arbitrator found that it was impossible to reimburse the unemployment insurance fund for benefits that were properly paid to a claimant, it was nevertheless held that the employer was not entitled to a deduction. Arbitrator Wagner's reasoning is reflective of the position of arbitrators who have ruled that management cannot have back pay reduced by unemployment compensation:

> To the employee who receives them, the benefits are income. To the employer of the employee, they represent costs since the fund from which they are paid [is] built up by employer contributions. Yet the payments are made by a public agency to carry out a public policy. In this sense they are not payments made by the employer for work performed by an employee. They are collateral benefits and are not earnings and therefore should be disregarded in a situation in which an employee is to be made whole by the employer just as collateral costs are disregarded for the same purpose.[183]

Similarly, Arbitrator Ralph Roger Williams, in *Union Carbide Corp.*,[184] found that a prior award directing that im-

---

[180]Metro E. Disposal, 88-2 ARB ¶8497 (Clifford, 1988); Sparklett Devices, 88-2 ARB ¶8388 (Fowler, 1988); Communication Corp. of Am., supra note 175; Air Treads of Atlanta, 85-2 ARB ¶8431 (Yancy, 1985); Vaco Prods. Co., 77 LA 432 (Lewis, 1981); Zapata Indus., 76 LA 467 (Woolf, 1981); Wehr Corp., 76 LA 399, 403 (Hunter, 1981) (adjusting unemployment compensation of $480 upward by 25 percent to reflect nontaxable status, resulting in "true economic offset" in favor of employer of $600); Central Foundry Co., 72 LA 531 (Rutherford, 1979); Air France, 71 LA 1113 (Turkus, 1978); Ocean Spray Cranberries, 71 LA 161 (Stern, 1978); Western Airlines, 67 LA 486 (Christopher, 1976); Farmer Bros. Co., 64 LA 901 (Jones, 1975); Bamberger's, 59 LA 879 (Glushien, 1972); Supreme Wire & Metal Prods. Co., 58 LA 531 (Kelliher, 1972); United States Steel Corp., 52 LA 1210 (Dybeck, 1969) (public assistance); Hawaiian Tel. Co., 45 LA 336 (Tsukiyama, 1965); Continental Can Co., 39 LA 821 (Sembower, 1962); Levinson Steel Co., 23 LA 135 (Reid, 1954); Bethlehem Steel Co., 16 LA 741 (Feinberg, 1951); Aviation Maintenance Corp., 8 LA 261 (Aaron, 1947).

[181]National Linen Serv., 74 LA 857 (Dunn, 1980); Advance Carbon Prods., 67 LA 1061 (Concepcion, 1976); Dubuque, Lorenz, Inc., 66 LA 1245 (Sinicropi, 1976); Brown & Williamson Tobacco Co., 62 LA 1211 (Davis, 1974); Union Carbide Corp., 56 LA 707 (Williams, 1971); National Rejectors, 38 LA 1091 (Wagner, 1962); Littleford Bros., 62-3 ARB ¶8840 (Warns, 1962); International Harvester Co., 16 LA 376 (Seward, 1951).

[182]Supra note 181.

[183]Id. at 1092, citing NLRB v. Gullett Gin Co., 340 U.S. 361, 27 LRRM 2230 (1951).

[184]Supra note 181.

properly discharged employees be reinstated and "made whole for all lost pay" does not permit the employer to deduct unemployment compensation received by the employees. According to the arbitrator:

> To be "made whole for all pay lost," the Grievants must be paid by the Company such pay as the Grievants would have earned had they not been discharged. The concept of making one whole for all pay lost is remedial rather than punitive, it being a device to restore the employee to a status extant prior to his unlawful discharge. "Whole" means total and entirely.
>
> If the fact that the Grievants were not working for any reason resulted in their being paid monies from any source which they would not have received had they been working at their regular jobs with the Company, the fact of such receipts of monies by the Grievants is immaterial to their entitlement to be made whole for all pay lost. The unemployment compensation benefits were not "pay" or wages, but were benefits earned by employment prior to the discharges. Whether or not the State moves to recoup such benefits, is a matter for the State and the Grievants; it cannot inure to the benefit of the Company, which cannot now deduct monies that it did not pay to the Grievants, but which they received from a collateral source.[185]

The NLRB has faced the same problem with unemployment compensation and other collateral benefits. At one time the Board, in providing for back-pay relief, directed employers to deduct from the payments to reinstated employees the amounts they had received from work-relief projects. Furthermore, to avoid a "windfall" to the employees, the NLRB directed the employers to pay over such amounts to the appropriate government agencies. The Supreme Court, in *Republic Steel Corp. v. NLRB*,[186] held that the Board exceeded its powers under the statute by mandating that the employer make such payments. In so holding, the Court stated:

> We think that affirmative action to "effectuate the policies of this Act" is action to achieve the remedial objectives which the Act sets forth. . . . To go further and to require the employer to pay to governments what they have paid to employees for services rendered to them is an exaction neither to make the employees whole nor to assure that they can bargain collectively with the employer through representatives of their own choice.

---

[185]Id. at 708.
[186]311 U.S. 7, 7 LRRM 287 (1940).

We find no warrant in the policies of the Act for such an exaction.[187]

Subsequent to *Republic Steel*, the Board disregarded the practice of deducting unemployment compensation payments from back pay and of similarly ordering employers to reimburse the appropriate agency for the amount of benefits. In this regard the current practice of the Board is not to deduct state unemployment compensation payments from back-pay orders. This policy was approved by the Supreme Court in *NLRB v. Gullett Gin Co.*,[188] where the Court held that failure to take them into account in ordering back pay does not make the employees more than "whole," as that phrase is understood and applied. The Court's reasoning is particularly instructive:

> Payments of unemployment compensation were not made to the employees by respondent [employer] but by the state out of state funds derived from taxation. True, these taxes were paid by employers, and thus to some extent respondent helped to create the fund. However, the payments to the employees were not made to discharge any liability or obligation of respondent, but to carry out a policy of social betterment for the benefit of the entire state. . . . We think these facts plainly show the benefits to be collateral.[189]

If any definite conclusion can be drawn from a study of this issue, it is that arbitrators should consider all operative factors in the particular jurisdiction where the award is to have effect. For example, in some states unemployment insurance benefits are paid out of the state's general tax revenues and not out of special employer and/or employee contributions.[190] This is an important factor if the arbitrator desires to avoid a windfall for the employer by reducing benefits from a back-pay award. A reduction in such a state may arguably result in a taxpayer subsidization in favor of an employer.

Another factor to consider is whether an employee has limited or exhausted his or her eligibility for future benefits during the layoff or suspension. To permit a deduction of ben-

---

[187]Id., 7 LRRM at 290.
[188]Supra note 183.
[189]Id. at 364, 27 LRRM at 2231. See also Marshall Field & Co. v. NLRB, 318 U.S. 253, 12 LRRM 519 (1943).
[190]See, e.g., the discussion of the Supreme Court in NLRB v. Gullett Gin Co., supra note 183, at 364. See also Gray, supra note 179.

efits may effectively force an employee to return benefits without a corresponding credit in eligibility. For this reason Arbitrator Charles Carnes, in *General Felt Industries*,[191] ordered an offset for unemployment compensation, but provided that in the event the grievants were required to repay any amount of unemployment compensation because of their reinstatement, the company should reimburse them.[192]

Finally, because unemployment benefits are administered by the individual states, it is possible that a state statute controls the outcome. Various states provide that if an individual receives a back-pay award that is not reduced by unemployment compensation benefits received, the employee becomes liable to the state agency. For example, the Connecticut statute provides:

> Whenever any person who has drawn benefits under this chapter subsequently receives retroactive pay without deduction for such benefits under an arbitration . . . he shall be liable to repay to the administrator the amount of benefits so drawn upon demand.[193]

Similarly, Virginia declares that:

> Whenever the Commission finds that a discharged employee has received back pay at his customary wage rate from his employer after reinstatement such employee shall be liable to repay the benefits, if any, paid to such person during the time he was unemployed . . . .[194]

Illinois provides that:

> Whenever, by reason of a back pay award . . . , an individual has received wages for weeks with respect to which he has received benefits, the amount of such benefits may be recouped

---

[191]74 LA 972 (1979).

[192]Other arbitrators have similarly ruled. See, e.g., City of Shawnee, Okla., 91 LA 93, 100 (Allen, 1988) ("deduction [from grievant's back pay] includes unemployment compensation unless the grievant is required to return it to the issuing agency."); Alvey, Inc., 74 LA 835, 840 (Roberts, 1980) ("in the event that Grievant is required to repay any such sum from which the Company was credited by virtue of this Award, the Company shall make him whole by such amount."); Schnuck Mkts., 73 LA 829, 832 (Holman, 1979) ("If, by reason of this award[,] Grievant is required by law to repay any unemployment benefits . . . and does repay same, the Company shall not be credited with that amount on the wages due."); Atlas Metal Parts Co., 67 LA 1230, 1238 (Kossoff, 1977) ("Should [grievant], as a result of this award, be required to return unemployment compensation or other benefits received and does, in fact, return the same, no deduction shall be made for what is returned.").

[193]Conn. Gen. Stat. §31-257 (1987).

[194]Va. Code §60.2-100 (1987).

or otherwise recovered as herein provided. An employing unit making a back pay award to an individual for weeks with respect to which the individual has received benefits shall make the back pay award by check payable jointly to the individual and to the Director.[195]

In *Armour-Dial*,[196] Arbitrator Benjamin Aaron discussed the Illinois statute and had this to say on the issue:

Unemployment compensation to an employee covering a period for which he or she subsequently receives full back pay is properly reimbursable by the employee to the state, not to the employer. The Illinois statute applicable in this case expressly provides that when an employee, by virtue of an arbitration award, has received wages for weeks in respect of which he has received unemployment benefits, such benefits may be "recouped or otherwise recovered" by procedures provided in the statute. I am unaware of any overriding policy that compels the employee to reimburse his or her employer instead of the state, and the weight of arbitral authority on this point seems to me irrelevant.[197]

Further, some states provide that the arbitrator must notify the appropriate agency after making an award of back pay.[198]

In an attempt to deal with the unemployment compensation problem, some arbitrators, in determining the amount of back pay, have ordered the employer to deduct any unemployment compensation benefits and remit them to the respective state agency.[199] Other arbitrators have ordered reinstatement with full back pay, less any interim earnings and other benefits, provided that the employee is not required by law to repay the interim compensation.[200] Still other arbitrators have ordered management to directly reimburse the unemployment commission.[201]

---

[195]Ill. Rev. Stat. ch. 48, §490 (1987).

[196]76 LA 96 (1981).

[197]Id. at 100.

[198]Colorado, for example, provides: "The person ordering any such award of back pay shall, within five days after the date of the order, notify the director of the division of employment and training of such award." Colo. Rev. Stat. §8-2-119 (1986 & Supp).

[199]Fruehauf Trailer Co., 16 LA 666 (Spaulding, 1951); Masonite Corp., 10 LA 854 (McCoy, 1948); National Lock Co., 4 LA 820 (Gilden, 1946); International Shoe Co., 3 LA 500 (Wardlaw, 1946).

[200]Wilshire Indus., 71 LA 56 (Mueller, 1978); Northern Ind. Pub. Serv. Co., 69 LA 201 (Sembower, 1977); Marathon Pipe Line Co., 69 LA 555, 563 (Brown, 1977).

[201]Cowlitz Redi-Mix, 85 LA 745, 750–751 (Boedecker, 1985) (employer to reimburse Department of Employment Security for any benefits agency paid to grievant during period in question to ensure that employee "benefit year ending" will be

One possibility is to remand the matter back to the parties for appropriate action. Thus Arbitrator John Sembower, in *Universal Producing Co.*,[202] drafted the following award:

> If there is a requirement of reimbursement . . . then the matter shall be consummated legally by a reimbursement payment jointly of the Grievant and the employer as outlined by the illustrative ruling of the Illinois administrator.
> If, upon advice of counsel, the parties are convinced that no reimbursement is required, then the gross payment of that pay to the Grievant shall have deducted from it the unemployment compensation she already has received.[203]

There is no question that the task of the arbitrator in formulating a "make whole" back-pay award is complicated by the fact that unemployment benefits are administered by the individual states. As one commentator has stated, in the end the arbitrator "makes his own law" in reaching a determination on this subject. Since the parties seek his "informed judgment," it is their obligation to bring to his attention the many factors that may affect his judgment on unemployment compensation.[204] We believe, however, that the NLRB's policy reflects the better view and that absent a statutory mandate to the contrary, unemployment benefits should be considered a collateral benefit that the employee receives from the state as a matter of social policy.[205] Employees are not compensated

---

properly extended); Eastern Prods. Corp., 43 LA 16, 20 (Rice, 1964) (ordering employer to reimburse Wisconsin unemployment compensation division); American Bakeries Co., 43 LA 1106, 1111 (Purdom, 1964) (ordering employer to remit benefits to state of Tennessee); Hub City Jobbing Co, 43 LA 907, 911 (Gundermann, 1964) (ordering company to pay to unemployment compensation fund amount paid to grievant).

[202]57 LA 1072 (1971).

[203]Id. at 1074.

[204]Wolff, supra note 31, at 185.

[205]Accord Whatley v. Skaggs Cos., 707 F.2d 1129, 31 FEP Cases 1202 (10th Cir. 1983); Kauffman v. Sidereal Corp., 695 F.2d 343, 32 FEP Cases 1710 (9th Cir. 1982) (unemployment benefits collateral source); EEOC v. Ford Motor Co., 645 F.2d 183, 25 FEP Cases 774 (4th Cir. 1981); Marshall v. Goodyear Tire & Rubber Co., 554 F.2d 730, 15 FEP Cases 139 (5th Cir. 1977); State, County & Mun. Employees Council 94 v. Rhode Island, 475 A.2d 200, 116 LRRM 2224 (R.I. 1984) (upholding arbitration back-pay award with no unemployment compensation offset); Michael v. Cole, 122 Ariz. 450, 595 P.2d 995, 997 (1979) (G.I. benefits collateral and not to be deducted from back-pay award); Hopcraft Art & Stained Glass Works, 258 NLRB 1392, 108 LRRM 1237 (1981); Sioux Falls Stock Yards Co., 236 NLRB 543, 99 LRRM 1316 (1978). But see EEOC v. Enterprise Ass'n Steamfitters Local 638, 542 F.2d 579, 13 FEP Cases 705 (2d Cir. 1976), cert. denied, 430 U.S. 911, 14 FEP Cases 702 (1977) (policy considerations allow for deduction of unemployment compensation in back-pay awards); Merriweather v. Hercules, Inc., 631 F.2d 1161, 26 FEP Cases 733 (5th Cir. 1980) (deduction within discretion of trial court). See generally Note, *The De-*

for collateral losses when they are wrongfully discharged and, similarly, collateral benefits, such as unemployment compensation, should not be considered a setoff in favor of management.

6. Undue Delay

Arbitrators support either complete denial of back pay or limiting the award to partial back pay in situations where there has been delay in bringing the grievance to arbitration or where one or both of the parties are found remiss in their duties under the contract.[206] For example, in *Dayton Tire & Rubber Co.*,[207] Arbitrator Harry Dworkin ruled that an employee has the obligation to initiate a grievance within a reasonable time period even though the contract sets forth no time limitation. Furthermore, the arbitrator declared:

> An employee may not passively observe conduct which if permitted to continue would give rise to a claim for monetary compensation, without acting in a reasonably prudent manner. A union, or an employee, may not sit idly by in the face of a contract violation with the expectation of reaping benefits inuring from the conduct of the employer. The foregoing principles have been enunciated in various forms; they are suggested by the phrases "equitable estoppel", "Rule of Laches", and "failure to make timely protest."

The contract terms are designed to provide relief to an innocent victim. The contract is not intended to invest an em-

---

duction of Unemployment Compensation for Back-Pay Awards under Title VII, 16 Mich. L. Rev. 643 (1983).

[206]Baltimore Sun, 91 LA 1133, 1139 (Wahl, 1988) (denying back pay for inordinate delay in pursuing grievance and closeness of issue); California Neon Prods., 91 LA 485, 489 (Kaufman, 1988) (back pay reduced where grievant " 'consciously' remained silent for over a year."); Simplex Prods. Div., 91 LA 356, 360 (Byars, 1988) (back pay limited to one-half unemployment period where grievant failed to notify company of medical status); Weyerhaeuser Co., 90 LA 870, 872 (Allen, 1988) (reinstated employee's back pay computed from discharge through two months before arbitration hearing, where employer attempted to expedite hearing and union rejected first arbitration panel); Genstar Bldg. Materials Co., 89 LA 1265 (Weisbrod, 1987) (reducing back pay where grievance delayed for more than one year and union partially responsible for delay); Air Carrier Engine Serv., 65 LA 666 (Naehring, 1975); General Cable Corp., 64 LA 978, 981 (Rauch, 1975) ("party to a contract who feels that some right under the contract is being violated by the other party, has an obligation to make a reasonable effort to minimize the damage caused by the violation"); Hawaiian Airlines, 60 LA 741 (Tsukiyama, 1973); WVUE Television, 69-1 ARB ¶8370 (Oppenheim, 1969); McLouth Steel Co., 23 LA 640 (Parker, 1954) (failure to respond to proper notice). See also, NLRB v. Cashman Auto Co., 223 F.2d 832, 36 LRRM 2269 (1st Cir. 1955).

[207]48 LA 83 (1967).

ployee with a claim for compensation, which liability could have been prevented by timely action on the part of the employee. An employee is generally charged with the responsibility of acting in a reasonably prudent manner so as to minimize damages where he has the power, the right and responsibility to act in the context of the employment relationship.[208]

Arbitrator Peter Kelliher has similarly stated:

> [T]he Grievant cannot sit back and let the financial liability of the Company mount. He has a duty to mitigate damages by promptly filing a Grievance . . . .[209]

Even where the liability of the employer is unaffected by a late filing, arbitrators have denied relief where the grievance is not filed within a reasonable time from the event giving rise to the complaint. Arbitrator Ronald Talarico, in *Housing Authority of Lawrence County, Pa.*,[210] stated the rule this way:

> It has been held that where a contract states no time limit for initially filing grievances but does state specific time limits for processing grievances to subsequent steps of the procedure, the evident intent of the parties is that grievances must be filed with reasonable promptness.[211]

Arbitrator Talarico ruled that a grievance filed more than five years after the union learned of the employer's failure to include cost-of-living adjustments was not arbitrable, even though in the interim the parties initiated several proceedings in court.

Similarly, in *Jacuzzi Brothers*,[212] an employee was discharged for leaving the plant to attend a union meeting, contrary to supervisory instructions to remain on the job. A grievance was filed, but the union requested a delay in the arbitration of the matter pending negotiation of a new agreement. A strike ensued and arbitration was delayed for six months. when the matter was finally brought to arbitration, the arbitrator, while ordering reinstatement, awarded no back pay because the initial delay was the responsibility of the

---

[208]Id. at 86. See also Cardinal Printing Co., 60 LA 1208 (Dworkin, 1973).
[209]Warner Elec. Brake & Clutch Co., 31 LA 219, 220 (1958).
[210]89 LA 452 (1987).
[211]Id. at 456.
[212]68-1 ARB ¶8193 (Bothwell, 1967).

union, and there was no reason that the matter could not have been arbitrated during the strike.

Arbitrator William B. Lockhart, in *Lavoris Co.*,[213] likewise concluded:

> [I]f the employer's wrongful practice is of a continuing character, which could be corrected and the cost to employer reduced by informing him of the Union's objections, failure to do so within a reasonable time is highly prejudicial to the employer. He should not be held financially responsible for the increased harm that has resulted from failure of the Union to protest within a reasonable time after learning of the employer's action. In such a case, at least where the employer's mistake was in good faith as it was here, the Union is equally responsible with the employer for the harm and must be held to have waived any claim to compensation of the employees it represents for injuries to their rights that could have been avoided by the employer had the Union filed the grievance within a reasonable time. . . .[214]

Many labor agreements utilize a progressive disciplinary system providing for dismissal when an employee accumulates a designated number of "occurrences" or "chargeable incidents," all meted out prior to the termination at issue. Suppose an employee fails to grieve a specific incident and is later discharged for an accumulation of "incidents." He now wants to challenge a prior incident. Can the grievant's failure to grieve reduce the back-pay liability of the employer if the dismissal is overturned by an arbitrator? Arbitrator Edgar Jones, Jr., in a 1985 unpublished case, ruled that back pay could be reduced because of the union's failure to challenge an employee's "occurrences" (any occasion of unexcused absences, tardiness, and early quits) at the time that management assessed them against the grievant. Jones stated that it is unrealistic to expect a union to expend limited financial resources investigating the circumstances and contesting to arbitration the issuance of a warning, or even a suspension, rather than waiting to see if the employee's later improved attendance record may cause the potential problem to dissipate with the passage of time. Jones' reasoning is noteworthy:

> But there is a potential problem of fair procedure evident

---

[213]16 LA 156 (1951).

[214]Id. at 161. Accord Cooper-Bessemer Corp., 68-2 ARB ¶8392 (Howlett, 1968) (union estopped from claiming 20 months' back pay as compensation for employer's failure to award pay increases to apprentices, where union should have been aware of the practice within six months of its being applied).

in this situation. Statutory and contractual limitations restricting the time for the filing of grievances are based in substantial part on the realization that the passage of time may impair the capacity of the people involved accurately to reconstruct the disputed events. Although it is now accepted that an employer has the burden of proof to demonstrate that misconduct both occurred and warrants the discipline imposed, in this situation, once the employer proves the happening of the final "occurrence," the burden must then be upon the union to demonstrate the extent to which any of the prior ungrieved "occurrences" should not have been assessed against the employee's attendance record; the risk of failure of proof created by the lapse of time should in fairness be imposed on the union, not the employer. Furthermore, the failure to grieve prior "occurrences" may also implicate the propriety of awarding back pay in a reinstatement from discharge that is consequent upon such proof by the union of the lack of a proper earlier "occurrence" as the contractual foundation for a final terminable "occurrence." By hypothesis, had the grievance against the earlier "occurrence" been filed in a timely manner and resolved on its merits on behalf of the employee, there would have been no terminable "occurrence" even if the final incident prompting discharge was validly assessed as an "occurrence." Depending on the surrounding circumstances, that fact may in fairness preclude financially penalizing the employer with an award of back pay even though reinstatement is proper and is awarded.

7. Reduction for "Self-Help"

The term "self-help" generally refers to a refusal to carry out a work order or other directive on the ground, whether real or imagined, that the order violates the collective bargaining agreement or is otherwise improper.[215] Absent unusually hazardous work, the general rule is that an employee must obey supervision even when he disagrees with an order.[216] Arbitrator Harry Platt has stated the rule this way:

---

[215]Albertson's, Inc., 65 LA 1042 (Christopher, 1975).
[216]The "obey now, grieve later" rule is discussed at length in Hill and Sinicropi, Management Rights, 507–513 (BNA Books, 1986). Besides the cases discussed in this section, see Niemand Indus., 88-1 ARB ¶8070 (Sergent, 1987) (no back pay where grievant uncooperative in production of documents and information relating to grievance); Southeastern Mich. Gas Co., 90 LA 307, 311 (Daniel, 1987) (employee improperly denied promotion for refusing to relocate residence, entitled to promotion but not back pay where grievant could have mitigated damages by accepting unreasonable condition under protest); Gulf Atl. Distribution Servs., 87-1 ARB ¶8013 (Williams, 1986) (reinstatement, but no back pay for insubordination and withholding information). But see EZ Communications, 91 LA 1097, 1101 (Talarico, 1988) (finding exception to self-help rule where grievant, incurring humiliating and degrading

It is a well established rule in industrial relations that where a collective bargaining agreement provides for the processing of employee grievances through a grievance procedure, employees may not resort to self-help but must abide by the terms of the contract and must process any grievance they may have under the grievance procedure and await the decision thereunder and accept it as final and binding.[217]

An often-quoted statement of this principle is that made by the late Dean Harry Shulman, of the Yale Law School, while serving as impartial umpire under the Ford Motor Co.-United Auto Workers agreement:

> No committeeman or other union officer is entitled to instruct employees to disobey supervision's orders no matter how strongly he may believe that the orders are in violation of agreement. If he believes that an improper order has been issued, his course is to take the matter up with supervision and seek to effect an adjustment. Failing to effect an adjustment, he may file a grievance. But he may not tell the employee to disregard the order.
>
> The employee himself must also normally obey the order even though he thinks it improper. His remedy is prescribed in the grievance procedure. He may not take it on himself to disobey. To be sure, one can conceive of improper orders which need not be obeyed. An employee is not expected to obey an order to do that which would be criminal or otherwise unlawful. He may refuse to obey an improper order which involves an unusual health hazard or other serious sacrifice. But in the absence of such justifying factors, he may not refuse to obey merely because the order violates some right of his under the contract. The remedy under the contract for violation of right lies in the grievance procedure and only in the grievance procedure. To refuse obedience because of a claimed contract violation would be to substitute individual action for collective

---

comments from co-employee, walked off job. In the arbitrator's words, "I would find it unreasonable to require the grievant to have remained on the job after being subjected to such vile and lewd insults and be expected merely to file a grievance."); Bronx-Lebanon Hosp. Center, 90 LA 1216, 1217 (Babiskin, 1988) (reducing one-day suspension to written warning with back pay for grievant who disobeyed "reasonable order" to work on Good Friday, stating that "[e]mployees may properly refuse orders that are (1) illegal, (2) require the performance of an illegal act, (3) are beyond the supervisor's authority to issue, and (4) subject the employee to an unreasonable risk of harm.").

The self-help principle is particularly relevant in the drug-testing area, where employees risk dismissal for refusing a drug test. See, e.g., Crescent Metal Prods., 91 LA 1129 (Coyne, 1989) (upholding discharge of shop steward for refusing drug test).

[217]Simplicity Pattern Co., 14 LA 462, 466 (1950).

bargaining and to replace the grievance procedure with extra-contractual methods.

. . .

[A]n industrial plant is not a debating society. Its object is production. When a controversy arises, production cannot wait for exhaustion of the grievance procedure. While that procedure is being pursued, production must go on. And some one must have the authority to direct the manner in which it is to go on until the controversy is settled. That authority is vested in supervision.[218]

In those cases where an employee can effectively protect his interest by filing a grievance, arbitrators have required that the employee pursue this route rather than resort to "self-help." An employee who forgoes this option risks loss of back pay for "failing to mitigate damages," even if it is subsequently determined that the employee's interpretation of the agreement was correct. For example, in *Jordanos' Markets*,[219] the arbitrator reinstated an employee who refused to comply with a company rule prohibiting long hair. Back pay was denied, however, because the employee failed to remain on the job and file a grievance. Arbitrator Marshall Ross declared:

Instead of complying and grieving the rule the Grievant stood fast on principle for which he should not be criticized. On the other hand management should not be penalized unless it acted in such a clearly unreasonable manner as to merit that treatment. . . . In this situation where the Employee could have protected his interest without too much inconvenience or expense the Arbitrator is loath to penalize management by a back pay award. We are persuaded by the rationale leading to this result used in United Parcel Service, 52 LA 1069, 1070, where the arbitrator rejecting the employer's grooming standards declared,
In the presence of the alternative of compliance with the order and resort to the grievance procedure to establish the propriety or the impropriety of the order, the grievant's resort to self-help by consistently refusing to comply was taken at his own risk. For these reasons no back pay is awarded.[220]

Arbitrator Lionel Richman similarly disqualified a grievant from a back-pay award because he engaged in "self-help"

[218]Ford Motor Co., 3 LA 779, 780–781 (1944).
[219]63 LA 345 (Ross, 1974).
[220]Id. at 350.

by refusing to shave his beard and later file a grievance. With regard to the "obey now, grieve later" rule, Arbitrator Richman outlined a limitation of the rule as follows:

> [T]he rule is no stronger than the underpinning upon which it rests. Generally speaking, one can obey and order and file a grievance without invading any fundamental personal right of the employee. Where, however, we deal with fundamental personal rights, the employee may not be compelled to surrender a fundamental right and then later prove that the surrender was improper.[221]

Wearing a beard was not a fundamental right, according to Arbitrator Richman.

Finally Arbitrator Dale Allen, Jr., has summarized this area of arbitral law as follows:

> In essence, if a worker knowingly disobeys his supervisor, and does not even bother to avail himself of the grievance procedure, then he subjects himself to the full range of penalties commensurate with his transgression. Of course, there is no guarantee when he files a grievance that it will be resolved in his favor, but at least he accords the Company a chance to work out a mutual settlement. Further, if his complaint should go to arbitration, the grievant comes with "clean hands" in so far as procedure and "self-help" are concerned.[222]

In summary, even when the grievant is ultimately successful on the merits arbitral authority supports the proposition that resort to "self-help," rather than to the grievance procedure, will disqualify an employee from the right to any "make whole" back-pay relief.

8. Reduction for Dishonesty

In *Alumbaugh Coal Corp. v. NLRB*,[223] the Eighth Circuit refused to enforce an order by the NLRB which, in part, provided for reinstatement with back pay. The record indicated that subsequent to an unlawful discharge, an employee will-

---

[221]Operating Eng'rs Local 501, 88-2 ARB ¶8395 (1988), at 5006. See also Riceland Foods v. Carpenters Local 2381, 737 F.2d 758, 116 LRRM 2948 (8th Cir. 1984) (vacating award reinstating employees discharged for refusing order to shave if certified to wear respirator; arbitrator not authorized under parties' agreement to evaluate propriety of discipline selected by management).
[222]Colgate-Palmolive Co., 64 LA 397, 401 (1975).
[223]635 F.2d 1380, 106 LRRM 2001, 2005 (8th Cir. 1980).

fully and unlawfully failed to report earnings to the Pennsylvania Bureau of Employment Security, for the purpose of obtaining unemployment compensation benefits to which he was not entitled. While the administrative law judge found the employee's misconduct "reprehensible," the judge nevertheless recommended that the employee be reinstated to his job with full back pay on the ground that, but for the discriminatory layoff by the employer, he would not have applied for unemployment compensation. The Board adopted this recommendation.

In refusing to enforce the back-pay order of the Board, the court of appeals stated that the employee's dishonesty, although not directed at the employer, nevertheless adversely affected the company's unemployment reserve account. Moreover, the court reasoned that the purposes and policies of the Act do not justify full reinstatement of an employee whose dishonesty has been established "and whose untruthful testimony abused the process he now claims should grant him full relief." As such, the court ruled that the employee should be reinstated with full back pay for only that period preceding his unlawful postdischarge conduct.

In *Wilks v. American Bakeries Co.*,[224] an employee charged with assaulting a company superintendent was reinstated and awarded back pay plus interest from the time of his discharge until his reinstatement. At the arbitration hearing the employee testified that his only income since his discharge had come from unemployment benefits. The company subsequently attempted to reopen the hearing when it was learned that the grievant had been arrested and charged with operating a lottery (for which he was later convicted). The evidence involving the lottery charge was intended to challenge the amount of back pay and to impeach the grievant's credibility. The arbitrator correctly refused to reopen the hearing, and the company again terminated the grievant for the same reasons giving rise to the first discharge. Declaring that "[t]he discovery of 'new evidence' is not grounds for vacating or refusing to enforce the Arbitrator's award," and finding that the company acted in "bad faith and without justification" for discharging the grievant in violation of the arbitrator's award,

---

[224]563 F. Supp. 560, 116 LRRM 2687 (W.D.N.C. 1983).

the federal court sustained the arbitrator and awarded the grievant expenses and attorney's fees for bringing the action to enforce the award.

Consistent with *Alumbaugh*, it may be appropriate for an arbitrator to consider the postdischarge conduct of a grievant in formulating a back-pay remedy. Once the award is issued, however, any setoff for dishonesty is beyond the jurisdiction of the arbitrator.

(1) Dishonesty and the federal sector. Under 5 U.S.C. §5596(b)(1)(A)(i), an award of back pay must be reduced by "any amount earned by the employee through other employment" during the relevant back-pay period. Following a removal action, management informed an employee that he was to provide evidence of any employment during the back-pay period. The employee then executed a notarized statement that indicated that he earned no wages during the relevant period. That statement was made notwithstanding the fact that he had, through other employment, earned almost $29,000 during the same period. As a result of the information the employee received a check for more than $78,000 in back pay. Based on these facts the Merit Systems Protection Board affirmed his subsequent removal, which was sustained by the Federal Circuit.[225]

9. Reduction for Comparative Fault

Somewhat related to reducing back pay for the grievant's dishonesty regarding interim earnings is a decision reported by Arbitrator Sol Yarowsky. In *Panhandle Eastern Pipeline Co.*,[226] the grievant falsely stated on his wife's medical-expense claim form that she was not insured through her own employer. The employer dismissed the grievant for receipt and retention of payments that exceeded the amount properly payable. Finding that the employee was careless and inattentive, but lacked the intent to deceive, Arbitrator Yarowsky ordered reinstatement but limited his back pay to half of what otherwise would be due him on the basis of *comparative fault*.

---

[225]Harp v. Department of the Army, 791 F.2d 161 (Fed. Cir. 1986).
[226]88 LA 725 (1987).

What is of note is that the parties' collective bargaining agreement provided that if the just cause was not found, the grievant was to be returned to work with full back pay. In
implementing the award the arbitrator required the grievant
and the union to execute a waiver to modify their rights to
full back pay. This, said the arbitrator, "is believed to be a
more equitable apportionment of fault among the parties."[227]
The decision was upheld by the federal district court against
an appeal by the union. The decision was appealed to the court
of appeals for the Eighth Circuit, but abandoned before brief-
ing.

Similar to Arbitrator Yarowsky's decision, we have found
precedent for conditioning an award on the grievant's waiving
a contract benefit where the grievant was reinstated on condition that he waive back pay.

---

[227]Id. at 729.

Chapter 9

Remedies for Procedural Violations

A. Introduction

Arbitrator Robben Fleming has called attention to the problems of procedural irregularities in the administration of the collective bargaining agreement.[1] In the discharge and discipline area, Fleming notes that contracts frequently include provisions that require the employer, prior to imposing disciplinary measures, to provide notice to the union. Other requirements include giving the employee a written statement of the charges and/or holding a predisciplinary hearing which the employee and the union representative are given the option of attending.[2] When the employer has not observed contractually mandated procedural requirements, or is found to have otherwise engaged in procedural irregularities inconsistent with a "just cause" standard,[3] arbitrators are faced with the problem of formulating a remedy.

Fleming notes that when there has ben a procedural violation in a discharge or discipline case, there are three pos-

---

[1]Fleming, The Labor Arbitration Process, 134–164 (Univ. of Ill. Press, 1967).

[2]The Bureau of National Affairs, Inc., reports that procedures for discharge are found in 64% of contracts in the 400-contract database. According to BNA, such provisions vary considerably and may require, for example, giving notice to the union in advance of the discharge, holding a predischarge hearing, or giving written notice to the employee, the union, or both. Basic Patterns in Union Contracts, 12th ed., 9 (BNA Books, 1989).

[3]See, e.g., the discussion of Arbitrator Carroll Daugherty in Enterprise Wire Co., 46 LA 539 (1966).

sible positions that arbitrators may adopt: (1) that unless there is strict compliance with the procedural requirements, the entire action at issue will be nullified; (2) that the requirements are of significance only where the employee can demonstrate that he has been prejudiced by failure to comply therewith; or (3) that the requirements are important, and that any failure to comply will be penalized, but that the action taken is not necessarily rendered null and void.[4] Depending upon the particular procedural violation, as well as the substantive facts, arbitrators have formulated various remedies, including the positions cited by Fleming.

B. Investigative Infirmities

Due process rights drawn from tenets of constitutional and criminal law are generally not applicable in the industrial setting.[5] As pointed out by Arbitrator John Flagler:

> Such concepts as the "fruit of the poisoned tree," the requirement for a "Miranda" warning, or the shelter of a Fifth Amendment plea, are rarely recognized under the "law of the shop" which is the heart of labor arbitration jurisprudence.[6]

Flagler went on to note that "fatal" or "irreversible" violations of due process may give rise to reversing management's actions. In the arbitrator's words, "[t]he deference arbitrators pay to due process is to vacate any result that is *substantially* tainted and *irreversible* because of procedural defects."[7]

The most commonly cited violation of "due process" standards in the arbitral forum revolves around the investigation of the incident giving rise to the penalty assessed.[8] Where management has failed to make a complete investigation prior to effecting discipline or discharge, arbitrators have invalidated discharges and ordered reinstatement of the aggrieved

---

[4]Supra note 1, at 139.

[5]The problem of evidence and due process considerations is treated at length in Hill and Sinicropi, Evidence in Arbitration, 2d ed., 242–255 (BNA Books, 1987).

[6]Steiger Tractor, 80 LA 219 (1982) (ruling that due process did not require setting aside discharge where management effected termination without first obtaining doctor's report). See also Southern Cal. Gas Co., 89 LA 393, 396 (Alleyne, 1987) (declaring "fruit of the poisonous tree" doctrine inapplicable in industrial setting).

[7]80 LA at 225.

[8]See Jennings and Wolters, "Discharge Cases Reconsidered," 31 Arb. J. 1645, 178 (1976).

employee.[9] This principle has been expressed by Arbitrator Michael Beck as follows:

An essential element of just cause is a requirement that the Employer, before administering discipline to an employee, particularly where the supreme penalty of discharge is being imposed, make an effort to discover whether the employee did in fact violate or disobey a rule or order of management. This requirement is really no more than what is known in our legal system as procedural due process. Arbitrators generally require

---

[9]Alpha Beta Co., 91 LA 1225, 1228 (Wilmoth, 1988) (grievant prematurely discharged without investigation entitled to back pay from date of dismissal to date eight days later where he had opportunity to discuss matter with employer); Dyer's Chop House, 82 LA 198, 202 (Ray, 1984) ("the failure to grant Grievant a hearing is serious. A hearing gives Grievant and the Union an opportunity to bring out important facts for the Employer's consideration *before* the decision is made."); American Bakeries Co., 77 LA 530 (Modjeska, 1981) (noncompliance with investigative requirements affords independent grounds for setting aside discharge); Gilman Paper Co., 61 LA 416 (Murphy, 1973) (discharge invalidated where employer violated settled principle of industrial process by not interrogating grievant before reaching decision to terminate); Flintkote Co., 59 LA 329, 330 (Kelliher, 1972) ("While this Arbitrator does not believe that all of the complexities of due process that exist in judicial proceedings are equally applicable in arbitration matters, certain 'basic notions of fairness or due process' must be followed. This is particularly true where the Company has made representations to its employees that disciplinary actions will be administered fairly and that employees will not be dismissed 'without having an opportunity for a fair and impartial hearing.' "); Missouri Research Laboratories, 55 LA 197, 209 (Erbs, 1970) ("Company bears the burden of the responsibility of having considered any and all facts, from whatever source, that could have an influence on the extent of the discipline . . . and for the Company only to give consideration to one side of a story before reaching a decision on the degree of disciplinary action is not fully living up to the responsibility imposed."); Aerosol Techniques, 48 LA 1278, 1279–1280 (Summers, 1967) ("There is an inherent unfairness in discharging employees first, and then determining whether they deserve it. The action, once taken, loads the scales with a desire to justify, and short of arbitration the burden is put on the employee and the Union to persuade the Company that the employee is entitled to his job back."); United States Steel Corp., 29 LA 272, 278 (Babb, 1957) ("The importance of affording employees charged with a crime a full and fair opportunity to be heard, as incidental to due process, has often been emphasized . . . as has been the duty to make appropriate inquiry, to act upon the true facts, and to adhere to contractual procedures."); American Iron & Mach. Works Co., 19 LA 417 (Merrill, 1952) (failure to afford employee notice and opportunity to rebut charges independent grounds for setting aside discharge).

But see Williams, White & Co., 67 LA 1181 (Guenther, 1977) (no requirement for ascertaining employee's story where agreement provided that employee shall be subject to immediate discharge if insubordinate); National Steel Corp., Weirton Steel Div., 60 LA 613 (McDermott, 1973) (failure to undertake extensive investigation does not invalidate suspension where employees indicted for drug possession; suspension proper action pending determination of guilt); Summers, *Individual Protection Against Unjust Dismissal: Time for a Statute*, 62 Va. L. Rev. 481, 504 (1976) ("The employee is not entitled to a hearing before discipline is imposed, unless the contract so provides. . . .").

See generally Elkouri and Elkouri, How Arbitration Works, 4th ed., 673–675 (BNA Books, 1985), especially the citations at notes 115–116; Fairweather, Practice and Procedure in Labor Arbitration, 2d ed., 272–276 (BNA Books, 1983); Holger, *Employee Discipline and Due Process Rights: Is There an Appropriate Remedy?*, Lab. L.J. 783 (Dec. 1982).

that an employee be afforded such due process. Further, the failure of an employer to make reasonable inquiry or investigation before assessing punishment is a factor, and in some cases the only factor, in an arbitrator's refusal to sustain a discharge.[10]

Particularly noteworthy in the investigative area is a decision by the Eighth Circuit. In *Teamsters Local 878 v. Coca-Cola Bottling Co.*,[11] the appellate court upheld an arbitrator's determination that the concept of just cause included not only the substantive elements of appropriate factual circumstances but also a procedural requirement that the employee be given some minimal, adequate opportunity to present his side of the case before the discharge. In so ruling, the Eighth Circuit noted that arbitrators have long been applying notions of "industrial due process" to "just cause" discharge cases.[12]

In further support of this principle is a decision by the Sixth Circuit, where it was held that an arbitrator did not exceed his authority in ordering reinstatement of an employee who struck a company inspector, despite a rule prescribing discharge as the penalty for such a violation. Although the agreement reserved to the employer "all customary and usual rights, power, functions, and authority of management," the court of appeals reasoned that it cannot follow from such reserved power that a legitimate dispute could not arise with respect to the method and manner in which the employer should exercise its managerial functions or the imposition of individual penalties.[13] The same court, in another decision, declared that "[t]he determination of procedural fairness is sufficiently integral to 'just cause' to sustain the arbitrator's decision to decide that issue, when the submission did not make it clear that procedural fairness was not in question."[14]

Where a termination was based upon a hearsay statement

---

[10]Osborn & Ulland, 68 LA 1146, 1151 (1977).

[11]613 F.2d 716, 103 LRRM 2380 (8th Cir.), cert. denied, 446 U.S. 988, 104 LRRM 2431 (1980).

[12]Id., 103 LRRM at 2383, citing Summers, supra note 9, at 500.

[13]Timken Co. v. Steelworkers, 492 F.2d 1178, 85 LRRM 2532 (6th Cir. 1974).

[14]Johnston Boiler Co. v. Boilermakers Local 893, 753 F.2d 40, 118 LRRM 2348, 2351 (6th Cir. 1985). See also Anaconda Co. v. Machinists Lodge 27, 693 F.2d 35, 37, 111 LRRM 2919 (6th Cir. 1982) (upholding decision of arbitrator finding that it was improper for company to deny union representation based on following language: "All employees shall be treated fairly and justly by the Company and/or any of its supervisory employees.").

(a letter charging the grievant with discourteous treatment), one arbitrator ruled that the airline had not established just cause until the arbitration hearing (where a witness to the incident was produced). As a remedy the arbitrator awarded back pay from the date of the discharge to the arbitration hearing, the date the grievant's due process rights were satisfied. Asserting that the arbitrator made an award not called for in the parties' collective bargaining agreement, the grievant filed a lawsuit to have the award overturned. The district court and the Tenth Circuit affirmed.[15]

Likewise, in *Gold Kist*,[16] Arbitrator Lloyd Byars ruled that an employer's failure in complying with procedural requirements of reviewing the grievant's entire work record before effecting a discharge warranted setting aside the discharge. The arbitrator pointed out that management's failure to comply with procedural requirements would not always result in refusing to uphold the dismissal. The arbitrator did note that "if there is a possibility, regardless of how remote, that the grievant was prejudiced by the employer's omission, the employer's action should be set aside."[17]

C. Predischarge Hearings in the Public Sector

In *Cleveland Board of Education v. Loudermill*,[18] the Supreme Court stated that "the root requirement" of the Due Process Clause is "that an individual be given an opportunity for a hearing *before* he is deprived of any significant property interest." However, the Court recognized that there are some situations in which a postdeprivation hearing will satisfy due process requirements, commenting, "In general, 'something

---

[15]Chernak v. Southwest Airlines, 778 F.2d 578, 120 LRRM 3483 (10th Cir. 1985). See also Meyer Prods., 91 LA 690 (Dworkin, 1988) (discharge reduced to suspension, even though conduct justified removal, where superintendent made decision within one hour after hearing foreman's secondhand report of on-duty fighting).

[16]89 LA 66 (1987).

[17]Id. at 70. Accord Bake Rite Rolls, 90 LA 1133, 1136 (DiLauro, 1988) (suspension and discharge reversed where employer failed to allow union representative to be present at meeting with purported eyewitness, citing NLRB v. J. Weingarten, 420 U.S. 251, 88 LRRM 2689 (1975) and Gold Kist, supra note 16).

[18]470 U.S. 532, 118 LRRM 3041 (1985).

less' than a full evidentiary hearing is sufficient prior to adverse administrative action."[19]

Case law clearly suggests that a public employer, in dismissing a nonprobationary employee, should provide either oral or written notice of the charges and an opportunity for a predetermination hearing of some kind. The hearing need not be a full adversarial hearing prior to governmental action,[20] but may simply be a request that the employee provide his or her side of the story in person or in writing to management. While the predetermination hearing "need not definitively resolve the propriety of the discharge," it should be constructed as an initial check against incorrect decisions. As stated by the Court in *Loudermill*, it should be "essentially, a determination of whether there are reasonable grounds to believe that the charges against the employee are true and support the proposed actions."[21]

What is the remedy where a probationary employee, contrary to the express terms of the contract, is not afforded any opportunity to respond with her side of the story?

Arbitrator Edgar Jones, Jr., in *Paramount Unified School District and Teachers Association of Paramount*,[22] addressed the problems with not sharing complaints with the grievant, a probationary teacher. The parties' collective bargaining agreement mandated that "no derogatory material shall be placed in an employees' file until the employee has had an opportunity to review and submit a response to it." The agreement further provided that when

> significant complaints or derogatory allegations are made against an employee . . . the following procedures shall be followed: . . . 2 . . . the site administrator shall advise the employee of it within a reasonable time, identifying the complainant if

---

[19]Id., 118 LRRM at 3046.

[20]The *Loudermill* Court noted that in only one case, Goldberg v. Kelly, 397 U.S. 254 (1970), has it required a hearing of this type.

[21]118 LRRM at 3046. See also Jones v. McKenzie, 628 F. Supp. 1501, 121 LRRM 2901 (D.D.C. 1986) (termination of school employee for drug abuse arbitrary and capricious where employment terminated on basis of unconfirmed initial urine test (EMIT test) and employee afforded no hearing prior to discharge, citing *Loudermill*); Letter Carriers v. Postal Serv., 625 F. Supp. 1527, 121 LRRM 2384 (D.D.C. 1986) (upholding reinstatement without back pay of letter carrier discharged after indictment for criminal abuse of minor, where grievant's branch manager accepted recommendations by Managerial Sectional Center outright and failed to make an independent judgment as to proper penalty).

[22]AAA Case No. 72-390-0334 (1988 unpublished).

known. . . . 3. If requested by the employee, the District shall make a reasonable effort to arrange a meeting between the employee, the complainant and the site administrator, in an effort to solve the problem. . . . 5. The site administrator shall make a fair and reasonable effort to verify the accuracy of any written complaint or allegation. 6. The employee shall have the right to submit a written response to any written complaint or allegation received.

Without knowledge of the grievant-teacher, the administration placed numerous complaints and derogatory memoranda in her file. All items were utilized in the administration's decision not to renew the contract of the teacher. While the Teachers did not challenge the administration's failure to re-elect the grievant at the end of her second probationary year (the association accepted the District's right, under California law, to make the decision on the merits without recourse by the probationary employee to the collective bargaining agreement's just cause provision), the union did grieve the employer's failure to follow the evaluation procedures. Arbitrator Jones' lengthy analysis is especially applicable in this case:

> There are two tangents of precaution that have to be kept in mind which were not in this instance.
> First, if the administration's negative perception is indeed an accurate one, careful attention must be given to assembling a solid and unassailable record that demonstrates the existence of the deficiencies. But *no record will be unassailable upon impartial scrutiny that has been put together without the opportunity of the affected employee to contribute to it by confronting accusers and responding to derogatory allegations with countervailing facts.*
> There are two sources for that fundamental reality. One is cultural: the American dedication to due process and fairness in the implementation of authority (which is reflected in various legal contexts, arbitration decisions, and in the terms of this collective bargaining agreement). The other source is pragmatic: the experiential awareness that untested factual allegations all too frequently turn out to have false proof, naively accepted or maliciously created.
> Second, and disconcertingly of course, it is not at all unusual for such a negative perception to turn out to be erroneous. The conclusion of irremediable incompetence may be discovered to have been due to the lack of available information that would counterbalance or rebut what has thus far been gathered. To think and act in anticipation of that possibility of error or incompleteness is to enhance the prospects both of achieving fairness toward the employee and of safeguarding the employer's

interests. The District, after all, has invested time and money in anticipation of the success of the employee. It also wants to avoid the prospect of liability in arbitral or judicial proceedings for having engaged in unwarranted adverse actions that have been prompted by inadequate investigations.

The ultimate effect in a particular case of utilizing this more balanced and skeptical process of gathering and appraising the facts of an employee's performance and potential are unpredictable, and properly so. *Educated guesses are no substitute for factfinding. What is produced may reinforce the negative information already at hand; it may disclose that the initial negative impression is no longer tenable; or it may indicate that the employee should be given further remediating counseling and more understanding support.* [Emphasis supplied.]

Finding a procedural violation, Arbitrator Jones went on to discuss the remedy:

The normal expectation of collective bargainers is that their arbitrator is empowered to fashion remedies that are realistically responsive to whatever contractual violations are found. That expectation, of course, is wholly subject to their control in negotiations. Collective bargainers may and frequently do expressly withhold from arbitrators the authority to fashion a particular remedy in specified circumstances that might otherwise be deemed appropriate. But so long as they have not expressly restricted the otherwise impliable authority to award a particular remedy, the presumption of appropriate remedial power necessarily remains operative. In this instance they have not done so.

The normal expectation is also that the nature and extent of the remedy will be dictated by the nature of the contractual mandate that has been violated. Here the violation manifestly resulted in the deprivation of the proper conditions for an evaluation of the employee's probationary year. That amounts to a serious deprivation of a right of the Association.

Rejecting a verbal reprimand as a "verbal wrist-slapping," Arbitrator Jones ordered the administration to purge the teacher's personnel file of all documents (other than those that were not physically disclosed and identified). Jones further "instated" the teacher to a second probationary year. The arbitrator found compensation "questionable in these circumstance of probationary status."

In separate decisions, Louis Zigman and Norman Brand, arbitrators in *Bellflower Unified School District* (1989) and *Merced City Elementary School District* (1989), respectively, found that reemployment for an additional second probationary year was an appropriate remedy for management's failure to evaluate an employee in accordance with contractual mandates. Arbitrator Zigman's *Bellflower* decision was vacated (no written decision) because the court felt he had granted a remedy that was not available, though it was appropriate. Disagreeing with arbitrators Jones, Zigman, and Brand, Arbitrator Joseph Gentile, in *San Bernardino Community College District* (1990), acknowledged that there are "rights without remedies" and that the remedy of reinstatement is not available should a violation of the parties' agreement be established. Gentile acknowledged that the remedy of reinstatement is appropriate (albeit "unavailable") where management fails to follow the contractual evaluation procedure.

D. Failure to Notify Employee or Union Representative

Some arbitrators have found that failure to provide contractual notice to the union prior to assessing discipline will warrant overturning the penalty. The rationale generally expressed is that it is far easier to convince a company representative not to discharge or discipline an employee during the deliberative stage than after the decision has been implemented.[23] In these cases, however, there is usually a finding that the absence of prior notice has, or is likely to have, some prejudicial effect on the aggrieved employee. For example, in *Piedmont Natural Gas Co.*,[24] the contract provided that in the event that an employee was to be discharged, the union representative was to be notified immediately. Arbitrator James Whyte found that the employer violated the agreement when it waited 10 working days before informing the union of its intent to discharge an employee, found that the delay let the

---

[23]See, e.g., Cuyahoga Metro. Hous. Auth., 90 LA 612, 616–617 (Bittel, 1988), (reversing five-day suspension and ordering back pay where contract conditions disciplinary suspensions on prior notice to employee and union, reasoning that violation of contract provision is denial of due process); Zenith Radio Corp., 47 LA 257, 258 (Griffin, 1966); Braniff Airways, 44 LA 417, 420 (Rohman, 1965) (discharge invalidated for failure to follow procedures; employer ordered to comply with agreement before discharge).

[24]59 LA 661 (1972).

case "grow cold" and deprived the union of the opportunity to gather "fresh evidence."

Some other arbitrators have distinguished between pre- or postdischarge notice, noting that different rights are at issue depending upon the type of notice required. As stated by Arbitrator William Eaton in *Wilson & Co.*:[25]

> What the Union is contending is that strict compliance is required for notice either before or after discharge, and that the remedy is the same in either case, namely that the discharge be voidable for failure of proper notice. The Union argues that immediacy of notice is required by the "facts of life" of labor relations. It is pointed out that decisions made on the spur of the moment "are reversible if people can bargain about controversial items before positions harden and 'face' needs to be saved." Surely, however, this is a description of what would occur in the "cooling-off" situation, and not what would result from notice after discharge. . . .
>
> The different operation of the two types of notice suggests very strongly that two different kinds of rights are at stake. In the "cooling off" situation there is a Union right to be heard before discharge occurs. In the case of notice afterwards the matter becomes one of review, and the employee is assured only that he will be furnished with a written statement as to why the action has been taken. It is questionable, therefore, whether the prevailing remedy for violation of a contract provision requiring notice prior to discharge, which is to hold such a discharge voidable, is appropriate to the situation in which the requirement is only for written notice after discharge.[26]

Arbitrator Peter Kelliher has likewise noted that the value of a predischarge hearing both to the employer and to the grievant is fully recognized "and the purpose cannot be served by an ex post facto determination as to whether the grievant was 'prejudiced' by the lack of 'due process.' "[27]

In *Safeway Stores v. Food & Commercial Workers Local 400*,[28] the federal court for the District of Columbia sustained an arbitrator's award that ordered reinstatement without back pay because of the employer's failure to disclose fully all reasons for the discharge of an employee otherwise guilty of insubordination and threatening a supervisor. The arbitrator

---

[25]50 LA 807 (1968).
[26]Id. at 809–810.
[27]Flintkote Co., supra note 9, at 330.
[28]621 F. Supp. 1233, 118 LRRM 3419 (D.D.C. 1985).

stated that had the employer properly notified the grievant and the union of its reasons for discharge, he would have affirmed the discharge. The court stated that the arbitrator's interpretation of the "good cause" provision "by its silence granted [the arbitrator] discretion to determine procedural requirements."

E. Failure to Have a Union Representative Present at Investigation

Following the decision of the Supreme Court in *NLRB v. J. Weingarten, Inc.*,[29] arbitrators have invalidated discipline or discharges where the grievant was denied assistance of a union representative during an investigatory interview. Moreover, discharges have been overturned where the employer did not "meet and confer" with the union prior to reaching a decision to discipline or discharge an employee.[30] Thus, where an agreement provided that "the Company agrees to meet and confer with representatives of the Union within three (3) working days prior to its decision to discharge or suspend any employee," Arbitrator Gerald Brown reasoned as follows:

> Sterile or archaic procedures should not be emphasized at the expense of equity or justice, but the right to participate and to consult before a decision is made is a very real and substantive right. Application of the concepts of due process varies widely

---

[29]Supra note 17, at 257 (holding that employee is entitled to union representation during investigatory phase of disciplinary proceeding where (1) employee "reasonably believes the investigation will result in disciplinary action," and (2) "where the employee requests representation.").

[30]See, e.g., Southern Cal. Gas Co., 89 LA 393 (Alleyne, 1987) (finding right to union steward in advance of requiring employee to undergo drug test rooted in parties' past practice); Ames Co., 88 LA 741 (Duda, 1987) (suspension without presence of union representative improper where contract required employee have representation at time of discipline); City of Sterling Heights, 80 LA 825, 829 (Ellmann, 1983) (holding that affirmative duty exists in management to secure *Weingarten* rights for grievant); Furr's, Inc., 70 LA 1036 (Gorsuch, 1978); Ward La France Truck Corp., 69 LA 29 (Levy, 1977); Combustion Eng., 67 LA 349 (Clark, 1976) (under contract provision requiring agreement to conform to U.S. or state laws, employer improperly discharged employee because it denied employee's request to be represented by union steward at meeting); Eaton Corp., 66 LA 581 (Emerson, 1976) (finding violation of contract and Taft-Hartley by denying employee's requests for union representation during disciplinary interviews; Babcock & Wilcox Co., 61 LA 360 (Ellis, 1973) (failure to permit grievant to phone steward); Kelsey-Hayes Co., 60 LA 9, 15–16 (Howlett, 1972) (discharge overturned where compliance with request for union representation would have prevented employee's conduct that led to discharge).

in our system of industrial democracy because of the nature of different agreements reached by the parties. The right to be heard before a decision is made is vastly different from trying to reverse a decision already made. Denial of such privilege, when guaranteed by an agreement, invariably warrants a remedy.[31]

Declaring that the discharge was without just cause "solely because of the Company's failure to comply with the requirements of [meeting with the union]," the arbitrator reinstated the grievant without back pay.

Ruling that the grievants were entitled under the parties' agreement to have representation at the earliest possible stage, Arbitrator Fred Denson, in ordering reinstatement because of due process violations, reasoned as follows:

> Whether earlier representation of the grievants would have changed the outcome of this matter is not important. What is important is that representation was not permitted by the Company for a period of time prior to the individual interviews. Equity requires that the Company not be permitted to fully enforce its contractual right to discharge employees without first fully complying with the contractual due process requirements regarding representation. Based on these considerations, the appropriate penalty is a suspension without pay, rather than discharge.[32]

An issue of concern to a federal-sector arbitrator is whether an employee is entitled to have the presence of a union representative at a reply meeting when the employee meets with management to respond orally or in writing to a possible disciplinary charge. Section 7114(a)(2)(A) of the Federal Service Labor-Management Relations Act (FLMRA) provides:

> (2) An exclusive representative of an appropriate unit in an agency shall be given the opportunity to be represented at—
> (A) any formal discussion between one or more representatives or more representatives of the agency and one or more employees in the unit or their representatives concerning any grievance or any personnel policy or practices or other general condition of employment.

Section 7114(a)(2)(B) provides:

> (B) An exclusive examination of an employee in the unit

---

[31]Cameron Iron Works, 64 LA 67, 70 (1975).
[32]Kraft, Inc., 82 LA 360, 366 (1984).

by a representative of the agency in connection with an investigation if—
    (i) the employee reasonably believes that the examination may result in disciplinary action against the employee; and
    (ii) the employee requests representation.

As pointed out by Judge (and former Arbitrator) Harry Edwards of the Court of Appeals for the District of Columbia Circuit, for an exclusive representative to have an independent right to be represented, each of the following elements must be present: there must be a "discussion," formal in nature, between one or more agency representatives and one or more bargaining unit employees, concerning a "grievance," "personal policy," or "other general condition of employment."[33] Applying the statute, Judge Edwards ruled that an employee, accused of sexual harassment, had no right to union representation in a meeting called by management to respond to the charge. The failure to provide a representative was not an unfair labor practice because the meeting did not concern a "grievance" under the statute. Moreover, since the employee did not request the presence of a union representative, the employee's *Weingarten* rights under Section 7114(a)(2)(B) were not violated.

F. Failure to Advise Employee That Union Representative May Be Present

Arbitrators have also invalidated discipline on procedural grounds where the grievant was not advised of his right to have a steward present during an investigatory interview.[34] This is especially prevalent in the federal sector, where Con-

---

[33]Government Employees (AFGE) Local 3882 v. Federal Labor Relations Auth., 865 F.2d 1283, 130 LRRM 2365 (D.C. Cir. 1989). See also Defense Criminal Investigative Serv. (DCIS) v. Federal Labor Relations Auth., 855 F.2d 93, 129 LRRM 2233 (3d Cir. 1988) (DCIS investigator of federal agency's subdivision, Defense Logistics Agency (DLA), is representative of DLA under statute entitling federal employee in bargaining unit to presence of union representative when questioned by representative of employing agency about matter that could lead to imposition of disciplinary sanctions).

[34]See, e.g., Maui Pineapple Co., 86 LA 907 (Tsukiyama, 1986) (sustaining discharge but awarding employee one month's wages for employer's violation of *Weingarten* rights); Briggs & Stratton Corp., 66 LA 758 (Grant, 1976); United States Steel Corp., 59 LA 1129 (Wolff, 1972). Contra Tampa Elec. Co., 88 LA 791 (Vause, 1986) (employer not required to notify grievant of *Weingarten* rights).

gress has codified employees' *Weingarten* rights in 5 U.S.C. Section 7114(a)(2)(B), and agencies are annually required to inform employees of their *Weingarten* rights.[35]

G. Other Procedural Infirmities

1. *Miranda* Warnings

In *Postal Workers v. Postal Service*,[36] the employer, at the arbitration proceeding, sought to introduce statements of the grievant made during a custodial interrogation by federal law enforcement officers. The arbitrator found that the statements were elicited before the grievant had been given a type of *Miranda*[37] warning and, on that account, ruled the statements inadmissible. The arbitrator then concluded that "[h]aving excluded the Grievant's statements which form the fundamental basis of the Postal Service charges, the removal action is not sustainable." Concluding that the arbitrator's award could not be enforced because it did not "draw its essence" from the contract, the trial court adopted an alternative interpretation of the agreement and vacated the award.[38] The D.C. Circuit reversed.

In finding that just cause was absent, the arbitrator cited the management rights provision which required that the discharge of a Postal Service employee must be "consistent with applicable laws and regulations." The court of appeals reasoned that it does not matter whether the arbitrator's construction and application of *Miranda* was correct as a matter of law. Even if the arbitrator's view of *Miranda* was wrong, his decision to exclude the grievant's statements did not violate the law or cause the employer to act unlawfully and, accordingly, the award had to be enforced under traditional standards of review.

With respect to the application of the *Miranda* rule in the

---

[35]Department of Treasury, 82 LA 1209 (Kaplan, 1984). See also Defense Mapping Agency Aerospace Center, 88 LA 651, 656 (Hilgert, 1986) (management ordered to publicize essence of arbitration award as remedy for *Weingarten* violation).
[36]789 F.2d 1, 122 LRRM 2094 (D.C. Cir. 1986).
[37]Miranda v. Arizona, 384 U.S. 436 (1966). See generally Hill and Sinicropi, supra note 5, at 229–240.
[38]118 LRRM 2472 (D.D.C. 1985).

workplace, the better rule is that the constitutional protection against self-incrimination has little application. Reflecting the thinking of most arbitrators on the issue, Willard Wirtz has stated that the privilege against self-incrimination enters into due process of arbitration, but its relevance is quite specific:

> [T]here is a fairly clear consensus in the arbitration opinions that this privilege, established in the criminal law, has no place, at least as such, in the arbitration of grievance cases (invariably discharge or disciplinary cases). The importance of this point is accordingly, as an illustration of the fact that "due process of arbitration" is a distinct concept, similar in its approach and purposes to "due process of law," but entirely independent in the conclusion it reaches.[39]

Addressing the public sector, Hill and Sinicropi, in *Evidence in Arbitration*,[40] summarize this area as follows:

> Similar to the private sector, most public-sector arbitrators will not credit arguments based on the constitution, especially those arguments based on *Miranda*, where constitutional rights are not explicitly contemplated in the parties' collective bargaining agreement. (The one exception seems to be in the federal sector where arbitrators are more sensitive to constitutional mandates.) Arbitrators' reasoning varies, but the result is the same. The fifth amendment does not guarantee that a person who invokes it will not be subject to an unfavorable inference or even discharge for insubordination, and arbitrators and courts have, with few exceptions, so held.[41]

2. Equitable Doctrines

In what appears to be a true "outliner," one arbitrator, seeking a remedy for an employer's failure to timely notify an employee of his failure to pass his probationary period, applied the common-law "unclean hands" doctrine[42] and or-

---

[39]Wirtz, *Due Process of Arbitration*, in The Arbitrator and the Parties, Proceedings of the 11th Annual Meeting, National Academy of Arbitrators, 1, 19 (BNA Books, 1958).

[40]Hill and Sinicropi, supra note 5.

[41]Id. at 240. Accord Anderson v. National R.R. Passenger Corp., 754 F.2d 202, 118 LRRM 2673 (7th Cir. 1984) (Amtrak not required to provide fifth amendment due process protection to employees discharged for disappearance of railroad funds).

[42]As defined by the district court, "The equitable maxim that he who comes into equity must come with clean hands provides that a party seeking relief from a court of equity will be barred if it has engaged in fraudulent, unconscionable, or bad faith conduct toward the party proceeded against." Daiichiya-Love's Bakery v. Longshoremen (ILW) Local 142, 121 LRRM 2459, 2462 (D. Haw. 1985).

dered reinstatement. The arbitrator found that management violated the agreement because it notified the grievant of his failure to pass his probationary period on December 28th, rather than on December 24th. (This occurred because the personnel manager did not wish to provide the grievant with the bad news on Christmas Eve and because the manager did not see the grievant until the 28th.) Substituting its judgment for that of the arbitrator, the federal court reversed, reasoning that the employer's failure to notify the grievant cannot be deemed such willful conduct as to warrant the application of the doctrine of unclean hands. The court stated that the arbitrator had no basis upon which to apply the doctrine of unclean hands.

3. Failure to Properly Evaluate an Employee

The question of the remedy to be applied when an employer fails to properly consider an employee for a position under a sufficient- or relative-ability seniority clause is discussed at length in Chapter 17. Arbitrator Walter Kaufman, in *Pacific Bell*,[43] reports a decision where management violated the terms of its attendance plan. Prior to the dismissal of an employee the plan mandated that a medical opinion be obtained "on whether the employee's ability to be at work in the future will improve, remain stable or deteriorate."[44] As a remedy for failing to obtain a current medical report before approving the discharge, Arbitrator Kaufman ordered a physical examination of the grievant and a review of her medical history between the date of discharge and the examination. The arbitrator ordered that the report include "an opinion as to whether Grievant will be able to report to work without falling below the standards set forth in the attendance plan with regard to disability absences." The grievant was ordered reinstated with back pay if the doctor indicated that the grievant was able to meet the plan's standards. Otherwise, the employer's procedural violation "shall be considered a tech-

---

[43]91 LA 653 (1988).
[44]Id.

nical violation" and in that case the grievant "shall neither be reinstated nor awarded a monetary remedy."[45]

4. Implementation of Procedurally Flawed Disciplinary Policies

What is the remedy when management unilaterally implements a rule in violation of its bargaining obligation under the parties' agreement? One remedy is simply to rescind the policy and order the parties to bargain the matter to impasse.

Difficult remedy problems arise when employees are disciplined under a unilaterally implemented policy and the policy is subsequently ordered rescinded, either by an arbitrator or the NLRB. There are situations where expunging discipline and providing back pay and reinstatement are not appropriate remedies for management's implementing a procedurally flawed disciplinary policy and assessing penalties under that policy. In a 1988 unpublished case reported by Arbitrator Richard Mittenthal, a federal agency implemented a disciplinary-attendance policy in three cities and refused to bargain with the union over such programs. In response to an adverse arbitration award (after the case was deferred to the arbitrator under the NLRB's *Collyer Insulated Wire* principle), the agency terminated the programs and argued that no further remedy was appropriate. The union submitted that any discipline meted out pursuant to these programs (or any discipline which relies on penalties meted out earlier pursuant to these programs) should be expunged. Reinstatement and back pay were requested. Management asserted that there was no justification for expunging the discipline under the terminated policy simply because of a procedural failure by the administration to negotiate with the union. Management believed it had a contractual right to implement the program without negotiations and it did so.

Arbitrator Mittenthal, focusing only on the remedy issue, observed that there are two distinct features to any disciplinary policy. The first concerns the misconduct for which employees are disciplined. The second deals with the penalties that may be invoked for such misconduct. The attendance

---

[45]Id. at 657.

policy at issue, reasoned Mittenthal, dealt only with the penalties for attendance-related misconduct. It made no attempt to change long-standing rules (or practices) that treated poor attendance as the kind of misconduct that warrants discipline. Mittenthal reasoned that the fact that the penalties chosen by management were determined by a program prematurely introduced in violation of the national agreement, does not diminish the existence of the alleged misconduct. The arbitrator's analysis of a difficult remedy issue is particularly instructive:

> [T]he purpose of a remedy is to place employees (and management) in the position they would have been in had there been no contract violation. The remedy serves to restore the *status quo ante*. Consider the employees who allegedly committed attendance-related offenses. Where would they be now if [the policy] had not been introduced . . ., if its introduction had been delayed a substantial period of time because of the need for prior negotiation? The answer is clear. They would be awaiting a judgment on their grievances based on whether they were innocent or guilty of the charged offense and whether, if guilty, the penalty imposed was reasonable under all the circumstances [excluding the policy] of their case. The remedy here should assure them that they will be exposed to a Management judgment, and an arbitral judgment, that is . . . free [of the former policy].

Mittenthal concluded by pointing out that the remedy sought—expunging discipline and consequently providing back pay and reinstatement—"would go far beyond the notion of a status quo ante. It would reward employees for management's procedural error by freeing them of any responsibility for their alleged misconduct."

H. Summary

There is no uniform solution or preferred remedy when a procedural violation is found in a discipline or discharge case. As suggested by Arbitrator Robben Fleming, it may be undesirable to rule that the entire action will be voided unless there is strict compliance with all procedural requirements for the following reasons: (1) the procedural infirmities may not have been prejudicial to the grievant, (2) the emphasis upon technicalities would be inconsistent with the informal atmosphere of the arbitration process, and (3) the end result could on many occasions be quite ludicrous. Fleming points out that if, for example, an employee becomes intoxicated on the job, and starts smashing valuable machinery with a sledge hammer, it would not be appropriate to nullify his discharge on the sole ground that it was in violation of a contractual requirement that the union be given advance notice.[46]

What, then, should be the remedy? The second position (procedural requirements are important where employee can demonstrate prejudice), notes Fleming, has considerable merit because it focuses on the facts of a particular case. If the affected grievant can demonstrate prejudice because of the procedural violation, it may be appropriate to invalidate the discharge. In this regard, some procedural defects are, on their face, prejudicial to an employee's case, as the situation where an employee is denied all opportunity to explain his side of the story. In light of these facts, an arbitrator may appropriately nullify such action based only on procedural infirmities. Still, as pointed out by Fleming, there may be a problem with this approach in that it tends to require value judgments as to when an action is actually prejudicial to an individual employee.

The third approach (that any failure to observe procedures will be penalized) recognizes that procedural requirements are important and that any failure to comply will be penalized, but will not thereby render the action void. This approach, argues Fleming, has been taken by most arbitrators. To encourage future compliance, one remedy is not to reinstate the grievant, but rather to order the employer to pay the grievant back pay from the date of the violation to the date of the award because it failed to follow the procedural requirements of the contract. According to Fleming, the outrage will most likely assure the company's making sure that the contract is followed in the future. Another remedy may be to assess the costs of the proceedings against the party who has not complied with the procedural mandates of the agreement.[47] In those cases

---

[46]Fleming, supra note 1, at 139–140. See also Hygrade Food Prods. Corp., 69 LA 414, 418–419 (Harter, 1977) (where arbitrator stated that "[a] discharge for just cause cannot be upheld unless the Employer provides due process," yet reduced discharge to four-week suspension); Grief Bros. Cooperage Corp., 42 LA 555 (Daugherty, 1964) (declaring that every employee in industrial democracy has right of "due process of law," but reinstating the grievant without back pay).

[47]See, e.g., City of Henderson, Nev., 91 LA 941, 946 (Morris, 1988) (employer that

where prejudice is demonstrated, for example, where the grievant has made incriminating statements in an investigatory interview while being denied the presence of a union steward, any evidence derived may properly be excluded by an arbitrator.[48]

I. Federal Sector

Many of the options suggested by Fleming may not be appropriate in the federal sector. Where a government agency has agreed to consult with a labor organization on a particular matter and expressed that intention in the bargaining agreement, two determinations are necessary for a back-pay remedy to be appropriate when the agency has failed to consult. The arbitrator must determine not only that the agency violated a contractual obligation to consult, but also that such improper action directly caused the grievant to suffer a loss of pay. For example, if an agency had consulted with a union concerning hours-of-work changes, there is no reason to believe the agency would have modified a proposed change in the work-week schedules to allow a grievant overtime work. And since it cannot be shown that the agency's failure to consult would have resulted in overtime to the grievant, an award of back pay would not be an appropriate remedy for this "procedural" violation.

In summary, under the Back Pay Act, the "causation" or "nexus" between the conduct and the remedy must be present before a grievant is entitled to restitution. Thus, before an employee is entitled to restitution as a remedy for an improper disciplinary action by an agency, it must be determined that the unjustified or unwarranted action directly caused the harm for which the employee seeks restitution.

---

failed to post notice and consider grievant when filling vacancy ordered to pay two-thirds of arbitration costs); Union Oil Co. of Cal., 91 LA 1206, 1210 (Klein, 1988) (employer that prevailed in discharge proceeding liable for reasonable value of union representatives' services in arbitration, union's portion of cost of transcript, and other direct and necessary expenses involved in processing grievance where union forced to arbitrate so as not to set precedent for waiver of procedural rights); Cameron Iron Works, 73 LA 878, 882 (Marlatt, 1979) (union reimbursed for actual costs of taking case to arbitration for employer's procedural violation of failing to meet with union prior to discharge of employee for theft).

[48]See *Individual Rights Issues* in Hill and Sinicropi, Evidence in Arbitration, 229 (BNA Books, 1987).

Chapter 10

Arbitral Authority to Reduce Discipline

A. Arbitration Awards

The question of the arbitrator's authority to convert a discharge to a lesser penalty is a vexing problem and is a much debated topic among arbitrators and advocates. Even in the absence of a specific contractual provision precluding the arbitrator from changing a penalty, various arbitrators have held that they should not substitute their judgment for that of management as to the appropriateness of a penalty. As noted by Arbitrator John Larkin in *White Pine Copper Co.*:[1] "The Arbitrator should not substitute his judgment for that of management in a case where there is a definite cause for discharge."[2]

Arbitrator Whitley McCoy articulated the rationale for this principle in the often-quoted *Stockham Pipe Fittings Co.*[3] decision as follows:

> Where an employee has violated a rule or engaged in conduct meriting disciplinary action, it is primarily the function of management to decide upon the proper penalty. If management acts in good faith upon a fair investigation and fixes a penalty not inconsistent with that imposed in other like cases, an arbitrator should not disturb it. The mere fact that management has imposed a somewhat different penalty or a somewhat more severe

---

[1] 63-2 ARB ¶8548 (1963).
[2] Id. at 4816.
[3] 1 LA 160 (1945).

penalty than the arbitrator would have, if he had had the decision to make originally is no justification for changing it. The minds of equally reasonable men differ. A consideration which would weigh heavily with one man will seem of less importance to another. A circumstance which highly aggravates an offense in one man's eyes may be only slight aggravation to another. If an arbitrator could substitute his judgment and discretion for the judgment and discretion honestly exercised by management, then the functions of management would have been abdicated, and unions would take every case to arbitration. The result would be as intolerable to employees as to management.[4]

Arbitrator McCoy conditioned this precept further by pointing out that there are circumstances where arbitral discretion may be exercised:

The only circumstances under which a penalty imposed by management can be rightfully set aside by an arbitrator are those where discrimination, unfairness, or capricious and arbitrary action are proved—in other words, where there has been abuse of discretion.[5]

Interpreting a standard "just cause" provision, Arbitrator Wilbur C. Bothwell similarly held that "the arbitrator should not substitute his judgment for that of management unless he finds that the penalty is excessive, unreasonable, or that management has abused its discretion."[6]

Arbitrator Milton O. Talent has ruled that once a violation of one of the company's plant rules is found, the arbitrator has no authority to modify the penalty called for under the rule:

Since there was a violation of the rule which called for a three day suspension, it is beyond the Arbitrator's authority to modify the penalty under the circumstances. The issuance of the rule and the failure of the Union to contest it leave the Arbitrator no choice but to sustain the penalty after a violation was found.[7]

Arbitrator Elwin Hadlock, in *North Star Steel Corp.*,[8] has likewise stated:

It is a function of management to decide upon a proper penalty.

---

[4]Id. at 162.
[5]Id.
[6]Franz Food Prods., 28 LA 543, 548 (1957).
[7]Wagner Castings and Allied Indus. Workers Local 728, Grievance No. 6846 (unpublished).
[8]68 LA 114 (1977).

It is not the province of the arbitrator to substitute his judgment for the judgment of the Company, if it is established that the management acted in good faith, upon a fair investigation, and fixed a penalty not inconsistent with that imposed in other like cases.[9]

Other arbitrators take the position that, where the agreement does not impose a clear limitation on the authority to modify a penalty, an arbitrator may reduce the amount of discipline even in the absence of arbitrary, capricious, or discriminatory behavior. In this regard Arbitrator Harry Platt noted:

> In many disciplinary cases, the reasonableness of the penalty imposed on the employee rather than the existence of proper cause of disciplining him is a question the arbitrator must decide. . . . In disciplinary cases generally, therefore, most arbitrators exercise the right to change or modify a penalty if it is found to be improper or too severe, under all the circumstances of the situation. This right is deemed to be inherent in the arbitrator's power to discipline and in his authority to finally settle and adjust the dispute beforehand.[10]

Arbitrator Adolph M. Koven has declared that the right to alter a penalty is "inherent in his power to decide the sufficiency of cause."[11]

Similarly, A. Howard Myers, in an address before the National Academy of Arbitrators, argued that in the absence of a contractual waiver of the right to review a penalty, the justification and the extent of the penalty fall within the scope of arbitration:

> [A]n arbitrator usually applies the equity concept in a di[s]cipline case so as to include the power to appraise penalties in terms

---

[9]Id. at 123.

[10]Platt, *The Arbitration Process and the Settlement of Labor Disputes*, 31 J. Am. Jud. Soc'y 54, 58 (1947), as cited at 66 LA 286, 294. See also Wolverine Shoe & Tanning Corp., 18 LA 809, 812 (Platt, 1952) (noting that an essential element of just cause is that the penalty "be fair and reasonable and fitting to the circumstances of the case.").

[11]Kaiser Steel & Gravel, 49 LA 190, 193 (1967). Accord Diversitech Gen., 85-2 ARB ¶8406 (Katz, 1985), at 4678 ("The right of an arbitrator to modify an employer's disciplinary penalty is deemed to be inherent in his authority to finally settle and adjust the dispute before him."); Davis Fire Brick Co., 36 LA 124, 127 (Dworkin, 1960) ("Inherent in the contractual provision that an employee may be disciplined for just cause, is the fairness and reasonableness of the penalty. While the basis for discipline may be clearly established, unless the penalty is reasonably commensurate with the improper conduct of the employee, then 'just cause' is wanting as regards the penalty imposed.").

of the fitness and fairness for the particular offense, since the extent of the penalty is logically reviewed as related to the action for which the employee is held responsible. Thus management rights, implied or expressed in an agreement, are qualified and reviewable by the need to be reasonable and fair, rather than arbitrary and capricious.[12]

Myers finds support for this principle even when the contract specifically designates the penalty:

> Reversing a penalty may make sense even where the schedule of penalties incorporated in the agreement by reference has been adhered to consistently. For example, the insubordination may have been stimulated by supervisory conduct, such as telling a generally cooperative worker to do as he's told or go home.[13]

Where an employer cited awards alleging that arbitrators should not interfere with discipline assessed by management if the collective bargaining agreement permits management to exercise judgment, Arbitrator Charles Spaulding responded as follows:

> Three answers to this line of argument seem appropriate. The first is that arbitrators very frequently do step in and upset the decisions of Management. The second is that, if arbitrators could not do so, arbitration would be of little import, since the judgment of management would in so many cases constitute the final verdict. Finally, the more careful statement of the principle would probably run to the effect that where the contract uses such terms as discharge for "cause" or for "good cause" or for "justifiable cause" an arbitrator will not lightly upset a decision reached by competent careful management which acts in the full light of all the facts, and without any evidence of bias, haste or lack of emotional balance. Even under these conditions, if the decision is such as to shock the sense of justice of ordinary reasonable men, we suspect that arbitrators have a duty to interfere.[14]

One federal court has endorsed this principle, stating that the just cause standard is not satisfied unless the penalty bears a reasonable relation to the offense:

> A decision of the company to discharge an employee for mis-

---

[12]Myers, *Concepts of Industrial Discipline*, in Management Rights and the Arbitration Process, Proceedings of the 9th Annual Meeting, National Academy of Arbitrators, 59, 67 (BNA Books, 1956).
[13]Id. at 66.
[14]Fruehauf Trailer Co., 16 LA 666, 670 (1951).

conduct, even if the employee is guilty, may or may not be for just cause. If the offense and the circumstances accompanying it are sufficient to warrant such a penalty, just cause would exist, but it is also true that in many cases such a penalty may be excessive and unwarranted.[15]

In this same regard, the Eighth Circuit has stated that the "just cause" standard of discipline may imply a "procedural" as well as a "substantive" element, and that it was permissible for an arbitrator to find that an employer did not have just cause to discharge an employee where the employer did not give the employee an adequate opportunity to present his side of the story.[16]

Modification of a penalty, however, should not be confused with the exercise of leniency (or clemency). As stated by Arbitrator James McBrearty:

> The distinction between these actions was emphasized by Arbitrator Whitley P. McCoy when he recognized the power of arbitrators to modify penalties found on the basis of mitigating circumstances to be too severe for the offense, but at the same time declared that arbitrators have no authority to grant clemency where the penalty assessed by management is not found too severe.[17]

Arbitrator McBrearty also posits that arbitrators' view of their function in reviewing discipline may vary according to the nature of the offense:

> For instance, Arbitrator Robert G. Howlett has stated that an arbitrator should be more hesitant to overrule penalties where the offense is directly related to the company's product than where it involves primarily the personal behavior of the employee and is only indirectly related to production. . . . Also, where the safety of the public is a direct factor in a discharge, Arbitrator Whitley P. McCoy would require the union to "show that the decision was arbitrary, made in bad faith, or clearly wrong."[18]

---

[15]Capitol Airways v. Airline Pilots Ass'n, 237 F. Supp. 373, 377, 54 LRRM 2326, 2329 (M.D. Tenn. 1963), modified on other grounds, 341 F.2d 288, 58 LRRM 2404 (6th Cir.), cert. denied, 381 U.S. 913, 59 LRRM 2240 (1965).
[16]Teamsters Local 878 v. Coca-Cola Bottling Co., 613 F.2d 716, 103 LRRM 2380 (8th Cir. 1980).
[17]Lear Siegler, Inc., 63 LA 1157, 1168 (1974), citing Chattanooga Box & Lumber Co., 10 LA 260, 261 (1948).
[18]Id. at 1167, citing Valley Steel Casting Co., 22 LA 520, 524–525 (Howlett, 1954) and United Air Lines, 19 LA 585, 587 (McCoy, 1952).

Arbitrator Gabriel Alexander has posed the question whether, in their proper function, arbitrators may carry their feelings of uncertainty as to the facts at issue into their assessment of a penalty:

> Traditionally it has been considered that the arbitrator was to execute the jury function, that is, determine guilt or innocence, before taking on the judicial function of determining the extent of penalty. I have no quarrel with this mode of approach. Indeed, in the present state of thinking of arbitrators and the parties to arbitration, I would be inclined to believe that the arbitrator who did not proceed in this manner was not meeting the expectations of the parties. I wonder, however, whether this is a realistic point of view in the light of experience in the lower steps of the grievance procedure. I suspect that, in many cases, companies and unions compromise disciplinary penalties as a means of circumventing the necessity for making a straight yes or no answer on questions of fact. If this be true, would it not be more realistic for the parties to permit, perhaps even to encourage, arbitrators to pursue the same line of reasoning.[19]

What can be concluded regarding an arbitrator's authority to change a penalty? Most arbitrators will change a penalty without hesitation if, given the facts and circumstances of the case including the grievant's seniority and work record, it is found to be clearly out of line with generally accepted industrial standards of discipline. Where the parties have contractually removed the arbitrator's power to change the penalty, however, arbitrators must respect this limitation. Thus, when a collective bargaining agreement explicitly provided that "the arbitrator may not modify disciplinary penalties," Arbitrator Ralph Williams correctly held that his only authority was to decide whether some disciplinary action should have been taken against the grievant.[20]

---

[19] Alexander, *The Concepts of Industrial Discipline: Discussion*, in Management Rights and the Arbitration Process, supra note 12 at 79.

[20] Allied Paper, 52 LA 957 (1969). In Wiley Mach. Co., 14 LA 770 (1950), Arbitrator Edgar Warren found that where the agreement provided that back pay would be awarded only if "an injustice has been dealt the employee with regard to his discharge without any fault on the part of the employee," an award of back pay would not be proper for an employee found to be partially at fault. See also Teamsters Local 784 v. Ulry-Talbert Co., 330 F.2d 562, 55 LRRM 2979 (8th Cir. 1964), where the agreement provided:

> [T]he arbitration board shall not substitute its judgment for that of management and shall only reverse the action or decision of the management if it finds that the Company's complaint against the employee is not supported by the facts, and that management has acted arbitrarily and in bad faith or in violation of the

Before arbitrators will recognize such limitations, the agreement must contain clear language that the arbitrator is not to have discretion to reduce a penalty. Language denying to the arbitrator "the power to add to, amend, or modify the agreement in any manner" will not preclude arbitral discretion.[21] Nor will language stating that the "arbitration committee shall be judicial rather than legislative" remove jurisdiction to revise a penalty.[22]

1. Modification of Penalties and "No-Fault" Absenteeism Provisions

Does an arbitrator have jurisdiction to reduce a penalty under either a "no-fault" or "last-chance" agreement? No-fault plans provide fixed disciplinary standards for excessive absenteeism regardless of whether the absences are the employee's fault. Arbitrators Howard Block and Richard Mittenthal,[23] discussing the argument that a "no-fault" plan is inconsistent with a just-cause provision, highlight the inherent conflict between both provisions:

[T]he concept of "just cause" requires the arbitrator to make two essential inquiries. They are: (1) whether the employee is guilty of misconduct, and (2) assuming guilt, whether the discipline imposed is a reasonable penalty under the circumstances of the case. A no-fault plan precludes either inquiry. For the arbitrator who accepts such a plan is concerned with two entirely different questions: (1) whether the employee was absent, and (2) if so, whether the absence falls within any of the plan's express exclusions. Should these questions be answered in management's favor, the arbitrator has no choice but to affirm the penalty prescribed in the plan. The crucial issues of whether the employee's absence is misconduct and whether the penalty is reasonable are removed from the arbitrator's reach. All that is left is a hollow mechanical function, a mere reading of the

---

express terms of the Agreement.
The Eighth Circuit had no trouble vacating an award where the arbitrator's opinion stated that while some discipline was warranted, discharge was too severe.
   [21]See, e.g., Lima Elec. Co., 63 LA 94 (Albrechta, 1974).
   [22]International Harvester Co., 53 LA 1197 (Seinsheimer, 1969).
   [23]*Arbitration and the Absent Employee: Absenteeism*, in Arbitration 1984: Absenteeism, Recent Law, Panels, and Published Decisions, Proceedings of the 37th Annual Meeting, National Academy of Arbitrators, 77 (BNA Books, 1985).

plan's listed penalty for a numbered "absence occurrence." Thus, the plan seems inconsistent with the "just cause" standard.[24]

The authors go on to argue that most arbitrators find no-fault plans to be reasonable in principle. Nevertheless, according to Block and Mittenthal, arbitrators approach the problem from a highly pragmatic point of view.

> They stress the damage caused by absenteeism, the need for objective attendance standards, and the actual experience under the plan. They have given considerable weight to proof by the employer that the plan has been reasonable in operation or to the absence of proof by the union that the plan has worked a hardship in particular cases.[25]

Block and Mittenthal, reflecting the better view, argue that arbitrators who have declared a plan reasonable have not hesitated to reject a "perverse application" of a no-fault rule. As summarized by the arbitrators:

> We cannot give unqualified approval to the typical no-fault plan because of its potential for inequitable results in exceptional cases and because such results cannot be harmonized with "just cause" requirements. Management cannot expect blind arbitral support for a mechanical application of penalties up to and including discharge. It is precisely this rigid, unbending application of penalties which gives us pause. But arbitral insistence of an appropriate degree of flexibility does not mean that the no-fault concept is rejected. We recognize that notice of realistic attendance standards can be beneficial to everyone. Such standards aid employees who are entitled to know what is expected of them; they aid supervisors who strive for uniformity in the enforcement of rules. In short, although the ordinary no-fault plan can provide a practical solution to the need for specific absentee criteria, it cannot fully comply with traditional notions of "just cause."[26]

With respect to "last chance" agreements, arbitrators have generally ruled that "last chance" agreements, executed as part of a settlement of a grievance, are binding on the parties and, accordingly, an arbitrator has no jurisdiction to modify a penalty once a violation of the last-chance agreement is

---

[24]Id. at 100–101.
[25]Id. at 101.
[26]Id. at 103. See also Union Camp Corp., 91 LA 749, 757 (Clarke, 1988) (holding "no-fault" plan unreasonable).

found. The rationale behind this position has been expressed by one arbitrator as follows:

> Arbitrators regularly have ruled that such "last chance" agreements are binding on the parties. . . . Such agreements are becoming more prevalent, especially in alcohol and drug abuse cases. They represent a novel means to permit an employee a "last chance opportunity," subject to the specific terms of such agreement to demonstrate that by his/her conduct to be worthy of the confidence placed on him/her by the parties which conditionally reinstated him/her to employment. Arbitrators should encourage and enforce such agreements as efforts to rehabilitate persons with alcohol and drug problems, especially since society now recognizes alcoholism and drug abuse as an illness rather than simply misconduct. If these last chance agreements are ignored or freely overturned by arbitrators, the parties will be discouraged from making such efforts. This would be a considerable disservice and injustice to the parties, including employees, who might benefit from "last chance opportunities."[27]

Arbitrator James Sherman, in a 1988 unpublished federal-sector decision, outlined the better view on last-chance agreements as follows:

> Oftentimes, management, the Union, and the individual employee enter into a "last chance agreement" designed to save the employee's job if he fulfills all obligations set forth in the agreement. Although these last chance agreements are open to criticism and even challenges to their validity, most Arbitrators will enforce them so long as a responsible Union official is made a party and the agreement appears to be essentially fair and equitable. The reasoning behind this recognition and acceptance of "side agreements" is it must be assumed their chances of "winning" in arbitration, and the agreement reflects their best estimate of the strength of their respective evidence and arguments. In other words, once the last chance agreement is signed, the Arbitrator has no reason to consider the original charge which raised the probability of discharge. Instead, he/she must look to the terms of the agreement and decide whether the grievant abided by its terms or violated them.

Citing arbitral authority, Sherman "voided" the last-chance agreement in part because of the absence of the union's signature.

---

[27]Inland Container Corp., 91 LA 544, 549 (Howell, 1988). See also PPG Indus., 90 LA 1033 (Edelman, 1988) (sustaining dismissal for failure to complete program required by last-chance agreement).

2. Increasing a Penalty Subsequent to Discharge

May an arbitrator increase a penalty assessed by management? Arbitrator Walter Kaufman, in *Pacific Southwest Airlines*,[28] considered an employer's request that the arbitrator, by way of formulating an appropriate remedy, *increase* the discipline initially imposed in view of the grievant's "continued insistence on dishonesty throughout the arbitration process." A flight attendant was suspended for three days for having "committed an act of dishonesty [cashing of both an allegedly lost check and its replacement issued by the company's credit union] by being untruthful in her response to [the company's] investigation." Although the arbitrator discredited the grievant's testimony and sustained the three-day suspension, he declined to act on the employer's request that the penalty be increased to a discharge. The arbitrator reasoned that the grievant's defense in the arbitration proceeding was substantially the same as her defense at the grievance meeting, yet in the interim management did not act to increase the penalty. Further, the offense for which the discipline was imposed—failure to respond honestly to questions concerning the cashing of both checks—was essentially the same before and after the suspension. The arbitrator found that it was for the company to impose discipline subject to the review under the parties' grievance procedure, and that it would be inappropriate for management to impose light discipline, thereby minimizing the risk of liability, and later, after the grievant's defenses are discredited by an arbitrator, to impose a more severe penalty for substantially the same offense.

3. Modification of Penalties in the Federal Sector

In *Douglas v. Veterans Administration*,[29] the Merit Systems Protection Board (MSPB) outlined 12 factors that are the litmus tests federal-sector arbitrators consider in determining whether a penalty is appropriate. They are listed as follows:

---

[28]85-1 ARB ¶8101 (1984).
[29]5MSPR 280 (1981).

(1) The nature and seriousness of the offense, and its relation to the employee's duties, position, and responsibilities, including whether the offense was intentional or technical or inadvertent, or was committed maliciously or for gain, or was frequently repeated;

(2) the employee's job level and type of employment, including supervisory or fiduciary role, contacts with the public, and prominence of the position;

(3) the employee's past disciplinary record;

(4) the employee's past work record, including length of service, performance on the job, ability to get along with fellow workers, and dependability;

(5) the effect of the offense upon the employee's ability to perform at a satisfactory level and its effect upon supervisors' confidence in the employee's ability to perform assigned duties;

(6) consistency of the penalty with those imposed upon other employees for the same or similar offenses;

(7) consistency of the penalty with any applicable agency table of penalties;

(8) the notoriety of the offense or its impact upon the reputation of the agency;

(9) the clarity with which the employee was on notice of any rules that were violated in committing the offense, or had been warned about the conduct in question;

(10) potential for the employee's rehabilitation;

(11) mitigating circumstances surrounding the offense such as unusual job tensions, personality problems, mental impairment, harassment, or bad faith, malice or provocation on the part of others in the matter; and

(12) the adequacy and effectiveness of alternative sanctions to deter such conduct in the future by the employee or others.[30]

The MSPB notes that not all of these factors will be pertinent in every case, and that it is not uncommon that some of the factors will weigh in the employee's favor while others may not constitute aggravating circumstances. According to the Federal Circuit, the key "is a responsible balancing of the relevant factors" in each case.[31]

B. Judicial Response to Discharge Awards

What is the response of the courts that have reviewed awards that find the employee at fault, but have revoked or

---

[30]Id. at 304–305.

[31]Kline v. FAA, 808 F.2d 43 (Fed. Cir. 1986) (applying *Douglas* factors in removal action).

modified discharge penalties? What contractual language restricts an arbitrator from reducing a penalty?

Cases involving rule violations are particularly troublesome for arbitrators, especially where the parties negotiate and incorporate into their agreement the disciplinary rules and resulting penalties for violation of the rules. In *S.D. Warren Co. Div. v. Paperworkers Local 1069 (Warren II)*,[32] the First Circuit ruled that an arbitrator exceeded her authority when overturning various discharges for violation of a rule prohibiting "possession, use or sale" of marijuana on company property.[33] Under the parties' agreement, management had the sole right to manage the business, including "the right to discharge employees for proper cause." The arbitrator found beyond a reasonable doubt that three grievants violated the marijuana rule, but nevertheless held that the discharges were not justified. In so concluding, the arbitrator rejected the company's argument that the plain meaning of the contract provided for immediate discharge for violation of the rule. The court of appeals gave lip service to the *Enterprise Wheel*[34] standard of review but reversed both the district court and the arbitrator, finding that the management rights provision and the rule in question did not contemplate that the arbitrator determine remedies for a marijuana violation. In the court's words:

> [T]he company and the union negotiated and incorporated into the collective bargaining agreement the disciplinary rules and the resulting penalties for violations of these rules. Nothing is left to the arbitrator's judgment except determining whether the rules are violated. An uncomplicated reading of the contract reveals that management has the *sole* right to discharge employees for cause, the definition of which includes possession of marijuana on Mill property. It is not a question of a strained interpretation by the arbitrator with which we might agree or disagree, but rather a reading of the plain language of the contract which removes from the arbitrator the authority to determine a remedy once she concludes that a certain rule has been

---

[32]845 F. 2d 3, 128 LRRM 2175 (1st Cir. 1988) (*Warren II*).
[33]Mill Rule 7(a) stated as follows:
    7. Causes for Discharge. . . . Violations of the following rules are considered causes for discharge: (a) Possession, use or sale on Mill property of . . . marijuana.
128 LRRM at 2177.
[34]Steelworkers v. Enterprise Wheel & Car Corp., 363 U.S. 593, 46 LRRM 2423 (1960).

breached. The parties negotiated and agreed to the remedy for violations of Rule 7(a). Here the arbitrator found a violation of that rule by reason of the employee's possession of marijuana on Mill property. The rule plainly states that such a violation is "cause for discharge." . . . In the face of the contract's unambiguous language to this effect, it cannot be said that the arbitrator even "arguably constru[ed] or appl[ied] the contract."[35]

In a companion case (*Warren III*),[36] the First Circuit similarly held that an arbitrator exceeded his authority in reversing the discharges of employees who violated contractually established disciplinary rules which declared that "possession, use or sale on Mill property of intoxicants, marijuana, narcotics or other drugs" is "considered cause for discharge." According to the court, the contract gave the company the sole right to discharge one who violates a particular company rule.

Rejecting the approach of the First Circuit, the Seventh Circuit, in *F.W. Woolworth Co. v. Teamsters Local 781*,[37] ruled that an arbitrator had the power to reduce a discharge to a suspension even though he found a "technical violation" of a rule and the contract provided that the violation of "any rule" is just cause for discharge. Finding ambiguity in the contract, the court of appeals reasoned that the arbitrator was not bound to read the contract literally.

In a 1989 decision the Sixth Circuit, citing the Supreme Court's *Misco* decision,[38] refused to vacate an arbitrator's decision reinstating an employee found guilty of violating a work rule against fighting on company time. The corresponding disciplinary action allowed for a first offense fighting violation was discharge (although the work rules were not mentioned in the agreement). And similar to *Warren I and II*, the parties' contract gave management the sole right to discharge. Finding nothing in the labor agreement "which expressly limits or removes from the arbitrator the authority to review the remedy," the court deferred to the arbitrator.[39]

---

[35]128 LRRM at 2178.
[36]S.D. Warren Co. Div. Paperworkers Local 1069, 846 F.2d 827, 128 LRRM 2432 (1st Cir. 1988) (*Warren III*). See also S.D. Warren Co. Div. v. Paperworkers Local 1069, 815 F.2d 178, 125 LRRM 2086 (1st Cir. 1987) (*Warren I*).
[37]629 F.2d 1204, 104 LRRM 3128 (7th Cir. 1980).
[38]Paperworkers v. Misco, Inc. 484 U.S. 29, 126 LRRM 3113 (1987).
[39]Eberhard Foods v. Teamsters Local 406, 868 F.2d 890, 130 LRRM 2830 (6th Cir. 1989).

Where the contract reserves to the employer the right to discipline or discharge for "just cause," and where the arbitrator finds the penalty excessive but not completely unjustified, an award reducing the penalty may not be enforced, especially in the Fourth and Sixth Circuits.[40] For example, the Sixth Circuit, in *Amanda Bent Bolt Co. v. Automobile Workers, Local 1549*,[41] vacated an arbitrator's award reinstating employees found to have participated in a "wildcat" strike. The court of appeals, substituting its judgment for that of the arbitrator, found that the arbitrator exceeded his jurisdiction under a contract that made employees participating in such a strike subject to discharge.

Similarly, in *Timken Co. v. Steelworkers Local 1123, (Timken I)*,[42] an agreement provided for reinstatement "in the event it should be decided that the employee is not guilty of the matter charged." An arbitrator ordered an employee who had been absent without excuse for more than seven days to be reinstated (the employee was serving a jail sentence), even though such an absence was defined as a "voluntary quit" under the contract. The court, in vacating the award, found that there was no need for the arbitrator "to go outside the record and consider other dimensions of the term 'quit.' " The court disagreed with the arbitrator's finding that the purpose of the voluntary quit provision was to discipline employees who had abandoned their jobs and not to individuals who were confined in jail.

In a subsequent decision *(Timken II)*,[43] the Sixth Circuit

---

[40]Walter Fogel reports that from 1960 to 1980 most challenged discharge awards were upheld by the courts; 18 of 66 (about one fourth of all final decisions) have been vacated. Eleven of the vacations have been at the circuit court level, six of these by the Sixth Circuit. One half of the 66 terminal court decisions were decided in the last five years of the 1960-1980 period. Fogel, *Court Review of Discharge Arbitration Awards*, 37 Arb. J. No. 2, 22, 33 (1982).

[41]451 F.2d 1277, 79 LRRM 2023 (6th Cir. 1971). In Aladdin Indus., 61 LA 896 (1973), Arbitrator Hilpert, citing the decision by the Sixth Circuit in *Amanda Bent Bolt*, refused to reduce a discharge for violating a "no strike" clause. In holding that he could not reduce the discharge penalty, the arbitrator stated:

> Amanda Bent Bolt governs in the instant case not only because it states the only now-available "federal" law on the reduction-of-penalty point but also because this instant case is one which arose in, and one in which the award will be effective in, an area that lies within the territorial jurisdiction of the Sixth Circuit Court which decided Amanda Bent Bolt. . . . and to decline, in any event, to disturb the discharge penalties which were imposed . . . . Id. at 900.

[42]482 F.2d 1012, 83 LRRM 2814 (6th Cir. 1973) *(Timken I)*.

[43]Timken Co. v. Steelworkers, 492 F.2d 1178, 85 LRRM 2532 (6th Cir. 1974) *(Timken II)*.

considered an arbitrator's award reinstating an employee found fighting with a fellow employee. Although the agreement prescribed discharge as the penalty for such a rule violation, the agreement also provided that if an employee "believes he has been discharged improperly, such discharge shall constitute a case arising under the method of adjusting grievances herein provided." In affirming the award the court stated that the arbitrator could fairly construe the contract to confer upon himself the power to determine whether the employee was guilty of committing the act charged. The court of appeals distinguished this case from earlier ones where awards were vacated on the premise that the contracts in those decisions limited the arbitrator to a finding of guilt or innocence and, accordingly, the arbitrator had no power to "measure the appropriateness of the penalty."[44]

This principle was further illustrated in *Falls Stamping & Welding Co. v. Automobile Workers*,[45] where the agreement provided that the employer "shall have the right to discharge or otherwise discipline any employee who does engage in a strike." The contract also provided that "any discipline or discharge as a result of the foregoing is subject to the grievance procedure." Upholding an arbitration award that reinstated 93 strikers, the court of appeals stated:

> [W]hen an employer reserves the unequivocal right to discharge employees who violate the no-strike provision of a collective bargaining agreement, an arbitrator has no authority to order reinstatement. In the present case, however, the company expressly agreed that the discharge of employees for participating

---

[44]Id., 85 LRRM at 2533. See also Butterkrust Bakeries v. Bakery Workers Local 361, 726 F.2d 698, 115 LRRM 3172 (11th Cir. 1984) (where agreement reposed sole control over employee discipline in employer and expressly prohibited modification of terms, once arbitrator found prerequisite for discharge present, authority over matter ceased and arbitrator without authority to reinstate employee upon successful completion of Dale Carnegie course); Morgan Servs. v. Clothing & Textile Workers Local 323, 724 F.2d 1217, 1224, 115 LRRM 2368 (6th Cir. 1984) (provision allowing employer right to dismiss employee "without redress" if guilty of insubordination unambiguously vested company with sole discretion to determine sanction, and arbitrator was without authority to modify penalty; "provision in a collective bargaining agreement cannot be treated as ambiguous and then ignored simply because it varies from the arbitrator's expectations."); Magnavox Co. v. Electrical Workers (IUE) 410 F.2d 388, 71 LRRM 2049 (6th Cir. 1969) (under agreement providing that company could discharge employee for refusing to work, once arbitrator found employee had refused, penalty could not be mitigated).
[45]575 F.2d 1191, 98 LRRM 2530 (6th Cir. 1978).

in a strike would be subject to the grievance procedure set forth in the contract. This procedure included arbitration.[46]

The Fifth Circuit reversed an award of reinstatement (but without back pay) of an employee found guilty of insubordination where the parties' agreement declared that "[s]hould it be determined by the arbitrator than an employee has been suspended or discharged for proper cause therefor, the arbitrator shall not have jurisdiction to modify the degree of discipline imposed by the Company." Prior to the arbitration the parties stipulated that the issue for resolution was whether there was "just cause" for the discharge and, if not, what shall be the remedy. The arbitrator, without specifically finding that just cause existed, nevertheless noted that "evidence of just cause for discharge . . . has been presented by the Company." According to the court, the arbitrator noted that he was following a school of thought allowing modification of a penalty even in a situation where just cause had been found. Under the limitation contained in the parties' collective bargaining agreement, this was sufficient for the appellate court to vacate the award. The remedy, said the court, was "*ultra vires.*"[47]

In another case, the Fourth Circuit found that the express provisions of a management prerogative clause to the effect that the employer's exercise of discipline may be the subject of a grievance, but not arbitration, meant that "the employer's established disciplinary practices were not to be upset by an arbitrator on the ground of inappropriateness."[48]

The Tenth Circuit, in *Mistletoe Express Service v. Motor Expressmen*,[49] held that an arbitrator had no authority to set aside a discharge for failing to follow billing procedures where the agreement provided: " 'Employees may be discharged for just cause, among which just causes are the following: . . . Failure to settle bills and funds collected for the company within twenty-four (24) hours.' "[50]

---

[46]Id., 98 LRRM at 2531.

[47]Container Prods. v. Steelworkers, 873 F.2d 818, 131 LRRM 2623, 2625 (5th Cir. 1989).

[48]Textile Workers Local 1386 (TWUA) v. American Thread Co. 291 F.2d 894, 48 LRRM 2534, 2539 (4th Cir. 1961).

[49]566 F.2d 692, 96 LRRM 3320 (10th Cir. 1977).

[50]Id.

In contrast, however, where the agreement stated only that "the right to . . . suspend or discharge employees for just cause . . . is vested exclusively in this Company," the Tenth Circuit, in *Machinists v. San Diego Marine Construction Corp.*,[51] held that an arbitrator could properly reduce a discharge to a suspension. In that case the court, in distinguishing *San Diego* from *Mistletoe*, upheld the award since the contract did not expressly define the grievant's misconduct as misconduct that constitutes just cause for firing.[52] While the arbitrator "cannot substitute his or her discretion for the discretion of the Company," the court stated "the arbitrator does have the power to determine when a matter is subject to Company discretion."[53]

Finally, in several cases courts have set aside arbitration awards, even though they arguably derived their essence from the collective bargaining agreement, on the basis that the award was in conflict with public policy. The bellwether case in this area is *Paperworkers v. Misco*,[54] a 1987 decision of the Supreme Court. *Misco* is discussed at length in Chapter 3.[55]

C. Summary

In the absence of a contractually specified penalty, both arbitrators and courts agree that the arbitrator may fashion a remedial award reducing the penalty imposed by management. A review of the published cases, however, reveals that arbitrators vary in the manner in which they state the limits on the exercise of discretion in this matter. Arbitrator Elmer Hilpert has summarized this principle as follows:

> Some [arbitrators] apparently believe that *they* are possessed of power to apply the Gilbert & Sullivan principle that the " punishment should be made to fit the crime"; others, while adhering to that same principle, grant that the initial discretion, as to the severity of the penalty to impose, rests with the employer but claim the power to reverse, by modification, employer "abuses

---

[51]Machinists Dist. 50, Local Lodge 389 v. San Diego Marine Constr. Corp., 620 F.2d 736, 104 LRRM 2613 (9th Cir. 1980).
[52]Id. at 2614–2615.
[53]Id. at 2615.
[54]Supra note 37.
[55]See, Chapter 3, at notes 63–70 and accompanying text.

of discretion" in that regard; while still others insist that they are to sustain the penalty imposed by the employer, unless, to do so, would "shock his [the arbitrator's] conscience". We believe the precise *verbal* formula to be applied to be unimportant, for some arbitrators' consciences "shock" more readily, and some less readily, than others.[56]

As suggested by Owen Fairweather in the first edition of his text, the difference in approach concerning the issue of substitution of judgment may be merely one of semantics. For example, when an arbitrator finds that the discipline imposed by management varies from the action which he himself believes would be justified, he can find that management acted in a capricious or arbitrary manner and reach the same result that would have been reached had he had the authority to modify the amount of discipline without such a finding.[57]

In the paradigm case where the contract explicitly states that the arbitrator has no power to review penalties,[58] discretion to reduce a penalty is absent, and the arbitrator's function under such an agreement may be to merely determine whether the employee engaged in the conduct giving rise to the discipline. Where the arbitrator finds that the conduct for which the employee was disciplined did not constitute the conduct specified in the contract, the arbitrator presumptively

---

[56]Aladdin Indus., supra note 40; at 898.

[57]Fairweather, Practice and Procedure in Labor Arbitration, 284 (BNA Books, 1973).

[58]In Riceland Foods v. Carpenters Local 2381, 737 F.2d 758, 760, 116 LRRM 2948, 2949 (8th Cir. 1984), the parties contract provided:

Any arbitration with respect to the exercise of a right to discharge or discipline . . . shall be limited to the question of whether or not there was just cause or whether or not the working rules were violated, and shall not include whether or not the type of discipline selected was appropriate.

The Eighth Circuit vacated an award ordering reinstatement of employees failing to obey rule requiring employees whose jobs necessitated wearing self-contained breathing apparatus to be cleanshaven.

See also Bridgford Frozen-Rite Foods, 91 LA 681, 681 (McKee, 1988), where the arbitrator, imploring the company to reinstate the grievant, nevertheless sustained the discharge of a 30-year employee for theft of hairnets worth $5.00 under the following provisions:

"[W]hile the arbitrator may rule on the merits of a grievance, the arbitrator may not award money for any time prior to ten (10) working days prior to the occurrence of the alleged dispute, nor for more than 30 days in any event, nor shall he have the power to mitigate penalties or disciplinary action assessed pursuant to the terms of this Agreement where the arbitrator has found that the employee did in fact commit the acts of which he was accused."

Arbitrator McKee stated that "If, under some alternative forum, I were empowered to decide equity and due process in this matter, the Grievant would be returned to work with substantial backpay." Id. at 685.

is on safe ground,[59] although a reviewing court may still decide to substitute its judgment for that of the arbitrator.

At the other extreme, where the agreement contains a "just cause" provision without more, it is clear that the arbitrator is not without jurisdiction to reduce the penalty. As stated by Arbitrator Harry Platt:

> Where a contract reserves to the employer the right to discipline or discharge for cause, I think the logical inference is that the parties meant that the right shall be exercised only when "good," "sufficient," "proper," or "just" cause exists. What is "good," etc., cause is, of course, subject to interpretation in an arbitration case and may depend, in the final analysis, on the arbitrator's background of experience, his training and education, his own or the community's standards of justice and fair treatment, and possibly, too (as Justice Douglas has said of judges in the exercise of the interpretive function), the "genes of the bloodstream of his ancestors." In essence, I think that what the parties intend when they adopt a clause such as above indicated, is that discipline will be imposed only when the employee is guilty of misconduct and that in that event, the penalty will be such a one as would appeal to fair-minded persons as just, under all the circumstances of the case, and not disproportionate to the offense.[60]

Between these two extremes are reported decisions holding that where the contract expressly provides for discharge for violation of a specific contractual provision, an arbitrator may not be at liberty to reduce a penalty from discharge to

---

[59]Teamsters Local 968 v. Sysco Food Servs., 838 F.2d 794, 127 LRRM 2925 (5th Cir. 1988) (arbitrator within jurisdiction in holding that no insubordination had occurred under rule providing for immediate termination for insubordination); Distillery Workers Local 186 v. E. & J. Gallo Winery, 847 F.2d 1384, 128 LRRM 2631 (9th Cir. 1988) (where employer had not reserved exclusive right to determine if strict-related conduct was "violent" under contract specifically excluding from grievance procedure strikers who had engaged in violence, appropriate for arbitrator to decide issue under "just cause" provision); Bechtel Constr. v. Laborers Local 1263 Dist. Council, 130 LRRM 2749 (E.D. Pa. 1988) (arbitrator's award reinstating with back pay four discharged employees not inconsistent with public policy against permitting drug users work access to construction site of nuclear plant, where employer failed to prove violation of work rule concerning use or possession of controlled substance).

[60]Letter from Harry Platt to Russell Smith (Sept. 9, 1949), reprinted in Collective Bargaining and Labor Arbitration, 416 (Bobbs-Merrill, 1970), See also State, County & Mun. Employees v. Illinois Dept. of Mental Health, 529 N.E.2d 534, 130 LRRM 2183, 2186 (Ill. Sup. Ct. 1988) ("Where a collective bargaining agreement does not define what 'just cause' is, it is left up to the arbitrator to determine if the grievants were discharged for 'just cause.' ").

suspension,[61] especially where the company's rules are divided into two sections: one listing discharge for a violation, and the other providing for disciplinary action.[62]

When the agreement appears to permit arbitrability of the discharge penalty, either by a specific contractual provision,[63] or by an independent submission,[64] there should be no jurisdictional objection even though the agreement may also contain a provision requiring discharge for a particular offense. In view of the purpose of the grievance and arbitration procedure, the federal policy in favor of arbitration should not, as stated by the Tenth Circuit, be frustrated because the arbitrator selects one of two possible interpretations of the agreement.[65] As argued, however, this view is not the law in all circuit courts of appeal.

Finally, when considering the policy implications of granting an arbitrator the power to reduce a penalty, the words of Arbitrator Peter Seitz are especially noteworthy: "The arbitrator is expected to save the parties from the consequences of their own extremism in the position taken before him by adjusting the scales of justice to balance."[66]

---

[61]Operating Eng'rs Local 670 v. Kerr-McGee Ref. Co., 618 F.2d 657, 103 LRRM 2988 (10th Cir. 1980); Automobile Workers Local 342 v. TRW, 402 F.2d 727, 69 LRRM 2524 (6th Cir. 1968), cert. denied, 395 U.S. 910, 71 LRRM 2253 (1969) (award reinstating seven employees who were discharged for striking was vacated, notwithstanding arbitrator's finding that discharge was "selective" and "lacking in fundamental fairness"; contract gave employer "the right . . . to take disciplinary action, including discharge, against any employee who participates in a [strike], whether such action is taken against all of the participants or against only selected participants . . ."); Litvak Packing Co. v. Meat Cutters Local 641, 455 F. Supp. 1180, 99 LRRM 2862 (D. Colo. 1978).

[62]See, e.g., Teamsters Local 968 v. Sysco Food Servs. supra note 59, 127 LRRM at 2928–2929; Georgia-Pacific Corp. v. Paperworkers Local 27, 864 F.2d 940, 130 LRRM 2208 (1st Cir. 1988) (reversing reinstatement award where agreement established two independent justifications for dismissal: (1) just cause, and (2) list of offenses, including dishonesty, for which immediate discharge is appropriate).

[63]Fireman & Oilers Local 935B v. Nestle Co., 462 F. Supp. 94, 100 LRRM 2927 (S.D. Ohio 1978).

[64]Carpenter's Dist. Council of Greater St. Louis v. Anderson, 619 F.2d 776, 104 LRRM 2188 (8th Cir. 1980); Steelworkers v. Sunshine Mining Co., 103 LRRM 2822 (D. Idaho 1980).

[65]Machinists Dist. 50, Local Lodge 389 v. San Diego Marine Constr. Corp., supra note 50, 104 LRRM at 2615.

[66]Seitz, Substitution of Disciplinary Suspension for Discharge (A Proposed "Guide to the Perplexed" in Arbitration), 35 Arb. J. 27, 28 (1980).

Chapter 11

Employers' Remedies for Breach of No-Strike Clause

A. Discharge of Strikers

Employees who elect to participate in a work stoppage in violation of a no-strike clause run the risk of being severely disciplined or even discharged. As stated by the Supreme Court in *Atkinson v. Sinclair Refining Co.*:[1]

> It is universally accepted that the no strike clause in a collective agreement at the very least establishes a rule of conduct or condition of employment the violation of which by employees justifies discipline or discharge.[2]

While it is a generally recognized principle of arbitration that assessment of penalties must be exercised consistently so that all employees who engage in the same kind of prohibited activity will be similarly treated, an employer who is the victim of an "illegal" strike is not necessarily required to dismiss all employees participating in the walkout. Arbitrators have reasoned that the effect of a no-strike clause would be defeated if an employer were required, in every instance, to discharge all participants.[3]

This proposition was recognized by Arbitrator Paul Lehoczky in *MSL Industries*,[4] where it was pointed out that it

---

[1]370 U.S. 238, 50 LRRM 2433 (1962).
[2]Id., 50 LRRM at 2437.
[3]Aladdin Indus., 61 LA 896, 899 (Hilpert, 1973); Kaye-Tex Mfg. Co., 36 LA 660, 663 (Horlacher, 1960).
[4]53 LA 75 (1969).

is not a practical solution for an employer to discharge all illegal strikers, and therefore the company does the next best thing: "It assigns penalties on the basis of some evaluation, such as presence on the illegal picket line, or perhaps personal activities or statements connected with the action."[5]

Selective discipline of employees has been upheld in the public sector against equal protection claims. In *Battle v. Illinois Civil Service Commission*,[6] a court upheld the dismissal of 33 employees who were found to have instigated a strike or engaged in picket-line misconduct against a claim that imposing differing punishment violated the equal protection doctrine. The court found that the state was not required to discharge all 280-plus employees who engaged in a strike, but could legitimately classify strikers in a manner that would benefit the public and fulfill the state's objective of deterring future strikes.

In most of the reported cases, however, the issue is not whether the employer may validly adopt a policy of selectively disciplining employees,[7] but rather whether the system used for assessing penalties is "rational" and has been applied in an "even-handed" manner. These standards were outlined by Arbitrator Elmer Hilpert in *Aladdin Industries*:[8]

> In the first place, there must be a "rational" basis—arbitrators, including this one, have held—for the "selectivity"; and the most obvious "rational" basis for discharging some employees and not others is their greater degree of participation. Here the Company purports to have discharged those employees who

---

[5]Id. at 77.

[6]78 Ill.App.3d 828, 396 N.E.2d 1321, 103 LRRM 2790 (1st Dist. 1979).

[7]For some of the many cases upholding the principle of selective discharge, see: Nottawa Gardens Corp., 90 LA 24 (Bendixsen, 1987); Super Valu Stores, 86 LA 622, 626 (Smith, 1986) (sustaining selective discipline "according to their observation of those employees it [management] observed during the day of the strike."); Quanex, 73 LA 9, 12 (McDonald, 1979); Homer Laughlin China Co., 67 LA 1250 (Jones, 1977); Dravo Corp., 68 LA 618 (McDermott, 1977); Herrud & Co., 66 LA 682 (Keefe, 1976); SCA Servs., 66 LA 1073 (Mayer, 1976); Philip Morris, U.S.A., 66 LA 626 (Beckman, 1976); Butler Mfg. Co., 55 LA 451 (Purdom, 1970); American Hoist & Derrick Co., 53 LA 45, 59 (Stouffer, 1969); Carmet Co., 52 LA 790 (Kramer, 1969) (employer justified in discharging union president and ship steward for leading walkouts); Philips Indus., 45 LA 943, 952 (Stouffer, 1965) (employer may select those for punishment as it sees fit, provided that such selection is not capricious); General Am. Transp. Co., 42 LA 142 (Pollack, 1964); Deere & Co., 43 LA 182 (Davis, 1964); Ford Motor Co., 41 LA 609 (Platt, 1963); Drake Mfg. Co., 41 LA 732 (Markowitz, 1963). See generally Elkouri and Elkouri, How Arbitration Works, 4th ed., 685–686 (BNA Books, 1985).

[8]61 LA 896 (1973).

"actively" participated vis-à-vis those who participated merely "passively"; and the proved association with the placards (which were carried by human pickets or were made to "stand up" as inanimate pickets) by these grieving employees is a wholly satisfactory index of such "active" *versus* "passive" participation in the strike. . . .

In the second place, the employer must not discriminatorily apply its "selective" index; rather, to meet the over-riding test of "just and proper" cause, the employer must apply such index to all employees, whom it knew, or, through the exercise of reasonable diligence, it should have known, engaged in the same, or substantially similar, conduct as did those employees whom it did discharge.[9]

Arbitrator David Keefe adopted the following line of reasoning in selective discharge cases:

In assessing discipline as the aftermath to an illegal work stoppage, Management is not constrained to issue penalties to everyone. However, when discipline is given, then it must be applied fairly and fall evenly in degree on those involved according to their complicity.[10]

The view of Arbitrator Harry H. Platt in *Ford Motor Co., Chicago Stamping Plant*,[11] was similar:

[N]o agreement provision and no obligation to justice compels the Company to discipline in every case of employee misconduct. Inequality of treatment in disciplinary matters does not amount to unjust discrimination if there are rational grounds for distinguishing between those to be disciplined and those not to be disciplined. It is only where the grounds for distinction are irrational, arbitrary [or] whimsical that disciplining of some employees and not of others may be looked upon as unjust and discriminatory.[12]

The delineations of the "rationality" of the employer's disciplinary measures when assessing penalties were ably set forth in *American Potash & Chemical Co.*:[13]

It is my holding that we are clearly obligated to accept the selection criteria chosen by the Company provided that they are within the bounds of [the agreement] and are nonarbitrary, that

---

[9]Id. at 899. Hilpert declares that a claim that discrimination occurred is in the nature of an affirmative defense, which the union has the burden of establishing.
[10]Allied Supermkts., 71-1 ARB ¶8041, at 3150 (1970).
[11]Supra note 7.
[12]Id. at 616. See also American Hoist & Derrick Co., supra note 7.
[13]67-2 ARB ¶8606 (Meyers, 1967).

is, based on some foundation of rationality. To illustrate, I do not think we would be obligated, even under this contract, to sustain choices made purely at random, nor do I think we would be obligated to sustain choices deliberately related inversely to the degree of strike activity and leadership. Such criteria would be nonrational, i.e., capricious or arbitrary. Once having determined that the selection criteria are within this definition of nonarbitrariness or noncapriciousness, I think we are bound to rectify a material mistake made by the Company in applying them, since to fail to do so would permit a nonrational, that is, arbitrary and capricious action to stand.[14]

The arbitrator also asserted that management is not prohibited from punishing the known instigators of a strike merely because other participants who may have been equally guilty are not known. Expressing the better rule in this regard, the arbitrator had this to say:

It will be noted that I have not defined arbitrary and capricious in such fashion as to require the Company to find every employee who fell within its selection criteria, at pain of voiding its entire course of disciplinary action. This is one argument, in effect, of the Union. I think the Company must act based upon its knowledge. Those employees of whom it had no knowledge can thank their fates for escaping; there should be no other consequences.[15]

In some situations, the agreement will preclude an arbitrator from ruling that the penalty assessed for participating in a strike in violation of the no-strike clause is too severe.[16] For example, in *General Tire & Rubber Co.*,[17] the collective bargaining agreement provided:

Any strike, stoppage, concerted or deliberate slowdown, or other interruption of work during the life of this Agreement shall constitute cause for discharge, suspension, or other disciplinary action of the employee or employee[s] who participate therein or are responsible therefor, as the Employer may determine.[18]

Under this language, Arbitrator Ernest Marlatt ruled that the employer had the "absolute and unlimited right to deter-

---

[14]Id. at 5113.
[15]Id. See also Hooker Chem. Corp., 36 LA 857 (Kates, 1961); Kaye-Tex Mfg. Co., 36 LA 660, 662 (Horlacher, 1960); Clinton Corn Processing Co., 71 LA 555, 567 (Madden, 1978); General Am. Transp. Corp., supra note 7, at 143.
[16]See Chapter 10, Arbitral Authority to Reduce Discipline.
[17]60 LA 787 (Marlatt, 1973).
[18]Id. at 788.

mine whether a given employee participated in or was responsible for a prohibited work stoppage." He further noted that once a determination was made that an employee had participated in a strike, the company could, at will, discharge, suspend, or impose any other punishment on the offender.

Arbitrator Thomas Gallagher, in *Rust Engineering Co.*,[19] reports a case where involving selective discipline under provision declaring that neither the union nor any employee shall "sanction, aid or abet, encourage or continue any work stoppage, strike, picketing or other disruptive activity" and that any employee "who participates in or encourages any activities which interfere with the normal operation of the project shall be subject to disciplinary action, including discharge." Finding that the agreement does not explicitly state a standard for determining when discharge is appropriate and when some lesser discipline is appropriate, Arbitrator Gallagher reviewed the line of arbitral thinking on the issue as follows:

> The arbitration decisions that have considered the appropriate penalty for violation of a no-strike clause fall into two categories. One group of cases holds that an employer may decide to discharge all, or any one or more, of those who participate in a wildcat strike and that the sole issue that the arbitrator must decide is whether the grievant was a participant. . . . The other group of cases holds that an employer may discharge less than all of the participants in a wildcat strike, but that, as in any other case of disparate discipline, there must be a rational basis for selecting those who are discharged. Elkouri and Elkouri summarize these arbitration decisions in *How Arbitration Works* (4th Ed., 1985) at page 685–686:
>
>> Particularly in cases involving illicit strikes or slowdowns, management may vary discipline on the basis of the degree of fault and is not required to assess uniform punishment against all participants; also, management may punish those who bear greater fault while not punishing other participants at all. Nor is management prohibited from punishing the known leaders of a stoppage or those employees detected in overt activities in connection with the stoppage merely because the company is unable to identify other participants who may have been equally guilty. [Citations omitted.]
>
> The rule applied in this second group of cases is that an employer may discharge some, but not all, participants in a

---

[19]89 LA 1296 (1987).

wildcat strike, but that the basis for selecting those to be discharged must be reasonable. I adopt the standard stated in this group of cases—the standard applied by most arbitrators.[20]

Arbitrator Gallagher rejected the union's argument that a third standard should be applied—that the discipline of all employees who did not work on the day in question should be the same, that is, that all of them or none of them should be discharged. The arbitrator found this standard unacceptable "because it would treat differences in conduct as unimportant," and also, "because application of this standard [would] require the Employer either to accept wildcat strikes without the option of discharging those responsible, or to close down the project after discharging most of the labor force." Gallagher concluded that management, when deciding whether to discharge a participant in an illegal strike, must have "a reasonable basis for distinguishing the conduct of those disciplined from the conduct of those who are not disciplined."[21]

Finally, some arbitrators have ruled that under a standard no-strike clause, there is no requirement for an employer to undertake an objective investigation, or to determine degrees of participation when imposing discipline.[22]

1. Special Status of a Union Representative

Arbitrators have been uniform in holding that a union representative, by virtue of his office occupies a position of responsibility and, thus, may be more severely disciplined than a mere unit employee for participating in an illegal work stoppage. Arbitrator Ralph Seward cited this principle in *International Harvester Co.*:[23]

> By virtue of his office a Union steward or committeeman has a special obligation to observe the Agreement. It is his contractually recognized function to protect employees in the grievance

---

[20]Id. at 1300–1301.
[21]Id. at 1301.
[22]Automobile Workers Local 342 v. TRW, 402 F.2d 727, 69 LRRM 2524 (6th Cir. 1968), cert. denied, 395 U.S. 910, 71 LRRM 2253 (1969) (nothing in contract calling for "objective investigation"); Acme Boot Co., 52 LA 1047, 1049–1050 (Oppenheim, 1969) (only criterion that employee instigate, actively support, give leadership to, or participate in strike); Randall Co., Div. of Textron, 66-2 ARB ¶8692 (Wissner, 1966) (employer need only establish participation, not degrees of participation).
[23]14 LA 986 (1950).

procedure against violations of that Agreement by Management. The Agreement gives him special rights and privileges in order that he may perform that function. He cannot with impunity turn his back on the very Agreement which it is his duty to defend.

By virtue of his office, further, a Union steward or committeeman is a leader: indeed, it is reasonable to assume that it is because he is a leader that he acquires his Union office. It follows inescapably that when a Union steward or committeeman participates in a work stoppage—making no effort to prevent it or bring it to a close—he is setting an example for the other employees and indicating by his action that the stoppage has his tacit approval and sanction. This is a graver offense than participation by an ordinary employee and justifies a more serious penalty.[24]

Arbitrator Eric Schmertz, in *United Parcel Service*,[25] outlined a steward's duties in the event of an illegal walkout as follows:

> If there is one principle that is universally recognized in the field of industrial relations, it is that shop stewards have the highest duty to faithfully adhere to all the provisions of the Collective Bargaining Agreement. . . . While it is improper for an ordinary employee to deliberately breach the Agreement, a similar act by a shop steward is untenable and grounds for his discharge. . . . Hence it is inconsistent in the extreme, for a shop steward to lead, or support, or participate in a work stoppage in violation of a "no strike" clause. . . . Indeed, a shop steward's duty in the face of an unauthorized work stoppage is well settled. Not only should he make a determined effort to prevent the stoppage before it begins, but upon its development must actively and unequivocally attempt to bring an end of the stoppage at the earliest possible moment. Moreover, he must set an example by either reporting to work himself or by clearly indicating a willingness to work if his Employer wishes him to do so. And obviously if he is either requested or directed to work, he must do so. Only in this way can the stewards comply with their responsibility to uphold the integrity of the contract and its orderly processes for dispute settlements.[26]

It should be stressed that while union officers are held to a higher degree of responsibility than unit employees, the better rule holds that merely because an individual is an of-

---

[24]Id. at 988. See also Mack Trucks, 64-1 ARB ¶8422 (Wallen, 1964); Skenandoa Rayon Corp., 21 LA 421, 424 (Feinberg, 1953).
[25]47 LA 1100 (1966).
[26]Id. at 1100–1101.

ficial of the union is not sufficient, by itself, to warrant the imposition of a penalty. This principle was cited by Arbitrator John Sembower in *Berg Airlectro Products Co.*,[27] as follows:

> On the one hand, arbitrators point out that violation of a no-strike clause is so serious that they should not be loath to sustain the supreme penalty of discharge it it is warranted. On the other, they say, however, that because of the seriousness of the wrong, one must not be "carried away" so that just anyone and everyone in a position of union responsibility is automatically found "guilty" without a dispassionate study being made of what happened and his role, if any. That is, no local union and no union officer can be considered as "an insurer" against an illegal walkout. Individual culpability must be considered. . . .[28]

Some arbitrators are of the view that simple participation in a strike by employees filling an official capacity in the union amounts to active participation per se when a no-strike clause is in effect.[29] This line of thinking, however, may be suspect after the Supreme Court's decision in *Metropolitan Edison Co. v. NLRB.*[30] Pursuant to contract language providing that "during the term of this agreement there shall be no strikes or walkouts of the Brotherhood or its members," the company disciplined union officials more severely than other participants for four unlawful work stoppages between 1970 and 1974. Twice the union filed a grievance because of the disparate treatment accorded its officials, and in both cases the arbitrators upheld management's actions, reasoning that union officials have an affirmative duty to uphold the bargaining agreement.

In August of 1977, the Operating Engineers, an unrelated union, set up an informational picket line at the entrance to the Three Mile Island construction site. When members of the Electrical Workers refused to cross the picket line, management requested the local union president to cross the line thus inducing other employees to follow. When the picket line was lifted, Edison disciplined all of its employees who refused to cross by imposing 5- to 10-day suspensions. Two union rep-

---

[27]46 LA 668 (1966).
[28]Id. at 674.
[29]Schult Homes Corp., 76-1 ARB ¶8062 (Boals, 1975).
[30]460 U.S. 698, 112 LRRM 3265 (1983).

resentatives, however, received 25-day suspensions for failing to make "every bona fide effort to prevent the unlawful work stoppage," specifically their failure to attempt to end the strike by crossing the picket line. The union filed an unfair labor practice and the administrative law judge (ALJ) ruled that selective discipline of union officials violates Sections 8(a)(1) and (3) of the National Labor Relations Act. The Board affirmed the ALJ's conclusions and findings.[31] The Third Circuit enforced the Board's order,[32] and the Supreme Court affirmed.

Declaring that the case does not present the question "whether an employer may impose stricter penalties on union officials who take a leadership role in an unlawful strike," the Court said that the question "is whether an employer unilaterally may define the actions a union official is required to take to enforce a no strike clause and penalize him for his failure to comply."[33] Absent an explicit contractual duty to prevent work stoppages, the Court ruled that the imposition of more severe sanctions on union officials for participating in an unlawful work stoppage violates the NLRA. Interestingly, the Court rejected the employer's argument that the prior arbitration awards and the union's acquiescence in the harsher sanctions imposed on its officials were sufficient to establish a clear contractual duty. The Court found that two arbitration awards and the history of bargaining between the parties was insufficient to establish a higher duty on union officials where the parties' agreement provided that "[a] decision [by an arbitrator] shall be binding . . . for the term of *this* agreement."

2. Breach-of-Contract Striker as a Voluntary Quit

There is some authority, arguably in the minority, that a breach-of-contract striker acquires essentially the same status as a quit.[34] Unless the agreement explicitly provides that employees who violate the no-strike clause shall be deemed

---

[31]252 NLRB 1030, 105 LRRM 1487 (1980).
[32]Metropolitan Edison Co. v. NLRB, 663 F.2d 478, 108 LRRM 3020 (3d Cir. 1981).
[33]460 U.S. at 699–670.
[34]Fairweather, Practice and Procedure in Labor Arbitration, 2d ed., 510–512 (BNA Books, 1983).

to have quit their employment,[35] the better rule is that an employee who engages in an improper walkout does not terminate the employment relation by that fact alone.[36] Arbitrators, in dealing with questions of whether an individual can be considered to have quit his employment, generally conclude that the matter is dependent primarily on the intent of the individual, and it has usually been held that there can be a volunatary quit only if there is an intention to quit.[37]

B. Awarding Monetary Damages

Arbitrator Robben Fleming, in a 1962 article,[38] observed that damage suits for violation of no-strike clauses have not traditionally come before arbitrators but that these claims are now being arbitrated with increasing frequency. Fleming further noted that arbitrators are not likely to welcome this development with open arms.[39] Notwithstanding the reluctance of some arbitrators to make damage awards for breach of the no-strike clause, the reported cases indicate that, however distasteful or distressing the task may be, arbitrators are often called upon to render monetary damages for improper strikes.

1. Arbitrator's Function When Awarding Damages for Breach of No-Strike Clause

The function of an arbitrator when awarding damages for breach of a no-strike clause is different from that of arbitrating mere grievance claims. As stated by Arbitrator David Feller:

> Arbitration of a claim for damages for breach of a no-strike clause, the adjudication of that claim, is obviously not a substitute for industrial strife but is a substitute for litigation. The "arbitrability" question, when an employer asks for damages

---

[35]See, e.g., Wells Mfg. Corp., 49 LA 1189 (Updegraff, 1968).
[36]See Gold Bond Stamp Co., 49 LA 27 (King, 1967); De Mello's Office Furniture, 45 LA 398 (Koven, 1965); National Gypsum Co., 34 LA 114 (Abernethy, 1960); cf. Wolff Shoe Mfg. Co., 33 LA 568, 571 (Klamon, 1959) ("It is not necessary for us to decide that the men had voluntarily quit their jobs or that there had been a constructive discharge instead. This question, while interesting, is entirely moot, for in either event the end result is the same.")
[37]See Edward Kraemer & Sons, 72 LA 684, 687 (Martin, 1979), for a discussion of arbitral authority in this area.
[38]Fleming, *Arbitrators and the Remedy Power*, 48 Va. L. Rev. 1199 (1962).
[39]Id. at 1220.

for breach of the no-strike clause, is: in what forum is he to try the suit for damages?[40]

A similar focus was adopted by Arbitrator H. Bryan in *Fortex Mfg. Co.*[41] Where the parties had withdrawn a court action for damages resulting from the breach of a no-strike clause and submitted the damage issue to arbitration, the arbitrator declared:

> In the case before us we do not have a grievance as defined in the contract and the grievance procedure therein is, therefore inapplicable. In view of the terms of submission we must be governed by decisions of courts in those cases where the courts decided questions of damages rather than decisions of arbitrators made pursuant to contract provisions.[42]

2. Arbitrability of Employers' Claims for Damages

There is no uniform rule for determining when a claim for damages arising out of a breach of the no-strike clause will be arbitrable since what is subject to arbitration depends upon the particular contract at issue. For example, where the parties' agreement provided for arbitration of all disputes and all grievances involving an act of either party, or any conduct of either party, the Supreme Court, in *Drake Bakeries v. Bakery & Confectionery Workers Local 50*,[43] held that an employer's LMRA Section 301 damage action against the union for breach of the no-strike clause should be stayed pending arbitration of the damage claims.[44] The Court found that the determination of damages may be particularly suited to arbitration:

> If the union did strike in violation of the contract, the company is entitled to its damages; by staying this action, pending arbitration, we have no intention of depriving it of those damages. We simply remit the company to the forum it agreed to use for processing its strike damage claims. That forum, it is

---

[40]Feller, *The Power of the Arbitrator to Make Monetary Awards—Remedies in Arbitration: Discussion*, in Labor Arbitration: Perspectives and Problems, Proceedings of the 17th Annual Meeting, National Academy of Arbitrators, 193, 199 (BNA Books, 1964).

[41]67 LA 934 (1976), enf'd sub nom. Fortex Mfg. Co. v. Clothing Workers Local 1065, 99 LRRM 2303 (M.D. Ala. 1978).

[42]67 LA at 939.

[43]370 U.S. 254, 50 LRRM 2440 (1962).

[44]For discussion of Section 301, see Chapter 3 at notes 8–12 and "Labor-Management Relations Act of 1947—Section 301."

true, may be very different from a courtroom, but we are not persuaded that the remedy there will be inadequate. Whether the damages to be awarded by the arbitrator would not normally be expected to serve as an "effective" deterrent to future strikes, which the company urges, is not a question to be answered in the abstract or in general terms. ... The dispute which this record presents appears to us to be one particularly suited for arbitration, if the parties have agreed to arbitrate.[45]

The Third Circuit has summarized the law in this area as follows:

> In those cases where some ambiguous language appears in the contract and the contract can be read to provide for the employer initiating arbitration, ... the strong presumption in favor of arbitration requires that the employer *must* arbitrate. ...
>
> However, when a contract contains no language which explicitly contemplates or permits the employer to initiate arbitration procedures, and the grievance structure is designed solely to afford the union the right to arbitrate, ... an employer, despite the presence of arbitration procedures in the collective bargaining agreement, is not bound to assert its [damage] claims before an arbitrator.[46]

While the parties are free to make such claims arbitrable, there is some authority to support the theory that an employer's claim for damages arising out of a breach of the no-strike clause is not accorded the traditional strong presumption in favor of arbitrability.[47] As pointed out by Arbitrator David Feller and others, adjudication of damage claims is not a substitute for industrial strife, but rather a substitute for litigation. The presumptions which apply to grievance arbitration under the *Steelworkers Trilogy* standards may simply

---

[45]50 LRRM at 2444–2445. See also Roadway Express v. Teamsters, Local 515, 642 F. Supp. 116, 122 LRRM 3155 (N.D. Ga. 1986) (union not enjoined from striking under contractual provision mandating arbitration for all disputes that parties have "agreed to submit") Eberle Tanning Co. v. Food & Commercial Workers Section 63L, 682 F.2d 430, 110 LRRM 3136 (3d Cir. 1982) (holding employer damage claim arbitrable under broad grievance procedure); Capital City Tel. Co. v. Communications Workers, 575 F.2d 655, 98 LRRM 2438 (8th Cir. 1978) (confirming arbitrator's decision denying employer compensatory damages arising from union's breach of no-strike clause); Pietro Scalzitti Co. v. Operating Engineers Local 150, 351 F.2d 576, 60 LRRM 2222 (7th Cir. 1965); Minnesota Joint Bd. Clothing Workers v. United Garment Mfg. Co., 338 F.2d 195, 57 LRRM 2521 (8th Cir. 1964).

[46]Lehigh Portland Cement Co. v. Cement Workers, 849 F.2d 820, 128 LRRM 2766, 2767–2768 (3d Cir. 1988).

[47]See, e.g., Welded Tube Co. v. Electrical Workers (UE) Local 168, 91 LRRM 2027 (E.D. Pa. 1975); Affiliated Food Distributors v. Teamsters Local 229, 483 F.2d 418, 84 LRRM 2043 (3d Cir. 1973), cert. denied, 415 U.S. 916, 85 LRRM 2465 (1974).

be inapplicable.[48] Absent a submission as to the issue of damages, an arbitrator ought to proceed with caution before concluding that the parties have in fact vested him with authority to make a monetary award for such a breach. Evidence that the parties' grievance procedure is "employee-oriented" may preclude arbitrability of an employer's claim for damages under a no-strike provision.[49]

Does the arbitrator need a special grant of authority to award damages to the employer? Arbitrator Sidney Wolff has argued that an arbitrator needs no special grant of authority to award an employer monetary damages for a breach of the no-strike agreement:

> If we justify an award of damages to an employee for a contract breach on the theory of implied power to formulate a remedy, why must we insist upon a specific grant of authority to award damages for violation of the no-strike covenant?
> When arbitration is properly invoked, no purpose can be gained by determining a breach had occurred and then remitting the parties to the courts to determine damages.[50]

Arbitrator William Hockenberry, in *Farrell Lines*[51] awarded $20,000 in compensatory damages to a vessel owner and a contractor it employed to perform stevedoring services during an illegal work stoppage by the Longshoremen's Association, despite the absence of provisions in the labor agreement authorizing the arbitrator to award damages. With respect to the authority issue, the arbitrator declared:

> As to the question of the authority of the arbitrator to award damages for a breach of the agreement, an award of damages for illegal work stoppages is a proper performance of an arbitrator's duties and inherent in his or her office. . . . Such authority of the arbitrator to fashion a remedy to a labor dispute is critical to the ultimate resolution of the parties' differences, and should be sustained absent contrary language in the agreement. . . .
> In the instant case, the parties' collective bargaining agree-

---

[48]Feller, supra note 40, at 198.
[49]See, e.g., Bliss & Laughlin Indus., Faultless Div. v. Machinists Local Lodge 2040, Dist. 153, 513 F.2d 987, 88 LRRM 3531 (7th Cir. 1975) (grievance procedure "wholly employee oriented.")
[50]Wolff, *The Power of the Arbitrator to Make Monetary Awards—Remedies in Arbitration*, in Labor Arbitration: Perspectives and Problems, supra note 40, at 185–186.
[51]86 LA 36 (1986).

ment is silent as to an arbitrator's authority to award damages, neither sanctioning nor limiting such an award. Under these circumstances, this arbitrator prefers to follow the long line of cases supporting an arbitrator's authority to award damages.[52]

One federal court stated the hornbook law this way:

> The [parties' collective bargaining agreement] contains a no-strike clause which the arbitrators in each case found to have been violated. It is certainly reasonable to infer, as was found by the arbitrators, that since an alleged breach of the no-strike clause was subject to arbitration, the arbitrator could fashion a remedy in the form of monetary damages once he finds there was a breach.[53]

3. Elements of Damages

A review of arbitral authority indicates that arbitrators have invariably applied damage principles adopted by the courts when awarding monetary relief for breach of no-strike clauses. Under both Sections 301 and 303 of Taft-Hartley,[54] the amount of damages recoverable are "actual" or "compensatory" damages, representing those damages directly caused by the breach of the collective bargaining agreement or other illicit activity. Both arbitrators and courts have required that these damages be foreseeable and within the reasonable contemplation of the parties. At the same time, however, it is not necessary that the damages be calculated with precise specificity so long as the existence of some damage is certain. Thus, in *Sterling Gravure Co.*,[55] Arbitrator David Kaplan, in computing damages for a breach of a no-strike clause and an illegal secondary boycott, stated this principle as follows:

> Once the threshold question of direct and proximate cause is answered in the affirmative, the amount claimed in damages demands a less rigid test. "Reasonable estimates" or "a fair and just approximation" are acceptable, and economic losses caused by a union's unlawful conduct or breach of contract need not be

---

[52]Id. at 41.

[53]National Elevator Indus. v. Elevator Constructors Local 5, 426 F. Supp. 343, 94 LRRM 2822, 2825 (E.D. Pa. 1977). See also Carpenters Dist. Council (Chattanooga, Tenn. & Vicinity) v. Rust Eng'g Co., 701 F.2d 181, 108 LRRM 3053 (E.D. Tenn. 1981) (upholding arbitration award granting company damages for amounts employer forced to pay in overtime expenses and for legal fees in securing injunction for illegal strike).

[54]29 U.S.C. §187 (a) and (b).

[55]79-2 ARB ¶8325 (1979).

proven with mathematical certainty. . . . However, while the wronged party need not establish damages with exactitude, a court will not allow damages to be recovered by mere indulgence, speculation or guesswork. . . .

Upon a determination that the injured party is entitled to recover for the breach of contract, the theory is that the resulting damages were presumed foreseeable by the offending party's unlawful conduct . . . .[56]

When direct and proximate cause has been established,[57] arbitrators have allowed recovery for a variety of economic losses sustained by employers as a result of an "illegal" strike or boycott. The most comprehensive review of damage awards is contained in the opinion of Arbitrator Joseph Gentile in *Dan J. Peterson Co.*,[58] and we cite at length selected components and corresponding cases analyzed by Arbitrator Gentile as a summary of the possibilities in this area:[59]

"*Abandonment of Independent Project Caused by Strike.*" In *Lewis v. Benedict Coal Corp.*,[60] the Court of Appeals for the Sixth Circuit considered, in a Section 301 action, an employer's claim for damages for losses sustained on [an] independent project abandoned during a strike. Although the court found that the strike contributed to the decision to abandon the project, the court nevertheless held that such abandonment was not a foreseeable consequence of the strike for which damages could be awarded.

"*Attorney's Fees.*" While recovery of attorney's fees incurred in prosecuting an action under Section 301 are generally not allowed, it may nevertheless be possible to obtain such fees in the arbitral forum.[61]

"*Consultant's Fees Expended as a Result of Strike.*" Where evidence exists that consultants were hired as a result of an improper strike, such fees may properly be awarded as compensatory damages.

"*Costs of Obtaining Goods Elsewhere to Sell to Customers During Strike.*" Arbitral authority supports awarding lost profits

---

[56]Id. at 4354.

[57]The leading case is Hadley v. Baxendale, 9 Exch. 341, 156 Eng. Rep. 145 (1854), cited by Arbitrator Kaplan in Sterling Gravure Co., supra note 55, at 4355.

[58]66 LA 388 (1976).

[59]For corresponding citations the reader is urged to review Arbitrator Gentile's decision in 66 LA at 392–398 n. 60. The headings are taken from Gentile.

[60]259 F.2d 346, 43 LRRM 2237 (6th Cir. 1958).

[61]See Chapter 20, section titled "Attorneys' Fees."

as well as the difference between the cost in obtaining goods from other suppliers and the lower price at which the employer then resells to customers. As an example cited by Arbitrator Eaton, in *Mercer, Fraser Co.*,[62] the arbitrator allowed an employer to recover from the union profits lost as a result of an illegal strike. In addition, the company was awarded the difference between the company's cost in obtaining concrete from other suppliers, and the lower price at which it was then resold to customers.

"Depreciation." Where it can be demonstrated that actual depreciation results from nonuse of tools or equipment, such depreciation may properly be awarded. While there is authority to the contrary, the better rule in this regard would appear to be that depreciation estimates for mere accounting purposes are not controlling as a measure of damages as a result of actual depreciation from nonuse of equipment. Thus in *Master Builders Association of Western Pennsylvania*,[63] the arbitrator disallowed a claim of depreciation of equipment idled during a strike. This denial was based on the fact that the tools and equipment were not in actual use during the strike, and the evidence did not establish any actual depreciation from nonuse.

"Destruction of Business." In the extreme case where a business has been completely destroyed, there is precedent for allowing recovery of the value of the business.

"Equipment (Owned by Company) Idled by Strike." Both arbitrators and courts have appropriately awarded the fair rental value of idled equipment. For example, in *Foster Grading Co.*,[64] Arbitrator Robert Jarvis ruled that an employer was entitled to recover damages for a two-day work stoppage in violation of a no-strike agreement called by a union steward at a construction site. As items of damages, the employer was awarded (1) labor costs for supervisors and office men; (2) the fair rental value of the employer's own equipment which sat idle for two workable days (the rental value to be computed from monthly rental figures based on the 18th Edition of Monthly Rental Rates by Associated Equipment Distributors);

---

[62]70-2 ARB ¶8615 (Eaton, 1970).
[63]67-1 ARB ¶8243 (Kates, 1967).
[64]52 LA 198 (1968).

(3) the actual rental value of six pickup trucks and other equipment rented from rental companies prorated on a daily basis; and (4) the prorated costs of maintenance and protection of traffic. And in *Denver Building & Construction Trades Council v. Shore*,[65] the Colorado Supreme Court stated: "[T]he rule has generally been adopted that where through unlawful or wrongful acts of defendants heavy equipment has been kept idle and the work expected to be accomplished thereby delayed, the fair rental value of such equipment during the period of prevention of its use is generally adopted as a proper measure for determination of the extent of damage."

"*Equipment Rented Idled by Strike.*" Where it is demonstrated that, because of an improper strike, rented equipment was not used or, alternatively, it was necessary to keep the equipment longer than was originally planned, an arbitrator may properly award damages for equipment idled by the strike.

"*Freight Loss and Damage.*" Costs for loss and damage to freight caused by strikers may properly be awarded in either the court or arbitral forum.

"*Inability to receive Shipments of Goods During Strike.*" An inability to receive deliveries of raw materials during a strike may result in a damage award to the employer.

"*Insurance.*" In *Vulcan Mold & Iron Co.*,[66] an arbitrator awarded the prorata portion of fire and other insurance for the period of the illegal strike. Similarly, in *Master Builders Association*,[67] Arbitrator Thomas McDermott awarded as damages the amounts paid to extend a builder's risk insurance to cover completion of a job delayed by an improper strike.

"*Interest on Judgment.*"[68]

"*Labor Cost.*" Arbitrators and courts have awarded various categories of labor costs as damages for a breach of a no-strike agreement. Such an award of damages may include compensation for any of the following:

"(*Direct Pay to Idle Workers*)." In *Mason-Rust v. Laborers Local 42*,[69] the federal district court awarded call-in pay for workers unable to work because of an illegal work stoppage,

---

[65]287 P.2d 267, 36 LRRM 2578, 2583 (Colo. Sup. Ct. 1955).
[66]70-1 ARB ¶8080 (Kates, 1969).
[67]50 LA 1018 (1968).
[68]See Chapter 20, topic titled "Awarding Interest."
[69]306 F. Supp. 934, 72 LRRM 2743 (E.D. Mo. 1969).

as well as fringe-benefit costs incurred as a result of the employees showing up for work.

"Labor Costs: (Increased Extra Time Necessary to Complete Job)." The Court of Appeals for the Fifth Circuit, in a damage action under Section 303 of Taft-Hartley, allowed recovery of overtime pay required to catch up on delayed work provided that the employer could demonstrate that such damages were purely compensatory. In so ruling, the court declared: "Section 303 is purely compensatory, all elements of damages must be directly related to or caused by the unlawful secondary activity."[70]

"Labor Costs: Recovery of Portion of Wages Paid to Workers Working at Reduced Efficiency Due to Strike." The District Court for the Eastern District of Missouri, in *Mason-Rust v. Laborers Local 42*,[71] stated that damages due to reduced efficiency could not be awarded where the job at issue was still in its planning stage, and hence any award would be speculative. However, in *A.I. Gage Plumbing Supply Co. v. Hod Carriers Local 300*,[72] the California District Court of Appeals ruled that, by virtue of an illegal strike, some plumbers had a more difficult time installing pipes and thus were made less productive. Damages were accordingly awarded to persons who worked at a reduced efficiency rate. In making such an award, the court stated the general principle which is applied in awarding damages: " 'In an action against a union under Section 301 for damages caused by a breach of a no-strike provision in a contract, the measure of damages recoverable is the actual loss sustained by the plaintiff as a direct result of the breach. . . . Such loss would be that which may reasonably and fairly be considered as arising naturally from the particular breach of contract involved and which may reasonably be supposed to have been in the contemplation of the parties at the time the agreement was entered into in the event of such violation'. . . . Damages stemming directly from a strike with which the collective bargaining contract was concerned and which contained a 'no-strike' clause are clearly within the contemplation of the parties."[73]

---

[70]Sheet Metal Workers Local 223 v. Atlas Sheet Metal Co. of Jacksonville, 384 F.2d 101, 110 65 LRRM 3115, 3122 (5th Cir. 1967).

[71]Supra note 69.

[72]20 Cal. Rptr. 860, 50 LRRM 2114 (Cal.App.2d, 1962).

[73]Id., 50 LRRM at 2117, 2119.

"Loss of Goodwill." An employer may appropriately claim loss of reputation resulting from the inability to deliver orders on time, or loss of company goodwill due to the inability to accept new orders or fill old ones.

"Overhead Expenses." In *Electrical Workers (UE) v. Oliver Corp.*,[74] the Court of Appeals for the Eighth Circuit stated: "Overhead expense is the necessary cost incurred by a company in its operations which cannot be easily identified with any individual product and which by accepted cost accounting procedure is spread over or allocated to the productive labor, which is labor performed in the processing of the company's products. Such expenses do not fluctuate directly with plant operations. They are expenses necessary to keep the company on a going concern basis and are based upon the company's production which is planned for a year in advance. They are constant regardless of fluctuations in plant operations. When productive labor in a plant is reduced for any period to less than the normal, the company sustains a loss in expenditure of necessary overhead for which it receives no production."[75] Finding that the plant had operated at 52.5 percent of normal production, the court concluded that a jury could indeed determine that its loss amounted to 47.5 percent of overhead for which no return was received in the form of productive labor.

Similarly, in *Canadian General Electric Co.*,[76] an employer was allowed to estimate its overhead by taking a percentage of overhead costs for a year determined by the ratio of a number of working hours lost during the strike to the total number of hours worked for the year. The arbitrator included in the calculation of overhead the following items: depreciation on fixed assets; insurance premiums, mainly for fire insurance; rent of outside property used for storage; salaries of office and managerial staff; local taxes; telephone and telegraph service; traveling expenses; and heat. In making such an award, the abitrator declared: "[I]t is axiomatic that the company is not entitled to double recovery," but, as summarized by Arbitrator Gentile, an award of these overhead expenses in conjunction with lost profits was allowable, because they were not overlapping.

---

[74]205 F.2d 376, 32 LRRM 2270 (8th Cir. 1953).
[75]Id. at 387, 32 LRRM at 2278.
[76]18 LA 925 (Gentile, 1952).

Another example cited by Arbitrator Gentile was *Belmont Smelting & Refining Works,*[77] where the employer requested damages for daily overhead expenses, including wages and salaries paid to non-bargaining-unit employees. The arbitrator suspended assessment of the requested damages, but indicated that breach of the conditions of suspension (i.e., another work stoppage) would result in the imposition of the requested damage on the union.

In *Vulcan Mold & Iron Co.,*[78] a wrongful work stoppage resulted in a 75 percent loss in production. The arbitrator awarded damages for utilities used during the strike, but reduced the employer's request by one third on the theory that utilities were used less during the strike. The arbitrator refused to make an award for supervisors' salaries where it was determined that the supervisors performed bargaining-unit work during the strike rather than regular supervisory functions.

"Penalties for Late Completion." Any penalty suffered as a result of an illegal strike may appropriately be awarded as compensatory damages. Thus, the District Court for the Western District of Kentucky, in *Wells v. Operating Engineers,*[79] allowed an employer to recover $35 per day for 35 days for a late completion. Where the employer has the option to extend the time for delivery, however, it may not be appropriate to award recovery of damages even where the delay was caused by a strike.

"Pension Liability." Any prorata portion of fringe benefits, including pension payments, that accrued during a strike may be awarded as damages. The arbitrator, however, should be satisfied that the lost benefits in fact relate to the strike period.

"Profit Loss." It is well settled that an arbitrator or a court may award lost profits as a result of illegal strike activity. In addition, an award may be made for profits likely to be lost in the future. For example, in *Abbott v. Plumbers Local 142,*[80] the Court of Appeals for the Fifth Circuit, in a Section 303 action, sustained a lower court award of $11,218 for profits lost as a result of illegal picketing. In that case the court stated:

---

[77]68-1 ARB ¶8342 (Turkus, 1968).
[78]Supra note 66.
[79]206 F. Supp. 414 (W.D. Ky. 1962).
[80]429 F.2d 786, 74 LRRM 2879 (5th Cir. 1970).

Having established disruption of the project and a lower than average rate of return on the project the plaintiffs introduced evidence showing that the low rate of profitability was not attributable to causes other than the picketing. Proof was introduced demonstrating that: (1) the project was bid in the customary manner; (2) the bid was neither excessively high nor inordinately low; (3) factors which had resulted in lower than average profits on other Abbott jobs (e.g., torrential rains, incompetent labor, unusually small size of project, discounts to religious institutions) were absent from this project; and (4) nothing about this job was especially complicated or challenging.[81]

The court sustained the lower court's determination that the loss of profits should be measured by calculating the difference between the actual profits on the picketed project and the average profit made by the employer.

Likewise, in *Canadian General Electric Co.*,[82] the employer was permitted to approximate lost profits by taking a percentage of the total profits of all operations of the company, as measured by the proportion of "shipping costs" attributable to the particular plant at issue. After a measure of the yearly profit attributable to that plant was so obtained, the amount of profits lost due to the strike was calculated by taking a percentage of the estimated total, determined by the ratio of working hours lost to the total available during the year.

"Protection of Freight During Strike." In *Overnite Transportation Co. v. Teamsters*,[83] the Supreme Court of North Carolina, in a Section 303 case, allowed recovery of $16,662 expended for guards necessary to protect freight service from strikers.

"Punitive Damages."[84]

"Recovery Where Business Is Operating at Loss Before the Strike." Arbitrator Gentile cited authority for the proposition that where the company is operating at a loss prior to an illegal strike, it is entitled to recover fixed charges until operations return to normal, but no more than the amount by which the overall loss is aggravated by the strike.

"Salaries of Non-Bargaining-Unit Personnel." Amounts paid to supervisory and nonbargaining-unit personnel nec-

---

[81]Id. at 790, 74 LRRM at 2881.
[82]Supra note 76.
[83]257 N.C. 18, 125 S.E.2d 277, 50 LRRM 2377 (1962), cert. denied, 371 U.S. 862, 51 LRRM 2267, rehearing denied, 371 U.S. 899 (1962).
[84]See Chapter 19, *Punitive Remedies.*

essarily retained by the company while the illegal strike is in progress may be awarded as compensatory damages. Before such an award is made, it should be clearly established that supervisors did not perform bargaining-unit work. Thus, in *Vulcan Mold & Iron Co.*,[85] the arbitrator refused to make an award for supervisory expenses during a strike where it was demonstrated that no supervisory functions were performed. And in *Master Builders Association*,[86] an arbitrator denied a claim for damages as a result of reduced efficiency of supervisors who had 26 rather than 36 workers to supervise during a strike. The arbitrator stated that the supervisors had to be paid the same no matter how many men had to be supervised. In addition, there was evidence that they performed unit work during the strike.

"*Telephone Charges.*" Additional telephone and telegraph expenses incurred as a result of a strike have been allowed by both arbitrators and courts.

"*Travel Expenses.*" Travel expenses incurred because of an improper strike may appropriately be awarded as compensatory damages.

4. Factors Used in Considering Damages

As a final note on this topic, arbitrators have generally relied on testimony of experts, including certified public accountants, in determining the amount of damages arising from a temporary shutdown.[87]

C. Individual Liability for Breach of No-Strike Clause

Section 301(b) of Taft-Hartley,[88] provides, in relevant part:

Any money judgment against a labor organization in a district court of the United States shall be enforceable only against the organization as an entity and against its assets, and shall not be enforceable against any individual member or his assets.

---

[85]Supra note 66.
[86]Supra note 67.
[87]See, e.g., the discussion of Arbitrator David Kaplan in Sterling Gravure Co., 79-2 ARB ¶8325 (1979).
[88]29 U.S.C. §185(b).

When a union is found liable for damages in violation of the no-strike clause of a collective bargaining agreement, its officers and members are not liable for those damages. The Supreme Court, in *Atkinson v. Sinclair Refining Co.*,[89] made it clear that "where the union has inflicted the injury, it alone must pay."[90] The Court, however, specifically did not reach the issue of whether the officers or members of the union could be individually liable for activity, not on behalf of the union, but in their personal and nonunion capacity.[91]

In *Complete Auto Transit v. Reis*,[92] the Court considered whether an employer had a cause of action for damages against individual employees for breach of a collective bargaining agreement's no-strike provision where the strike was unauthorized. In holding that individual members may not be held financially liable for the consequences of a wildcat strike conducted without union authorization or approval, the Court reasoned:

> Section 301(b) by its terms forbids a money judgment entered against a union from being enforced against individual union members. . . . It is a mistake to suppose that Congress thereby suggested by negative implication that employees *should* be held liable where their union is not liable for the strike. . . . Although lengthy and complex, the legislative history of Section 301 clearly reveals Congress' intent to shield individual employees from liability for damages arising from their breach of the no-strike clause of a collective-bargaining agreement, whether or not the union participated in or authorized the illegality. Indeed, Congress intended this result even though it might leave the employer unable to recover for his losses.[93]

Adopting this same line of reasoning, the better rule is for an arbitrator not to award damages against any individual for a breach of a no-strike agreement, but rather to limit such a monetary award to assessments against the union. The employer's remedy is discipline or dismissal of wildcat strikers

---

[89]370 U.S. 238, 50 LRRM 2433 (1962).
[90]Id. at 249. See also Carbon Fuel Co. v. Mine Workers, 444 U.S. 212, 102 LRRM 3017 (1979) (international union liable for damages only for strikes which they had authorized or ratified).
[91]Id. at 249 n.7.
[92]451 U.S. 401, 107 LRRM 2145 (1981).
[93]Id. at 409, 107 LRRM at 2147 (emphasis added).

or, alternatively, a *Boys Markets-Buffalo Forge*[94] injunction against the striking union.

D. Summary

Arbitrators exercise considerable discretion in awarding damages for a breach of the collective bargaining agreement. This is especially true when violations of the no-strike clause are found. As stated by Arbitrator William Eaton, however, merely because a violation is found does not necessarily imply that damages will be awarded:

> Finding a violation of the no-strike clause by the Union does not automatically bind an arbitrator to an award of full compensatory damages, any more than finding that an employee has been discharged without just cause automatically binds an arbitrator to award full back pay upon reinstatement. There are principles of equity as well as principles of contract to be considered. These principles must be applied in a manner designed to serve the best interests of the continuing collective bargaining relationship.[95]

A review of recent cases indicates that monetary damages have been denied where the arbitrator has determined that: there was no basis for establishing actual damages,[96] the monetary claim was not part of the original grievance,[97] the employer did not have "clean hands,"[98] or the work stoppage was of short duration.[99]

As an alternative to awarding monetary damages, some arbitrators have ordered the wildcat strikers to work extra hours without overtime compensation.[100] Where the parties have not requested such a remedy, the better rule is not to assess damages but to remand the issue to the parties and, if deemed proper, retain jurisdiction for a specific period of time.

---

[94]Boys Mkts. v. Retail Clerks, Local 770, 398 U.S. 235, 74 LRRM 2257 (1970); Buffalo Forge Co. v. Steelworkers, 428 U.S. 397, 92 LRRM 3032 (1976).

[95]Mercer, Fraser Co., 70-2 ARB ¶8615 (Eaton, 1970), at 5037.

[96]AG Proctor Co., 67 LA 505, 508 (Krislov, 1976).

[97]Truck Transport., 66 LA 60 (Seidman, 1976).

[98]Smitty's Glass & Lock Serv., 68 LA 1102 (Conway, 1977); Buchholz Mortuaries, 69 LA 623, 628–629 (Roberts, 1977).

[99]Thiokol Corp., 63 LA 633 (Rimer, 1974).

[100]Gamble-Skogmd, Inc., 71 LA 1151 (Weiss, 1978). Cf. Southern Ohio Coal, 66 LA 446 (Lubow, 1976) (illegal striker given suspension equal to loss of days of production that employer sustained).

Chapter 12

Injunctions and Other
Interim Relief

Since an arbitration award does not have the force of law, the term "injunction" as applied to labor arbitration is somewhat misleading. It is nevertheless settled that an arbitrator, in the exercise of his power, may include injunctive-type relief in the award.[1] Thus, awards in the nature of "mandatory injunctions,"[2] such as an order that an employer reinstate a

---

[1]See generally Fairweather, Practice and Procedure in Labor Arbitration, 2d ed., 543–549 (BNA Books, 1983); Feller, *Remedies: New and Old Problems: I. Remedies in Arbitration: Old Problems Revisited*, in Arbitration Issues for the 1980s, Proceedings of the 34th Annual Meeting, National Academy of Arbitrators, 109–133 (BNA Books, 1982); Wolff, *The Power of the Arbitrator to Make Monetary Awards—Remedies in Arbitration*, in Labor Arbitration: Perspectives and Problems, Proceedings of the 17th Annual Meeting, National Academy of Arbitrators, 176, 188–189 (BNA Books, 1964); Feinberg, *Interim Relief and Provisional Remedies in Arbitration*, in NYU 24th Annual Conference on Labor, 49 (1964); Fleming, *Arbitrators and the Remedy Power*, 48 Va. L. Rev. 1199, 1210–1213 (1962); Annotation, Power of Arbitrators to Award Injunction or Specific Performance, 70 A.L.R.2d 1055 (1960).

See also, e.g., Butler Paper Co., 91 LA 311 (Weiss, 1988) (employer ordered to cease and desist from restricting union agent's access to plant); Pacific Maritime Ass'n, 52 LA 1189 (Kagel, 1969); New Orleans S.S. Ass'n, 45 LA 1099 (Oppenheim, 1965), enf'd sub nom. New Orleans S.S. Ass'n v. Longshoremen (ILA) Local 1418, 389 F.2d 369, 67 LRRM 2430 (5th Cir. 1968) ("cease-and-desist" order to striking union was proper under contract providing that arbitrator may "prescribe appropriate relief, including an order to desist therefrom"); Ford Motor Co., 41 LA 619 (Platt, 1963); United Parcel Serv., 41 LA 560 (Turkus, 1963); General Am. Transp. Corp., 41 LA 214 (Abrahams, 1963); ("cease and desist from engaging in strike" and officers to "use their best efforts to secure the return of the striking employees to their jobs"); Macy's New York, 40 LA 954 (Scheiber, 1962) (injunction against sympathetic picketing); Brynmore Press, 7 LA 648 (Rains, 1947) (permanent injunction awarded for remainder of contract).

[2]A "mandatory injunction" is a court order "which (1) commands the defendant to do some positive act or particular thing; (2) prohibits him from refusing (or

309

discharged employee, bargain with a union, change a method of allocating overtime, or reopen a plant and return machinery, are common where the parties' contract or submission agreement indicates an intention that such relief may be awarded. Likewise, injunctions to cease doing certain acts, such as directing a union to refrain from picketing, are less common but are generally considered to be within the arbitrator's jurisdiction when necessary for the proper resolution of the matter in dispute.[3] As stated by one arbitrator, "the question is not one of authority in general but whether, upon a reading of the entire agreement, it may fairly be concluded that the parties contemplated that a remedy be provided where there has been a violation."[4]

A. Awarding an Injunction Against Strikes, Slowdowns, or Lockouts

Section 4 of the Norris-LaGuardia Act provides in relevant part:

> No court of the United States shall have jurisdiction to issue any restraining order or temporary or permanent injunction in any case involving or growing out of any labor dispute to prohibit any person or persons participating or interested in such dispute . . . from doing, whether singly or in concert, any of the following acts:
>
> (a) Ceasing or refusing to perform any work or to remain in any relation of employment.[5]

In *Boys Markets v. Retail Clerks Local 770*,[6] the Supreme Court, recognizing that the peaceful resolution of labor disputes is a fundamental principle of national labor policy, reversed *Sinclair Refining Co. v. Atkinson*,[7] which held that the

---

persisting in a refusal) to do or permit some act to which the plaintiff has a legal right; or (3) restrains the defendant from permitting his previous wrongful act to continue operative, thus virtually compelling him to undo it." Black's Law Dictionary, 5th ed. 705 (1979), citing Bailey v. Schnitzius, 45 N.J.Eq. 178, 16 A. 680 (1889).
[3]San Antonio Packing Co., 68 LA 893 (Bailey, 1977).
[4]Lucky Stores, 70-1 ARB ¶8271 (1969).
[5]29 U.S.C. §104.
[6]398 U.S. 235, 74 LRRM 2257 (1970). An excellent analysis of case law relating to the issuance of injunctions is contained in Bulgar, Boys Markets *Injunctions: A Brief Overview of Injunctions to Prevent Breaches of Collective Bargaining Agreements*, 69 Ill. B.J. 94 (1980).
[7]370 U.S. 195, 50 LRRM 2420 (1962).

Norris-LaGuardia Act precluded a federal court from enjoining a strike in breach of a collective bargaining agreement, even where the agreement contains a provision for final and binding arbitration. The Court ruled that a federal district court, subject to traditional equitable considerations, may properly enjoin a strike over a grievance where the parties are contractually bound to arbitrate.

The Supreme Court further delineated the boundaries of the *Boys Markets* exception in *Buffalo Forge Co. v. Steelworkers*[8] by holding that a federal court could not enjoin a sympathy strike in support of sister unions negotiating with the employer since it "had neither the purpose nor the effect of denying or evading an obligation to arbitrate . . .." Accordingly, when a strike is not called over an arbitral issue, there is no need to accommodate the policies of Norris-LaGuardia to the federal policy favoring arbitration, because such a strike does not frustrate the arbitration process. Again giving Norris a broad interpretation, in 1982 the Supreme Court held in *Jacksonville Bulk Terminals v. Longshoremen (ILA)*[9] that a strike called in protest of the Soviet Union's invasion of Afghanistan (the Longshoremen refused to handle any cargo bound to, or coming from, the Soviet Union or carried on Russian ships) involved a "labor dispute" under Norris-LaGuardia and, therefore, could not be enjoined pending arbitration of the legality of the work stoppage under the parties' collective bargaining agreement. Although several states have also enacted anti-injunction statutes, the principles announced in *Boys Markets*, *Buffalo Forge*, and *Jacksonville Bulk Terminals* are applicable to state courts.[10]

Where a collective bargaining agreement requires arbitration, and a strike is in violation of the contract, an employer may proceed to arbitration requesting an "injunction" or cease-and-desist order against the union rather than petition a court for equitable relief. Unless specifically prohibited by the agreement,[11] an arbitrator may properly grant such relief, and

---

[8]428 U.S. 397, 92 LRRM 3032 (1976).
[9]457 U.S. 702, 110 LRRM 2665 (1982).
[10]Textile Workers v. Lincoln Mills, 353 U.S. 448, 40 LRRM 2113 (1957); Teamsters Local 174 v. Lucas Flour, 369 U.S. 95, 49 LRRM 2717 (1962).
[11]Some agreements may explicitly authorize the arbitrator to grant "injunctive" relief. See, e.g., F & A Painting, 74 LA 106, 107 (Christopher, 1980) ("The Joint Judicial Committee and/or designated arbitrator shall . . . be empowered to impose

a court may enforce the award, notwithstanding federal anti-injunction legislation.[12] Thus, in the often-quoted *Ruppert* decision,[13] Arbitrator Theodore Kheel "enjoined" a union from continuing to engage in a slowdown in violation of the agreement. In challenging the award before the New York Court of Appeals, the union argued that, even though arbitration-issued injunctions are not necessarily unlawful, the injunction issued by Arbitrator Kheel was unlawful, since it was issued contrary to a state anti-injunction statute. The appellate court rejected the union's argument, holding that nothing short of an injunction would have accomplished the evident intent of the parties that there be speedy and effective relief against strikes, lockouts, and slowdowns.[14] More important, the court stated that the parties' contract contemplated the inclusion of an injunction, even though the agreement was silent on that matter, speaking only of "complaints and disputes."[15]

When an arbitrator does grant the employer's request for an order enjoining a strike, and the union refuses to honor it, the employer may proceed to state or federal court for enforcement of the award under section 301 of the Taft-Hartley Act. Once the award is confirmed by the court, an injunctive decree incorporating the arbitral award will properly issue.

B. Preliminary Relief to Determination on the Merits

Arbitrators and courts have granted injunctive-type relief in cases other than wildcat strikes and while these cases usually involve a union seeking a remedy against management, it is instructive to consider status quo orders in this section.

In *Giffords Oil*,[16] Arbitrator Burton Turkus granted a temporary injunction restraining the employer from further subcontracting bargaining-unit work, pending final determination of the merits of the case. Where the employer had

---

such judgments, monetary, injunctive or both, as in its opinion would tend to cure the breach of contract and to make such decisions which in its opinion would most accurately reflect the intent and meaning of the Agreement.").

[12]See, e.g., General Dynamics Corp. v. Marine & Shipbuilding Workers Local 5, 469 F.2d 848, 81 LRRM 2746 (1st Cir. 1972).

[13]In re Ruppert, 3 N.Y.2d 576, 148 N.E.2d 129, 29 LA 775 (1958).

[14]Id., 148 N.E.2d at 130.

[15]Id. at 131.

[16]59 LA 959 (1972).

requested and had received numerous delays in the hearing, Arbitrator Turkus ruled that the union had established a *prima facie* case of entitlement to an interim stay or injunction as a condition to the granting of another adjournment. Attention is called to the arbitrator's reasoning:

> [A] balance of the equities involved requires that the Union obtain at least interim relief to prevent further depletion and/ or erosion of the bargaining unit and to preserve the work opportunities of the employees covered by the agreement; that the employer was granted every fair opportunity to attend the scheduled hearing to preserve its position and argue in support of the requested adjournment; and that greater injury would result to the Union and the contractually agreed bargaining unit from the denial of the request for interim relief than would be realized by the employer by the grant [of another delay].[17]

In granting the restraining order, Arbitrator Turkus nevertheless provided that the employer would be able to move, within 48 hours, for an expedited hearing, which could include an application to modify or vacate the interim stay or injunction.[18]

Similarly, Arbitrator Thomas McDermott, at the close of an arbitration hearing, issued a "temporary restraining order" directing the employer from continuing to conduct time studies. The arbitrator determined that such a remedy was appropriate, pending resolution of the ultimate merits, since there would be no way that the arbitrator could undo the effects of the time studies or prevent the use of the results obtained if it was subsequently determined that the employer did not have the right under the agreement to conduct the studies.[19]

Where interim relief pending final resolution on the merits has been denied, arbitrators have stressed the absence of "irreparable harm" to the complaining party. Thus, Arbitrator Raymond Goetz refused to issue an order restraining the employer from using another employer's employees to perform clean-up work. Refusing to direct the employer to return to the status quo, pending a final decision, Arbitrator Goetz expressed "grave doubts whether the interim order requested is

---

[17]Id. at 961.
[18]Id.
[19]McCall Printing Co., 63 LA 627, 629 (1974).

within the scope of his authority. Instead of providing temporary relief, any such order would probably only invite further dispute and perhaps litigation over its propriety."[20] The arbitrator further stressed that caution ought to be exercised in issuing these types of remedies:

> Even if it could be assumed that the Arbitrator does have some inherent power to do whatever is necessary to provide relief, much like a court of equity, he would be constrained to exercise this power with restraint. This is because any temporary restraining order, issued pending determination of the merits of the case, temporarily at least, decides the case against the party being restrained—before there has been a full hearing and decision on the merits of the claim of the complaining party. Accordingly, even where the parties have by advance agreement given arbitrators the needed authority, a showing of irreparable harm is required as a condition to granting any such temporary restraining order.[21]

In determining whether to grant injunctive-type relief prior to conducting a full hearing on the merits, a major consideration cited by arbitrators is the course of action contemplated (or enacted) by the employer or union and the difficulty of undoing that action once it has taken place. As noted by one commentator, it is much more difficult to undo a plant transfer, a sale of an employer's business,[22] or a subcontracting agreement, than to undo the alteration of a work schedule.[23] Similar to the standards established by the federal courts, a review of the few arbitration awards that have been reported in this area indicates that before an "injunction" will be issued, the complaining party will be required to demonstrate, at the very least, a potential for irreparable harm and a probability of success on the merits. And while some commentators may validly argue that injunctive-type relief has little utility in the arbitral forum,[24] the better rule, as seen by the authors, is to grant such relief where the facts so warrant.

---

[20]Armour & Co., 68 LA 1076, 1077 (1977).
[21]Id. See also Postal Serv., 67 LA 133 (Garrett, 1976); Oakland Tribune Publishing Co., 60 LA 665 (Koven, 1973).
[22]See, e.g., Hosanna Trading Co., 74 LA 128 (Simons, 1980) (sale of assets).
[23]Kratze, *Enjoining Employers Pending Arbitration: Some Misconceptions and Clarifications*, 24 St. Louis U.L.J. 92, 114 (1979).
[24]As noted by Arbitrator Stein: "I fail to see any real benefit to anyone in an injunction issued by an arbitrator. And, if it were disobeyed, as is quite likely in an emotion-charged situation, the result might well be to discredit arbitration and collective bargaining." Stein, *Remedies in Labor Arbitration*, in Challenges to Arbitra-

In the drug-testing area, courts have entered the arena and have issued status quo injunctions pending arbitration when management has enacted random testing plans. Ruling that when the issue is arbitrable an injunction can issue notwithstanding the Norris-LaGuardia Act, Judge Harold Greene, in *Electrical Workers (IBEW) Local 1900 v. PEPCO*,[25] concluded that the arbitral process stood to be harmed irreparably if management's unilateral drug-testing program were allowed to take effect. In granting a temporary restraining order, Judge Greene found "that absent arbitration the employees whose privacy will be invaded by these proposed actions could not be made whole" and further declared:

> I am not aware of any organization similar to this one, government or private, that has gone this far, and has sought unilaterally, without consultation or without negotiation, to impose these kinds of drastic measures. . . .
> I don't denigrate at all the importance of electric supply needs and electric power, but that does not mean that it's vital that these drastic measures must be imposed on everyone, including clerks and secretaries, or even on anyone. On the other hand, it's clear that plaintiffs will be severely injured. Pending outcome of the arbitration they must undergo invasions of privacy which are almost unheard of in a free society or they will be summarily fired.[26]

Judge Greene pointed out the infirmities of the employer's program:

> [Under management's program] an employee "shall be discharged" on the first offense if he as much as refuses to submit to urine and blood tests. An employee shall be discharged on the first offense if he refuses the search not only of his locker or his lunchbox or other possessions but also of his person, again on the first offense.
> He is discharged on the first offense if he is found to have any detectable quantity of drugs in his system, even if they were acquired during his private time such as weekends or vacations.[27]

Judge Greene concluded:

---

tion, Proceedings of the 13th Annual Meeting, National Academy of Arbitrators, 3, 47 (BNA Books, 1960).
[25]121 LRRM 3071 (D.D.C. 1986).
[26]Id. at 3072.
[27]Id. at 3073.

> The drug menace is certainly a terrible menace as the court is well aware, having had the unfortunate experience of having to try many drug cases . . . , but that does not mean that we must resort to hysterical measures, particularly by a company which, while important certainly to safety and well-being and welfare of our city and of our society, is hardly in the forefront of the danger as would be, for example, airline pilots or CIA operatives.[28]

Judge Greene accordingly issued a temporary restraining order for five days, the maximum allowable under Norris-LaGuardia. When this order expired, the union returned to court to seek another injunction.[29] Judge Louis Oberdorfer heard the union's motion for a preliminary injunction. Noting that "a court may issue an injunction if, in addition to the usual equitable concerns, the integrity of the arbitration process would be threatened absent interim relief," Judge Oberdorfer disagreed with Judge Greene's holding. According to Oberdorfer,

> Temporary loss of employment by the employees represented by a plaintiff union does not usually threaten the integrity of the arbitral process, since back pay and reinstatement can in most instances provide complete relief. . . . But, if a union can demonstrate that its members have special current needs which could not be fully redressed by an arbitration award, preliminary relief can be justified.[30]

What is particularly noteworthy is that Judge Oberdorfer required management to satisfy certain conditions, the most important of which was to adhere to its prior policy of testing only when there are "compelling circumstances." Judge William D. Stiehl of the Southern District of Illinois, in *Stove Workers Local 185 v. Weyerhaeuser Paper Co.*,[31] adopted Judge Greene's analysis and preliminarily enjoined management from implementing an alcohol and drug testing plan at its Belleville, Illinois, plant. Finding irreparable harm to the union and a likelihood of success on the merits, and no irreparable harm to the employer if its program was delayed pending arbitration, Judge Stiehl credited the union's argument that

---

[28]Id.
[29]Electrical Workers (IBEW) Local 1900 v. PEPCO, 634 F. Supp. 642, 121 LRRM 3287 (D.D.C. 1986).
[30]Id., 121 LRRM at 3288.
[31]650 F. Supp. 431, 126 LRRM 2184 (S.D. Ill. 1986).

the program was an invasion of privacy and would cause a "black mark" on employees' records.

Other federal district courts have similarly enjoined drug and alcohol testing programs pending arbitration where (1) the underlying dispute is arbitrable, (2) the union is likely to prevail on the merits, (3) there is a showing of irreparable harm and (4) the balance of hardship favors a restraining order.[32] The appellate courts are less receptive to union arguments, at least in the drug testing area.[33]

C. Use of Interim Awards

In an address before the 17th Annual Meeting of the National Academy of Arbitrators, Arbitrator Peter Seitz proposed that many cases arguably call for the issuance of rulings or interlocutory or interim decisions requiring that certain things be done, or for additional facts to be reflected by the record of the case, before an arbitrator undertakes a final decision.[34]

Despite a general reluctance by arbitrators to issue an interim award, except when specifically requested to do so by the parties, Seitz defended his thesis by noting that the labor arbitrator is frequently asked to perform functions which are not purely "judicial" in the conventional sense:

> The parties may delegate to the arbitrator the power to determine a crew size for a new or changed operation or equipment;

---

[32]See, e.g., Steelworkers v. USX Corp., 130 LRRM 3089 (E.D. Pa. 1989) (union entitled to preliminary injunction enjoining implementation of across-the-board drug testing of safety employees pending arbitration); Machinists Dist. Lodge 120 v. General Dynamics Corp., No. 86-2244 (C.D. Cal., Apr. 9, 1986); Electrical Workers (IBEW) Local Sys. Council 409 v. Metropolitan Edison, No. 86-4426 (E.D. Pa., Aug. 6, 1986) (granting injunction pending arbitration for drug-testing programs for "in-house" employees at Three Mile Island, finding that irreparable injury would result from invasion of privacy, humiliation, and damage to reputation). See also Murray v. Brooklyn Union Gas Co., 122 LRRM 2057 (N.Y. Sup. Ct. 1986) (restraining gas company from implementing drug-testing program pending expedited arbitration); Railway Labor Executives Ass'n v. Port Auth. Trans-Hudson, 695 F. Supp. 124, 130 LRRM 2043 (S.D.N.Y. 1988) (enjoining program, holding that RLA does not prohibit drug testing by carriers but requires negotiation with employers prior to instituting any "major" change in working conditions).

[33]See, e.g., Utility Workers Local 246 v. Southern Cal. Edison Co., 852 F.2d 1083, 129 LRRM 2077 (9th Cir. 1988) (holding lower court erred in issuing preliminary injunction against implementation of drug-testing program absent implicit or explicit promise that status quo would be preserved pending arbitration).

[34]Seitz, *Problems of the Finality of Awards, or Functus Officio and All That—Remedies in Arbitration*, in Labor Arbitration: Perspectives and Problems, supra note 1, at 169.

or to determine a rate for a new classification; or to determine whether it is safe to operate certain printing presses at a given speed; . . . or to determine whether an individual has the mental capacity to perform a job efficiently, or the physical capacity to perform it without injury to himself or danger to others.[35]

Seitz further stated that these are not the types of decisions conventionally made by a judge in a court of law. The arbitrator is not asked to interpret and apply standards but, in effect, to legislate them. The difficulties arise when the arbitrator feels that the record before him is inadequate. Should he ask for additional facts, he does so at considerable risk. According to Seitz:

> For one thing, he is delaying a prompt and expeditious conclusion of the controversy which is one of the objectives of arbitration. For another, he may be adding materially to the cost of arbitration: a consideration, frequently of considerable weight, particularly if he is from distant parts. Further, counsel have been known to resent the arbitrator's request for facts which they had not regarded as necessary to present, some even feeling that it suggests to their clients that the presentation was not as brilliant as it was hopefully represented to be. Finally (although arbitrators, as much as the next man, like to be loved), it is sad to relate that the asking of questions which go beyond the mere comprehension of what is being placed in front of him and the request that additional data be furnished by one of the parties, frequently does not facilitate or promote affection. Such requests by an arbitrator may be resented on the ground that he is engaged in making a case for the other side.[36]

Other commentators have voiced concern over the unrequested service of interim awards. In an appearance before the National Academy in 1964, Jesse Freidin stated:

> [W]hat the parties expect and what they ask an arbitrator to provide is a final resolution of their grievance, of their difference; not a temporary one; not a partial one, not an interim one, but a final one; and I submit to you that this finality is itself a quality of worth, for it accomplishes a most useful purpose—it brings a difference to an end—the very purpose that the parties intended the arbitration procedure to provide.[37]

---

[35]Id. at 172.
[36]Id. at 173.
[37]Freidin, *The Power of the Arbitrator to Make Monetary Awards—Remedies in Arbitration: Discussion*, in Labor Arbitration: Perspectives and Problems, supra note 1, at 203.

When the grievant requests arbitration, declares Freidin, he assumes the obligation of persuading the arbitrator to that end. By refusing to act finally on that claim, the arbitration process is cheapened by encouraging the "shoot-from-the-hip" grievance and the "try-it-on-for-size" award. Absent agreement from the parties, Friedin argues that the arbitrator's duty is to decide the case before him because, if the parties believe the facts can yield a decision, it is not the place of the arbitrator to say that the facts cannot.[38]

Another practitioner has similarly argued that interim decisions generally prove unsatisfactory to the parties and may foster discord between them:

> The very things in issue, most often factual disputes, remain unresolved, and the parties merely find themselves where they started—haggling over the facts. The consequence is usually a prolongation of the dispute and further friction between the parties.
>
> From management's point of view these interim arbitration decisions are particularly disconcerting because in all but discipline cases, the burden of proof rests with the union. If the grievance has not been proved, it should be denied; it's as simple as that. All too often the interim award encourages trial grievances and provides the other party with an opportunity to rehabilitate a weak position or a losing case. In short, such decisions frustrate the state of finality which arbitration was designed to provide the parties.[39]

Despite the controversy, arbitrators have issued interim awards, especially in those cases where the record is incomplete. For example, in *Silas Mason Co.*,[40] Arbitrator Pearce Davis withheld final decision on the propriety of a discharge of an employee who had become emotionally unstable from her job of handling highly explosive materials. Although the arbitrator found that it would be improper to reinstate her to her prior job, he reserved making a final decision in view of the absence of evidence as to whether there was an alternative job that the employee could perform. The interim decision directed the parties to undertake a comprehensive investi-

---

[38]Id. at 204.
[39]Mekula, *Implementation of Arbitration Awards: The Ford Experience*, in Arbitration and the Public Interest, Proceedings of the 24th Annual Meeting, National Academy of Arbitrators, 110, 121–122 (BNA Books, 1971).
[40]59 LA 197 (1972).

gation of alternative job opportunities and to make a written report to the arbitrator within 10 days of the award. The arbitrator further provided that if the parties were unable to agree on the facts, either or both could petition for further hearings.[41]

Where a discharged state trooper was under investigation for illegal importation of alcoholic beverages into a "dry" town, one arbitrator, after hearing arguments on the matter, issued an "intermediate award" ruling that the dismissal had been untimely, reasoning that it was the intent of the legislature to grant the grievant a hearing before discharge despite the nature of the misconduct (it is unclear where the arbitrator found this "legislative guarantee") and, accordingly, ordered the grievant's discharge reduced to a suspension. The arbitrator later issued a supplemental award after the grievant had been convicted in his criminal trial holding the dismissal justified. Reversing a trial court, the Supreme Court of Alaska found no infirmity in issuing an interim remedy.[42]

Arbitrator Charles Mullin, Jr., in *Babcock & Wilcox Co.,*[43] reserved making a final award in a discharge case where the grievant's alleged mental health problems were found to underlie the case. The arbitrator ordered the employer to provide for, and the grievant to submit to, an examination by a psychiatrist. The results of the examination would then serve as the basis for a final determination which would involve return to work, further consideration after treatment, or separation. Jurisdiction was retained in the event that the parties did not reach agreement with regard to the details of the order.

Similarly, Arbitrator A.Q. Sartain, in *Molycorp, Inc.*[44] remanded disposition to the parties in the case of an underground lead miner who was certified by his doctor as being able to return to his job following a work-related injury, but who was not reinstated by management based on the opinion of its doctor. In this case the agreement provided that when disagreement exists between the parties' doctors, a third medical doctor should be selected for an opinion. The arbitrator

---

[41]Id. at 200.
[42]Public Safety Dep't (Alaska) v. Public Safety Employees Ass'n, 732 P.2d 1090, 125 LRRM 2116 (Alaska 1987).
[43]72 LA 1073 (1979).
[44]82 LA 693 (1984).

remanded the case to the parties, stating that he could neither uphold nor deny the grievance. With respect to retaining jurisdiction, Arbitrator Sartain stated that he was not retaining jurisdiction, believing that jurisdiction should be conferred by the parties and not the arbitrator.

There is arbitral precedent for issuing an interim award under circumstances where various situations must be examined and individual decisions are required to determine whether an employee can be reinstated. Arbitrator Bert Luskin reported to the authors an unpublished decision involving an agreement among the parties that permitted an interim award, with the understanding that the final award would be issued to the parties together with a full written opinion at some subsequent point in time. The hearing (involving the dismissal of several hundred employees for honoring a picket line of a sister local engaged in an unauthorized strike) extended over a period of seven days. Arbitrator Luskin's instincts proved to be correct; the parties ultimately adopted the interim award reinstating the employees with no loss of seniority, but without back pay, and agreed that there would be no need to issue a full opinion. (The parties were able to work out among themselves the procedures to be followed in the restoration of seniority rights.) According to the arbitrator, the interim award resulted in saving the jobs of several hundred people who, at the time of the issuance of the award, had already been replaced by newly hired or former employees who had been rehired in the interim period.

In situations where an arbitrator believes that the record is insufficient to allow determination of (1) the nature and the extent of a disciplinary suspension to be imposed in lieu of discharge, (2) the period of back pay, or (3) who shall bear the costs of excessive delay in bringing the case to arbitration, Peter Seitz has proposed that the arbitrator issue an interim, rather than a final, award:[45]

> In that interim award, he might order prompt reinstatement of the grievant in his employment and job classification to stop the running of time and the accumulation of damages; but, in so doing, he should state that he makes no determination as to

---

[45]Seitz, *Substitution of Disciplinary Suspension for Discharge (A Proposed "Guide to the Perplexed" in Arbitration)*, 35 Arb. J. 27, 30 (1980).

the subjects of back pay, seniority rights, or other beneficial rights in respect of that period between the date of discharge and the date of reinstatement because the record made in the case is inadequate for that purpose. He should reserve jurisdiction, expressly, as to such matters.[46]

Arbitrator Seitz goes on to argue:

The interim award should proceed to order the parties to meet and to seek to reach agreement as to such matters and to report the results of their efforts to the arbitrator within a stated period of time. Should they report that agreement has been reached he should offer the parties the opportunity to choose one of the following procedures: (a) the holding of additional hearings at which the parties could present him with their positions as to the matters on which jurisdiction had been reserved and the facts supporting such positions; or (b) an "in chambers" discussion between the arbitrator and the advocates of the parties as to matters referred to in (a), supra. At such discussion the parties would inform the arbitrator of all facts and considerations bearing upon the disciplinary practices in the employing establishment, which should guide him in deciding the nature and extent or severity of the disciplinary suspension he will order.[47]

Arbitrator Edgar Jones, Jr., effectively used an interim order, in part, to avoid the possibility of multiple claims being filed in numerous forums against the union and/or the employer. Thus, in *Michaelson's Food Service*,[48] Arbitrator Jones issued an interim award holding that a back-pay dispute was arbitrable, provided that a number of conditions were subsequently satisfied. Two conditions worth noting were that the grievant be formally designated as a "party" to the proceeding, along with any other employees who elected to press claims against the employer, the union, or both, and that the union petition the court for enforcement of the interim award. Arbitrator Jones' remedy was reversed by the Ninth Circuit,[49] which held that the arbitrator was without power to allow other employees similarly situated to join in the proceeding for the first time at the arbitration stage. The court of appeals also found that Jones exceeded his authority under the collective bargaining agreement by ordering arbitration of an

---

[46]Id.
[47]Id. at 30–31.
[48]61 LA 1195 (1973).
[49]Hotel & Restaurant Employees v. Michelson's Food Servs., 545 F.2d 1248, 94 LRRM 2014 (9th Cir. 1976).

employee's claim against the union where there was no agreement between the union and the employee to arbitrate his claim.

Where the time limits that an employer allowed an apprentice as part of a test to qualify him as a machinist was unreasonable, rather than directing any particular time limit and ordering the grievant qualified, Arbitrator Peter Henle, in *Bethlehem Steel Corp.*[50] remanded the case to the parties' grievance procedure for reconsideration.

D. A Note on Cease-and-Desist Orders: Rights Without Remedies?

While it is clear that an arbitrator can appropriately issue an order directing the union or the employer to stop violating the agreement, arbitrators have questioned whether these remedies are more shadow than substance in relation to arbitration. Arbitrator Louis Crane, addressing the National Academy of Arbitrators,[51] has observed that when a court issues an injunction requiring someone to cease and desist from engaging in a course of conduct, it has the power to issue a contempt citation, either civil or criminal, to compel compliance. In contrast to an equity court, arbitrators' remedy power, after someone disobeys their order to cease and desist from violating the agreement, is the same as it was when they first issued the cease-and-desist order. Crane further points out that before issuing a cease-and-desist order, an arbitrator must first find that the conduct in question violates the agreement. Expanding on this argument, Arbitrator Crane states:

> If he lacks the power to do anything about the violation, any relief must of necessity be declaratory. Issuing a cease-and-desist order in these circumstances makes him no less a paper tiger if the offender insists upon following the same course of conduct after the decision is issued. On the other hand, if the arbitrator has the power to redress the violations he finds, is it

---

[50]84 LA 1105 (1985). See also Kraft, Inc., 86 LA 882 (Sabghir, 1986) (grievance challenging wage rate for filler classification returned to parties for negotiations; grievance to be resubmitted if not settled by specific date).

[51]Crane, *The Use and Abuse of Arbitral Power*, in Labor Arbitration at the Quarter-Century Mark, Proceedings of the 25th Annual Meeting, National Academy of Arbitrators, 66–75 (BNA Books, 1973).

not a better course to do so then and there instead of issuing a cease-and-desist order?[52]

Crane expands his thesis to include the situation where an arbitrator, while not immediately granting affirmative relief, may nevertheless want to forewarn the parties that any repetitive violation of the agreement will result in an affirmative remedy:

> In a permanent umpire system, the arbitrator can withhold affirmative relief, explain why he is doing so, and tell the parties they may expect different treatment in the future if the same situation occurs again. A cease-and-desist order is unnecessary. In an ad hoc situation, such a warning from an arbitrator could very well resolve any question about whether he would be the mutual choice of the parties if the same thing happens again. Besides, he has no assurance that the arbitrator the parties may subsequently choose would arrive at the same conclusion. Consequently, a cease-and-desist order would be no more effective than the other relief the first arbitrator could have granted.[53]

Stuart Bernstein has likewise argued that cease-and-desist orders are generally not useful as a remedy:

> The problem with cease-and-desist orders is that they are something like gratuitous advice in the award. They both tend to have impact on future conduct where there may be serious and honest disagreement on whether the future conduct, when it occurs, is really within the framework of the original condition which gave rise to the award.[54]

Bernstein does concede, however, that this type of remedy may be appropriate where the cease-and-desist order is directed at conduct that is continuing at the time of the hearing, as opposed to conduct which has ceased but is expected to recur:

> It may be appropriate to direct an employer to cease what he is then doing, or to tell a union to stop a strike which violates a no-strike provision. It may not be appropriate to tell a party that something he did in the past—but is not then doing—was wrong and that he should never do it again. The again may not be the same thing. Circumstances change results. It is one thing

---

[52]Id. at 73–74.

[53]Id. at 74. It should not be overlooked, however, that in an ad hoc situation where the parties may opt not to use the same arbitrator in a subsequent hearing, it is well understood that a different arbitrator, while not bound by the decision of another arbitrator, may be influenced and persuaded by the reasoning of the first neutral.

[54]Bernstein, *The Use and Abuse of Arbitral Power: Comment*, supra note 51, at 79–80.

to rely on an earlier case as precedent and quite another to charge a party with being in violation of an outstanding cease-and-desist order.[55]

If the parties specifically request a cease-and-desist order or, alternatively, a declaratory judgment that the agreement has been violated, the better weight of authority is to incorporate such a remedy into the award if the facts so warrant. It must be recognized that not all violations of a collective bargaining agreement can, or even should, be remedied with a monetary award. In numerous situations, the only viable remedy is an order directing the breaching party to honor the agreement.[56] Arbitration awards, similar to orders of administrative agencies, are not self-enforcing, but this factor should not preclude an order directing a union or an employer to cease violating the contract. Once such an award is issued, if the breaching party continues to ignore the order, the award may be enforced in a subsequent court proceeding.

E. Summary: Injunctions and Arbitral Authority to Grant Specific Performance

In an address before the National Academy of Arbitrators, Arbitrator David Feller[57] argued what we believe is the better perspective regarding the arbitrator's authority to issue injunctive-type relief. Asserting that the primary authority im-

---

[55]Id. at 80.

[56]See, e.g., Naval Air Rework Facility, North Island, 72 LA 129, 133 (Kaufman, 1979) (employer to refrain from prohibiting union representative from visiting facility); Federal Aviation Admin., 71 LA 1138 (Tsukiyama, 1978) (order to recognize union); Hempstead Pub. Schools Bd. of Educ., 69 LA 808, 811 (Gootnick, 1977) (ordering management to provide clerical assistance); Social Sec. Admin., 67 LA 766 (Smith, 1976) (order to cease using dress code); Headquarters XVIII Airborne Corps., 67 LA 91, 93 (Carson, 1976) (employee not to be excluded from participation in policy meetings); Internal Revenue Serv., 67 LA 403 (Sinicropi, 1976) (union to be allowed use of bulletin board); Hawaii Dep't of Educ., 66 LA 1221 (Tsukiyama, 1976) (policy against showing of R-rated films to be rescinded); North Shore Cent. School Dist. Bd. of Educ., 64 LA 1312 (Silver, 1975) (discussion recommended); U.S. Army Publications Center, 65 LA 564, 572 (Fitzsimmons, 1975) (employer to allow union representatives reasonable time to assist employees in processing grievances); Anaconda Co., 63 LA 259 (Daughton, 1974) (allowance of company officials in grievance steps); Otis Elevator Co., 60 LA 1332 (Silver, 1973) (dirty restrooms; employer to take affirmative action to remedy effects of violation); American Flyers Airline, 70-2 ARB ¶8724 (Sembower, 1970) (cease and desist proper remedy where employer failed to remedy admitted violations of assigning too much overtime).

[57]Feller, supra note 1.

plicitly granted to the arbitrator is the authority to grant specific performance of the provisions of the agreement, Feller submits that the discussion as to the authority of an arbitrator to issue an injunction is "foolish" because that is all that an arbitrator ever does, or should do. In Feller's words, "[w]hen an arbitrator orders the company to reinstate a grievant, he is issuing an injunction. When an arbitrator directs the company to remedy a condition that is unsafe, he is issuing an injunction. He is ordering the company to take specific action."[58]

In support of this view, Feller goes on to point out that common law courts have no such power in breach of contract cases, being limited to a finding that the defendant, because of the breach, is indebted to the plaintiff for a specific sum of money, otherwise known as damages. The usual meaning of a collective bargaining agreement, however, is different. Unless otherwise stated, when the parties execute a labor agreement they intend that the employer will perform in accordance with the contract, not the option of performing or paying damages. Feller argues that "the remedy power which the parties give to the arbitrator is the authority to order the performance that the contract requires." Absent an instantaneous grievance and arbitration procedure, in which all violations of the rules set forth in the agreement could be instantly grieved and decided, the only remedy power of the arbitrator would be to order the employer to do that which the contract specifies he should do.

We see no particular infirmity in an arbitrator issuing a so-called injunction under the circumstances described in this section. There are times, however, when an arbitrator will not order a cease-and-desist remedy, especially in the federal sector where the remedy may conflict with a constitutional or statutory right.[59]

---

[58]Id. at 117.
[59]See, e.g., Luke Air Force Base, 90 LA 1065 (Cohen, 1988) (holding that arbitrator lacks authority to grant federal agency prior restraint against union publication).

Part III

Remedies in Nondisciplinary Cases Selected Topics

Chapter 13

Subcontracting and Improper Transfer of Operations

A. Introduction

In arbitration terminology, as well as in general business parlance, subcontracting carries a connotation of third persons being hired to perform work. More specifically, it is work performed by employees that are not part of the bargaining unit, whether or not such work is actually performed inside or outside the premises of the employer.[1] In *American Air Filter Co.*,[2] Arbitrator David Dolnick suggested that no fixed guidelines can be applied in subcontracting disputes. Quoting the arbitrator:

> Subcontracting is one of the most troublesome and perplexing problems in labor-management relations. It affects the concern of the recognized collective bargaining agent and the

---

[1]Food Marketing Corp., 83 LA 671 (Chapman, 1984); Overhead Door Corp., 77 LA 619, 621 (Herrick, 1981); Rockwell Int'l, 71 LA 1024, 1025 (Cox, 1978). See also Elkouri and Elkouri, How Arbitration Works, 4th ed., 537–547 (BNA Books, 1985); Fairweather, Practice and Procedure in Labor Arbitration, 2d ed., 469–493 (BNA Books, 1983); Miscimarra, The NLRB and Managerial Discretion: Plant Closings, Relocations, Subcontracting, and Automation (Labor Relations and Public Policy Series, No. 24) (Philadelphia: Industrial Research Unit, the Wharton School, University of Pennsylvania, 1980).

See generally Hill and Sinicropi, Management Rights: A Legal and Arbitral Analysis, 449 (BNA Books, 1986), and the related discussions: "Transfer or Relocation of Unit Work," Chapter 15, at notes 45–64, and accompanying text; "Work Preservation Clauses and Transfer of Operations," Chapter 15, at notes 103–112, and accompanying text; and "Supervisors Performing Bargaining-Unit Work," Chapter 17, at notes 31–83, and accompanying text.

[2]54 LA 1251 (1970).

329

preservation of the bargaining unit. It triggers the fear of job loss and unemployment. Although Arbitrators have extensively dealt with this subject, and although many excellent scholarly treatises have been written, there is no fixed guideline which may be applied in every subcontracting dispute. Each case must be examined in the light of the applicable agreement, from the fixed, undisputed practices of the parties, from the implications that stem from either or both the contract and practice where they do not conflict, and from the circumstances and the evidence in each dispute.[3]

Grievances alleging improper subcontracting arise in situations where the contract is silent on the issue of contracting out or, alternatively, where the parties have incorporated guidelines on subcontracting in their agreement. Although many of the standards that arbitrators use in resolving subcontracting disputes and formulating remedies are applicable in either situation, it is useful to examine both categories separately.

B. Court Decisions and NLRB Policy on Duty to Bargain in Subcontracting Disputes[4]

At one time the bellwether case controlling the policy in this area was *Fibreboard Paper Products Corp. v. NLRB,*[5] where the Supreme Court held that an employer's decision to subcontract plant maintenance work formally performed by the bargaining unit was a mandatory subject of bargaining, despite the fact that the decision was economically motivated. The decision also required that the bargaining be carried to impasse. The case is significant, but it must be stressed that it was restricted to its own facts, which included the following conditions: (1) the subcontracting did not alter the basic operation of the business; (2) the subcontracting occurred in the plant under situations which were similar to those that prevailed prior to the subcontracting; (3) employee jobs were

---

[3]Id. at 1254.

[4]This section is taken, in part, from a paper delivered by one of the authors at the 32d Annual Meeting of the National Academy of Arbitrators, and from Hill and Sinicropi, supra note 1. See Sinicropi, *Revisiting an Old Battle Ground: The Subcontracting Dispute,* in Arbitration of Subcontracting and Wage Incentive Disputes, Proceedings of the 32d Annual Meeting, National Academy of Arbitrators, 125–166 (BNA Books, 1980); Hill and Sinicropi, supra note 1, at 451–453.

[5]379 U.S. 203, 57 LRRM 2609 (1964).

eliminated and were taken over by the subcontractor's employees; (4) reasons for the subcontracting were related to the costs of labor, which might have been adjusted by negotiation with the union, thereby avoiding the need to subcontract; and (5) the employer was still in the same business-risk situation under the subcontracting, because the subcontracting was done on a cost-plus basis.

One year later, in *Westinghouse Electric Corp.*,[6] the NLRB set forth five factors that it would consider in determining whether an employer must bargain with the union over the decision to subcontract: (1) whether the contracting out was motivated solely by economic considerations; (2) whether it comported with the traditional methods by which the company conducted its business; (3) whether the subcontracting varied significantly from what had been customary under past practice; (4) whether it had a demonstrable adverse impact upon the employees in the unit; and (5) whether the union had the opportunity to bargain about changing existing subcontracting practices at negotiations.

Fibreboard and *Westinghouse* made it clear that management is not obligated to consult and bargain with the union over every subcontracting decision. While no hard and fast rules exist, under these decisions subcontracting of unit work without notice to and consultation with the union is arguably permissible unless it results in a "significant detriment" to the bargaining unit.[7]

Recent Board decisions indicate that "the critical factor in determining whether a management decision is subject to mandatory bargaining [under Section 8(d) of Taft-Hartley] is the essence of the decision itself, i.e., whether it turns upon a change in the nature or direction of the business, or turns upon labor costs; *not* its effect on employees nor a union's ability to offer alternatives."[8] Thus, in *Griffith-Hope Co.*,[9] a three-member Board held that a company violated the Act by

---

[6]150 NLRB 1574, 58 LRRM 1257 (1965).
[7]See, e.g., Olinkraft, Inc. v. NLRB, 666 F.2d 302, 109 LRRM 2573 (5th Cir. 1982).
[8]UOP, Inc., Bostrom Div., 272 NLRB 999, 117 LRRM 1429, 1429 (1984), citing Otis Elevator Co., 269 NLRB 891, 115 LRRM 1281 (1984) (critical factor in determining whether management decision is mandatory is "the essence of the decision itself, i.e., whether it turns upon a change in the nature or direction of the business, or turns upon labor cost") (plurality opinion).
[9]275 NLRB 487, 119 LRRM 1197 (1985).

unilaterally subcontracting unit work without bargaining over the decision to do so and its effects on the bargaining unit. The Board, citing its decision in *Otis Elevator Co.*[10] stated that "when a particular management decision turns upon labor costs, it falls within the scope of Section 8(d) and concerns a mandatory subject of bargaining."[11] A fair reading of management's bargaining obligation is that a subcontracting decision that turns on labor costs, and does not alter the basic nature of the business, is subject to bargaining with the union if it results in a "significant detriment" to the unit.[12] Less clear is management's obligation when the decision alters the basic nature of the business and, at the same time, turns on labor costs.[13] An essential fact is whether labor problems contributed to the employer's decison to subcontract.[14]

C. NLRB Remedies for Improper Subcontracting

When subcontracting violations have been found, the Board may order resumption of the discontinued operations along with reinstatement with back pay, so long as the order will not impose an undue or unfair burden on the company.[15] As an example, the Supreme Court in *Fibreboard* sustained the Board's order requiring (1) termination of the subcontract,

---

[10]Supra note 8.

[11]119 LRRM at 1198.

[12]See, e.g., Ausable Communications, 273 NLRB 1410, 118 LRRM 1295 (1985) (subcontracting of increased installation work without affording union opportunity to bargain not violative of Act); Pennsylvania Energy Corp., 274 NLRB 1153, 119 LRRM 1042 (1985) (finding violation when company laid off employees from strip-mining operation and thereafter subcontracted work; contracting out based on labor costs, did not involve change in nature of business, and was amenable to resolution through bargaining process without significant burden on employer); P.W. Supermkts., 269 NLRB 839, 115 LRRM 1315 (1984); Gottfried v. Echlin, Inc., 113 LRRM 2349 (E.D. Mich. 1983); Liberal Mkts., 264 NLRB 807, 111 LRRM 1326 (1982). Cf. Nurminco, 274 NLRB 764, 119 LRRM 1059 (1985) (layoff of unit employees and transfer of work to nonunit employees violative of Act where decision based in substantial part on labor costs).

[13]In Griffith-Hope Co., supra note 9, Chairman Donald L. Dotson and Members Robert P. Hunter and Patricia Diaz Dennis pointed out that the management "viewed the subcontracting program as a temporary one that did not effect a fundamental change in the nature of its operation." Id., 119 LRRM at 1198.

[14]NLRB v. Eltec Corp., Plymouth Stamping Div., 870 F.2d 1112, 130 LRRM 3080, 3082 (6th Cir. 1989).

[15]UFI Razor Blades v. Distributive Workers Dist. 65, 610 F.2d 1018, 102 LRRM 2759 (2d Cir. 1979), citing Fibreboard Paper Products Corp., supra note 5, at 214–217.

(2) reinstatement of the former maintenance operation within the plant, and (3) back pay for the terminated employees.[16]

Board and court decisions suggest, however, that restoration of production will not be required when it would be financially burdensome for the employer. For example, when severe economic hardship was demonstrated by a small employer, the Seventh Circuit refused to enforce a Board order requiring reestablishment of delivery operations. And since reinstatement without resumption of the operations would have been impossible, the court of appeals found that the proper remedy was to order bargaining on the issue and to pay the discharged employees the wages they would have received had they continued working from the date of their discharge until the date that a bargain or impasse was reached.[17]

The Eighth Circuit has also stated that an employer will not be required to reinstate workers if their jobs no longer exist.[18] Similarly, while several courts suggest that a reinstatement order may be enforced despite the assertions that the jobs no longer exist, these holdings are arguably premised on the assumption that the employer will have a later opportunity to demonstrate that reinstatement is no longer possible.[19]

D. Arbitration Decisions in Subcontracting Disputes

1. Situations Where the Agreement Is Silent

Arbitrator Anthony V. Sinicropi reported in an address before the National Academy of Arbitrators that situations of this kind have been studied and researched with greater frequency than any other area of subcontracting. Citing studies

---

[16]On remand, the Board ordered back pay for a 10-year period in accordance with a formula that provided an increasing amount of back pay each year.

[17]NLRB v. Townhouse TV & Appliances, 531 F.2d 826, 91 LRRM 2636, 2641 (7th Cir. 1976); see also NLRB v. American Mfg. Co. of Tex., 351 F.2d 74, 60 LRRM 2122 (5th Cir. 1965); NLRB v. Major, 296 F.2d 466, 48 LRRM 2595 (7th Cir. 1961).

[18]UFI Razor Blades v. Distributive Workers Dist. 65, supra note 15, citing NLRB v. Kostilnik, 405 F.2d 733, 735, 70 LRRM 3102 (3d Cir. 1969); NLRB v. Vail Mfg. Co., 158 F.2d 664, 667, 19 LRRM 2177 (7th Cir.), cert. denied, 331 U.S. 835, 20 LRRM 2185 (1947).

[19]See citations in UFI Razor Blades v. Distributive Workers Dist. 65, supra note 15, at 2762.

by G. Allen Dash,[20] Marcia Greenbaum,[21] Saul Wallen,[22] and others,[23] Sinicropi found that the following considerations are those that are most frequently considered by arbitrators when they examine the merits of a subcontracting dispute in cases where the labor agreement does not contain a subcontracting clause:[24]

> "1. *The discussion or treatment, if any, of the subject of subcontracting during contract negotiations.*" (Is one party attempting to obtain in arbitration something that could not be obtained at the bargaining table? In other words, does the history of negotiations between the parties indicate that the union has tried unsuccessfully to insert a provision in the parties' agreement prohibiting the company from subcontracting unit work?)[25]
>
> "2. *The "good faith" of the employer in subcontracting the work.*" (Was the decision to subcontract motivated by antiunion bias or, alternatively, sound economic reasons? Was it designed to discriminate against the union? Is it aimed at the union's ability to enforce the union-security clause? Did management subcontract because of the union's unwillingness to surrender rights secured under the labor agreement?)[26]

---

[20]Dash, *Arbitration of Subcontracting Disputes*, 16 Indus. & Lab. Rel. Rev. 208 (1963).

[21]Greenbaum, *Arbitration of Subcontracting Disputes: An Addendum*, 16 Indus. & Lab. Rel. Rev. 221 (1963).

[22]Wallen, *How Issues of Subcontracting and Plant Removal Are Handled by Arbitrators*, 19 Indus. & Lab. Rel. Rev. 265 (1966).

[23]Jacobs, *Subcontracting Arbitration: How the Issues are Decided*, 21 Clev. St. L. Rev. 162 (1972); McEachern, *The Arbitration of Subcontracting Disputes*, 19 Me. L. Rev. 55 (1967); Crawford, *The Arbitration of Disputes Over Subcontracting*, in Challenges to Arbitration, Proceedings of the 13th Annual Meeting, National Academy of Arbitrators, 51–72 (BNA Books, 1960).

[24]Sinicropi, supra note 4 at 140–141.

[25]See, e.g., Pacific Tel. & Tel. Co., 78 LA 68, 69 (Koven, 1982); Burger Iron Co., 78 LA 57, 59 (Van Pelt, 1982) ("The evidence shows that there was an attempt to include a provision against subcontracting by the Union in the contract negotiations without success."); Chrysler Corp., 59 LA 629, 634 (Alexander, 1972) ("[T]he fact that no protest was voiced with respect to such divestitures . . . must be taken to mean that the Union never previously believed that Chrysler was obligated by implication not to contract out the operation of plant cafeterias."); Phillips Chem. Corp., 44 LA 102, 104 (Sartain, 1965) ("An important consideration in this case, however, is what the Union has tried without success to secure in previous years. . . .").

[26]See, e.g., City of Detroit, 79 LA 1273, 1277–1278 (Mittenthal, 1982); Town of

"3. *Any layoffs resulting from subcontracting.*" (Were regular employees deprived of work? Alternatively, did the subcontracting result in employees who were already on layoff not being recalled by the employer?)[27]

"4. *The effect or impact that subcontracting will have on the union and/or bargaining unit.*" (Was the required work part of the main operation of the plant?)

"5. *Possession by the company of the proper equipment, tools, or facilities to perform the subcontracted work.*" (Did the employer own or lease the equipment that was used to perform the disputed work?)

"6. *Was the required work an experiment into a specialty line?*" Was it sufficiently unique to require outside expertise? Is the contracting out a one-time contract or does it involve a regular, continuing service?[28]

"7. *Any compelling business reasons, economic considerations,* or *unusual circumstances justifying the subcontracting.*" (Was the work subcontracted out performed at a substantially lower cost? Is the contracting out simply an attempt to find another person to do the same work at less pay? Or, alternatively, is the subcontractor charging lower prices simply because it is more efficient?)[29]

"8. *Any special skill, experience, or techniques required to perform the required work.*" (Does the employer have qualified supervisors to oversee the project?)[30]

"9. *The similarity of the required work to the work regularly performed by bargaining-unit employees.*" (In this respect, one arbitrator commented that "Parties and arbitrators alike should have little trouble dis-

---

Van Buren, Me., 80 LA 105, 109 (Chandler, 1982) (finding bad faith where management negotiated subcontract while contractual negotiations were in progress with the union).

[27]Super Valu Stores, 84 LA 738, 743 (Heinsz, 1985) ("Here there is no new venture in the form of increased business but rather a different method of performing prior tasks which had been accomplished by refrigeration mechanics. Moreover, the bargaining unit classification of refrigeration mechanics has been depleted and effectively eliminated as a result of this substitution . . ..").

[28]General Metals Corp., 25 LA 118 (Lennard, 1955).

[29]See, e.g., Continental Tenn. Lines, 72 LA 619 (Cocalis, 1979); White Bros., 32 LA 965 (Hogan, 1958).

[30]National Distillers Prod. Co., 79 LA 1216, 1220 (Katz, 1982).

tinguishing between integral and ancillary functions, and prohibiting subcontracting of the former while permitting the latter.")[31]

"10. *Past practice in the plant with respect to subcontracting this type of work.*" (Has the union accepted the contracting out of work by the employer in the past?)

"11. *The existence of any emergency conditions*" such as a special job, a strike, or an unusual situation requiring special expertise. (Were properly qualified bargaining-unit employees available to complete the work within the required time limits? Would management experience a "penalty" for not completing work on time?).[32]

"12. *Was the required work included within the duties specified for a particular job classification?*"

A paradigm case in this area is *Dreis & Krump Manufacturing v. Machinists District 8*,[33] a decision by the Seventh Circuit. An employer, who was having financial problems, laid off a welder. Management later decided as a cost-saving measure that rather than recall the welder it would subcontract the welding work he had been doing. The agreement neither permitted nor prohibited subcontracting. An arbitrator ordered the company to stop subcontracting welding as long as its welders were on layoff, to recall the laid-off welder, and to make him whole for the wages and benefits that he lost as a result of the violation. The company argued that the management rights clause withdrew the subject of subcontracting from the scope of the arbitration clause as to deprive the arbitrator of jurisdiction. The arbitrator rejected this argument and declared:

"The position of the company is untenable. It has been rejected by most arbitrators who hold that as a general rule an employer does not have an unqualified right to subcontract bargaining unit work to outsiders. This position is based on the theory that a collective bargaining relationship impliedly imposes an obligation on management to not enter upon a unilateral course of conduct, the effect of which would render the contractually protected scope of the bargaining unit null and void. . . . The

---

[31]Uniroyal, Inc., 76 LA 1049, 1053 (Nolan, 1981).
[32]Commercial Constr. Co., 80 LA 565, 567 n.2 (Nicholas, 1983).
[33]802 F.2d 247, 123 LRRM 2654 (7th Cir. 1986).

cases are legion in which arbitrators have implied limits on subcontracting from the recognition, seniority, wage and other contract clauses similar to those found here. The essence of these cases is that the employer must act reasonably and in good faith in exercising its right to subcontract."[34]

Applying a "reasonableness" test, the arbitrator applied the following criteria in determining whether the agreement was violated:

"1. Past subcontracting practices; who normally performed the work;
"2. Whether there were sound business reasons for subcontracting . . . ;
"3. The effect on the bargaining unit; whether there is anti-union animus or deliberate undermining of the Union;
"4. The effect on members of the bargaining unit in terms of job opportunities, layoffs or overtime;
"5. Whether the work is subcontracted regularly or intermittently or for long, short or indefinite periods of time;
"6. The history, if any, of negotiations regarding subcontracting."[35]

Writing for the majority, Judge Richard Posner sustained the award and commented as follows on the employer's management rights argument:

Read literally and by itself this language [of the management rights provision] is certainly broad enough to make subcontracting a prerogative of management, yet really it does no more than spell out the implications of the contractual provision held insufficient in United Steelworkers of America v. Warrior & Gulf Navigation Co., . . . , to bar arbitration of a dispute over subcontracting—the provision that "matters which are strictly a function of management shall not be subject to arbitration." And the clause must not be read in isolation from the rest of the agreement, the main purpose of which is to fix wages and benefits for the workers and give them job security in accordance with their relative seniority, in exchange for their promise not to strike. If the company encounters hard times it can lay off unneeded workers, in reverse order of seniority; but, equally, if it has work it can't terminate workers without cause and replace them with other workers to whom it pays lower wages. One method of avoiding the central obligations of the agreement would be to lay off workers and subcontract their work to per-

---

[34]Id. at 253, 123 LRRM at 2659.
[35]Id. at 254, 123 LRRM at 2659.

sons who would perform the identical work and on company premises but paid less for it.[36]

The Ninth Circuit has also spoken on the use of a "balancing test" under an agreement that is silent on subcontracting. During the economic recession of 1979–1982 when logging and other similar industries were heavily hit, an employer incurred losses which led to the closing of a sawmill and related logging operations. Motivated by economic considerations, the employer decided that the mill could not be opened unless the logging operations were subcontracted. Management reopened the mill but eliminated the logging crews and replaced them with unrepresented subcontractors. An arbitrator ruled in favor of the union, reasoning that the employer's right to subcontract was limited by the implied covenant not to seriously erode the bargaining unit found in every collective bargaining agreement. The award was vacated by the district court.

The court of appeals, reversing the district court, ruled that a balancing of interests test was appropriate when an agreement is silent on the subcontracting issue. The court's reasoning is particularly instructive since it approved the use of the criteria noted by Sinicropi.

> To consider whether an award drew its essence from the collective bargaining agreement, the court must ensure that the arbitrator looked to the words of the contract and to the conduct of the parties. . . .
>
> In the case at bar the arbitrator did so. He examined the past practices of the parties. He noted that the employer had never before used subcontractors to the complete exclusion of bargaining unit loggers. He clearly based his decision in large part on the employer's undisputed historical practice of maintaining a 60-40 ratio [of company loggers to subcontractors] as indicated above. He discussed in his award past arbitral decisions favoring the employer and past negotiations, but found them to be distinguishable since none before had involved a permanent loss of so many bargaining unit positions. Additionally, the arbitrator found that other clauses, such as wages, recognition, union security, and seniority, taken together, constituted an implied covenant that the employer would not seriously erode the bargaining unit by subcontracting. The

---

[36]Id. at 252, 123 LRRM at 2658.

arbitrator considered the reserved rights theory of management, but rejected it after reviewing the applicable authorities.[37]

Perhaps the best summary of what has occurred in this area and what may be expected to continue was made by Arbitrator Saul Wallen:

> [T]he predominant approach to subcontracting by arbitrators in cases where the contract is silent on the subject appears to involve application of the implied-obligations approach. But the obligation is not to refrain from innovation or change if they have a limited impact on jobs. It is to avoid unreasonable reductions in the scope of the unit and to refrain from nullifying the terms of the contract by means of the contracting-out device. Much more often than not, contracting out is upheld.[38]

Where the contract is silent, arbitrators accord great deference to the decision to subcontract, especially where management has discussed the matter with the union before contracting out. Even when the agreement is completely silent on the matter of contracting out, arbitrators balance the interests of management against those of the bargaining unit in deciding whether the collective bargaining agreement has been violated. The balance is usually struck in favor of the employer, especially when the contract is silent, but an arbitrator faced with a subcontracting grievance when the agreement is silent is unlikely to reason that since the contract does not contain a subcontracting limitation, the company must win. Most arbitrators require that management demonstrate some basis in fact for the decision to pass muster under the agreement. A finding that a subcontract deprives the union or its members of the contractual gains or benefits is especially suspect. The better view was summarized by one arbitrator as follows:

> "Arbitrators recognize that there is implied covenant of fair dealing between contracting parties, and that one of the parties cannot subvert an agreement by conduct seeking to deprive the other party of the bargain that was struck. The published awards

---

[37]Edward Hines Lumber Co. v. Lumber & Sawmill Workers Local 2588, 764 F.2d 631, 119 LRRM 3210, 3213 (9th Cir. 1985). See also Ford Motor Co. v. Plant Protection Ass'n, 770 F.2d 69, 120 LRRM 2008 (6th Cir. 1985) (enforcing award ordering employer to return guards to original positions and restore any loss in wages or security). But see Sears, Roebuck & Co. v. Teamsters Local 243, 683 F.2d 154, 110 LRRM 3175 (6th Cir. 1982), cert. denied, 460 U.S. 1023, 112 LRRM 2896 (1983).
[38]Wallen, supra note 22, at 271.

dealing with this problem indicate a subcontract that deprives the Union or its employed members of any contractual gains or benefits is suspect and will be denied unless an employer can demonstrate a special business need that outweighs the loss caused by the members of the bargaining unit."[39]

2. Subcontracting Clauses in Collective Bargaining Agreements

In 1960, the late Donald Crawford categorized four types of subcontracting clauses found in collective bargaining agreements:

> 1. The weakest limitation on contracting out is the "discussion before contracting out" type of clause. The company shall inform the union of any construction or repair work, or bargaining-unit work, to be contracted out prior to the writing of the contract, and discuss it with the union.
> 2. The strongest prohibition against contracting out is found in this type of clause: "There shall be no regular work performed by any employee not covered by the contract except in emergencies or when work must be performed for which regular employees are not qualified." Here the probability of layoff or demotion as a consequence of the subcontracting is not required.
> 3. More common is the limitation of reasonableness: "The Company will make every reasonable effort to use its available working force and equipment in order to avoid having its work performed by outside contractors" or "The Company will use its own employees whenever possible."
> 4. Finally, the most common clause is the prohibition against contracting out unit work when the firm's own employees are on layoff or when the layoff or demotion of unit employees would result.[40]

In 1989, the Bureau of National Affairs, Inc., reported that subcontracting is mentioned in 54 percent of contract samples—51 percent in manufacturing agreements and 59

---

[39]Federal Wholesale Co., 86 LA 945, 957 (Cohen 1985), quoting Campbell Truck Co., 73 LA 1036, 1039 (Russ, 1979). See also Fruehauf Corp., 62 LA 37, 47 (McBrearty, 1974) ("In the absence of contractual language relating to contracting out of work, the general arbitration rule is that management has the right to contract out work as long as the action is performed in good faith, it represents a reasonable business decision, it does not have the effect of seriously weakening the bargaining unit or important parts of it. This general right to contract out may be expanded or restricted by specific contractual language."), citing Shenango Valley Water Co., 53 LA 741, 744–745 (McDermott, 1969).

[40]Crawford, supra note 23, at 52, as cited in Sinicropi, supra note 4, at 126.

percent in nonmanufacturing contracts. BNA further reports that in 48 percent of the subcontracting clauses, advance discussion with the union is required, in 26 percent subcontracting is prohibited if a layoff currently exists or would result from such action. Furthermore, in 36 percent of the sample contracts subcontracting is allowed only if the necessary skills and equipment are not available, and in 22 percent only if contracting standards are met. Finally, in under 18 percent of subcontracting clauses, contracting out must be in accordance with past practice.[41]

Whether a remedy is forthcoming will depend, in part, on the type of management limitation the parties negotiate and whether the union can show a resulting economic loss from management's conduct. Court cases indicate that the parties' contract must be accorded greater weight than the later consideration. Illustrative is *Sears, Roebuck & Co. v. Teamsters Local 243*,[42] where the agreement stated that the employer had "[t]he right to subcontract any type of work . . . provided however, that such right to subcontract shall be restricted to work that can be performed more efficiently and economically outside of the bargaining unit . . . . The agreement also provided that the employer would "substantiate such action by submitting facts and figures that the work involved can be done more efficiently and economically."[43]

The arbitrator recognized that the agreement did not, on its face, limit Sears' authority to subcontract in the interest of efficiency and economy. Moreover, he specifically found that Sears acted in good faith in entering the subcontract at issue. (Sears had contracted out the work of its entire "MA" sales employees who sell Sears maintenance contracts by telephone, thereby eliminating 90 jobs.) Nevertheless, the arbitrator applied a "balancing" test and concluded that the costs to the union of the disputed subcontract outweighed its benefits to the employer. On this rationale, reinstatement of the MA sales unit with back pay was ordered.

In concluding the arbitrator "exceeded his authority by

---

[41]Basic Patterns in Union Contracts, 12th ed., 80 (BNA Books, 1989).
[42]Supra note 37.
[43]Id., 110 LRRM at 3176.

amending the express terms of the agreement," the appellate court distinguished between those contracts that are silent and those that contain a subcontracting provision:

> The authorities cited by the arbitrator in support of his use of a "balancing test" in this case are inapposite. There is, as the District Court explained, a critical distinction in arbitration cases between collective bargaining agreements which are silent on the question of subcontracting and those which specifically address the issue.
>
> In the former instance, it is accepted practice for arbitrators to infer a "reasonableness" limitation on the employer's right to subcontract; "reasonableness" is determined by a "balancing test" or cost-benefit analysis. . . .
>
> On the other hand, when the parties to a collective bargaining agreement have negotiated a clear, unambiguous subcontracting provision, an arbitrator lacks discretion to alter the effect of that provision by performing, *sua sponte*, a "balancing test." The weight of authority supports this conclusion.[44]

Other courts have taken a similar approach where the agreement vests subcontracting decisions with management.[45]

A decision of special note is *Jones Dairy Farm v. Food & Commercial Workers Local P-1236*,[46] a case reported by the Seventh Circuit. The contract provided that with respect to subcontracting of work, each party retained its legal rights in effect prior to execution of the agreement. When the company contracted out janitorial work that was formerly performed by the union, Arbitrator John Flagler reasoned that any limitations on the employer's right to subcontract must be found in external law. Looking at the Board's first decision in *Milwaukee Spring I*[47] the arbitrator ruled that the parties' contractual language prohibited this subcontracting. On appeal, the majority found the law to be that absent agreement to the

---

[44]Id. at 3177, citing Laclede Gas Co., 67 LA 461 (Davis, 1976); Timken Co. v. Steelworkers Local 1123, 482 F.2d 1012, 1014, 83 LRRM 2814 (6th Cir. 1973); Electric Storage Battery Co., 44 LA 782 (Koven, 1965). Contra Consolidated Aluminum Co., 66 LA 1170 (Boals, 1976).

[45]See, e.g., Lever Bros. v. Oil Workers Local 7-336, 555 F. Supp. 295, 113 LRRM 2615 (N.D. Ind. 1983), rev'd without opinion, 745 F.2d 61, 118 LRRM 3232 (7th Cir. 1984); Clinchfield Coal v. Mine Workers Dist. 28, 736 F.2d 998, 116 LRRM 2884 (4th Cir. 1984). Cf. Lone Star Indus. v. Teamsters Local 291, 119 LRRM 2121 (N.D. Cal. 1985) (vacating award holding that company was precluded from transferring work outside jurisdiction of bargaining unit where contract was silent regarding transfers).

[46]755 F.2d 583, 118 LRRM 2841 (7th Cir. 1985).

[47]Illinois Coil Spring Co., Milwaukee Spring Div., 265 NLRB 206, 111 LRRM 1486 (1982).

contrary management was free to subcontract, even if the motivation for the decision is to pay lower labor costs. Since the arbitrator followed *Milwaukee Spring I*, which was then on appeal and later repudiated by the Board, his award did not draw its essence from the collective bargaining agreement. The court went on to state that the arbitrator was simply "expressing his opinion on a legal question, and courts (the bearers of expertise in such matters) are free to correct a mere mistake of law . . . ."[48]

The position of the majority in *Jones Dairy* is incorrect under the federal standard of court review of arbitrators' awards. As pointed out by Judge Richard Posner in his dissent, the arbitrator looked at the parties' subcontracting clause, determined that it required him to look at *Milwaukee Spring*, and then interpreted that case, although, according to the dissent, his interpretation was too broad. As stated in his dissent:

> The arbitrator read Milwaukee Spring too broadly in thinking that it decides this case. He should have asked whether the clause in the collective bargaining agreement in this case was intended to give Jones Dairy Farm an absolute right to contract out, which would be permissible under Milwaukee Spring, or whether it merely incorporated current Board doctrine, whatever that might be, on collective bargaining agreements that are silent on the matter of contracting out. He did not ask the right question, and it is impossible to say therefore whether he came up with the right answer.[49]

Although the arbitrator may have "looked through rather than at the contracting-out clause," it is submitted that this did not justify a decision that the arbitrator's award did not draw its essence from the agreement. As noted by the dissent, courts have frequently deferred to the legal determinations of arbitrators and, on its face, the decision of the arbitrator did not require the parties to do something in violation of a statute.[50]

---

[48]118 LRRM at 2842.

[49]Id. at 2843.

[50]On rehearing, the Seventh Circuit ruled that its initial decision was wrong and that the district court should not have set aside the arbitrator's award. The case was remanded with directions to enforce the award. Jones Dairy Farm v. Food & Commercial Workers Local P-1236, 760 F.2d 173, 119 LRRM 2185 (7th Cir.), cert. denied, 474 U.S. 845, 120 LRRM 2632 (1985).

E. Arbitration Remedies for Improper Subcontracting

A review of arbitration awards and court cases indicates that where subcontracting violations are found (even under so-called "silent" agreements), no one remedy is preferred. Rather the remedy ordered will depend upon the facts and circumstances of each case and, in particular, the specific contractual provisions at issue. Preferred remedies include "cease-and-desist" orders, mandates to return the improperly contracted work to the bargaining unit, and traditional "make-whole" relief for employees displaced or denied work.[51] A common monetary remedy is to award an amount equal to the lost earnings of the employees laid off as a result of the subcontracting, or the amount paid to the employees performing the contracted-out work.[52] A sampling of these remedies are discussed as follows:

1. Meet-and-Discuss Limitations

What is the remedy when management fails to discuss with the union plans to contract-out bargaining-unit work? Arbitrator Harold Wren, in *Rockwell International Corp.*,[53] found that, as a result of management's failure to discuss with the union a plan to contract out electrical work on a new facility, the union was denied the opportunity to prove the number of work hours that plant electricians might have worked on the project. Finding that there were 1,049 hours of electrical

---

[51]See, e.g., Dreis & Krump Mfg. v. Machinists Dist. 8, supra note 33 (upholding arbitrator's award ordering cancellation of subcontract and recall of employees under "silent" contract).

[52]Champion Int'l Corp., 91 LA 245 (Duda, 1988) (awarding each of 10 affected employees one-tenth of $1,581, representing rate multiplied by hours subcontractor expended on job); Sea-Land Freight Serv., 87 LA 633 (D'Spain, 1986) (awarding 42 employees equal shares of $476,524 for loss of work opportunity for improper subcontracting of trucking work to nonunion carriers); American Standard, 82-1 ARB. ¶8125 (Cabe, 1982) (employer's liability for improper subcontracting not based on work hours involved in contracting-out work but, rather, on basis of total wages that laid-off employees would have earned); Central Ill. Pub. Serv. Co., 82-1 ARB. ¶8135 (Bernstein, 1982) (granting grievants compensation for hours that subcontractor's employees worked, noting that for some it will represent windfall); Falstaff Brewing Corp. v. Teamsters Local 153, 479 F. Supp. 850, 103 LRRM 2008 (D.N.J. 1978) (upholding cease-and-desist order and "damages" of lost earnings of laid-off employees). But see W.H. Kiefaber Co., 87 LA 396, 398 (Modjeska, 1986) (denying monetary remedy for "good-faith" violation of subcontracting provision).

[53]85-1 ARB ¶8217 (1985).

work at issue, and that it was now too late to allow bargaining-unit employees to work on the project, the arbitrator awarded the unit an equivalent number of hours of work opportunity on overtime.

Arbitrator Alan Rothstein reports a 1987 decision involving management's failure to bargain the effects of a subcontracting decision that eliminated an employee's position and forced him to accept a demotion. Concluding that the company violated the recognition clause by not giving notice of a decision that would abolish a unit position (the recognition clause was silent on the issue of notice), the arbitrator, citing NLRB precedent[54] and a decision by the Seventh Circuit,[55] found that it would be inappropriate to restore the status quo at the time the company's obligation arose "because such a reinstatement would be an unfair burden on the Company." The arbitrator ordered the parties to bargain "until an agreement is reached on what should have taken place or until an impasse is reached." Further, the grievant was awarded a remedial amount equivalent to the wages he was earning in his prior position until an agreement or impasse is reached (less any wages actually paid in his current position).

In *Kaiser Foundation Hospitals*,[56] the contract required 30-day notice of the company's intention to subcontract. On eight separate occasions the hospital failed to do so. Arbitrator Arthur Jacobs found that the employer's failure to give notice was a violation of the agreement. He reasoned that the notice was a condition precedent to subcontracting and, if that condition were met, then the balancing factors with regard to the subcontracting decision itself would determine whether a remedy was in order and what such a remedy would be. Alternatively, if the condition precedent were not met (the 30-day notice), then again the remedy would depend on the balancing

---

[54]The arbitrator, citing NLRB v. Ingersoll Rand Co., 247 NLRB 801, 103 LRRM 1224 (1980) and Westinghouse Elec. Corp., 150 NLRB 1574, 58 LRRM 1257 (1965), referenced the rule requiring bargaining on the *effects* of contracting-out services even when the decision itself may not be negotiable. Witco Chem. Corp., 89 LA 349, 351 (Rothstein, 1987).

[55]NLRB v. Townhouse TV & Appliances, 531 F.2d 826, 91 LRRM 2636, 2641 (7th Cir. 1976) (refusing to order reinstatement of delivery operations, but ordering bargaining on issue and payment to affected employees wages they would have received had they continued working from date of change until date parties reached agreement or impasse).

[56]61 LA 1008 (1973).

of management responsibilities against union rights. His words on the notice requirement were as follows:

> In effect, this is a definite restriction on the right of the Hospital to subcontract work. Unless this condition precedent shall have been fulfilled, there is no contractual right to subcontract work. If the required thirty day notification is given, and because there are no other restrictions against the subcontracting of work in the contract, then the criteria and standards generally applicable to the various aspects of subcontracting become applicable to any work subcontracted by the Hospital. If, on the other hand, this condition precedent is not fulfilled the subcontracting of work by the Hospital constitutes a breach of the contract.[57]

In this case, the arbitrator found management's rights to be prevailing on one occasion and the union's rights to be violated on another. Where the hospital failed to use fully its existing bargaining-unit employees (including the offering of reasonable overtime), Arbitrator Jacobs awarded to all the qualified bargaining-unit employees who were available for overtime an amount of money equal to the actual amounts expended by the hospital for the subcontracted work. Such monies were to be prorated among the employees, not as an award of overtime pay, but as "damages for the breach of the contract by the Hospital."[58] In those cases where existing personnel were fully utilized, including the assigning of reasonable overtime, the arbitrator awarded no monetary damages even though the hospital violated the notice provision.[59]

In *Indian Head*,[60] a similar clause in the agreement required management to meet and confer with the union prior to subcontracting.[61] The company in this case conceded that it had not met and discussed the subcontracting matter with the union prior to resorting to subcontracting. Given those events, the arbitrator focused on what he considered the sole

---

[57]Id. at 1012.
[58]Id. at 1014.
[59]Id.
[60]65 LA 706 (Foster, 1975).
[61]It reads as follows: "Before major sub-contracts of bargaining unit work are made, the plant involved will give the Local Union advance notice before the contract is let. Local management will discuss the work to be performed with the Local Union upon request, but if the Company decides to subcontract, the decision will be subject to the applicable provisions of the labor agreement, including the grievance procedure and arbitration." Id. at 706.

question—the appropriate remedy, if any, to be applied. Arbitrator Robert Foster reasoned that if the discussions had proved to be futile, there would not have been any restriction on management's decision to subcontract. Since the employer had not given the notice mandated by the agreement, the arbitrator provided that the remedy "should be governed by the general principle that the aggrieved party ought to be put in as good a position as if the contract had been fully performed." Declaring "that the Company's breach precluded grievants from the opportunity to perform the work assigned to the subcontractors," the arbitrator awarded the grievants the pay that they would have received had they been assigned the work (which amounted to 410 man hours of compensation divided equally among five employees).[62]

In yet another case involving contractually mandated notice, Arbitrator Thomas Erbs ruled that there should not be a remedy where an employer had not notified the union before subcontracting because the contract did not authorize the arbitrator to penalize the employer for such a required-notice breach. Arbitrator Erbs reasoned that even after discussions, the parties' labor agreement did not state that the company could not subcontract, nor did it provide that an arbitrator would have the authority to assess a penalty against management for a violation of the notice provision. The arbitrator found that "the [notice] provision was inserted in order to give the Company and the Union time to discuss the letting of a contract and if the Union felt that there was a need to grieve that it could grieve before the letting of the contract."[63]

In *National Distillers Products Co.*,[64] the agreement provided that no bargaining-unit work would be contracted out "except upon due consultation with the Union." The agreement further provided that "any disagreement not satisfactorily resolved shall be subject to arbitration." Even though management consulted with the union, the union argued that such consultation alone does not excuse the contracting out, unless the implied limitations of good faith and reasonableness were met. Arbitrator Jonas Katz ruled that, where due

---

[62]Id. at 708.
[63]Grain Processing Corp., 65 LA 431, 435 (1975).
[64]79 LA 1216 (Katz, 1982).

consultation occurs, such bargaining-unit work may still be contracted out. In the words of the arbitrator, " 'consultation' requires more than notification, but less than agreement."[65]

Kimberly-Clark[66] presents a situation where another factor came into play under a meet-and-confer provision. Although the meet-and-confer issue was not the focal point of the decision, the union argued that it had not received from the employer the data regarding the subcontracting decision and that such information was essential for the union to make an informed judgment on whether to contest the action. The arbitrator ruled that there was no such requirement, although he predicated that answer on the fact that he requested the data to be turned over to him and, after examining the information, concluded that it would not alter the decision.

Is the meet-and-discuss provision a condition precedent to the actual subcontracting? If so, is management still required under an "implied-obligation" theory to justify its subcontracting decision? Alternatively, does the union waive its right to challenge the merits of management's subcontracting decision by agreeing to a meet-and-discuss provision? If arbitrators adopt the former view, management may argue that the meet-and-discuss provision is a further limitation than the implied obligation, and that for a company to agree to a meet-and-confer clause in addition to the implied-obligation concept is a penalty to which it would not agree if it knew beforehand that the other constraints were to remain. A union, on the other hand, could argue that if the meet-and-discuss clause cancels out implied obligation to act reasonably, it is a meaningless clause, since all management would be required to do is discuss the matter until impasse is reached.

There is support for both positions in the reported cases. For example, it might be argued that the primary purpose of the meet-and-confer clause is to allow the union an opportunity to persuade management to accede to the union's arguments. On the other hand, proponents of the view that meet-and-confer provisions do not cancel the implied-obligation standard argue that, after the condition precedent of the meeting and discussing is met, the arbitrator might limit man-

---

[65]Id. at 1218.
[66]69-2 ARB. ¶8577 (Rill, 1969).

agement's action only if it is "reasonable" and does not cause a "serious detriment" to the unit.

It would appear that the predominant view is that the meet-and-discuss clause absolves management of any further obligation once an impasse is reached, but, as evidenced by the cited awards, there is authority to the contrary. Similarly, when the agreement contains a meet-and-discuss provision and the employer subcontracts without discussing the matter with the union, the better rule is that the union should be provided a remedy even though the contracting out was reasonable.[67]

2. Significance of Recognition Clause When There Is a Subcontracting Clause

Arbitrators have uniformly rejected claims that a recognition clause, standing alone, limits management's right to make changes in the operation of its business.[68] Does the existence of a weak subcontracting clause or a management-rights provision make a difference? A review of cases in this area indicates that reliance on recognition, seniority, and other such clauses has not been persuasive to arbitrators as a limitation on subcontracting, especially where there is a weak subcontracting clause in the agreement.[69] Rather than focus on recognition or seniority provisions, arbitrators tend to predicate decisions on an implied-obligation residual-rights theory

---

[67]See, e.g., Witco Chem. Corp., 89 LA 349 (Rothstein, 1987) (discussed at supra note 54); Rockwell Int'l Corp., supra note 53 (providing overtime remedy); North Star Steel Co., 83-2 ARB ¶8532 (Gallagher, 1983). But see Ideal Elec. Co., 88-2 ARB ¶8543 (Coyne, 1988) (noting that failure to notify does not presuppose award to employee if no harm is demonstrated); Macomb Intermediate School Dist., 79-2 ARB ¶8620 (Roumell, 1979) (upholding grievance but denying monetary relief for failure to meet).

[68]See, e.g., Leeds-Dixon Laboratories, 74 LA 407, 410 (Kramer, 1980); American Sugar Ref. Co., 37 LA 334, 336 (Beatty, 1961); Carbide & Carbon Chems. Co., 24 LA 158, 159–160 (Kelliher, 1955). See generally Hill and Sinicropi, supra note 1, at 443–454.

[69]See Fruehauf Corp., 62 LA 37, 41 n.7 (McBrearty, 1974); Jos. Schlitz Brewing Co., 58 LA 653 (Lande, 1972) (routine recognition clause in itself cannot serve to inhibit employer from effecting contemplated shutdown and transfer of operations); National Cash Register Co., 48 LA 1025, 1026 (Beatty, 1967) (contracting out not limited by usual recognition clause, seniority provision, or listing of jobs, classifications, occupations, or labor grades in back of contract); American Sugar Ref. Co., 61-3 ARB ¶8773 (Beatty, 1961); Columbus Bolt & Forging Co., 35 LA 397, 402 (Stouffer, 1960). But see Advertiser Co., 89 LA 71, 76 (Baroni, 1987) (finding that recognition, wages, and seniority clauses, when taken together, implicitly prohibit subcontracting that eliminated 50% of bargaining-unit jobs).

to determine the substantive issue. For example, in *Sealtest Foods*,[70] Arbitrator Rolf Valtin, while not specifically repudiating the recognition clause, chose to examine the subcontracting issue on the "good-faith" efforts of the employer[71] and the residual-rights implied-obligation concept of management rights. Since the employer had merely announced a decision to subcontract and had not implemented it at the time of the hearing, the only "remedy" was a declaration that the proposed action would be disallowed.

3. Restrictions Where Parts and Products Are Customarily Made by Unit Employees

Generally, arbitrators confronted with a clause restricting management from subcontracting for work involving production of parts and equipment normally made by unit employees[72] will hold for the union if there is significant detriment to the unit as a result of the subcontracting. Such a situation was present in *Consolidated Aluminum*,[73] where Arbitrator Bruce Boals ruled that an employer did not have the right unilaterally to contract out unit work during a time that maintenance mechanics were on layoff. As a remedy the arbitrator awarded $800 to be divided equally among eight general maintenance mechanics on layoff at the time of the subcontracting. This award was based on the estimated labor costs to the subcontractor of that minimum portion that should not have been subcontracted out.[74]

---

[70]48 LA 797 (1966).

[71]Arbitrator Valtin did indicate, however, that "good faith" was, in itself, not enough to sustain the subcontracting: "I do not believe that a 'good clause' showing is itself enough to sustain a subcontracting-out action. (If it were, bad faith would be the only ground for overruling Management.) It is, rather, by a balancing process of all the pertinent considerations on both sides of the coin that a decision is to be formulated." Id. at 801. See also Consolidated Aluminum Co., 66 LA 1170, 1178 (Boals, 1976) ("caveat overlooked by the Company was that if the effect tended to deprive and undermine, even with no ill-will, then the original 'good intentions,' the wag says, 'pave the road to hell.' ").

[72]For a discussion of what constitutes "work normally performed," see Climax Mfg. Co., 82 LA 992 (Gross, 1984).

[73]66 LA 1170 (1976).

[74]Id. at 1179.

4. Restrictions Except Where Company Lacks Equipment and Facilities

Under these clauses subcontracting is restricted except in instances where the employer lacks the equipment or facilities to do the work. A challenging idea was offered by Arbitrator Peter Carmichael in *Ashland Chemical Co.*[75] In that case the agreement provided that the bargaining unit should be permitted to do all maintenance and repair work whenever they had the facilities and training to perform the duties in an efficient manner. The arbitrator concluded that under such an agreement the employer was prohibited from subcontracting even if that required renting part of the equipment and training the affected employees to operate the machinery. The remedy provided was overtime compensation for the time the work required, paid to each of the two members of the bargaining unit who were the first entitled to any overtime work on the dates the contract was performed.

Similarly, in *Hi-Ram*,[76] the agreement provided that there would be no subcontracting "where the work has customarily been performed by employees in this bargaining unit and appropriate equipment and qualified employees are available to do such work." Arbitrator William Daniel ruled it was improper to subcontract circuit-breaker work, which could have been done by a salvage crew following a layoff had the employer not assigned the crew to perform alternative work at the time of the subcontracting. As a remedy, the arbitrator directed that the parties attempt to determine which individuals would compose that work crew and to divide between them the amounts of money, at straight time rates, that they would have earned by doing the contracted-out work.[77]

---

[75]64 LA 1244 (1975).

[76]68 LA 54 (Daniel, 1977).

[77]Id. at 57. Jurisdiction was retained for the purpose of specifically directing the remedial action outlined above. See also Norris Indus., 67 LA 357 (Howard, 1976) (payment was ordered at same rate of pay, including overtime if necessary, and in same manner as if work had been performed "in house"); Hi-Ram, Inc., 67 LA 549 (Allen, 1976) (back-pay settlement to be worked out by parties for any employees who were laid off or who experienced reduction in wages as result of improper subcontracting).

5. Restrictions Where Work Is Normally Performed by Unit Employees

Several issues arise in this area. Does work "normally performed by unit employees" include work of a similar nature but of a far greater magnitude than that which was previously performed? In *Merck, Sharp, & Dohme*,[78] Arbitrator William Loucks held that it does not. He reasoned that the phrase refers to all significant aspects of past work and is not to be applied in terms of abilities and skills of the employees:

> [T]he words "normally performed" [are] related to past practice and, in the instant case, means that contracting-out is contractually prohibited only if the contemplated flooring job in all of its significant aspects has previously been performed by Carpenter employees of the Company. The Arbitrator feels that he can not validly deny the Company's position that "magnitude" of the flooring job in question is one of these significant aspects . . ..[79]

Full-employment and overtime questions are also included in these situations. For example, in *Ideal Electric & Manufacturing Co.*,[80] the agreement provided that the company would not subcontract work normally performed by unit employees "with the intent that such act would result in less than full employment to employees currently in the classification." Arbitrator F. Wilson Chockley ruled that the contract did not provide that full employment include overtime.

In *Buhr Machine Tool Corp.*,[81] Arbitrator John Sembower ruled that the employer did violate the agreement by subcontracting where the employees were available for further overtime. Although there were attritions in the unit, the arbitrator found that the employees on the job could have worked additional overtime. As stated by Arbitrator Sembower:

> By far the most significant and novel issues presented by this arbitration is the question of whether so-called "attrition" can constitute an "erosion" of the bargaining unit. Here again, we have a head-on collision of basic concepts. On the one hand, it is axiomatic that an employer cannot be required to fill a job

---

[78]44 LA 262 (1965).
[79]Id. at 266.
[80]67 LA 227 (Chockley, 1976).
[81]61 LA 333 (1973).

which because of economic reasons he thinks is no longer needed. To the contrary, from the very beginning of the Wagner Act days, deliberate erosion of a bargaining unit has been eschewed. Perhaps for the best economic motives imaginable, the Company here seems to have adopted a course of letting the bargaining unit "wither on the vine," by not replacing employees who leave for whatever reason. The Unit has consequently shrunken considerably in recent months during the pendency even of this arbitration. At the same time, sub-contractors have come into the plant itself and performed work which has historically been performed by the Company's own employees. It seems clear that the employer cannot disable himself to perform the customary work of his shop simply by letting his Unit members die off.[82]

Arbitrator Sembower ruled that, although nothing could be done for the unit employees who had left, "attrition" could not be used to reduce the bargaining unit, while work customarily performed by its members was taken over by subcontractors, either outside or inside the plant, either union or nonunion.

In a subsequent hearing called solely for purposes of fixing the damages, Arbitrator Sembower ordered all unit employees to be paid as though they had worked a 55-hour week. In addition, the arbitrator ordered the employer to "return the bargaining unit's size to approximately 210 as long as work exists which can be done by bargaining unit employees, reinstating former employees and/or recalling any employees who may be on layoff status."[83]

To implement this remedy, Sembower further provided:

The company shall reinstate and actively promote the apprenticeship program as provided in the Agreement. The Company will hire apprentices as part of an affirmative hiring program set out herein. When the journeyman-apprentice ratio, as specified in the contract, is attained, the Company shall hire temporary employees.

The Company shall run reasonable help-wanted advertisements which specify that a 55-hour work week is in view and that permanent openings exist for both apprentices and journeymen.

The Company also shall seek referrals from [employment] offices ... and it shall notify local area high schools that applications are being accepted on the apprenticeship program.

The Company shall provide the Union with lists, on a weekly basis, of all prospective job seekers, showing names, position

[82]Id. at 339.
[83]Id. at 341.

sought and telephone numbers, and no qualified applicants shall be refused employment.[84]

F. Improper Transfer of Operations

Not infrequently an employer will transfer operations in whole or in part, formerly manned by bargaining-unit employees. In a typical transfer or relocation of bargaining-unit work situation, two or more facilities are involved, although the operational independence between the facilities may vary from complete control to complete independence. An employer may operate more than one unionized plant and, for whatever reasons, decide to transfer work from one unionized location to another. Alternatively, and perhaps more common, an employer may wish to transfer work from a union facility to a facility that is not organized. A variant of either of the above situations involves a transfer or relocation that, on its face, appears to be a transaction between two separate and distinct business entities but in reality is an exchange between an employer and its "alter ego." Since these actions are often challenged as a form of improper subcontracting, it is appropriate to consider remedies for improper transfers in this section.[85]

1. Arbitrability of Plant Removals or Transfer of Operations

Consistent with the presumption of arbitrability established by the Supreme Court in *Warrior & Gulf*,[86] where the collective bargaining agreement provides for arbitration of "any controversy whatsoever" or of "all disputes arising under the agreement," courts and arbitrators have found little dif-

---

[84]Id. at 341–342. See also Dubuque Packing Co., 69 LA 999 (Carter, 1977) (second shift); Goodyear Atomic Corp., 66 LA 598 (Volz, 1976); Kaiser Found. Hosp., 61 LA 1008 (Jacobs, 1973); United States Steel Corp., 54 LA 1207 (Duff, 1970); Lehigh Portland Cement Co., 49 LA 967 (Crawford, 1967).

[85]Besides the cases discussed in this section, see Schaper Mfg. Co., 87 LA 907, 913 (Jacobowski, 1986) (ordering return of work for improper transfer of writing-up of production receipts from unionized production plant to nonunion distribution center to extent such receipts are needed and used by production).

[86]Steelworkers v. Warrior & Gulf Navigation Co., 363 U.S. 574, 46 LRRM 2416 (1960).

ficulty in ordering arbitration of disputes involving plant removals or transfers of operations.[87] Even where the agreement is completely silent on the issue of plant relocation or subcontracting, the better weight of authority holds that unless the issue is specifically excluded from the arbitration clause, an order to arbitrate will not be denied.[88] As stated by the Ninth Circuit:

> Although arbitration is a matter of mutual agreement between the parties, and they may choose to exclude certain areas of contention from the arbitration process, the standard set by the [Supreme] Court for finding a dispute nonarbitrable is a strict one: There must be either an "express provision excluding a particular grievance from arbitration" or "the most forceful evidence of a purpose to exclude the claim from arbitration."
> . . .
> . . . [E]xplicit language in collective bargaining agreements covering each specific claim alleging to be arbitrable is not required. We have held that the complete silence of an agreement on the issues sought to be arbitrated is not sufficient evidence to meet the rigorous standard set by the Steelworkers Trilogy for a finding of nonarbitrability.[89]

Illustrative of the extent to which the judiciary has accommodated arbitration in this area is a decision by the First Circuit. In *Mobil Oil Corp. v. Oil Workers Local 8-766*,[90] a union filed a grievance after Mobil had unilaterally decided to subcontract all delivery of fuel oil and gasoline at its Bangor, Maine, facility. Management argued that the dispute was not arbitrable because there was no express provision regarding subcontracting in the labor agreement and the arbitration clause in the contract limited the scope of the arbitrator's power to the "express provisions of the agreement." Finding

---

[87]Clothing Workers v. Ratner Corp., 602 F.2d 1363, 102 LRRM 2571 (9th Cir. 1979) (consignment of manufacturing and sales to subsidiaries); Typographical Union No. 101 (Columbia) v. Evening Star Newspaper Co., 100 LRRM 2394 (D.C. Cir. 1978) (union entitled to *Boys Market* (Boys Mkts. v. Retail Clerks Local 770, 398 U.S. 235 (1970)) injunction enjoining publisher from ceasing publication of newspaper); Lever Bros. Co. v. Chemical Workers Local 217, 554 F.2d 115, 95 LRRM 2438 (4th Cir. 1976) (transfer of operations); Bressette v. International Talc Co., 527 F.2d 211, 91 LRRM 2077 (2d Cir. 1975) (plant closing and termination of employees); Advertiser Co., 89 LA 71 (Baroni, 1987); Pantsmaker, Inc., 83 LA 753 (Roberts, 1984); Union Oil Co. of Cal., 81 LA 540 (Richman, 1983).

[88]Machinists v. Howmet Corp., 466 F.2d 1249, 81 LRRM 2289 (9th Cir. 1972) (plant closure); Mobil Oil Corp. v. Oil Workers Local 8-766, 600 F.2d 322, 101 LRRM 2721 (1st Cir. 1979) (subcontracting).

[89]Machinists v. Howmet Corp., supra note 88, at 2290–2291.

[90]Supra note 88.

that the subcontracting could undercut the express terms of the agreement dealing with recognition, seniority, job classification, and wage scales, the arbitrator determined that the dispute was arbitrable. Mobil commenced an action in federal court to vacate the award. The district court denied the motion, and the court of appeals affirmed the decision making the following statement:

> [A] dispute is arbitrable unless it can be said "with positive assurance that the arbitration clause is not susceptible of an interpretation that covers the asserted dispute" and unless there is an "express provision excluding a particular grievance from arbitration."[91]

Since the arbitration clause did not expressly exclude subcontracting from arbitration, the dispute was deemed arbitrable.[92]

2. Balancing Approach

Arbitrators have generally rejected the proposition that absent a specific restriction in the parties' contract, an employer has an inherent absolute right to determine the questions of corporate ownership, subcontracting, termination or transfer of operations, and other changes of operations.[93] The policy supporting this view has been expressed by the Supreme Court as follows:

> The objectives of national labor policy, reflected in established principles of federal law, require that the rightful prerogative of owners independently to rearrange their businesses and even eliminate themselves as employers be balanced by some protection to the employees from a sudden change in the employment relationship. The transition from one corporate organization to another will in most cases be eased and industrial strife avoided if employees' claims continue to be resolved by arbitra-

---

[91]Id., 101 LRRM at 2725, quoting Steelworkers v. Warrior & Gulf Navigation Co., supra note 86, at 582–583, 585, 46 LRRM at 2421.

[92]See also George Day Constr. Co. v. Carpenters Local 354, 722 F.2d 1471, 115 LRRM 2459 (9th Cir. 1984); Teamsters Local 117 v. Washington Employers, 557 F.2d 1345, 96 LRRM 2096 (9th Cir. 1977); Electrical Workers (IBEW) Local 323 v. Coral Elec. Corp., 576 F. Supp. 1128, 116 LRRM 2790 (S.D. Fla. 1983).

[93]See, e.g., Teledyne Monarch Rubber, 89 LA 565 (1987), where Arbitrator Morris Shanker, applying a "balancing test," ruled that management could not transfer assembly operations to a nonunion, out-of-state facility during the term of a collective bargaining agreement, where the transfer would result in the elimination of 15 to 30% of the unit jobs.

tion rather than by "the relative strength . . . of the contending forces."[94]

A review of the published cases indicates that arbitrators have formulated a wide variety of remedies where improper transfers are found.

3. Return of Plant or Machinery to Original Location

The usual NLRB remedy for failing to bargain about a decision to close a facility and transfer work elsewhere is an order to restore the status quo ante. Such an order will be modified, however, when restoration of the status quo is considered unduly burdensome to the company. An illustrative case is *Reece Corp.*,[95] where the NLRB found that a company violated Taft-Hartley by unilaterally implementing a decision to close one of its plants and transfer unit work to other facilities, but refused a reopening order where (1) the company paid to unit employees over $1 million in severance pay, (2) total costs related to closing were over $2.3 million, (3) more than half of the machinery was transferred to other facilities, and (4) the employer sold the office, plant, and land. The remedy devised was an order requiring management to offer the affected employees reinstatement to their former positions at the facilities to which the company unlawfully transferred unit work, dismissing, if necessary, any person hired after the closing of the plant. In addition, Reece was ordered to pay employees' travel and moving expenses. The Board further provided that if there was sufficient work for all employees to be offered reinstatement, the company should place the employees on a preferential hiring list. Finally, the employees were to be paid what they normally would have earned from the date of the termination to the date of reinstatement or, for employees who decided not to relocate, until the date they secured substantially equivalent employment with other employers. Back pay was based on the earnings that employees

---

[94]John Wiley & Sons v. Livingston, 376 US 543, 549, 55 LRRM 2769, 2772 (1964), citing Steelworkers v. Warrior & Gulf Navigation Co., supra note 86, at 580. See also the discussion of Arbitrator Jerome Lande in Jos. Schlitz Brewing Co., 58 LA 653, 659–660 (1972).
[95]294 NLRB No. 33, 131 LRRM 1413 (1989).

normally would have received during the applicable period less any net interim earnings, computed in that manner set forth in *F.W. Woolworth Co.*[96] (back pay period by quarter), with interest computed in the manner set forth in *New Horizons for the Retarded*[97] ("short-term" federal rate for underpayment of taxes).

Arbitrators, similar to the NLRB, may direct an employer to return machinery and equipment and, in the case of a "runaway shop," even an entire plant, to the original location and to resume operations at that site.[98]

Where an agreement provided for arbitration of all cases "whatsoever" and also stated that an award "may contain provisions directing and restraining acts and conduct of the parties," the federal district court for the Southern District of New York sustained an arbitrator's award directing the reopening of a garment factory. The employer had terminated all work at its New York City facility, while continuing to have garments manufactured at its Savannah, Georgia, plant. Pursuant to a clause prohibiting subcontracting as long as the shop was not fully supplied with work, the arbitrator ordered full and complete resumption of the factory operations in New York City even though the collective bargaining agreement had already expired at the time of the award. In addition, the arbitrator awarded the union "certain sums" for lost earnings and supplemental benefits for employee members from the time they were laid off until the date of their reinstatement.[99]

When the parties' agreement contains explicit language

---

[96]90 NLRB 289, 26 LRRM 1185 (1950), discussed in Chapter 8, at notes 52–53 and accompanying text.

[97]283 NLRB 1173, 125 LRRM 1177 (1987). Interest on and after January 1, 1987, computed at the short-term federal rate for underpayment of taxes set out in 1986 amendment to 26 U.S.C. §6621. Interest on amounts accrued prior to January 1, 1987 (the effective date of 26 U.S.C. §6621), shall be computed in accordance with Florida Steel Corp., 231 NLRB 651, 96 LRRM 1070 (1977); Reece Corp., supra note 95, 131 LRRM at 1419 n.11.

[98]Besides the cases discussed in this section, see Greif & Co., 78 LA 825, 836 (Seibel, 1982) (recognizing that arbitration awards may direct an employer to reopen a closed facility "provided that it is still practicable and economically feasible to reopen the operations (i.e., the machinery and building are still in existence)").

[99]Atomic Uniform Corp. v. Ladies' Garment Workers Local 10, 86 LRRM 2331 (S.D.N.Y. 1973). See also Ladies' Garment Workers Joint Bd. of Cloak, Skirt & Dressmakers v. Senco, Inc., 289 F. Supp. 513, 69 LRRM 2142 (D. Mass. 1968) (return of caging operation and recall of affected employees with restored seniority and back pay); White Motor Co., 43 LA 682 (McGury, 1964) (transfer of accounting work back to bargaining unit).

limiting the right of an employer to move the plant,[100] arbitrators have ordered the return of operations as a remedy for a contractual violation. For example, where the contract provided that the employer would not remove his plant outside a 15-cent fare zone of greater New York, Arbitrator Sidney Wolff ruled that the contract was violated when the employer diverted a portion of the jobs covered by the agreement. As a remedy, the arbitrator directed (1) recovery of all machinery sold, (2) cessation of transferring work to another company, and (3) reinstatement with "damages" for lost time for all laid off employees.[101] Arbitrator G. Allan Dash, Jr., in *Sidele Fashions*,[102] found that the employer's surreptitious establishment of a new plant in a different locality and subsequent movement of bargaining-unit work to that plant were violative of the agreement providing that "no member of the association during the life of this agreement shall move his factory or factories outside the City of Philadelphia." Arbitrator Dash ordered the employer to pay all affected employees any wages lost from the time of the move until the expiration of the agreement. The company was also directed to reimburse the union for any dues lost during the same period and to make contributions to the union's health, welfare, and retirement funds on the basis of the wages lost by the employees, plus a 10-percent "penalty" if such contributions were not made before a specific date. Finally, in ruling on the issue whether the employer should be ordered to return its operations from the South Carolina to the Philadelphia area, the arbitrator concluded that the company must reestablish and operate a factory in Philadelphia of substantially the same size and character as the one which it operated prior to the improper closing. If the employer refused to follow this order, it was given the option of repaying the union and the retirement funds any losses that had been suffered over the past year—and would be suffered in the coming years—as a consequence of setting up its southern plant.[103]

---

[100]See, e.g., Fisher-Stevens, 89 LA 556, 557 (Kramer, 1987) (where agreement provided that "the Employer shall not remove its plant beyond a radius of forty-four (44) miles from Grand Central Station, New York City").
[101]Address-O-Mat, 36 LA 1074 (1961).
[102]36 LA 1364 (1961).
[103]Id. at 1381.

Similarly, the Third Circuit reports a case where the parties' agreement prohibited management from moving its plant "beyond the radius of twenty-five (25) miles without the written consent of the Union." Finding that this provision prohibited the elimination of the entire work force by a move of production to a distance that would make employees' transfer infeasible (management unilaterally transferred all its production to its existing out-of-state plants), the arbitrator ordered the plant "re-opened," the workers recalled, and back pay from the date of the closing to the date each employee was recalled. The court of appeals, reversing the district court, stated that the question for the court was not whether the remedy was the best remedy, but rather, whether the remedy is rational and justified. With regard to the argument that the remedy was futile (the district court concluded that the reopening costs outweighed whatever bargaining power a plant reopening would restore to the union), the court declared that this is a question for the arbitrator, not the court.[104]

In *Jack Meilman*,[105] the parties' contract provided that "[d]uring the term of this Agreement the Employer agrees that he shall not, without the consent of the New York Joint Board, remove or cause to be removed his present plant or plants from the city . . .." As a remedy for a total shutdown of operations, Arbitrator Herman Gray ordered the employer to cease manufacturing operations outside the state, to reestablish facilities in the city from which they were initially removed, and to pay to the union damages for lost wages of the displaced employees and other contractual benefits that would have been earned had the relocation not taken place.[106]

In *Selb Manufacturing Co.*,[107] Arbitrator Joseph Klamon ruled that an employer, by shipping machinery from its St. Louis location to plants in Arkansas and Colorado, violated the following subcontracting provision: "The Companies will not, so long as equipment and personnel are available, sub-

---

[104]Teamsters Local 115 v. DeSoto, Inc., 725 F.2d 931, 115 LRRM 2449 (3d Cir. 1984).

[105]34 LA 771, 773 (1960).

[106]See also Centra Leather Goods, 25 LA 804 (Kheel, 1956) (ordering "injunction" against plant removal).

[107]37 LA 834 (1961), enf'd sub nom. Selb Mfg. Co. v. Machinists Dist. 9, 305 F.2d 177, 50 LRRM 2671 (8th Cir. 1962). See also UFI Razor Blades v. Distributive Workers Dist. 65, 610 F.2d 1018, 102 LRRM 2759 (2d Cir. 1979).

contract work which is customarily performed by employees in the bargaining unit to any other Company." As a remedy, the arbitrator ordered the employer (1) to return to their plants in St. Louis all machinery, equipment, and work that had been improperly transferred to the out-of-state plants, and (2) to recall all St. Louis employees who had been laid off and to reinstate them without any loss of seniority or any other rights. The employees were also to be made whole financially "so that none shall suffer any loss of money as a result of being laid off."[108] In fashioning this remedy, Arbitrator Klamon reasoned:

> [A] Company may discontinue in whole or in part a totally unprofitable operation; we do not believe that a Company may avoid an agreement or any part thereof by moving such operations in order to increase the degree of profitability. If this could be done, such clauses [the subcontracting provision] would mean very little.[109]

Arbitrator Marshall Ross, in ordering the employer to return maintenance and repair work it had improperly subcontracted, found the employer's "undue hardship" argument unpersuasive:

> The remedy applied by arbitrators and the Labor Board in this type of case is to restore the status quo. The Employer contends that this would be expensive and therefore impractical. But this situation was created by the Employer, and the difficulties it created cannot be an obstacle to remedying the damage done by its breach of contract. The only way this can be accomplished is by restoring the status quo and returning the work of maintenance and repair to [unit employees].[110]

In *Houston Publishers Association*,[111] Arbitrator Charles Milentz similarly ordered a newspaper to "cease immediately" the practice complained of (computer interfacing eliminating the need for restroking ads by unit employees before delivery to nonunit ad takers) and to return the disputed work to the bargaining unit. Concluding that management's conduct amounted to a 10 percent out-of-unit transfer of unit work, Arbitrator Milentz nevertheless refused to order any "make

---

[108]37 LA at 842.
[109]Id. at 843.
[110]Campbell Truck Co., 73 LA 1036, 1040 (1979).
[111]83 LA 767 (1984).

whole" relief (including costs and attorney's fees) for the improper transfer and the violation of the "status quo" provision, reasoning that there was no prescribed penalty for noncompliance and that he would be "adding to" the parties' agreement by adding a "penalty."

Many agreements will contain "work preservation" clauses that, under certain fact situations, will prevent management from effecting structural changes in its business.[112] In *Pabst Brewing Co.*,[113] the contract provided that management "shall not reassign any work presently being performed by employees . . . to other personnel to do such work who are not in the Bargaining Unit at this plant . . . ."[114] Arbitrator Sidney Wolff ruled that in transferring for economic reasons its brewery operation from its Peoria, Illinois, to its Milwaukee, Wisconsin, plant, the company violated the above work preservation clause. The arbitrator rejected the employer's argument that the clause prohibited the company from using nonbargaining unit personnel at the Illinois plant only. As a remedy Arbitrator Wolff ordered the employer to reopen the Peoria facility and reinstate the displaced employees.

A similar result was reported by Arbitrator William Ellmann in *Douwe Egberts Superior Co.*,[115] under the following provision:

> For the purpose of preserving work and job opportunities for the employees covered by this agreement, the Employer agrees that no work or services presently performed by the collective bargaining unit for customers located in the State of Michigan will be subcontracted, transferred, assigned, leased or conveyed, in whole or part to any other plant, vendor, person or non-union employees except if equivalent work or services are substituted.[116]

The arbitrator found the employer, in closing its Detroit facility and moving to Chicago, violated the above-cited subcontracting provision. As a remedy the arbitrator ordered reinstatement with back pay, fringe benefits, and seniority.

---

[112]Besides the cases cited in this section, see Food Fair Stores, 71 LA 873, 874 (Hardy, 1978); MacFadden-Bartell Corp., 58 LA 1061 (Friedman, 1972); Selb Mfg. Co., supra note 107.
[113]78 LA 772 (1982).
[114]Id. at 774.
[115]78 LA 1131 (1982).
[116]Id. at 1131.

The arbitrator could not rule out the possibility that the Detroit facility should be reopened and the work returned (the matter was remanded to the parties with the arbitrator retaining jurisdiction for one year).

The Eighth Circuit sustained Arbitrator Richard Ross' award holding that the following language precluded an employer from transferring its payroll and accounting work to an out-of-state facility operated by its parent company while employees were on layoff status:

> "The Employer agrees that no function or service presently performed, or hereafter assigned, to the bargaining unit shall be subcontracted, leased, assigned or conveyed in whole or in part to any other person or organization, if any member of the bargaining unit is, at the time of such action, on layoff due to lack of work. . . .
>
> "The above language shall not be construed or interpreted to prohibit the Employer from adding or discontinuing manufacture, packaging, or processing of a product or performance of a service based on sound business considerations."[117]

Arbitrator Ross ordered the company to cease transferring the office bargaining-unit work to another plant and awarded the grievant back pay from the date she filed the grievance.

Not infrequently, there will not be a remedy for the union in work preservation cases. Arbitrator Lynn Griffith, in *Liquid Carbonic Corp.*,[118] reports a decision where an employer, with operations in the Canton, Ohio, area, established a new terminal some distance from Canton to better compete with other companies who had terminals in that area. Wages in the new area were substantially lower than in Canton. The union filed a grievance alleging that the employer violated the parties' agreement when it assigned drivers to make deliveries in the new territory to perform work previously performed by the Canton bargaining unit. It was argued that the loss of work from the assignment of delivery duties violated the representation clause of the contract.

The arbitrator declared that if there are clauses according exclusive recognition of the union for employees performing work of the categories covered by the contract, then there is

---

[117]Manhattan Coffee Co. v. Teamsters Local 688, 743 F.2d 621, 117 LRRM 2530, 2531 (8th Cir. 1984).
[118]79 LA 180 (1982).

an implied prohibition against performance of work by management personnel or other persons outside the bargaining unit. This was not the situation in the instant case and the arbitrator, in ruling against the union, balanced the rights of management against the rights of the bargaining unit.

> Obviously, if the Company had unlimited management rights and the representation clause had no force other than a mere identification of the representative agent, the Company could withdraw all the jobs from the bargaining unit personnel and render the contract a nullity. On the other hand, if the Union could freeze the work of the bargaining unit, the Company's right to determine the location of the plants and the continuance of any departments would be a nullity. . . . I believe this answer must be found as in most of the cases in which these two provisions of the contract (Management Rights Clause v. Union Representation Clause) come into conflict in a determination of reasonable and prudent business practice. The bad faith that would tip the scale in favor of the Union is absent in this case.[119]

4. Preferential Hiring

If restoration of the plant or the equipment to the original situs will impose an undue hardship or would otherwise be impracticable, an arbitrator may appropriately order the employer to offer employment to the displaced employees at the new site, plus all costs of moving. Superseniority is also a possible remedy, although this remedy may give rise to integration problems at the new site.[120]

In *Ex-Cello Corp.*,[121] the employer closed two of its plants in Detroit and subsequently transferred some of the work performed at Detroit to plants located some 125 miles from the area. Finding that the employer had exacted bargaining concessions from the union by promising that the Detroit plants would be kept open, Arbitrator John Sembower ordered that the affected employees be given preferential transfer rights

---

[119]Id. at 182.
[120]Warehousemen Local 767 v. Standard Brands, 560 F.2d 700, 96 LRRM 2682 (5th Cir. 1977).
[121]60 LA 1094 (Sembower, 1973).

to the relocated operations, with full seniority and pension rights.[122]

Similarly, in *John B. Stetson Co.*,[123] Arbitrator Joseph McGoldrick stated that the employer's unilateral decision to move its plant was "unwise and morally wrong," and, as a remedy, directed the company to set aside $100,000 to cover moving expenses for those employees desiring to transfer.

When management failed to give proper notice that it would be opening a new terminal, Arbitrator Alexander Cocalis, in *Bowman Transportation*,[124] ordered a transfer remedy for laid-off employees who had requested transfer to the new terminal and to assign them seniority greater than employees initially hired there.

5. Reimbursement of Union Dues and Assessments

Another remedy employed by arbitrators in subcontracting, plant, and equipment-removal cases is to order the reimbursement of union dues and assessments lost to the union as a result of the employer's breach. This remedy may be partially appropriate when the union is also alleging a breach of the union security clause.[125]

6. Other Remedies for Improper Transfer of Operations

In *Leona Lee Corp.*,[126] the employer entered into an agreement, recognized by the union, binding the company to transfer its assets to a "successor" and to require the successor-employer to sign a standard union contract. When the em-

---

[122]See also Holiday Inn/Town Square, 90 LA 67, 72 (Cooper, 1987) (ordering employer to redetermine appropriate order of layoff and to reinstate with back pay employees who should have been retained to provide services improperly transferred); Federal-Mogul Corp., 61 LA 745 (Cole, 1973).

[123]28 LA 514 (1957).

[124]88 LA 711 (1987). See also Mack Trucks, 89 LA 1101 (Schmertz, 1987) (management improperly placed short time limit of exercise of employees' transfer rights).

[125]See, e.g., Jones Dairy Farm, 83-2 ARB ¶8389 (Flagler, 1983) (payment of lost wages and lost dues as result of improper subcontracting); Campbell Truck Co., 73 LA 1036 (Ross, 1979); Sam Garvin & Co., 58 LA 1 (Howlett, 1971); Fifth Wheel Cafe, 55 LA 1228 (Zimring, 1969).

[126]60 LA 1310 (Gorsuch, 1972), enf'd sub nom. Asbestos Workers Local 66 v. Leona Lee Corp., 84 LRRM 2165 (W.D. Tex. 1973), aff'd, 489 F.2d 1032, 85 LRRM 2446 (5th Cir.), cert. denied, 419 U.S. 829, 87 LRRM 2397 (1974).

ployer transferred its assets to various contractors who did not adopt the standard union agreement, the union commenced a civil suit which was subsequently stayed pending arbitration.[127] Stating that a company cannot transfer its assets when a major basis is to abrogate a collective bargaining agreement and that the activities of the employer were a subterfuge to avoid carrying on business under a collective bargaining agreement, the arbitrator fashioned the following remedies: (1) loss of income from dues, initiation fees, assessments, and the like, equal to $9,215; (2) assessment against the employer for the costs of the hearings, reporters' fees, transcripts, and the arbitrator's fees; and (3) $25,000 in damages as a result of the "weakening of the union's bargaining position." With respect to the third remedy, the arbitrator stated:

> Finally, with respect to the weakening of the union's bargaining power, capacity to represent employees effectively and impairment of its prestige and reputation, this the arbitrator feels is a major element of damage. The defendants by their conduct in lulling the plaintiff [union] into the belief that it would be dealing with a successor corporation to Leona Lee, which had a union contract, and then depriving the union of this right, has truly weakened the union's bargaining power and its standing with its members. This is borne out by the fact that many members had to leave the jurisdiction to obtain work elsewhere, and must of necessity, have ramifications in the area of contract negotiations and the like with other union employers. The concept of bargaining power and reputation is an extremely important element to the union and fundamental to its dealings, both with its members and with other employers. The undersigned feels that the evidence was overwhelming to show that this loss to the union was a substantial one and affected its entire course of industrial relations during the period from 1967 on. Such a loss cuts directly at the heart of the union's ability to effectively achieve its fundamental objectives, and in this regard the arbitrator is convinced that the evidence sustains an award of compensatory damages in the amount of $25,000.00.[128]

In enforcing the award, the federal district court declared:

> Federal Case Law requires that an Arbitrator have latitude

---

[127]Asbestos Workers Local 66 v. Leona Lee Corp., supra note 126.
[128]60 LA at 1319–1320. It is noteworthy that the arbitrator rejected any claim of punitive damages.

and flexibility in applying remedies for breach of collective bargaining agreements. Since each and every alternative cannot be covered for breach of contract in a collective bargaining agreement, an Arbitrator chosen by both parties should have wide latitude in awarding damages.[129]

An issue frequently associated with a sale or transfer of assets is the remedy to be applied when the company fails to give the union the required notice of sale.[130] In one case involving notice and a promise to negotiate severance pay, *Industrial Workers (AIW) Local 879 v. Chrysler Marine Corp.*,[131] Arbitrator Byron Yaffe had found that the company violated a letter of understanding requiring six-months' notice in case of a closing, as well as an agreement to negotiate a severance-pay plan upon such notice, when Chrysler sold its assets to U.S. Marine with only 22 days' notice to the union. As a remedy he ordered several adjustments, including a directive to attempt to agree upon a severance-pay plan similar to plans in comparable relationships. He reasoned that had such negotiations occurred prior to the sale, the union would be in an advantageous bargaining position, since the company would probably have sought a waiver of the six-months' notice requirement which would have enabled it to meet the purchaser's demands with respect to the timing of the transaction. The union, stated Yaffe, would in all likelihood have been able to negotiate a severance plan which provided benefits comparable with the more generous of such plans in existence at that time in comparable employee-union relationships. The parties were given 90 days to negotiate, after which the arbitration would be reconvened at the request of either party.

Chrysler brought an action seeking to set aside the award, the parties did not negotiate, and the arbitrator reconvened the proceeding. A supplemental award was issued that included, among other things, "a fair and generally comparable severance-pay plan" for all former Chrysler employees, regardless of whether the employees continued employment with the new purchaser (the dissent argued that the remedy pro-

---

[129]Asbestos Workers Local 66 v. Leona Lee Corp., supra note 126, 84 LRRM at 2171.

[130]See the discussion under "Meet-and-Discuss Limitations," at supra notes 53–67, and accompanying text.

[131]819 F.2d 786, 125 LRRM 2681 (7th Cir. 1987).

vided a windfall to some 223 of the 272 former Chrysler employees who were rehired by U.S. Marine). Arbitrator Yaffe observed that no lesser or traditional remedy, such as a cease and desist order or a direction to bargain, could be effected because the parties no longer had a bargaining relationship and Chrysler had no incentive to reach an agreement with the union. The district court enforced both awards, and the Seventh Circuit, in a split decision, affirmed against a claim that the arbitrator exceeded his authority by creating a duty "out of whole cloth" to provide severance pay. The Seventh Circuit declared that the arbitrator could resolve doubts as to the remedy against the party that breached the agreement. Adopting the view of most courts, the appellate court stated that the authority to decide the meaning and application of the agreement necessarily implies the authority to find a breach and "further implies the authority to prescribe a remedy which can be said reasonably to cure the breach."[132]

---

[132]Id., 125 LRRM at 2683–2684.

Chapter 14

Overtime

A. Introduction

The Bureau of National Affairs, Inc., reports that nearly all agreements (97 percent of the 400 contracts in the relevant database) provide premium pay for overtime work.[1] Distribution of overtime work is discussed in 67 percent of the sample contracts—78 percent in manufacturing agreements and 48 percent in nonmanufacturing contracts. Of the provisions for distributing overtime, BNA also reports that 34 percent distribute overtime equally among all employees; 17 percent assign overtime on a strict seniority basis; 12 percent provide for a cumulative equalization of overtime; and 9 percent distribute overtime by rotation of turns.[2]

Where it has been found that an employer has improperly distributed overtime assignments in violation of the agreement or a past practice (as opposed to the situation where management simply neglects to call in an employee on overtime),[3] the reported cases indicate that arbitrators either award monetary compensation for the opportunity lost or issue quasi-injunctive relief providing the employee the opportunity to work overtime at some later date.[4]

While a majority of the arbitrators prefer a monetary award rather than a "make-up" remedy for improper distri-

---

[1]Basic Patterns in Union Contracts, 49 (BNA Books, 1989).
[2]Id. at 51.
[3]See, e.g., American Cyanamid Co., 93 LA 361 (Bernstein, 1989).
[4]Gorske, *Arbitration Back-Pay Awards*, 10 Lab. L.J. 18, 22 (1959); Pittsburgh Plate Glass Co., 32 LA 622 (Sembower, 1958).

bution of overtime, a study of the reported cases indicates that the remedy has varied depending upon the specific context of the violation. The most important variable in the arbitrator's decision to award monetary damages is the relevant contractual provision at issue. In many instances the contract will explicitly provide the remedy[5] and, as pointed out by Arbitrator Neil Bernstein, "if the parties have done so, the Arbitrator's jurisdiction and duties are limited to applying that remedy to the facts before him. The responsibility of an arbitrator is only to answer those questions that the parties have failed to answer for themselves."[6]

Where the remedy is not specified, the cases indicate that arbitrators are more likely to award monetary relief where the parties' contract or past practice[7] provides for distribution of overtime on a strict seniority basis, as opposed to the situation where the agreement compels distribution of overtime on an equalization basis.

B. Equalization Clauses

Recognizing that contractual clauses requiring that overtime be equalized "as far as practicable," or "to the best ability

---

[5]See, e.g., Kelly Springfield Tire, 59 LA 413, 413 (Jacobs, 1972) ("In the event errors occur in the distribution of hours of work . . . the error will be corrected by offering work to those by-passed at the first opportunity when work is available"); Diamond Nat'l Corp., 52 LA 33 (Chalfie, 1969) ("Should an error be made . . . the man bypassed shall become due for the next call-in, or overtime when available. If the employee calls the alleged error to the attention of the foreman and he refuses to correct the situation, the above shall not apply"); Potash Co. of Am., 47 LA 865 (Block, 1966) ("If through error or oversight overtime has been improperly allocated, available overtime will be allocated to the affected employee or employees in order to remedy the indicated error or oversight"); Vulcan Mold & Iron, 41 LA 59 (Brecht, 1963) ("In the event of inequitable distribution of overtime, opportunity for correction shall be made in scheduling future overtime"); Kimberly-Clark Corp., 34 LA 792 (Hawley, 1960) ("Any errors in the future assignment of overtime hours shall be corrected through the assignment of future overtime hours. this assignment shall be made at the first opportunity, and shall give the employee at least as favorable treatment as he would have received had the error not been made.").

[6]American Cyanamid Co., supra note 3, at 363 (crediting argument that following language relieves employer of monetary obligation for improper overtime assignment, i.e., where employer gave overtime to wrong employee, as distinguished from not calling employee on overtime: "If any error occurs in the distribution of overtime, such error will be corrected by adjusting the overtime records of the employees concerned.").

[7]Johnson Controls, 84 LA 553, 561 (Dworkin, 1985) (holding practice of payment to employees for inadvertent or intentional failure to assign overtime on basis of seniority ripened into contractual obligation).

of the supervisor," or requiring in the employer some flexibility in the distribution of overtime, Arbitrator John Sembower nevertheless states that the general aim of such clauses is for overtime to be equalized "and this imposes a duty upon the Company to meet an appropriate test of diligence under the particular circumstances of each instance."[8] In those cases where the employer's efforts have fallen short of the contractual standard, arbitrators have advanced several theories for granting back pay at overtime rates.[9]

Arbitrator Robert G. McIntosh has emphasized the deterrent effect of an award of money damages:

> Generally, however, the rule has been to permit employees to recover the amount of overtime lost without having to work therefor. The arbitrator feels that to permit such recovery is more fair and just and in keeping with the proper adjustment of disputes under contracts. To permit one party to violate a contract and then to give him additional consideration equal to the amount of the damage he has caused would be in effect to permit a person to benefit by the violation of his contract. Such would also weaken the desire for observance of contractual obligations, because if a person knows that he is actually not going to lose anything by virtue of violation he is less likely to be careful in the observance of his contractual obligations.[10]

In *Bendix Aviation Corp.*,[11] Arbitrator Peter Kelliher, in construing a contract providing that overtime be equalized

---

[8]Pittsburgh Plate Glass Co., supra note 4, at 624.

[9]Besides the cases discussed in this section, see Morton-Norwich Prods., 78-2 ARB ¶8556, at 5574 (Allen, 1978) (finding offer of make-up overtime not appropriate remedy under provision stating "[t]he practice of equalizing overtime will be followed to the fullest possible extent."); Phillips Petroleum Co., 76-2 ARB ¶8476 (Wann, 1976) (finding no past practice for opportunity to perform compensatory overtime and ordering make-up pay at overtime rates for overtime-deprived grievant under equalization clause); Mason & Hanger-Silas Mason Co., 36 LA 425 (Hale, 1961) (concluding that pay for lost overtime does not constitute penalty against employer); John Deere Dubuque Tractor Works, 35 LA 495, 498 (Larkin, 1960) ("Offering an employee an opportunity to make up improperly lost hours at a later date is not an adequate remedy. . . . The one sure way of putting an end to foremen's inadvertent errors, or their favoritism in making overtime assignments under the round-robin system, is to hold the Company liable for these breaches of contract by awarding pay to the employee who failed to get his proper assignment.").

Under certain circumstance arbitrators may award monetary compensation for failure to equalize overtime opportunities, but at "straight time" rates. See, e.g., Neches Butane Prods., 63-2 ARB ¶8433 (Coffey, 1963). At other times a cease-and-desist order will issue. See Del Monte Corp., 86 LA 134 (Denson, 1985) (cease-and-desist order is appropriate remedy where union's acquiescence in employer's failure to evenly distribute overtime precludes it from enforcing its rights without first giving company notice).

[10]W.R. Grace Co., 64-2 ARB ¶8457, at 4626 (1964).

[11]26 LA 540 (1956).

"within a classification on a shift insofar as practicable," reasoned that the "make-up" remedy would not prevent future violations of the agreement. Stated Kelliher: "A right is of no value unless an adequate remedy exists. The Company cannot 'create' work."[12]

Arbitrator Samuel Nicholas, Jr., in *ARCO Chemical Corp.*,[13] rejected the argument that compensating a bypassed employee for an overtime assignment with a monetary award represents a punitive award, especially where management had been repeatedly warned of its improper conduct:

> Remedies may consist of admonition or injunction against the wrongdoing and/or be viewed as monetary relief, e.g., backpay. Indeed, the decision to merely warn the wrongdoer, as opposed to allowing for specific monies to be granted to the aggrieved, is often a difficult task for an Arbitrator. But, when dealing with a situation as seen herein, where Management has been duly and repeatedly warned of its incorrect decision making, something more than a reprimand is warranted. To hold otherwise is to discount the importance of [the parties' agreement].[14]

Some arbitrators have held that an employee is entitled to compensation on a principle of damages, and not earnings. Thus Arbitrator Whitley McCoy noted:

> Where damages are proved the Company must pay damages instead of merely offering to permit a man to work at another time and thus earn pay for such work. Giving the right to earn pay is not equivalent to paying damages.
> The argument sometimes made that "we don't pay for time not worked" overlooks the many instances where a company concededly pays for time not worked—holidays, vacations, reporting pay, call-in pay, time during which an employee was improperly suspended or discharged, time during which he was laid off out of seniority on a curtailment of force, etc. Further, that argument mistakes the essential nature of the payment when awarded by an arbitrator, which is damages, not pay for time not worked. The time not worked may or may not be the measure of the damages, in arbitration just as in courts of law.[15]

In *Phillips Chemical Co.*,[16] the arbitrator rejected the sug-

---

[12]Id. at 541.
[13]82 LA 146 (1984).
[14]Id. at 148.
[15]Hercules Powder Co., 40 LA 526, 529 (1963).
[16]17 LA 721 (Emery, 1951).

gestion that make-up of lost overtime was a proper remedy, ruling that the aggrieved is entitled to compensation "on a principle of damages, not earnings, and his right to compensation arose at the instant that the contract was breached."

Where an employee was improperly denied an opportunity to work overtime, Arbitrator Samuel Edes, in *Cities Service Petroleum Co.*,[17] stressed the restitution nature of a monetary award:

> [T]he practice of the Company [of not paying for lost overtime] is so widely at odds with what is generally held to be orthodox remedial restitution in such cases that it cannot be viewed as controlling in the absence of fixed contract language so providing or, in the alternative, strong and positive evidence of an understanding between the parties so providing. Fundamental contract law, as applied in the area of labor-management relations, provides that persons who suffer monetary loss due to contract breach shall be made whole for the loss suffered by such breach.[18]

Robert Gorske's study of arbitration cases indicates that the decision to fashion monetary relief may rest on any of the following grounds:

> (1) that the company deserves a "penalty" for its violations; (2) that the employee is entitled to work the overtime hours when they are available, not at some later time; (3) that the employee might never be given the opportunity to make up the lost time, for example, because of termination of employment; (4) that the contractual guarantee of equal distribution would be valueless unless compensation is provided to its breach; (5) that the employee is entitled to compensation on the principle of damages, not earnings, his right to compensation arising at the instant the contract is breached.[19]

A qualified view of the remedy for failure to "equalize" was offered in *A.O. Smith Corp.*,[20] where the arbitrator held that in the absence of definite contract language, an award of lost overtime pay must be based upon a clearly established past practice or a showing that the employee actually suffered damages rather than temporary postponement of an overtime

---

[17]37 LA 888 (1961).
[18]Id. at 891.
[19]Gorske, supra note 4, at 22.
[20]33 LA 365 (Updegraff, 1959).

work opportunity.[21] Absent language and a past practice, a make-up remedy is generally ordered.[22]

Arbitrator Fredric Richman, in *Liquid Carbonic Corp.*,[23] found that a monetary remedy was not appropriate and outlined the following reasons for his decision:

> The Union asks for a monetary award to grievant, that he be paid for time not worked, in effect a penalty payment. While arbitrators have certainly recognized situations wherein this type of award would be equitable, those criteria have not been met here. First, there is no contractual specified punitive assessment for failure to properly implement the overtime and seniority provisions in the contract. Second, there has been no allegation of repeated abuses of overtime/seniority provisions or of inconsistent or selective distribution of overtime by management. . . . Third, including unjustified labor costs where the situation may be equitably resolved in other ways is inconsistent with the contractually stated objectives of both parties regarding efficient operations.[24]

Richman pointed out that, under similar circumstances, Arbitrator Morris Shanker declared:

> "Such might be the situation where assigning the lowman a future overtime assignment is no longer feasible by reason of a job change, transfer to another work location, etc. But, absent these kinds of special circumstances, this Labor Agreement does not prevent the Company from remedying the error caused a lowman, who inadvertently was passed over in making an overtime assignment by offering him a future overtime opportunity."[25]

Of note in this area is a 1986 decision by the federal court for the Eastern District of Wisconsin which vacated an arbitrator's decision because the court disagreed with the remedy. In an attempt to correct an assignment error, management

---

[21]Akron Brass, 67 LA 267 (Morgan, 1976); Dow Chem. Co., 71-1 ARB ¶8264 (Williams, 1971).

[22]Additional cases holding that a make-up remedy is preferred include: Scotts Branch Coal Co., 87 LA 881, 883 (Feldman, 1986) (ordering one day at shift premium and make-up remedy for two days); A.O. Smith, supra note 20 (stating that law is opposed to penalties and holding that absent language and showing that employee suffered damages rather than temporary postponement of overtime work opportunity, make-up remedy is awarded); Fruehauf Trailer Co., 27 LA 834 (Seligson, 1957); North Am. Aviation, 17 LA 320 (Komaroff, 1951); B.F. Goodrich Co., 8 LA 883 (McCoy, 1947).

[23]84 LA 704 (1985).

[24]Id. at 707.

[25]Id., quoting Price Bros. Co., 76 LA 10, 13 (Shanker, 1980).

offered the grievant make-up work at her overtime rate. The grievant refused, contending that as the senior bypassed employee she was entitled to overtime back pay. Arbitrator Neil Gundermann ruled for the company and the union filed an action to vacate the award. Concluding that "it is 'almost unimaginable' that the remedy devised was within the contemplation of the parties during negotiation of their collective bargaining agreement," the federal court reasoned:

> By allowing the elimination of backpay as a remedy for [a contractual] violation, the arbitrator has effectively destroyed any incentive for the Company to comply with that provision of the collective bargaining agreement. Remedying violations with make-up work, rather than backpay, permits the Company to assign overtime work without regard for seniority and without fear of true retribution. The worst that could result . . . would be "forcing" the Company to . . . perform make-up overtime work when such work was available. This type of "remedy" does little to discourage [contractual] violations and would likely not have been approved by the Union had the issue been dismissed in negotiations.[26]

The logic of the federal court is reflective of the views of most arbitrators, but in reaching this result the court, in no uncertain terms, substituted its judgment for that of Arbitrator Gundermann.

C. Significance of the Overtime-Equalization Unit

Some arbitrators, in formulating a remedy, have distinguished whether the overtime was assigned to the wrong employee within the overtime-equalization unit or if the overtime was improperly assigned out of the classification or out of the department. In the former situation, Arbitrator Wilber Bothwell found inappropriate any award of back pay. In making that award, he reasoned as follows:

> When the error in assignment of overtime work is to another employee within the overtime equalization unit, or the

---

[26]Independent Employees' Union of Hillshire Farm Co. v. Hillshire Farm Co., 638 F. Supp. 1154, 1157, 122 LRRM 3374, 3376–3377 (E.D. Wis. 1986). Contra Bic Pen Corp. v. Rubber Workers Local 134, 183 Conn. 579, 440 A.2d 774, 112 LRRM 3165 (1981) (upholding monetary remedy for misassignment of overtime under equalization clause).

roster, the overtime earnings are not lost to the employee who should have received the assignment. The employee who actually does the work is charged with the hours and will receive that much less work in the long run among the members of the overtime equalization unit. The individual employee on an overtime equalization roster is only entitled to his approximately equal share of the overtime work properly available to employees in that overtime equalization unit. So long as he receives his share over a period of time of reasonable duration he has not lost any earnings. The remedy of overtime work opportunity at the convenience of the employee is a better remedy than the next available overtime work opportunity, which is often the remedy provided. This is true because the employee can select the most convenient time to work the overtime.[27]

Arbitrator Harry Dworkin has reasoned differently where overtime was improperly assigned outside of the equalization unit:

When through an error, overtime work is assigned to employees of another department, such loss can never be rectified through make-up overtime. Such overtime work, when assigned to the aggrieved employees, would necessarily come from the same department, thereby depleting the overtime potential in which all employees are entitled to share equally. This in turn could logically generate other grievances on the part of classified employees claiming that their right to an equal share in the overtime has been diminished by the assignment of extra overtime to the grievants.[28]

Arbitrator J. Earl Williams, in *General Foods Manufacturing Corp.*,[29] ruled that management was obligated to pay whenever overtime is improperly assigned outside the overtime equalization category, unless the company can demonstrate that make-up overtime is possible which will not affect the overtime entitlement of the grievant or any other employee.

Where the agreement provided that "the work in each department or classification will be distributed equally among the employees in that department or classification insofar as possible," Arbitrator Paul Hebert took a "middle position" and

---

[27]Kaiser Alum. Chem. Corp., 54 LA 613, 617–618 (1970).
[28]Aetna Portland Cement Co., 41 LA 219, 223 (1963). See also Midland-Ross Corp., National Castings Div., 76-1 ARB ¶8187 (Fish, 1976); Rubatex Corp., 74-1 ARB ¶8036 (Reel, 1974); Trane Co., 52 LA 1144 (Cahn, 1969); Dayton Tire & Rubber Co., 48 LA 83 (Dworkin, 1967).
[29]83 LA 889 (1984).

ordered that the employer's improper assignment of overtime could be remedied by offering the grievant his choice of an overtime assignment within some designated period. The arbitrator further provided that the work offered the employee must be work which would not otherwise be offered to other employees on an overtime day. In formulating this remedy, the arbitrator's comments with respect to the reported decisions are especially noteworthy:

> While the many decisions in this field cannot be easily harmonized, the central theme of all the decisions is to make the employee whole to the extent that this can be done without affecting the rights of other employees. Sometimes this will mean that only an award of damages or lost pay is appropriate as, for example, when the assignment is to the wrong group of employees who were never entitled to the overtime at all. Sometimes it will mean that an employer can, as here, create overtime work that would not have been created but for the error and, in such cases, a make-up of the overtime can be a proper remedy.[30]

Arbitrator William P. Murphy, in *Internal Revenue Service, Memphis Service Center & Treasury Employees, Chapter 90*, an unpublished 1986 decision, considered the following issues in connection with an overtime equalization case: (1) What is the period of time for determining whether overtime has been distributed as equitably as possible? (2) Does the agency have the obligation to contact employees on jury duty and annual leave to offer them the opportunity to work overtime? and (3) What is the proper remedy for a violation of an overtime equalization provision mandating overtime assignments "as equitably as possible?"

Both parties accepted the proposition, outlined in 1978 by Arbitrator Clair Duff at the Philadelphia Service Center, that the phrase "as equitably as possible" does not mean that on a day-to-day basis there must be precise mathematical equality. The wording implies that over a reasonable period of time, management will take reasonable steps to provide a fair and equitable apportionment of the available overtime among all employees qualified to perform the work that generated the overtime opportunities. Noting that arbitrators have found

---

[30]Morton Salt Co., 42 LA 525, 531 (1964); American Viscose Corp., 38 LA 70 (Crawford, 1962).

reasonable equalization periods varying from one month to one year, Arbitrator Murphy concluded that a six-month period was reasonable. Murphy rejected the union's argument that the equalization period should be on a biweekly basis to conform with the biweekly time and attendance records used by the Service. The arbitrator reasoned that all employees in the unit have the ability to perform the work and there is high stability of employment, both of which support a longer period since they minimize the possibility of "lost" overtime. Since the agency has the contractual obligation to equalize and the authority to make work assignments, a proper approach is to accept the agency's judgment as to a reasonable period unless that judgment is clearly unreasonable.

With respect to the remedy for an improper equalization (this question was not made contingent upon a finding of a violation), Arbitrator Murphy, holding that a monetary remedy is proper, reasoned that a make-up remedy is inconsistent with the establishment of an equalization period. In Murphy's words: "If a failure to equalize within a prescribed period can simply be corrected during the next period, and so on successfully, then the duty to equalize is indefinite in duration rather than a duty related to a fixed period. Under this theory, in effect there would never be a contract violation, since the contract obligation would be repeatedly continued into the next period." Murphy pointed out that "the standard remedy for a contract violation which results in lost earnings is back pay" and "the fact that employees may be paid for work not performed is no bar to a monetary award. That occurs in many other situations, e.g., reinstatement after a discharge without just cause, improper denial of a promotion, etc."

The submission did not include the question of how much deviation is acceptable without a contract violation. That question, reasoned Murphy, should be determined by the parties.

Arbitrator Murphy found no duty on the part of management to contact and offer overtime to employees while on annual leave or jury duty. There would be no obligation on the part of the employees to accept the work offer, and a denial of the offer would not be charged against the employees for equalization purposes.

Where arbitrators have awarded a make-up remedy in equalization cases, the theories cited have been the "punitive" nature of awarding compensation for work not performed, the "intent of the parties' agreement," and the fact that such overtime opportunity would not affect the overtime rights of other employees.[31]

D. Illustrative Problems in Equalization Cases

Assume the following contractual provision is operative at a particular plant:

> It is recognized that overtime cannot always be offered to the man entitled to the same at the time overtime is needed, but the company will attempt insofar as practical to equalize the same during the (1) year term of this contract.[32]

At the end of the relevant time period—within which the equality of overtime was to be measured—the record indicated that 200 hours of overtime were distributed as follows: employee A (100 hours); B (50 hours); C (25 hours); D (25 hours). Employees B, C, and D filed a grievance and requested "make whole" relief as a remedy. What should be the result?

According to one view, since 200 hours were available during the relevant time period, each employee should have been assigned 50 hours. Employee B received 50 hours (his equal share); employees C and D, however, were 25 hours short. In the authors' opinion, a remedy providing C and D with the next available opportunity would not make them whole, since both employees would have worked additional overtime in the next period in any case. Under this set of facts,

---

[31]General Mills Chems., 66 LA 1012 (Cox, 1976); Kimberly-Clark Corp., 61 LA 1094, 1102–1103 (Fellman, 1973) (holding make-up overtime appropriate provided it was at a time where employee would not otherwise be working and it would not take away from co-employee's opportunity); Kelly Springfield Tire Co., 59 LA 413 (Jacobs, 1972); Olin Corp., Indiana Army Ammunition Plant, 70-2 ARB ¶8733 (Sullivan, 1970); Houston Chem. Corp., 70-2 ARB ¶8688 (White, 1970); Olin Mathieson Chem. Corp., 67-1 ARB ¶8081 (Davis, 1966); Morton Salt Co., 42 LA 525, 529–530 (Hebert, 1964) (allowing make-up overtime as long as it was on a day where grievant's crew not scheduled to work).

Where it was shown that the grievant did not accept a majority of the overtime opportunities offered to him, Arbitrator Walter Seinsheimer, in Goodrich Chem. Co., 67 LA 517 (1976), denied a monetary remedy. A partial adjustment was made by Arbitrator Lester Bergeson, in Menasco Mfg. Co., 69 LA 759 (1977), upon a showing that the grievants refused 80% of the overtime assignments. Accord Colt Indus., 73 LA 1087, 1091 (Belshaw, 1979); B.F. Goodrich Chem. Co., 73 LA 603, 604–605 (Tharp, 1979).

[32]Standard Lime & Cement Co., 26 LA 468, 469 (Dworkin, 1956).

the better weight of authority would remedy the employer's violation with an award of back pay at overtime rates of 25 hours for C and D.[33]

According to a second view, since A had already received 100 hours, B, C, and D should be allowed to work 50, 75, and 75 hours, respectively, during the next overtime period. Once B, C, and D "caught up" to A, the equalization record would start anew. C and D, however, would still not be "made whole" by this remedy since they would have been assigned overtime hours in the second period regardless of the employer's breach.

A third view would award employees C and D each 25 hours of overtime pay on the theory that if available overtime assignments had been equalized each employee would have worked 50 hours. In view of the prior assignment of 100 hours to A, however, A should not be allowed to compete in the second period on the same ground as B, C, and D. A should be "credited" with 50 hours (i.e., the number of hours he received improperly). Once B, C, and D each accumulated 50 hours, A would again become eligible for overtime assignments.[34]

E. Seniority Provisions

Where the overtime allocation scheme is based upon strict seniority, an award of compensation is also the preferred remedy for an improper assignment of overtime.[35] Arbitrators may differ, however, when the bypass was inadvertent, where the parties' past practice mandates otherwise, or when the make-up work does not prejudice the rights of other employees.[36]

---

[33]Logemann Bros. Co., 66 LA 1105 (Berteau, 1976); Olin Corp., Indiana Army Ammunition Plant, 70-2 ARB ¶8504 (Uible, 1970); Caterpillar Tractor Co., 67-1 ARB ¶8223 (Brown, 1967).

[34]Giant Tiger Super Stores Co., 43 LA 1243 (Kates, 1965).

[35]See, e.g., Lever Bros. Co., 86 LA 234, 237 (Gordinier, 1986) (stating that providing grievant with opportunity to work overtime on a make-up basis is illusory remedy); American Carco of Ind., 86 LA 19, 20 (Grohsmeyer, 1986) (recognizing that offering an overlooked employee make-up overtime work deprives someone of overtime, possibly that same grievant); Olmsted Community Hosp., 81 LA 560 (Kapsch, 1983) (ordering that grievant be paid for overtime worked by junior employee); Hamilton Indus., 76-2 ARB ¶8342 (Millious, 1976) (monetary compensation for senior employee passed over in overtime assignment, but noting that make-up overtime would be proper if error had been excusable if emergency existed).

[36]See, e.g., National Serv. Indus., 89 LA 781 (Chandler, 1987) (make-up remedy

Within the seniority context, by far the most difficult problems arise in cases where the bypassed grievant, although senior to the employee who was assigned the overtime, was nevertheless not next in line on the basis of proper overtime allocation.

F. Remedy for the "Junior" Bypassed Employee

Arbitrator James Taylor considered a case where an employee who was fifth in seniority standing was bypassed in favor of an employee who was sixteenth in seniority standing. Although the agreement provided that an employee who lost an overtime opportunity should be paid an amount "equal to that paid to the employee who did take advantage of the opportunity," the employer argued that since four other employees were senior to the grievant, the grievance should be defeated. In making an award of back pay at overtime rates, Arbitrator Taylor reasoned as follows:

> To hold as the Company contends would enable supervision to prostitute the explicit terms of the Agreement without fear of effective recourse. If the Company's theory by some remote chance should be adopted by the arbitrator, the net effect could be an unenforceable Agreement except in those cases where the grievant was the most senior employee. If the Company's philosophy were adopted it could distribute overtime to any individual in the Electrical Department it chose without fear of penalty or recourse unless . . . the most senior employee in the Electrical Department, filed a grievance.[37]

Arbitrator Taylor further provided:

> Carrying the Company's ridiculous theory one step further, [the most senior employee] who was on record of declining all overtime except in extreme emergencies would not have a bona fide grievance in the event he was not called because of such declinations and certainly would not file a grievance. Further, it is conceivable to conclude that the most eligible employee to work overtime could be persuaded not to file a grievance by

---

proper where practice existed and agreement silent as to remedy for improper assignments); Webb Co., 85-1 ARB ¶8157 (Bognanno, 1984) (finding that practices of the parties supports remedy of make-up time).

[37]Celotex Corp., 63 LA 521, 524 (1974).

unscrupulous Company officials. While this is not the situation in this dispute, such could occur if the Company's contentions were upheld.[38]

A different result was reached by Arbitrator Harold Jones in *ITT Rayonier*.[39] In that case 32 employees filed grievances when the company allowed a junior employee to work overtime (another 20 employees grieved a separate assignment). The employer offered to settle the matter by paying overtime to the two employees who had the first right to work overtime, but this settlement was rejected on the basis that the offer did not properly remedy the violations. Finding that overtime was actually lost by only two employees, and that the union's remedy would result in a cost to the company of $13,619, the arbitrator held that the employer's remedy was proper.

The authors submit that the better weight of authority supports the viewpoint of Arbitrator Taylor.

G. Summary

A review of published decisions indicates that arbitrators have been on both sides of the issue with respect to awarding monetary compensation to employees who have been improperly denied overtime assignments. Arbitrator Howard Block has aptly noted that the various opinions in this area, however diverse, do contain consistent elements:

> Decisions as to the proper remedy generally turn on analysis of, among other things, the particular provisions of the contract, past practice of the parties, the nature of the breach, and the availability of the makeup work.[40]

Absent contractual language specifying the exact remedy to be applied, the predominant view expressed by arbitrators is to award back pay at overtime rates where overtime assignments are to be allocated according to seniority. In those cases where overtime opportunities have been lost under an

---

[38]Id. See also Harris Bros. Co., 53 LA 293 (Solomon, 1969) (award of lost overtime awarded to employee, although not next in line in seniority, where evidence was present that only other employee senior to grievant would not have accepted assignment).

[39]83-2 ARB ¶8351 (1983).

[40]Kalamazoo Spice Co., 73-2 ARB ¶8444 (1973), at 4633.

overtime equalization scheme, the decisions are split. The better weight of authority holds that if equalization is still possible within the time frame for equalizing assignments, an employee is not really damaged and an order to permit a grievant to make up lost overtime before the equalization period expires is an appropriate remedy. If, on the other hand, the overtime is forever lost, either as a result of an assignment outside of the equalization unit or because the period of equalization has expired, a monetary award may be appropriate.

Chapter 15

Work Assignments

Work assignment cases present situations where a contractual violation injures a group of identifiable employees but it is impossible to determine which employee has been injured and to what degree. The most common violations occur when work is assigned to the wrong classification of employees, or when a supervisor improperly performs bargaining-unit work. In these cases an identifiable group of workers have had their rights infringed, but it is difficult or impossible to show that any particular individual would have received the additional work, and resultant pay, if the agreement had not been violated.[1] The cases indicate that arbitrators have decided both ways with regard to awarding monetary damages. The better rule holds that when a violation is established the burden shifts to the employer to demonstrate that the breach did not cause a loss of earning opportunity measured by the amount of time, either straight or overtime.[2]

A. Assigning Work to Wrong Classification

Unless the parties provide otherwise in their agreement, a monetary remedy is appropriate where an employee can demonstrate economic loss as a result of management's assignment of work to the wrong job classification or to the

---

[1]See, e.g., Lucky Stores, 70-1 ARB ¶8271, at 3902 (Feller, 1969).
[2]Id.

wrong employee within a classification.[3] As noted by Arbitrator C. Allen Foster, in *Celanese Fibers Co.*,[4] arbitrators agree that when misassigned work is performed on overtime or employees are on layoff at the time the work is done, the affected class suffers an economic loss of work, and an award for compensatory damages by the loss of wages must be granted.[5]

Arbitrators disagree, however, in situations involving misassignment where no economic loss can be claimed by the grievants. In this respect, Arbitrator Foster states:

> One view, apparently in the minority, is illustrated by Lockheed Aircraft Corp., 55 LA 964, (1970), where the arbitrator awarded back pay to the slighted employees as if they, and not the members of the rival craft, had actually done the work. The disadvantage of this approach is that it does more than merely make the grievants whole, the traditional justification for compensatory damages. It pays employees for work not done, a bonus in addition to their undiminished regular pay. The company in effect has been made to pay a penalty, or smart money, for violating the contract.[6]

As seen by Arbitrator Foster, the majority view avoids this inequity and instead contents itself with the fact that the agreement has been violated. Since no damage has been done to employees, no money can change hands:

> This analysis has its own problems. The contract has been broken, apparently with impunity. Thus, although the employees may not have suffered harm, their Union has—a provision negotiated by it and for which concessions in other fields may have

---

[3]See, e.g., Unitog Co., 85 LA 740 (Heinsz, 1985); Grinnell College, 83 LA 39 (Nathan, 1984) (ordering college to reinstate position of telephone operator and to make whole employees performing work in that position); Bard Mfg. Co., 83 LA 749 (Feldman, 1984) (overtime for employee improperly denied during assignment leading to overtime). But see A.E. Staley Mfg. Co., 85 LA 880 (Kates, 1985) (special circumstances justifies no monetary remedy); Central Ill. Pub. Serv. Co., 84 LA 1065 (Feldman, 1985) (denying monetary remedy where none requested by union); City of Minneapolis, 84-2 ARB ¶8530 (Ver Ploeg, 1984) (applying past practice of four hours' compensatory time off for improper scheduling).

[4]72 LA 271 (1979).

[5]Id. at 275. See, e.g., United States Steel Corp., 68 LA 829 (Hales, 1977); American Shipbldg., 69 LA 234 (Morgan, 1977); Mahoney Plastics Corp., 69 LA 1017 (King, 1977); Autocon Indus., 66 LA 73 (Marshall, 1976); General Cable Corp., 52 LA 229 (Feller, 1968). But cf. Mallinckrodt Chem. Works, 68-2 ARB ¶8511 (Goldberg, undated), discussed infra notes 9–11.

[6]72 LA at 275. Contra Borden, Inc., 71-1 ARB ¶8263 (Lanna, 1971); WFMJ Broadcasting Co., 69-2 ARB ¶8612 (Belkin, 1969); Pace Corp., 69-2 ARB ¶8696 (Jones, 1969); Kennecott Copper Corp., 69-2 ARB ¶8469 (Sartain, 1968); Record Files, 66-3 ARB ¶8927 (Geissinger, 1966); Light Metals Corp., 64-1 ARB ¶8354 (Cole, 1964); Manufacturers & Repairers Ass'n, 61-3 ARB ¶8793 (Owen, 1961).

been made has been ignored. Even a well-intentioned company has no incentive to work harder to prevent misassignment of work under these circumstances, and a company seeking to avoid in practice what it cannot eliminate in bargaining is undeterred from efforts to shirk its bargain. This weakness becomes more apparent as the number of violations mounts, even though each seems to be made in perfect good faith.[7]

In the instant case, Arbitrator Foster, finding no evidence that any overtime work had been performed or that employees in the aggrieved classifications had been laid off or had otherwise suffered a loss in earning opportunities, nevertheless awarded the union $400 in damages where the agreement had been repeatedly violated.[8]

In a similar case, Arbitrator Stephen B. Goldberg found that the union's failure to show monetary loss to any employee would not prevent a monetary award, at least in the case where it was shown that the employer had deliberately made an improper assignment. The arbitrator's reasoning in this matter is especially instructive:

> The arguments in favor of an award of damages despite the Union's failure to show monetary loss to any employee are three-fold. Initially, it can be argued that unless management is subject to a monetary penalty for a knowing breach of the agreement relating to assignment of work, it will be free to ignore those provisions whenever all employees in the disfavored classification are working a full forty hour week. Conversely, a damage award for a knowing breach of contract will encourage a good faith effort to abide by the contract. . . .[9]

Arbitrator Goldberg also stressed the status of the union as representative of the individual employees:

> [T]he vice of an unremedied misassignment of work, at very least a knowing misassignment, is that it reflects adversely on the Union and injures the Union's standing among the employees. "What good is the Union if the Company can ignore the Union contract whenever it wishes and the Union can't do anything about it?", a typical employee might ask. Arguably, the Union is entitled to protection against this type of injury to its reputation, as well as to the monetary injury incurred by it in policing the agreement through the grievance and arbitration

---

[7]72 LA at 275.
[8]Id. at 276.
[9]Mallinckrodt Chem. Works, supra note 5, at 4762. See also Emerson Elec. Co., 69-2 ARB ¶8457 (Lesar, 1969).

procedure, even if it cannot show a loss of wages to any individual employee.[10]

The potential adverse monetary consequences were also noted:

> Finally, the argument can be made (wholly without regard to whether the misassignment of work was knowing or not) that where work is wrongfully assigned to employees in one classification rather than employees in another classification, an award of damages measured by the amount of wages that might have been earned had the work been properly assigned is justified on the theory that even though the union cannot show a loss of earnings by any employee in the disfavored classification, such a loss might well have occurred. The employer, if forced to assign the work within the proper classification, might have had the work done on an overtime basis. Alternatively, the employer's action in assigning the disputed work to another classification, rather than to an employee in the proper classification might mean that at some indefinite date in the future, an employee in the disfavored classification will be laid off sooner than he would otherwise have been. It is extraordinarily difficult for the union to prove either of these facts since the former rests on speculation as to how management would have reacted in a hypothetical situation and the latter on speculation as to whether or not the future holds any prospect of layoffs or short work weeks for employees in the disfavored classification. Yet the difficulty of proof does not wholly negate the possibility that there either was or will be a loss of work for these employees.[11]

In *Freeman United Coal*,[12] Arbitrator Jack Clarke denied a monetary award where the injured employee accepted make-up work for management's improper assignment of an idle-day shift. The arbitrator rejected the union's argument that it, and not the grievant, had the authority to settle a grievance. Reasoning that the grievant, having accepted the make-up work, waived any claim to an additional remedy, the arbitrator applied a "make-whole" principle to the facts of the case and stated that any additional remedy would be "grossly excessive compensation." In the arbitrator's words:

> The purpose of any remedy directed in labor arbitration is to place the injured party, that is, the grievant and union, in the same position each would have been had the employer not violated the collective bargaining agreement. The purpose of

---

[10]68-2 ARB ¶8511, at 4762–4763.
[11]Id. at 4763.
[12]86-1 ARB ¶8026 (Clarke, 1985).

such a remedy is not to punish the employer or to give any bonus to the grievant/union. If the Arbitrator were to direct an additional remedy in the present case, the Grievant would be in a much better position as a result of the Arbitrator's decision than he would have been had the Company scheduled him properly in the first place.[13]

B. Supervisors Performing Bargaining-Unit Work[14]

Generally the issues that arise in cases where work is improperly assigned to the wrong classification of employees are also present in cases where supervisors have violated the agreement by performing bargaining-unit work. Where the work that has been performed by nonbargaining unit personnel results directly in an economic loss to an individual or bargaining unit, arbitrators have not hesitated to award monetary compensation either to those employees who would have performed the work or, alternatively, to the union.[15] A common remedy is to pay employees who would have performed the work an amount equal to the time worked by the nonunit supervisor at the employee's applicable rate.[16]

Numerous employers have argued that a monetary remedy for a supervisor performing a small amount of unit work is "punitive" and should not be awarded. This argument was rejected by one arbitrator in a case involving the sorting of bolts by a supervisor. When it was pointed out that the supervisor was performing unit work, management ordered a unit employee to remix the bolts. The arbitrator stated that it would be a "total travesty" to find that either party could

---

[13]Id. at 3111.

[14]For an expanded discussion of the substantive issues on nonunit personnel performing unit work see Hill and Sinicropi, Management Rights: A Legal and Arbitral Analysis, 494–503 (BNA Books, 1986); Elkouri and Elkouri, How Arbitration Works, 4th ed., 550–551 (BNA Books, 1985). See also the discussion of Arbitrator J. W. Murphy in Tenneco Chems., 59 LA 357, 360–362 (1972).

[15]NCR-Worldwide Serv. Parts Center, 74 LA 224 (Mathews, 1980) (monetary award to unit employee who would have performed required work); Pemcor, Inc., 68 LA 63 (Grant, 1977) (time and one-half to three most eligible unit employees for average number of hours worked by nonunit personnel); Stanray Corp., 63 LA 332 (Kelliher, 1974) (monetary award to successful bargaining-unit bidder once contractual procedures are implemented); United States Steel Corp., 62 LA 743 (Fisfis, 1974) (two hours' pay to employee who lost opportunity to work); General Cable Corp., supra note 5.

[16]Canada Post Corp., 83 LA 330 (Adams, 1984).

violate the contract and then nullify such violation by reversing their procedures. Because the bargaining unit brought the grievance for its loss of unit work (the union did not designate the employee who was entitled to receive pay), the arbitrator ordered the employer to compensate the union treasury in the amount of one-half hour pay.[17]

Where the length of time it took management to perform the work in question (construction of expanded office space) could not be determined, Arbitrator Marvin Feldman, in *Randall Bearings, Inc.*,[18] awarded a "token payment of wages of three hours each of straight time" for supervisory personnel performing unit work. Another arbitrator found four hours call-in pay an appropriate remedy for two grievants where the work performed by management did not exceed eight hours. The arbitrator rejected management's argument that one of the grievants should not receive payment since he was not next in line for the work. Since no other classified employees filed grievances, and the time for filing had passed, the arbitrator found that other potential grievants waived their rights to file.[19] Still another arbitrator awarded a union twice the amount it would have paid union members for the hours that nonunit employees operated equipment within the union's jurisdiction.[20]

Monetary awards have been denied where it is not clear that the work would have ever been performed had supervisory personnel not completed the work;[21] where there is no evidence that any identifiable unit employee sustained loss of earnings or damages;[22] where the grievants were not necessarily the ones who would have performed the work;[23] or where

[17]Cadillac Gage Co., 87 LA 853 (Van Pelt, 1986). See also Boy's Mkt., 82 LA 45 (Wilmoth, 1983) (ordering payment at overtime rates for three senior unit employees under supervisor who improperly performed work).
[18]84 LA 357 (1985).
[19]Island Creek Coal Co., 84 LA 623, 627 (Mittlelman, 1985).
[20]Parsons Contractors, 91 LA 73 (DiLauro, 1988).
[21]Hemstock Bros., 67 LA 113 (Yaffe, 1976).
[22]Columbus Jack Corp., 82 LA 179, 183 (Kindig, 1984) (pointing out that union did not request back pay and that no employee suffered any loss); Germain's, Inc., 82 LA 1022 (Pollard, 1984) (no retroactive remedy, noting that no unit employee was laid off or lost wages because of employer's violation); Atlanta Wire Works, 66 LA 365 (Roberts, 1976); Harley-Davidson Motor Co., 63 LA 1149 (Kossoff, 1974); Eaton Corp., 61 LA 410 (Ellmann, 1973).
[23]Standard Oil Co., 63 LA 445 (Kates, 1974).

the union has acquiesced in the practice of having supervisors perform bargaining-unit work.[24]

One option exercised by some arbitrators is to remand the issue of damages to the parties, retaining jurisdiction in case of disagreement.[25] This is one area, however, where any arbitral remedy (short of monetary "damages") is illusory. As pointed out by union advocate Ben Fischer at the 1971 meeting of the National Academy of Arbitrators:

> Management says: "Foreman won't work." And when they do work, management says: "That's wrong. We're going to look into this and do something about it." They do, and the foreman is told not to work—and this keeps going on and on until you go to arbitration, and then you've got a new kind of remedy. Now the arbitrator says that the foreman shouldn't work.
>
> And the way you implement this is by giving the foreman a copy of the award, and if he can read he knows he violated the contract. Perhaps management takes him aside, if he can't read, and explains it to him. But nothing happens. If you think it's a great deal of satisfaction to a union member to say, "We won!" when it costs us $1,200 to get this little lecture to the foreman, you are quite wrong. People are not that concerned with that sort of elusive victory.
>
> I don't know that this is the arbitrator's problem. I think it is the parties' problem. It seems to me that in responsible collective bargaining at this late date, if you're going to say that there is a rule, then you ought to say that there should be some penalty for its violation. When a member of the union violates a rule, there's a penalty; there's not much of a problem involved with that. When management violates a rule, there ought to be a penalty, and it is not primarily—in my judgment—the responsibility of the arbitrator to fashion such a remedy. If he can do so, God bless him—and I'll help him if I can—but I'm not going to lose sight of the fact that it is the contract itself that really fashions the remedy.[26]

---

[24]Ralph's Grocery Store, 63 LA 845 (Petrie, 1974).

[25]See, e.g., Avis Rent A Car Sys., 83 LA 294, 297 (Schedler, 1984) (returning to employer to resolve question of damages); Northwest Automatic Prods., 83 LA 913 (Reynolds, 1984) (leaving to good judgment of parties wages lost from date of grievance); Grand Valley Coop., 74 LA 326 (Daniel, 1980); Bethlehem Steel Corp., 57 LA 299 (Harkless, 1971) (grievance returned to determine which employee should have received work).

[26]Fischer, *Implementation of Arbitration Awards*, in Arbitration and the Public Interest, Proceedings of the 24th Annual Meeting, National Academy of Arbitrators, 110, 132 (BNA Books, 1971).

C. The *De Minimis* Doctrine

In fashioning remedies arbitrators frequently apply the legal principle of *de minimis non curat lex*, which means that the law does not care for, or take notice of, very small or trifling matters.[27] This doctrine is applied in denying any remedy because the violation is considered trivial or, alternatively, is evoked to dismiss a grievance altogether because the conduct complained of is so minor that it cannot reasonably be considered a violation of the parties' contract. One commentator has stated, in what appears to be the better reasoning, that the *de minimis* doctrine ought to be reserved only to determine the amount of damages and not as a reason for dismissing the grievance.[28] Although the law does not concern itself with trifles, the institution of collective bargaining does. Arbitrator Whitley McCoy makes this point:

> In explanation of my having discussed issues and contentions upon which the ultimate decision is not to be based, I may say that parties do not spend many days of preparations, three days of hearings, and thousands of dollars worth of the time of important officers and attorneys, for the purpose of finding out whether one girl should or should not have got a trivial promotion. They are interested in principles. They are entitled, for their future guidance in various respects, to the arbitrator's findings upon the evidence and the various contentions.[29]

By far the most common application of the *de minimis* rule is where supervisors have performed bargaining-unit work. The reported decisions, however, do not lend themselves to the formulation of any set guidelines as to when the *de minimis* doctrine will defeat a grievance. At one extreme is the view expressed by Arbitrator Elmer Hilpert:

> There is a "*de minimis*" rule; and it is to be applied in a proper case; but the de minimis rule does not mean that ascertainable sums of money, by way of "damages", are not to be recovered merely because they are small—or even "tiny"—in size. Such

---

[27]See generally Elkouri and Elkouri, supra note 14, at 355–356; Fairweather, Practice and Procedure in Labor Arbitration, 2d ed. (BNA Books, 1983), 521–525; Nolan, Labor Arbitration Law and Practice, 190–191 (West, 1979).
[28]Nolan, supra note 27, at 191.
[29]Southern Bell Tel. & Tel., 16 LA 1, 9 (1951). See also Minneapolis-Honeywell Regulator Co., 31 LA 213, 216–217 (McCormick, 1958).

an application of the rule of de minimis would be a travesty on justice. . . .

The *de minimis rule* is to be applied ONLY when there is no *measurable* damage; i.e., where "damages" are only "nominal." Here "damages", though small and, under one view, even "tiny", are *measurable*.[30]

An example of a "true" *de minimis* situation, stated Hilpert, would be the case where a nonunit employee merely provided "a hand in passing" so that no unit employee lost a work opportunity. The arbitrator accordingly awarded one-half hour at overtime rates as the proper measure of damages where a nonunit employee worked approximately 15 minutes unloading pallets.

Under an agreement that stated that "supervisory employees shall perform no production, classified or other work" and, where a dispute arose under this section, "the burden of proof will be on the employer to prove that the supervisory employee has not performed such work," Arbitrator Bernard Cantor found the *de minimis* rule inapplicable where a nonunit employee performed two or three minutes of work in cranking a welding machine onto a ball-headed connection on a truck. In finding the rule inapplicable, the arbitrator focused on the parties' intent as evidenced in their agreement:

> To an outsider, it would seem to be unspeakably minor.
> But the parties do not see it so. Of course, management now argues that it was trivial, and suggests the lawyers' concept of *de minimis*, something too small to invite the consideration of judge or arbitrator, but they are, directly, and through the agents who negotiated this agreement, parties to a document that evidences a much different attitude out of historical perspective. Somewhere back down the line, some management has so abused the situation as to outrage the people. The union has demanded, and the management people have acquiesced, that on a complaint of this nature, the management must prove the negative, an almost impossible task. Not that alone, they have imposed a penalty provision [one shift's pay to the individual who should have performed the work] which requires far greater restitution than the offense might occasion. That contract provision is most notable. . . . There is no concept of *de minimis* here. The contract does not allow for it. The contract controls.[31]

---

[30]Acme Paper Co., 47 LA 238, 242 (1966).
[31]Roberts & Schafer Co., 72 LA 624, 626 (1979). Accord Wheland Co., 34 LA 904 (Tatum, 1960) (10-second period of performing unit work was sufficient to make out violation under strict agreement).

Arbitrator James Altieri, in *Westinghouse Electric Corp.*,[32] ruled that the *de minimis* doctrine could not properly be applied where the work at issue, constituting no more than one minute of the supervisor's time, was a "principal" activity of the unit employees. In discussing the problems in evaluating *de minimis* claims on the basis of the time involved, Arbitrator Altieri offered the following hypothesis:

> Supposing the Company determines that it will increase production and make for a more efficient operation if, instead of ringing the bell at 10:30 A.M., that it do so at 10:31 A.M., and answers the Union's protest by saying that the extra minute is de minimis . . . .
>
> The foregoing analysis, of course, stems necessarily from the conclusion that the tasks involved are integrally related with and constitute a part of the principal activity. Once this conclusion is arrived at, there is no room, in the opinion of the undersigned, for application to unilateral Company action [nonunit personnel getting tools ready for use on assembly line] of the principle of "de minimis non curat lex" without doing gross violence to the contractual relationship between the parties.[33]

Where arbitrators have held that the *de minimis* rule operated to deny either a grievance or a remedy for a proven violation, they have stated that the work was of insignificant nature and short duration or that there were no measurable damages.[34]

---

[32]43 LA 84 (1964).
[33]Id. at 90.
[34]National Lead Co., 62 LA 190 (High, 1974) (rule was applicable where work lasted 10–15 minutes); superior Fiber Prods., 58 LA 582 (Johnson, 1972) (*de minimis* nature of work); Oxford Paper Co., 45 LA 609 (Cahn, 1965) (damages insignificant for 10–15 minutes of work); Columbian Carbon Co., 65-1 ARB ¶8008 (Oppenheim, 1964) (work *de minimis*); Pullman, Inc., Trailmobile Div., 63-2 ARB ¶8661 (Stouffer, 1963) (minor nature of work); General Chem., 61-3 ARB ¶8609 (McConnell, 1961) (work was minimal); Acheson Dispersed Pigments Co., 36 LA 578 (Hale, 1960) (pay lost was inconsequential).

Chapter 16

Scheduling Vacations

A. Introduction

Suppose that an agreement specifies that employees shall be given a choice of vacation periods and that vacations, once scheduled, shall not be changed except when proper notice is effected. When the employee's grievance cannot be heard and decided before the effective date of the changed schedule, what is the remedy when management reschedules that vacation to a different time or, as sometimes happens, assigns a plant shutdown period as the designated vacation time for employees?

Arbitrators and courts are split in their views concerning the remedy that should apply to an employee who improperly has been denied a preference in vacation time. One view is that monetary damages should be assessed against the employer since by forcing an employee to take vacation at a rescheduled time it caused an inconvenience to the employee. On the other hand, a significant number of arbitrators have held that no effective remedy is possible in such a case because the employee is not damaged merely by being forced to take a vacation (as opposed to a denial of a vacation) at a different period. Still other arbitrators have reasoned that if there are any damages, they are not the type that can be compensated in the arbitral forum.

B. Altering Scheduled Vacations—Failure to Give Contractual Notice

In *Combustion Engineering*,[1] the collective bargaining agreement provided that "a scheduled extended vacation shall not be changed without at least 60 days' notice to the employee, unless the employee consents to the change in the schedule." The arbitrator held that the employer was not justified in rescheduling extended vacations of six employees for a poststrike period and, as a remedy, ordered payment for the unscheduled vacation weeks the grievants were forced to take.

Arbitrator Lewis Gill, in *Bethlehem Steel Corp.*,[2] found that back pay was a proper remedy when the employer, contrary to the explicit terms of the contract, failed to give timely notice of a change in the employees' vacation preference. In making the award, the arbitrator explained that there was a problem of timing with regard to the remedy:

> For those grievants whose preferred dates have already passed, by the time this decision is issued, it is of course impossible to grant their requests, and back pay is the obvious alternative. . . .
> Some of the grievants' preferences are still chronologically possible to grant, however, calling for specified weeks in late November or early December. In those cases, I think management should be given the alternative of granting those weeks *or* pay in lieu thereof. It would not be proper, in my view, simply to direct that the weeks be granted, since that might create severe operational problems.[3]

Arbitrator Gill rejected the employer's argument that an award of back pay is improper since that remedy had not been discussed in the earlier steps of the grievance procedure. Finding that all but one of the grievants asked to be "made whole," the arbitrator reasoned that this was an effective request for back pay and that it is well within an arbitrator's discretion to award back pay as an alternative to the requested weeks if granting those weeks is inappropriate or impossible.[4]

---

[1]61 LA 1061 (Altrock, 1973).
[2]48 LA 223 (1966).
[3]Id. at 226–227.
[4]Id. at 227. See also Multimedia of Ohio, 87 LA 927, 932 (Kindig, 1986) (ordering make-whole relief for employees who suffered actual loss); Hoover Co., 85 LA 41 (Shanker, 1985); Reynolds Metals Co., 83 LA 221 (White, undated).

Arbitrator John Gentry, in *Bethlehem Steel Corp.*,[5] found a monetary remedy improper for the company's failure to abide by notice requirements for scheduling vacations. Pointing out that this was not a case involving "forced" vacation time nor a case where the company was guilty of repeat violations, Arbitrator Gentry refused a remedy of a paid make-up vacation.

In *Lucky Stores*,[6] Arbitrator David Feller considered what remedy should apply for an employer's failure to secure the union's permission before allowing employees to take vacations outside of a stipulated vacation period. In this type of case noted Feller, no employee is injured, monetarily or otherwise. The injury is to the labor organization and the collectivity it represents. Feller, in not awarding monetary damages, reasoned as follows:

> In such a case it seems to me that the premise that my authority is remedial rather than punitive requires that I reject the contention that I order second vacations, or pay in lieu thereof, to the four individuals who received vacations prior to the contractual vacation period. Under no theory could such an award be regarded as remedial. It would provide the four individuals with additional pay or paid vacation time for having received a favorable response to what I am entitled to assume were their own requests.[7]

The appropriate remedy, stated Feller, is one that will correct the situation that caused the violation: lack of awareness of the requirement for securing the union's consent before making changes in the schedule. The employer was accordingly ordered to issue a notification to the appropriate supervisor at each store covered by the agreement to prevent similar violations in the future.

C. Rescheduling During Shutdowns

In *South Carolina Industries*,[8] an employer required senior employees to take their vacations during a shutdown to prevent having their absences charged to its unemployment

---

[5]81 LA 1272 (1983).
[6]70-1 ARB ¶8271 (1969).
[7]Id. at 3903.
[8]65 LA 745 (1975).

experience rating. Arbitrator Cary Williams ordered the employer to allow the grievants to reschedule their vacations. In making that award the arbitrator held that the so-called vacations were actually layoffs for lack of work. The arbitrator refused to make any monetary award, including an award for unemployment compensation payments the grievants would have been entitled to if the employer had merely laid off the employees. However, he did declare that this was an issue for the state unemployment compensation agency to decide.[9]

A number of arbitrators have directed employers to compensate employees for unemployment compensation payments lost as a result of improperly scheduled vacations during a shutdown. Arbitrator Lewis Gill, in *Philip Carey Manufacturing Co.*,[10] after finding that an employer violated the agreement by requiring employees to take vacations during a two-week plant shutdown, ordered lost unemployment compensation payments to the affected employees. In making that award, the arbitrator reasoned that the claim for unemployment compensation is for a "distinctly monetary and measurable loss":

> Looking at the situation from a realistic rather than a technical point of view, however, there is simply no doubt that the men lost out on unemployment compensation benefits *because of the Company's violation of the contract in the first place.* This was a definite monetary loss, and I think it falls squarely within the language of the Award which is here to be applied—"The appropriate employees shall be made whole by the Company for whatever losses, if any, they suffered because of this action by the Company.[11]

It is noteworthy that 21 employees were affected during the first week of the shutdown and 38 during the second week, yet only two employees actually filed claims with the unemployment compensation bureau. Arbitrator Gill, nevertheless, did not find it improper to award all employees relief, since the claims of the employees who had filed were rejected by

---

[9]Accord Park-Ohio Indus., 56 LA 142 (Keefe, 1971); Phoenix Iron & Steel Co., 32 LA 378 (Crawford, 1959); Baldwin-Lima-Hamilton Corp., 31 LA 37 (Fleming, 1958) (employer ordered to notify unemployment compensation agency); Ford Motor Co., 3 LA 829 (Shulman, 1946).

[10]37 LA 134 (1961).

[11]Id. at 137. Accord Cone Mills Corp., 29 LA 346 (McCoy, 1957); Caterpillar Tractor Co., 23 313 (Fleming, 1954).

the bureau and it was reasonable to assume that the other employees had concluded that their claims would similarly be denied.[12]

A contrary result was ordered by Arbitrator Sam Jaffe in *Scovill Manufacturing Co.*[13] Where employees were required to take a second week of plant shutdown as a vacation period, Arbitrator Jaffe provided an extra week of vacation with pay. His reasoning in that decision is instructive:

> [I]t may be argued that giving them another week's vacation (with pay), as requested, would have the effect of giving them an *extra* week off with pay. But this argument loses sight of the fact that these girls suffered damage, and the question before us is how we ascertain the amount. And there *was* damage, even if it is difficult to assess its precise amount. What the Company did in violation of the Agreement did cause them inconvenience which may be inferred to be substantial, and presumably some monetary loss as well. One of the difficulties in fixing the precise amount of loss is, of course, the fact that it would undoubtedly vary to some extent from girl to girl. But although the Company acted in good faith in what it did . . . the fact remains that it was *its* breach which has created the uncertainty.
>
> . . .
>
> On the whole, I believe that it is not unreasonable to infer that the resulting inconvenience plus some monetary loss was in general equivalent to one week's pay for each of the twelve employees with whom we are presently concerned. Even if there be an element of uncertainty as to the scope of the damages, as distinguished from its existence, it would be more speculative to try to assess an offsetting credit to the Company. Moreover, the monetary assessment of an imponderable like inconvenience is hardly more difficult than trying to assess the value of pain and suffering to an injured plaintiff in an accident case.[14]

Some arbitrators have refused to award monetary damages of any kind where employees are forced to take a vacation during a shutdown but, nonetheless, have ordered that the

---

[12]37 LA at 139.
[13]31 LA 646 (1958).
[14]Id. at 651. Accord United States Steel Corp., 33 LA 82 (Garrett, 1959). Of interest is Parchment Co. v. Paterson Parchment Paper Co., 282 U.S. 555 (1931), a decision cited by Arbitrator Jaffe, where the Court stated that the wrong having been proven, the risk of uncertainty as to the scope of damage is on the party who committed the breach, and recovery may be had even if the extent of the damage is only an approximate inference.

employees be rescheduled for an unpaid vacation of their choosing.[15]

D. Absence of a Remedy

Where employees were not allowed to exercise their contractual preference for vacation, Arbitrator Thomas McDermott, reflecting the views of most arbitrators, held that there could not be an effective remedy because "damages" are impossible to determine:

> An arbitrator is authorized to assess damages, but these damages must be related to the losses suffered by the aggrieved party. In the instant case the difficulty in determining a proper remedy lies in making a determination of just what damages an individual employee has suffered, when he was forced to take his extended vacation at a time other than his original first preference. With some employees it will make no real difference, as the time selected was one of personal preference, rather than one based upon particular needs. For some others there may be circumstances, such as personal needs, family requirements or long range plans, which might actually cause a real injury to the employee. . . .
> Therefore, for those grievants who have already received their extended vacation, I cannot find any effective remedy.[16]

Arbitrator McDermott rejected the union's request that each grievant be given another extended vacation at a time of his own choosing financed by the employer.

In a 1958 case, Umpire Ralph Seward also denied a union request for monetary damages where vacations had been accelerated to avoid layoffs. Umpire Seward reasoned as follows:

> The complaint in these grievances was not against a *denial* of vacations; it was concerned entirely with the *dates* on which the grievants were required to *take* their vacations. And though the grievants may justly feel that—because of the change in dates—their vacations in 1957 were less happy and enjoyable than they otherwise would have been, the Umpire does not see how he can hold that they had no vacations at all or how—for

---

[15]Harlo Prods., 59 LA 613, 620–621 (Howlett, 1972); Interstate Indus., 46 LA 879 (Howlett, 1966) (fixing of vacation period); Huebsch Originators, 47 LA 635 (Merrill, 1966) (no specific relief awarded absent request for remedy by union).
[16]Pittsburgh Steel Co., 42 LA 1002, 1008 (1964).

that matter—he can assign a monetary value to the grievants' mental discomfort.[17]

Although the arbitrator declined to award damages, he did point out that the employer's actions in accelerating the vacations were taken in the good-faith belief that the contract permitted such action—a belief to which the union had contributed by its failure to protest such accelerations in the past. Arbitrator Seward made it clear that in cases of "repeat" violations, deliberately forcing an employee to take an accelerated vacation, an award of back pay would be appropriate.[18]

Arbitrator Rolf Valtin similarly found no effective remedy where employees were forced to take one week of vacation during a period of work shortages. Rejecting the union's claim for another week of vacation with full vacation pay, at a time of their choice, Valtin declared:

> As to "another week of vacation," the reality of the situation is that, at the time of the writing of this decision, the 1959 vacation year is over. It is clearly not for the Arbitrator to order that the vacation year be elongated. The most that he could hold is that the grievants be reimbursed a week's vacation pay in lieu of taking a vacation. Even this, however, would be "too much." As a result of the Agreement violation here found, the grievants did *not* lose a week's vacation pay—for there is no disputing the fact that they could not have worked on their scheduled Iron Powder Plant operations during the week in question.[19]

Still, the arbitrator found that the employees did lose "whatever they would have been entitled to had they been laid off from their jobs." Valtin noted that the record did not reveal whether the grievants would have been laid off "to the streets" or merely demoted to other jobs. The parties were accordingly directed to "reconstruct the situation as best they can," paying each grievant the sum to which he would have been entitled had there been a layoff.[20]

One arbitrator has characterized a monetary award for

---

[17]Bethlehem Steel Co., 31 LA 857, 858, cited in Bethlehem Steel Corp., supra note 2, at 225.

[18]31 LA at 858.

[19]Alan Wood Steel Co., 33 LA 772, 775 (1960).

[20]Id. at 775. But see Bethlehem Steel Co., 37 LA 821, 823–824 (Valtin, 1919) (vacation pay appropriate with past awards under similar contract where employer failed to give employee first choice of vacation, and failed to offer employee second opportunity to state preference).

improper changing of vacations as "punitive" in nature and, accordingly, refused to award a remedy of additional vacation pay:

> The union asserts that the remedy in this case should be additional vacation pay for all those employees who took their vacations at the time scheduled by the company under the pressure of the company.
>
> The legal principles concerning damages and remedies, however, cannot justify any such remedy. The company correctly says adopting the proposed remedy would be a punitive rather than a compensatory matter. . . .
>
> The short answer concerning damages in this case is that no damage has been shown. The board of arbitration has no power to award damages where damage has not been shown.[21]

Arbitrator Walter Kaufman similarly denied a monetary remedy in *Southern California Permanente Medical Group*,[22] although he found that management improperly denied an employee a vacation day to prepare for a trip to her daughter's graduation. Rejecting a request for an additional vacation day to compensate for the day she was unreasonably denied, the arbitrator pointed out that the violation was not "willful" and there was no evidence of any financial loss.[23]

E. Awards of Vacation Days and "Punitive" Remedies

The Eighth Circuit, reflecting the better view on the subject, has spoken on the issue whether an award of additional vacation days is a "punitive" award not subject to enforcement. In *Electrical Workers (UE) Local 1139 v. Litton Systems*,[24] management forced employees to either work during a plant shutdown (for taking of inventory), or to take their vacations at a time not provided for in the parties' agreement. The arbitrator ordered Litton to grant all employees who were improperly required to take their vacations a second vacation

---

[21]ACF Indus., 39 LA 1051, 1057 (Williams, 1962). Accord Lucky Stores, supra note 6 (no authority to issue punitive sanction); Pittsburgh Steel Co., supra note 16, at 1008 (no punitive remedy); Philip Carey Mfg. Co., supra note 10 (employees not entitled to one week's pay as "punitive" damages for "inconvenience" resulting from employer's designation of plant shutdown as vacation period in violation of contract).
[22]90 LA 900 (1988).
[23]See also Town of Hamberg, 73 LA 906 (Denson, 1979) (sustaining grievance but not ordering monetary remedy).
[24]728 F.2d 970, 115 LRRM 2633 (8th Cir. 1984).

with pay. The district court had agreed that a second vacation should be granted, but refused to enforce that portion of the award directing that the second vacation should be a paid vacation. Reversing the lower court, the court of appeals, in a split decision, stated that it could not say "that that arbitrator clearly exceeded his authority or violated the collective-bargaining agreement, when he resolved doubts as to the remedy against the party that had broken its promise."[25]

A different result, however, was reached by the Fourth Circuit. In *Westinghouse Electric Corp. v. Electrical Workers (IBEW) Local 1805*,[26] the appellate court ruled that the arbitrator exceeded his authority in awarding three additional days of paid vacation for employer's failure to provide sufficient time for negotiating with the union concerning its contractually permitted shutdown for vacations. The court found that the conduct was neither willful nor wanton, and the employees did not suffer any monetary loss, inconvenience, or hardship due to employer's infraction. In the court's view, "with respect to vacation shutdowns, compensatory damages may be awarded only when a breach of the bargaining agreement causes a monetary loss." The court found that "[t]hough nominally compensatory, the award was actually punitive."[27]

F. Summary

Apart from unemployment compensation losses, most claims arising out of rescheduled vacation periods are for nonmonetary losses, such as inconvenience to employees. Absent special circumstances, such as the case where a rescheduling is made with full knowledge that the agreement is being violated, the better view is not to award monetary damages for the mere inconvenience of employees. This view is best supported by an analogy offered by Arbitrator Lewis Gill:

> I think it can hardly be doubted that an employee who is fired from his job is subjected to much greater "inconvenience," to put it mildly, than an employee who is forced to take his vacation at a time not of his own choosing. The uncertainty

---

[25]Id. 115 LRRM at 2634.
[26]561 F.2d 521, 96 LRRM 2084 (4th Cir. 1977).
[27]Id. 96 LRRM at 2085, 2086.

about his future status, the worry over whether a serious blot on his record will be removed, the problem of keeping financially afloat while his case is being adjudicated (presumably with no unemployment compensation payments to cushion him in the meantime)—these matters and others all add up to a vastly more impressive catalogue of inconvenience and hardship than anything we are talking about here. And yet it has never to my knowledge been the practice to go beyond back pay for actual loss of wages in fashioning a remedy for unjust discharges.

. . .

[T]here is no established concept of which I am aware to the effect that contract violations involving no monetary loss to employees are to be remedied by payments based on inconvenience or designed as punitive damages.[28]

The arbitrator does state, however, that this view would be different in a case where an employer is shown to be engaging in deliberate or repeated violations, relying on the absence of any effective remedy. The authors feel that in such a case an arbitrator may appropriately award monetary compensation, since the employee did not receive the vacation required by the agreement and the remedy is designed to accomplish more than merely compensate inconvenience.[29]

---

[28]Philip Carey Mfg. Co., supra note 10, at 136.

[29]See the related discussion of Feller, *The Remedy Power in Grievance Arbitration*, 5 Indus. Rel. L.J. 128, 141–142 (1982) (arguing that awards refusing to compel management to provide, in effect, two paid vacations, or pay in lieu thereof, depart from traditional judicial relief for breach of contract where willful breaches have not been distinguished from other breaches).

Chapter 17

Promotion Decisions

A. Introduction

A survey of collective bargaining agreements made by The Bureau of National Affairs, Inc., indicates that seniority[1] provisions are found in 91 percent of contracts. Seniority is assigned a role in determining promotions in 74 percent of the contracts. Of these, seniority is the sole factor for determining promotions in 5 percent of the agreements. In 43 percent of the contracts, seniority is the determining factor if the employee is qualified for the job ("sufficient ability" clauses). Twenty-five percent of the agreements provide that seniority will be a secondary factor to be considered where other factors are equal ("relative ability" clauses). Seniority is given equal consideration with other factors in determining promotions in only three of the 400 contracts sampled.[2] One area of controversy involves the appropriate remedy to be applied for breach of the promotion-transfer provisions of the collective bargaining agreement.

---

[1]The term "seniority" is commonly understood to mean the length of service with the employer or in some division of the enterprise. With few exceptions, seniority rights derive their scope and significance exclusively from union contracts. Accordingly, employees have no inherent, constitutional, or natural right to seniority. For a comprehensive treatment of the subject, see Healy, *The Factor of Ability in Labor Relations*, in Arbitration Today, Proceedings of the 8th Annual Meeting, National Academy of Arbitrators, 45 (BNA Books, 1955). See generally Hill and Sinicropi, Management Rights: A Legal and Arbitral Analysis, 350–369 (BNA Books, 1986).
[2]Basic Patterns in Union Contracts, 12th ed., 86–88 (BNA Books, 1989).

B. Relative-Ability Clauses

Under this type of seniority provision, seniority is the determining factor only if the qualifications of competing employees are "relatively" equal. The question of "relative ability" involves comparing competing employees on all the qualities that indicate capacity to perform the work at issue. Some examples of relative ability clauses include:

> Promotions of employees within the Bargaining Unit shall be made on the basis of the necessary qualifications to perform the work, and seniority. If qualifications to perform the work of the job classification are considered equal, the senior employee shall be given preference.[3]
>
> Seniority, ability and efficiency are considered and so long as ability and efficiency are reasonably equal, then seniority shall apply to all promotions in the prevailing lines of progression.[4]
>
> It is understood and agreed that in all cases of: (A) promotion . . . the following factors as listed below shall be considered; however, only where factors "b" and "c" are relatively equal shall length of continuous service be the determining factor:
> a. Continuous service.
> b. Ability to perform work.
> c. Physical fitness.[5]

The reported cases indicate that management has the responsibility of making the initial determination as to which employee is better qualified and awarding that employee the position. However, unless otherwise limited by the parties' agreement, management's decision is subject to challenge through the grievance-arbitration procedure.

When comparing two employees under a "relative ability" clause, Arbitrator D.L. Howell reflected the thinking of most arbitrators when he stated that,

> Even with the use of tests, one must be mindful that a seniority clause is being construed, which is intended to grant certain preferences to the senior employee. This comparison is at best inexact. Human beings are different and cannot be inspected and measured as finished products from the assembly line. Doubt must be resolved in favor of the senior employee. The words "relative ability" do not suggest exactness or absolute equality.

---

[3]ARO, 69-2 ARB ¶8466 (Boothe, 1969).
[4]Gulf States Paper Corp., 68-1 ARB ¶8260 (Hardy, 1967).
[5]Interlake Steel Corp., 46 LA 23 (Luskin, 1965). See also Erie Mining Co., 49 LA 390 (Dworkin, 1967); Mead Corp., 68-1 ARB ¶8075 (Volz, 1967).

An approximate or near equality is sufficient. Since the nod is to be given to the senior in close cases, it is usually held by arbitrators that the junior must demonstrate more than slight superiority. His greater ability should be clearly discernible to outweigh the factor of seniority.[6]

This principle is also termed the "head and shoulders" rule. That is, other considerations equal, unless an employee is proved by management to be "head and shoulders" above the senior employee in ability, the employee is not entitled to a promotion under a "relative ability" clause. Similar standards include "substantially and demonstrably superior," "significantly, measurably and demonstrably greater," or "measurably and substantially superior."[7] Even under a "head and shoulders" rule, the nature of the job is a key variable influencing the thinking of many arbitrators. Comparative ability plays a greater role in the higher-skilled jobs and in these disputes a "slight" edge in a junior employee's ability may normally suffice.

Similarly, when the seniority provision at issue uses the terms "equal" or "relatively equal," ability need not be exactly equal for the seniority factor to be operative.[8] Still, in absence of qualifying language in the parties' agreement, arbitrators have applied the ability factor differently in promotion cases than to movements down the scale. Harry Edwards points out that there may be a presumption that employees in the upper level jobs can always perform the lower-classified work:

> [I]t is important to recall that seniority does not always apply comparably in all kinds of job movements. Thus, for example, seniority may be a more weighty factor in job movements downward than in promotion situations. If the employing enterprise has a relatively narrow upward path of jobs and employees at the upper end of the job progression generally are able to perform the work in jobs below them, the parties may rely on seniority alone for regression and layoffs. In other words, there is a convenient presumption that employees in the upper level jobs can always perform lower level work.[9]

---

[6]Screw Conveyor Corp., 72 LA 434, 436–437 (1979). See also Lancaster School Dist., 72 LA 693 (Raymond, undated); British Overseas Airways Corp., 61 LA 768, 769 (Turkus, 1973).
[7]Mountain States Tel. & Tel. Co., 70 LA 729, 741 (Goodman, 1978).
[8]See the review of case authority by Arbitrator Roger Tilbury in Washington County, Or., 78 LA 1081, 1085 (1982).
[9]Edwards, *Seniority Systems in Collective Bargaining*, Arbitration in Practice, 129 (Cornell Univ., ILR Press, 1984).

Another well-known arbitrator, James Hill, noted that "[i]t was a general viewpoint and experience that the competitive standard applies to promotions, while capacity to do the work applies in down-grading and transfers associated with layoff," but again, "it all depends on the particular agreement at issue."[10]

The remedy problems in this area are illustrated by reference to a decision by Arbitrator Peter Kelliher. In *Sun Chemical Corp.*,[11] the collective bargaining agreement provided that in the matter of permanent promotions or transfers, the employer shall, in evaluating candidates, consider the following factors: plant seniority; ability to learn the job; physical fitness and condition; past performance record; and attendance record. The contract further stated that, in making the selection from among qualified candidates, "if the above mentioned factors are relatively equal then plant seniority shall be controlling." The three employees who applied for the job included C, who was awarded the position, and the grievant M, who was senior to C.

If it is found that employees C and M have relatively equal ability, what remedy should be applied? A review of the published decisions indicates that most arbitrators, upon finding a violation of the contract, will award the position to M, with back pay,[12] without recognizing that there may be problems with such a remedy if there were other employees senior to M with the same ability.

The difficulties in applying "relatively" or "substantially" equal provisions have been reported by Robert Gorske:

> For example, assume that employees A, B, C, and D have 20, 15, ten, and five years' seniority respectively. Assume, however,

---

[10]Hill, *Seniority and Ability: Workshop No. 1: Summary*, in Management Rights and the Arbitration Process, Proceedings of the 9th Annual Meeting, National Academy of Arbitrators, 44, 46 (BNA Books, 1956).

[11]69-2 ARB ¶8642 (1969).

[12]See, e.g., County of Stearns, 90 LA 1181 (Kapsch, 1988); Ralph M. Parsons Co., 69 LA 290 (Rule, 1977); British Overseas Airways Corp., 61 LA 768 (Turkus, 1973); Sun Chem. Corp., supra note 11; City of Fond Du Lac, 69-2 ARB ¶8520 (Moberly, 1969); Pacific Press & Shear Corp., 69-1 ARB ¶8422 (Davey, 1969) (next opportunity for senior grievant); Orgill Bros. & Co., 68-1 ARB ¶8301 (Williams, 1968); Mead Corp., supra note 5; United States Plywood, 67-2 ARB ¶8528 (Jones, 1967); Bemis Co., 66-2 ARB ¶8513 (Moore, 1966); Patterson Steel Co., 66-3 ARB ¶8949 (Logan, 1966); National Steel & Ship Bld., 61-3 ARB ¶8762 (West, 1961). See also Tobacco Workers Local 317 v. P. Lorillard Corp., 448 F.2d 949, 78 LRRM 2273 (4th Cir. 1971) (sustaining award of retroactive pay for employees who were not properly awarded job vacancy).

that C has the greatest merit, ability and capacity, that B ranks next, and that A and D are relatively equal in these respects, or in lack of these respects. Clearly, an erroneous promotion of D is a violation of the labor agreement. However, suppose that A is the only one who files a grievance, and suppose that the union takes A's case to arbitration. The arbitrator, of course, will find a contract violation pointing out that as between the two there is relative equality of merit, ability and capacity, and that A is the senior. However, what should his award be?[13]

Gorske argues that many arbitrators will order the employer to replace D with A and to issue appropriate back pay. This remedy, however, may be inappropriate since employee C would clearly win out over A. An alternative remedy, and one adopted by arbitrators,[14] both in the private and public sector, is to order the wrongful promotion set aside, with directions to management to fill the vacancy consistent with the labor agreement.

There is merit in the argument that an aggrieved employee must fail in his claim for promotion unless it can be demonstrated that he, as an individual, was entitled to the job by the terms of the collective bargaining agreement. In many instances, this requirement of proof is not satisfied merely by showing that the grievant was superior to the employee promoted, for there are other considerations that must be taken into account in formulating a remedy. Gorske reasons as follows:

> First of all, unless the employer's rights of allocating the work force and of hiring from the outside to fill vacancies have been relevantly restricted in the collective agreement, it is readily apparent that the position wrongfully filled could have been filled in a number of ways, consistently with the labor agreement but not involving the aggrieved, though his superiority to the actual transferred employee is unquestioned. . . .
>
> Second, the fact that the aggrieved has been found by the arbitrator to be equal or superior to the promoted employee is certainly insufficient to show an essential fact—that is, that he is superior to the other by-passed employees in the unit of consideration for promotion.[15]

---

[13]Gorske, *Arbitration Back-Pay Awards*, 10 Lab. L.J. 18, 23–24 (1959).

[14]See, e.g., ARO, supra note 3; Gulf States Paper Corp., 68-1 ARB ¶8260 (Hardy, 1967); National Distillers Co., 49 LA 918, 920–921 (Volz, 1967) (rejecting argument that qualifications of senior bidder are to be matched against requirements of job and are not to be compared with qualifications of other bidders).

[15]Gorske, supra note 13, at 23.

Gorske goes on to argue that it should not matter that the other employees have "waived" their rights to the promotion by failing to file a grievance. The employer also has the right, recognized in the agreement, to promote qualified junior employees and to pass over unqualified employees in the exercise of its contractual rights. He further points out that if the arbitrator, after finding a contract violation, directs the employer to promote the grievant, the union and not the employer becomes the selector of promotees in all cases where the company has made an error in its original selection.[16]

C. Sufficient-Ability Clauses

"Sufficient ability" clauses require management to assign, promote, or retain the employee with the longest continuous service if the employee is qualified to perform the job. The fact that the junior employee is more qualified is of no effect. In cases involving sufficient ability clauses, most arbitrators place the burden on the employer to show that the bypassed senior employee is not competent. As pointed out by Judge Harry Edwards, where the work at issue is of semi-skilled or low-skilled nature, a sufficient ability standard is virtually the same as a straight seniority approach.[17] Examples of "sufficient" or "mere ability" clauses include:

> If in a department an opening or vacancy occurs in a classification, which has a classification grade below it in the same group, then the opening or vacancy shall be filled by an employee from the next lower classification grade, provided each employee has the ability to do the work.[18]
> Promotions, assignments and displacements under these articles shall be based on seniority, fitness and ability; fitness and ability being sufficient, seniority shall prevail.[19]
> The Company subscribes generally to the principle of seniority; that is, the oldest employee in length of service, if qualified, shall be entitled to priority in promotions and other seniority rights and privileges, including the right to more desirable jobs within the same classification.[20]

---

[16]Id. at 24.
[17]Edwards, supra note 9, at 126.
[18]Baker, American Platinum & Silver, 67-1 ARB ¶8011, at 3037 (Trotta, 1967).
[19]Northwest Airlines, 46 LA 238, 239 (Elkouri, 1966).
[20]Continental Oil Co., 8 LA 170, 171 (Carmichael, 1947).

> Seniority shall govern and control all cases of promotion, demotion, permanent, non-rotating shift assignment, layoffs, recall or new jobs within the bargaining unit, providing the employee is qualified to perform the work.[21]

In the case where the collective bargaining agreement mandates that seniority shall control in promotions or assignments if an employee is shown to have the mere ability to perform the job, a grievance by the most senior employee in the relevant job classification should not preclude the arbitrator from ordering the grievant to be promoted where it is shown that the employer improperly promoted a junior employee.[22] Similarly, under a minimal-ability provision an arbitrator may properly order a single grievant placed in a position improperly awarded to a junior employee, even though the aggrieved is not the most senior employee in the relevant classification.[23] In such a case the question before the arbitrator is whether the grievant is merely capable of performing the job in question. A finding that the grievant is qualified should entitle him to the position, absent evidence that a nongrieving employee desires the job. The better rule in this respect is that once a grievant has established that he is entitled to a job by virtue of seniority the burden shifts to the employer to establish that other employees more senior to the grievant desire to be placed in the position.

Where multiple grievants challenge the promotion of a single employee under a "sufficient" or "mere ability" clause, the arbitrator is left with the problem of drafting a remedy once it has been determined that the agreement was violated. One option is to award the position to the most senior qualified employee, or alternatively, to direct the employer to offer the position to the most senior grievant. The latter approach was used by Arbitrator Lennart Larson, in *Mack Trucks*,[24] where 10 employees, all senior to the individual improperly pro-

---

[21]Southwest Airmotive Co., 41 LA 353, 357 (Elliott, 1963).

[22]See, e.g., Cook County, Ill., Oak Forrest Hosp., 90 LA 905, 910 (Wolff, 1988) (ordering employee promoted under sufficient ability provision; back pay computed as difference between what was earned on old job and what he would have earned in new position); Turbine Support Div., 73-2 ARB ¶8618 (Fox, 1974); North Am. Philips Co., 69-2 ARB ¶8561 (Hogan, 1968); Hughes Aircraft Co., 43 LA 1248 (Block, 1965).

[23]Warner Cable of Akron, 91 LA 48 (Bittel, 1988).

[24]55 LA 813 (1970).

moted, filed grievances requesting that the employer be directed to promote the senior qualified individual. The arbitrator, holding that only five of the ten were qualified (some more than others), directed only that the employer offer the job to one of the employees in order of their seniority and pay the selected employee retroactive pay.[25]

Arbitrator William P. Murphy, in an unreported decision, considered the situation where other nongrieving employees were more senior than two unit employees who had filed grievances protesting the promotion of a junior employee. The employer argued that, even if the arbitrator held that the promotion of a junior employee was improper, neither of the grievants was entitled to a remedy because there were nongrieving employees who were more senior than the grievants; thus an award to either of them would be a "windfall." The union argued that, even though the grievants would not have received the position originally, they were the only ones who had filed a grievance. In holding for the union, the arbitrator declared that the grieving employees were not disqualified as beneficiaries of an award:

> There is no doubt that they [the grievants] were senior to X [the junior employee], there is no doubt on their employment records that they were qualified for the Utility-man job, there is no doubt that they had standing to file the grievance. While it may be true that an award in their favor would be a windfall, the alternative is to permit improper conduct to go unremedied. It should also be noted that cases like this are brought not only to obtain individual relief but to vindicate the principle of seniority which is involved.[26]

The above award aside, in many instances it may be improper for an arbitrator to direct an employer to promote a successful grievant, especially where the employer has noted concern that other employees, although nongrievants, have greater claim to the position. The better rule would appear to be if it is established that the senior grievant is more entitled to the job than the junior employee, the senior grievant is

---

[25]Interstate Metal Prods., 38 LA 1072 (Howlett, 1962) (reposting of job ordered where nongrieving employees could possibly have qualified for position improperly awarded to junior employee).

[26]See Employer (name deleted by request) and Machinists (1978), as cited in Teple and Moberly, Arbitration and Conflict Resolution, 270 (BNA Books, 1979).

presumptively entitled to the position, absent a bona fide showing that other employees should be considered in the promotion decision, as outlined in the agreement.

D. Improper Evaluation or Failure to Consider an Employee for Promotion

What is the remedy where management performs an improper evaluation and another employee is awarded the contested position? Suppose an employer simply fails to consider an employee for promotion or transfer? Arbitrator Robben Fleming has addressed this problem as follows:

> Suppose the contract provides, as it frequently does, that the senior man shall receive the promotion provided that he has the qualifications for the job. When the company fails to promote the senior man a grievance is filed and the issue ultimately comes to arbitration. At the hearing considerable evidence is adduced to show that the senior man was interviewed and carefully considered, but that in the judgment of management he did not have the qualifications. Having concluded that the senior man could not qualify, the company, according to its evidence, looked elsewhere and finally found the man who was given the job. When it comes time for the union to present its evidence, it calls, as a hostile witness, the man who got the job. He then testifies that he was in fact offered the job some time before the company evidence shows that it interviewed the senior applicant. Finally, the senior man takes the stand and it is proven to the satisfaction of the arbitrator that he does not have the qualifications for the job.[27]

In summary, at issue is (1) a "mere ability" clause; (2) with the senior applicant not fairly evaluated or considered for the job, since it was offered to the junior employee before the senior employee was considered—if he ever was; and (3) the senior person, on the evidence presented, is unqualified for the position.

Fleming notes that, on substantially the above facts, he ruled that the grievant was not entitled to the job, but that because he had been denied a fair opportunity to prove his qualifications until the date of the arbitration, he was entitled to be paid at the higher rate from the time the job was filled

---

[27]Fleming, *Arbitrators and the Remedy Power*, 48 Va. L. Rev. 1199, 1218–1219 (1962).

to the date of the arbitration. In defense of this remedy, Arbitrator Fleming points out the conflicting considerations at issue in this type of case:

> The grievant was not qualified for the job. Since he was not qualified he could not have been damaged by being denied a job to which he was entitled only if qualified. What appears to have been an unfair procedure on the part of the company may, in fact, only have reflected intimate knowledge of the grievant gained in day-to-day contacts without going through the formal interview process except in a perfunctory manner. And even if there was bad faith it is regrettable but none of the arbitrator's business. On the other hand, one can argue that the grievant, though not qualified, was entitled by contract to a fair opportunity for the job. Since management has the initiative in making promotions and its decision is entitled to respect, the process of decision making must be free of doubt. The more traditional remedy of vacating the job was not applicable since the grievant was now proven not qualified. Penalizing the company for improper procedure might have the effect of forcing good faith compliance with the contract in the future, and this is what the parties bargained for.[28]

Case law indicates that charges of procedural infirmities surrounding a promotion or transfer decision are not uncommon. Where it is not clear that the grievant would have been selected but for the improper evaluation, a common remedy is to declare the position vacant and order management to reevaluate all candidates.[29]

Should the arbitrator credit arguments that an improper transfer should not be remedied by ordering the grievant placed in the position because it will result in the displacement of the incumbent? The general assumption is that an arbitration award will result in moving the incumbent to the status he would have occupied absent violation of the agreement.[30] Accordingly, where a clear violation is found, arguments in-

---

[28]Id. at 1219–1220.

[29]See, e.g., Montana Dep't of Highways, 91 LA 766, 772 (Corbett, 1988) (declaring position vacant and ordering reevaluation of candidates; no back pay where it was not clear that grievant would have been awarded position had proper procedure been followed); Michigan State Employees Ass'n, 90 LA 413, 423 (Borland, 1987) (discussing remedy for department's failure to consider grievant for special assignment). See also Miller Brewing v. Brewery Workers Local 9, 739 F.2d 1159, 1163, 116 LRRM 3130 (7th Cir. 1984) (vacating remedy ordering employer to hire 39 former employees for management's violation of hiring preference clause).

[30]Jefferson Smurfit Corp., 91 LA 41 (Abrams, 1988).

volving the impact on incumbent employees should be given little, if any, weight.

Is a reevaluation remedy illusory or does it have some substantive utility? Arbitrator Dennis Nolan, in a 1988 unpublished decision involving a dispute between a federal agency and its union, ruled that management could not dismiss an employee for an inaccurate but not deceptive job application (the grievant mischaracterized a prior criminal conviction in his job application) but that it could reevaluate the application in light of newly discovered facts, provided it did so in complete good faith. Concluding that if it had known the facts it would not have hired the employee in the first place, management reinstated the grievant with back pay (as the arbitrator ordered), but terminated him as soon as the new decision was made. The union returned the case to the arbitrator pursuant to his retention of jurisdiction.

In determining that the reevaluation was made in "good faith," Arbitrator Nolan reasoned that the union offered no evidence suggesting that the procedure and judgment of the evaluator was anything less than professional. Nolan pointed out that the decision was made by a person who "was far away from those involved in the first decision, and by someone who had had no prior connection with the Grievant." The arbitrator also found it significant that before making up its mind management consulted with several other experienced labor relations persons, all of whom reached the same conclusion. Satisfied that the decision was reasonable and made in good faith, the second grievance was denied.

E. Promotion in the Federal Sector

On October 13, 1978, President Jimmy Carter signed into law the Civil Service Reform Act of 1978 (CSRA) which, as stated by one arbitrator, "almost makes the Constitution look simple."[31] The law, which went into effect January 11, 1979, split the Civil Service Commission into two bodies: The Office of Personnel Management (OPM) and the Merit Systems Pro-

---

[31]Nolan, *Federal Sector Labor Arbitration: Differences, Problems, Cures*, 14 Pepperdine L. Rev. 805, 807 (1987).

tection Board (MSPB). The Act further provided that any grievance not satisfactorily settled under the negotiated procedure be subject to binding arbitration. Further, the Act provided that removals for performance or conduct may be submitted to binding arbitation if such a provision is included in the parties' labor agreement. Exceptions to awards may be taken to the Federal Labor Relations Authority (FLRA), and awards involving performance removals or adverse actions may be taken to the Court of Appeals for the Federal Circuit.[32] The statute provides for FLRA review only to determine if an award is deficient as contrary to law, rule, or regulation, or deficient on other grounds similar to those applied by federal courts in private-sector labor relations.[33]

The parties to a negotiated contract in the federal sector are permitted to include in that agreement a provision mandating arbitration of grievances. A 1977 report by the U.S. Civil Service Commission[34] and recent studies[35] lists promotions as the issue most frequently addressed in federal sector arbitrations. As reported by the Commission, a series of decisions issued by the Federal Labor Relations Council articulate some of the limits of arbitral authority to order corrective remedies when an arbitrator finds that such action is appropriate. These constraints are summarized as follows:

1. An agency may not be constrained to select a particular candidate from a promotion certificate as a corrective action. The only exception to this is when it has been demonstrated that the candidate would have been promoted but for the violation of law, regulation, or negotiated agreement that occurred. Under these circumstances, the promotion should be made retroactive and the employee accorded back pay.
2. An agency may be required to reconstruct or reprocess a promotion action in which an error or violation has occurred. The position(s) should not be vacated or any previously successful candidate(s) removed in advance of the reconstruction unless it has been determined that, absent the violation found

---

[32]5 U.S.C. §7121 (1982).

[33]5 U.S.C. §7122(a)(1)–(2).

[34]Grievance Arbitration in the Federal Service (U.S. Civil Serv. Comm'n, July 1977).

[35]Charles Feigenbaum reports that during the years 1980–1984, the total number of federal-sector arbitration awards received was 3,966. Slightly more than 25% of the total (1,007) involved promotion actions. Feigenbaum, *Arbitrating Promotion Actions*, in Grievance Arbitration in the Federal Service, 281 (Federal Personnel Management Inst., 1987).

by the arbitrator, the incumbent could not have been considered or selected. When such a determination has not been made, the incumbent must be allowed to compete in the second round and no action should be taken with regard to him/her until the results of that competition are known. The arbitrator may limit reconsideration to those candidates who were eligible for consideration or selection when the initial action was taken. In conducting the reconstruction, neither the successful candidate nor the other competitors may be selected. If the incumbent is not reselected, he/she must be removed from the position by a method to be determined by the agency in accordance with law, regulations and negotiated agreements.

3. While an arbitrator can order a re-running of the promotion action with consideration limited to those who could have been selected had the violation not taken place, the arbitrator cannot order the selection of a candidate from the second referral list since that order would abridge management's right to non-select.

4. Unless the agency limits its discretion through regulation or negotiated agreement, it cannot be ordered by an arbitrator to offer a position at a particular grade even when the position is advertised at multiple grade levels.

5. An arbitrator may rule on a prospective non-competitive promotion provided such promotion is directly related to the injury sustained and is conditioned upon the meeting of relevant FPM [Federal Personnel Manual] requirements. For example if an arbitrator rules that an employee was wrongfully denied appointment to a trainee position, the arbitrator could order that the employee be placed in such position and be given the usual noncompetitive promotion upon completion of the training period, provided all relevant requirements are met.[36]

As noted, many of the principles established by arbitrators in the private sector have been applied when formulating remedies in the promotion area. Back pay, however, is not an appropriate remedy when a governmental agency, in violation of a contract, has failed to consider an employee for a promotion unless it can be said that "but for" the wrongful action, the employee would have received the promotion.

One researcher, in reviewing arbitration awards involving promotion issues, outlined in summary form the body of case law fashioned by the FLRA:

---

[36]Id. at 29–30.

1. An arbitrator may not require management to use a particular process to fill a position.
2. An arbitrator may not require management to make selections from among a certain group of employees.
3. An arbitrator may not require that a particular employee be selected for promotion, notwithstanding improper agency action, unless the arbitrator finds that the improper action was directly connected to (i.e., was the direct cause of) the failure of that employee to be selected.
4. An arbitrator's award may not violate the FPM [Federal Personnel Manual], even if the award is based on clear contract language.
5. An arbitrator may order that a person selected for promotion must vacate the position to which promoted, only if the arbitrator determines that the selectee could not have been selected properly for the promotion.
6. An arbitrator may not order the promotion of an employee, including a temporary promotion, if the employee does not meet the OPM minimum qualification requirements for the position.
7. An arbitrator's authority to order a retroactive promotion in cases where a promotion was delayed is limited to situations in which the delay occurred after an authorized official made the decision to promote.[37]

In summary, an arbitrator is permitted to award retroactive promotions with back pay where a direct, casual connection exists between a violation of a relevant law, regulation, or collective bargaining agreement and the nonpromotion of the employee. A common remedy is to order priority or special consideration for the next appropriate vacancy. Another remedy is to order an agency to vacate the selection when it is found that the process is defective and to order it to rerun the selection process.[38]

---

[37]Id. at 284–286.

[38]Department of Agric., 89 LA 35, 40 (Aronin, 1987) (ordering rerun of selection process for failure to consider grievant for promotion); Department of Labor, 85 LA 841 (Byars, 1985) (denying remedy where it could not be shown that grievant would have been selected but for management's action); National Weather Serv., 83 LA 689 (Gaunt, 1984) (discussing "harmful error" rule in removal case); United States Army, 78 LA 62 (Bernstein, 1982) (denying remedy where actual loss not demonstrated); Library of Congress, 79 LA 158, 163 (Mullin, 1982) (ordering vacation of position and reposting); Mine Safety & Health Admin., 74 LA 741 (Dean, 1980) (ordering transfer); Internal Revenue Serv., 71 LA 1018, 1021 (Harkless, 1978) (finding violation but denying remedy where individual grievants not damaged).

See generally Ferris, *Federal Sector Promotion Remedies: Rambo's Newest Challenge*, in Grievance Arbitration in the Federal Service, supra note 35, at 263.

Chapter 18

Remedies for Mistake

A. Introduction

Professor Robert Hillman, in his text on contract remedies, writes:

> One of the more confusing areas of remedial law involves
> the remedies available for mistake. The confusion stems par-
> tially from the fact that the threshold question—has a mistake
> been made—is not always easily determined. In addition, there
> are many types of mistakes which can arise in various stages
> of a transaction. The remedies vary depending on the type of
> mistake and the stage of the transaction.[1]

So, too, in labor-management relations. While the number
of reported mistake cases is not large, it is well established that
arbitrators have encountered problems where claims of "mistake" are at issue. A review of arbitration awards and of the
literature indicates that with respect to genuine issues of mistake, the law of contracts has been influential, if not controlling,
in the arbitration of collective bargaining contracts where issues
of mistake are alleged.[2]

---

[1]Hillman, Contract Remedies, Equity, and Restitution, 105 (Iowa Law School,
1979).
[2]Goetz, *The Law of Contracts—A Changing Legal Environment: Comment*, in
Truth, Lie Detectors, and Other Problems in Labor Arbitration: Proceedings of the
31st Annual Meeting, National Academy of Arbitrators, 218, 224–225 (BNA Books,
1979).

B. What Is a Mistake?

A bona fide issue of mistake should not be confused with ignorance, inability, or poor judgment. An arbitrator should not grant relief merely because one of the parties feels that the contract is a "bad deal" or that it "made a mistake" or exercised "bad judgment" in agreeing to a particular contractual provision.

Likewise, mistake should be distinguished from the concept of misunderstanding. This problem, generally arising in contract formation, involves faulty communication between the parties, so that each one reasonably believes that the contract is different in material respect. Arbitrator Raymond Goetz notes that problems of misunderstanding are not uncommon in labor negotiations and provides the following example of how principles of contract law may be helpful to the arbitrator:

> In a recent case involving the Internal Revenue Service and the National Treasury Employees Union, the issue was the meaning of the term "Office of the District Director," as used in the last step of the grievance procedure to designate the managerial participant at that step. During the negotiations, the union was under the impression that this meant the individual holding the office of district director or assistant director. The agency, on the other hand, intended it to include any person clothed with the authority of the office of the district director, and assumed that the district director or assistant director did not have to be present personally. When the agency presented this language in writing as a compromise proposal, it offered no explanation or illustration of what was meant, and the union asked for none. Evidence of bargaining history was fairly convincing that in the negotiations each side subjectively had the intention argued for in the arbitration, but neither one had clearly manifested that intention outwardly to the other. The words themselves seemed reasonably susceptible to either interpretation.[3]

Arbitrator Goetz, searching for a way out of this predicament, turned to the rule on misunderstanding in the *Restatement* (Second) of Contracts. The rule, as stated in Section 227 of the *Restatement*, provides in essence that the term is to be interpreted according to the meaning attached to it by one of the parties if that party had no reason to know of any

---

[3]Id. at 225–226.

different meaning attached to it by the other, and the other did not have reason to know the meaning attached by the first party. Applying this rule, Goetz concluded that the agency's interpretation should prevail, since the union should have realized that the agency did not intend the restricted meaning ascribed by the union.

This rule was applied by Arbitrator William Corbett in *Potlatch Corp.*[4] In that case the parties' contract provided that "[e]mployees will be paid for hours worked on three (3) designated days within an announced shutdown period as they would normally be paid for hours worked on July 3, 4 and 5." When rotating shift employees claimed double time for work performed during the three-day shutdown, management argued that the language is limited to day maintenance employees, not rotating shift employees. Sustaining the grievance, the arbitrator reasoned that the fact that the company intended the language to apply only to one classification does not make the language ambiguous. In the arbitrator's words:

> A well-accepted principle of contract interpretation is that it "is incumbent upon the proponent of a contract provision either to explain what is contemplated or to use language which does not leave the matter in doubt." . . .
> In the instant case the Company created the ambiguity. The Company proposed contract language that in its normal usage had one meaning, yet the Company intended a quite different meaning. The evidence supports the conclusion the Company did not adequately articulate that the other meaning was intended. Accordingly, the Union could not have agreed to the Company's intention. There was no mutuality between the parties regarding the meaning of [the language at issue]. The ambiguity created by the Company must be construed against it.[5]

Mistake differs from misunderstanding in that the latter involves a different assumption of facts, while a true mistake case deals with the parties operating under the same faulty assumption of facts. As stated by Professor Hillman:

> In misunderstanding cases, often a two-step analysis is made. First, was the term in the contract ambiguous to a reasonable person—that is, was the agreement objectively ambiguous? (There is no relief for a party whose own use of a term differs from

---

[4]88 LA 1184 (1987).
[5]Id. at 1187, quoting Elkouri and Elkouri, How Arbitration Works, 4th ed., 362 (BNA Books, 1985).

what is reasonably understood to be the usage of the term.)
Second, if the term was objectively ambiguous, did the parties
actually have different interpretations of the clause in mind?
The latter, a subjective test, when answered affirmatively, is
often explained by stating that there was no meeting of the
minds. When both questions are answered affirmatively, there
was a misunderstanding so that there was never a contract, and
mistake analysis need not be utilized.[6]

C. Proving a Mistake Has Been Made

In proving a bona fide mistake has taken place, the parol
evidence rule is often urged as a bar to crediting any evidence
that would contradict the parties' written agreement. It should
be recalled that parol evidence is any evidence, whether oral
or in writing, which is extrinsic to the written contract and
is not incorporated therein by reference.[7] The rule forbids the
use of extrinsic parol to "add to," "vary," or "alter" the written
agreement. This rule, however, should not properly operate
to bar evidence that a mistake was made, since parol evidence
is admissible even where an unambiguous, integrated, written
agreement is operative if there is a bona fide issue of fraud,
duress, or mistake.

Illustrative is *Town of North Haven*,[8] where Connecticut
Board of Mediation and Arbitration Chairman Howard Sacks
found no infirmity in crediting oral evidence against a claim
that the parol evidence operated to preclude consideration:

> Union has argued that we may not consider evidence (other
> than the contract itself) as to the intentions of the parties be-
> cause of the parol evidence rule. That rule states that, in in-
> terpreting a written contract, evidence of prior understandings
> and negotiations cannot be considered. However, it is elemen-
> tary law that parol evidence can be introduced and considered
> in cases of fraud, duress and mistake. (See *Williston on Contracts*
> (3rd Ed'n., Jaeger, 1961 at p. 948.) Since this is a case which
> might involve mistake, we are free to consider, and we do con-
> sider, evidence as to what happened during the negotiations.[9]

---

[6]Hillman, supra note 1, at 106–107.
[7]The parol evidence rule is covered at length in Hill and Sinicropi, Evidence in Arbitration, 2d ed., 335–337 (BNA Books, 1987).
[8]71 LA 983 (1978).
[9]Id. at 987.

Arbitrator Sacks declared that for the employer to prevail on a mistake theory, it must demonstrate, by clear and convincing evidence (not by the lower standard of "a preponderance of the evidence"), that there was a variance between the agreement reached by the parties during negotiations and what finally emerged in the written contract.

Arbitrator Goetz has similarly stated:

> It also is probably true that no arbitrator of sound mind needs such a rule or contractual limitation to keep from giving effect to evidence of a claimed oral agreement or understanding that would contradict the writing. Obviously, the later written expression should supersede earlier contradictory expressions on the same subject—whether oral or written. In the absence of mistake or something of that sort, few responsible unions or employers would even suggest such contradiction of the written agreement.[10]

D. Types of Mistakes

It is important to distinguish unilateral from mutual mistake, for arbitrators, like courts, will grant relief only in cases of mutual mistake. Absence evidence of fraud or deceit by a party, there is no remedy for a unilateral mistake.

1. Unilateral Mistake

A mistake is unilateral if only one party is in error as to the existence or nonexistence of a material fact. As a general rule, a person who makes a mistake to his own injury will be required to show that he was free from negligence before he can assert the invalidity of the agreement.

This principle was applied by Arbitrator Peter Seitz in *Kasser Distillers Products Corp.*,[11] where an employer, without checking any other sources, adopted an insurance plan based solely upon the union's cost estimates. When the company discovered that the true cost of the plan it agreed to implement was significantly greater than that quoted by the union, it refused to adopt the agreed-upon program. Arbitrator

---

[10]Goetz, supra note 2, at 222.
[11]69-1 ARB ¶8219 (1968).

Seitz, in ruling for the union, rejected the employer's argument that there was a "mutual mistake of fact" as to the cost of the plan. Attention is called to the arbitrator's reasoning:

> The Company in this case certainly made a mistake. Manifestly, it agreed to a health and welfare plan including dependents in its coverage under a miscalculation of its cost. But was this mistake and miscalculation made under circumstances which relieve it from the bargain it struck? Or is it bound by an improvident undertaking? The Company clearly was competent to deal with the subject matter of health and welfare funds, and even lacking the special technical expertise in insurance matters, it had the resources to obtain such services which are readily available.[12]

Arbitrator Seitz did note, however, that had the union deliberately misled the employer in the matter, a different result might have been reached. This view, of course, represents the general doctrine that if one of the parties knows, or should know, that the other is mistaken in his belief that certain facts exist, and enters into a contract taking advantage of the situation, the agreement will properly be rescinded.[13]

Similarly, in *Klein Tools*,[14] a dispute arose over the meaning of the term "actuarial cost" and whether management could increase the insurance rates during the term of the labor agreement. Ruling that the union is presumed to know the significance of the terms that are used in the labor agreement, the arbitrator pointed out that the union's argument is essentially one of mistake and, absent evidence of fraud or deceit, there could be no reformation of a collective bargaining agreement unless a mutual mistake were made.[15]

2. Mutual Mistake

A mistake is mutual when it is held by both contracting parties. In these cases the general rule in contract law has been that courts will provide relief for mutual mistake, but

---

[12]Id. at 3758.

[13]W.R. Grace & Co., 66 LA 517 (Hebert, 1976); United Drill & Tool Corp., 28 LA 677 (Cox, 1957). Cf. Calhoun Dry-Wall Co. v. Bernard, 333 F.2d 739, 56 LRRM 2392 (9th Cir. 1964).

[14]90 LA 1150 (Poindexter, 1988).

[15]See also Primeline Indus., 88 LA 700, 702 (Morgan, 1986) ("Union was mistaken in its understanding of the rule, but this . . . is a unilateral mistake and does not form a basis for a reformation of the rule").

not for unilateral mistake. To properly come within the rule, both parties must have contracted in the mistaken belief that certain material facts existed, and, as noted by Arbitrator Goetz, labor arbitrators have followed this doctrine.[16]

A true mutual-mistake situation was found by Arbitrator Clair Duff in *Overhead Door Corp.*[17] Where the record indicated that the parties had executed two different signed copies of a bargaining agreement, each having differing versions of a retirement plan, Arbitrator Duff ruled that this was a classic case of mutual mistake. Holding that no agreement was ever consummated, the issue was remanded back to the parties for bargaining.

Cases involving mutual mistake in the formation stage of a contract are rare. As stated by Arbitrator John Sembower:

> There are two other possible areas of contract interpretation which may be cited; those of so-called "unilateral mistake" and "mutual mistake." If it appears that the parties were so totally at variance that their minds did not meet, in effect, upon the matter at all, courts and arbitrators usually rule that the agreement is null and void. The doctrine is applied very restrictively, and usually in such bizarre instances as, say, when two men are discussing buying and selling an automobile, one thinks they are discussing the seller's Buick while the other is thinking of his Oldsmobile. Even this sometimes is not sufficient, if the mistaken inference seems to be entirely on one side—i.e., "unilateral mistake"—and there is no fraud or bad faith on the part of the other.[18]

As opposed to cases involving mistake in formation, cases dealing with mistake in integration involve situations where the parties have reached an agreement but, for whatever reason, the final integration does not reflect the true agreement reached. Both courts and arbitrators will generally grant relief in the form of reformation when it is demonstrated that what was agreed to in negotiations and what was written do not reflect the true intent of the parties. Such a remedy of reformation, however, must clearly be built on mutuality. As stated by Arbitrator Joseph Gentile in *Los Angeles Meat Co.*:[19]

---

[16]Goetz, supra note 2, at 225.
[17]61 LA 1229 (1973).
[18]Peoria Malleable Castings Co., 43 LA 722, 727 (1964).
[19]59 LA 1067 (1972).

It is well established that the remedy of reformation to correct a mistake in the agreement is a remedy utilized by arbitrators to resolve disputes. . . . However, it is equally clear that such a remedy must be built upon the foundation of mutuality. The party alleging that a mutual mistake has occurred in the drafting of a document has the burden of showing that both parties intended that the language read as alleged. It is not enough to show that one party intended the agreement to read as alleged.[20]

When management argued that the words "during working hours" were inadvertently omitted from the published contract and, thus, union representatives should not be paid the time spent adjusting grievances that extended beyond their regular working hours, Arbitrator Arvid Anderson, in *Jacobsen Manufacturing Co.*,[21] ruled that a contract, which by reason of a mutual mistake of the parties, does not express accurately the agreement consummated, could be reformed to reflect the true intention of the parties. According to Arbitrator Anderson, a collective bargaining relationship "would seem to give greater urgency to the need to relieve the parties of an agreement they didn't make." The mistake was mutual, said Anderson, "and neither party should be in a position to take advantage of any benefits to be derived from an error to which it was a party as much as anyone else." Arbitrator Anderson accordingly reformed the agreement to reflect what the parties had originally intended. He stated that to rule otherwise would place undue emphasis on the letter of the contract without regard to the intent of the parties. Such a result would, in turn, encourage sharp bargaining practices requiring the parties to be overly cautious in their bargaining efforts.[22]

Integration problems are found in *Town of North Haven*.[23] Arbitrator Howard Sacks ruled that an employer improperly refused to allow employees to take their vacations between December 21, 1978, and December 31, 1978, under a contract provision allowing employees to complete their vacations between January 1 and December 31 of each year. The employer

---

[20]Id. at 1071, citing Abex Corp., Railroad Prods. Group, & Steelworkers Local 1285, 70-2 ARB ¶8479 (Krimsly, 1970).
[21]43 LA 730 (1964).
[22]Id. at 733–734.
[23]Supra note 8.

argued that inclusion of December 31 in the agreement was a typographical error and, in support of this position, noted that the past agreement provided that vacations were to be taken between January 1 and December 21. Arbitrator Sacks held that for the employer to prevail on its mistake theory, it must demonstrate that there was a variance between an agreement reached between the parties during negotiations and what finally emerged in the written contract. Finding that the parties did not express mutual assent to the December 21 date, the arbitrator ruled that the agreement could not be "reformed."

Arbitrator Sacks also analyzed the facts under a unilateral-mistake theory and attention is called to the test cited by Sacks:

> If one party to a contract is mistaken as to some aspect of the contract, he can secure avoidance of the contract (but not reformation) if he can show:
> 1. Enforcement of the contract as written would be oppressive, or at least, result in an "unconscionably unequal exchange of values" (be substantially burdensome).
> 2. Rescission (voiding) of the contract would impose no substantial hardship on the other party.
> . . .
> To prevail on a unilateral mistake theory, [the proponent] must prove three things:
> 1. Existence of a typographical error.
> 2. Rescission would impose no substantial hardship on Union.
> 3. Enforcement of the contract as written would be oppressive, or at least substantially burdensome.[24]

Rejecting the employer's argument that the arbitrator should consider that management did a poor job in proofreading the agreement, Arbitrator Sacks declared that "[i]t is a basic rule of contract law that a party who signs a document manifests his assent to it, and may not later complain that he did not read the instrument or that he did not understand its contents."[25] Exceptions to the rule include where enforcement would be oppressive and substantially burdensome, and rescission of the contract would impose no substantial hardship on the other party.

---

[24]Id. at 988.
[25]Id.

In yet another example, Arbitrator William Dolson, in *Dura Corp.*,[26] ordered reformation of an agreement's insurance package. The arbitrator found that the parties made a mutual mistake by negotiating an insurance package calling for a prescription drug plan, where the provision did not appear in an insurance booklet and the parties did not discuss such a plan when negotiating the package.

Finding a true typographical error, Arbitrator Walter Kaufman, in *Food Employers Council*,[27] reformed a contract excluding from coverage "employees or suppliers engaged in handling." According to the arbitrator, the actual agreement

[26]61 LA 372 (1973).

[27]87 LA 514 (1986). See also Cleveland Pneumatic Co., 91 LA 428 (Oberdank, 1988) (refusing to enforce typographical transposition of Consumer Price Index figure resulting from mutual mistake). St. Louis Post Dispatch, 92 LA 23 (Heinsz, 1989) (Employees who worked overtime on eve of July 4 holiday are entitled only to regular overtime rate rather than holiday "duplicate" premium rate, despite side agreement providing premium rate for work on eve of holiday, where current contract changed definition of holiday to morning and night shifts of holiday itself, and *retention of contrary language in side agreement was mutual mistake.*); Pillowtex Corp., 92 LA 321 (Goldstein, 1989) (Contract that changed incentive rate to compensate for introduction of new technology was not "mistakenly" ratified and void, despite union's claim that Spanish-speaking bargaining unit misunderstood impact of contract, where union negotiating committee fully understood impact of proposed changes and had meaning fully explained to it, union had sole responsibility to explain new contract to unit, management was not derelict in its duty to present and discuss proposed changes during bargaining, and impact of provision was not so unfair to employees that employer was put on notice constructively that both union and membership erred in agreeing to it.); Cleveland Twist Drill Co., 92 LA 105 (Strasshofer, 1989) (Employees who took early retirement and accepted settlement resolving dispute over severance pay may not allege that they were discriminated against in light of subsequent court decisions that denial of severance pay to eligible retirees violated Age Act, where full performance of settlement agreement discharged contract, law at time settlement negotiated did not recognize such discrimination, and arbitrator does not have power to reform contract where *no mutual mistake.*); Continental Maritime of San Francisco, 91 LA 1115 (Koven, 1989) (Employer bound by grandfathering date in footnote to contractual wage schedule, despite contention that failure to insert date specified in previous contract was mutual mistake, where employer proofread contract containing challenged date, it failed to object although it knew or should have known of "mistake," and it paid affected employees for several weeks at higher rate specified in footnote.); Augsburg College, 91 LA 1166 (Gallagher, 1989) (Failure of employer's negotiator to point out that "snow-day" compensation was not covered in contractual wage provisions or specifically incorporated from precontract employee handbook does not entitle union to equitable relief; negotiator had no legal or equitable duty to point out absence of provision, omission was *mutual mistake*, and union's subsequent misunderstanding of contract coverage did not result from any intentional misstatement by employer.). Cf. City of Bethany, Okla., 87 LA 309 (Levy, 1986) (Arbitrator need not decide whether city improperly passed ordinance changing firefighters' work period to 212 hours in 28-day period to comply with what city and union believed were requirements of Fair Labor Standards Acts, where city failed to bargain with union, union acquiesced in changes, both parties made "mistake of law" concerning applicability of FLSA, and arbitrator lacks authority to abrogate ordinance.).

reached by the parties extended coverage to "employees of suppliers." The change from "of" to "or" was held to be a typographical error, especially where the parties applied the exclusion as originally intended for twelve years.

E. Mistake in Performance—Problems of Overpayment

When an employer mistakenly overcompensates an employee, he has committed a mistake in performance. Since restitution for mistake in performance is based on unjust enrichment principles,[28] the better rule in this area is to allow recovery by the employer. As stated by Arbitrator Robert McIntosh:

> Good faith is a basic requirement in all contracts and should be more inherent in labor contracts than in others. These contracts not only define the economic relations between the parties, but their daily conduct toward each other as well. Certainly, since the employees had ratified and authorized the execution of a contract giving them 18 cents an hour increase, they must have been aware that a payment in excess thereof was not according to the agreement. There is no question that if the pay had been 5 cents less, instead of 5 cents more, there would have been a prompt protest. . . . To a reasonable person it was obvious that someone "goofed." The facts prove this, unfortunately, only after excess pay had been given for several months. To refuse to permit the Company to correct the mistake of an employee would be grossly unfair and in violation of the contract.[29]

Some arbitrators, however, have conditioned the employer's right to recover payments made in error, especially when the employee was without knowledge of the mistake. As declared by one arbitrator:

---

[28]Hillman, supra note 1.

[29]Richmond Screw Anchor Co., 59 LA 867, 868 (1972). Accord Aeolian Corp., 72 LA 1178 (Eyraud, 1979) (unjust enrichment for employer to retain amount that in error was not paid to grievant); Ingram Mfg. Co., 67 LA 780 (Davis, 1976) (wage increase paid in error); Kaiser Aluminum & Chem. Corp., 68 LA 970 (Roberts, 1977) (employer may properly recover portion of cost-of-living increase due to error by Bureau of Labor Statistics); Kennecott Copper Corp., 69 LA 52 (Platt, 1977) (overpayment in cost-of-living increase recovered where error was made by BLS); Bay Shipbld. Corp., 63 LA 556 (Fleischli, 1974) (error in wages); Mobil Chem. Co., 61 LA 117 (Rose, 1973) (jury-duty pay properly recoverable when paid in error). Contra Food Employers Council, 64 LA 862 (Karasick, 1975) (employees allowed to retain overpayment as a result of BLS error in cost-of-living data).

A company does have the right to correct errors in wage rates. However, the right to recover overpayments is not absolute. Where the mistake was an (sic) unilateral one on the company's part and the employee could reasonably believe that he was being properly paid, the company should be the one to suffer for its mistake and not the employee.[30]

Where it demonstrated that an employee was aware of a mistake in overpayment, but remained silent on the matter, discipline or even discharge has been sustained by arbitrators.

F. Delay in Discovering Error

Where the evidence indicates that the mistake in integration was continued for any length of time, a reformation remedy may be denied. As stated by one arbitrator, "the point may be reached where it has become too late to be awarded relief from even a mutual mistake in an agreement."[31] Thus, in *Peoria Malleable Castings Co.*,[32] Arbitrator John Sembower refused to credit evidence that a printer, in error, had omitted language in the printed agreement where the alleged error was made three years past and was continued in two subsequent extensions of the contract without being discovered.[33]

Likewise, if one party had sufficient opportunity to examine the collective bargaining agreement and fails to catch an error, that fact will work against an award of reformation. One arbitrator stated this principle as follows:

> The main problem, however, that this arbitrator has with the prospect of reformation is the fact that Management perpetuated the so-called error seven times in both the final draft and printed copy of the Agreement. If it wasn't the intent of the parties to observe the holiday in the first year of the Contract, why didn't Management reform the Contract before it became

---

[30]Peabody Galion Corp., 63 LA 144, 147 (Stephens, 1974). See also Olin Corp., 86 LA 1193 (Penfield, 1986) (Employer improperly made deductions from wages to recoup holiday pay that it mistakenly paid, since general rule is that money paid under mistake of law may not be recovered, and neither contract nor Illinois law permits deduction of holiday pay from wages.)

[31]San Diego Community College, 77 LA 1153, 1155 (Kaufman, 1981).

[32]43 LA 722 (1964).

[33]See also Universal Printing Co., 67 LA 456 (Kubie, 1976); Dura Corp., supra note 26; Glendale Mfg. Co., 28 LA 298 (Maggs, 1957).

final? This may appear to be an academic question, but it is a major stumbling point for this arbitrator.[34]

Intervening events from the effective date of the agreement to the time the arbitrator hears the matter may preclude reformation.

G. Jurisdiction to Change Award Based on Mistake

Once an award has been issued, the arbitrator's jurisdiction is at an end and no power exists for reopening the hearing based on evidence that a mistake occurred.[35] This principle was well illustrated in *Pressmen & Platemakers Local 28 v. Newspaper Agency Corp.*,[36] where a federal court considered the validity of an amended award based on evidence submitted to the arbitrator after a first award had issued. In his first award, the arbitrator ruled that the employer could unilaterally discontinue overtime payments to night shift employees who were required to report to work early, and that the arbitrator had no power to change management's decision. Subsequently, counsel for the union moved the arbitrator to reconsider and reverse his decision because his findings were "significantly in error with respect to material facts" (the arbitrator had incorrectly held that a "zone" shift began at 4:00 p.m. and ended at 11:30 p.m.; the shift actually began at 6:00 and ended at 1:45 a.m.). The arbitrator agreed to reconsider his original decision and requested the parties to submit evidence regarding hours worked. While the employer did not agree that the arbitrator still had jurisdiction to consider the matter, it nevertheless made available the information requested.

As a result of the new information, a second award was

---

[34]Transit Mgmt. of Se. La., 88 LA 1055, 1058 (Baroni, 1987).
[35]However, if both parties agree to rearbitrate a matter based on new evidence, an arbitrator may properly take jurisdiction. Branch v. American Freight Sys., 586 F. Supp. 184, 115 LRRM 2619 (W.D. Mo. 1983) (reopening of hearing by joint arbitration board). Moreover, "an arbitrator can correct a mistake which is apparent on the face of his award, complete an arbitration if the award is not complete, and clarify an ambiguity in the award. . . . Recommiting an issue to an arbitrator for clarification and interpretation does not effect an appeal to the arbitrator, a new trial, or an opportunity to relitigate the issue." McClatchy Newspapers v. Typographical Union 46 (Central Valley), 686 F.2d 731, 111 LRRM 2254, 2256 n.1 (9th Cir. 1982).
[36]485 F. Supp. 511, 104 LRRM 2326 (D. Utah 1980).

issued, reversing the earlier decision. In that award the arbitrator stated that he did not consider the additional information as new evidence but a clarification of the actual work and pay practice central to the issue.[37] When the employer refused to abide by the second decision, the union filed an action for enforcement. In granting summary judgment for the employer, the federal district court declared that when the arbitrator renders his final award, his power under the agreement is exhausted. The fact that the arbitrator's findings were in error cannot by itself constitute sufficient grounds for reconsideration.

Similarly, the federal court in *Food & Commercial Workers Local P-9 v. George A. Hormel & Co.*,[38] vacated an award that was amended by the arbitrator. In that case the union filed a grievance challenging a newly issued work schedule. The issue submitted before the arbitrator (an industrial engineer) was whether the work schedules were based on the benchmark level of normal effective effort as defined in the parties' agreement. More specifically, the issue was the calculation of "steeling time" (knife sharpening) in the overall work schedule. On May 17, 1983, the arbitrator issued an award in favor of the union. In a letter accompanying the award, the arbitrator stated that if the parties desired to discuss the decision, he would be available to do so on May 26, 1983. A meeting was held on that date, at which time the company introduced evidence that the arbitrator's calculation of steeling time was contrary to past practice. The past practice argument had not been made at the first arbitration. Over the objection by the union, on June 16, 1983, the arbitrator issued an amended opinion, this time upholding the company. The arbitrator reasoned that he could retain authority to reconsider or change an award "where it has been determined that an error on the face of the award may have been made."

Vacating the amended award, the federal court correctly reasoned that the *functus officio* doctrine prohibited the arbitrator from amending the first award, and the original award was accordingly reinstated. It is of special note that the court

---

[37]Id., 104 LRRM at 2328.
[38]599 F. Supp 319, 118 LRRM 2142 (D. Minn. 1984), rev'd and remanded, 776 F.2d 1393, 120 LRRM 3283 (8th Cir. 1985).

found inappropriate the arbitrator's affidavit that the May 17th award was only intended as a draft. In the words of the court: "the postaward comments by arbitrators such as the ones made in the instant case are improper and inconsistent with the fundamental goals of finality and labor peace underlying the federal law of arbitration."[39]

A decision that seriously undermines the finality of arbitration awards and ignores the doctrine of *functus officio* is *Red Star Express Lines v. Teamsters Local 170*.[40] On May 4, 1983, Bishop, a Red Star truck driver, was hurt when his truck was involved in an accident. The issue before the arbitrator was whether Bishop had driven recklessly. The parties' agreement forbade the employer from dismissing or suspending an employee without "at least one warning notice." But, it allowed a discharge without a warning notice "if the cause for such discharge is . . . recklessness resulting in serious accident while on duty. . . ." The arbitrator decided in the union's favor and ordered reinstatement, less a five-day suspension (beginning May 27). He also held that Red Star must pay the grievant "what he would have earned" while has was recuperating, minus what he received under workers' compensation during that time. The award was issued on July 18, 1983; the employer claimed it received the award on July 22.

Within five days of receiving the award, the employer reinstated the grievant, but also wrote to the arbitrator pointing out errors in his finding and the remedy ordered. Management argued that the arbitrator should not have ordered it to pay Bishop the difference between what he would have earned and his workers' compensation payments from May 4 to May 27 because Bishop was "disabled and unavailable for work" during that time. Accordingly, Red Star requested that it "be allowed to hold in abeyance any payment of back wages ordered to Mr. Bishop due to the difficulties in reclaiming those monies should you find it proper to reverse the original remedy." The arbitrator agreed and scheduled another hearing, but the union, on August 1, went on strike in protest of the employer's failure to comply with the award. When the

---

[39]Id., 118 LRRM at 2145.
[40]809 F.2d 103, 124 LRRM 2361 (1st Cir. 1987).

employer sought a *Boys Markets*[41]injunction (the parties' contract prohibited strikes except when the company failed to comply with a "final decision" of the arbitrator), the union responded that its strike was lawful under the agreement since the company failed to comply with the "final decision" of the arbitrator. Red Star obtained a temporary restraining order, and the union ended its strike the next day. On August 9, the arbitrator reaffirmed his award. Red Star continued its court suit, asking the court to set aside the protested portion of the arbitration award as well as to award damages for the strike. The court affirmed the award, but held the strike illegal.[42]

The First Circuit upheld the injunction, ruling that the union's strike did not fall within the exception to the no-strike clause. According to the court, the application of *functus officio* to labor disputes is not absolute, and the arbitrator may interpret or amplify his award, *functus officio* notwithstanding. In this case, said the court, the arbitrator had the power to suspend an issued order temporarily while he considers a request that he do so. Red Star, in asking for a reopening while holding the grievant's money "in abeyance," did not fail to comply with a final award.

Red Star aside, the better rule is that when the award is issued, an arbitrator has no authority to revise it merely because it may have been based on a mistaken view of fact.[43] The only option available to a dissatisfied party would be a suit to set aside the award based on gross error or mistake.[44] However, when a clerical error or other miscalculation is apparent to a reviewing court, the error may be corrected by the court's resubmission to the arbitrator.[45]

---

[41]Boys Mkts. v. Retail Clerks Local 770, 398 U.S. 235, 74 LRRM 2257 (1970).

[42]Red Star Express Lines v. Teamsters Local 170, 587 F. Supp. 1243 (D. Mass. 1984).

[43]But see the discussion in Beaunit Corp., 64 LA 917 (Mathews, 1975).

[44]Gross error or mistake is an accepted common-law ground for setting aside an arbitration award. See, e.g., Northwest Airlines v. Air Line Pilots, 530 F.2d 1048, 91 LRRM 2304 (D.C. Cir. 1976); Electronics Corp. of Am. v. Electrical Workers (IUE) Local 272, 492 F.2d 1255, 85 LRRM 2534 (1st Cir. 1974).

[45]See Annotation: *Comment Note—Power of Court to Resubmit Matter to Arbitrators for Correction or Clarification, Because of Ambiguity or Error in, or Omission From, Arbitration Award*, 37 A.L.R. 3d 200 (1971). As stated:
    Section 9 of the Uniform Arbitration Act, read in conjunction with §13, provides that on application of a party, or if an application to the court is pending

H. Summary

In summarizing this area, one may appropriately call attention to the much-quoted langauge of Judge Learned Hand in *Hotchkiss v. National City Bank of New York*:[46]

> A contract has, strictly speaking nothing to do with the personal, or individual, intent of the parties. A contract is an obligation attached by the mere force of law to certain acts of the parties, usually words, which ordinarily accompany and represent a known intent. If, however, it were proved by twenty bishops that either party, when he used the words, intended something else than the usual meaning which the law imposes upon them, he would still be held, unless there was some mutual mistake, or something else of the sort. . . .[47]

Another arbitrator stated the rule this way:

> The so-called "intention of the parties" to an agreement does not ordinarily refer to the subjective intention of either party, but to the expressed intention. Absent any ambiguity, an agreement is ordinarily taken to mean what it says.[48]

When, then, will an arbitrator award a remedy of reformation? Although the distinction between unilateral and mutual mistake is frequently blurred and difficult to apply in practice, the time-honored approach of providing a remedy only for a mutual mistake has generally been followed by arbitrators.[49] Arbitrators ought to search for, and then enforce, the real agreement between the parties, regardless of the words used in the contract.[50] When the facts indicate that a mutual mistake was made, an arbitrator is likely to reform the words to correspond to the parties' intent.

In cases involving mistake of performance, however, the

---

under §§11, 12, or 13 (providing, respectively, for confirming, vacating, and modifying or correcting an award), on submission to the arbitrators by the court under such conditions as the court may order, the arbitrators may modify or correct the award if there was an evident miscalculation of figures or an evident mistake in the description of any person, thing, or property referred to in the award.
Id. at 217.
[46]200 F. 287 (1911), as cited in Peoria Malleable Castings Co., supra note 32, at 729.
[47]Id.
[48]San Diego Community College, supra note 31, at 1155.
[49]Goetz, supra note 2, at 225.
[50]Town of North Haven, 71 LA 983, 989 (Sacks, 1978).

better rule is to disregard the mutuality of mistake requirement. Restitution for mistake of performance is based on unjust enrichment principles, and an employee should not be
permitted to retain payments that were clearly not authorized
by the parties' agreement.

Chapter 19

Punitive Remedies

The generally accepted rule in labor arbitration is that a monetary award should be limited to the amount necessary to make the injured employee whole. As such, with few exceptions, arbitrators have ruled that an award of punitive damages, or any other such penalty, is inappropriate in the arbitral forum.[1]

A. Policy Against Awarding Punitive Remedies

The traditional unavailability of punitive or exemplary damages in arbitration can, in part, be traced to the common law notion that punitive damages are not available in the standard action for breach of contract, unless a tort is in some

---

[1]See generally Elkouri and Elkouri, How Arbitration Works, 4th ed., 405–406 (BNA Books, 1985); Fairweather, Practice and Procedure in Labor Arbitration, 2d ed., 303–309 (BNA Books, 1983); Feller, *Remedies: New and Old Problems: I. Remedies in Arbitration: Old Problems Revisited*, in Arbitration Issues for the 1980s, Proceedings of the 34th Annual Meeting, National Academy of Arbitrators, 109, 112–114 (BNA Books, 1982); Hackett, *Punitive Damages in Arbitration: The Search for a Workable Rule*, 63 Cornell L. Rev. 272 (1978); Wolff, *The Power of the Arbitrator to Make Monetary Awards—Remedies in Arbitration*, in Labor Arbitration: Perspectives and Problems, Proceedings of the 17th Annual Meeting, National Academy of Arbitrators, 176, 187–191 (BNA Books, 1964); Stutz, *Arbitrators and the Remedy Power*, in Labor Arbitration and Industrial Change, Proceedings of the 16th Annual Meeting, National Academy of Arbitrators, 54 (BNA Books, 1963); Sirefman, *Rights Without Remedies in Labor Arbitration*, 18 Arb. J. 17, 32–35 (1963).
See also Chapter 11, *Employer's Remedies for Breach of No-Strike Clause*; Chapter 20, at notes 59–61, and topic titled "Awarding Costs for Successful Court Actions"; and notes 81–93 and topic titled "Attorney's Fees in Federal-Sector Arbitration."

way associated with the wrongdoing.[2] Further, the federal courts have disallowed punitive damages under virtually every federal labor statute against both unions and employers.[3] Arbitrators, similar to the legal community, have seriously questioned whether punitive remedies are appropriate in awarding "make whole" relief. Arbitrator Harry J. Dworkin, in ordering a monetary remedy for management's failure to properly assign overtime, stated the general rule regarding relief as follows:

> In the absence of contract language controlling the arbitrator's authority, or specifying the precise form of relief, the determination must rest with the arbitrator's judgment and discretion, which in turn must fairly reflect the provisions of the contract and the evidence. Under such circumstances it must be implied that the parties intended to vest in the arbitrator the authority to fashion the form of relief which would be fair and equitable, and which would accord content and meaning to the agreement. Where the contracting parties have solemnly concluded a labor agreement through the process of negotiation, it must necessarily follow that a breach of its terms will require such relief as will reasonably approximate restitution to the injured party. The guiding principle in such cases is that the person deprived of a contract benefit should be made whole for his loss. Such persons are therefore entitled to compensatory "damages" to the extent required, no more, and no less. An award in such form is designed to make the employee whole to the extent practicable, it is not intended as a penalty, or as a

---

[2]Sullivan, *Punitive Damages in the Law of Contract: The Reality and Illusion of Legal Change*, 61 Minn. L. Rev. 207 (1977).

[3]See, e.g., Electrical Workers (IBEW) v. Foust, 442 U.S. 42, 101 LRRM 2365 (1979) (denying punitive damages in breach of fair representation suit under Railway Labor Act); Republic Steel Corp. v. NLRB, 311 U.S. 7, 7 LRRM 287 (1940) (no punitive remedy for violation of unfair labor practice under NLRA); Delaware Coca-Cola Bottling Co. v. Teamsters Local 326, 474 F. Supp. 777, 102 LRRM 2727 (D. Del. 1979), rev'd on other grounds, 624 F.2d 1182, 104 LRRM 2776 (3d Cir. 1980) (no punitive damages against union for breach of labor agreement); Shoe Workers Local 127 v. Brooks Shoe Mfg. Co., 298 F.2d 277, 49 LRRM 2346 (3d Cir. 1962) (no punitive award against employer for breach of collective bargaining agreement); Dian v. Steelworkers, 486 F. Supp. 700, 103 LRRM 3023 (E.D. Pa. 1980) (no punitive damages under LMRA against union for breach of duty of fair representation). But see Electrical Workers v. Foust, supra at 59 (Blackmun, J., concurring) (noting circuit courts have awarded punitive damages against unions for violations of Landrum-Griffin Act, 29 U.S.C. §§411, 412. See generally Deboles v. Trans World Airlines, 552 F.2d 1005, 1019, 94 LRRM 3237 (3d Cir.), cert. denied, 434 U.S. 837, 96 LRRM 2514 (1977) (discussing case law under various federal labor statutes denying punitive damage awards and stating that in some circumstances punitive awards under the RLA might be maintainable against employers); Harrison v. United Parcel Serv., 119 LRRM 2163 (C.D. Cal. 1984) (holding that punitive damages may not be assessed against employer in §301 action except where employer's conduct has been egregious).

deterrent to discourage future violations. The concept of a punitive award is inconsistent with the underlying philosophy of the arbitration process.[4]

Arbitrator Peter Seitz, rejecting a request for punitive damages when a union refused to direct employees to operate printing presses at speeds directed by management, stated that *lex talionis*, or "the law of retaliation," is not part of the arsenal of remedies normally available to an arbitrator. In Seitz's words, "such blood-letting and sword-wielding might better be done in other tribunals and authorities than by arbitrators."[5]

And Arbitrator David Feller, finding that an arbitrator has the authority, even when the agreement is silent as to the remedy, to devise an appropriate remedy without requiring the union to prove an identifiable individual loss, has nevertheless cautioned: "This does not, of course, end the inquiry or even, indeed, advance it very far, since it is also my view that "a grievance is not a traffic ticket." I have no authority to impose a punitive sanction."[6]

As seen by the authors, the better rule in this area has been stated by Arbitrator M.S. Ryder:

> Remedies that are punitive in monetary or exemplary nature should be avoided, on the ground that parties bargaining collectively in a more or less perpetual relationship should not seek that one or the other partner be punished for a mistake. To so seek and to obtain punishment is putting a mortgage on the future happiness of the joint relationship. The trauma and embarrassment of an exposed error should be enough. Engaging in a mistake and acting accordingly should not be in a setting of perilous consequences.[7]

B. What Is a Punitive Remedy?

While the cases indicate that arbitrators universally refuse to award any remedy that appears to be punitive in na-

---

[4]Aetna Portland Cement Co., 41 LA 219, 222–223 (1963).
[5]Publishers' Ass'n of New York City, 37 LA 509, 520 (1961).
[6]Lucky Stores, 70-1 ARB ¶8271, at 3902 (1969). See also WFMJ Broadcasting Co., 69-2 ARB ¶8612 (Belkin, 1969); California Brewers Ass'n, 65-2 ARB ¶8603 (Roberts, 1965); Sears, Roebuck & Co., 61-1 ARB ¶8084 (Miller, 1960).
[7]Ryder, *Discussion—Arbitrators and the Remedy Power*, in Labor Arbitration and Industrial Change, supra note 1, at 69.

ture, arbitrators, as well as the courts, are not in agreement as to what constitutes a punitive award. Both arbitrators and courts use the term punitive two ways. First, it is used to describe a monetary award where there is no provable financial loss. The party has suffered some type of injury, but proof of calculable loss is uncertain or nonexistent. When a monetary award is made under these circumstances, it may have overtones of punitive damages. Second, a punitive award may refer to situations where the nonbreaching party is fully compensated, but the arbitrator issues an additional award intended solely to punish and deter the breaching party. The latter type of awards are uncommon in labor arbitration, but nevertheless appear from time to time. In one case the union requested that the company be directed to pay to other members of the bargaining unit an incentive bonus that the employer improperly paid to one employee. In denying the grievance, the arbitrator stated:

> The remedy sought is in the nature of a penalty. It does not seek to make the other employees whole for what they have lost. As a general rule, and in the absence of clear language granting that authority, an arbitrator does not have the power to impose a penalty as distinguished from damages for a loss directly sustained. This view is consistent with the interpretation given the Labor Management Relations Act.[8]

In *A.O. Smith Corp.*,[9] the collective bargaining agreement required that overtime be distributed evenly within departments but did not require payment for an improper assignment. In response to a demand for monetary damages, the arbitrator stated:

> The words of the current agreement do not expressly authorize an award of money payment at the overtime rate in cases where men have not received their exactly correct turns at working overtime. In the absence of such an express under-

---

[8]Servomation of Chattanooga, 60 LA 402, 404 (Rayson, 1973), citing Teamsters Local 20 v. Morton, 377 U.S. 252, 56 LRRM 2225 (1964). One court has summarized the law in this area as follows: "[C]ourts have consistently rejected award of punitive damages in other areas of the Labor Management Relations Act, including unfair labor practices, actions for recovery of tortious damages under §303, and actions under §301." Dian v. Steelworkers, supra note 3 (punitive damages not allowed in fair representation suit). See also Electrical Workers (IBEW) v. Foust, supra note 3 (punitive damages not recoverable for breach of union's duty of fair representation under Railway Labor Act).

[9]33 LA 365 (Updegraff, 1959).

taking, it would be necessary to rest an award favorably to the contention of the Union upon clearly established past practice or upon a showing that the grievant-claimant actually did suffer damages rather than temporary postponement of an overtime work opportunity.

It is well-known that the law is opposed to penalties. Consequently, it cannot be assumed that an arbitrator in any case has the authority to impose a penalty upon any party without clear and express authority in the contract or in the submission agreement leading to the arbitration.[10]

Arbitrator John Caraway, in *Day & Zimmerman*,[11] found that an award of a day's pay for a misassignment of pipefitter work to another craft would be punitive in nature where there was no evidence that any pipefitter lost any wages by reason of the erroneous work assignment.

In *International Paper Co.*,[12] the arbitrator found that the employer had violated the contract by scheduling a general vacation shutdown. Nonetheless, he rejected an award of additional vacation time with pay as an appropriate remedy. Attention is called to his reasoning:

> I see no justification for such a remedy. Though the vacation shutdown interfered with certain valuable employee rights, no employee lost any vacation time because of the shutdown. Such an award would be punitive in nature, and there is nothing in the record to justify a punitive sanction. The Company acted in good faith, with advance notice and made a sincere effort to reach an understanding of its rights under the Agreement. . . . I can find no basis for calculating any monetary damages in this case or for devising an effective affirmative remedy.[13]

While there are arbitrators who have characterized a remedy as compensatory and not punitive, the mere fact that the arbitrator declares that a remedy is nonpunitive does not mean it will pass muster with the courts. For example, in *Westinghouse Electric Corp. v. Electrical Workers (IBEW) Local 1805*,[14]

---

[10]Id. at 366. Accord Refinery Employees of Lake Charles Area v. Continental Oil Co., 268 F.2d 447, 44 LRRM 2388 (5th Cir.), cert. denied, 361 U.S. 896, 45 LRRM 2131 (1959); Celanese Fibers Co., 64-2 ARB ¶8585 (Howard, 1963).

[11]70-2 ARB ¶8624 (1970).

[12]76-1 ARB ¶8214 (Carnes, 1976).

[13]Id. at 5449. See also Pittsburgh Steel Co., 42 LA 1002, 1008 (McDermott, 1964); ACF Indus., 39 LA 1051, 1057 (Williams, 1962); Philip Carey Mfg. Co., 37 LA 134 (Gill, 1961).

[14]561 F.2d 521, 96 LRRM 2084 (4th Cir. 1977), cert. denied, 434 U.S. 1036, 97 LRRM 2341 (1978).

an arbitrator found that the company had violated the agreement by failing to provide sufficient time for negotiations in advance of a deadline for designating a time for vacation shutdowns. As a remedy, the arbitrator ordered three additional paid vacation days to each employee. Although the arbitrator stated that his remedy was nonpunitive, the court of appeals disagreed. In affirming the judgment of the lower court vacating the award, the Fourth Circuit stated:

> With respect to vacation shutdowns, compensatory damages may be awarded only when a breach of the bargaining agreement causes a monetary loss. In the absence of willful or wanton conduct, punitive damages should not be awarded.[15]

In the court's eyes, "[t]hough nominally compensatory, the award was actually punitive," at least in the case where no employee testified that he suffered any monetary loss, inconvenience, or hardship, and no provision of the contract warranted this punishment.

In another decision, the Fourth Circuit held that an arbitrator exceeded his authority in ordering a clothes manufacturer, who had violated the collective bargaining agreement by failing to obtain the union's consent before subcontracting, to pay the union $80,000 for distribution among a group of employees who had been laid off following a shutdown of the plant. The arbitrator determined that the union had suffered a payroll loss of $80,000 as a result of the improper subcontracting, although the district court accepted as undisputed facts that the plant was operating at full capacity with some overtime at the time that the improper subcontracting took place. In vacating the award, the court reasoned:

> It is clear that in order to be entitled to compensatory damages for contract breach, a party must have suffered some legally cognizable loss, be it manifestly monetary or measurable in monetary terms. . . .
> . . . The award of damages in the present case does not draw its essence from the bargaining Agreement, for the Agreement's essence does not contemplate punitive, but only compensatory, awards. Though not termed punitive, the award here given can only be such, for there is nothing in the record showing it validly compensatory, and it is manifestly not nominal. In the absence of any provision for punitive awards, and of any substantiating

---

[15]Id., 96 LRRM at 2085.

proof of willful or wanton conduct, an arbitrator may not make
an award of punitive damages for breach of a collective bargaining agreement. . . . There being no provision in the Agreement here for an award of punitive damages, the arbitrator's
award is not sustainable.[16]

Operating Engineers Local 450 v. Mid-Valley,[17] is a classic
case where a court denied an arbitrator the power to impose
(as determined by the court) a punitive remedy. In *Mid-Valley*
the arbitrator awarded wage payments, in two time segments,
equal to salaries that would have been earned by union members if the employer had complied with the agreement by
maintaining a prescribed crew. The first period extended from
the initial date of the violation until the date of the award.
The second segment, commenced on the decision date, was to
terminate upon the employer's compliance with the contract.

The district court found that the award of future unearned
salaries for each week the employer refused to comply with
the contract after the award had issued (second segment) was
not punitive, since it was a reasonable means of effectuating
the intent of the agreement. The award for the first time
segment, however, was unenforceable since it "bears no reasonable relationship to encouraging compliance with the award
and is punitive in nature." The court's reasoning is noteworthy:

> The first time segment of the award cannot be considered
> compensation for damage because no compensable injury oc-
> curred to Union, either before or after the decision. The arbi-
> trator found that Company had breached the contract by not
> hiring men to work the pumps. However, Union neither alleged
> nor proved damage to itself resulting from that breach. Union
> did not suffer any loss of wages or other money damages because
> of the breach.[18]

The court further noted that contracting parties do not normally agree to assess exemplary damages for a breach of contract and that agreement to such a drastic remedy for a simple
breach cannot be implied. In this case the court, substituting
its judgment for the arbitrator's, found that neither the con-

---

[16]Clothing Workers Baltimore Regional Joint Bd. v. Webster Clothes, 596 F.2d
95, 100 LRRM 3225, 3227 (4th Cir. 1979).
[17]347 F. Supp. 1104, 81 LRRM 2325 (S.D. Tex. 1972).
[18]Id., 81 LRRM at 2328.

tract clause nor the parties' submission suggested authority to issue exemplary damages. Thus, except as to nominal damages of one dollar per day, that part of the arbitrator's award of damages for the period of the first segment was unenforceable.

Taking a noncompensatory approach, the New York Court of Appeals has offered the following analysis in determining whether a remedy is punitive:

> Merely because an arbitrator's award is not arrived at by precise mathematical computations does not make it punitive. Indeed, much of the laudatory value of arbitration lies in the arbitrator's power to construct a remedy best suited to the situation without regard to the restrictions on traditional relief in a court of law. . . . Merely because the computation of damages may be so speculative as to be unsupportable if awarded by a court does not make the award infirm, for, as we have firmly stated, arbitrators are not bound by rules of substantive law or, indeed, rules of evidence. . . .[19]

In upholdng an award of monetary damages for a school teacher who was improperly discriminated against in not being considered for a guidance counselor position, the court declared that "ritualistic incantations of 'punitive damages' will not suffice to vacate an arbitration award where discretion is used in the computation of damages." It is only where the damages are genuinely intended to be punitive that the courts should vacate the award.[20]

While it is difficult to generalize in this area, a fair statement of the law is that a compensatory award becomes punitive and arguably beyond the jurisdiction of an arbitrator if there is no causal connection between the award and the conduct of the employer.[21] The better view is that the award

---

[19]Niagara, Wheatfield, Lewiston & Cambria Cent. School Dist. No. 1 Bd. of Educ. v. Niagara-Wheatfield Teachers Ass'n, 46 N.Y.2d 553, 415 N.Y.S.2d 790, 101 LRRM 2258, 2259 (1979).

[20]Id.

[21]See, e.g., Howard P. Foley Co. v. Electrical Workers (IBEW) Local 639, 789 F.2d 1421, 122 LRRM 2471 (9th Cir. 1986) (holding back-pay award against contractor punitive where employee of contractor is barred from premises of utility by the utility); Berklee College of Music v. Teachers Local 4412, 127 LRRM 2908, 2909 (D. Mass. 1987) (arbitrator not free to interpret unambiguous language to fashion remedy, reasoning "where the Agreement does not specify the consequence of a missed deadline the 'arbitrator has the power to fashion a remedy which is compensatory, not punitive.' "); CBS v. Electrical Workers (IBEW) Local 1241, 1986 WL 11469 (E.D. Pa. 1986) (rejecting as punitive award ordering employer to pay union an amount equal to prevailing wages that would have been paid to union technician where

need not be arrived at by precise mathematical computation to pass muster if challenged in court. However, cases where arbitrators issue awards genuinely intended to be punitive in character are especially suspect. Although not dispositive of the issue, awards that exceed the monetary loss suffered by the injured party may be considered punitive, even though arbitrators routinely make monetary awards when no damages have been sustained by the grieving party.[22]

C. Cases Where Punitive or Exemplary Remedies Have Been Imposed

Despite the strong arbitral sentiment against awarding punitive remedies, some arbitrators, with court approval, have held that punitive sanctions may be appropriate in labor arbitration. For example, Arbitrator Elmer Hilpert has declared:

> Where repetitive violations of a collective bargaining agreement are shown to have occurred and "damages" were only *nominal*, there is some arbitral authority for imposing a money "penalty," as a deterrent to recurrent violations, on the theory that a mere arbitral "cease and desist" directive . . . would be ineffectual.[23]

---

management performed work during radio call-in program); Desert Palace v. Local Joint Executive Bd. of Las Vegas, 486 F. Supp. 675, 105 LRRM 3053 (D. Nev. 1980) (ruling award granting servers approximately seven to ten times amount of gratuity usually received is punitive and outside essence of labor contract). See also Delta Air Lines v. Airline Pilots Ass'n, 686 F. Supp. 1573, 127 LRRM 2530 (N.D. Ga. 1987) (rejecting argument that award ordering employer to pay costs of private alcohol treatment that employee sought after his discharge for cause amounts to punitive damages).

[22]Where an employer assigned bargaining-unit work to nonunit employees, Arbitrator Stephen Goldberg, in Mallinckrodt Chem. Works, 50 LA 933, 938 (1968), had this to say regarding the argument that he was without authority to award damages absent a showing of monetary loss:

> [T]he Company asserts there is nothing in the Agreement that authorizes the Arbitrator to award damages absent a showing of monetary loss. This argument is not convincing. It is equally true that there is nothing in the collective agreement authorizing the Arbitrator to award damages where there *is* a showing of monetary loss, yet the Company concedes the Arbitrator's power to do so. The Agreement simply does not deal with the question of the circumstances under which damages are to be awarded or the principles on which they are to be computed. This is a matter as to which the parties have given the Arbitrator no explicit guidance, but rather have left him with the task of ascertaining their implicit intent. Hence the absence of language in the Agreement explicitly authorizing the Arbitrator to award damages absent a showing of monetary loss is not fatal to his power to do so.

[23]Acme Paper Co., 47 LA 238, 242 n.2 (1966). See also Bethlehem Steel Co., 37 LA 821, 824 (Valtin, 1961); Bethlehem Steel Co., 31 LA 857, 858 (Seward, 1958).

Where an employer improperly established a new policy relating to personal leaves, one arbitrator held that a punitive remedy was appropriate. Finding that the company knowingly attempted to "rewrite the leave of absence conditions," Arbitrator Martin Conway reasoned as follows:

> I agree with the theory and rationale of the "obey and grieve rule," however, I hasten to observe that employers who put themselves in the position of unilaterally establishing extra-contractual, unreasonable, or arbitrary "administrative policies" as substitutes for agreed and settled language or practices and avoid or refuse to bargain with the Union on such matters, leave penalties as the only possible and appropriate pressure on their actions. As in this case, unless some penalty is imposed the employer breaks the bargaining and administration rules and suffers not one whit.[24]

As exemplary damages, the arbitrator directed the employer to pay to each of three grievants the amount of wages that each would have given up had their requested leaves been granted.[25]

Arbitrator Burton Turkus' award in *Belmont Smelting & Refining Works*,[26] made it clear that a second work stoppage would result in the assessment of both compensatory and punitive damages against the union:

> Any future indulgence in a wildcat strike or work stoppage in violation of the proscribed no-strike commitment of the labor Agreement . . . may not only subject the Union to an assessment of punitive as well as compensatory damages for such action of its members but also expose the Union to such assessment for the contractually violative strike of August 15th, under the fully preserved right in the award to renew the demand for such relief in the instant case in the event of such a contingency. In plain and blunt language, it is the purpose and intendment of this award to have the memory of August 15, 1967, like Banquo's Ghost, long persist—so that it just doesn't happen again.[27]

In *Electrical Workers (IBEW) Local 1842 v. Cincinnati Electronics Corp.*,[28] the Sixth Circuit affirmed an arbitrator's

---

[24]John Morrell & Co., 69 LA 264, 281 (1977).
[25]Compare to Walker Mfg. Co., Plant & Int'l Union, UAW, 64-2 ARB ¶8634 (Anderson, 1964) (union denied $50,000 in damages for employer's improper refusal to grant leave; proper remedy was cease-and-desist order).
[26]50 LA 691 (1968).
[27]Id. at 696.
[28]808 F.2d 1201, 124 LRRM 2473 (6th Cir. 1987).

decision under a procedural forfeiture clause in the parties' collective bargaining agreement. The Union argued that the company had assigned bargaining-unit work to salaried engineering employees in violation of the agreement. During processing of the grievance management failed to present a timely answer in accordance with the agreement's provision that "the grievance shall be deemed to have been granted for such a failure." The arbitrator held that the agreement's forfeiture provision applied and, accordingly, ruled for the union. What is especially interesting is that the arbitrator also awarded the Union approximately $3,000 to "deter temptation to default in response to grievances instead of complying with the negotiated time limits." Both the district court and appellate court upheld that the award drew its essence from the collective bargaining agreement and that the arbitrator had granted a remedy which was within his broad authority to fashion.

Similarly, in *Electrical Workers (UE) Local 1139 v. Litton Systems*,[29] the Eighth Circuit, in a split decision, upheld a decision by an arbitrator granting employees a second paid vacation when an employer required employees to take their paid vacations at a time not permitted by the agreement. The dissent argued that the award was punitive in nature and based on an unsupported factual assumption.

Sometimes the agreement explicitly permits an award of punitive damages. In *Northshore Investments v. Directors Guild*,[30] the collective bargaining agreement gave the arbitrator the power to award "money damages" and "any other relief the Arbitrator deems appropriate in the circumstances." A federal district court upheld Arbitrator Edward Mosk's award of $25,000 to an movie director and $20,000 to his Guild as compensation for the violation of a "creative rights" clause of a collective bargaining agreement. The court reasoned that since the agreement made no distinction between an award of compensatory and punitive damages, "an award of damages, whatever it may be labeled, is not beyond the scope of the arbitrator's power and must be upheld."[31]

Similarly, in *Asbestos Workers Local 34 v. General Pipe*

---

[29]728 F.2d 970, 115 LRRM 2633 (8th Cir. 1984).
[30]108 LRRM 3010 (C.D. Cal. 1981).
[31]Id. at 3013.

Covering,[32] the union filed a grievance alleging a violation of a trade agreement when management transferred work to a nonunion shop. The grievance was brought before a trade board made up of employers and union members pursuant to the collective bargaining agreement. General was ordered to pay $75,000 to the American Lung Association in punitive damages. The district court and Eighth Circuit affirmed the award under a contract that expressly provided that where either party violated any of its provisions, "[t]he Trade Board [would] have the power to impose fines or other penalties." The court remanded for determination of whether the $75,000 exceeded the Board's authorization.

While at one time a punitive award, even if authorized in the parties' agreement, would not be enforced,[33] the better view is that the courts will not consider a punitive award per se unenforceable, especially in the situation where willful and repetitive violations are found.[34] There may also be a requirement that a punitive remedy must be put at issue from the beginning of the grievance procedure.[35]

D. Federal Sector

A punitive remedy is not available to a federal-sector arbitrator under the Back Pay Act of 1970.

E. Summary

One problem in this area is the tendency of both arbitrators and courts to characterize remedies either punitive or compensatory as a bootstrap to reaching a desired result. If

---

[32]792 F.2d 96, 122 LRRM 2816 (8th Cir. 1986).

[33]Publishers Ass'n v. Newspaper & Mail Deliverers of New York, 280 App. Div. 500, 114 N.Y.S.2d 401, 18 LA 855 (1952).

[34]See, e.g., Bakery & Confectionery Workers Local 369 v. Cotton Baking Co., 514 F.2d 1235, 89 LRRM 2665 (5th Cir. 1975) (upholding award to union of one year's wages for employee who should have been assigned work against claim that award was punitive); Sheet Metal Workers Local 416 v. Helgesteel Corp., 335 F. Supp. 812, 80 LRRM 2113 (W.D. Wis. 1971). But see Operating Eng'rs Local 450 v. Mid-Valley, supra note 17 (holding that, absent compensable injury, award constitutes unauthorized penalty against employer).

[35]Hotel & Restaurant Employees v. Michelson's Food Servs., 545 F.2d 1248, 94 LRRM 2014, 2019 (9th Cir. 1976).

an arbitrator or a reviewing court finds that a particular remedy is inappropriate, it may be labeled as punitive and not fit for arbitral consumption.[36] A better focus is to consider monetary compensation as it relates to the overall function of the arbitrator as the parties' contract reader. Absent a specific directive or mandate in the agreement with respect to remedies, the question, as stated by one court, should not be whether an award is punitive but rather whether it was reasonable in light of the findings of the arbitrator.[37] In the words of another court, "[h]aving chosen arbitration as their forum, the parties must recognize that an award may differ from that expected in a court of law without being subject to attack for that reason alone."[38]

In an address before the National Academy of Arbitrators, Arbitrator Sidney Wolff observed that public policy may frown on punitive awards, but it also frowns on certain aspects of improper labor relations. Wolff pointed out that a breach of the labor contract can result in costly industrial instability and warfare. Thus, any tool or process that can help to maintain labor peace is in the public interest, and its use should accordingly be encouraged.[39] Is a punitive remedy such a tool? One commentator has argued that a punitive remedy is necessary to protect intangible expectations under collective bargaining agreements, and in certain situations a monetary award

---

[36]See, e.g., Lockheed Space Operations Co., 91 LA 457, 465 (Richard, 1988) ("no evidence of damages to any of those grievants from the employer's breach of duty was presented, and no basis for punitive damages or any other monetary award was presented"); E.A. Norris Plumbing Co., 90 LA 462 (Christopher, 1987) (rejecting employer's request for a $1,000 fine against the grievant for insubordination as punitive); Great Atl. & Pac. Tea Co., 88 LA 430, 434 (Lipson, 1986) (rejecting compensatory remedy for breach of agreement requiring stores to be closed on Christmas and New Year's Day, reasoning that "the Arbitrator is not inclined to award punitive damages such as quadruple pay for the employees who worked or high exemplary damages as requested by the Union"); Cadillac Gage Co., 87 LA 853, 856 (Van Pelt, 1986) (noting that arbitrator could award compensatory, but not punitive, damages for management performing bargaining-unit work; employer ordered to pay union one-half hour's pay); ITT Higbie Mfg. Co., 83 LA 394, 398 (Edes, 1984) ("where both parties are properly assessed some degree of fault, the punitive imposition of interest payments is not appropriate"); ACF Indus., 62 LA 364, 366 (Williams, 1974) (holding no authority to award punitive damages of eight hours' pay to production crew for management's performance of unit work, citing de minimis rule).
[37]Sheet Metal Workers Local 416 v. Helgesteel Corp., supra note 34, 80 LRRM at 2116.
[38]Niagara, Wheatfield, Lewiston & Cambria Cent. School Dist. No. 1 Bd. of Educ. v. Niagara-Wheatfield Teachers Ass'n, supra note 19, 101 LRRM at 2259.
[39]Wolff, supra note 1, at 188.

will contribute to industrial peace.[40] Perhaps the best thought in this area has been expressed in 1958 by Chief Justice Earl Warren, dissenting in *Automobile Workers v. Russell*,[41] when he stated:

> The parties to labor controversies have enough devices for making one another "smart" without this Court putting its stamp of approval upon another. I can conceive of nothing more disruptive of congenial labor relations than arming employee, union and management with the potential for "smarting" one another with exemplary damages. Even without the punitive element, a damage action has an unfavorable effect on the climate of labor relations. Each new step in the proceedings rekindles the animosity.[42]

Judge Richard Posner of the Seventh Circuit has likewise observed:

> Now arbitrators are rarely thought authorized to award punitive damages. It is not the kind of remedy that the parties probably would have agreed to authorize if they had thought about the matter, because of the great power it would give the arbitrator (subject to virtually no judicial review), and the bitter note a claim for punitive damages could inject into the parties' relationship, which is a continuing one.[43]

The reasoning of Justice Warren and Judge Posner express the better position with respect to awarding punitive remedies in the arbitral forum. While the arbitrator has the authority to read into the contract those provisions which the arbitrator finds can reasonably be assumed to exist by the parties even if they fail to signify it by words,[44] absent extraordinary circumstances, the authority to award a true penalty is not considered part of the arbitrator's sweeping remedial authority. An arbitrator should not, however, reject as punitive a monetary award simply because of a party's inability to prove damages precisely.

---

[40]Note, *Protecting Intangible Expectations Under Collective Bargaining Agreements—Overcoming the Proscription of Arbitral Penalties*, 61 Minn. L. Rev. 126 (1976).
[41]356 U.S. 634, 42 LRRM 2142 (1958).
[42]Id. at 653, 42 LRRM at 2149.
[43]Miller Brewing Co. v. Brewery Workers Local 9, 739 F.2d 1159, 1164, 116 LRRM 3130, 3134 (7th Cir. 1984), cert. denied, 469 U.S. 1160, 118 LRRM 2192 (1985).
[44]Feller, supra note 1, at 114.

Chapter 20

Interest, Costs, and Attorney's Fees

A. Awarding Interest

Arbitrators traditionally have been reluctant to grant an award of interest on back pay or other monies owed for a breach of a collective bargaining contract primarily because (1) the parties rarely request it in the submission, and (2) it is not considered customary in the industrial relations forum.[1] The absence of awarding interest in arbitration can, in part, be attributed to the one-time and now abandoned practice of the NLRB of not awarding interest on back-pay awards. Since Board and court actions frequently spill over into the arbitration area,[2] attention is called to the reasoning of the Board when, in 1962, it changed its practice of not awarding interest:

> "Back pay" granted to an employee under the Act is considered as wages lost by the employee as the result of the re-

---

[1]See, e.g., Cowlitz Redi-Mix, 85 LA 745, 753 (Boedecker, 1985) (noting that interest on back pay is exception rather than rule); Nevada Resort Ass'n, 56 LA 1263 (Cohen, 1971) (failure to demand interest in grievance); Fremont Hotel, 60-2 ARB §8588 (Block, 1968) (no statute and nothing in contract authorizing interest); American Chain & Cable Co., 40 LA 312 (McDermott, 1963) (interest awarded only in special circumstances); Intermountain Operators League, 26 LA 149 (Kadish, 1956) (failure to authorize arbitrator to award interest).

See generally Elkouri and Elkouri, How Arbitration Works, 4th ed., 406–407 (BNA Books, 1985); Fairweather, Practice and Procedure in Labor Arbitration, 2d ed., 518–520 (BNA Books, 1983); Youngdahl, *Awarding Interest in Labor Arbitration Cases*, 54 Ky. L.J. 717 (1966).

[2]Fleming, *The Labor Arbitration Process: 1943–1963*, in Labor Arbitration: Perspectives and Problems, Proceedings of the 17th Annual Meeting, National Academy of Arbitrators, 33, 50 (BNA Books, 1964).

spondent's wrong. It is not a fine or penalty imposed on the respondent by the Board. "It is an indebtedness arising out of an obligation imposed by statute—an incident fixed by law to the employer-employee relationship. A liability based on quasi-contract. . . .

"Accordingly, under accepted legal and equitable principles, interest should be added to backpay awards made to employees who have been discriminatorily separated from their employment."[3]

In *Kaiser Permanente Medical Care Program*,[4] Arbitrator Reginald Alleyne confronted the interest issue head on and had this to say on the matter:

How arbitral practice developed so as not to award interest on back pay as a matter of equity and consistent with the term "make whole," may be an unsolved mystery, but that is no reason to ignore reason.[5]

In *Kaiser*, the arbitrator relied heavily on the National Labor Relations Board's routine practice of awarding interest on back pay in his decision to grant such relief, and on the basis that the employer-employee relationship is one of debtor-creditor. Alleyne further cited Arbitrator Hilpert's decision in *Allied Chemical Co.*,[6] where interest was awarded in the absence of contract language in the agreement, on the ground that the arbitration process should, and does, recognize the common-law relief. Alleyne maintained that in the absence of a rational reason for not awarding interest on back pay, it should be awarded, at least if it is requested. He noted that because, in *Kaiser*, the grievant had requested interest, their was no reason to address the general question of whether interest should be awarded even when it is not requested by the grievant.

In a case of first impression, Arbitrator Benjamin Aaron held that under the National Postal Service Agreement arbitrators have discretionary authority to grant interest on back-pay awards when sustaining disciplinary grievances. Arbitrator Aaron's reasoning is particularly instructive:

---

[3]Isis Plumbing & Heating Co., 138 NLRB 716, 51 LRRM 1122, 1124 (1962), rev'd on other grounds, 322 F.2d 913, 54 LRRM 2235 (9th Cir. 1963). See also Florida Steel Corp., 231 NLRB 651, 96 LRRM 1070 (1977) (adoption of Internal Revenue Service's "adjusted prime interest rate" sliding scale).
[4]89 LA 841 (1987).
[5]Id. at 845.
[6]47 LA 686 (1966).

A phrase commonly employed in reference to arbitral remedies for wrongful disciplinary suspensions or terminations is that the grievants should be "made whole" for what they have lost in wages, seniority, and other benefits. When a successful grievant is forced to wait a long time before recovering back pay he has lost as a result of an unjust disciplinary penalty, denial of interest means that he cannot be "made whole." Although, generally, interest on a back-pay award has been neither asked for nor granted in the bulk of disciplinary cases in which the grievants have been sustained, I can see no logical reason why it should not be granted in circumstances in which the penalty was excessive or vindictive, or imposed in bad faith or in violation of an established public policy, particularly when the grievant has had to wait a long time before being paid. Indeed, at least one reason for the practice of denying interest on back pay in arbitration cases may be that the average length of time between the filing of a grievance and the arbitrator's decision used to be considerably less than it is today, and the denial of interest did not significantly affect the "made-whole" remedy of reinstatement with back pay.[7]

Over the years, some arbitrators have awarded interest on back-pay awards only where special circumstances—such as the company acting in an arbitrary and capricious manner—warrant such relief. Interest has also been awarded where emotional factors appear to accentuate the "injustice" which the particular discharge embodied.[8] Arbitrator Thomas McDermott has observed:

> The demand for payment of interest on the monies due is one that is only occasionally raised in arbitration cases, which involve damages. It is, however, a demand that can only be granted under very special circumstances. As an example, if it can be shown that a Company acted in a very arbitrary fashion in its handling of a case, so that the logical conclusion could be drawn that the Company was deliberately trying to injure the affected employees, an arbitrator might find cause for inclusion of interest as a part of damages.[9]

In *Sunshine Convalescent Hospital*,[10] Arbitrator Melvin

---

[7]Postal Serv. (Case No, HLN-5-FD-2560, 1984), (unpublished. See also Postal Serv. (Case No. WLN-5G-D-25655, 1985) (unpublished decision by Carlton Snow awarding interest).

[8]Youngdahl, supra note 1, at 725, citing All States Trailer Co., 44 LA 104 (Leflar, 1965).

[9]American Chain & Cable Co., supra note 1, at 315.

[10]62 LA 276 (1974).

Lennard ordered payment of interest and reasonable attorney's fees where the employer's conduct in withholding vacation pay was known by it to be without merit. Similarly, in *Markle Manufacturing Co.*,[11] Arbitrator J. Williams found an award of interest proper where the employer engaged in "extreme dilatory tactics" with respect to offers of reinstatement and settlement of obligations. In this way, an award of interest may be seen as punitive-type relief and, indeed, many parties have argued this as a basis for denial of interest.

Markle is especially illustrative of this point. In that case, the union filed a grievance on behalf of two employees who were discharged in 1974. In 1985, Arbitrator Williams found the company violated its agreement with the employees, and the employees were ordered reinstated and awarded back pay. The company refused to comply with the award, and the union accordingly sought judicial enforcement in the U.S. District Court. In 1976, the district court upheld the award as valid and enforceable, and the company appealed. In 1978, the Court of Appeals for the Fifth Circuit affirmed the trial court, but the parties could not agree on the amount of back pay due the grievants. Thus, in 1979 the union filed a motion, which the company joined, seeking remand to the arbitrator for determination of its back-pay liability.

On remand, the company contended that in determining the amount of liability, the arbitrator should not include an award of interest in his computations, since the original finding did not include interest, and to do so now would be punitive in effect. In rejecting the company's argument, Arbitrator Earl Williams reasoned that the awarding of interest is on solid legal ground and is distinct from punitive relief. Williams articulated his analysis as follows:

> [D]espite the fact that arbitrators . . . have been awarding interest to a greater extent in recent years, this arbitrator has maintained a consistent standard in that there must not be reasonable doubts in regard to a company's tactics and/or actions. Consequently, in twenty years of arbitrating, I have never awarded interest. However, the entire history of this case, from the original charges against the Grievants to the extreme di-

---

[11]73 LA 1292 (1980).

latory tactics in regard to the offer of reinstatement and settlement of obligations, leaves not one scintilla of doubt in the mind of the Arbitrator that, for the first time, I must assess interest.[12]

Interest was awarded at a rate of 10 percent per annum, but calculation of the interest was held to start from the date of the original award in 1975 (not the date of injury) and continue until the date of reinstatement in 1978 (not the date of payment).

Similarly, in *Coppes, Inc.*,[13] Arbitrator Sinclair Kossoff, citing *Markle*, awarded interest. In the *Coppes* decision, the company failed to pay its employees vacation pay required by the parties' bargaining agreement. The company, a manufacturer of wood cabinets, maintained that it was in financial difficulty because of the depressed condition of the building trades industry. This hardship precluded distribution of the vacation pay at the time due. By the hearing date, the company had shown signs of recovery, but had still not paid vacation pay. The arbitrator said that the only real issue is whether interest, as required by the union in the grievance, should be granted. The arbitrator's reasoning is particularly instructive:

> I recognize that financial exigency caused the Company to withhold vacation pay distribution. However, what the Company did here, in effect, was to obtain a forced loan from the employees in the amount of the vacation pay. . . . As a business enterprise the Company must be prepared to pay interest for business related loans.[14]

Arbitrator Kossoff, in awarding interest for the first time, rejected the company's contention that because there was no mention of interest in the collective bargaining agreement, an award of interest would be improper:

> No significance, however, may be attached to the fact that there is no reference to interest in the collective bargaining agreement. The contract does not address the question of remedy for breach thereof. For example, it does not state what amends shall be made to an employee discharged without just cause. This does not mean that in an appropriate case an arbitrator may not order reinstatement and back pay for the discharged indi-

---

[12]Id. at 1300.
[13]80 LA 1058 (1983).
[14]Id. at 1059.

vidual. Similarly, the absence of any mention of interest in the contract does not mean that in a proper case an arbitrator may not award such a remedy.

. . .

There is, moreover, substantial arbitral authority supporting the award of interest where the employer, in denying payment to employees, acted intentionally and with knowledge that its withholding of payment was without any legal basis.[15]

Kossoff went on to find an appropriate case for an award of interest on the vacation pay, noting that he did not recall any other case wherein an employer intentionally withheld monies due an employee without any claim of right on the employer's part.

Some arbitrators seem more willing to grant an award of interest in cases where the parties have previously and expressly contracted for such remedy in the event of a dispute. For example, in *Dutko Wall Systems*,[16] interest was awarded because the parties had contracted that, in the event of an arbitral dispute, an award of interest on any monies owed would be appropriate. In *Dutko*, a collective bargaining agreement provided for contributions on the part of certain employees to a fringe benefit fund, and matching contributions by the employer. It was found that the employer failed to negotiate matching contributions, and the company was ordered to pay to the fund the amount necessary to satisfy the deficiency, as well as interest on the stated amount at a rate of eight percent, from the time such contributions were due. The contract also provided the stated interest rate.

Perhaps one of the most liberal awards of interest is gleaned from *Sterling Colorado Beef Co.*,[17] where Arbitrator Jerome Smith held that numerous laid-off employees of an employer forced to shut down its plant were entitled to back pay, insurance for the period, a prorated vacation, and interest on all the payments. In so holding, Arbitrator Jerome Smith stated that, while awards of interest are of relatively recent origin, interest is proper even in the absence of special circumstances.

Arbitrator Smith found that because a failure to award interest would unjustly enrich the employer and would leave

---

[15]Id. at 1059–1060.
[16]89 LA 1215 (Weisinger, 1987).
[17]86 LA 866 (1986).

the employees less than whole, an award of interest on all wages and vacation benefits was appropriate. The arbitrator further held that the accrual period of the interest commenced on the date of the injury to the employees and ran until the date of payment of the award. The grievants were accordingly awarded both pre- and postjudgment interest.

Awarding interest for the period after the award has issued may be a proper remedy for the employer's dilatory tactics, as held by Arbitrator Edgar Jones, Jr., in *Farmer Brothers*.[18] In a second postaward hearing, Arbitrator Jones found:

> That this futile indulgence in dilatory tactics would be financially harmful to Grievants is so patently obvious in the circumstances of this case and the depressed economy that it must be presumed to have been intentional. That being so, the Employer has purposely retained and converted to its own use monies long overdue, that are rightfully Grievants. It should pay for that use and it should do so at the rate of interest which Grievants themselves would have to pay in order to borrow the monies withheld from them by the Employer. With their credit status, that rate in the period 1974–1976 certainly would not be less than ten percent which shall be the rate of interest to be paid by the Employer for its continued use of their monies.[19]

Arbitrator Michael Beck has also distinguished prejudgment from postjudgment interest:

> Arbitrators have generally been more willing to grant interest, when none is set forth in the Agreement, for periods after the award, i.e., postjudgment interest. The rationale in this regard is that prior to an award only a claim for relief is involved, while the award is in the nature of a judgment constituting a "liquidated" amount or an amount reasonably certain of ascertainment by computation upon which interest is normally awarded.[20]

The arbitrator awarded interest at the legal rate (6 percent) for the period between the discharge and the receipt of the award and payment to the grievant.

In *Synergy Gas Co.*,[21] Arbitrator Jesse Simons awarded simple interest at 16 percent as one element of damages for the employer's refusal to comply with a prior arbitrator's award

---

[18]66 LA 354 (1976).
[19]Id. at 356.
[20]Osborn & Ulland, 68 LA 1146, 1153 (1977). See also Sears, Roebuck & Co., 35 LA 757, 783 (Miller, 1960) (interest granted from date of award).
[21]91 LA 77 (1987).

ordering a grievant reinstated. The Arbitrator's thoughts are particularly instructive on the matter of a make-whole remedy:

> In essence, the Employer has argued that the Undersigned should ignore, and is required to ignore, the passage of six years when measuring the scope of relief to be accorded to Grievant pursuant to the 1981 Cashen Award. . . .
>
> . . . [T]his award will accord to Grievant the justice to which he is now entitled to redress the balance for the past injustices imposed on him.
>
> The first injustice occurred when, in 1980, Grievant, in violation of the Contract, was discharged without just cause. The second injustice occurred when he was denied reinstatement in 1981 as directed by Arbitrator Cashen, also in violation of the Agreement. The third injustice occurred when Grievant was denied the full fruits of that Award for almost six years because of unfounded claims that Arbitrator Cashen acted improperly.
>
> An arbitrator's remedial authority is not limitless. Here, however, the refusal to comply with the Cashen Award and the Employer's breach of contract has extended from 1980 to date. Therefore, the remedy awarded Grievant necessarily has to be co-extensive.
>
> It is only by granting interest, as urged by the Union, on the sums due Grievant for wages and profit sharing benefits will he be fully made whole.[22]

Arbitrator Simons also directed management to pay to the union reasonable attorney's fees incurred as a result of litigating the employer's refusal to honor the first award. Both the interest and fee remedy were sustained by the Second Circuit.[23]

Of special note in this line of cases is *Falstaff Brewing Corp. v. Teamsters Local 153*,[24] where a federal district court held that an arbitrator did not exceed his authority in imposing interest on the amount of damages assessed against an employer that violated the collective bargaining contract. The court rejected the employer's arguments that an award of interest is barred since the collective bargaining agreement is silent on the imposition of interest in a damage award and

---

[22]Id. at 91.

[23]Synergy Gas Co. v. Sasso, 853 F.2d 59, 129 LRRM 2041 (2d Cir. 1988), cert. denied, 57 USLW 3412, 129 LRRM 3072 (1988), discussed in Chapter 4 at notes 12–16 and accompanying text.

[24]479 F. Supp. 850, 103 LRRM 2008 (D.N.J. 1978).

that assessing interest is punitive and unwarranted. The court stated that "interest is within the traditional inherent power of an arbitrator to award in order to make an employee whose rights have been violated reasonably whole."[25]

Notwithstanding the decisions in favor of awarding interest on awards of back pay and other benefits, decisions to the contrary continue to be the norm. In *Oil Transport Co. & Gypsum Transport*,[26] Arbitrator Albert Carter held that employee drivers were not entitled to an award of interest on amounts accruing as a result of their employers' improper exclusion of a fuel surcharge from revenues in computing the drivers' pay. According to the arbitrator, interest could be denied because the actions of the employers were not arbitrary and capricious and willful. Arbitrator Carter reasoned that there was no proof that the employers deliberately withheld the fuel surcharge from revenues in determining the drivers' pay in order to "enrich their own treasures."

Similarly, in *Cowlitz Redi-Mix*,[27] a concrete company that was found liable under a prior arbitration award to a former truck driver for more than 400 hours of lost work over a 15-month period of his discharge, was not liable for interest on the original back-pay award because the employer had not committed "egregious acts" in the interim. The arbitrator maintained that, even in 1985, an award of interest on back pay is the exception rather than the rule.

Arbitrator Mark L. Kahn, in *City of Pontiac, Michigan*,[28] ruled that absent a showing that monetary remedies previously included interest, such an award would not issue, at least where the union did not make the proposal prior to its

---

[25]Id., 103 LRRM at 2017.

[26]79 LA 1285 (1982).

[27]85 LA 745 (Boedecker, 1985).

[28]91 LA 830, 835 (1988). See also, Allis-Chalmers Corp., 84-1 ARB ¶8291 (Goetz, 1983), (denying interest, citing no authorization in collective bargaining agreement and absence of precedent in arbitration cases between parties); City of Vallejo, 86 LA 1082 (Bogue, 1986) (Back pay order against city that erroneously interpreted contractual formula for police officers' pay increases will not require payment of interest on amounts withheld, where city acted in good faith and award results in pay increase significantly greater than that contemplated.); Summit City Brewers & Distribs. Ass'n, 84 LA 840 (Kates, 1985) (denying request for interest at statutory rate of 10% per annum on COLA wage payments which may be found due in arbitration of grievance in which arbitrator ruled that union is entitled to cost-of-living wage increase; evidence does not establish that union made demand for interest prior to filing of posthearing brief, or that employer acted in bad faith in refusing to acknowledge liability for more than 15 cents per hour COLA increase).

posthearing brief. Arbitrator Kahn also denied attorney's fees and costs because the union cited no precedent in the parties' bargaining relationship for such relief.

Finally, in *Shell Oil Co.*,[29] an improperly discharged employee was found not entitled to attorney's fees or interest on back pay. In support of this holding, the arbitrator articulated only the following:

> [T]he remedy cannot include interest or Attorney's fees. To be sure, each party is responsible for preparing its case and providing the necessary representation for same. The fact that Grievant chose to be represented by an Attorney is not a matter that [the] Company should have to bear in connection with an Order to duly compensate him for an unjust termination. However, this arbitrator has honored Motions for Attorneys' fees when same was tied to a dispute where the employer was "obdurately obstinate" and, therefore, purposely sought to do injury to the aggrieved via the grievance/arbitral process. But such is not the case here. . . .[30]

The arbitrator made no reference to any support for denial of an award of interest, and dismissed the issue cursorily.

1. Summary

Awarding interest in arbitration has been the exception rather than the rule.[31] When it has been awarded, it resulted because it had been requested or because there had been such dilatory or bad-faith action by the employer that the arbitrator concluded some penalty in the form of interest was due. The calculation of the interest rate when interest has been found appropriate has taken on several aspects. Some regard it to be the current market rate while others use other yardsticks

---

[29]87 LA 473 (Nicholas, 1986).

[30]Id. at 478.

[31]For whatever it's worth, in the Cumulative Digest and Index (CDI) of BNA's Labor Arbitration Reports, there are six cases cited in Volumes 41–50, of which four requests for interest were denied. In the CDI of Volumes 51–60, there are two cases cited, in one of which the request for interest was denied and interest at "the legal rate" for a limited period was awarded in the other. Three cases are cited in Volumes 61–65; two of which were awarded interest. More recently, Volumes 71–80 cite four cases, all of which awarded interest; Volumes 80–85 report just one interest case (interest was awarded). Is there a trend? We're not sure. The problem with making a comparison between past and present based on the cases reported in the CDIs is that BNA does not headnote all issues in the select cases it publishes. See, e.g., ITT Higbie Mfg. Co., 83 LA 394 (Edes, 1984), a case in which the interest issue is discussed and not indexed under interest in Volumes 81–85 of CDI.

such as the state "legal" rate. While interest in arbitration awards traditionally has not been granted, there is reason to believe that a contrary trend has developed.

B. Costs and Fees

In the absence of an express contractual agreement to the contrary, there is an implied agreement on the part of the parties to pay an arbitrator for the expenses incurred and services rendered. Arbitrator J. Jenkins has expressed this notion as follows:

> The authority to award fees and expenses, and the authority to determine who shall pay them, is incident to and necessarily implied from the authority of the arbitrator to determine full [sic] the matters in controversy.[32]

Additional support for this rationale can be found in Section 10 of the Uniform Arbitration Act, which states:

> Unless otherwise provided in the agreement to arbitrate, the arbitrators' expenses and fees, together with other expenses, not including counsel fees, incurred in the conduct of the arbitration, shall be paid as provided in the award.[33]

Rule 44 of the Voluntary Labor Arbitration Rules of the American Arbitration Association, in relevant part, provides:

> Expenses of the arbitration, other than the costs of the stenographic record, including required traveling and other expenses of the Arbitrator and of AAA representatives, and the expenses of any witness or the costs of any proofs produced at the direct request of the Arbitrator, shall be borne equally by the parties unless they agree otherwise, or unless the Arbitrator in the award assesses such expenses or any part thereof against any specified party or parties.[34]

Perhaps the most common situation where arbitrators

---

[32]Associated General Contractors, 58 LA 162, 163 (1972), citing Bernstein v. Perlmutter, (Sup) 37 N.Y.S.2d 95.

[33]See Uniform Arbitration Act (adopted by the National Conference of the Commissioners on Uniform State Laws in 1955 and amended in 1956, and approved by the House of Delegates of the American Bar Association, August 26, 1955, and August 30, 1956).

[34]The Bureau of National Affairs reports that in 91% of the contracts sampled, provisions for arbitration expenses were cited. Under 92% of these provisions, the fee is shared equally by the parties; in 4% the fee is paid by the losing party. Basic Patterns in Union Contract, 12th ed., 39 (BNA Books, 1989).

have assessed costs and expenses of arbitration, including, at times, attorney's fees, is where the employer has initially refused to arbitrate and the union, at its own expense, is forced to secure a court order compelling the company to arbitrate. Such an award, however, is usually made only after a finding that the employer's refusal was merely a delaying tactic rather than a good faith belief that the dispute was not arbitrable.[35] Other arbitrators have ruled that, absent contractual authorization, such a remedy is clearly punitive, and hence not appropriate in the arbitral forum.[36]

Some arbitrators have suggested that in a case where the employer knowingly and/or repeatedly violates the contract, the arbitrator might appropriately charge the employer with the entire cost of the arbitration. Thus, Arbitrator Sidney Wolff has proposed:

> I suggest that, should a case arise that might tempt the arbitrator to impose a penalty when not authorized by the contract, he consider assessing the costs of the proceedings upon the intentional violator, be it the company or union unless barred by the contract. This might tend to prevent a repetition of a violation that does not cause monetary loss.[37]

A particularly troublesome situation may occur when the arbitrator feels that a party has engaged in egregious conduct and should have the costs of the proceedings assessed against it, but the agreement provides that costs should be shared equally. Arbitrator Edgar Jones, Jr., in a postaward hearing, hinted that, under certain circumstances, such an assessment might be proper:

> The Union seeks an award of its costs, including $350.00 in attorney's fees, on the ground that the Company has unwarrantably and unreasonably abused the post-award procedure provided in the May 7 Award, thereby damaging the Union to the extent of all of its costs in making its appearance. But the Agreement is explicit in its direction that arbitral expenses shall be borne equally "except, however, *each party shall bear*

---

[35]See, e.g., High & Mighty Farms, 63 LA 992 (Rose, 1974); Munsingwear, Inc., 65 LA 997 (Blum, undated); Jacuzzi Bros., 49 LA 760 (Bothwell, 1967). Cf. Vancouver Plywood Co., 62 LA 133 (Williams, 1974) (employer not assessed costs where it acted in good faith); Fort Smith Couch & Bedding Co., 64-1 ARB ¶8210 (Emery, 1963).
[36]M & T Co., 69-1 ARB ¶8085 (Caraway, 1968).
[37]Wolff, *The Power of the Arbitrator to Make Monetary Awards*, in Labor Arbitration: Perspectives and Problems supra note 2, at 191. See also Mallinckrodt Chem. Works 50 LA 933, 937 n.4 (Goldberg, undated).

the entire cost, if any, of their representative in the arbitration proceeding.". . . The Arbitrator cannot in the face of that language imply the power, itself not a common provision of collective bargaining agreements, to award all costs against one of the parties, at least in the circumstances of this case. Once again, if it may be argued that there could conceivably occur such an egregious abuse of a grievance procedure as to warrant a punitive allocation of costs, the evidence here . . . falls considerably short of the blatant bad faith that might justify such a punitive award.[38]

Where the agreement mandates that the costs are to be shared equally, the published awards uniformly hold that the arbitrator is without power to make a different allocation.[39] One arbitrator stated the rule this way:

[The agreement] expressly provide[s] each party will equally share the expenses of the arbitrator and all other expenses are to be borne by the party incurring them. It is significant that this provision is found generally within the provisions describing the arbitrator's authority. Thus if the parties had intended to give the arbitrator the authority to assess damages in certain limited situations . . . , the parties must expressly provide such authority in the collective bargaining agreement.[40]

An arbitrator who orders a different allocation than that provided in the labor agreement is subject to reversal by a reviewing court.[41]

1. Costs of Producing Transcripts

In situations where the agreement is silent as to whether the arbitration hearing must be transcribed, there is no legal infirmity when neither the arbitrator nor the parties have it transcribed.[42]

Suppose a party orders a transcript where the agreement

---

[38]Farmer Bros. Co., 65 LA 884, 886 (1975). It is noteworthy that a second postaward hearing was necessary and Arbitrator Jones did not award costs. See Farmer Bros. Co., supra note 18.

[39]American Chain & Cable Co., 58 LA 724 (Dunne, 1972); Memphis Pub. Co., 48 LA 554 (Oppenheim, 1967); Allied Chem. Corp., 47 LA 686 (Hilpert, 1966). But see the discussion of Arbitrator Clair Duff in Litton Systems v. Shopmen Local 522, infra, at note 55 and accompanying text; Fortex Mfg. Co., 67 LA 934 (Bryan, 1976).

[40]Melvindale Schools, 79 LA 27, 33 (Grossman, 1982).

[41]See, e.g., Fortex Mfg. Co. v. Clothing Workers Local 1065, 99 LRRM 2303 (M.D. Ala. 1978).

[42]Mine Workers Dist. 5 v. U.S. Steel Mining Co., 596 F. Supp. 1041 (W.D. Pa. 1984).

provides for sharing of costs? In *Nuturn Corp.*,[43] the parties' agreement provided that "[t]he expense and fees of the Arbitrator shall be shared equally by the Company and Union." The company ordered a court reporter to appear, take and transcribe the hearing before the arbitrator. The company contended that this was a reasonable expense, if not a necessary expense and, accordingly, the union should share in the cost of producing a transcript of the hearing by the reporter.

In ruling for the union, Arbitrator Marshall Seidman pointed out that the proceeding was governed by the Rules of the Federal Mediation and Conciliation Service and the common law of industrial relations for the conduct of the arbitration hearing. Nowhere in the rules or the "common law" is there a requirement that a transcript be provided. The arbitrator stated the rule as follows:

> When a court reporter is present he or she appears at the request of one of the parties. That party is bound to pay his or her full cost, unless the other party volunteers to participate in such payment. It is not for the Arbitrator to compel such payments. The normal meaning of the word "expense" of an Arbitrator is limited to transportation, hotel and meals. It does not include the costs of producing a transcript of the hearing.[44]

Where one party hires a court reporter, and the other does not, the better practice is to allow the nonpaying party to examine, but not reproduce, a copy of the transcript.[45] What remedy is available to the paying party against the other side that uses the transcript? In *Twin Coast Newspapers*,[46] Arbitrator Mei Bickner ordered a union that acquired a copy of the arbitration-hearing transcript from the arbitrator for use in preparing its posthearing brief to pay the company one-half of the difference between the cost of the transcript ($1,242) and the cost of photocopying ($33.40), even though the agree-

---

[43]84 LA 1058 (Seidman, 1985).

[44]Id. at 1060. See also General Tel. Co. of Sw., 79 LA 102 (Holman, 1982) (union not obligated to order copy of transcript or share in cost if copy not ordered, under contract requiring that each party bears expenses of presenting its own case and shall share expenses of arbitrator); Cleveland Pneumatic Tool Co., 42 LA 722 (Dworkin, 1964) (seven-year practice of having transcript did not warrant conclusion that practice was contractual).

[45]See Hill and Sinicropi, Evidence in Arbitration, 2d ed., 301–302 (BNA Books, 1987).

[46]90 LA 1157 (1988).

ment protected the union from any obligation to share in the cost of a transcript without its express consent. The arbitrator found that the intent of the contract is that either party can elect to forsake the advantages of a transcript and, in return, avoid its costs. The union, in using the transcript, freely obligated itself to pay.

2. Late Awards

When the arbitrator's award was issued six weeks late, Arbitrator Otis King, in *Ingram Manufacturing Co.*,[47] ruled that the company could not withhold payment to the arbitrator of his fees and expenses. Management argued that the arbitrator's delay caused additional liability of $1,692 to a reinstated grievant. Further, the employer argued that not only does it not have to pay its share of the costs of the arbitration, but the arbitrator is responsible for a portion of the liability that it has incurred as a result of its discharge of the grievant. Although the contract provided that "[t]he Arbitrator's decision shall be in writing to the Company and the Union within 30 days after the parties have been . . . " fully heard, the Arbitrator ruled that the company was not entitled, without precedent, to give this provision its own particular interpretation. In the arbitrator's words:

> While the parties are free to provide a time limitation upon the issuance of an arbitrator's decision, such provisions are so incongr[u]ous and detrimental to the process of arbitration that they should never be found to exist unless the parties have so provided in the clearest language. Additionally, it is for the arbitrator and not the Company to determine whether he has been ousted of jurisdiction under the terms of the contract.[48]

Arbitrator King went on to note that if the company's view were the rule, an arbitrator could have, in many instances, violated the contract before he ever attempted to write an opinion, for rarely do arbitrators read the contract and briefs until such time as they begin to work on their opinion. Arbitrator King articulated what we believe is the better rule:

> Certainly, if a party is going to contend for so severe a result,

---

[47]77 LA 1198 (1982).
[48]Id. at 1199.

there is an obligation to bring this position to the arbitrator's attention at the hearing. No such courtesy was shown the arbitrator in this case.[49]

3. Loser-Pay-All Provisions

Many agreements contain "loser-pays-all" provisions whereby the losing party is assessed all costs of the proceeding. The reason for such provisions is to prevent a party from proceeding to arbitration with frivolous or nonmeritorious positions. When the award, however, is a compromise settlement—for example, when an employee is reinstated, but without back pay—arbitrators have split the costs, sometimes even making assessments according to some determined degree of fault.[50] On this point, one arbitrator has stated that a distinction should be made between contract interpretation cases where one party may win or lose, and a discharge case, where the union may be compelled under its duty of fair representation to proceed to arbitration. Thus, in *Ocean Spray Cranberries*,[51] Arbitrator John Sembower ruled:

---

[49]Id. at 1200.

[50]See, e.g., Grossmont Union High School, 91 LA 917 (Weiss, 1989) (school district and union are liable, under clause providing that costs are to be shared if decision is "split," for one-half of arbitrator's fees and expenses, where arbitrator upheld union's arbitrability claims as to three grievances involved in dispute but then denied all of them on merits; arbitrability of grievances is not "minor or peripheral issue," since substantial amount of hearing time and of posthearing briefs were devoted to this question and entire dispute could have been dismissed on that basis); Northern Ohio Red Cross Blood Serv., 90 LA 393 (Dworkin, 1988) (costs shared equally where no clear "loser" or "winner"); Elyria Bd. of Educ., 89 LA 477 (Dworkin, 1987) (expenses of arbitrating grievance protesting posting of inaccurate drive times will be shared by parties despite contract requiring payment by "loser," where union's request for renewed selection process for following school year is granted, but request for monetary relief is denied, and arbitrator cannot identify "winner" or "loser" with meaningful certainty); City of Cheyenne, 89 LA 133, 136 (Allen, 1987) (employer assessed two-thirds and union one-third of costs, where employer's position, although not sustained, was "substantive and quite worthy of argument"); Security Contractor Servs., 90 LA 228 (Riker, 1987) (costs of arbitration assessed two-thirds against employer, one-third against union where arbitrability and improper discharge claims sustained but union failed to prove violation of NLRA); McGill Mfg. Co., 67 LA 1135 (Rezler, 1976); Eagle Beverage Co., 60 LA 684 (Andrews, 1973); Selas Corp., 68-2 ARB ¶8732 (Galfand, 1967) (fee was split where neither party could be determined "loser"); W.O. Larson Foundry Co., 42 LA 1286 (Kates, 1964) (union was "heavy loser" and 80% of costs were assessed against labor organization); Tyson Bearing Co., 38 LA 385 (Dworkin, 1962) (reinstatement without back pay warrants assessment against employer, since grievance was sustained to greater degree in favor of union); Atlas Chain & Mfg. Co., 32 LA 117 (Crawford, 1959) (employer to pay two-thirds, union one-third of expenses for five grievances where two were sustained, two denied, and one sustained in part).

[51]68-1 ARB ¶8252 (1968).

The contract contains a clause providing that the party which "loses" shall pay the expenses of the arbitrator, but that if there is a "compromise settlement," the expense is to be divided. There was no "compromise settlement" of this matter, for while the grievances of the two disciplined employees were carried along together, the management made it clear that it modified its action with respect to [V] in light of its own examination of his clear record. However, the arbitrator construes this clause as giving him the prerogative to assign costs to one party as the "loser." While the Union vigorously presented the best possible case on behalf of the Grievant, in a case of this nature it has a legal as well as perhaps a moral obligation to do so. Thus it is not like a controversy over a contract interpretation when indeed one party may "win" and the other "lose," because strictly the Union may not be said to have been the "loser" in this instance. Therefore, the arbitrator should assess the costs evenly.[52]

Arbitrator Jonathan Dworkin, in *Northern Ohio Red Cross Blood Service*,[53] has stated that loser-pay-all provisions are only applicable when a clear loser can be identified:

The contractual penalty for arbitrating a losing case controls only when the prevailing party can be clearly identified. The positions of the parties in this case were completely opposite to one another. The Employer sought dismissal of the grievance and an affirmation that the penalty imposed on Grievant was proper. The Association requested that the penalty be overturned entirely, on the finding that Grievant was not a candidate for discipline. The remedy sought by the Association was expungement of the record with full back pay and benefits. The award is a "split decision." It grants neither the Employer's position nor the Association's. It stems from a finding that Grievant's infraction was serious and warranted commensurately serious corrective discipline, but that the two-month suspension was too long to be reasonable or corrective. Accordingly, the Arbitrator is unable to identify the "winner" or the "loser." It follows that costs and fees must be shared equally, notwithstanding the "loser-pay" provision. . . .[54]

4. Assessing Costs Against the Winning Party

An example of awarding costs and attorney's fees to the unsuccessful party is found in a supplemental award of Arbitrator Clair Duff, which is an appendix to the opinion of a

---

[52]Id. at 3880–3881.
[53]90 LA 393 (1988).
[54]Id. at 398.

federal court in *Litton Systems v. Shopmen Local 522*.[55] An employer's grievance was involved in this case, and although the company did not prevail on the merits, Arbitrator Duff awarded the employer $5,000 in damages as reimbursement for legal services, arbitration fees, and expenses incurred in connection with the hearing and the filing of briefs. The damages were awarded because of "the willful delay in the proceedings caused by the Union's authorized representatives in their persistent attempts to frustrate the arbitration of this grievance."[56] The District Court for the Southern District of Ohio upheld the award, finding "no basis to overturn the arbitrator's decision" even though the agreement was apparently silent on the issue of awarding costs. Attention is called to Arbitrator Duff's reasoning for awarding damages in the form of costs and attorney's fees:

> "The Company and the Union agree that the grievance procedures provided herein are adequate to provide a fair and final determination of all grievances arising under the terms of this contract." Upon mutual selection and appointment of the arbitrator to preside at the arbitration hearing, it becomes incumbent upon him to assure that the negotiated arbitration tribunal affords each party full and complete opportunity for a fair hearing. It is directly contrary to the parties joint promise to resolve disputes by arbitration for one side to flout the whole arbitration process by deliberately engaging in dilatory tactics antithetical to dispute resolution in the orderly fashion bargained for. The contractual grievance machinery is designed to provide an appropriate remedy for all of the various types of contractual violations that may occur. An arbitrator would be rendered powerless to redress clear contractual violations if he would be denied the power to fashion an appropriate and reasonable monetary remedy. Likewise, if no compensatory damages could be awarded for losses occasioned by obvious attempts to frustrate access to the contractually created arbitration forum, an arbitrator would simply be unable to fulfill his obligation to conduct a fair trial of the issue in dispute. If arbitration is to provide an alternative to lockouts and strikes it must remain effective in the face of novel challenges. We believe it is a necessary corollary that where mockery is openly made of the arbitration process, it is implied from the creation of the arbitration tribunal and the authorization of the arbitrator to make a binding decision that he has the power of compensating the party who by

---

[55]90 LRRM 3176 (S.D. Ohio, 1975).
[56]Id. at 3178.

such perversion of the process has been subjected to unnecessary costs that have no reasonable connection with the underlying controversy.

In the Court's Conclusions, reference is made to "awarding damages in the nature of punitive damages." Perhaps a clarification of our intent would be helpful. We directed payment of only those damages necessary to compensate the Company for its actual expenses incurred in those preliminary proceedings where the Union conducted its vigorous and unsuccessful campaign to defeat the exercise of the Company's contractual right to seek relief in the proper contractual forum. Any other claims for damages, either punitive in nature, or amount, or, having any causal connection with the adjudication of the basic dispute, were rejected. The bedrock of our authority is *Section 20* which establishes arbitration and in order to keep the arbitral process a viable institution for the resolution of disputes, we deemed it both reasonable and appropriate to award compensatory damages for conduct that went a vast distance beyond mere foot dragging and produced direct and demonstrable losses.[57]

5. Assignment of Costs Where Hearing Untimely Postponed

Unless the collective bargaining agreement or past practice provides otherwise, where a party has acknowledged responsibility for an untimely postponement of a hearing, that party should be assessed any postponement fee. Indeed, such fees are sometimes assessed against the postponing party even when the contract provides that costs are equally shared.[58]

6. Awarding Costs for Successful Court Actions

Courts are increasingly awarding costs of defending an arbitrator's award against a party asserting frivolous arguments for overturning the award.[59] Similarly, arbitrators have awarded damages represented by a party's actual expendi-

---

[57]Id. at 3179–3180.

[58]Florida Staff Org., 91 LA 1094 (Mase, 1988) (holding that employer should bear expense of arbitrator's cancellation fee where continuance granted); Denver Pub. Schools, 88 LA 507 (Watkins, 1986).

[59]See, e.g., Posadas de P.R. Assocs. v. Asociacion de Empleados de Casino de P.R., 821 F.2d 60, 125 LRRM 3137 (1st Cir. 1987) (awarding double costs to union contesting employer's action to vacate award).

tures incurred over the years to secure an employer's compliance with the agreement.[60]

7. Summary

Absent specific contractual authority, the better rule in grievance arbitration is to reserve awarding of costs for those situations where extreme bad faith is shown. (The better test may be "brazen," or "palpably without merit.") In this regard, such an award should not be made on the arbitrator's own motion, nor should it be granted if not alleged in the lower steps of the grievance procedure. Further, in view of the consequences of a union breaching its duty to fairly represent bargaining-unit employees, there is good reason to refrain from awarding costs against a union, even though the grievance may be considered frivolous. As stated by one arbitrator, "[h]indsight may provide the parties with many reasons for contending that resort to arbitration in a particular case was unwarranted and without justification,"[61] but rarely does a union have the benefit of such clairvoyance.

C. Attorney's Fees

1. Background

Under the prevailing American rule, in a federal action, attorney's fees may not be recovered absent contractual or statutory authorization. The justification for this rule is that "since litigation is at best uncertain one should not be pen-

---

[60]Service Employees Local 722 v. Children's Hosp. Nat'l Medical Center, 117 LRRM 2488, 2490 (D.D.C. 1984) (union entitled to recover expenses incurred in effort to compel employer to comply with court order enforcing award; employer's failure to reinstate grievant pending appeal was "without justification," "without a basis," "vexatious" and, as to the employee, "oppressive"; Wayne County Bd. of Comm'rs v. Police Officer Local 502-M, 254 N.W.2d 896, 95 LRRM 3396, 3397 (Mich. Ct. App. 1977) (upholding arbitrator's award of $27,816 representing arbitration costs borne by union during contract years 1972–1974 to secure contractual compliance by employer, attorney's fees incident to grievance arbitration, and "unusual and excessive administration costs incurred by the union to process and appeal grievances through arbitration to the courts.").

[61]See, e.g., Chattanooga Gas Co., 83 LA 48, 51 (Mullin, 1984) (refusing to assess costs of arbitrating last-chance agreement on union, reasoning that violation of duty of fair representation may result in dire consequences for union's failure to pursue matter to arbitration).

alized for merely defending or prosecuting a lawsuit, and that the poor might be unjustly discouraged from instituting actions to vindicate their rights if the penalty for losing included the fees of their opponents' counsel."[62] In *Alyeska Pipeline Co. v. Wilderness Society*,[63] the Supreme Court reaffirmed the American tradition, but recognized that the general rule is subject to certain narrow exceptions. Thus, a court may "permit the trustee of a fund or property, or a party preserving or recovering a fund for the benefit of others in addition to himself, to recover his costs, including his attorneys' fees, from the fund or property itself or directly from the other parties enjoying the benefit" (common benefit exception).[64] The Court also stated that attorney's fees may be assessed "for the 'willful disobedience of a court order . . .' or when the losing party has 'acted in bad faith, vexatiously, wantonly, or for oppressive reasons . . . .' "[65]

While the exceptions are firmly established, the limits of the bad-faith exception are unclear, especially when applied to arbitration. Generally, three types of cases fall within the bad-faith exception: (1) bad faith occurring during the litigation, (2) bad faith in bringing the action or in causing an action to be brought, and (3) bad faith in the acts giving rise to the substantive claim.[66] The Fourth Circuit has ruled that "[i]n an appropriate case attorneys' fees should be awarded against a party who, without justification, refuses to abide by the award of an arbitrator."[67] The Court of Appeals for the District of Columbia has stated that an "action 'without justification' may be 'vexatious' within the meaning of *Alyeska*, thereby drawing the case within the equitable exception recognized by the Court in that case."[68] The Ninth Circuit discussed the policy reasons for allowing an award of attorney's fees against an employer who refuses to comply with an arbitration award:

---

[62]Fleishmann Distilling Corp. v. Maier Brewing Co., 386 U.S. 714, 718 (1967).

[63]421 U.S. 240, 10 FEP Cases 826 (1975).

[64]Id. at 257.

[65]Id. at 258–259.

[66]Shimman v. Operating Eng'rs Local 18, 744 F.2d 1226, 117 LRRM 2579, 2582 (6th Cir. 1984).

[67]Automobile Workers Local 149 v. American Brake Shoe Co., 298 F.2d 212, 49 LRRM 2480, 2482 (4th Cir.), cert. denied, 369 U.S. 873, 50 LRRM 2170 (1962).

[68]Letter Carriers v. Postal Serv., 590 F.2d 1171, 100 LRRM 2008, 2013 n.11 (D.C. Cir. 1978).

It is generally recognized that labor arbitration advances the goal of industrial stabilization. . . . Engaging in frivolous dilatory tactics not only denies the individual prompt redress, it threatens the goal of industrial peace. Therefore, the deter[r]ence aspect of an award of attorneys' fees is particularly served where a party, without justification, refuses to abide by an arbitrator's award.[69]

In another case the Ninth Circuit stated that the policy concerns raised by frivolous or bad-faith refusals to arbitrate or appeals of district court orders compelling arbitration are the same as those raised by frivolous or bad-faith refusals to comply with an award.[70]

Case law suggests that courts, applying the "vexatiousness" standard of *Alyeska*, will not award attorney's fees simply because it is subsequently determined that a party was incorrect in refusing to abide by an arbitrator's award. To come within the "equitable" exception of *Alyeska*, a party must show that the refusal to abide by an arbitral order amounted to "acts taken 'in bad faith, vexatiously, wantonly, or for oppressive reasons.' "[71] It is an action without any foundation in law that will give rise to an award of attorney's fees. There is some indication, however, that in light of the federal policy favoring labor arbitration, a more relaxed standard for fee requests is operative. As observed by Judge Richard Posner of the Seventh Circuit, "because there are so few grounds for attacking arbitration awards, it is easy to pronounce most such attacks utterly groundless."[72]

---

[69]Petroleum & Indus. Workers v. Western Indus. Maintenance, 707 F.2d 425, 428, 113 LRRM 3010, 3012 (9th Cir. 1983).

[70]Food & Commercial Workers Local 197 v. Alpha Beta Co., 117 LRRM 2326, 2335 (9th Cir. 1984) (upholding district court's denial of attorney's fees, stating that employer's arbitrability defense was not frivolous).

[71]Letter Carriers v. Postal Serv., 590 F.2d 1171, 100 LRRM 2008, 2012 (D.C. Cir. 1978). See also Washington Hosp. Center v. Service Employees Local 722, 241 App.DC 186, 746 F.2d 1503, 117 LRRM 2887 (D.C. Cir. 1984); Boston Univ. Trustees v. American Ass'n of Univ. Professors, 746 F.2d 924, 117 LRRM 2885 (1st Cir. 1984) (assessing double costs but no attorney's fees); Manhattan Coffee Co. v. Teamsters Local 688, 571 F. Supp. 347, 117 LRRM 3129, 3133 (E.D. Mo. 1983) (denying attorney's fees, concluding that employer's contentions were "essentially meritless but not quite frivolous"); Fabricut, Inc. v. Teamsters Local 523, 597 F.2d 227, 101 LRRM 2148 (10th Cir. 1979); Nursing Home & Hosp. Employees Local 1115 Joint Bd. v. Krest View Nursing Home, 100 LRRM 2174 (S.D.N.Y. 1978).

[72]Miller Brewing Co. v. Brewery Workers Local 9, 739 F.2d 1159, 1168, 116 LRRM 3130, 3137 (7th Cir. 1984), cert. denied, 469 U.S. 1160, 118 LRRM 2192 (1985) ("some courts have applied what appears to be a less demanding standard to fee requests in labor arbitration cases than in other cases, by giving the party successfully defending the award his attorney's fees if the opposition was 'without justification' "). See also

2. Arbitral Response

As a general proposition, arbitrators, like the courts, do not award attorney's fees for a simple breach of the collective bargaining agreement. For example, in *Montgomery County Community Action Agency*,[73] Arbitrator Harry Dworkin, denying the union's request for attorney's fees, stated:

> The instant arbitrator therefore concludes that he is prohibited from considering attorney fees as an element of damages and a form of relief inasmuch as, 1) the instrument providing for the arbitration of employee grievances contains no language that expressly, or by clear implication grants such authority; 2) the submission of the grievance to arbitration does not encompass attorney fees as an element of relief; 3) the authority of an arbitrator to award costs against either party, does not extend to attorney fees; 4) the "common law" of labor arbitration, as enunciated by arbitrators in their reported decisions is to the effect that exemplary damages including attorney fees will not be awarded by way of relief; 5) an arbitrator is without authority to award attorney fees absent express language empowering him to consider such, even where there is a finding that the employer's actions were tainted by fraud, malice, wantonness, or caprice, since arbitrators may not award punitive damages against the wrongdoer.[74]

Some arbitrators, however, have held that jurisdiction does exist for awarding attorney's fees. In support of this view, Arbitrator Wilbur Bothwell has held:

> The arbitrator believes that an arbitrator does have jurisdiction and authority to award damages, including attorneys' fees, under appropriate circumstances, even though the Agreement contains no language authorizing the arbitrator to award damages. The award of legal costs and attorneys' fees should not be made in cases where there is evidence of good faith. It should be pointed out that an award of attorneys' fees is not an award of punitive damages when the damages are limited to

---

Automobile Workers Local 1165 v. United States Farm Tools, 762 F.2d 76, 119 LRRM 2559 (8th Cir. 1985) (questioning employer's honest disagreement as to validity of award where employer did not act to have award set aside).

[73]62 LA 1278 (1974).

[74]Id. at 1281. Accord City of San Antonio, 69 LA 541 (Caraway, 1977); George Ellis Co., 68 LA 261 (Sacks, 1977); Westinghouse Transp. Leasing Corp., 69 LA 1210 (Sergent, 1977); Farmer Bros., 65 LA 884 (Jones, 1975); Hampton Corp., 39 LA 177 (Davis, 1962).

the actual expenses incurred in the unnecessary legal proceedings.[75]

Where one arbitrator awarded $200 in attorney's fees for an employer's simple breach involving payment of holiday pay, the First Circuit affirmed a lower court's determination that the remedy was improper. The court pointed out that arbitrator cited no provision in the agreement authorizing such an award and did not provide any rationale for the remedy. The court further reasoned that there was no showing that the union made a claim for such damages, or alleged willful, wanton, or bad faith conduct that could justify such an award of attorney's fees.[76]

In cases where the employer is claiming monetary damages for breach of the no-strike clause, arbitrators have frequently awarded attorney's fees.[77] Thus, in *Fortex Manufacturing Co. v. Clothing Workers Local 1065*,[78] a federal district court upheld an arbitrator's award of attorney's fees because the parties stipulated that the arbitrator was to base his decision upon federal law as if the action were brought in federal court. Since the employer voluntarily withdrew its Section 301 suit from district court and agreed to submit the dispute over damages to arbitration, and because the arbitrator did not stray from the scope of the submission (e.g., the arbitrator's powers would equal the court's powers), the court deferred to the arbitrator's grant of legal fees based upon his conclusion that the union failed to undertake every reasonable means to end the strike.

Arbitrators have also come down hard on unions that engage in deliberate dilatory tactics aimed at frustrating the grievance procedure. In *Litton Systems v. Shopmen Local 522*,[79]

---

[75]Leavenworth Times, 71 LA 396, 409 (1978). Other cases awarding attorney's fees include, Synergy Gas Co., 91 LA 77 (Simons, 1987); Basic Vegetable Prods., 64 LA 620 (Gould, 1975); Sonic Knitting Indus., 65 LA 453, 469 (Helfand, 1975); Sunshine Convalescent Hosp., 62 LA 276 (Lennard, 1974).

[76]Bacardi Corp. v. Congreso de Uniones Indus. de P.R., 692 F.2d 210, 111 LRRM 2923 (1st Cir. 1982).

[77]See Chapter 11, *Employers' Remedies for Breach of No-Strike Clause.* For a comprehensive review of the issue of attorney's fees and recent litigation, see Sterling Gravure Co., Div. of Sterling Regal, 79-2 ARB ¶8325 (Kaplan, 1979). See also Rust Eng'g Co., 77 LA 488 (Williams 1981); Fortex Mfg. Co., 67 LA 934 (Bryan, 1976), enf'd, Fortex Mfg. Co. v. Clothing Workers Local 1065, 99 LRRM 2303 (M.D. Ala. 1978).

[78]99 LRRM 2303 (M.D. Ala. 1978).

[79]90 LRRM 3176 (S.D. Ohio 1975).

a federal district court upheld an award by Arbitrator Clair V. Duff of attorney's fees and expenses to the employer caused by a union's unjustified delay in proceeding through arbitration. The court concluded that the award drew its essence from the contract because it agreed with the arbitrator's supplemental decision. In the supplemental decision the arbitrator had found that the grievance arbitration procedure was totally frustrated and essentially abandoned by the union's deliberate dilatory tactics aimed at avoiding the speedy and efficient dispute resolution procedure provided for in the contract. The arbitrator reasoned that if no compensatory damages could be awarded for losses occasioned by attempts to frustrate the grievance procedure, an arbitrator would be unable to fulfill his obligation to conduct a fair trial of the issue in dispute.

3. Sanctions Under Federal Rule 11

Rule 11 of the Federal Rules of Civil Procedure provides for sanctions (including reasonable attorney's fees) against pleadings that do not reflect the signing attorney's "belief formed after reasonable inquiry [that the pleading] is well grounded in fact and is warranted by existing law or a good-faith argument for the extension, modification, or reversal of existing law."[80]

4. Summary

The decisions indicate that attorney's fees are appropriate, not as a matter of course for simply arbitrating a particular case but, rather, as an element of damages resulting from a party's bad-faith refusal to comply with the terms of a collective bargaining agreement or the mandates of a prior arbitration award. An award of attorney's fees in a labor dispute as an appropriate amount of damages should not be seen as a punitive remedy, especially when the arbitrator finds conscious, deliberate, and egregious wrongdoing by a party.

---

[80]Dreis & Krump Mfg. Co. v. Machinists Dist. 8, 802 F.2d 247, 255, 123 LRRM 2654 (7th Cir. 1986) (holding union entitled to attorney's fees in employer's unsuccessful action to vacate).

D. Attorney's Fees in Federal-Sector Arbitration[81]

Two separate provisions for awarding attorney's fees are included in the Civil Service Reform Act (CSRA) of 1978: first, an amendment to Section 702 of the Back Pay Act and, second, 5 U.S.C. Section 7701(g) establishing standards for awarding fees by the Merit System Protection Board (MSPB). Both provisions are relevant since the amendments of the Back Pay Act incorporate by reference the standards established by the MSPB.

The Back Pay Act Amendment,[82] of the CSRA outlines the threshold requirement for any award of attorney's fees. In relevant part the Act provides:

> (b)(1) An employee of an agency who, on the basis of a timely appeal or an administrative determination (including a decision relating to an unfair labor practice or a grievance) is found by appropriate authority under applicable law, rule, regulation, or collective bargaining agreement, to have been affected by an unjustified or unwarranted personnel action which has resulted in the withdrawal or reduction of all or part of the pay, allowances, or differentials of the employee—
>
> (A) is entitled, on correction of the personnel action, to receive for the period for which the personnel action was in effect—
>
> . . .
>
> (ii) reasonable attorney fees related to the personnel action which, with respect to any decision relating to an unfair labor practice or a grievance processed under a procedure negotiated in accordance with chapter 71 of this title, . . . shall be awarded in accordance with standards established under section 7701(g) of this title; . . .
>
> . . .
>
> (3) This subsection does not apply to any reclassification action nor authorize the setting aside of an otherwise proper promotion by a selecting official from a group of properly ranked and certified candidates.

In brief, the amendment provides that when an "appro-

---

[81]See generally Reischl, *Attorney Fees in Arbitration: Law and Practice*, in Grievance Arbitration in the Federal Service (Federal Personnel Mgmt. Inst., 1987); Bufe and Ferris, *A Second View of Awarding Attorney's Fees in Federal Sector Arbitration*, 38 Arb. J. 21 (1983); Moore, *Awarding Attorney's Fees in Federal Sector Arbitration*, 37 Arb. J. 38 (1982); Kagel, *Grievance Arbitration in the Federal Service: Still Hardly Final and Binding?*, in Arbitration Issues for the 1980s, Proceedings of the 34th Annual Meeting, National Academy of Arbitrators, 178–206 (BNA Books, 1982).
[82]5 U.S.C. §5596 (Supp. II 1979).

priate authority" (the arbitrator) determines that an employee has been affected by an "unjustified or unwarranted personnel action" resulting in the "withdrawal or reduction" of pay, the employee is entitled to back pay and, in certain circumstances, attorneys' fees. An "unjustified or unwarranted personnel action" is defined as "an act of commission or an act of omission" that is "unjustified or unwarranted under applicable law, Executive Order, rule, regulation, or mandatory personnel policy established by an agency, or through a collective bargaining agreement." Absent a finding that "pay, allowances, or differentials" were improperly withdrawn or withheld, there can be no entitlement to attorney's fees, regardless of whether there has been any other violation.

1. Entitlement Under 5 U.S.C. Section 7701(g)

Satisfying the criteria of the Back Pay Act is the first step in securing an award of attorney's fees in a federal-sector arbitration. The second set of criteria governing an arbitral award of fees is outlined in 5 U.S.C. Section 7701(g). That section provides that the MSPB may award attorney's fees when it determines that (1) an agency has discriminated on the basis of race, color, religion, sex, national origin, age, handicapping condition, marital status, or political affiliation; or (2) the grievant is a "prevailing party" in a nondiscrimination appeal and attorney's fees are warranted "in the interest of justice." In the latter case, the party requesting such fees must satisfy both conditions. Attorney's fees do not automatically accompany success on the merits. A fee award is discretionary.

Who is a "prevailing party?" A "prevailing party" is a grievant who obtains all or a significant part of the relief sought. It is not necessary that the grievant obtain 100 percent of the relief he or she seeks in order to qualify as a prevailing party. For example, a discharge that is later reduced to a suspension by an arbitrator may, under certain circumstances, qualify for attorney's fees.[83] Moreover, an individual grievant

---

[83]Hines Veterans Admin. Hosp., 85 LA 239 (Wolff, 1985) (discharge reduced to suspension); Customs Serv., 79 LA 284, 287 (Rocha, 1982) ("significant result was reinstatement with about $22,000 in back pay; this remedy was substantially all the relief sought").

may be awarded fees as a "prevailing party" even though he is represented by a union.[84]

The leading case on the meaning of the term "in the interest of justice" is *Allen v. Postal Service*,[85] where in 1980 the MSPB formulated the following circumstances for determining when "justice" warrants an award of fees:

> 1. Where the agency engaged in a "prohibited personnel practice";
> 2. Where the agency's action was "clearly without merit," or was "wholly unfounded" or the employee is "substantially innocent" of the charges brought by the agency.
> 3. Where the agency initiated the action against an employee in "bad faith," including:
> a. Where the agency's action was brought to "harass" the employee;
> b. Where the agency's action was brought in "exert improper pressure on the employee to act in certain ways";
> 4. Where the agency committed a "gross procedural error" which "prolonged the proceeding" or "severely prejudiced" the employee;
> 5. Where the agency "knew or should have known that it would not prevail on the merits" when it brought the proceeding.[86]

The MSPB in *Allen* emphasized that the list was not exhaustive, but illustrative and "should serve primarily as directional markers toward the 'interest of justice.'"

More recently, *Naval Air Development Center and Government Employees (AFGE) Local 1968*,[87] cites six instances in which the "interest of justice" requirement may be served:

> "a. Instances where the agency presents little or no evidence to support its actions or demonstrates either a lack of or negligent preparation of the case. This includes instances where the agency's action lacks substantial justification or is totally unfounded and clearly without merit. For example, a situation where the agency's careful reading of the relevant statutes and regulations would have promptly shown that its interpretation was erroneous.
> "b. Instances where agency ill will, or negligence, tainted

---

[84]Veterans Admin., 88 LA 554, 563 (Byars, 1986) ("multiplicity and complexity of issues involved in this case establishes the Grievant's need to employ outside legal counsel").

[85]2 MSPB 582, 80 FMSR 7015 (1980).

[86]Id. at 587.

[87]21 FLRA 131 (1986), cited in Williams Air Force Base, 89 LA 671 (Smith, 1987).

the action against the employee to an unconscionable degree. This may be inferred from agency action or inaction throughout the proceedings.

"c. Instances where the agency initiated action against any employee in disregard of prevailing law, regulations, or negotiated agreement provisions on federal policy. Examples include actions based on improper denial of overtime, environmental differential pay, shift differentials, hazardous duty pay, annual leave, administrative leave, or official time for representational functions.

"d. Instances where the employee is ultimately found to be substantially innocent of the charges brought by the agency. This determination is made on the basis of the result of the appeal rather than on the evidence and information available to the agency at the time the agency effected the action. This standard is not met, however, where the employee believes that he or she is substantially innocent, can prove his or her innocence, and deliberately does not communicate all of the facts to the agency deciding official where the employee's disclosure would reasonably have caused the agency official to modify or overturn the action. Such an employee deliberately and improperly prolongs the agency's legal proceedings and cannot be regarded as an innocent victim who is entitled to attorney fees in the interest of justice.

"e. Instances where the agency fails to inquire into facts presented by the employee or fails to conduct a prudent inquiry into the employee's contradictory facts presented by the employee, the agency would or should have ascertained at the outset that the charges against the employee were without merit or that the grievance should have been sustained.

"f. Instances where there is either a service rendered to the federal work force or there is a benefit to the public derived from maintaining the action. For example, situations where an employee's grievance leads to correction of workplace problems affecting a segment of the workforce, as in the instant case."[88]

One arbitrator, interpreting the "interest of justice" standard, noted that "[d]etermining whether conduct is 'clearly without merit' or 'tainted . . . to an unconscionable degree' or 'totally unfounded' requires the arbitrator to establish the point separating fault from extreme fault in agency performance."[89] The arbitrator went on to note that in considering problems of employer fault, the neutral must be mindful of

---

[88]89 LA at 674.
[89]Williams Air Force Base, supra note 87, at 674.

the purpose of fee awards: "to minimize the burden upon the employee—not to punish the agency."[90]

Finally, any fee that is awarded must actually have been incurred by an attorney or someone working under the direction of an attorney,[91] and the amount must be "reasonable."[92] In *Federal Correctional Institution*,[93] Arbitrator Harold White concluded that costs for photocopying, court reporters, transcripts, and the fees and costs of the arbitrator could not be awarded under the Back Pay Act and section 7701. As correctly stated by the arbitrator, under federal law "attorney's" fees are not synonymous with "all expenses."

---

[90]Id. at 675.

[91]See the discussion in Reischl, supra note 81, at 186–188.

[92]The MSPB has adopted a substantial body of law from the federal courts to define a "reasonable fee." See the discussion by Moore, supra note 81 at 45–47.

[93]90 LA 942 (1987).

Chapter 21

Miscellaneous Problem Areas

A. Remedy for Noncompliance with Arbitrator's Award

What is the remedy when a party does not abide by an arbitrator's award? In *American Chain & Cable Co.*,[1] the union requested that the employer put into effect an arbitration award issued by another arbitrator involving job classifications. When the company refused, rather than bring suit under Section 301 of Taft-Hartley to compel compliance with the award,[2] the union filed another grievance alleging a violation of that part of the agreement providing that an arbitration award, once issued, should be final and binding upon both parties. The union also requested the costs of processing the grievance, as well as interest on the money involved in the prior award "until such time as the award is finally made effective so far as the new rates of pay are concerned." In returning the case to the parties, Arbitrator James Dunne found that no appropriate remedy existed in the arbitral forum for this type of violation. Attention is called to his reasoning:

> In any event, it is clear that the power and authority to enforce or set aside another arbitrator's award does not lie with this (or any other) arbitrator, even though the parties allowed the question to be heard by him without challenge to the propriety of it being presented to him. An arbitrator simply does not, under the law, possess enforcement powers, nor does he

---

[1]58 LA 724 (Dunne, 1972).
[2]See the discussion of Textile Workers v. Lincoln Mills, 353 U.S. 448, 40 LRRM 2113 (1957), in Chapter 3, at notes 16–25 and accompanying text.

possess the power to modify or set aside arbitration awards. This is clearly a function of a court of competent jurisdiction whose power flows from the law, not from a contract.[3]

The arbitrator also denied the union's request for the costs of the arbitration and any interest on the money owed under the prior award, reasoning that the parties' collective bargaining agreement required that the parties share equally the fees and expenses of arbitration.

The reasoning of the arbitrator in *American Chain* does not represent the better weight of authority. Numerous arbitrators have properly held that jurisdiction exists to interpret the terms of a prior award, especially when the contract provides that the decision of the arbitrator shall be final and binding.[4]

B. Remedies Where Grievance Procedure Fails to Provide Relief

As noted in an earlier chapter,[5] in those cases where employees can effectively protect their interests by filing a grievance, arbitrators have required that employees pursue that route rather than resort to "self-help." Cases arise, however, where the grievance procedure may not provide an adequate remedy for a violation of the agreement. Paul Prasow and Edward Peters have considered this issue within the context of an employee who is improperly forced to work overtime. If, consistent with the "self-help" rule, the employee "obeys now and grieves later," what is an appropriate remedy for that employee? Stated another way, what protection does an employee have against continued managerial action detrimental to contract rights where invoking the grievance procedure

---

[3]58 LA at 732.

[4]See, e.g., Duquesne Light Co., 90 LA 860 (Probst, 1988) (holding two-week delay in complying with reinstatement order not unreasonable); Synergy Gas Co., 91 LA 77 (Simons, 1987) (interpreting prior award, and awarding interest and attorney's fees for employer's delaying tactics); National Cash Register Co., 90 LA 252 (Krislov, 1987) (finding that employer complied with remedy mandated by another arbitrator); Northwest Airlines, 89 LA 484 (Flagler, 1987) (interpreting prior award and subsequent settlement agreement); Willamette Indus., 88 LA 11, 17 (Hayford, 1986) (holding that employer acted improperly in failing to reinstate employee pursuant to prior award).

[5]See Chapter 8, at notes 215–222 and topic titled "Reduction for 'Self Help.' "

would arguably fail to provide appropriate relief? Prasow and Peters offer the following thoughts on this issue:

> There is no simple answer to this perplexing question. However, several observations are warranted. In the first place, the immediate objective in all such cases is to remove the detriment to which the employee was improperly subjected by issuing a "cease and desist" order, to prevent recurrence in the future. The Arbitrator can direct that the improper conduct be stopped.
> In the second place, where the remedy is at the heart of the dispute, the parties have a number of approaches they can follow. They could limit the authority of the Arbitrator to determine whether or not the Agreement was violated, reserving to themselves the fixing of the remedy. An extension of this method is to provide that if the Arbitrator should find that a violation occurred, a specific remedy could be stipulated in the submission agreement. . . . Where the parties reserve the right to negotiate their own remedy, they could also provide that, in the event of failure to agree, the matter may be referred back to the Arbitrator for resolution of this problem.[6]

They specifically urge the parties to consider using a submission to solve this problem:

> The submission agreement is especially well adapted to a definition of the Arbitrator's authority on remedies. Where the remedy is important and the contract seems to make no provision for it, the parties may very well include in the submission their views on the remedy. This should be done before the hearing, when the outcome on the substantive issue has not yet been determined.[7]

As a final note on the matter of those who resort to self-help where no remedy is possible for the employee to be made whole, Prasow and Peters argue that, in these exceptional cases, two basic criteria applied by the courts when considering petitions for injunctive relief may be resorted to:

> 1. Will the damage suffered by the petitioner be irreparable if he is subsequently proved to be the victim of an illegal wrongful action?
> 2. Will the damage to the petitioner be substantial enough to warrant restraining the other party, who might be subsequently proved to be in the right, and in turn suffer needless

---

[6]Prasow and Peters, Arbitration and Collective Bargaining, 223 (McGraw-Hill, 1970), citing Globe-Union, 42 LA 713, 721 (Prasow, 1962).
[7]Prasow and Peters, at 223–224.

harassment, perhaps irreparable damage, by the restraining order?[8]

They argue that if the aggrieved employee could meet these tests, it would seem inappropriate for an arbitrator to take an inflexible position against self-help.

When security employees (represented by the AFGE) filed a harassment charge against a supervisor (requesting that the harassment stop and that the grievants receive a written apology), Arbitrator James Sherman, in a 1986 unpublished decision, had this to say about the function of an arbitrator:

> The instant grievance contains allegations of misconduct which, if fully supported by the evidence, would call for a remedy consisting of a cease and desist order and possibly more specific directions designed to remedy the situation. However, the arbitrator finds serious problems with the evidence and with the remedy requested.
>
> . . . [T]he arbitrator is concerned that the remedy requested by the Union involves matters which the contracting parties never intended the Arbitrator to consider and adjudicate. . . . [T]he only effective remedy would be a system of monitoring the relationship which involves immediately investigating each and every communication that was less than ideal. Of course, this Arbitrator would not interject himself into the relationship in this manner. If this is to be done it will have to be done by agreement of the parties and the role of the investigator will have to be filled by someone more readily accessible to the parties than this Arbitrator, perhaps someone who is trusted by all interested parties and is assigned to this work location in a capacity unrelated to the security function.

As implied by Arbitrator Sherman, sometimes the cure is worse than the disease.

C. Granting a Remedy not Requested by a Party

While it is generally understood that the arbitration of a substantive issue empowers an arbitrator to issue an appropriate remedy, it is not always certain that an arbitrator will order a remedy that has not been requested or discussed, either in the lower steps of the grievance procedure or at the hearing. This is especially the case where a particular remedy cannot

---

[8]Id. at 224.

be implied from the nature of the grievance. For example, the fact that an employee does not request back pay in a grievance alleging an improper discharge should not preclude an arbitrator from making a back-pay award if the facts otherwise indicate that such a remedy is warranted.[9] However, the same cannot be said of monetary damages for a breach of the no-strike clause, or reinstatement to a position other than the one from which a grievant was discharged. Thus it should be emphasized that even after the parties have empowered the arbitrator with jurisdiction to decide the substantive issue, they should specifically outline the requested relief, either in the grievance itself or at the hearing, in order to ensure that an appropriate remedy will issue. In most cases submission of the question, "What is the appropriate remedy?" will suffice.[10] Failure to do so may result in an award with inappropriate relief, or no relief, being granted.[11]

D. Extending a Remedy to a Nongrievant: The Class-Action Concept in Arbitration

Arbitrators are in disagreement concerning the circumstances, if any, that would warrant extending relief to an employee who is not properly designated as an aggrieved in the case before the arbitrator. While many arbitrators declare that no jurisdiction exists to extend a remedy to an employee not named as a grievant,[12] situations may exist that justify

---

[9]See, e.g., Board of Junior College Dist. 508, County of Cook and State of Illinois, 70-1 ARB ¶8262 (Sembower, 1969).

[10]Amana Refrigeration, 86 LA 827, 832 (Kulkis, 1986) ("The failure of the parties to discuss the potential issue . . . is not binding upon the Arbitrator or limit his jurisdiction insofar as considering a remedy is concerned. . . . [T]he parties placed the matter before the Arbitrator by asking, 'What is the appropriate remedy?' ").

[11]Cf. Westinghouse Air Brake Co., 8 LA 772 (Blair, 1947).

[12]United States Steel Corp., 89 LA 300 (Dybeck, 1987) (no authorization for "class grievance" where agreement generally contemplates initiation of grievances by complaint forms signed by aggrieved employees, and alleged violation not violation owed by employer to union as such); Delmarva Power & Light Co., 72 LA 501, 502 (Coburn, 1979) ("It may well be, as the Union argues, that other employees similarly situated to [grievant] have also filed grievances raising the same issue as in this case, but none of these grievances has been submitted to this arbitration. Therefore, it seems to me that I would be exceeding my authority as the arbitrator to find that those grievances are to be included within the scope of the decision rendered here."); American Bakeries Co., 67 LA 474 (Bowles, 1976) (no remedy for nongrieving employees where it is uncertain whether others are similarly situated); Monongahela Power Co., 64 LA 1210 (Blue, 1975) (arbitrator deciding merits of one grievance does not

providing relief to a nongrieving employee. Where, for example, the grievance on its face is a complaint by the union as representative of a group of similarly situated employees, an arbitrator may appropriately grant class relief. Similarly, if the grievance clearly is intended to apply to all employees, relief should not be denied merely because all similarly affected employees have failed to sign unless, of course, the contract mandates otherwise.[13] As stated by one arbitrator,

> Arbitration is or should be a cost-and-time effective process. If an arbitrator had to be hired for every employee affected by identical circumstances, productivity per person hour at the plant could suffer materially, and union and company coffers would suffer financially.[14]

In these situations, by joining multiple—or potentially multiple—complaints into one grievance, similar or identical issues can be decided in one hearing, thus permitting the expeditious, efficient, and inexpensive handling of the matter at issue.[15]

Where it was unclear whether a remedy applied to some unnamed employees, Arbitrator Marlin Volz ordered the parties to return the case to the original arbitrator for a clarification of his award.[16]

There should be no question regarding the union acting as a representative for a properly designated class. In *Teams-*

---

have authority to decide that two other grievances be forfeited in future); United Tel. Sys., 64 LA 525, 527 (Cohen, 1975) (only those grievants who specifically filed complaints are entitled to redress; to do otherwise would convert hearing into species of class action); Colorpac, Inc., 62 LA 1029 (Chalfie, 1974) (no authority to extend award to similarly situated employees).

[13]Gates Rubber Co., 90 LA 1045, 1048 (Cohen, 1988) (stating "for a class action for a union grievance to be permissible, the facts must apply to all employees with very little variation"); South Cent. Bell Tel. Co., 72 LA 333 (Morris, 1979); Continental Tenn. Lines, 72 LA 619, 621 (Cocalis, 1979); Ohio State Univ., 69 LA 1004 (Bell, 1977); West Allis-West Milwaukee Joint City School Dist., 68 LA 644 (Yaffe, 1977); ASG Indus., 68 LA 304 (Elkouri, 1977); Weyerhaeuser Co., 65 LA 1061 (Foster, 1975); American Art Clay Co., 64 LA 34 (Fish, 1975) (remedy extended to 38 employees who were not advised that they had option of waiting and receiving overtime); Allegheny Ludlum Steel Corp., 62 LA 859 (Porter, 1974); S.S. Kresge Co., 61 LA 975 (Groty, 1973); McDonnell Douglas Corp., 60 LA 1300 (Sembower, 1973); Bethlehem Steel Co., 54 LA 445 (Gill, 1969) (retroactive relief for all affected employees); Philip Carey Mfg. Co., 37 LA 134 (Gill, 1961).

[14]Lake Erie Screw Corp., 90 LA 204, 206 (Coyne, 1987) (holding back-pay award to machine operator improperly denied higher rate when assigned to higher classification applicable to all machine operators even though grievance signed by single operator).

[15]Fort Wayne Community Schools, 61 LA 1159, 1163–1164 (Doppelt, 1973).

[16]Peabody Coal Co., 90 LA 201 (1987).

ters Local 744 v. Skokie Valley Beverage Co.,[17] a federal district court held that even though a contractual grievance procedure omitted any reference to "union," it was proper for a labor organization to file a grievance in its own name on behalf of aggrieved employees. Given the presumption of arbitrability and the union's authority as exclusive bargaining representative to control the grievance process, the court correctly ruled that the union could act for a group of employees, even though the grievance form required an employee to execute a written signed statement. In another case, the union claimed nonarbitrability to avoid the requirement that it exhaust contractual remedies before pursuing a claim against management in court. In support of its claim, the union argued that contract's grievance procedure only allowed individual employees to file grievances. The contract provided:

> "Should any dispute or grievances arise under any of the terms of this Agreement, the aggrieved employee or employees must file the grievance in writing within five (5) working days of the occurrence of said grievance in order for the grievance to be timely."[18]

The federal court reasoned that the union was the exclusive bargaining agent for the unit and the grievance procedure was an element of the continuous bargaining process. Noting the presumption of arbitrability, the court concluded that the union, as a party to the parties' contract, had the authority to file a grievance as agent of the employees.[19]

E. Remedies and Forfeiture Clauses

Many collective bargaining agreements contain forfeiture clauses that provide that if a written answer is not given by

---

[17]644 F. Supp. 213, 123 LRRM 3175 (N.D. Ill. 1986).

[18]Painters Dist. Council No. 2 v. Tiger Stripers, 582 F. Supp. 860, 117 LRRM 3021, 3023 (E.D. Mo. 1984).

[19]Id. See also Teamsters Local 657 v. Stanley Structures, 735 F.2d 903, 117 LRRM 2119 (5th Cir. 1984) (rejecting claim that grievance was not procedurally arbitrable because union filed grievances on employees' behalf, contrary to provision that requires employees themselves to file); Southern Fla. Hotel & Motel Ass'n, 245 NLRB 561, 102 LRRM 1578 (1979) (unlawful frustration of arbitration procedure where employers that terminated large number of employees insisted that union's multiple grievances be tried as separate grievances before different arbitrators); Arkansas State Highway Employees Local 1315 v. Smith, 585 F.2d 876, 99 LRRM 3168 (8th Cir. 1978) (holding grievance procedure under which employer will not consider grievance unless employee submits written complaint directly to employer representative deprives union of first amendment right).

management within the time limits specified in the grievance procedure, the grievance should be considered granted as requested. Suppose a grievant requests a remedy that is clearly outlandish and, through oversight, management does not deny the grievance within the time limits outlined in the agreement. Does the existence of the forfeiture clause mandate that the remedy requested should be granted? One arbitrator, addressing a class grievance which, if granted, would result in an award of $300,000 (if the grievance were a true class action), remarked that the burden which the grievant sought to impose on management was manifestly unjust and contrary to the allegedly good faith negotiations that preceded it. He went on to note, however, that his concept of what is just or unjust is not at issue, that no arbitrator is empowered to reform a contract to better fit what he believes is reasonable. The arbitrator's reasoning is especially noteworthy:

> The decision-making process in this and every other case must be premised on contract reading, interpretation, and application. This principle is applied time and again to grievances protesting wrongful discharges, which are commenced outside contractual time limits. In such instances, it is held that contractually required forfeitures govern regardless of the merit of an aggrieved employee's position. There is little conceptual difference between upholding, for procedural default, the unjust discharge of an employee who perhaps has many years of seniority and is virtually unemployable elsewhere, and allowing this Grievant to unjustly extract an enormous amount of money from the Company for the same reason.[20]

The arbitrator finally held that the grievance was never a "legitimate class action" since "the other members of the unit were not included in the grievance at the start, were not represented by this Employee [the grievant], and could not subsequently join in the grievance through their shirttail petition."[21]

Arbitrator Anthony Sinicropi, in an unpublished decision, held that a forfeiture clause could not work against management when the grievance at issue was filed seven years after the time limit. In a prior arbitration the arbitrator ruled that a forfeiture provision applied to some 16 grievances that the company had failed to timely answer (the merits of the griev-

---

[20]AVCO New Idea, 86 LA 27, 31 (Dworkin, 1985).
[21]Id. at 32.

ances or the remedies to be applied were not discussed at the first hearing). The question before Arbitrator Sinicropi in a second arbitration was whether the company was liable for seven years' back pay (the pay differential between the grievant's position and the position the grievant claimed she should have been awarded seven years before) in one of the grievances management had failed to timely deny. In denying any monetary remedy, the arbitrator reasoned that no remedy could be awarded for a bad faith attempt to slip by management a grievance which the union knew was untimely. The grievance, as well as the remedy, must have a foundation in reason and fact.[22]

In *Electrical Workers (IBEW), Local 1842 v. Cincinnati Electronics Corp.*,[23] a grievance protested the assignment to salaried employees of certain production work and requested as relief that such work " 'be placed on the production floor immediately [and] . . . [a]ll monies due and owing.' " The arbitrator determined that management had failed "to present a timely answer" to the grievance, which under the forfeiture provision of the contract required that " 'the grievance shall be deemed to have been granted.' " The arbitrator found that he was required by that provision to sustain the grievance, but further held that the union still had the burden of establishing the relief to which it was entitled, which was limited to that proximately resulting from the contractual violations claimed. Both the district court and the Sixth Circuit upheld the award, even though the arbitrator awarded the union approximately $3,000 " 'to deter temptation to default in response to grievances instead of complying with negotiated time limitations.' "

F. Remedies for Deliberate and Continued Violations of the Agreement

As noted in prior sections, arbitrators have justified the imposition of costs,[24] attorneys' fees,[25] and even "punitive type"

---

[22]Cf. Teamsters Local 657 v. Stanley Structures, supra note 19 (upholding award based on employer's failure to notify union of dismissal of employees within time limits prescribed by agreement).
[23]808 F.2d 1201, 124 LRRM 2473, 2474–2475 (6th Cir. 1987).
[24]See Chapter 20, notes 32–41 and accompanying text.
[25]Id. at notes 62–93 and accompanying text.

remedies[26] where a party deliberately and repeatedly ignores specific obligations under the agreement. Where breaches of the no-strike clause are found, monetary damages may also be appropriately assessed against a labor organization.[27] In those situations where repeated violations characterize the parties' relationship, there may be no effective remedy that can restore the status quo and make the injured party whole, and it should be so recognized by an arbitrator. In this regard, the better rule has been well summarized by Arbitrator Paul Prasow as follows:

> The real problem [in cases where a party deliberately and repeatedly ignores certain provisions] is the breakdown in the relationship between the parties. Arbitration is not designed to deal with such problems. If an Arbitration Board finds a deliberate violation of the Agreement, it should say so. However, it would seem inappropriate for the Board to fashion a remedy to deal with intentional violations on exactly the same basis as unintentional ones. If one party or the other appears determined to evade the provisions of the contract, the best approach is for the parties to face the issue frankly, rather than expect the arbitration process to deal with a situation which is beyond its purpose.[28]

G. Awarding Damages for Mental Distress

In *Segarra v. Sea-Land Service*,[29] the Court of Appeals for the First Circuit held that compensation for mental distress in the context of labor disputes is warranted only in the exceptional case of extreme misconduct. The court of appeals, reversing a judgment of $30,000 against a union in a fair representation suit, stated:

> The district court's award was not based on any finding that appellee suffered actual, though intangible, mental injury. . . . The element of speculation is a necessary evil inherent in valuation of the emotional harm caused by violation of a federal right. Special caution against excessive awards is counseled in the labor law context where a carefully conceived and administered balance between the rights, powers and duties of

---

[26]See Chapter 19, at notes 23–25 and accompanying text.
[27]See Chapter 11, at notes 54–86 and accompanying text.
[28]Globe-Union, 42 LA 713, 721 (1963), as cited in Prasow and Peters, supra note 6, at 224.
[29]581 F.2d 291, 99 LRRM 2198 (1st Cir. 1978).

union, management and individual employee has been established by Congress on a national scale. . . . For that reason, damages for mental distress are only appropriate in cases of extreme misconduct.[30]

While mental distress damages are now recoverable in some breach-of-contract actions,[31] in the labor arbitration context there is strong argument that an arbitrator should never award damages for mental distress, even when there is no question of actual injury to the grievant. The question is not one of power generally, but rather whether it can reasonably be concluded that the parties, in negotiating their agreement, contemplated that such relief could be secured in the arbitral forum. The absence of reported decisions in the area[32] arguably indicates that the better rule is to refrain altogether from making awards for emotional distress arising out of an employer's breach of contract. Such relief is better left to the expertise of the courts than the labor arbitrator.

H. Dues Withholding

When an employer improperly deducts union dues from an employee, "back pay" in the amount of dues improperly deducted may be ordered as a remedy. If an improper deduction of dues results in overpayment to a labor organization, an employer should be permitted the right to recoup from the union the amount of overpayment by reducing the current payment of the dues by the specified amount.[33] In those cases where an employee has been reinstated with full or partial

---

[30]99 LRRM at 2204.

[31]See Hillman, Contract Remedies, Equity, and Restitution, 143 (Iowa Law School, 1979).

[32]See, e.g., Stone Container Corp., 91 LA 1186, 1192 (Ross, 1988) (denying compensation for grievant's "embarrassment, humiliation and anxiety" resulting from negligence of company in drug testing); Klamath County, Or., 90 LA 354, 360 (Levak, 1987) (ruling that employee was justifiably suspended, but ordering employer to return one half of lost wages where management improperly embarrassed and humiliated grievant; agreement provided that discipline shall be imposed in manner that will not unduly embarrass or humiliate employee before other employees and public).

[33]Machinists Lodge 2424 v. United States, 564 F.2d 66, 96 LRRM 2720 (Ct. Cl. 1977) (holding that arbitrator exceeded authority in ruling that "self-help" remedy resorted to by government in recouping erroneously withheld and remitted union dues of employee after promotion to position not covered by agreement was improper under agreement).

back pay, it is expected that the employer will, pursuant to the check-off agreement, deduct and remit payment to the union.

Suppose management, pursuant to a belief that employees are not part of the bargaining unit, fails to deduct dues? In *Broadway Cab Cooperative v. Teamsters Local 281*,[34] management, asserting that certain "owner-drivers" were not part of the unit, failed to check off union dues. The submission agreement under which the matter was arbitrated read, in part, as follows: "If Art. 2.3 [which includes the 'owner-drivers' within the union] is enforceable as to the 'owner-drivers,' what is the appropriate remedy?" Ruling for the union, the arbitrator ordered the employer to make restitution to the union of $18,195, representing back union dues which management refused to withhold from the pay of the owner-drivers. Management then commenced an action to vacate the award, arguing that it did not intend to submit the issue of back dues for arbitration, and that the "appropriate remedy" language was not sufficient to put it on notice that the dues issue would be arbitrated. The federal court rejected this argument, and had this to say concerning the scope of a submission agreement:

> When the Submission Agreement requires the arbitrator to determine the "appropriate remedy," it need not spell out every conceivable remedy which the arbitrator might choose, in order to fairly put the parties on notice of the parameters of the issues to be arbitrated.[35]

Where an employer has failed to honor a valid check-off provision, an amount equal to dues and assessments the employer failed to deduct and remit to the union may properly be ordered as a remedy.[36] The employer may, however, effect a double deduction from an employee's check until the deficit is satisfied.[37]

---

[34]110 LRRM 2171 (D. Or. 1982).

[35]Id. at 2174.

[36]See, e.g., City of Maumee, Ohio, 90 LA 946, 949 (Graham, 1988) (employer violated agreement in permitting employees to cease paying dues; employer ordered to pay amount that union would have received in dues payments); Shore Manor, 71 LA 1238 (Katz, 1978); Schnadig Corp., 71 LA 228 (Marcus, 1978); Valmac Indus., 66 LA 1002 (Moore, 1976); Warren Petroleum Co., 63 LA 1246 (Merrill, 1974); Big Ten Taxicab, 58 LA 672 (Goodman, 1971).

[37]See, e.g., Asarco, Inc., 71 LA 730 (Roberts, 1978); Allied Maintenance Corp., 66

Few arbitrators order the termination of an employee for failure to tender union dues pursuant to a valid union shop agreement. The preferred remedy is outlined in a 1988 unpublished decision reported by Arbitrator James Sherman, who rejected the union's argument that management was contractually required to terminate employees who have not tendered an initiation fee and dues required as a condition of acquiring and retaining membership in the union. Based on the nature of the work (maintaining security for an airline at a specified international airport) and its relationship to the airline involved, the National Mediation Board held that the bargaining unit was to be governed not by the Labor Management Relations Act but by the Railway Labor Act (under RLA case law it is legal for the parties to enter into a union security agreement which makes union membership, or payment of dues, a condition of membership even in a "right to work" state).

Ruling that he had no choice but to uphold the union's right to have all employees pay initiation fees and dues, Arbitrator Sherman nevertheless found that it would create a hardship on the employees and upon the company if he were to award "complete damages, payable immediately," since no one was absolutely certain that the union security provision was valid and enforceable. The company was directed to notify all employees that they must make arrangements to pay initiation fees and dues, and that failure to do so will result in their termination. The grievants were accordingly given "one last chance" to comply with the contractual mandates.

I. Consequential Damages and the Foreseeability Rule

It is generally expected that before a remedy is awarded by an arbitrator, the individual grievant or the union must establish a causal relationship between the breach of the collective bargaining agreement and the loss of some contractual

---

LA 875 (Richman, 1976) (employer ordered to check-off one additional month's dues in any successive month until employee's arrears are liquidated). But see Synergy Gas Corp., 91 LA 77 (Simons, 1987) (arbitrator lacks authority to condition backpay award upon grievant's payment to union of sum equal to dues that employer failed to forward on his behalf during period in which it wrongfully denied him employment; dues claim as formulated is between union and grievant).

benefit. If it can be demonstrated that the grieving party would have incurred "damages" regardless of the breach, they should not be recoverable as consequential damages. It is likewise the rule in the federal sector that a remedy under the Back Pay Act[38] is not available unless it can be established that, "but for" an "unwarranted or unjustified personnel action," the withdrawal of "pay, allowances, or differentials" would not have occurred. The term "pay, allowances, or differentials" includes, in addition to the usual salary and premium pay benefits, a number of monetary benefits which are usual to federal employment. Thus, annual and sick leave and health insurance benefits could be included in a make-whole award; but benefits not directly attributable to a person's status as a federal employee (e.g., access to public transportation, making a car unnecessary) would not.[39]

With few exceptions, arbitrators follow the common-law requirement that "damages" are not recoverable unless they arise naturally from the breach or were contemplated by the parties as a probable result of the breach at the time the contract was made. Sometimes, however, questionable applications of this principle are reported. In *Southwestern Bell*,[40] the arbitrator found that an employee was improperly forced to work overtime on an unscheduled day. The record indicated that, because of working overtime, the employee was absent from home during a rainstorm and was unable to protect her furniture from rain damage resulting from a roof that had been split to move the house from one location to another. Finding that the employer knew that the roof had been split, the arbitrator awarded the employee $225 for water damage to a Victorian couch. The analysis of the arbitrator is particularly interesting:

> So what the opinion should do for the parties is to allow them to relax and enjoy the feeling of oneness with each other in a common enterprise and to strive to bring a little bit more of the Golden Rule to play in their overtime relations—which I daresay most of the Company officials, Union officials and employees

---

[38]5 U.S.C. §5596 (1982).
[39]See Manual on Remedies Available to Third Parties in Adjudicating Federal Employee Grievances, Appendix IX–1 (Government Accounting Office, 1977).
[40]61 LA 202 (Wolff, 1973).

would agree is a pretty good way to seek to balance each other's needs.[41]

One commentator has argued that the function of grievance arbitrators is not to do justice, much less to allow the parties "to relax and enjoy the feeling of oneness with each other." An arbitrator's function is to read the parties' collective bargaining agreement and tell the parties what those provisions mean as applied to a particular case.[42]

The authors submit that a remedy should not be granted by an arbitrator unless it can reasonably be concluded that the parties, in negotiating the contract, contemplated that a particular form of relief could be secured through the grievance-arbitration procedure.

J. Perjury

Is there a remedy for an award that is secured by perjury? While an employer, governed by the National Labor Relations Act, may not discharge an employee for testifying at an arbitration hearing, testifying dishonestly is not a protected activity and management is free to effect discipline or discharge against an employee who deliberately gives false statements in a hearing.[43]

While an arbitrator cannot reopen a hearing based on the discovery of new evidence (once the award is issued), there is a possibility that the award can be vacated if the other party's evidence was perjured. In *Dogherra v. Safeway Stores*,[44] the Ninth Circuit held that (1) obtaining an award by perjured testimony constitutes fraud, and (2) fraud is a ground for va-

---

[41]Id. at 219.

[42]Feller, *The Remedy Power in Grievance Arbitration*, 5 Indus. Rel. L.J. 128, 154 (1982).

[43]See, e.g., Wright-Bernet, Inc., 81-1 ARB ¶8071, at 3321 (1981), where Arbitrator Roland Strasshofer, Jr., in upholding a discharge for giving false testimony, stated: "It is clear that the false testimony during the [prior] March arbitration was an act of dishonesty and that the promulgation of the humiliating lies given during that testimony and spread about the plant knowingly and deliberately by the grievant, constitute abusive and indecent conduct toward a supervisor." See also the discussion of Arbitrator Gerald Cohen in Defense Mapping Agency, 92 LA 653 (1989) (overturning discharge of federal-agency employee for making false sexual harassment charge).

[44]679 F.2d 1293, 110 LRRM 2790 (9th Cir.), cert. denied, 459 U.S. 990, 111 LRRM 2856 (1982).

cating an award under either the United States Arbitration Act or federal common law fashioned by the courts pursuant to *Textile Workers v. Lincoln Mills*.[45] In so ruling, however, the court of appeals cautioned that courts must be slow to vacate an award and that in order to protect the finality of arbitration decisions, "[t]he fraud must not have been discoverable upon the exercise of due diligence prior to the arbitration." Moreover, the fraud "must materially relate to an issue in the arbitration."[46] Generally, courts have been reluctant to vacate awards based on a claim of perjury, and a party that is convinced that perjured testimony is being offered faces an uphill battle in vacating the award.[47]

K. Changing a Remedy Based on Posthearing Conduct

Hill and Sinicropi discuss at length the relevance of postdischarge conduct in *Evidence in Arbitration*.[48] May an arbitrator change a remedy (which would otherwise apply) based on the grievant's postdischarge conduct? Arbitrator Marshall Ross, in *Bib Bear Stores*,[49] held that if a grievant engaged in misconduct (justifying discharge) after the first hearing, it was not necessary for management to return him to the payroll.

In an undated, unpublished decision reported by Arbitrator Martin Cohen, a security guard for a large Chicago "loop" building was dismissed. After the hearing the guard approached a tenant who testified against him at the hearing, and was rude. Management requested that the hearing be reopened and that the arbitrator accept the evidence as part of management's just cause case. Over a vigorous protest by

[45]353 U.S. 448, 457, 40 LRRM 2113 (1957), discussed in Chapter 2.
[46]110 LRRM at 2793. See also Fireman & Oilers Local 261 v. Great N. Paper Co., 118 LRRM 2317, 2323 (D. Me. 1984) ("Courts have been reluctant to vacate arbitration awards on claims of perjury. In cases involving alleged perjury or willful nondisclosure of evidence, a 'due diligence' requirement has been imposed.").
[47]See generaly Tidwell, *The Effects of Perjury Committed at an Arbitration Hearing*, 38 Arb. J. No. 3, 44–52 (1983).
[48]Hill and Sinicropi, Evidence in Arbitration, 2d ed., 318–329 (BNA Books, 1987). Besides the cases discussed in this section, see Continental Tel. Co. of Va., 86 LA 274 (Rothschild, 1986) (Grievant's postdischarge attempts to prevent witnesses from testifying relevant to his entitlement to relief. Arbitrator directs parties to confer on remedies and, if unable to agree within 10 days, to provide arbitrator with anwers to questions that he raised regarding entitlement to reinstatement and other issues).
[49]90 LA 634 (1988).

the union, Arbitrator Cohen reopened the hearing with the ruling that this was postdischarge conduct and would not go toward the merits of the discharge case, but could impact the remedy. The arbitrator awarded reinstatement with full back pay contingent upon the grievant apologizing to the tenant.

Arbitrator Marvin Hill, in a 1990 unpublished decision, ruled that the employer was without just cause to terminate the grievant's employment under an ambiguous "no fault" attendance policy, but denied all back pay because of the grievant's postdischarge conduct (the employee picked a fight with a supervisor and also attempted to induce a wildcat strike at the plant).

L. Detrimental Reliance

There are situations that arguably call for a remedy even when the collective bargaining agreement has not been violated. Arbitrator J.C. Fogelberg reports a case where a company superintendent overruled shift bosses and safety personnel by removing a small refrigerator purchased by coal miners to cool beverages within the mine. Finding no violation of the agreement, the arbitrator ordered management to offer the employees the option of selling the refrigerator to the company based on a detrimental reliance theory.[50]

M. Agreements to Split Damages

There are potential problems with adjusting grievances in arbitration where it is known prior to the hearing that any monetary award will be divided among interested employees. To illustrate, Arbitrator Bernard Cantor, in *United States Steel Corp.*,[51] considered a grievance alleging that a supervisor was improperly performing bargaining-unit work. The employee who filed the grievance disclosed at the hearing that he was not claiming the work for himself, since he was not in the proper classification to do so; rather, he had made an agreement with other members of the union to split any recovery

---

[50]Homestake Mining Co., 90 LA 720 (Fogelberg, 1987).
[51]66 LA 925 (1976).

arising out of the complaint five ways with other union members. Although the arbitrator denied the grievance on the merits, he nevertheless found the agreement to split damages disturbing. Arbitrator Cantor explained:

> The whole case was colored by the statement that there had been an agreement amongst employees to share any dollar recovery that might result from processing this grievance. An agreement like this tends to cast doubt on the veracity of witnesses. I find, as a matter of fact, that all these witnesses spoke the truth; but if, however, there had been a dispute as to the details of what had happened, this agreement would place a pall over the witnesses. This type of an agreement should be condemned. The grievance procedures may be used for no purpose except the direct, proper protecting of the contract.[52]

N. Prospective Application of Remedies

Under what conditions will an arbitrator's remedy apply prospectively? The res judicata effect of an arbitrator's award is discussed by the authors in *Evidence in Arbitration*.[53] One particular case of note in the remedies area is *Oil Workers Local 4-367 v. Rohm & Haas, Texas*,[54] a case reported by the Fifth Circuit. An arbitrator ordered management to pay overtime pay to an employee who had lost the opportunity to earn additional pay as a result of the implementation of a new procedure for filling temporary shift vacancies. The Fifth Circuit held that the award would not be enforced prospectively as to similar occurrences where the issue of future application of the award was not submitted to the arbitrator. The court reasoned that collateral questions about the scope or application of an award are themselves questions for arbitration.

The Eleventh Circuit has similarly declared that "whether or not the award is 'final' in a stare decisis sense is an issue for further arbitration."[55] The court reasoned that it was "unnecessary to protect the arbitral process from repetitive grievances because the arbitral process is quite capable of protecting itself." Further, in the court's words:

---

[52]Id. at 928.
[53]Hill and Sinicropi, supra note 48, at 390–395.
[54]677 F.2d 492, 111 LRRM 2361 (5th Cir. 1982).
[55]Electrical Workers (IBEW) Local 199 v. United Tel. Co. of Fla., 738 F.2d 1564, 117 LRRM 2094, 2100 (11th Cir. 1984).

[A] judicially-created system of arbitral precedent would be likely to impair the flexibility arbitrators require to respond to changing conditions or new factual situations that may arise in the shop, an environment with which the arbitrator has a special familiarity foreign to the courts.[56]

O. Estoppel

Arbitrators may deny a monetary remedy even though a contract violation is found and even though it is possible to compute a monetary award. Arbitrator Walter Kaufman reports two decisions applying "estoppel" as a basis for denying a monetary remedy. In *Snowflake Bakery,*[57] a salaried engineer was a member of the bargaining unit and was therefore entitled to all employee benefits under the parties' collective bargaining agreement. When the employee filed a grievance requesting overtime pay, Kaufman, finding a violation, nevertheless credited management's estoppel argument and denied retroactive payment. The arbitrator reasoned that the grievant should not be allowed to receive overtime pay as if he were an hourly employee when he had asked for and accepted raises substantially greater than the contractual minimum. In the arbitrator's words, "Grievant not only seemed to give up overtime pay computed on an hourly basis pursuant to the Union contract, but also requested and accepted a salary increase far exceeding the contractual formula and otherwise conducted himself apparently in line with an understanding that he was being 'fully compensated for all hours which he worked.' "[58]

In *Oilfield Electrical Co.,*[59] an electrical contractor relied on the advice of its local business manager that fringe benefit contributions did not have to be made on the employees' travel time to and from an offshore drilling platform. Arbitrator Kaufman ruled that no monetary remedy was due even though a violation was found. The arbitrator reasoned that in conducting labor relations management must deal with the rep-

---

[56]Id., 117 LRRM at 2100 n.11.
[57]73 LA 75 (1979).
[58]Id. at 79.
[59]81-2 ARB ¶8449 (1981).

resentations of its employees, "and the employees take the benefit or burden from those dealings."[60]

P. Protective Remedies

Arbitrators have frequently implemented protective remedies when necessary to shield a witness from undue influence or possible retaliatory measures, such as fines, demotions, or other sanctions. While some of the measures cited may seldom be imposed, when a valid issue of possible retaliation is raised, an arbitrator may properly order any of the following remedies:

1. Excluding or Sequestering Witnesses

Under the rules of the American Arbitration Association,[61] an arbitrator has the power to require the exclusion of any witness during the testimony of other witnesses.[62] Since the rules provide that a person having a direct interest in the outcome of the arbitration is entitled to attend the hearing, an arbitrator is not expected to exclude the grievant, especially in a discharge case. Accordingly, an order sequestering witnesses may have limited utility in providing any degree of protection to a witness who is fearful of harassment by other unit employees.

2. Withholding Identity of Witness Until the Hearing

In *Max Factor & Co.*,[63] Arbitrator Edgar Jones, Jr., ruled that a union was not entitled, until after the hearing convened, to the name and address of a former employee who was to serve as a company witness to the grievant's alleged theft. In refusing prearbitral disclosure, Arbitrator Jones stated:

---

[60]Id. at 4975.

[61]Rule 22, in relevant part, provides: "The Arbitrator shall have the power to require the retirement of any witness or witnesses during the testimony of other witnesses." See generally Hill and Sinicropi, Evidence in Arbitration, 2d ed., 89–90 (BNA Books, 1987).

[62]See Seattle-Post Intelligencer, 66 LA 717 718–719 (Stephan, 1976).

[63]61 LA 886 (1973).

The trouble with this script is that it does not take account of a situation, like this one, in which there exists a combination of a cr[e]dibility confrontation pitting sworn testimony of accused and accusers wholly incompatible one with another—meaning someone obviously is lying—which is also coupled with an obviously strong sense—regardless of whether it be reasonably perceived or not—of fear by one of the accusers of physical retaliation against her by friends of the accused. Pre-arbitral disclosure of the identities, more particularly of the home addresses and current employers—as requested by the Union before the arbitral hearing—in those circumstances had the real and substantial prospect for the intimidation of an already fearful and crucial Company witness. To avoid that prospect the Company was entitled to withhold the requested information until the arbitration convened.[64]

3. Direct Appeal to Arbitrator

Arbitrator George Connolly, in *High Point Sprinkler Co. of Boston*,[65] provided as follows:

Company employees who appeared as witnesses, voluntarily or otherwise, at the hearings are hereby protected and authorized to petition directly to the Arbitrator for relief from sanctions imposed due to the testimony or appearance of the employee.[66]

It is unclear from the award how the arbitrator, independent of the parties, could provide any degree of protection against reprisals against a witness.

4. Granting "Immunity"

Where a union officer refused to reveal the names of employees who allegedly made threatening statements to him without an "assurance of immunity" from the named employees, Arbitrator John Sembower ruled that he had no power to grant this type of order. Attention is called to Arbitrator Sembower's statements:

Not only is the Arbitrator, and the Company's counsel for that matter, unable to give a guarantee of so-called "immunity" to any persons the Grievant might name in his testimony or

---

[64]Id. at 889–890.
[65]67 LA 239 (1976).
[66]Id. at 248–249.

implicate as wrongdoers in any sense, but the Arbitrator also does not have any power . . . to hold a witness in contempt, if the Grievant persists in his refusal to answer a question. Under such circumstances there may be other possible sanctions, such as that invoked by some NLRB examiners to disregard the entire testimony of such a witness who balks, but the appropriateness or inappropriateness of this would have to remain for later consideration, in light of argument to be offered by respective counsel.

. . .

It seems quite possible that any employer who launched upon a wholesale reprisal campaign against persons named by such a witness . . . would be held guilty of an "unfair labor practice." Although there is no specific authority to support the proposition, it seems reasonable that the parties to a voluntary arbitration, such as this, include in their subscription to the arbitration process a clear implication that all their witnesses will testify frankly, freely and completely, and that by the same token, they will not engage in reprisals against witnesses for the opposite party or persons named by them.[67]

5. Redress Through the NLRB

Section 8(a)(4) of the National Labor Relations Act, as amended,[68] provides that it is an unfair labor practice for an employer "(4) to discharge or otherwise discriminate against an employee because he has filed charges or given testimony under this Act."

In *NLRB v. Scrivener*,[69] the Supreme Court rejected the view that this section serves only to protect against reprisal for filing an unfair labor practice charge or for giving testimony at a formal hearing. Eschewing a literal interpretation of Section 8(a)(4), the Court held that this section afforded broad protection to an employee who participates in the investigative stage of an NLRB proceeding, including giving a written statement to a field examiner. The NLRB, expanding this doctrine, has found a violation where an employee was disciplined because the employer suspected that a charge was about to be filed.[70]

---

[67]Berg Airlectro Prods., Co., 46 LA 668, 675–676 (1966).
[68]29 U.S.C. §158(a)(4).
[69]405 U.S. 117, 79 NLRB 2587 (1972).
[70]First Nat'l Bank & Trust Co., 209 NLRB 95, 85 LRRM 1324 (1974).

Related to the arbitral process is *Ebasco Services*,[71] where a three-member Board held that an employer violated the statute by demoting three foremen who testified at an arbitral proceeding. Consistent with the rationale of *Scrivener*, the three-member Board declared:

> "General Counsel argues that the same rule should apply [protecting employees from reprisal for giving testimony] where employees resort to contract grievance procedures to vindicate their rights under such contract, and supervisors take it on themselves to appear before tribunals created under those procedures. This argument has merit, for the Act itself recognizes and favors employees' right to use, and actual use of, contract grievance procedures to settle labor disputes, and so do the courts. The Board has specifically protected employees from employer interference with their right to resort to such procedures under contracts, as well as procedures before outside tribunals, to enforce contract rights, on the theory that the filing of claims by employees in either instance was a form of implementation of the collective bargaining agreement and thus an extension of the concerted activity which gave rise to that agreement. In addition, the Board has long followed the statutory policy by withholding its processes in deference to an arbitrator's award under contract procedures where the arbitral process meets certain standards of fairness and regularity. Therefore, it appears to be no more than a reasonable extension of the above principle and Board policy to say that employees have a corollary right to a full and fair hearing on their grievances under contract procedures which must likewise be protected from interference or limitation."[72]

Accordingly, an employee who is subject to discriminatory treatment because he has given testimony at an arbitration proceeding may be granted relief under the Taft-Hartley Act.

---

[71] 181 NLRB 768, 73 LRRM 1518 (1970).
[72] Id., 73 LRRM at 1519.

Conclusion

Chapter 22

Are There Remedial Patterns?

For the most part collective bargaining agreements do not expressly define or limit an arbitrator's remedial powers. At the same time most labor agreements contain boilerplate provisions expressly prohibiting the arbitrator from adding to, modifying, or ignoring the terms of the agreement. Within that broad limitation, arbitrators enjoy great, but not unlimited, freedom to fashion remedies when a party breaches the labor agreement. Arbitrators may be a conservative lot (as demonstrated by their continued reluctance to grant interest on a back-pay award), but with respect to most contract violations they have a good sense of what it will take to remedy an employer's breach of the labor agreement. This "good sense," when exercised, is accorded great deference by reviewing courts.

Is there a synthesis or a preferred approach to the area of remedies?

The general rule followed by arbitrators is that for a breach of contract a remedy is required. In fashioning a remedy, arbitrators, with few exceptions, attempt to make whole the "damaged" party. Sometimes an arbitrator's remedy will simply consist of a declaration that the agreement has been breached and that the offending party "cease and desist" from future violations. More often, the arbitrator will order a party to undertake certain conduct (reinstatement, posting a vacancy, return of machinery) and/or to pay money damages to the nonbreaching party, either the union or the grieving employee. Some arbitrators view the presence of an identifiable grievant and specific, measureable damages as prerequisites to recovery of a monetary award. Our sense is that arbitrators require more specificity with respect to the amount of damages than identification of a specific injured employee. When management violates the collective bargaining agreement, the injury is to the union, whether or not an individual grievant can be identified.

When the parties elect to submit a dispute to an arbitrator they are not engaged in an academic exercise. They desire a solution to an issue (not infrequently the grievance involves a recurring issue) and a directive restoring the *status quo ante*. With few exceptions this mandate requires that money change hands. Whether the arbitrator drafts the award in a lettered manner and declares that, as the parties' official "contract reader," he is explicating what is implicit in the agreement when he awards a specific remedy, or simply states that, like any contract, there ought to be a remedy for a breach of the agreement (even though, admittedly, a collective bargaining agreement is not quite like a commercial agreement), makes no difference in terms of what the arbitrator is hired to do. The power to formulate a remedy, as seen by the courts and the parties themselves, does not change because the arbitrator holds one view over the other.

There are discernible themes in the area of remedies. Arbitrators frequently talk about "preserving the parties' collective bargaining relationship" when formulating remedies. Most neutrals give lip service to the notion that a remedy should "flow from the collective bargaining agreement," and that an arbitrator should never grant a remedy that the parties themselves have not contemplated. Rarely do the parties discuss remedies at the bargaining table or the hearing, but this does not preclude or inhibit arbitrators from determining "what the parties would have concluded" had the issue of breach been brought up during bargaining. Another pattern ascertained from the decisions is that arbitrators will rarely grant a remedy not requested by a party. A party may not get what it asks for, but if a remedy is not requested, a party can expect that it will not be granted. When in doubt over the remedy, arbitrators will remand the question to the parties, at times retaining jurisdiction to resolve any disputes over the matter.

The predominant recurrent theme echoed by arbitrators and the preferred approach in the remedies area is the almost uniform declaration that when a violation of the agreement is found, "make-whole" relief is the telstar. The parties may argue as to that will place the nonbreaching party in the same position, financial or otherwise, it would have occupied had the agreement not been violated,[1] but they will not seriously contest the applicability of the make-whole doctrine in the arbitral forum. The principle of make-whole relief has guided common-law judges for some 700 years. Arbitrators have followed the same tenet and we see no reason why the make-whole principle, along with the other trends noted, should not continue to govern when the agreement is violated.

---

[1]Like Prohibition, the solution may be worse than the disease.

Appendices

Appendix A

Voluntary Labor Arbitration Rules of the American Arbitration Association*

1. Agreement of Parties

The parties shall be deemed to have made these rules a part of their arbitration agreement whenever, in a collective bargaining agreement or submission, they have provided for arbitration by the American Arbitration Association (hereinafter the AAA) or under its rules. These rules and any amendment thereof shall apply in the form obtaining at the time the arbitration is initiated.

2. Name of Tribunal

Any tribunal constituted by the parties under these rules shall be called the Voluntary Labor Arbitration Tribunal.

3. Administrator

When parties agree to arbitrate under these rules and an arbitration is instituted thereunder, they thereby authorize the AAA to administer the arbitration. The authority and obligation of the administrator are as provided in the agreement of the parties and in these rules.

---

*As amended and in effect January 1, 1988.

4. Delegation of Duties

The duties of the AAA may be carried out through such representatives or committees as the AAA may direct.

5. Panel of Labor Arbitrators

The AAA shall establish and maintain a Panel of Labor Arbitrators and shall appoint arbitrators therefrom, as hereinafter provided.

6. Office of Tribunal

The general office of the Voluntary Labor Arbitration Tribunal is the headquarters of the AAA, which may, however, assign the administration of an arbitration to any of its regional offices.

7. Initiation under an Arbitration Clause in a Collective Bargaining Agreement

Arbitration under an arbitration clause in a collective bargaining agreement under these rules may be initiated by either party in the following manner:

(a) By giving written notice to the other party of intention to arbitrate (Demand), which notice shall contain a statement setting forth the nature of the dispute and the remedy sought, and

(b) By filing at any regional office of the AAA three copies of said notice, together with a copy of the collective bargaining agreement, or such parts thereof as relate to the dispute, including the arbitration provisions. After the arbitrator is appointed, no new or different claim may be submitted except with the consent of the arbitrator and all other parties.

8. Answer

The party upon whom the Demand for arbitration is made may file an answering statement with the AAA within seven days after notice from the AAA, simultaneously sending a copy to the other party. If no answer is filed within the stated time, it will be assumed that the claim is denied. Failure to file an answer shall not operate to delay the arbitration.

9. *Initiation under a Submission*

Parties to any collective bargaining agreement may initiate an arbitration under these rules by filing at any regional office of the AAA two copies of a written agreement to arbitrate under these rules (Submission), signed by the parties and setting forth the nature of the dispute and the remedy sought.

10. *Fixing of Locale*

The parties may mutually agree upon the locale where the arbitration is to be held. If the locale is not designated in the collective bargaining agreement or Submission, and if there is a dispute as to the appropriate locale, the AAA shall have the power to determine the locale and its decision shall be binding.

11. *Qualifications of Arbitrator*

No person shall serve as a neutral arbitrator in any arbitration in which he or she has any financial personal interest in the result of the arbitration, unless the parties, in writing, waive such disqualification.

12. *Appointment from Panel*

If the parties have not appointed an arbitrator and have not provided any other method of appointment, the arbitrator shall be appointed in the following manner: Immediately after the filing of the Demand or Submission, the AAA shall submit simultaneously to each party an identical list of names of persons chosen from the Panel of Labor Arbitrators. Each party shall have seven days from the mailing date in which to cross off any names to which it objects, number the remaining names to indicate the order of preference, and return the list to the AAA. If a party does not return the list within the time specified, all persons named therein shall be deemed acceptable. From among the persons who have been approved on both lists, and in accordance with the designated order of mutual preference, the AAA shall invite the acceptance of an arbitrator to serve. If the parties fail to agree upon any of the persons named, if those named decline or are unable to act, or if for any other reason the appointment cannot be made from the submitted lists, the administrator shall have the power to make the appointment from among other members of the panel without the submission of any additional list.

13. Direct Appointment by Parties

If the agreement of the parties names an arbitrator or specifies a method of appointing an arbitrator, that designation or method shall be followed. The notice of appointment, with the name and address of such arbitrator, shall be filed with the AAA by the appointment party.

If the agreement specifies a period of time within which an arbitrator shall be appointed and any party fails to make such appointment within that period, the AAA may make the appointment.

If no period of time is specified in the agreement, the AAA shall notify the parties to make the appointment and if within seven days thereafter such arbitrator has not been so appointed, the AAA shall make the appointment.

14. Appointment of Neutral Arbitrator by Party-Appointed Arbitrators

If the parties have appointed their arbitrators, or if either or both of them have been appointed as provided in Section 13, and have authorized such arbitrators to appoint a neutral arbitrator within a specified time and no appointment is made within such time or any agreed extension thereof, the AAA may appoint a neutral arbitrator who shall act as chairperson.

If no period of time is specified for appointment of the neutral arbitrator and the parties do not make the appointment within seven days from the date of the appointment of the last party-appointed arbitrator, the AAA shall appoint such neutral arbitrator, who shall act as chairperson.

If the parties have agreed that the arbitrators shall appoint the neutral arbitrator from the panel, the AAA shall furnish to the party-appointed arbitrators, in the manner prescribed in Section 12, a list selected from the panel, and the appointment of the neutral arbitrator shall be made as prescribed in that section.

15. Number of Arbitrators

If the arbitration agreement does not specify the number of arbitrators, the dispute shall be heard and determined by one arbitrator, unless the parties otherwise agree.

16. Notice to Arbitrator of Appointment

Notice of the appointment of the neutral arbitrator shall be mailed to the arbitrator by the AAA and the signed acceptance of the arbitrator shall be filed with the AAA prior to the opening of the first hearing.

17. Disclosure by Arbitrator of Disqualification

Prior to accepting the appointment, the prospective neutral arbitrator shall disclose any circumstance likely to create a presumption of bias or that the arbitrator believes might disqualify him or her as an impartial arbitrator. Upon receipt of such information, the AAA shall immediately disclose it to the parties. If either party declines to waive the presumptive disqualification, the vacancy thus created shall be filled in accordance with the applicable provisions of these rules.

18. Vacancies

If any arbitrator should resign, die, withdraw, refuse, be unable, or be disqualified to perform the duties of office, the AAA shall, on proof satisfactory to it, declare the office vacant. Vacancies shall be filled in the same manner as that governing the making of the original appointment, and the matter shall be reheard by the new arbitrator.

19. Time and Place of Hearing

The arbitrator shall fix the time and place for each hearing. At least five days prior thereto, the AAA shall mail notice of the time and place of hearing to each party, unless the parties otherwise agree.

20. Representation by Counsel

Any party may be represented at the hearing by counsel or by another authorized representative.

21. Stenographic Record

Any party wishing a stenographic record shall make arrangements directly with a stenographer and shall notify the other parties of such arrangements in advance of the hearing. The requesting party or parties shall pay the cost of such record. If such transcript is agreed by the parties to be, or in appropriate cases determined by the arbitrator to be, the official record of the proceeding, it must be made available to the arbitrator and to the other party for inspection, at a time and place determined by the arbitrator.

22. Attendance at Hearings

Persons having a direct interest in the arbitration are entitled to attend hearings. The arbitrator shall have the power to require the retirement of any witness or witnesses during the testimony of other witnesses. It shall be discretionary with the arbitrator to determine the propriety of the attendance of any other person.

23. Adjournments

The arbitrator for good cause shown may adjourn the hearing upon the request of a party or upon his or her own initiative, and shall adjourn when all of the parties agree thereto.

24. Oaths

Before proceeding with the first hearing, each arbitrator may take an oath of office and, if required by law, shall do so. The arbitrator may require witnesses to testify under oath administered by any duty qualified person and, if required by law or requested by either party, shall do so.

25. Majority Decision

Whenever there is more than one arbitrator, all decisions of the arbitrators shall be by majority vote. The award shall also be made by majority vote unless the concurrence of all is expressly required.

26. Order of Proceedings

A hearing shall be opened by the filing of the oath of the arbitrator, where required; by the recording of the place, time, and date of the hearing and the presence of the arbitrator, the parties, and counsel, if any; and by the receipt by the arbitrator of the Demand and answer, if any, or the Submission.

Exhibits may, when offered by either party, be received in evidence by the arbitrator. The names and addresses of all witnesses and exhibits in order received shall be made a part of the record.

The arbitrator may vary the normal procedure under which the initiating party first presents its claim, but in any case shall afford full and equal opportunity to all parties for the presentation of relevant proofs.

27. Arbitration in the Absence of a Party

Unless the law provides to the contrary, the arbitration may proceed in the absence of any party who, after due notice, fails to be present or fails to obtain an adjournment. An award shall not be made solely on the default of a party. The arbitrator shall require the other party to submit such evidence as may be required for the making of an award.

28. Evidence

The parties may offer such evidence as they desire and shall produce such additional evidence as the arbitrator may deem necessary to an understanding and determination of the dispute. An arbitrator authorized by law to subpoena witnesses and documents may do so independently or upon the request of any party. The arbitrator shall be the judge of the relevance and materiality of the evidence offered and conformity to legal rules of evidence shall not be necessary. All evidence shall be taken in the presence of all of the arbitrators and all of the parties except where any of the parties is absent in default or has waived the right to be present.

29. Evidence by Affidavit and Filing of Documents

The arbitrator may receive and consider the evidence of witnesses by affidavit, giving it only such weight as seems proper after consideration of any objection made to its admission.

All documents that are not filed with the arbitrator at the hearing, but arranged at the hearing or subsequently by agreement of the parties to be submitted, shall be filed with the AAA for transmission to the arbitrator. All parties shall be afforded opportunity to examine such documents.

30. Inspection

Whenever the arbitrator deems it necessary, he or she may make an inspection in connection with the subject matter of the dispute after written notice to the parties, who may, if they so desire, be present at such inspection.

31. Closing of Hearings

The arbitrator shall inquire of all parties whether they have any further proofs to offer or witnesses to be heard. Upon receiving negative replies, the arbitrator shall declare the hearings closed and a minute thereof shall be recorded. If briefs or other documents are to be filed, the hearings shall be declared closed as of the final date set by the arbitrator for filing with the AAA. The time limit within which the arbitrator is required to make an award shall commence to run, in the absence of another agreement by the parties, upon the closing of the hearings.

32. Reopening of Hearings

The hearings may for good cause shown be reopened by the arbitrator at will or on the motion of either party at any time before the award is made, but, if the reopening of the hearings would prevent the making of the award within the specific time agreed upon by the parties in the contract out of which the controversy has arisen, the matter may not be reopened unless both parties agree upon the extension of such time. When no specific date is fixed in the contract, the arbitrator may reopen the hearings and shall have thirty days from the closing of the reopened hearings within which to make an award.

33. Waiver of Oral Hearings

The parties may provide, by written agreement, for the waiver of oral hearings. If the parties are unable to agree as to the procedure, the AAA shall specify a fair and equitable procedure.

34. Waiver of Rules

Any party who proceeds with the arbitration after knowledge that any provision or requirement of these rules has not been complied with and who fails to state an objection thereto in writing shall be deemed to have waived the right to object.

35. Extensions of Time

The parties may modify any period of time by mutual agreement. The AAA may for good cause extend any period of time established by these rules, except the time for making the award. The AAA shall notify the parties of any such extension of time and its reason therefor.

36. Serving of Notice

Each party to a Submission or other agreement that provides for arbitration under these rules shall be deemed to have consented and shall consent that any papers, notices, or process necessary or proper for the initiation or continuation of an arbitration under these rules; for any court action in connection therewith; or for the entry of judgment on an award made thereunder may be served upon such party by mail addressed to such party or its attorney at the last known address or by personal service, within or without the state wherein the arbitration is to be held.

37. Time of Award

The award shall be rendered promptly by the arbitrator and, unless otherwise agreed by the parties or specified by law, no later than thirty days from the date of closing the hearings or, if oral hearings have been waived, from the date of transmitting the final statements and proofs to the arbitrator.

38. Form of Award

The award shall be in writing and shall be signed either by the neutral arbitrator or by a concurring majority if there be more than one arbitrator. The parties shall advise the AAA whenever they do not require the arbitrator to accompany the award with an opinion.

39. Award upon Settlement

If the parties settle their dispute during the course of the arbitration, the arbitrator may, upon their request, set forth the terms of the agreed settlement in an award.

40. Delivery of Award to Parties

Parties shall accept as legal delivery of the award the placing of the award or a true copy thereof in the mail by the AAA, addressed to such party at its last known address or to its attorney; personal service of the award; or the filing of the award in any other manner that may be prescribed by law.

41. Release of Documents for Judicial Proceedings

The AAA shall, upon the written request of a party, furnish to such party, at its expense, certified facsimiles of any papers in the AAA's possession that may be required in judicial proceedings relating to the arbitration.

42. *Judicial Proceedings and Exclusion of Liability*

(a) Neither the AAA nor any arbitrator in a proceeding under these rules is a necessary party in judicial proceedings relating to the arbitration.

(b) Neither the AAA nor any arbitrator shall be liable to any party for any act or omission in connection with any arbitration conducted under these rules.

43. *Administrative Fees*

As a not-for-profit organization, the AAA shall prescribe an administrative fee schedule to compensate it for the cost of providing administrative services. The schedule in effect at the time of filing shall be applicable.

44. *Expenses*

The expenses of witnesses for either side shall be paid by the party producing such witnesses.

Expenses of the arbitration, other than the cost of the stenographic record, including required traveling and other expenses of the arbitrator and of AAA representatives and the expenses of any witness or the cost of any proof produced at the direct request of the arbitrator, shall be borne equally by the parties, unless they agree otherwise, or unless the arbitrator, in the award, assesses such expenses or any part thereof against any specified party or parties.

45. *Communication with Arbitrator*

There shall be no communication between the parties and a neutral arbitrator other than at oral hearings. Any other oral or written communication from the parties to the arbitrator shall be directed to the AAA for transmittal to the arbitrator.

46. *Interpretation and Application of Rules*

The arbitrator shall interpret and apply these rules insofar as they relate to the arbitrator's powers and duties. When there is more than one arbitrator and a difference arises among them concerning the meaning or application of any such rule, it shall be decided by a majority vote. If that is unobtainable, the arbitrator or either party may refer the question to the AAA for final decision. All other rules shall be interpreted and applied by the AAA.

Appendix B

Code of Professional Responsibility for Arbitrators of Labor-Management Disputes*

Foreword

This "Code of Professional Responsibility for Arbitrators of Labor-Management Disputes" supersedes the "Code of Ethics and Procedural Standards for Labor-Management Arbitration," approved in 1951 by a Committee of the American Arbitration Association, by the National Academy of Arbitrators, and by representatives of the Federal Mediation and Conciliation Service.

Revision of the 1951 Code was initiated officially by the same three groups in October, 1972. The Joint Steering Committee named below was designated to draft a proposal.

Reasons for Code revision should be noted briefly. Ethical considerations and procedural standards are sufficiently intertwined to warrant combining the subject matter of Parts I and II of the 1951 Code under the caption of "Professional Responsibility." It has seemed advisable to eliminate admonitions to the parties (Part III of the 1951 Code) except as they appear incidentally in connection with matters primarily involving responsibilities of arbitrators. Substantial growth of third party participation in dispute resolution in the public sector requires consideration. It appears that arbitration of new contract terms may become more significant. Finally, during the interval of more than two decades, new problems have emerged as private sector grievance arbitration has matured and has become more diversified.

---

*Adopted by the National Academy of Arbitrators, the American Arbitration Association, and the Federal Mediation and Conciliation Service. As amended and in effect, May 29, 1985.

JOINT STEERING COMMITTEE
. . .
November 30, 1974

Preamble

Background

Voluntary arbitration rests upon the mutual desire of management and labor in each collective bargaining relationship to develop procedures for dispute settlement which meet their own particular needs and obligations. No two voluntary systems, therefore, are likely to be identical in practice. Words used to describe arbitrators (Arbitrator, Umpire, Impartial Chairman, Chairman of Arbitration Board, etc.) may suggest typical approaches but actual differences within any general type of arrangement may be as great as distinctions often made among the several types.

Some arbitration and related procedures, however, are not the product of voluntary agreement. These procedures, primarily but not exclusively applicable in the public sector, sometimes utilize other third party titles (Fact Finder, Impasse Panel, Board of Inquiry, etc.). These procedures range all the way from arbitration prescribed by statute to arrangements substantially indistinguishable from voluntary procedures.

The standards of professional responsibility set forth in this Code are designed to guide the impartial third party serving in these diverse labor-management relationships.

Scope of Code

This Code is a privately developed set of standards of professional behavior. It applies to voluntary arbitration of labor-management grievance disputes and of disputes concerning new or revised contract terms. Both "ad hoc" and "permanent" varieties of voluntary arbitration, private and public sector, are included. To the extent relevant in any specific case, it also applies to advisory arbitration, impasse resolution panels, arbitration prescribed by statutes, fact-finding, and other special procedures.

The word "arbitrator," as used hereinafter in the Code, is intended to apply to any impartial person, irrespective of specific title, who serves in a labor-management dispute procedure in which there is conferred authority to decide issues or to make formal recommendations.

The Code is not designed to apply to mediation or conciliation, as distinguished from arbitration, nor to other procedures in which the third party is not authorized in advance to make decisions or recommendations. It does not apply to partisan representatives on tripartite boards. It does not apply to commercial arbitration or to other uses of arbitration outside the labor-management dispute area.

Format of Code

Bold Face type, sometimes including explanatory material, is used to set forth general principles. *Italics* are used for amplification of general principles. Ordinary type is used primarily for illustration or explanatory comment.

Application of Code

Faithful adherence by an arbitrator to this Code is basic to professional responsibility.

The National Academy of Arbitrators will expect its members to be governed in their professional conduct by this Code and stands ready, through its Committee on Ethics and Grievances, to advise its members as to the Code's interpretation. The American Arbitration Association and the Federal Mediation and Conciliation Service will apply the Code to the arbitrators on their rosters in cases handled under their respective appointment or referral procedures. Other arbitrators and administrative agencies may, of course, voluntarily adopt the Code and be governed by it.

In interpreting the Code and applying it to charges of professional misconduct, under existing or revised procedures of the National Academy of Arbitrators and of the administrative agencies, it should be recognized that while some of its standards express ethical principles basic to the arbitration profession, others rest less on ethics than on considerations of good practice. Experience has shown the difficulty of drawing rigid lines of distinction between ethics and good practice and this Code does not attempt to do so. Rather it leaves the gravity of alleged misconduct and the extent to which ethical standards have been violated to be assessed in the light of the facts and circumstances of each particular case.

I. Arbitrator's Qualifications and Responsibilities to the Profession

A. General Qualifications

1. Essential personal qualifications of an arbitrator include honesty, integrity, impartiality, and general competence in labor relations matters.

An arbitrator must demonstrate ability to exercise these personal qualities faithfully and with good judgment, both in procedural matters and in substantive decisions.

a. Selection by mutual agreement of the parties or direct designation by an administrative agency are the effective methods of appraisal of this combination of an individual's potential and performance, rather than the fact of placement on a roster of an administrative agency or membership in a professional association of arbitrators.

2. An arbitrator must be as ready to rule for one party as for the other on each issue, either in a single case or in a group of cases. Compromise by an arbitrator for the sake of attempting to achieve personal acceptability is unprofessional.

B. *Qualifications for Special Cases*

1. An arbitrator must decline appointment, withdraw, or request technical assistance when he or she decides that a case is beyond his or her competence.

a. An arbitrator may be qualified generally but not for specialized assignments. Some types of incentive, work standard, job evaluation, welfare program, pension, or insurance cases may require specialized knowledge, experience, or competence. Arbitration of contract terms also may require distinctive background and experience.

b. Effective appraisal by an administrative agency or by an arbitrator of the need for special qualifications requires that both parties make known the special nature of the case prior to appointment of the arbitrator.

C. *Responsibilities to the Profession*

1. An arbitrator must uphold the dignity and integrity of the office and endeavor to provide effective service to the parties.

a. To this end, an arbitrator should keep current with principles, practices, and developments that are relevant to his or her own field of arbitration practice.

2. An experienced arbitrator should cooperate in the training of new arbitrators.

3. An arbitrator must not advertise or solicit arbitration assignments.

a. It is a matter of personal preference whether an arbitrator includes "Labor Arbitrator" or similar notation on letterheads, cards, or announcements. *It is inappropriate, however, to include memberships or offices held in professional societies or listings on rosters of administrative agencies.*

b. *Information provided for published biographical sketches, as well as that supplied to administrative agencies, must be ac-*

curate. Such information may include membership in professional organizations (including reference to significant offices held), and listings on rosters of administrative agencies.

II. Responsibilities to the Parties

A. Recognition of Diversity in Arbitration Arrangements

1. An arbitrator should conscientiously endeavor to understand and observe, to the extent consistent with professional responsibility, the significant principles governing each arbitration system in which he or she serves.

> a. Recognition of special features of a particular arbitration arrangement can be essential with respect to procedural matters and may influence other aspects of the arbitration process.

2. Such understanding does not relieve an arbitrator from a corollary responsibility to seek to discern and refuse to lend approval or consent to any collusive attempt by the parties to use arbitration for an improper purpose.

B. Required Disclosures

1. Before accepting an appointment, an arbitrator must disclose directly or through the administrative agency involved, any current or past managerial, representational, or consultative relationship with any company or union involved in a proceeding in which he or she is being considered for appointment or has been tentatively designated to serve. Disclosure must also be made of any pertinent pecuniary interest.

> a. The duty to disclose includes membership on a Board of Directors, full-time or part-time service as a representative or advocate, consultation work for a fee, current stock or bond ownership (other than mutual fund shares or appropriate trust arrangements), or any other pertinent form of managerial, financial, or immediate family interest in the company or union involved.

2. When an arbitrator is serving concurrently as an advocate for or representative of other companies or unions in labor relations matters, or has done so in recent years, he or she must disclose such activities before accepting appointment as an arbitrator.

An arbitrator must disclose such activities to an administrative agency if he or she is on that agency's active roster or seeks placement on a roster. Such disclosure then satisfies this requirement for cases handled under that agency's referral.

a. It is not necessary to disclose names of clients or other specific details. It is necessary to indicate the general nature of the labor relations advocacy or representational work involved, whether for companies or unions or both, and a reasonable approximation of the extent of such activity.

b. *An arbitrator on an administrative agency's roster has a continuing obligation to notify the agency of any significant changes pertinent to this requirement.*

c. When an administrative agency is not involved, an arbitrator must make such disclosures directly unless he or she is certain that both parties to the case are fully aware of such activities.

3. An arbitrator must not permit personal relationships to affect decision-making.

Prior to acceptance of an appointment, an arbitrator must disclose to the parties or to the administrative agency involved any close personal relationship or other circumstance, in addition to those specifically mentioned earlier in this section, which might reasonably raise a question as to the arbitrator's impartiality.

a. Arbitrators establish personal relationships with many company and union representatives, with fellow arbitrators, and with fellow members of various professional associations. There should be no attempt to be secretive about such friendships or acquaintances, but disclosure is not necessary unless some feature of a particular relationship might reasonably appear to impair impartiality.

4. If the circumstances requiring disclosure are not known to the arbitrator prior to acceptance of appointment, disclosure must be made when such circumstances become known to the arbitrator.

5. The burden of disclosure rests on the arbitrator. After appropriate disclosure, the arbitrator may serve if both parties so desire. If the arbitrator believes or perceives that there is a clear conflict of interest, he or she should withdraw, irrespective of the expressed desires of the parties.

C. *Privacy of Arbitration*

1. All significant aspects of an arbitration proceeding must be treated by the arbitrator as confidential unless this requirement is waived by both parties or disclosure is required or permitted by law.

a. Attendance at hearings by persons not representing the parties or invited by either or both of them should be permitted only when the parties agree or when an applicable law requires or permits. Occasionally, special circumstances may require that an arbitrator rule on such matters as attendance and degree of participation of counsel selected by a grievant.

b. *Discussion of a case at any time by an arbitrator with persons not involved directly should be limited to situations where advance approval or consent of both parties is obtained or where the identity of the parties and details of the case are sufficiently obscured to eliminate any realistic probability of identification.*

A commonly recognized exception is discussion of a problem in a case with a fellow arbitrator. *Any such discussion does not relieve the arbitrator who is acting in the case from sole responsibility for the decision, and the discussion must be considered as confidential.*

Discussion of aspects of a case in a classroom without prior specific approval of the parties is not a violation provided the arbitrator is satisfied that there is no breach of essential confidentiality.

c. *It is a violation of professional responsibility for an arbitrator to make public an award without the consent of the parties.*

An arbitrator may ask the parties whether they consent to the publication of the award either at the hearing or at the time the award is issued.

(1) *If such question is asked at the hearing it should be asked in writing as follows:*

> *"Do you consent to the submission of the award in this matter for publication?*
>
>
> *( )*   *( )*
> *YES*   *NO*
>
> *If you consent you have the right to notify the arbitrator within 30 days after the date of the award that you revoke your consent."*

It is desirable but not required that the arbitrator remind the parties at the time of the issuance of the award of their right to withdraw their consent to publication.

(2) If the question of consent to the publication of the award is raised at the time the award is issued, the arbitrator may state in writing to each party that failure to answer the inquiry within 30 days will be considered an implied consent to publish.

d. It is not improper for an arbitrator to donate arbitration files to a library of a college, university, or similar institution without prior consent of all the parties involved. When the circumstances permit, there should be deleted from such donations any cases concerning which one or both of the parties have expressed a desire for privacy. As an additional safeguard, an arbitrator may also decide to withhold recent cases or indicate to the donee a time interval before such cases can be made generally available.

e. *Applicable laws, regulations, or practices of the parties may permit or even require exceptions to the above noted principles of privacy.*

D. *Personal Relationships With the Parties*

1. An arbitrator must make every reasonable effort to conform to arrangements required by an administrative agency or mutually desired by the parties regarding communications and personal relationships with the parties.

a. *Only an "arm's length" relationship may be acceptable to the parties in some arbitration arrangements or may be required by the rules of an administrative agency. The arbitrator should then have no contact of consequence with representatives of either party while handling a case without the other party's presence or consent.*

b. *In other situations, both parties may want communications and personal relationships to be less formal. It is then appropriate for the arbitrator to respond accordingly.*

E. *Jurisdiction*

1. An arbitrator must observe faithfully both the limitations and inclusions of the jurisdiction conferred by an agreement or other submission under which he or she serves.

2. A direct settlement by the parties of some or all issues in a case, at any stage of the proceedings, must be accepted by the arbitrator as relieving him or her of futher jurisdiction over such issues.

F. *Mediation by an Arbitrator*

1. When the parties wish at the outset to give an arbitrator authority both to mediate and to decide or submit recommendations regarding residual issues, if any, they should so advise the arbitrator prior to appointment. If the appointment is accepted, the arbitrator must perform a mediation role consistent with the circumstances of the case.

a. Direct appointment, also, may require a dual role as mediator and arbitrator of residual issues. This is most likely to occur in some public sector cases.

2. When a request to mediate is first made after appointment, the arbitrator may either accept or decline a mediation role.

a. *Once arbitration has been invoked, either party normally has a right to insist that the process be continued to decision.*

b. *If one party requests that the arbitrator mediate and the other party objects, the arbitrator should decline the request.*

c. *An arbitrator is not precluded from making a suggestion that he or she mediate. To avoid the possibility of improper pressure, the arbitrator should not so suggest unless it can be discerned that both parties are likely to be receptive. In any event, the arbitrator's suggestion should not be pursued unless both parties readily agree.*

G. *Reliance by an Arbitrator on Other Arbitration Awards or on Independent Research*

1. An arbitrator must assume full personal responsibility for the decision in each case decided.

a. *The extent, if any, to which an arbitrator properly may rely on precedent, on guidance of other awards, or on independent research is dependent primarily on the policies of the parties on these matters, as expressed in the contract, or other agreement, or at the hearing.*

b. When the mutual desires of the parties are not known or when the parties express differing opinions or policies, the arbitrator may exercise discretion as to these matters consistent with acceptance of full personal responsibility for the award.

H. *Use of Assistants*

1. An arbitrator must not delegate any decision-making function to another person without consent of the parties.

a. *Without prior consent of the parties, an arbitrator may use the services of an assistant for research, clerical duties, or preliminary drafting under the direction of the arbitrator which does not involve the delegation of any decision-making function.*

b. *If an arbitrator is unable, because of time limitations or other reasons, to handle all decision-making aspects of a case, it is not a violation of professional responsibility to suggest to the parties an allocation of responsibility between the arbitrator and an assistant or associate. The arbitrator must not exert pressure on the parties to accept such a suggestion.*

I. Consent Awards

1. Prior to issuance of an award, the parties may jointly request the arbitrator to include in the award certain agreements between them, concerning some or all of the issues. If the arbitrator believes that a suggested award is proper, fair, sound, and lawful, it is consistent with professional responsibility to adopt it.

    a. *Before complying with such a request, an arbitrator must be certain that he or she understands the suggested settlement adequately in order to be able to appraise its terms. If it appears that pertinent facts or circumstances may not have been disclosed, the arbitrator should take the initiative to assure that all significant aspects of the case are fully understood. To this end, the arbitrator may request additional specific information and may question witnesses at a hearing.*

J. Avoidance of Delay

1. It is a basic professional responsibility of an arbitrator to plan his or her work schedule so that present and future commitments will be fulfilled in a timely manner.

    a. *When planning is upset for reasons beyond the control of the arbitrator, he or she, nevertheless, should exert every reasonable effort to fulfill all commitments. If this is not possible, prompt notice of the arbitrator's initiative should be given to all parties affected. Such notices should include reasonably accurate estimates of any additional time required. To the extent possible, priority should be given to cases in process so that other parties may make alternative arbitration arrangements.*

2. An arbitrator must cooperate with the parties and with any administrative agency involved in avoiding delays.

    a. *An arbitrator on the active roster of an administrative agency must take the initiative in advising the agency of any scheduling difficulties that he or she can foresee.*

    b. *Requests for services, whether received directly or through an administrative agency, should be declined if the arbitrator is unable to schedule a hearing as soon as the parties wish. If the parties, nevertheless, jointly desire to obtain the services of the arbitrator and the arbitrator agrees, arrangements should be made by agreement that the arbitrator confidently expects to fulfill.*

c. *An arbitrator may properly seek to persuade the parties to alter or eliminate arbitration procedures or tactics that cause unnecessary delay.*

3. Once the case record has been closed, an arbitrator must adhere to the time limits for an award, as stipulated in the labor agreement or as provided by regulation of an administrative agency or as otherwise agreed.

a. *If an appropriate award cannot be rendered within the required time, it is incumbent on the arbitrator to seek an extension of time from the parties.*

b. If the parties have agreed upon abnormally short time limits for an award after a case is closed, the arbitrator should be so advised by the parties or by the administrative agency involved, prior to acceptance of appointment.

K. Fees and Expenses

1. An arbitrator occupies a position of trust in respect to the parties and the administrative agencies. In charging for services and expenses, the arbitrator must be governed by the same high standards of honor and integrity that apply to all other phases of his or her work.

An arbitrator must endeavor to keep total charges for services and expenses reasonable and consistent with the nature of the case or cases decided.

Prior to appointment, the parties should be aware of or be able readily to determine all significant aspects of an arbitrator's bases for charges for fees and expenses.

a. *Services Not Primarily Chargeable on a Per Diem Basis*

By agreement with the parties, the financial aspects of many "permanent" arbitration assignments, of some interest disputes, and of some "ad hoc" grievance assignments do not include a per diem fee for services as a primary part of the total understanding. *In such situations, the arbitrator must adhere faithfully to all agreed upon arrangements governing fees and expenses.*

b. *Per Diem Basis for Charges for Services*

(1) *When an arbitrator's charges for services are determined primarily by a stipulated per diem fee, the arbitrator should establish in advance his or her bases for application of such per diem fee and for determination of reimbursable expenses.*

Practices established by an arbitrator should include the basis for charges, if any, for:

(a) hearing time, including the application of the stipulated basic per diem hearing fee to hearing days of varying lengths;

(b) study time;

(c) necessary travel time when not included in charges for hearing time;

(d) postponement or cancellation of hearing by the parties' and the circumstances in which such charges will normally be assessed or waived;

(e) office overhead expenses (secretarial, telephone, postage, etc.);

(f) the work of paid assistants or associates.

(2) *Each arbitrator should be guided by the following general principles:*

(a) *Per diem charges for a hearing should not be in excess of actual time spent or allocated for the hearing.*

(b) *Per diem charges for study time should not be in excess of actual time spent.*

(c) *Any fixed ratio of study days to hearing days, not agreed to specifically by the parties, is inconsistent with the per diem method of charges for services.*

(d) *Charges for expenses must not be in excess of actual expenses normally reimbursable and incurred in connection with the case or cases involved.*

(e) *When time or expense are involved for two or more sets of parties on the same day or trip, such time or expense charges should be appropriately prorated.*

(f) *An arbitrator may stipulate in advance a minimum charge for a hearing without violation of (a) or (e) above.*

(3) *An arbitrator on the active roster of an administrative agency must file with the agency his or her individual bases for determination of fees and expenses if the agency so requires. Thereafter, it is the responsibility of each such arbitrator to advise the agency promptly of any change in any basis for charges.*

Such filing may be in the form of answers to a questionnaire devised by an agency or by any other method adopted by or approved by an agency.

Having supplied an administrative agency with the information noted above, an arbitrator's professional responsibility of disclosure under this Code with respect to fees and expenses has been satisfied for cases referred by that agency.

(4) *If an administrative agency promulgates specific standards with respect to any of these matters which are in addition to or more restrictive than an individual arbitrator's standards,*

an arbitrator on its active roster must observe the agency standards for cases handled under the auspices of that agency or decline to serve.

(5) When an arbitrator is contacted directly by the parties for a case or cases, the arbitrator has a professional responsibility to respond to questions by submitting his or her bases for charges for fees and expenses.

(6) When it is known to the arbitrator that one or both of the parties cannot afford normal charges, it is consistent with professional responsibility to charge lesser amounts to both parties or to one of the parties if the other party is made aware of the difference and agrees.

(7) If an arbitrator concludes that the total of charges derived from his or her normal basis of calculation is not compatible with the case decided, it is consistent with professional responsibility to charge lesser amounts to both parties.

2. An arbitrator must maintain adequate records to support charges for services and expenses and must make an accounting to the parties or to an involved administrative agency on request.

III. Responsibilities to Administrative Agencies

A. General Responsibilities

1. An arbitrator must be candid, accurate, and fully responsive to an administrative agency concerning his or her qualifications, availability, and all other pertinent matters.

2. An arbitrator must observe policies and rules of an administrative agency in cases referred by that agency.

3. An arbitrator must not seek to influence an administrative agency by any improper means, including gifts or other inducements to agency personnel.

   a. It is not improper for a person seeking placement on a roster to request references from individuals having knowledge of the applicant's experience and qualifications.

   b. Arbitrators should recognize that the primary responsibility of an administrative agency is to serve the parties.

IV. Prehearing Conduct

1. All prehearing matters must be handled in a manner that fosters complete impartiality by the arbitrator.

a. The primary purpose of prehearing discussions involving the arbitrator is to obtain agreement on procedural matters so that the hearing can proceed without unnecessary obstacles. If differences of opinion should arise during such discussions and, particularly, if such differences appear to impinge on substantive matters, the circumstances will suggest whether the matter can be resolved informally or may require a prehearing conference or, more rarely, a formal preliminary hearing. When an administrative agency handles some or all aspects of the arrangements prior to a hearing, the arbitrator will become involved only if differences of some substance arise.

b. *Copies of any prehearing correspondence between the arbitrator and either party must be made available to both parties.*

V. Hearing Conduct

A. *General Principles*

1. An arbitrator must provide a fair and adequate hearing which assures that both parties have sufficient opportunity to present their respective evidence and argument.

a. *Within the limits of this responsibility, an arbitrator should conform to the various types of hearing procedures desired by the parties.*

b. An arbitrator may: encourage stipulations of fact; restate the substance of issues or arguments to promote or verify understanding; question the parties' representatives or witnesses, when necessary or advisable, to obtain additional pertinent information; and request that the parties submit additional evidence, either at the hearing or by subsequent filing.

c. *An arbitrator should not intrude into a party's presentation so as to prevent that party from putting forward its case fairly and adequately.*

B. *Transcripts or Recordings*

1. Mutual agreement of the parties as to use or nonuse of a transcript must be respected by the arbitrator.

a. *A transcript is the official record of a hearing only when both parties agree to a transcript or an applicable law or regulation so provides.*

b. An arbitrator may seek to persuade the parties to avoid use of a transcript, or to use a transcript if the nature of the case appears to require one. *However, if an arbitrator intends to make his or her appointment in a case contingent on mutual agreement to a transcript, that requirement must be made known to both parties prior to appointment.*

c. If the parties do not agree to a transcript, an arbitrator may permit one party to make a transcript at its own cost. The arbitrator may also make appropriate arrangements under which the other party may have access to a copy, if a copy is provided to the arbitrator.

d. Without prior approval, an arbitrator may seek to use his or her own tape recorder to supplement note taking. The arbitrator should not insist on such a tape recording if either or both parties object.

C. *Ex Parte Hearings*

1. In determining whether to conduct an ex parte hearing, an arbitrator must consider relevant legal, contractual, and other pertinent circumstances.

2. An arbitrator must be certain, before proceeding ex parte, that the party refusing or failing to attend the hearing has been given adequate notice of the time, place, and purposes of the hearing.

D. *Plant Visits*

1. An arbitrator should comply with a request of a party that he or she visit a work area pertinent to the dispute prior to, during, or after a hearing. An arbitrator may also initiate such a request.

a. *Procedures for such visits should be agreed to by the parties in consultation with the arbitrator.*

E. *Bench Decisions or Expedited Awards*

1. When an arbitrator understands, prior to acceptance of appointment, that a bench decision is expected at the conclusion of the hearing, the arbitrator must comply with the understanding unless both parties agree otherwise.

a. *If notice of the parties' desire for a bench decision is not given prior to the arbitrator's acceptance of the case, issuance of such a bench decision is discretionary.*

b. *When only one party makes the request and the other objects, the arbitrator should not render a bench decision except under most unusual circumstances.*

2. When an arbitrator understands, prior to acceptance of appointment, that a concise written award is expected within a stated time period after the hearing, the arbitrator must

comply with the understanding unless both parties agree otherwise.

VI. Post Hearing Conduct

A. Post Hearing Briefs and Submissions

1. An arbitrator must comply with mutual agreements in respect to the filing or nonfiling of post hearing briefs or submissions.

a. An arbitrator, in his or her discretion, may either suggest the filing of post hearing briefs or other submissions or suggest that none be filed.

b. When the parties disagree as to the need for briefs, an arbitrator may permit filing but may determine a reasonable time limitation.

2. An arbitrator must not consider a post hearing brief or submission that has not been provided to the other party.

B. Disclosure of Terms of Award

1. An arbitrator must not disclose a prospective award to either party prior to its simultaneous issuance to both parties or explore possible alternative awards unilaterally with one party, unless both parties so agree.

a. Partisan members of tripartite boards may know prospective terms of an award in advance of its issuance. Similar situations may exist in other less formal arrangements mutually agreed to by the parties. In any such situation, the arbitrator should determine and observe the mutually desired degree of confidentiality.

C. Awards and Opinions

1. The award should be definite, certain, and as concise as possible.

a. When an opinion is required, factors to be considered by an arbitrator include: desirability of brevity, consistent with the nature of the case and any expressed desires of the parties; need to use a style and form that is understandable to responsible representatives of the parties, to the grievant and supervisors, and to others in the collective bargaining relationship; necessity of meeting the significant issues; forthrightness to an extent not harmful to the relationship of the parties; and avoidance of gratuitous advice or disclosure not essential to disposition of the issues.

D. Clarification or Interpretation of Awards

1. No clarification or interpretation of an award is permissible without the consent of both parties.

2. Under agreements which permit or require clarification or interpretation of an award, an arbitrator must afford both parties an opportunity to be heard.

E. Enforcement of Award

1. The arbitrator's responsibility does not extend to the enforcement of an award.

2. In view of the professional and confidential nature of the arbitration relationship, an arbitrator should not voluntarily participate in legal enforcement proceedings.

Appendix C

The United States Arbitration Act[*]
Chapter 1.—General Provisions

Section 1. "Maritime Transactions" and "Commerce" Defined; Exceptions to Operation of Title

"Maritime transactions," as herein defined, means charter parties, bills of lading of water carriers, agreements relating to wharfage, supplies furnished vessels or repairs of vessels, collisions, or any other matters in foreign commerce which, if the subject of controversy, would be embraced within admiralty jurisdiction; "commerce," as herein defined, means commerce among the several States or with foreign nations, or in any Territory of the United States or in the District of Columbia, or between any such Territory and another, or between any such Territory and any State or foreign nation, or between the District of Columbia and any State or Territory or foreign nation, but nothing herein contained shall apply to contracts of employment of seamen, railroad employees, or any other class of workers engaged in foreign or interstate commerce.

Section 2. Validity, Irrevocability, and Enforcement of Agreements to Arbitrate

A written provision in any maritime transaction or a contract evidencing a transaction involving commerce to settle by arbitration a controversy thereafter arising out of such contract or transaction, or the refusal to perform the whole or any part thereof, or an agreement in writing to submit to arbitration an existing controversy arising out of such a contract, transaction, or refusal, shall be valid, irrevocable, and enforceable, save upon such grounds as exist at law or in equity for the revocation of any contract.

---

[*]9 U.S.C.§§1–15 (1988).

538

Section 3. Stay of Proceedings Where Issue Therein Referable to Arbitration

If any suit or proceeding be brought in any of the courts of the United States upon any issue referable to arbitration under an agreement in writing for such arbitration, the court in which such suit is pending, upon being satisfied that the issue involved in such suit or proceeding is referable to arbitration under such an agreement, shall on application of one of the parties stay the trial of the action until such arbitration has been had in accordance with the terms of the agreement, providing the applicant for the stay is not in default in proceeding with such arbitration.

Section 4. Failure to Arbitrate Under Agreement; Petition to United States Court Having Jurisdiction for Order to Compel Arbitration; Notice and Service Thereof; Hearing and Determination

A party aggrieved by the alleged failure, neglect, or refusal of another to arbitrate under a written agreement for arbitration may petition any United States district court which, save for such agreement, would have jurisdiction under Title 28, in a civil action or in admiralty of the subject matter of a suit arising out of the controversy between the parties, for an order directing that such arbitration proceed in the manner provided for in such agreement. Five days' notice in writing of such application shall be served upon the party in default. Service thereof shall be made in the manner provided by the Federal Rules of Civil Procedure. The court shall hear the parties, and upon being satisfied that the making of the agreement for arbitration or the failure to comply therewith is not in issue, the court shall make an order directing the parties to proceed to arbitration in accordance with the terms of the agreement. The hearing and proceedings, under such agreement, shall be within the district in which the petition for an order directing such arbitration is filed. If the making of the arbitration agreement or the failure, neglect, or refusal to perform the same be in issue, the court shall proceed summarily to the trial thereof. If no jury trial be demanded by the party alleged to be in default, or if the matter in dispute is within admiralty jurisdiction, the court shall hear and determine such issue. Where such an issue is raised, the party alleged to be in default may, except in cases of admiralty, on or before the return day of the notice of application, demand a jury trial of such issue, and upon such demand the court shall make an order referring the issue or issues to a jury in the manner provided by the Federal Rules of Civil Procedure, or may specially call a jury for that purpose. If the jury find that no agreement in writing for arbitration was made or that there is no default in proceeding thereunder, the proceeding shall be dismissed. If the jury find that an agreement for arbitration was made in writing and that there is a default in proceeding thereunder, the court shall make an order summarily directing the parties to proceed with the arbitration in accordance with the terms thereof.

Section 5. Appointment of Arbitrators or Umpire

If in the agreement provision be made for a method of naming or appointing an arbitrator or arbitrators or any umpire, such method shall be followed; but if no method be provided therein, or if a method be provided and any party thereto shall fail to avail himself of such method, or if for any other reason there shall be a lapse in the naming of an arbitrator or arbitrators or umpire, or in filling a vacancy, then upon the application of either party to the controversy the court shall designate and appoint an arbitrator or arbitrators or umpire, as the case may require, who shall act under the said agreement with the same force and effect as if he or they had been specifically named therein; and unless otherwise provided in the agreement the arbitration shall be by a single arbitrator.

Section 6. Application Heard as Motion

Any application to the court hereunder shall be made and heard in the manner provided by law for the making and hearing of motions, except as otherwise herein expressly provided.

Section 7. Witnesses Before Arbitrators; Fees; Compelling Attendance

The arbitrators selected either as prescribed in this title or otherwise, or a majority of them, may summon in writing any person to attend before them or any of them as a witness and in a proper case to bring with him or them any book, record, document, or paper which may be deemed material as evidence in the case. The fees for such attendance shall be the same as the fees of witnesses before masters of the United States courts. Said summons shall issue in the name of the arbitrator or arbitrators, or a majority of them, and shall be signed by the arbitrators, or a majority of them, and shall be directed to the said person and shall be served in the same manner as subpoenas to appear and testify before the court; if any person or persons so summoned to testify shall refuse or neglect to obey said summons, upon petition the United States court in and for the district in which such arbitrators, or a majority of them, are sitting may compel the attendance of such person or persons before said arbitrator or arbitrators, or punish said person or persons for contempt in the same manner provided on February 12, 1925, for securing the attendance of witnesses or their punishment for neglect or refusal to attend in the courts of the United States.

Section 8. Proceedings Begun by Libel in Admiralty and Seizure of Vessel or Property

If the basis of jurisdiction be a cause of action otherwise justiciable in admiralty, then, notwithstanding anything herein to the contrary the party claiming to be aggrieved may begin his proceeding hereunder by libel and seizure of the vessel or other property of the other party according to the usual course of admiralty proceedings, and the court shall then have jurisdiction to direct the parties to proceed with the arbitration and shall retain jurisdiction to enter its decree upon the award.

Section 9. Award of Arbitrators; Confirmation; Jurisdiction; Procedure

If the parties in their agreement have agreed that a judgment of the court shall be entered upon the award made pursuant to the arbitration, and shall specify the court, then at any time within one year after the award is made any party to the arbitration may apply to the court so specified for an order confirming the award, and thereupon the court must grant such an order unless the award is vacated, modified, or corrected as prescribed in sections 10 and 11 of this title. If no court is specified in the agreement of the parties, then such application may be made to the United States court in and for the district within which such award was made. Notice of the application shall be served upon the adverse party, and thereupon the court shall have jurisdiction of such party as though he had appeared generally in the proceeding. If the adverse party is a resident of the district within which the award was made, such service shall be made upon the adverse party or his attorney as prescribed by law for service of notice of motion in an action in the same court. If the adverse party shall be a nonresident, then the notice of the application shall be served by the marshal of any district within which the adverse party may be found in like manner as other process of the court.

Section 10. Same; Vacation; Grounds; Rehearing

In either of the following cases the United States court in and for the district wherein the award was made may make an order vacating the award upon the application of any party to the arbitration—

(a) Where the award was procured by corruption, fraud, or undue means.

(b) Where there was evident partiality or corruption in the arbitrators, or either of them.

(c) Where the arbitrators were guilty of misconduct in refusing to postpone the hearing, upon sufficient cause shown, or in refusing to hear evidence pertinent and material to the controversy; or of any other misbehavior by which the rights of any party have been prejudiced.

(d) Where the arbitrators exceeded their powers, or so imperfectly executed them that a mutual, final, and definite award upon the subject matter submitted was not made.

(e) Where an award is vacated and the time within which the agreement required the award to be made has not expired the court may, in its discretion, direct a rehearing by the arbitrators.

Section 11. Same; Modification or Correction; Grounds; Order

In either of the following cases the United States court in and for the district wherein the award was made may make an order modifying or correcting the award upon the application of any party to the arbitration—

(a) Where there was an evident material miscalculation of figures or an evident material mistake in the description of any person, thing, or property referred to in the award.

(b) Where the arbitrators have awarded upon a matter not submitted to them, unless it is a matter not affecting the merits of the decision upon the matter submitted.

(c) Where the award is imperfect in matter of form not affecting the merits of the controversy.

The order may modify and correct the award, so as to effect the intent thereof and promote justice between the parties.

Section 12. Notice of Motions to Vacate or Modify; Service; Stay of Proceedings

Notice of a motion to vacate, modify, or correct an award must be served upon the adverse party or his attorney within three months after the award is filed or delivered. If the adverse party is a resident of the district within which the award was made, such service shall be made upon the adverse party or his attorney as prescribed by law for service of notice of motion in an action in the same court. If the adverse party shall be a nonresident then the notice of the application shall be served by the marshal of any district within which the adverse party may be found in like manner as other process of the court. For the purposes of the motion any judge who might make an order to stay the proceedings in an action brought in the same court may make an order, to be served with the notice of motion, staying the proceedings of the adverse party to enforce the award.

Section 13. Papers Filed with Order on Motions; Judgment; Docketing; Force and Effect; Enforcement

The party moving for an order confirming, modifying, or correcting an award shall, at the time such order is filed with the clerk for the entry of judgment thereon, also file the following papers with the clerk:

(a) The agreement; the selection or appointment, if any, of an additional arbitrator or umpire; and each written extension of the time, if any, within which to make the award.

(b) The award.

(c) Each notice, affidavit, or other paper used upon an application to confirm, modify, or correct the award, and a copy of each order of the court upon such an application.

The judgment shall be docketed as if it was rendered in an action.

The judgment so entered shall have the same force and effect, in all respects, as, and be subject to all the provisions of law relating to, a judgment in an action; and it may be enforced as if it had been rendered in an action in the court in which it is entered.

Section 14. Contracts Not Affected

This title shall not apply to contracts made prior to January 1, 1926.

Section 15.* Inapplicability of the Act of State doctrine

Enforcement of arbitral agreements, confirmation of arbitral awards, and execution upon judgments based on orders confirming such awards shall not be refused on the basis of the Act of State doctrine.

Section 15.* Appeals

(a) An appeal may be taken from—
  (1) an order—
    (A) refusing a stay of any action under section 3 of this title,

---

*So in original. There are two sections designated "15."

(B) denying a petition under section 4 of this title to order arbitration to proceed,

(C) denying an application under section 206 of this title to compel arbitration,

(D) confirming or denying confirmation of an award or partial award, or

(E) modifying, correcting, or vacating an award;

(2) an interlocutory order granting, continuing, or modifying an injunction against an arbitration that is subject to this title; or

(3) a final decision with respect to an arbitration that is subject to this title.

(b) Except as otherwise provided in section 1292(b) of title 28, an appeal may not be taken from an interlocutory order—

(1) granting a stay of any action under section 3 of this title;

(2) directing arbitration to proceed under section 4 of this title;

(3) compelling arbitration under section 206 of this title; or

(4) refusing to enjoin an arbitration that is subject to this title.

Appendix D

Uniform Arbitration Act*

Act Relating to Arbitration and to Make Uniform The Law With Reference Thereto

Section 1. (Validity of Arbitration Agreement.)

A written agreement to submit any existing controversy to arbitration or a provision in a written contract to submit to arbitration any controversy thereafter arising between the parties is valid, enforceable and irrevocable, save upon such grounds as exist at law or in equity for the revocation of any contract. This act also applies to arbitration agreements between employers and employees or between their respective representatives (unless otherwise provided in the agreement.)

Section 2. (Proceedings to Compel or Stay Arbitration.)

(a) On application of a party showing an agreement described in Section 1, and the opposing party's refusal to arbitrate, the Court shall order the parties to proceed with arbitration, but if the opposing party denies the existence of the agreement to arbitrate, the Court shall proceed summarily to the determination of the issue so raised and shall order arbitration if found for the moving party, otherwise, the application shall be denied.

(b) On application, the courts may stay an arbitration proceeding commenced or threatened on a showing that there is no agreement to arbitrate. Such an issue, when in substantial and bona fide dispute, shall be forthwith and summarily tried and the stay ordered

---

*Adopted by the National Conference of the Commissioners on Uniform State Laws, August 20, 1955, as amended August 24, 1956. Approved by the House of Delegates of the American Bar Association, August 26, 1955, and August 30, 1956.

Brackets and parenthesis enclose language which the Commissioners suggest may be used by those States desiring to do so.

if found for the moving party. If found for the opposing party, the court shall order the parties to proceed to arbitration.

(c) If an issue referable to arbitration under the alleged agreement is involved in action or proceeding pending in a court having jurisdiction to hear applications under subdivision (a) of this Section, the application shall be made therein. Otherwise and subject to Section 18, the application may be made in any court of competent jurisdiction.

(d) Any action or proceeding involving an issue subject to arbitration shall be stayed if an order for arbitration or an application therefore has been made under this section or, if the issue is severable, the stay may be with respect thereto only. When the application is made in such action or proceeding, the order for arbitration shall include such stay.

(e) An order for arbitration shall not be refused on the ground that the claim in issue lacks merit or bona fides or because any fault or grounds for the claim sought to be arbitrated have not been shown.

Section 3. (Appointment of Arbitrators by Courts.)

If the arbitration agreement provides a method of appointment of arbitrators, this method shall be followed. In the absence thereof, or if the agreed method fails or for any reason cannot be followed, or when an arbitrator appointed fails or is unable to act and his successor has not been duly appointed, the court on application of a party shall appoint one or more arbitrators. An arbitrator so appointed has all the powers of one specifically named in the agreement.

Section 4. (Majority Action by Arbitrators.)

The powers of the arbitrators may be exercised by a majority unless otherwise provided by the agreement or by this act.

Section 5. (Hearing.)

Unless otherwise provided by the agreement:

(a) The arbitrators shall appoint a time and place for the hearing and cause notification to the parties to be served personally or by registered mail not less than five days before the hearing. Appearance at the hearing waives such notice. The arbitrators may adjourn the hearing from time to time as necessary and, on request of a party and for good cause, or upon their own motion may postpone the hearing to a time not later than the date fixed by the agreement for making the award unless the parties consent to a later date. The arbitrators may hear and determine the controversy upon the evidence produced notwithstanding the failure of a party duly notified to appear. The court on application may direct the arbitrators to proceed promptly with the hearing and determination of the controversy.

(b) The parties are entitled to be heard, to present evidence material to the controversy and to cross-examine witnesses appearing at the hearing.

(c) The hearing shall be conducted by all the arbitrators but a majority may determine any question and render a final award. If, during the course of the hearing, an arbitrator for any reason ceases to act, the remaining arbitrator or arbitrators appointed to act as neutrals may continue with the hearing and determination of the controversy.

Section 6. (Representation by Attorney.)

A party has the right to be represented by an attorney at any proceeding or hearing under this act. A waiver thereof prior to the proceeding or hearing is ineffective.

Section 7. (Witnesses, Subpoenas, Depositions.)

(a) The arbitrators may issue (cause to be issued) subpoenas for the attendance of witnesses and for the production of books, records, documents and other evidence, and shall have the power to administer oaths. Subpoenas so issued shall be served, and upon application to the Court by a party or the arbitrators, enforced, in the manner provided by law for the service and enforcement of subpoenas in a civil action.

(b) On application of a party and for use as evidence, the arbitrators may permit a deposition to be taken, in the manner and upon the terms designated by the arbitrators, of a witness who cannot be subpoenaed or is unable to attend the hearing.

(c) All provisions of law compelling a person under subpoena to testify are applicable.

(d) Fees for attendance as a witness shall be the same as for a witness in the _____Court.

Section 8. (Award.)

(a) The award shall be in writing and signed by the arbitrators joining in the award. The arbitrators shall deliver a copy to each party personally or by registered mail, or as provided in the agreement.

(b) An award shall be made within the time fixed therefor by the agreement or, if not so fixed, within such time as the court orders on application of a party. The parties may extend the time in writing either before or after the expiration thereof. A party waives the objection that an award was not made within the time required unless he notifies the arbitrators of his objection prior to the delivery of the award to him.

Section 9. *(Change of Award by Arbitrators.)*

On application of a party or, if an application to the court is pending under Sections 11, 12, or 13, on submission to the arbitrators by the court under such conditions as the court may order, the arbitrators may modify or correct the award upon the grounds stated in paragraphs (1) and (3) of subdivision (a) of Section 13, or for the purpose of clarifying the award. The application shall be made within twenty days after delivery of the award to the applicant. Written notice thereof shall be given forthwith to the opposing party, stating he must serve his objection thereto if any, within ten days from the notice. The award so modified or corrected is subject to the provisions of Sections 11, 12 and 13.

Section 10. *(Fees and Expenses of Arbitration.)*

Unless otherwise provided in the agreement to arbitrate, the arbitrators' expenses and fees, together with other expenses, not including counsel fees, incurred in the conduct of the arbitration, shall be paid as provided in the award.

Section 11. *(Confirmation of an Award.)*

Upon application of a party, the court shall confirm an award, unless within the time limits hereinafter imposed grounds are urged for vacating or modifying or correcting the award, in which case the court shall proceed as provided in Sections 12 and 13.

Section 12. *(Vacating an Award.)*

(a) Upon application of a party, the court shall vacate an award where:

(1) The award was procured by corruption, fraud or other undue means;

(2) There was evident partiality by an arbitrator appointed as a neutral or corruption in any of the arbitrators or misconduct prejudicing the rights of any party;

(3) The arbitrators exceeded their powers;

(4) The arbitrators refused to postpone the hearing upon sufficient cause being shown therefor or refused to hear evidence material to the controversy or otherwise so conducted the hearing,

contrary to the provisions of Section 5, as to prejudice substantially the rights of a party; or

(5) There was no arbitration agreement and the issue was not adversely determined in proceedings under Section 2 and the party did not participate in the arbitration hearing without raising the objection;

But the fact that the relief was such that it could not or would not be granted by a court of law or equity is not ground for vacating or refusing to confirm the award.

(b) An application under this Section shall be made within ninety days after delivery of a copy of the award to the applicant, except that, if predicated upon corruption, fraud or other undue means, it shall be made within ninety days after such grounds are known or should have been known.

(c) In vacating the award on grounds other than stated in clause (5) of Subsection (a) the court may order a rehearing before new arbitrators chosen as provided in the agreement, or in the absence thereof, by the court in accordance with Section 3, or, if the award is vacated on grounds set forth in clauses (3), and (4) of Subsection (a) the court may order a rehearing before the arbitrators who made the award or their successors appointed in accordance with Section 3. The time within which the agreement requires the award to be made is applicable to the rehearing and commences from the date of the order.

(d) If the application to vacate is denied and no motion to modify or correct the award is pending, the court shall confirm the award.

Section 13. (Modification or Correction of Award.)

(a) Upon application made within ninety days after delivery of a copy of the award to the applicant, the court shall modify or correct the award where:

(1) There was an evident miscalculation of figures or an evident mistake in the description of any person, thing or property referred to in the award;

(2) The arbitrators have awarded upon a matter not submitted to them and the award may be corrected without affecting the merits of the decision upon the issues submitted; or

(3) The award is imperfect in a matter of form, not affecting the merits of the controversy.

(b) If the application is granted, the court shall modify and correct the award so as to effect its intent and shall confirm the award as so modified and corrected. Otherwise, the court shall confirm the award as made.

(c) An application to modify or correct an award may be joined in the alternative with an application to vacate the award.

Section 14. (Judgment or Decree on Award.)

Upon the granting of an order confirming, modifying or correcting an award, judgment or decree shall be entered in conformity therewith and be enforced as any other judgment or decree. Costs of the application and of the proceedings subsequent thereto, and disbursements may be awarded by the court.

[Section 15. (Judgment Roll, Docketing.)

(a) On entry of judgment or decree, the clerk shall prepare the judgment roll consisting, to the extent filled, of the following:

(1) The agreement and each written extension of the time within which to make the award;

(2) The award;

(3) A copy of the order confirming, modifying or correcting the award; and

(4) A copy of the judgment or decree.

(b) The judgment or decree may be docketed as if rendered in an action.]

Section 16. (Applications to Court.)

Except as otherwise provided, an application to the court under this act shall be by motion and shall be heard in the manner and upon the notice provided by law or rule of court for the making and hearing of motions. Unless the parties have agreed otherwise, notice of an initial application for an order shall be served in the manner provided by law for the service of a summons in an action.

Section 17. (Court, Jurisdiction.)

The term "court" means any court of competent jurisdiction of this State. The making of an agreement described in Section 1 providing for arbitration in this State confers jurisdiction on the court to enforce the agreement under this Act and to enter judgment on an award thereunder.

Section 18. (Venue.)

An initial application shall be made to the court of the (county) in which the agreement provides the arbitration hearing shall be held or, if the hearing has been held, in the county in which it was held. Otherwise the application shall be made in the (county) where the adverse party resides or has a place of business or, if he has no residence or place of business in this State, to the court of any (county). All subsequent applications shall be made to the court hearing the initial application unless the court otherwise directs.

Section 19. (Appeals.)

(a) An appeal may be taken from:

(1) An order denying an application to compel arbitration made under Section 2;

(2) An order granting an application to stay arbitration made under Section 2(b);

(3) An order confirming or denying confirmation of an award;

(4) An order modifying or correcting an award;

(5) An order vacating an award without directing a rehearing; or

(6) A judgment or decree entered pursuant to the provisions of this act.

(b) The appeal shall be taken in the manner and to the same extent as from orders or judgments in a civil action.

Section 20. (Act Not Retroactive.)

This act applies only to agreements made subsequent to the taking effect of this act.

Section 21. (Uniformity of Interpretation.)

This act shall be so construed as to effectuate its general purpose to make uniform the law of those states which enact it.

Section 22. (Constitutionality.)

If any provision of this act or the application thereof to any person or circumstance is held invalid, the invalidity shall not affect other provisions or applications of the act which can be given without the invalid provision or application, and to this end the provisions of the act are severable.

Section 23. (Short Title.)

This act may be cited as the Uniform Arbitration Act.

Section 24. (Repeal.)

All acts or parts of acts which are inconsistent with the provisions of this act are hereby repealed.

Section 25. (Time of Taking Effect.)

This act shall take effect _____

Appendix E

Tests Applicable for Learning Whether Employer Had Just and Proper Cause for Disciplining Employee*

Few if any union-management agreements contain a definition of "just cause." Nevertheless, over the years the opinions of arbitrators in innumerable discipline cases have developed a sort of "common law" definition thereof. This definition consists of a set of guidelines or criteria that are to be applied to the facts of any one case, and said criteria are set forth below in the form of questions.

A "no" answer to any one or more of the following questions normally signifies that just and proper cause did not exist. In other words, such "no" means that the employer's disciplinary decision contained one or more elements of arbitrary, capricious, unreasonable or discriminatory action to such an extent that said decision constituted an abuse of managerial discretion warranting the arbitrator to substitute his judgment for that of the employer.

The answers to the questions in any particular case are to be found in the evidence presented to the arbitrator at the hearing thereon. Frequently, of course, the facts are such that the guidelines cannot be applied with precision. Moreover, occasionally, in some particular case an arbitrator may find one or more "no" answers so weak and the other "yes" answers so strong that he may properly, without any "political" or spineless intent to "split the difference" between the opposing positions of the parties, find that the correct decision is to "chastise" both the company and the disciplined employee by decreasing but not nullifying the degree of discipline im-

---

*Enterprise Wire Co., 46 LA 359 (1966).

posed by the company—e.g., by reinstating a discharged employee without back pay.

It should be clearly understood also that the criteria set forth below are to be applied to the employer's conduct in making his disciplinary decision before same has been processed through the grievance procedure to arbitration. Any question as to whether the employer has properly fulfilled the contractual requirements of said procedure is entirely separate from the question of whether he fulfilled the "common law" requirements of just cause before the discipline was "grieved."

Sometimes, although very rarely, a union-management agreement contains a provision limiting the scope of the arbitrator's inquiry into the question of just cause. For example, one such provision seen by this arbitrator says that "the only question the arbitrator is to determine shall be whether the employee is or is not guilty of the act or acts resulting in his discharge." Under the latter contractual statement an arbitrator might well have to confine his attention to Question 5 below—or at most to Questions No. 3, 4 and 5. But absent any such restriction in an agreement, a consideration of the evidence on all seven Questions (and their accompanying Notes) is not only proper but necessary.

The Questions

1. Did the company give to the employee forewarning or foreknowledge of the possible or probable disciplinary consequences of the employee's conduct?

Note 1: Said forewarning or foreknowledge may properly have been given orally by management or in writing through the medium of typed or printed sheets or books of shop rules and of penalties for violation thereof.

Note 2: There must have been actual oral or written communication of the rules and penalties to the employee.

Note 3: A finding of lack of such communication does not in all cases require a "no" answer to Question No. 1. This is because certain offenses such as insubordination, coming to work intoxicated, drinking intoxicating beverages on the job, or theft of the property of the company or of fellow employees are so serious that any employee in the industrial society may properly be expected to know already that such conduct is offensive and heavily punishable.

Note 4: Absent any contractual prohibition or restriction, the company has the right unilaterally to promulgate reasonable rules and give reasonable orders; and same need not have been negotiated with the union.

2. Was the company's rule or managerial order reasonably related to (a) the orderly, efficient and safe operation of the company's business and (b) the performance that the company might properly expect of the employee?

Note: If an employee believes that said rule or order is unreasonable, he must nevertheless obey same (in which case he may file a grievance thereover) unless he sincerely feels that to obey the rule or order would seriously and immediately jeopardize his personal safety and/or integrity. Given a firm finding to the latter effect, the employee may properly be said to have had justification for his disobedience.

3. Did the company, before administering discipline to an employee, make an effort to discover whether the employee did in fact violate or disobey a rule or order of management?

Note 1: This is the employee's "day in court" principle. An employee has the right to know with reasonable precision the offense with which he is being charged and to defend his behavior.

Note 2: The company's investigation must normally be made before its disciplinary decision is made. If the company fails to do so, its failure may not normally be excused on the grounds that the employee will get his day in court through the grievance procedure after the exaction of discipline. By that time there has usually been too much hardening of position. In a very real sense the company is obligated to conduct itself like a trial court.

Note 3: There may of course be circumstances under which management must react immediately to the employee's behavior. In such cases the normally proper action is to suspend the employee pending investigation, with the understanding that (a) the final disciplinary decision will be made after the investigation and (b) if the employee is found innocent after the investigation, he will be restored to his job with full pay for time lost.

Note 4: The company's investigation should include an inquiry into possible justification for the employee's alleged rule violation.

4. Was the company's investigation conducted fairly and objectively?

Note 1: At said investigation the management official may be both "prosecutor" and "judge," but he may not also be a witness against the employee.

Note 2: It is essential for some higher, detached management official to assume and conscientiously perform the judicial role, giving the commonly accepted meaning to that term in his attitude and conduct.

Note 3: In some disputes between an employee and a management person there are not witnesses to an incident other than the two immediate participants. In such cases it is particularly important that the management "judge" question the management participant rigorously and thoroughly, just as an actual third party would.

5. At the investigation did the "judge" obtain substantial evidence or proof that the employee was guilty as charged?

Note 1: It is not required that the evidence be conclusive or "beyond all reasonable doubt." But the evidence must be truly substantial and not flimsy.

Note 2: The management "judge" should actively search out witnesses and evidence, not just passively take what participants or "volunteer" witnesses tell him.

Note 3: When the testimony of opposing witnesses at the arbitration hearing is irreconcilably in conflict, an arbitrator seldom has any means for resolving the contradictions. His task is then to determine whether the management "judge" originally had reasonable grounds for believing the evidence presented to him by his own people.

6. Has the company applied its rules, orders, and penalties evenhandedly and without discrimination to all employees?

Note 1: A "no" answer to this question requires a finding of discrimination and warrants negation or modification of the discipline imposed.

Note 2: If the company has been lax in enforcing its rules and orders and decides henceforth to apply them rigorously, the company may avoid a finding of discrimination by telling all employees beforehand of its intent to enforce hereafter all rules as written.

7. Was the degree of discipline administered by the company in a particular case reasonably related to (a) the seriousness of the employee's proven offense and (b) the record of the employee in his service with the company?

Note 1: A trivial proven offense does not merit harsh discipline unless the employee has properly been found guilty of the same or other offenses a number of times in the past. (There is no rule as to what number of previous offenses constitutes a "good," a "fair," or a "bad" record. Reasonable judgment thereon must be used.)

Note 2: An employee's record of previous offenses may never be used to discover whether he was guilty of the immediate or latest one. The only proper use of his record is to help determine the severity of discipline once he has properly been found guilty of the immediate offense.

Note 3: Given the same proven offense for two or more employees, their respective records provide the only proper basis for "discriminating" among them in the administration of discipline for said offense. Thus, if employee A's record is significantly better than those of employees B, C, and D, the company may properly give A a lighter punishment than it gives the others for the same offense; and this does not constitute true discrimination.

Note 4: Suppose that the record of the arbitration hearing establishes firm "Yes" answers to all the first six questions. Suppose further that the proven offense of the accused employee was a serious one, such as drunkenness on the job; but the employee's record had been previously unblemished over a long, continuous period of employment with the company. Should the company be held arbitrary and unreasonable if it decided to discharge an employee? The answer depends of course on all the circumstances. But, as one of the country's oldest arbitration agencies, the National Railroad Adjustment Board, has pointed out repeatedly in innumerable decisions on discharge cases, leniency is the prerogative of the employer rather than of the arbitrator; and the latter is not supposed to substitute his judgment in this area for that of the company unless there is compelling evidence that the company abused its discretion. This is the rule, even though an arbitrator, if he had been the original "trial judge," might have imposed a lesser penalty. Actually the arbitrator may be said in an important sense to act as an appellate tribunal whose function is to discover whether the decision of the trial tribunal (the employer) was within the bounds of reasonableness above set forth—in general, the penalty of dismissal for a really serious first offense does not in itself warrant a finding of company unreasonableness.

Table of Court Cases

Index

Q

R

About the Authors

Marvin F. Hill, Jr., is currently Professor of Industrial Relations at the College of Business Administration and Adjunct Professor of Law, Northern Illinois University, and an Iowa attorney. A member of the National Academy of Arbitrators, Hill is actively engaged in arbitration and mediation in the public and private sectors. He has contributed articles to many journals, including *The Arbitration Journal, Labor Law Journal, Indiana Law Review, DePaul Law Review*, and *Oklahoma Law Review*. He has also co-authored (with A. V. Sinicropi) two other books, *Management Rights: A Legal and Arbitral Analysis* and *Evidence in Arbitration*, both published by The Bureau of National Affairs, Inc. (BNA).

Anthony V. Sinicropi is John F. Murray Professor of Industrial Relations at The University of Iowa and University Ombudsperson. In the past he has served the university in several administrative positions. He has also served as a consultant for several government organizations. He is an arbitrator and umpire serving extensively in the private sector including basic industries, airlines, and major league sports and in the public sector, serving at all levels—federal, state, and local. He is a member of the National Academy of Arbitrators, having served as a member of the Board of Governors, Vice President, and is now President-Elect. He is a past president and founder of the Society of Professionals in Dispute Resolution. Among his publications are *Iowa Labor Laws*, "The Legal Status of Supervisors in Public Sector Labor Relations," "The Legal Framework of Public Sector Dispute Resolution," "Excluding Discriminational Grievances From Grievance and Arbitration Procedures: A Legal Analysis," and "Subcontracting in Labor Arbitration."